About the Author

Photo by Michael Harter.

John Renard received his doctorate in Islamic Studies from Harvard University's Department of Near Eastern Languages and Civilizations in 1978. Since then he has been teaching courses in Islam, Buddhism, and Hinduism, religion and the arts, and comparative theology at the Department of Theological Studies at Saint Louis University. Earlier publications include *All the King's Falcons: Rumi on Prophets and Revelation* (SUNY, 1994); *Seven Doors to Islam and Windows on the House of Islam* (California, 1996, 1998); and *Islam and the Heroic Image: Themes in Literature and the Visual Arts* (Mercer, 1999), as well as volumes on Islam, Buddhism, and Hinduism for Paulist Press's "101 Questions" series. His most recent books are *Friends of God: Islamic Images of Piety, Commitment, and Servanthood* (California, 2008), *Tales of God's Friends: Islamic Hagiography in Translation* (California, 2009), *Islam and Christianity: Theological Themes in Comparative Perspective* (California, 2011), *Fighting Words: Religion, Violence, and the Interpretation of Sacred Texts* (California, 2012), and *Islamic Theological Themes: A Primary Source Reader* (California, 2014).

Also from Visible Ink Press

The Handy African American History Answer Book
by Jessie Carnie Smith
ISBN: 978-1-57859-452-8

The Handy American History Answer Book
by David Hudson
ISBN: 978-1-57859-471-9

The Handy Anatomy Answer Book
by James Bobick and Naomi Balaban
ISBN: 978-1-57859-190-9

The Handy Answer Book for Kids (and Parents),
    2nd edition
by Gina Misiroglu
ISBN: 978-1-57859-219-7

The Handy Art History Answer Book
by Madelynn Dickerson
ISBN: 978-1-57859-417-7

The Handy Astronomy Answer Book, 3rd edition
by Charles Liu
ISBN: 978-1-57859-190-9

The Handy Bible Answer Book
by Jennifer Rebecca Prince
ISBN: 978-1-57859-478-8

The Handy Biology Answer Book, 2nd edition
by Patricia Barnes Svarney and Thomas E. Svarney
ISBN: 978-1-57859-490-0

The Handy Chemistry Answer Book
by Ian C. Stewart and Justin P. Lomont
ISBN: 978-1-57859-374-3

The Handy Civil War Answer Book
by Samuel Willard Crompton
ISBN: 978-1-57859-476-4

The Handy Dinosaur Answer Book, 2nd edition
by Patricia Barnes-Svarney and Thomas E. Svarney
ISBN: 978-1-57859-218-0

The Handy Geography Answer Book, 2nd edition
by Paul A. Tucci
ISBN: 978-1-57859-215-9

The Handy Geology Answer Book
by Patricia Barnes-Svarney and Thomas E. Svarney
ISBN: 978-1-57859-156-5

The Handy History Answer Book, 3rd edition
by David L. Hudson, Jr.
ISBN: 978-1-57859-372-9

The Handy Investing Answer Book
by Paul A. Tucci
ISBN: 978-1-57859-486-3

The Handy Law Answer Book
by David L. Hudson Jr.
ISBN: 978-1-57859-217-3

The Handy Math Answer Book, 2nd edition
by Patricia Barnes-Svarney and Thomas E. Svarney
ISBN: 978-1-57859-373-6

The Handy Military History Answer Book
by Samuel Crompton
ISBN: 978-1-57859-509-9

The Handy Mythology Answer Book,
by David A. Leeming, Ph.D.
ISBN: 978-1-57859-475-7

The Handy Nutrition Answer Book
by Patricia Barnes-Svarney and Thomas E. Svarney
ISBN: 978-1-57859-484-9

The Handy Ocean Answer Book
by Patricia Barnes-Svarney and Thomas E. Svarney
ISBN: 978-1-57859-063-6

The Handy Personal Finance Answer Book
by Paul A. Tucci
ISBN: 978-1-57859-322-4

The Handy Philosophy Answer Book
by Naomi Zack
ISBN: 978-1-57859-226-5

The Handy Physics Answer Book, 2nd edition
By Paul W. Zitzewitz, Ph.D.
ISBN: 978-1-57859-305-7

The Handy Politics Answer Book
by Gina Misiroglu
ISBN: 978-1-57859-139-8

The Handy Presidents Answer Book, 2nd edition
by David L. Hudson
ISB N: 978-1-57859-317-0

The Handy Psychology Answer Book
by Lisa J. Cohen
ISBN: 978-1-57859-223-4

The Handy Religion Answer Book, 2nd edition
by John Renard
ISBN: 978-1-57859-379-8

The Handy Science Answer Book®, 4th edition
by The Carnegie Library of Pittsburgh
ISBN: 978-1-57859-321-7

The Handy Supreme Court Answer Book
by David L Hudson, Jr.
ISBN: 978-1-57859-196-1

The Handy Weather Answer Book, 2nd edition
by Kevin S. Hile
ISBN: 978-1-57859-221-0

Please visit the "Handy" series website at www.handyanswers.com.

THE
HANDY
ISLAM
ANSWER
BOOK

John Renard, Ph.D.

VISIBLE
INK
PRESS

Detroit

THE HANDY ISLAM ANSWER BOOK

Visible Ink Press®
43311 Joy Rd., #414
Canton, MI 48187–2075
Visible Ink Press is a registered trademark of Visible Ink Press LLC.

Most Visible Ink Press books are available at special quantity discounts when purchased in bulk by corporations, organizations, or groups. Customized printings, special imprints, messages, and excerpts can be produced to meet your needs. For more information, contact Special Markets Director, Visible Ink Press, www.visibleinkpress.com, or 734–667–3211.

Managing Editor: Kevin S. Hile
Art Director: Mary Claire Krzewinski
Typesetting: Marco Di Vita
Proofreaders: Larry Baker and Aarti Stephens
Indexer: Shoshana Hurwitz

Cover images: Shutterstock.

Library of Congress Cataloging–in–Publication Data

Renard, John.
  The handy islam answer book / John Renard.
    pages cm
  ISBN 978-1-57859-510-5 (paperback)
  1. Islam. I. Title.
  BP161.3.R465 2014
  297–dc23   2014033780

Printed in the United States of America

10 9 8 7 6 5 4 3 2 1

Contents

Acknowledgments

I owe special thanks to Jacob Van Sickle of Saint Louis University for invaluable editorial assistance in the completion of this book, and to Mary Ganser of Saint Louis University for editorial assistance in final proofreading. To David Oughton, I am grateful for generous permission to use several of his photographs, as so acknowledged in the captions. My thanks also to Roger Jänecke, publisher of VIP, for inviting me to do this book, and to Kevin Hile for his superb editorial management of the project. Thanks, also, to indexer Shoshana Hurwitz, Visible Ink Press proofers Larry Baker and Aarti Stephens, typesetter Marco Di Vita, and page and cover designer Mary Claire Krzewinski.

Portions of this work were previously published in *101 Questions and Answers on Islam* by John Renard, published by Paulist Press, Mahwah, New Jersey. Copyright © 1998 by John Renard. Used with permission of Paulist Press, Inc. (www.paulistpress.com).

Portions of this work were previously published in *In the Footsteps of Muhammad: Understanding the Islamic Experience* by John Renard, published by Paulist Press, Mahwah New Jersey. Copyright © 1992 by John Renard. Used with permission of Paulist Press, Inc. (www.paulistpress.com).

Photo Credits

AryanSogd: p. 341.

Bal'ami: p. 26.

Atilim Gunes Baydin: p. 47.

James Dale: p. 24.

David Edwards: p. 197.

Ed Ford: p. 103.

Foreign and Commonwealth Office, United Kingdom: p. 254.

James Gordon from Los Angeles, California, USA: p. 283.

Milpitas Graham: p. 83.

Kevin Hile: pp. 245, 302.

Tony Hisgett: p. 91.

Gunawan Kartapranata: p. 129.

John N. D. Kelly: p. 36.

Khalid78: p. 242.

Firdaus Latif: p. 55.

Munsha'at al Akhdar lil Alwan: p.41.

Nmkuttiady: p. 273.

David Oughton: pp. 97, 229.

Pew Research Center: p. 68.

Toni Castillo Quero: p. 57.

John Renard: p. 363.

Sandstein: p. 49.

Seeroos123BigBoy: p. 228.

Selbymay: 94.

David Shankbone from USA: p. 332.

Andrew Shiva: 290.

Shutterstock: pp. 2, 4, 6, 13, 16, 20, 22, 43, 63, 69, 71, 73, 75, 76, 89, 93, 95, 99, 102, 109, 112, 113, 116, 127, 137, 148, 149, 153, 155, 157, 160, 164, 167, 168, 172, 173, 176, 177, 179, 182, 183, 186, 190, 198, 202, 203, 205, 208, 214, 216, 225, 226, 233, 235, 237, 258, 260, 262, 264, 280, 287, 288, 292, 294, 299, 304, 306, 314, 316, 318, 319, 321, 324, 338, 353, 381.

Eric Stoltz: p. 10

Acquired by Henry Walters: p. 188.

Xxedcxx: p. 166.

Public domain: 35, 79, 90, 162, 163, 195, 232, 255, 284, 296, 344, 348, 361, 373, 376, 378.

Introduction

Winston Churchill once described Soviet Russia as "a riddle wrapped in a mystery inside an enigma." Many "Westerners" these days might be inclined to consider Churchill's comment equally applicable to the global religious tradition of Islam. For some, sadly, the characterization does not go nearly far enough—mere "inscrutability" hardly accounts for the threat of "evil" with which they associate Islam and Muslims. When Sir Winston added hopefully, "But perhaps there is a key," he had in mind a way of countering Stalin's geo-political designs.

Is there also a "key" for people who find Islam impossibly opaque, or perhaps simply intolerable? Actually, there are two: one too-seldom provided, the other too-often overlooked. The first is the need for reliable *information* about Islam and Muslims; the second has to do with the simple consideration of the *shared humanity* that joins Muslims and non-Muslims far more deeply than cultural or religious differences separate them. It is my hope that readers will find both in some measure in this volume's twelve chapters. Let me begin by responding to several large, general background questions I have been asked often over the forty-five years or so since I began turning toward the academic study of Islam.

How and why did I get seriously interested in Islamic religious studies? As a result of teaching high school and college-level courses on comparative religion during the late 1960's, I found myself increasingly intrigued by "other" faith traditions as a potential professional focus. Buddhism and Hinduism were especially interesting, colorful, and exotic. But mention of these major traditions raised few alarms, perhaps because Americans generally thought of them as "somewhere else," and thus unthreatening, if not simply irrelevant. Islam, however, was another matter altogether. This second-largest religious tradition began breaking into "western" awareness more concretely when the so-called "Six Day War" of 1967 thrust the Israel–Palestinian conflict into the news. A few years later, the "Arab Oil Embargo" had Americans lining up for blocks at gas stations and fuming at whoever they imagined was inconveniencing them so annoyingly.

The mere mention of Islam and Muslims became a source of potential misunderstanding and rancor, while the "Middle East" was fast becoming the very symbol of volatility and global threat. After completing a Master's degree in Biblical Studies, I decided to "test" my growing inclination to dive into Islamic Studies by combining the study of Arabic with a chance to visit biblical sites in the "Holy Land." With no reasonable future in Islamic Studies if I didn't like Arabic, I enrolled in a ten-week, intensive introductory Arabic course at the Hebrew University in Jerusalem, with time on weekends for the biblical connection. I loved Arabic and made many friends among Palestinian Arabs, both Christian and Muslim, and that was all the evidence I needed to pursue what has become a challenging and satisfying profession.

Many Muslims have asked me whether I have ever considered becoming a Muslim as a result of my professional commitment; and Christians have wondered whether, as a Roman Catholic, I wasn't perhaps putting my religious convictions in jeopardy. The short response to the first query is that I have never been moved to consider converting. That is not because I do not find Islam an attractive tradition, but because I regard my faith and my membership in the worldwide community of Roman Catholics as a gift to be cherished and nurtured. As a result, my answer to the second is simply that although I find the study of Islam immensely rewarding and even spiritually engaging and enriching, the study of Islam has never subverted my Christian beliefs or commitments. On the contrary, that study has encouraged me to dig more deeply into my own traditions. Neither, on the other hand, have I ever suggested to any student that he or she might consider becoming Muslim, or to any of my Muslim friends and acquaintances that they would be better off as Christians. First and foremost, the study of Islam is much more than a dry academic exercise for me. Islam is, for me, one of God's "signs" to believers of all perspectives. Islam is a challenge, a source of encouragement, and a call to take a bigger view of what life on this planet is about.

But surely my own religious convictions bias my study of the Islamic tradition, people wonder? Do I really think I can offer anything like an accurate, balanced assessment? True "objectivity" is indeed almost by definition impossible for any human being, but aiming at both accuracy and balance is of the utmost importance. My goal here is a good-faith attempt to present a faith tradition other than my own in a way that a significant percentage of members of that faith will find acceptable. Islam is a huge reality, and, like their counterparts in other faith traditions, Muslims also represent a vast spectrum of views about Islam.

And what sort of "larger perspective" do I see in my own faith traditions? Jesus challenged the people of his time not to be complacent about being the "chosen" people; he challenged them to read the signs of the times. The question for me is, how large am I prepared to allow God to be? How inclusive is God's love? If my religious affiliation comes between me and God's other children, it may very well come between me and

God, too. Risk often goes hand in hand with challenge. Jesus says to the Samaritan woman in the Gospel of John: "The hour is coming when neither on this mountain nor in Jerusalem will you worship the Father.... The hour is coming, and it is now, when the true worshippers will worship the Father in spirit and truth, for such the Father seeks to worship Him" (Jn. 4:21, 23). I believe the study of Islam has been part of my call, not to a diminished personal commitment to my faith, but to the risk of living in the uncharted territory "between" Gerizim and Jerusalem.

My experience as a student of Islam has been one of hope, encouragement, and often of profound spiritual consolation. I have found the beauty of the scripture and the literary and visual expression of the tradition's religious values deeply moving and uplifting. The increasingly evident fact of religious pluralism in our world convinces me more daily of the need to seek a more adequate understanding of what motivates Muslims, as well as members of other faith communities. Instead of being discouraged that the vast majority of people are not Christian and are not likely to become Christian, I am encouraged that so vast a multitude who call themselves Muslims seek God with a sincere heart.

Finally, the very fact of Islam calls me to a conversion more radical than any transfer of confessional allegiance. It is a call to expanded awareness. Islam is part of my world, a world about which, over fifty years ago, the Second Vatican Council called for a new vision: "Over the centuries many quarrels and dissensions have arisen between Christians and Muslims. The sacred Council now pleads with all to forget the past and urges that a sincere effort be made to achieve mutual understanding; for the benefit of all, ... let them together preserve and promote peace, liberty, social justice and moral values." Isaiah calls to mind God's global vision as well: "I will say to the north, Give them up; and to the south, Do not hold back. Bring my sons from afar and my daughters from the ends of the earth, everyone who is named as mine, whom I created for my glory, whom I formed and made" (Is. 43: 6–7).

In more recent years, many people have asked whether I recall what I was doing when I heard the tragic news of "9/11" and whether my study of Islam has offered any insight into those and subsequent related events. For most Americans, it was September 11, 2001. For me, it was the year 970, as I visited with Abu Talib al-Makki. Drifting back into tenth-century Mecca, I was engaged in my *jihad* of the lexicon, striving to translate the large chapter on Knowledge of God in Abu Talib's amazing but dauntingly difficult Arabic work, *The Sustenance of Hearts*. Into my sometime-medieval study, my wife, Mary Pat, stepped in as she returned from errands with a look of utter disbelief on her face. "Have you listened to any news yet?" she asked. And she described the shocking events as we tuned in for the latest grim tidings. We talked for a while and then tried to get back to work, I to reconnect with Abu Talib. Needless to say I was seriously distracted, but I thought about what Abu Talib might say about that sad day.

Abu Talib was a shrewd observer of the human condition. He minced no words as he talked about people who abused religion for their own purposes. Yes, he knew plenty of them. Abu Talib was particularly hard on hypocrites, people who feign authority only to be seen as important while they care only about the trappings that they hope will deceive others into following them. He talked often of Hudhayfa ibn al-Yaman, a Companion of Muhammad whom the Prophet had noticed because of his unique insight into the evils of hypocrisy. Muhammad even informally designated Hudhayfa as the young Muslim community's "expert" on hypocrisy. One day a Muslim approached Hudhayfa with a personal concern related to Hudhayfa's specialty. He said, "I fear I am becoming a hypocrite." "Nothing to worry about," said Hudhayfa, "hypocrites are not afraid of hypocrisy." Hudhayfa could pick a hypocrite out of any crowd.

If Abu Talib were here today, he would tell a lot of Hudhayfa stories. If Hudhayfa were here today, he would not hesitate to call a hypocrite a hypocrite, and would describe all forms of bigotry—religious and otherwise—as arising from hypocrisy. He would characterize our world as suffering a crisis of knowledge: the greatest tribulation of all is to be presented with good and evil and not know which one to choose. In just such a time, when moral ambiguity abounds, those whose hypocritical design involves distorting religious values mold those starved for genuine learning like putty in their hands. It is time for us all to use the "H-word" to make it crystal clear to all those with terror on their minds, hatred in their hearts, and blood on their hands that they do not speak for any of the faith traditions that *any* of us treasure.

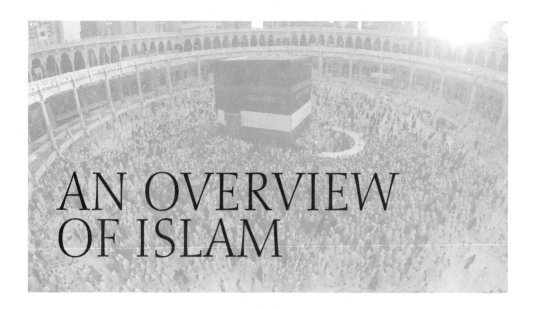

AN OVERVIEW OF ISLAM

What is "Islam"?

An Abrahamic monotheistic faith tradition that sees itself as a culmination, completion, and correction of Judaism and Christianity.

Who are Muslims?

Muslims comprise some 1.6 billion people living across the globe, representing scores of ethnicities, nationalities, and major language families.

What's the basic meaning of the terms "Islam" and "Muslim"?

"Islam" means "surrender to God" and "Muslim" refers to an individual who "does Islam"—note the shared letters S-L-M, signifying a root that connotes a "peace that comes from having all one's priorities in order."

Where did Islam originate?

In the west-central Arabian Peninsula region known as the Hijaz, in the city of Mecca.

When did Islam begin?

In the early seventh century, officially beginning Islam's lunar calendar in 622.

Why is that year significant?

An event called the *Hijra* ("emigration"), during which the small Muslim community left Mecca for a northwestern Arabian city now known as Medina.

Who is Islam's central/foundational figure?

Muhammad (c. 570–632), son of a member of the Hashimi clan of the Quraysh tribe. Said to have received a commission as Prophet in 610 with his first auditory revelation.

1

Muhammad is a preeminent example of humanity, but purely human.

What is Islam's principal source?

The Quran ("recitation"), c. 6200 Arabic verses, 114 "chapters," delivered orally by Muhammad over some twenty-three years (610–632) in the cities of Mecca and Medina.

What's the language of the Quran?

Arabic, the most important surviving Semitic language, is the language of revelation, Islam's "sacred" tongue.

Are there any other sacred texts?

Yes, the Hadith (tradition, saying), now many volumes in many authoritative collections enshrining the words and deeds of Muhammad.

Arabic is a Semitic language spoken by about three hundred million people today. It is also the sacred language of the Quran and Islam. This sample of written script reads "Muhammad the Prophet of Allah."

What are some central beliefs?

Faith in one transcendent deity (Allah), creator of all things, revealer of divine truth through "signs"—on the "horizons" (creation), in the prophetic scripture, and within the individual soul—and who has communicated via angelic heralds to an unbroken line of "warners" (prophets/messengers) beginning with Adam, including many "Old Testament" figures as well as John the Baptist and Jesus, and culminating in the definitive message through Muhammad. All will be held personally accountable for their choices in judgment, leading either to reward or punishment, and there will be a bodily resurrection. God's mercy always outweighs the divine wrath/justice.

Are there any core ritual practices?

The so-called Five Pillars—Profession of faith (*Shahada*), five daily ritual prayers (*salat*), pilgrimage once in lifetime to Mecca (*Hajj*), almsgiving (*zakat*), and fasting (*sawm*, during lunar month of Ramadan). Central emphasis in all these and other religious and devotional deeds is the priority of intention: without "presence of the heart," all such acts are spiritually empty.

What country has the largest Muslim population?

Indonesia, a nation of some three thousand islands in Southeast Asia, with a population of over two hundred million people, about 90 percent Muslim.

What countries have the largest Muslim population after Indonesia?

The next three largest Muslim populations are in Pakistan, Bangladesh, and India—with a combined total of nearly five hundred million.

Aren't most Muslims Arabs?

Approximately one in five Muslims are Arabs, the remaining 80 percent represented by dozens of ethnicities, nationalities, cultural backgrounds, as well as scores of different languages.

Are all Middle Eastern Muslims Arabs?

Though Arabs do comprise the ethnic majority of the "Middle East" and North Africa, Turks, Kurds, and Iranians of varied ethnic origins represent important non-Semitic peoples whose languages are unrelated to Arabic.

Do all Muslims believe and express their faith in exactly the same ways?

There is considerable unity concerning the core beliefs and ritual practices but also some variation due to internal diversity. This includes, for example, majority Sunni and minority Shi'i communities, as well as a broad spectrum of attitudes to what additional rules are "essential" and how strictly religious law must be enforced, and considerable variety in the interaction of religion and cultures across the globe.

ORIGINS AND EARLY EXPANSION

How did Islam begin?

Five hundred years after the Roman destruction of the Temple in Jerusalem dramatically altered the history of Judaism, an equally momentous event occurred in the Arabian Peninsula. According to tradition, Muhammad was born around 570 c.e. in the trading town of Mecca. When he was about twenty-five, Muhammad married a businesswoman named Khadija, fifteen years his senior. Muhammad developed the habit of seeking prayerful solitude in the hills and caves surrounding Mecca. One day around the year 610, he began to undergo some troubling auditory and visual experiences. Encouraged by Khadija not to dismiss the experiences, Muhammad came to understand them as divine revelations that he was meant to communicate to his fellow Meccans. He was to be a messenger of God, a prophet charged with delivering a message that would set straight misinterpretations of earlier revelations given through the prophets God had sent to the Jews and Christians.

What and where is Arabia?

The Arabian Peninsula is an enormous land mass that makes up the south-central portion of western Asia, also known as the Middle East. It is now home to the nations of Saudi Arabia, Yemen, Oman, and United Arab Emirates, and several other small so-called

3

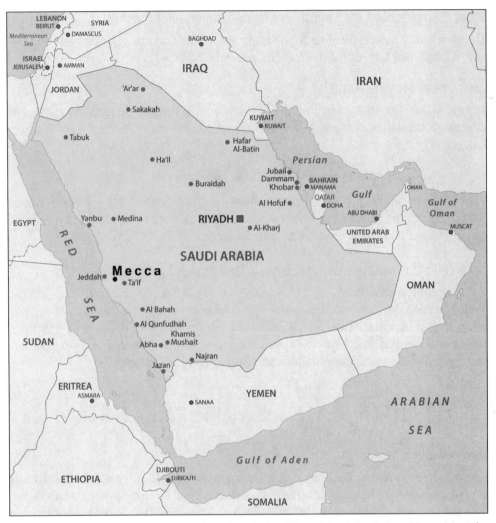

The Arabian Peninsula, just east of Africa, is where the holy city of Mecca is located and where Islam originated.

Gulf States. Arabia is bordered on the west by the Red Sea, on the south by the Arabian Sea, and on the east by the Persian Gulf. Mostly desert, the peninsula is larger than Iran and Iraq combined, twice the size of Egypt, and about 10 percent larger than Alaska. Total population today is just over twenty million. Riyadh is the capital of Saudi Arabia, the peninsula's largest nation state. Jeddah is the Red Sea port that serves the holy city of Mecca, Muhammad's home town. Medina, the second holy city, is about two hundred miles north of Mecca.

What was pre-Islamic religion like and did Islam retain any of its features?

Pre-Islamic Arabian tribes believed that the universe was animated by innumerable spirits, each inhabiting its own distinctive elements and natural features. They called each of these minor deities an *ilah*, "god," but tribespeople in many regions singled out one particular local power as the chief spiritual force. That power they called the god, *al-ilah*, or *allah* (ah-LAH). Mecca was one of several major cultic sites over which such a chief deity ruled.

There, a peculiar cubic-shaped structure called the Ka'ba stood for perhaps centuries at the center of pilgrimage traffic associated with a lively caravan trade. Pre-Islamic beliefs also acknowledged the existence of numerous troublesome beings called jinns, as well as downright diabolical spiritual forces. Muhammad's ancestors emphasized the importance of following the moral code of tribal custom unquestioningly and did not believe in an afterlife. In his early preaching the Prophet focused on the need to behave morally and justly in light of the coming judgment. He taught that a divine will was more important than tribal custom, however ancient, and gradually increased his condemnation of the cult of many spiritual powers (called polydaemonism). The Ka'ba remained an important symbol, as did the practice of pilgrimage, but Muhammad appropriated those aspects of tradition by underscoring their association with Abraham and Ishmael especially.

Why is Mecca a holy city for Muslims?

Mecca, in western Saudi Arabia, is the birthplace of the prophet Muhammad (c. 570) and was his home until the year 622, when those who opposed him forced him to flee to Medina (a city about 200 miles north of Mecca). Muhammad later returned to Mecca and died there in 632. Mecca is also the site of the Great Mosque, which is situated in the heart of the city. The outside of the mosque is an arcade, made up of a series of arches enclosing a courtyard. In that courtyard is the most sacred shrine of Islam, the Ka'ba, a small stone building that contains the Black Stone, which Muslims believe was sent from heaven by Allah (God). When Muslims pray (five times a day, according to the Five Pillars of Faith), they face the Ka'ba. It is also the destination of the hajj, or pilgrimage.

What is the Ka'ba and why is it important?

According to tradition, Abraham and his son Ishmael built (or perhaps rebuilt) a simple cube-like structure in what came to be the center of the city of Mecca. During Muhammad's time the Ka'ba was a relatively small structure, about fifteen feet tall, with a black stone, the size of a bowling ball, of (perhaps) meteoric origin built into one of its corners. Rebuilt several times since Muhammad's day, the Ka'ba now stands about forty-three feet high, with irregular sides ranging from thirty-six to forty-three feet. During Muhammad's lifetime, the building is said to have housed some 360 idols. In 630, Muhammad cleansed the Ka'ba, and it has since remained empty except for some lamps. Its holiness as a symbol of divine presence derives largely from its associations with the lives of Abraham and Muhammad.

Why did Mecca stand out as a religious center?

By the late sixth century, Mecca had achieved the status of the principal cultic center, attracting large numbers of traders and pilgrims to its regular religious and cultural

5

The cube-shaped building called the Ka'ba marks the end of the Hajj for many Muslims. Located in the center of Mecca, the inside of the building contains little more than a few lamps, but it serves as a symbol of God's divine presence.

festivities. At the heart of the city was—and still is—the Ka'ba, which in Muhammad's time was a simple, nearly cube structure of dark stone. In one of its four corners was set a black stone, an ovoid somewhat larger than a bowling ball, now fractured into seven pieces and framed in a collar of silver. Such stones had long been part of local religious centers not only in the Arabian Peninsula, but throughout the greater Middle East. In the Hebrew Scriptures, stone pillars had been both signs of contention, when they were at the center of idolatrous cults, and altogether acceptable symbols of help and witness. When Joshua, for example, gathered the people of Israel together to renew their special relationship with God, he set up a stone and called upon it to witness in its mute integrity how the people had reaffirmed the covenant (Joshua 24). Popular tradition has it that the Ka'ba's black stone has likewise been taking note of momentous events—the rise and fall of the powerful, the making and breaking of oaths—since the very dawn of Creation. At the appropriate moment, it will reveal all.

Where does the word "Muslim" come from? Is it the same as "Moslem"?

Arabic is a Semitic language, as is its distant cousin Hebrew. Both languages are based on roots made up of three consonants. For example, many words can be derived from the root S-L-M (Sh-L-M in Hebrew). Keep your eye on the upper case letters to follow the root. A basic verb from that root, SaLiMa, means to be safe or whole. A related Arabic noun is *salaam*, meaning "peace" (like the Hebrew ShaLoM), is part of a standard greeting among Muslims. When Arabic speakers want to build further meanings on a particular root, they do so by modifying the root with either prefixes, infixes (modifying interior letters), or suffixes. For example, to convey the notion of "causing someone to be safe or at peace," one modifies the root SaLiMa so that it becomes aSLaMa. In religious terms, to bring about a state of safety, peace, and wholeness, one has to get one's relationship to God in perfect order. That means letting God be God and giving up all pretense at trying to do what only God can do—in short, surrendering to the supreme power. That state of surrender is called iSLaaM, and a person who acts in such a way as to cause that state is called a muSLiM. One of the first major non-Semitic languages early Muslim conquerors encountered was Persian, in which the "u" was pronounced as an "o," and the "i" as an "e." Hence the variation so common today, "Moslem." Both mean exactly the same thing; the variations are entirely due to differences in pronunciation.

HISTORICAL CONTEXT

What was the religious tradition in the Arabian Peninsula before Islam?

At a little over fourteen hundred years old, Islam is one of the world's younger major religious traditions. It began in the early seventh century near the western edge of the Arabian Peninsula in a city called Mecca, an important stop along the caravan route from Syria to the north to the Yemenite kingdoms of southwestern Arabia. Some Christian and Jewish families and tribes had long before taken up residence in various parts of Arabia, but the prevailing religious climate was a kind of animism sometimes called "polydaemonism," the worship of "many spiritual beings" thought to inhabit natural phenomena. Features of landscape, such as stones and springs, could take on a numinous aura and gradually become the focus of a sacred place. Some sites developed as the centers of cultic worship and pilgrimage, with one of the several local deities (*ilahat*) rising to prominence as the chief among them (*al-ilah*, "the" god, elided into *allah*).

What were some of the most important things happening in the Mediterranean world and especially the Middle East and the environs of the Arabian Peninsula when Islam began?

In pre-Islamic times the Arabian Peninsula had rarely been at the center of Middle Eastern events. An immense coastline made the land accessible to and from the Red Sea on the west, the Persian Gulf on the east, and the Indian Ocean on the south, but the real estate of that vast, inhospitable ocean of sand held little strategic interest for the regional powers. Local kingdoms had ruled to the north, in Syria, and to the southwest, in Yemen. Although the Greeks and Romans knew about the place and liked its incense, they never set their sights on the territory. Soon after the Roman Empire divided into West and East in the fourth century, Byzantium began to consolidate its power in the Eastern Mediterranean, taking control of much of the central Middle East and North Africa. By the time Rome fell in 476, the Byzantine Empire was well established in its own right. Along its southeastern fringe, a line that ran northeast from southern Egypt through Syria and Iraq and across the Caucasus almost to the Caspian Sea, the Byzantines had developed a "buffer state" in the Monophysite Christian Arab tribe called the Ghassanids. Meanwhile, the Sasanian Persian Empire that ruled from eastern Iraq toward the east across what is now Iran also had its own buffer state in the Arab tribe called the unchurched Lakhmids. Through their Arab surrogates these two powerful "confessional empires" (Christian and Zoroastrian) struggled back and forth across the region to the north of the Arabian peninsula, an area covering much of present-day Syria and Iraq, engaged in a protracted tug-of-war over the Fertile Crescent with its enormous river systems.

Are there any important connections between ancient Middle East and European powers?

The Sasanian Persian empire had supplanted the last major Roman Middle Eastern successor state, the Parthians, in the early third century. Before the end of that century the Sasanians had reestablished Zoroastrianism as the creed of the realm. Just around the

Was there anything like "monotheism" in Arabia at the origins of Islam?

At Muhammad's time the Meccan cult revolved around a principal deity called Allah ("the" god, or simply God), whose three "daughters" (Allat, Manat, and Uzza) also figured in local piety. The Quraysh tribe had become the ruling authority over the city's affairs and exercised considerable control over the Ka'ba. The Ka'ba and its stone had many meanings to the Meccans of Muhammad's day, and they would play an important role, sometimes negative and sometimes more positive, in the Prophet's life. According to one account, when the structure had to be rebuilt, the Meccans asked Muhammad the Trustworthy to replace the stone in its socket. Ever aware of the symbolic value of his public actions, and looking for ways to unify local factions, Muhammad placed the stone in the center of his cloak and had representatives of the chief interests lift it with him by grabbing a corner of the cloak. Some estimates date that event at around the year 604 C.E., prior to the beginning of Muhammad's prophetic career. As the Quraysh came more and more to disapprove of his new preaching, they applied the ultimate social pressure, denying Muhammad access to the sacred precincts to pray. Eventually the Ka'ba would become the center of the world of Islam. In the classic Islamic interpretation of history, the birth of Islam marked the death of the "age of ignorance" (*jahiliya*).

time of Muhammad's birth both of the confessional empires reached the zenith of their powers, Byzantium under Emperor Justinian (527–565) and Sasanian Persia under Nushirvan (531–579). An important trade route ran up and down the western coastal region, a highway for exchange from Abyssinia (Ethiopia) and Yemen, to Syria and points north by way of Mecca. And as the Muslim community was beginning to grow in size and strength, the Byzantine and Sasanian regimes were embroiled in a protracted war (603–628) via their Arab clients that would virtually exhaust the capability of both empires to project their control over the central Middle East. The resulting political vacuum set the stage for the emergence of the Muslim forces as a dominant power in the region. By the time Muhammad died, Byzantium and Persia had all but spent themselves into bankruptcy and had so worn each other down that neither would mount serious resistance when the Muslim tribes advanced out of Arabia in a conquering mood.

PROPHET AND EARLY COMMUNITY

Who was Muhammad? What is known about his early life?

Muhammad was born in Mecca around 570 C.E. to a rather poor family of the clan of Hashim, one of the branches of the Quraysh tribe. His father died before Muhammad was born and the boy's mother died when he was six years old. According to Arabian custom, the child was sent to be reared for a time among the Bedouin. Tradition names his nurse Halima. After his mother's death, Muhammad grew up in the custody first of grandfather Abd al-Muttalib and later in the house of his uncle Abu Talib, whose son Ali would later become a major religious and political figure as well. Tradition has it that the young Muhammad travelled with his uncle on business. One story tells how in Syria they met an old Christian monk named Bahira, who discerned the marks of prophetic greatness in the boy.

Did Muhammad have any siblings?

He had no "blood" siblings but a total of eight "foster" siblings. His family tree was thus a bit more complex than many, in the sense that very early on Muhammad's family relations included intertribal connections. The practice of engaging the services of wet nurses from among the Bedouin meant that children often grew up with peers from outside their family of origin's lineage.

What is known about Muhammad's family life as an adult? Was polygamy a new development with Islam?

When Muhammad was about twenty-five, he married a widow fifteen years his senior. Khadija ran her own caravan business, and Muhammad went to work for her. They were married for over twenty years, and while Khadija lived, Muhammad married no other women. He remained unmarried, it appears, for another two years after her death. Over the following seven years, Muhammad contracted marriages with a total of eleven other women under a wide variety of circumstances. Polygamy was already a very ancient practice in the Middle East, as is clear from the Hebrew Scriptures. Abraham and subsequent "patriarchs," as well as David, Solomon, and assorted other kings of Israel, had multiple wives, including some who were very young when first married. Given such a long-standing cultural precedent, Muhammad's practice was not at all unusual. Muhammad's subsequent wives were Sawda, Aisha (daughter of major Companion and first Caliph Abu Bakr), Hafsa (daughter of Companion and second Caliph Umar), Zaynab (daughter of Khuzayma), Umm Salama, Zaynab (daughter of Jahsh), Juwayria, Umm Habiba, Safiya, Maymuna, and Maria (a Coptic Christian). Many of these relationships were the result of concerns for the security of individual women as well as means of cementing social bonds within the community.

The Tomb of Abraham in Hebron is a Muslim holy site.

What does tradition tell us about Muhammad's personal spiritual life?

Apparently Muhammad occasionally liked to retreat to mountain solitude, in a cave on Mt. Hira above Mecca, to meditate and seek within the source of life. He was very likely aware of traditions about previous "seekers after the One God," stories of whom had long been the shared patrimony of ancient Middle Eastern oral cultures. He may have learned of the practice of solitary meditation, at least indirectly, from Christian monks who lived in the region. Around 610 C.E., when Muhammad had reached the age long considered in the Middle East a necessary precondition for the imparting of wisdom and ministry, he began to experience troubling visitations that sent him in turmoil to ask for Khadija's counsel. She encouraged Muhammad to pay close heed to these experiences as authentic spiritual encounters, however bewildering they might be.

What's the Islamic understanding of the origins of Muhammad's experience of revelation?

Here is the traditional account: On the "Night of Power" in the year 610, now generally commemorated on the twenty-seventh day of Ramadan, the earliest message commanded him to "Recite!" (literally, "make *Quran*," i.e., "recitation") that which no human being could know unaided. The encounter left him confused and uncertain. Not until almost a year later did Muhammad hear a follow-up message of confirmation: "Indeed your Lord is the one who best knows who has strayed from His path, who best knows those who are guided" (Quran 68:7). Assured that he was not losing his sanity, Muhammad persisted in his attitude of attentiveness to the messages from the unseen world. From then on revelations came more frequently. During the next several years, Muhammad slowly gathered a circle of "converts" who would form the nucleus of a faith community. Leaders of the Quraysh grew increasingly unhappy at the effects of Muhammad's preaching on caravan and pilgrim traffic to the Ka'ba and at the prospect of a rival leader in their midst. Around 615 C.E., under growing pressure and amid threats to the safety of his community, Muhammad sent a group off to seek asylum across the Red Sea with the Christian rule of Abyssinia (Ethiopia). Muhammad remained in Mecca.

What were some critical events in Islam's earliest years?

Over the next twenty-two years or so (610–632), Muhammad continued to preach the word God had spoken directly to him. At the heart of the message was the notion of "surrender" (the root meaning of the Arabic word *islam*, is-LAAM) to the one true God. His early preaching called for social justice and equality and condemned oppression of the poor by the wealthy and powerful. Muhammad belonged to a powerful tribe called the Quraysh, who exercised considerable control over the lives of the Meccans generally. But Muhammad's family and the clan of which they were a part were among the poorer and less influential within the tribe. Muhammad's preaching did not endear him to the Quraysh, who made life difficult for the small community of Muslims. In 622, Muhammad and his followers made the crucial decision to move north to the city of Yathrib, whose representatives had offered the young community sanctuary. This "emigration," or *Hijra*, marked the official beginning of the Muslim calendar. Muhammad the prophet became a statesman as well, and Yathrib became known as Madinat an-Nabi, the City of the Prophet, or Medina for short. The Muslim community grew rapidly, doing battle with the Meccans and eventually regaining access to Mecca in 630.

What place does Muhammad occupy in Islamic tradition?

Muslims consider Muhammad the last in a line of prophets commissioned to act as God's spokesmen to humankind. Beginning with Adam and continuing down through Jesus,

Did Muhammad have any children?

Muhammad and Khadija had six children together, and Khadija had two children from a prior marriage. Muhammad's first six children included two boys (neither of whom lived past the age of two) and four girls, all of whom lived into young adulthood. Fatima, their fifth child, went on to become the most influential and important of all Muhammad's children. His seventh child was born to his Coptic wife, Maria, and died at about eighteen months. Fatima was thus the sole offspring of the Prophet to survive his death. Muhammad knew more than his share of parental grief.

the pre-Islamic prophets preached the same fundamental message of belief in one sovereign transcendent God. But because successive generations invariably found the message difficult and inconvenient, people sometimes corrupted or diluted the revelation. Hence, God chose upright individuals to reassert the original revelation. Muhammad was a man singled out for his natural virtue and integrity to fulfill the role of final and definitive intermediary of the divine communication. As a human being, Muhammad naturally had his faults. But Muslims regard him as the finest our species has yet produced, the ideal family man and leader of humanity. Muhammad himself never claimed to be a wonder-worker. His sole miracle was the Qur'an (kur-AAN, and hereafter transliterated as Quran), the Muslim sacred scripture. Popular tradition has nevertheless sometimes idealized Muhammad, expanding his powers and prerogatives to include various kinds of marvels. One dual experience, called the Night Journey and Ascension, stands out. According to tradition, God conveyed Muhammad by night from Mecca to Jerusalem, and from there through the various levels of heaven and hell. Popular lore has attributed other wonders to Muhammad, but it is most important to appreciate the enormous affection and reverence Muslims universally feel for their Prophet.

Do Muslims worship Muhammad?

Muslims have never considered Muhammad any more than a very special human being, particularly favored by God. They universally revere him, hold him in the greatest esteem, and feel enormous depth of affection for him. Muhammad provides first and foremost the ultimate model of what God wants every human being to strive for. Of course, Muhammad was what he was by God's grace and power; one can neither aspire to, let alone achieve, the status of prophet by one's own effort. Muslims are quick to point out that Muhammad himself considered the Quran his only "miracle," but tradition and popular lore over the centuries have attributed a number of extraordinary experiences to the Prophet.

Do Muslims attribute any special powers to the Prophet? What is his spiritual status?

Nevertheless, in order to understand Muhammad's lofty spiritual status, one needs to appreciate some of the experiences he is said to have gone through. Tradition reports that on the twenty-seventh night of the month of Rajab in the year 621 C.E., Muhammad underwent a two-fold mystical experience. In the first part, God "carried his servant by night, from the Mosque of the Sanctuary to the Farther Mosque" (Quran 17:1). Later interpreters would equate the first site with the shrine of the Ka'ba in Mecca, the second with the southern end of the temple platform in Jerusalem, where now stands an early eighth-century structure called "the Farther Mosque" (al-masjid al-aqsa). This "Night Journey" (isra) was already clearly a kind of otherworldly experience, for ancient narratives place Muhammad in the company of earlier prophets in the Farther Mosque, and they naturally ask him to lead them in the ritual prayer. The second phase of the journey, however, called the "Ascension" (mir'aj), finds the Prophet riding a winged human-faced steed named Buraq and led by Gabriel toward the very throne of God. Marvelously embellished tales have developed around this experience. Vivid descriptions of Muhammad's excursion follow him through the various levels of heaven, where he meets all of his major prophetic forebears, down to the dark circles of hell where Gabriel shows him the horrors of the damned. This is truly the picture of a heroic journey of initiation in the mysteries of the unseen world. Many Muslims believe the journey involved physical locomotion, but a strong tradition of non-literalistic interpretation has always regarded it as a spiritual and inward experience. However one interprets these moments in Muhammad's life, the power of the link tradition forged between the Prophet and Jerusalem remains as great as ever and continues to be part of the mix in current events in the Middle East.

What events led to the Muslim community's understanding of the "official" beginning of Islam?

Under pressure from the leading Meccans, Muhammad had been investigating the possibility of moving his community from the increasingly hostile environment of Mecca to a safer haven. Hopeful prospects arrived in 621 C.E. with a delegation from Yathrib, a city several hundred miles north of Mecca. Looking for someone to help

When Muhammad led his followers to the city of Medina it marked the beginning of the Muslim calendar in 621 C.E. Today, Medina is an important city that many pilgrims visit as part of the Hajj.

them negotiate a peaceful settlement to factional problems in their city, the representatives invited Muhammad to come and apply his already renowned talent for arbitration. Arrangements were finalized, and in 622 c.e. the Muslims headed north to Yathrib, whose name would soon change to Madinat an-Nabi ("City of the Prophet"), or simply Medina. That crucial journey was called the *Hijra* or Emigration. It marked the birthday of Islam, so to speak, and the beginning of the Muslim calendar (with dates marked A.H., "after the *Hijra*").

What are some key events during the Medina period?

Muhammad's years in Medina, as reflected in the text of the Quran as well as in later historical writing, witnessed major changes in his style of leadership and in the shape of the community of believers. Muhammad's prominence in the new setting gave prestige to the community. As the group increased, so did the demands on Muhammad's administrative time and skill, so that what began as spiritual leadership gradually grew into a more comprehensive oversight. During the Medinan period the Muslims also took up arms against the Quraysh and fought a number of serious military engagements with the Meccan forces. After nearly eight years of bitter conflict, the two sides struck a truce. The Muslims would be allowed to return to Mecca without opposition. In 630, Muhammad led a triumphal band to claim the city for the Muslims. Two years later, Muhammad returned to Mecca for what would be his farewell pilgrimage to the Ka'ba. He died in Medina in 632 after an illness of several months.

What happened when Muhammad died? Did Muslims develop religious institutions to carry on the leadership Muhammad had begun?

Muhammad's death thrust the young community into a protracted debate over the criteria of legitimate succession. According to sources compiled as many as two or three centuries after Muhammad's death in 632 c.e., two predominant solutions to the problem of succession emerged. One group maintained that the Prophet had explicitly designated his son-in-law Ali to be his Caliph (literally, "successor" or "vicegerent"). The other, convinced that Muhammad had made no such appointment, opted for the procedure of choosing from among a group of elder Companions of Muhammad. They chose Muhammad's father-in-law, Abu Bakr. The group that supported Ali's candidacy came to be called the Shia (party, faction, supporters) of Ali, popularly known as Shi'ites. Those who backed Abu Bakr were in the majority and formed the nucleus of what came to be called the "People of the Sunna and the Assembly," Sunnis for short. Ali's backers continued to insist that Ali was unfairly passed over three times, gaining only in 656 c.e. the leadership role that had been his by right for nearly thirty-five years. The well-known distinction between Sunni and Shi'i identifies only the largest institutional division within the Muslim community. Muslims are quick to point out that none of these so-called "divisions" indicates any noteworthy variations in belief and practice among the world's 1.6 billion Muslims. Still, major classical sources from within the tradition have seen fit to describe their own history in terms of these allegiances.

Is Mecca the only Islamic holy city?

As the birthplace of Muhammad and the site of the Ka'ba, Mecca, and its immediate en-virons, is naturally the holiest place on earth for Muslims. According to tradition, other prophets and important holy people passed through Mecca as well. Abraham nearly sac-rificed his son Ishmael at Arafat (the valley just outside Mecca) and built the Ka'ba. God rescued Abraham's consort, Hagar, and their son Ishmael from dying of thirst in the desert by causing the well of Zamzam to bubble forth. In 622 Muhammad traveled with his young community to Medina and there established Islam as an all-encompassing social entity. From Medina, the Prophet secured access to Mecca for Muslims and in Medina he died. Muhammad's house and earliest mosque remain a regular stop for most pilgrims who make Hajj and Umra. For these reasons and more, Medina ranks as the sec-ond-holiest city for Muslims. But Muhammad and a number of the other prophets also have important connections to Jerusalem. Muslim tradition has it that God carried Muhammad from Mecca to Jerusalem, to the "farther mosque," where he met and led the other major prophets in prayer. From a spot nearby, Muhammad began his Ascen-sion or *Mi'raj* (mi-RAAJ). For a time members of the young Muslim community in Med-ina faced Jerusalem when they prayed, but the orientation for prayer changed to Mecca in connection with a falling-out with the local Jewish tribes. Nevertheless, Jerusalem has retained a lofty place in Muslim piety and remains politically sensitive real estate.

FOUNDATIONS OF THE FAITH

What is the principal Muslim sacred text?

In about the year 610, Muhammad began to deliver orally the messages he believed were of divine origin. His "recitation" (qur'an) of the revelation was initially held in memory by his followers, and, according to traditional accounts, was not produced in full written form until some years after Muhammad's death in 632. Scholars distinguish between the "Meccan period" (610–622) and the "Medinan period" (622–632), and they note various significant differences in the tone and content of the revelations from one to the other. What began as "an Arabic recitation" retained that name even after it was written down, and the resulting book is still known as "The Recitation" or Quran.

How have Muslims preserved the teachings of Muhammad? Is the Hadith literature anything like the New Testament Gospels in which the words of the founding figure are enshrined?

Second only to the Quran in sacred authority are the "sayings" of Muhammad, enshrined in a large body of literature called Hadith. The Hadith literature is similar to the Gospels to the extent that it preserves the words and deeds of the religious founder. But the two sources are very different in a number of ways. First of all, the four Gospels developed

15

as conscious literary-theological endeavors. Their authors (or schools of thought associated with individuals whose names the Gospels bear) carefully designed works that would convey the meaning of Jesus's life from a particular perspective. They include many things Jesus is reported to have said, but those sayings are woven into the fabric of a larger narrative structure. They depended a great deal on oral reports, to be sure, but the written record was complete by about seventy years after Jesus's death.

The Quran (sometimes spelled Koran or Qur'an) is the holy book of Islam. It was delivered orally by the Prophet Muhammad as divine revelation.

How did the process of formalizing "tradition" about Muhammad unfold?

A remarkable enterprise known as the "search for Hadith" took scholar-collectors across the central Islamic lands, interviewing countless individuals known for reliable powers of recollection. But collecting was not the end of the process. Scholars then subjected the material to intense scrutiny, inquiring into the background and trustworthiness of every individual named among the "chains" of transmitters (*isnad*) associated with each saying. Analysis of such personal characteristics as veracity, intellect, uprightness, and devotion, along with other data concerning the times and places individuals had lived, allowed scholars to classify transmitters as part of the emerging "science of men." A single weak link in a chain would indicate an unreliable Hadith.

What were the first major results of the "search for the Hadith"?

By the end of the ninth century, a group of six major collections had come to be regarded as authoritative among Sunni Muslims, each containing thousands of sayings with assessments of their reliability. There are dozens of others, as well, and Shi'i Muslims also developed several major collections of their own. Like the Gospels, the Hadith are considered divinely revealed. But whereas Muslims consider the Quran the direct literal word of God, the Hadith represent content of divine origin couched in Muhammad's own unique expression.

Who were the Companions of the Prophet and why are they important?

Muslims have long known their tradition's earliest stalwart and exemplary figures as the Companions (*sahaba* [sa-HAA-ba]) of the Prophet. Classical sources from biographical dictionaries such as Ibn Sad's *Greater Book of Generations* identify fifty or sixty as the most intimately acquainted with the Prophet. Tradition credits some with being key sources of oral tradition, and thus with preserving the Sunna of the Prophet.

Did the Hadith material come into being in as short a time as the Quran?

The record of Muhammad's words and deeds evolved more gradually. For several generations at least, Muslims hesitated to put the words into writing, perhaps out of concern that the words of the Prophet be kept separate from the Word of God in the Quran. Some Hadiths were written down, but memory of Muhammad's sayings and actions remained alive largely through oral transmission, recollections passed on from one generation to another. Curiously, the early Muslims sought to remember not only *what* Muhammad had said and done, but *who transmitted* the material as well. Some members of local communities came to be known as particularly important living repositories of the tradition. Several generations along, religious scholars were becoming increasingly concerned that the living link might eventually weaken to the breaking point. So toward the end of the eighth and beginning of the ninth century, nearly two hundred years after Muhammad's death, traditionists mounted a vast concerted effort to gather all available evidence of the living record.

Representing high Muslim ideals, the Companions are listed prominently among religious authorities following Muhammad in Quranic interpretation.

Are there any important honorific distinctions among the Companions?

Of the total group, tradition further identifies a group of the "Ten Blessed Companions," among whom are the Four Rightly Guided Caliphs, Abu Bakr, Umar, Uthman, and Ali. The remaining six are: Zubayr ibn al-Awwaam, Abd ar-Rahman ibn Awf, Sad ibn Abi Waqqas, Sayyidina Said ibn Zayd, Talha ibn Ubaydallah, and Amr ibn Abu Ubayda. The Companions included, naturally, the elect cadre of first converts to Islam, but eventually embraced a much broader variety of people. Beneath the retrospective listing of Companions that began to take shape some seventy to eighty years after Muhammad's death (632) lies a skein of inter-related criteria that characterize an authentic Companion. In addition to having "seen" the Prophet, Companions were ranked first in terms of chronological order in conversion (the earliest known as the *sabiqun*, SAA-bi-koon, the predecessors). Other criteria included, for example, accompanying Muhammad in the *Hijra* to Medina (622), fighting in the Battle of Badr (624), participation in the treaty of Hudaybiya (628), or presence among the early converts in Medina known as the Prophet's "Helpers" (*Ansār*, an-SAAR). A host of other qualifications, mostly related to pin-pointing date of conversion, include participation in the battles of Uhud and the Ditch, for example, and relatively late conversion to Islam during Muhammad's visit to Mecca after the Muslims reclaimed it in 630. These were such signal events in the life of Muhammad and the early community that participation in them became

17

roughly analogous to the presence of leading first-generation Christians at major moments in Christ's life.

Christians talk about an "apostolic age" that extended beyond the lifetime of Jesus. Do Muslims have anything similar, a kind of idealized period that lives on as a time uniquely informed by the spirit of the founder?

Islamic tradition early on developed an intense interest in the importance of direct links to the Prophet. First generation Muslims, who had enjoyed the great blessing of living in Muhammad's presence, came to be called the Companions (*sahaba*, sa-HAA-ba). Their authority in matters of religious judgment ranks second only to that of the Prophet. In matters of dispute about how to interpret the Quran and sayings of Muhammad, the views of the Companions became the first recourse. As a group, the Companions have come to be revered much as Christians revere the apostles of Jesus. Christians need only recall how eager Paul was to establish his rank among the apostles, even though he had never met Jesus, to appreciate the importance of such a socio-religious classification.

Was there a core group among the Companions?

Four of the most important Companions are those who, in the Sunni view, were Muhammad's earliest successors in leadership—the first "caliphs." Muhammad's father-in-law Abu Bakr (d. 634) was chosen first. His first task was to bring back to the Islamic fold a number of Bedouin tribes for whom Muhammad's death triggered a return to their ancestral ways. Already advanced in age, Abu Bakr was among the few to hold his rank who died of natural causes. Umar ibn al-Khattab succeeded Abu Bakr and ruled for about ten years (d. 644). Umar was especially noted for his firm administrative style and is perhaps most famous for wresting the city of Jerusalem from Byzantine control. (The Dome of the Rock is popularly but erroneously called "The Mosque of Umar.") After Umar was

How did Ali's life end?

Ironically, it was a dissident who had originally been among Ali's Shia who would murder this fourth and last of the "Rightly Guided" caliphs, thus effectively ending the Islamic analog to Christianity's "apostolic age." Lest anyone be shocked at the sanguinary nature of some of these early events, it may help to recall that Peter and Paul both died violent deaths as well. The immediate descendants of the Companions came to be known as the Followers (*tabiun*, taa-bee-OON), and their views on substantive issues rank next in authority. Together with the previous and succeeding generations (called the "Followers of the Followers"), they comprise the category of the "predecessors" (*salaf*, SA-laf). As in most traditional views of religious history, Muslims regard the time of Muhammad himself as the pinnacle after which all else is spiritual entropy.

killed, a council appointed Uthman ibn Affan, a member of the Quraysh family, and he administered the growing Islamic sphere of influence until he was murdered in 656. During the twenty-four years following Muhammad's death, the caliphs administered from the city of Medina, but that would soon change.

How did Muhammad's cousin and son-in-law Ali rise to prominence?

Muhammad's cousin Ali ibn Abi Talib came to the fore definitively about twenty-four years after the Prophet's death. His supporters, the "Shia" or "faction" of Ali now known collectively as Shi'i Muslims, would argue that the first three caliphs had been usurpers. At last, they believed, the man who should have been the first caliph could assume his rightful place. Ali's stormy five-year tenure witnessed deepening fissures within the community and a heightened level of strife. Ali had built a base of support in the Iraqi garrison town of Kufa and so moved the capital there. Stiffest opposition came from Muawiya, the recently appointed governor of Damascus, who was a cousin of Uthman, the third caliph. Muawiya and his clan were convinced Ali had been complicit in the murder of Uthman and determined to avenge their kinsman's death.

ISLAM IN THE CENTURY AFTER MUHAMMAD

What were the first great Muslim dynasties?

Relatives of Uthman, called the Umayyads, brought Ali down for his complicity in the murder of Uthman. They established a new seat of power in the ancient city of Damascus (Syria), thus inaugurating the first of a series of Muslim dynasties. Under the Umayyads the map of Islamdom expanded dramatically. By the year 711, Muslim armies had claimed ground across North Africa to Spain, and as far east as the Indus River in present-day Pakistan. Consolidation and some further expansion continued under the Abbasid dynasty, which ruled from its newly founded capital, Baghdad, after supplanting the Umayyads in 750. But the early plan for a single unified Islamic domain soon began to unravel. Increasingly aware that Baghdad could not continue to hold its far-flung empire together, regional governors and princes at the fringes began to declare independence. Although the Abbasid caliph would continue to claim nominal allegiance until 1258, the future belonged to countless successor states, from Spain to central and south Asia.

How did Islam spread under Mohammad's immediate successors?

Muhammad's immediate successors, called caliphs (KAY-liffs), inherited an expanding but loose-knit social fabric. The Prophet had united the Bedouin tribes under the banner of Islam, but tribal loyalties cooled quickly when the leader died. When Muslim elders in Medina chose Muhammad's father-in-law, Abu Bakr, as the first caliph, the initial

Azem palace in Damascus, Syria, the city where the Umayyads established power in the mid-seventh century C.E.

challenge was to regather the tribes already reverting to their pre-Islamic ways. Umar (reigned 634–644), the second caliph, then mobilized tribal forces to move northward into Syria and Mesopotamia (Iraq), westward into Egypt, and eastward into Persia. Next, Umar instituted important policies in the conquered lands, allowing the subjected peoples to retain their religion and law, and levied taxes often lower than what had been paid previously to Byzantium and Persia. Muslim armies remained apart in garrisons that eventually became cities in their own right. Umar's successors, Uthman (reigned 644–656) and Ali (reigned 656–661), compassed the downfall of the last Sasanian emperor but had to deal with disastrous internal strife as well.

How else did Islam develop and spread during those first decades after Muhammad's death?

Very soon after the Prophet's death, in 632, Muslim forces began to move out of the Arabian Peninsula effectively for the first time. After Abu Bakr managed to unite most of the Arab tribes under the banner of Islam, Umar spent much of his ten-year rule conquering the regions that now constitute the heart of the central Middle East. To the north, his forces ended the Byzantine domination of the Fertile Crescent, including Iraq, greater Syria, and the holy city of Jerusalem. Further to the west, Umar established garrisons in Egypt. And to the east, he made serious inroads into the realm of the Zoroastrian Sasanian dynasty of Persia. Umar was responsible for the initial establishment of the military and financial mechanisms that would form the basis of subsequent expansion. This included the practice of setting up garrison cities in the subjugated territories. Growing out of a policy designed to allow maximum self-determination of the subject populations, the use of garrison cities was meant to keep the conquering forces apart except when needed to keep order. Two ancient garrisons that went on to become important Iraqi cities, for example, are Kufa and Basra. Conquered peoples were allowed to continue practicing their ancestral faiths; the Muslims did not follow a policy of forced conversion. There is considerable evidence that Christian communities fed up with oppressive Byzantine rule cooperated broadly with the invading Muslims.

Was there steady progress under the early caliphs?

During the twelve-year tenure of Uthman, Muslim forces made further decisive gains against the Byzantine empire to the north as far as the Caucasus. To the west he expanded into what is now Libya and developed naval forces capable of challenging Byzantine control of the Mediterranean. He brought an end to the Sasanian empire and pushed the Eastern border of Islamdom well into Persia. At Uthman's order, an official "standardized" written version of the Quran was produced. When Uthman was murdered in 656, the first of two disastrous civil wars that would mark the second half of the seventh century broke out. For the next five years or so, Ali fought a losing battle to establish his legitimacy as universal Muslim leader. His power base gradually eroded while that of his chief rival, Muawiya, grew to such an extent that Muawiya had himself proclaimed caliph in Jerusalem in 660. The following year Ali was murdered by a disaffected former supporter, Ali's son Hasan capitulated to Muawiya, and the first of the great dynasties, the Umayyad, came to birth with its capital in Damascus.

Did Muslims found Damascus?

In the mid-seventh century, Damascus had already been inhabited for at least two millennia. At the center of the region called Syria, Damascus had long been an important stop on north-south caravan routes originating all over Southwest Asia, also called the Middle or Near East. Stories of early Muslim origins provide accounts of trading journeys to the environs of Damascus, including one in which a Christian monk recognized prophetic greatness in the boy Muhammad, who had traveled there with his relatives. During Old Testament times the city had figured in the political history of several major Near Eastern powers such as the kingdom of Aram, whose two-century rule of the region left the Semitic language of Aramaic as one of its legacies. During the early Christian era, Damascus figured prominently in the lives of various apostles of Jesus, and perhaps most notably St. Paul. Damascus was a natural choice for Muslim administrative purposes and Muslims had begun to rule Syria from there by the mid-seventh century. Among the many interesting features of Muslim appropriation of the ancient Christian city is that governors and eventually caliphs of the Umayyad dynasty enlisted the services of old Christian families for high administrative office alongside Muslim officialdom. John of Damascus, often called the last Father of the Church, was one such figure, whose father and grandfather had also served in earlier Muslim administrations.

21

What is known about how the Muslim conquerors treated those whom they conquered?

Early documents from the seventh century suggest that Muslim administrators allowed non-Muslims in the conquered territories to live unmolested, provided they rendered the taxes required of non-Muslim inhabitants of the territories and abided by the terms of a peace accord. One early document records the agreement of the Christians of Syria, an accord in which they listed the conditions to which they acquiesced. They would not teach the Quran to their children, build new institutions of religion, harbor anyone who intended harm to Muslims, make public displays of religion, engage in proselytizing, dress as Muslims did, carry weapons, sell intoxicating beverages, display crosses or books or other religious symbolism in Muslim public spaces, or attack a Muslim. They agreed that they would give lodgings for three days to any traveler, including Muslims, and dress in recognizably Christian attire. And in exchange for these and a handful of other very benign considerations, the Christians would receive "safe conduct" in all aspects of their daily lives. These contents of the so-called Pact of Umar, the caliph who was then in power, represent a policy remarkably similar in its general terms to European Christian treatment of non-Christians.

What was the general picture of Islam's westward spread?

Rapid as Islam's spread was during the reigns of Muhammad's four immediate successors, the Rightly Guided Caliphs, it enjoyed still more dramatic expansion during the

Makkah *Masjid* is one of the oldest mosques in Hyderabad, India. Islam expanded quickly into what is now Pakistan, and over several centuries into much of present-day India.

subsequent fifty years or so. Under the earliest caliphs of the Umayyad dynasty, Muslim armies pushed westward across North Africa, rooting out the last vestiges of Byzantine power in Carthage, and had crossed the Straits of Gibraltar by 711. In Spain they encountered and defeated the Arian Visigoths of King Roderick. Within eight years they had established an administrative center in the city of Cordoba, and by 732 the Muslim armies had crossed the Pyrenees into France. There Charles Martel halted their advance at the Battle of Tours and Poitiers and forced an eventual retreat into Spain. But the Muslim foothold in Andalusia (Southern Iberia) was firm and marked the beginning of a significant presence lasting nearly eight centuries.

What are some key events in Islam's eastward expansion?

The very year the Muslims crossed into Spain, far to the east the Umayyad armies had conquered Sind in present-day Pakistan. The eastern campaign had consolidated earlier gains in Persia and moved further into Central Asia and on east through what is now Afghanistan. Muslim armies stood near the northwestern quarter of present-day India, but it would be several centuries before Islam would become a presence in India proper. Most importantly the process of Islamization was well under way in ancient urban centers of West and Central Asia such as Samarqand and Bukhara along the Great Silk Road.

Why were the early Muslims so successful in spreading Islam? Was it a political rather than "missionary" movement?

Back in the center of the caliphate, the Umayyads, buoyed by their capture of Sicily and the historic city of Chalcedon, laid a protracted but unsuccessful siege to Constantinople. Surviving yet another Umayyad attack thirty years later, that city would stand for more than another seven centuries. The first great Muslim dynasty had made extraordinary gains in one of the most spectacular three-front advances ever mounted. However, the rapidity of military conquest and expansive political domination should not lead one to conclude that suddenly the whole of the known world had converted to Islam. It was not primarily missionary zeal that motivated the troops, but the promise of adventure and booty. That is not to say that their leaders entirely avoided the rhetoric of heavenly reward for bringing the world into the embrace of Islam. But on the whole, desire for conversion was secondary at best. In fact the Umayyads established a system of taxation under which non-Muslims paid a revenue over and above that expected of Muslims; while it may have encouraged non-Muslims to convert for financial reasons, it gave the conquerors a like incentive to leave the subject (conquered) peoples a measure of religious liberty.

How did the early Muslim administrations deal with non-Muslim subjects? Did they allow freedom of religion?

Under the Umayyads Muslim rule developed a policy begun under Umar that defined the socio-religious category of *dhimmi* (also *ahl adh-dhimma*, protected minority). Non-

23

The Great Umayyad Mosque of Damascus was built on the site where once stood a Christian basilica dedicated to John the Baptist (whose shrine is the small domed structure). Muslims consider John the Baptist to be a prophet.

Muslims who chose not to convert enjoyed basic rights and freedom of worship so long as they paid a "poll tax" (*jizya*, JIZ-ya) in addition to the universally levied land tax (*kharaj*, KHA-raj). The poll tax was a carryover from both the Roman and Sasanian practices. In addition, Muslims were required to pay the *zakat*, legally prescribed alms and one of the "Five Pillars," while non-Muslims were not. For legal purposes this protected status meant that Jews and Christians were answerable to their own religions' jurisdictions rather than to Islamic religious law. In the Iranian territories, the *dhimmis* included Zoroastrians as well, and eventually Hindus too were brought under the umbrella of "dhimmitude" because they possessed their own sacred scriptures.

How much freedom did non-Muslims enjoy under Muslim rule?

Non-Muslims were—and still are in some places—under a number of significant restrictions. They were forbidden to proselytize and had to wear clothing that identified their confessional membership. They could repair their ritual sites but could not build new ones, ride horses, or bear arms. In some historical settings the restrictions were enforced onerously, but in many cases *dhimmis* enjoyed considerable latitude. *Dhimmis* were distinguished from idolaters, who were indeed treated without religious toleration and left the choice of fleeing, converting, or fearing for their lives. Jews and Christians did not enjoy what is now considered wide open religious freedom under Islamic rule. Even so, it was in general a far better state of affairs than what Jews or even Christian minority groups often experienced at the hands of majority Christian regimes such as the Byzantine or Spanish Catholic.

What specific role did the Shia play in the fortunes of the Umayyad dynasty?

Animosity intensified between the Umayyads and the Shia, those who had supported the caliphate of Ali. Problems dated back at least to the suspicion that Ali had been involved in the murder of the third caliph, Uthman, who belonged to the Umayyad clan. But in 680, Shia-Umayyad relations degenerated still further. Ali's son Husayn had decided to press his claim to rule by marching a small armed band out to meet the troops of the Umayyad Caliph Yazid. The Umayyad army slaughtered the badly outnumbered Shia entourage at Karbala just south of Baghdad and in the process made Husayn the Shi'i protomartyr.

Were the Shia the only major opposition to the Umayyad dynasty?

Still another faction had earlier separated from the Shia and were becoming a thorn in the side of the Umayyads. When Ali had contested the original Umayyad governor of Syria, Muawiya, to establish his legitimacy as fourth caliph in 657, the two sides fought to an apparent draw. At that point Ali decided to submit the case to human arbitration, inciting the ire of a group that insisted that the conflict should be decided by God through an appeal to the Quran alone. In anger the group decided to withdraw its support and came to be known as the "Seceders" (*khawarij*, kha-WAA-rij, plural of *khariji*,

After such a spectacular beginning, why did the first major dynasty last less than a century?

Amazing as the Umayyad dynasty was in so many ways, it suffered an untimely demise because it ultimately failed to contend with a number of social, religious, and political constituencies. The players in the drama of the fall of the Umayyad dynasty represent a fascinating cross-section of religious interests that have remained alive virtually throughout Islamic history in some form or another. First, the Umayyads had come to power largely as a result of their Meccan connections and were thus associated with a kind of Arab aristocracy. As the Muslim sphere expanded, however, the status of non-Arabs who chose to convert to Islam soon became a thorny issue. As a class they were known as "clients" (*mawali*), and as such they did not quite enjoy equality with Arab Muslims. According to some sources, Ali and the Shia had rejected such ethnic distinctions, thus winning the allegiance of some of the *mawali* and reinforcing their discontent with the Umayyads.

"those who secede"). The Kharijites had argued a hard line on membership in the community, claiming only non-sinners were true Muslims. They would come to regard the Umayyads as godless rulers, and hence as un-Muslim and unfit to lead.

What other forces worked to undermine the Umayyad dynasty?

In their military operations, the Umayyads had always had to depend on Arab tribal forces. But that in turn meant choosing sides between traditionally implacable enemies, the northern Qays tribes and the southern Kalb tribes. Opting to bring the Qays with them to Damascus, the Umayyads earned the undying enmity of the Kalb forces then encamped in the garrison cities of Iraq. One of those garrisons was Kufa, a stronghold of the Shia; another was Basra, a stronghold of the Khawarij. In such places discontent fed on itself. Medina, meanwhile, remained the home of prophetic tradition and of religionists convinced they had inherited the custody of Muhammad's authentic legacy. They looked on the Umayyads with suspicion and shared the view of other groups that the rulers were religiously unfit. So, for very different reasons, did small but increasingly important groups of ascetics. From their perspective, the Umayyads had assumed the mantle of royalty and

attempted to justify a lifestyle utterly incompatible with the simplicity they associated with Muhammad's leadership. Add to this volatile mix a new group of claimants to authority, and the die was cast for the Umayyads. The Abbasids, a faction that traced its lineage to an uncle of Muhammad's named Abbas, now emerged to take advantage of the internal strife. Using a network of propagandists spread across the impossibly extended Umayyad realm, the Abbasids succeeded in making allies among enough of the disaffected parties to eventually undermine the caliphate. By the mid-740s, the caliphate was doomed and in 750 the Abbasids stepped in to inaugurate a regime that would last, at least nominally, for over five centuries.

Were there any other important internal conflicts during the very early years of Islamic history?

Transitions in leadership are rarely orderly. That is especially true when the struggle involves forging the very institutions that alone can insure orderly transfer of power.

An early forteenth-century folio from the *Book of History* by Balami shows the election of Uthman ibn Affan as the third "rightly guided caliph." Under his leadership, Islam spread into Iran, Afghanistan, and Armenia.

Early Islamic history saw the development of numerous factions squaring off with claims to succession. Most notably, a series of four "civil wars" were testimony to considerable intra-Muslim fragmentation during the seventh and early eighth centuries. Lasting some five years (656–661), the "first *fitna*" ("dissension") began with the death of Uthman (third "rightly guided" caliph) and saw protracted struggle between his relatives and supporters over Ali's legitimacy as fourth caliph. An even more extended conflict (second *fitna*) began in 680 when a resurgent Shi'i community sought to overthrow the second caliph of the (Sunni) Umayyad dynasty (661–750). After the Shia suffered a catastrophic defeat at Karbala (southern Iraq), and the martyrdom of Ali's son Husayn, twelve years of strife saw further conflict both between the Shia and the Umayyads and within the Shia, with the Kharijites continuing their rebellious ways. This war ended in 692, and for the next fifty years or so, the Umayyad caliphs in Damascus managed to hold the expanding Muslim realm together. But as their ability to maintain control over an increasingly far-flung administration dwindled, the Umayyads came under duress from various Muslim factions in the third civil war (744–750). The result was the rise of the Abbasids, ruling from their newly founded capital, Baghdad. But within seventy years or so, the Abbasids too began to suffer from internal factionalism, involving vicious infighting within the caliph's own family as well as rebellion featuring the Shia, the Kharijites, and a host of other special interests. The fourth civil war had begun in 809, with the death of the famous Caliph Harun ar-Rashid and ended in 819 when his son Mamun wrested power from the rebels as well as his own brother.

How did early leadership of the Shia unfold?

Major differences between what evolved into the two largest segments of Shi'ites began to crystallize around the second half of the eighth century. Until that time, Shi'i Muslims were in general agreement in recognizing the leadership authority of a hereditary succession of six descendants of Muhammad, beginning with Ali and his two sons, Hasan and Husayn. They called these figures *imams*. All Shi'ites acknowledged these first three *imams*, as well as the following three. Jafar as-Sadiq, the sixth in that line, designated his son Ismail to be his successor, but when Ismail pre-deceased his father (in 760), a crisis arose. Despite the fact that Jafar then designated a younger son, Musa, some continued to insist on Ismail's legitimacy even though he had died. Others pledged their allegiance to Musa and a rift in the Shi'ite community opened. Followers of Ismail regarded him as the "final" imam and saw his death as a temporary departure. This group came to be called the "Seveners" or "Ismailis." They in turn eventually divided into more than one subgroup. Today Seveners live, for example, in East Africa, Pakistan, and India. The largest of the groups acknowledges the Aga Khan as its leader.

How did the alternative interpretation of Shia history develop?

The majority of Shi'ites hold another interpretation of the events of the 760s, arguing that Jafar's designation of younger son Musa abrogated his earlier designation of the deceased Ismail. Those who acknowledged Musa's leadership would follow a line of suc-

In addition to the central notion of spiritual descendants from the Prophet (*imams*), both Twelver and Sevener views of history are distinctly millennialist in tone. Though there are some important differences in how they have elaborated their theologies, both have historically looked forward to the return or reemergence of the last (i.e., seventh or twelfth) imam. He will establish then an age of justice in which all believers will reap the rewards of the redemptive suffering of the imam's extended family (especially for Twelvers) or from the imam's healing arcane knowledge (a classical Sevener notion). Sunni tradition also looks forward to the advent of a *Mahdi* (guided one) at the end of time, but there the idea is not so fundamental as in Shi'i tradition.

cession all the way to a twelfth imam. Their theological interpretation of history says that in about 874 C.E., the twelfth imam went into a "lesser concealment," a period during which he communicated to his followers through a series of four representatives (*wakil*, wa-KEEL). In 940 C.E., the last of those spokespersons died without having appointed a successor. Since the imam was no longer actively communicating, Twelver Shi'ites call that date the beginning of the "greater concealment," a condition that obtains to this day. These Twelvers, also called imamis or Jafaris, constitute by far the largest Shi'ite group and account for over ninety per cent of Iran's population and just over half the population of Iraq. Twelver Shi'ism became the state religion of Iran in the early sixteenth century.

In brief, what are the most important early Islamic sectarian movements?

Immediately upon Muhammad's death Muslims had to face the question of succession to leadership of the community. One faction claimed that the Prophet had designated his cousin and son-in-law, Ali, as his successor. They were to become known as the Party or Faction (*Shi'a*) of Ali, and today their various sub-communities are called Shi'i Muslims or Shi'ites. But a majority held that Muhammad had made no such appointment and that it was up to the elders to choose from among themselves. They considered their course of action to be both in keeping with the example of Muhammad (called his *Sunna*, SUN-na) and in the spirit of the needs of the whole community (*jama'a*, ja-MAA-ah) of Muslims. This majority group came to be known as the People of the Sunna and the Assembly (*Ahl as-sunna wa-l'jama'ah*), or Sunni Muslims for short.

Several other sects made their views known early on. When Ali was doing battle with the Umayyads to claim his rights to the caliphate, a number of his troops seceded on the grounds that Ali was too lax in his appeal to religious principles in the conduct of battle. They judged Ali a serious sinner who was no longer worthy of the name Muslim. That group became known as the Kharijites (or *Khawarij*, "those who secede"), and a small remnant of their several factions live today largely in Oman on the Persian Gulf. A variety of other groups also expressed their opinions as to how far one might go in judging another person's suitability for true membership in the Muslim community. One of the more influential believed that only God could judge a person's soul and that it was therefore best to postpone judgment on the matter. They were known as the Mur-ji'ites or "Postponers," because they "put off" until God's judgment any attempt to evaluate other people's spiritual status before God.

Major Figures in Early Islamic History

Name	Significance
Muhammad (d. 632)	Son of Amina and Abd Allah, clan of Hashim, last prophet
Khadija (d. 619)	Muhammad's first wife (and only wife during her lifetime), mother of Fatima
Fatima (d. 633)	Most important of Muhammad's children, wife of Ali, matriarch of the Shia, mother of the first two *imams* (Hasan, Husayn)
Abu Bakr (d. 634)	Father-in-law of Muhammad, first Rightly Guided Caliph
Aisha (d. 678)	Daughter of Abu Bakr, youngest wife of the Prophet, influential in early "civil war" episodes
Ali (d. 661)	Cousin of Muhammad, husband of Fatima, first Shia imam, fourth Rightly Guided Caliph (Sunni view)
Umar (d. 644)	Important Companion, second Rightly Guided Caliph
Uthman (d. 656)	Important Companion, third Rightly Guided Caliph
Muawiya (d. 680)	Brother-in-law of Muhammad, "founder" of Umayyad dynasty in Damascus
Husayn (d. 680)	Grandson of Muhammad, most-revered Shia martyr killed at Karbala (Iraq)

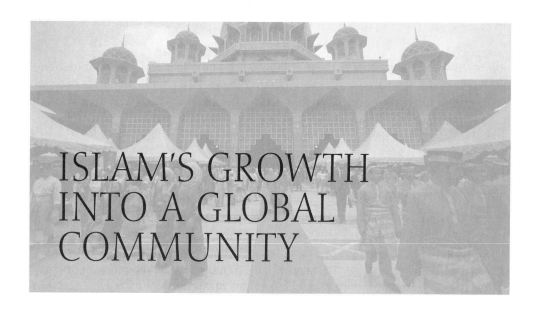

ISLAM'S GROWTH INTO A GLOBAL COMMUNITY

Many non-Muslims seem to assume (if not insist) that Islam was, and continues to be, always and everywhere "spread by the sword." Is this historically accurate?

Unfortunately, even highly placed and influential non-Muslims, such as Pope Benedict XVI in 2006, still make dramatic pronouncements to the effect that everything Muhammad taught was evil and inhumane and that it is a simple historical fact that Islam was spread by violence. A great deal of concrete historical data tells a very different story. The assumption that Islam spread so dramatically because Arab-Muslim armies moving out of Arabia, northward into the central Middle East (Syria, Iraq, Jordan, and Palestine), eastward into present-day Iran, and westward across North Africa, offered conquered peoples the stark option of conversion or death, is seriously flawed. It presupposes an equation between military domination and subjugation to *governance by Muslim invaders* on the one hand, and being forced to *become Muslim* on the other hand. On the contrary, Muslim military policy did not force conversion and in fact mandated that once the invaded territory's authorities accepted terms of peace (often without major loss of life to the general populace), the Muslim armies retreated to newly established garrison cities rather than leave a large footprint on existing cities and towns. Muslim taxation policy also made it financially advantageous for the conquerors *not* to convert subject peoples *en masse*, since that would remove the poll tax imposed on non-Muslims.

If Muslims didn't systematically force the conversion of peoples they conquered, how did these conquered territories become predominantly Muslim?

Recent studies concerning rates of conversion suggest nothing like a meteoric acceptance of Islamic faith. By around 750, 130 years after the death of Muhammad, the population of Persia (Iran) appears to have been around 10 percent Muslim, while at about the same time the populations of much of the Central Middle East (Greater Syria and Iraq) were no more than 20 percent Muslim. A century later (c. 850), Persia's Muslims numbered around 50 percent of the population. Two-and-a-half centuries later (c. 1096), on the eve of the first Crusade, the population of the central (Arab) Middle East was evidently still less than 50 percent Muslim. In other words, it seems to have taken nearly half a millennium for Muslims to become the clear religious majority in the lands conquered in the earliest invasions by Muslim armies.

How can one organize the huge topic of global Islamic history to make this difficult topic more manageable?

One good organizing concept is that of "culture spheres." It makes it possible to imagine large swaths of history and geography by thinking of somewhat overlapping areas of the globe, but recognizing each by its distinctive characteristics in a group of shared categories. For example, all of the five Islamic "culture spheres" have unique configurations of the following: First, a dominant religious school of law or "denomination"; second, a distinctive tone of popular spirituality or dominant Sufi order(s); third, signature racial or ethnic elements; fourth, a unique history or understanding of the region's past; fifth, special geography or demography; and finally, languages that predominate in culture or administrative structures.

What are these culture spheres?

The five spheres, or realms, are as follows: 1) the Arabicate, the oldest historically, in which the Arabic language has been a strong influence on other tongues (such as Swahili), even when Arabic is no longer the dominant tongue; 2) the Persianate, second in antiquity, with Persian casting as long a shadow as Arabic in its sphere; 3) the Turkic, originating in Central Asia and expanding westward with Turkish migrations; 4) the Southeast Asian Malay, where in addition to a blend of Arabicate and Persianate features, Malayo-Polynesian languages predominate; and 5) the Black African, with a host of indigenous sub-Saharan languages. A sixth large, more generic and amorphous sphere, whose Muslim populations are distinctly minorities, would be "Europe and the Americas," and will be treated separately below and in other chapters.

THE ARABICATE SPHERE

How would one describe the Arabicate culture sphere? And why not just call it "Arabic"?

With its center more or less in Egypt, the Arabicate sphere stretches eastward across the Central Middle East nations of Jordan, Syria, Lebanon, Palestine, Iraq, and the numerous nation-states of the Arabian Peninsula, the land of Islam's birth. Toward the west, it stretches across North Africa, encompassing Libya, Tunisia, Algeria, Morocco, with their Berber and Tuareg ethnicities and non-Semitic languages, as well as the historically crucial cultures of Islamic Spain, or Andalusia. South of Egypt, it includes not only Arabic speaking lands, such as Sudan and Somalia, but also the Swahili populations of Kenya and other parts of East Africa. Numerous smaller Islam-related communities such as the Alawis, Nusayris, and Druze are largely unique to the central part of this sphere, and significant Shi'i populations, including a slight majority in Iraq, are important in the religious mix, especially on the eastern fringe of the sphere. In this very diverse sphere, all four Sunni law schools are well-represented: the Maliki dominant in the western reaches, the Shafi'i and Hanafi more prevalent in the central areas, the Hanbali in the Arabian Peninsula, and the Shi'i schools important in Iraq and parts of the Persian Gulf coast. Finally, why not just "Arabic"? Because Arab(ic) *influence* in this sphere extends far beyond the actual dominance of Arabic as a language and pure Arab ethnicity and includes regions deeply *influenced* by Arab language and culture over many centuries.

How did the first Islamic "dynasty," the Umayyads, come into being?

In 656, after the murder of Uthman, the third Rightly Guided Caliph, Muhammad's cousin and son-in-law, Ali, acceded to the office of caliph, but not to universal acclaim. One group that opposed him was led by Aisha, one of the Prophet's wives, but this relatively weak faction was defeated in 656. Members of the Umayyad clan also refused to acknowledge Ali as caliph, thus sparking the first of several civil wars within the young Muslim community. A member of that clan, named Muawiya, a cousin of Uthman, was governor of the ancient city of Damascus when Ali and Muawiya's forces engaged in battle at Siffin. After fighting to a draw, Ali agreed to human mediation, thus alienating a group of his supporters who insisted that anyone who thus failed to trust in God alone was not a true Muslim. They "seceded" from the Shia, and these "seceders" (or Kharijites) became set on overthrowing Ali. In 659, a council of elders (*shura*) ruled against Ali's claims, thus further sealing a shift in which the Sunnis leaned decisively toward Muawiya's counterclaim. The First Civil War (*fitna*, dissension) ended in 661 when a Kharijite murdered Ali, clearing the way for Muawiya to become the first Umayyad caliph. Previously, the first three Rightly Guided Caliphs had ruled from their capital in Medina, after which Ali shifted his center of power to the former garrison town of Kufa in Iraq. Wanting to establish their own seat of authority, the Umayyads moved the capital to Damascus, thus signaling an important departure from Islam's land of origin and a deliberate opening to the greater Middle East.

How did the Abbasid dynasty originate?

Within the early years of Abbasid rule, the first two caliphs consolidated power against rivals, some of whom had been their collaborators against the Umayyads. Then there was the problem of the Umayyads themselves, which the first Abbasid caliph tried to solve by exterminating the dynasty's surviving elites. One of them, the story goes, managed to escape to Iberia, and there laid the foundation for an Andalusian extension of Umayyad rule in Spain. Meanwhile, back in Iraq, by 756 the Abbasid family had been firmly established as the ruling dynasty. The family traced its ancestral legitimacy to Muhammad's uncle Abbas, hence the name Abbasids, descendants of Abbas. It was Caliph

What were some of the greatest achievements of the Umayyads?

Muawiyah (r. 661–680) appointed strong governors over newly conquered territories, developed a highly refined system of diplomacy to keep the peace, and slowly increased the expanse of military expeditions. The caliph exchanged his power base in the tribal coalitions for a centralized monarchy and further expanded the military and administrative power of the state. Numerous factions continued to undermine his rule, however, and upon his death in 682, the Second Civil War (682–692) broke out with several groups fighting for power against Muawiya's son, Yazid (r. 680–683) and later by Caliph Abd al-Malik ibn Marwan (r. 685–705). Again the Shia reasserted themselves and promoted the cause of Ali's younger son, Husayn, but he became the first Shi'i martyr in 680 against the Umayyad general Yazid at Karbala (in southern Iraq). Again the Kharijis also rebelled, engaging in guerilla warfare with small armed bands, arguing that they were the only true Muslims. In time, Abd al-Malik brought the empire under Umayyad control through force, in turn weakening the dynasty further by stimulating still more factional discontent. Abd al-Malik remains, however, best known for creating the stunningly beautiful Dome of the Rock mosque in Jerusalem, completed in 692. His successors also expanded the empire westward all the way to Gibraltar and southern Iberia by 711 and inland to France by 732; and eastward as far as the Indus River in what is now Pakistan. During a Third Civil War in 743, anti-Umayyad forces gathered steam, undermining the regime and ending it definitively in 750.

al-Mansur (r. 754–775) who decided he needed a distinctive seat of power by distancing the Abbasids from the first dynastic capitol of Damascus. Emulating the royal dynasties of Sasanian (and Zoroastrian) Persia, he selected a site not far from Ctesiphon, a Persian royal palace in central Iraq—a statement not only that they would act like kings (though they had denounced the Umayyads for that very affectation), but that Islamic rule was now to be centered squarely in conquered territory in very new surroundings. There they founded the new city of Baghdad, proclaiming with its innovative round plan that it would be a symbol of openness to the wider world. It soon outgrew not only its Persian archetype, Ctesiphon, but Constantinople as well.

What are some of the signature features of the Abbasid dynasty?

The Abbasids looked back to the example of the legendary Umayyad Caliph Umar II in promoting the equality of all Muslims. Recruiting capable bureaucrats from across the empire, they organized new armies and new groups of administrators with the specific intent of weakening a prior pattern of privileging the Arab elite. Since the Umayyad armies had already expanded Muslim administrative control across an enormous expanse of territory, the Abbasids could replace a huge expeditionary capability with a smaller force at the center and a structure of frontier forces sufficient to maintain far-flung holdings. The Abbasid shift to a new expression of global diversity manifested itself in administrative appointments: Nestorian Christians, Shi'ites, Jews, and non-Arab Muslims, were given considerable authority in an increasingly complex centralized governmental structure. For example, the Abbasids created a chancery to deal with records and correspondence, bureaus for tax collection, and a kind of "exchequer" to manage expenses of the caliphs, including the army, court, and pensioners.

How long did the Abbasid dynasty last, and how did the Abbasids manage such a vast empire?

With conquered territories stretching from North Africa through the Middle East, across Persian and Central Asia and into South Asia, the administrative task facing the Abbasids was mind-boggling in scope. The logistical challenges soon manifested themselves in the slow undermining of Baghdad's control at the periphery. Governors in the outlying provinces took advantage of the caliph's increasing inability to extract taxes to pay mounting bills in the capital and immediately surrounding lands. This included challenges maintaining the loyalty of mercenary Turkic slave-soldier troops the Abbasids preferred as palace guards (since using Arab troops would have made them vulnerable to age-old inter-tribal feuding and mutiny). Within a scant seventy-five years of its founding, the Abbasid dynasty began to lose frontier provinces as governors refused to pay taxes and declared de facto independence. By the mid-tenth century, effective Abbasid control had

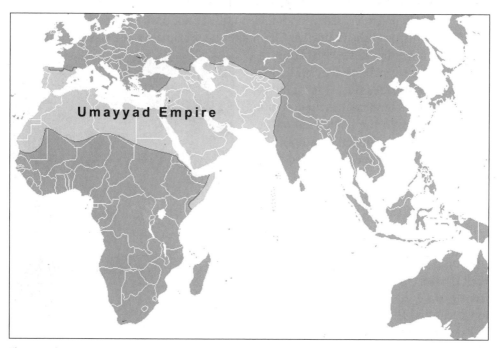

This map shows the widest extent of the Umayyad Empire around the year 750 C.E. (The country boundaries indicated are modern).

shrunk to the Central Middle East—and not the whole of that—as governors proclaimed themselves *emirs*, and *emirs* claimed the "universal" authority as caliphs and thus direct rivals to Baghdad's rule. Though some regions continued to mention the name of the "reigning" Abbasid at Friday prayers, the nod was largely an empty formality. More ominously still, in 945 a powerful Shia family called the Buyids managed to assume effective control, becoming the power behind the throne in Baghdad.

What are some of the key turning points in Abbasid history?

In 1055, invading Saljuqid Turks took Baghdad and created a two-track administrative structure in which a (Saljuqid Turkish) Sultan wielded actual temporal power, reducing the (Abbasid Arab) caliph to the role of a largely symbolic spiritual authority. The Saljuqids had converted to Sunni Islam in Central Asia and had as one of their goals the eradication of Shi'i power, and to that end they began a system of higher educational institutions called *madrasas*, a development that spread rapidly in other political regimes as well. A succession of smaller dynasties continued to rule a much diminished Baghdad, all nominally acknowledging the Abbasid caliph's authority, until an invasion by Mongol descendants of Genghis Khan in 1258 sealed the fate of the Abbasids. Various other dynasties continued to claim the title of caliph until the early twentieth century, but the office remained largely ceremonial.

What are the origins and early history of the Crusades?

Muslims had occupied Jerusalem since 638, but it was not until 1095 that Pope Urban II called for a crusade at the Council of Clermont. One proximate cause was the defeat of a

Byzantine force by a Turkish army at Manzikert in eastern Anatolia in 1071. That Saljuqid Turkish expeditionary force represented the first significant incursion of a Muslim power into the home land of the Byzantine Empire. Under Muslim rule, Christians were allowed to practice their faith. Stories that the invaders had desecrated Christian spaces and mistreated Christians gradually fueled conviction that Christians needed to respond in force. Then Emperor Alexis I of Constantinople asked the pope for help, and his call led to the First Crusade. Composed largely of knights from France and Italy, the first Crusader force set off in 1096 and eventually arrived in Palestine. The force captured Antioch in 1098 and Jerusalem in July 1099. A slaughter of Muslims and Jews ensued, and the

Pope Urban II (r. 1088 to 1099) was the first Christian leader to call for a crusade to the Holy Land. The First Crusade lasted from 1096 to 1099 C.E.

Crusaders established the so-called Latin Kingdom of Jerusalem. When Turkish troops moved into Edessa, Syria, Christian Europe responded with the ultimately unsuccessful Second Crusade in 1147. Christian hold on the Latin Kingdom began to weaken and finally fell to a Kurdish Muslim general named Saladin (Salah ad-Din). He retook Jerusalem in 1187, beginning the Ayyubid dynasty. He treated the Christians there very well and historical sources suggest that the non-Muslim population held Saladin in high regard. Christian loss of Jerusalem led to the Third Crusade in 1189, in which Christian forces made limited territorial gains, but Christian pilgrims were granted free access to Jerusalem. During the following century or so, Christian forces suffered steady erosion and considerable defeats, and by the Sixth Crusade, the Mamluk dynasty had driven all remaining Crusaders out of Syria-Palestine.

Major Crusades in Middle East/North Africa/Spain
Seven from 1095 to 1291, others later [not formally numbered]

Campaigns in	Dates	Crusaders/Land	Main Leaders	Battles/Results
Palestine	1099–1101	Lorrain and Provençe	Godfrey, Raymond	Jerusalem/Latin Kingdom 1099–1189
Syria	1147–1149	France, Germany	Louis VII, Conrad III	Damascus
Palestine	1191–1192	England, France	Richard I, Philip II	Acre truce 1191, Christian access to Jerusalem
Meant to take Jerusalem via Egypt	1202–1204	Western Europe esp. Venice and France	Enrico Dandolo, Boniface I,	Constantinople becomes center of Latin Empire 1204–1261
Egypt	1218–1221	France	Jean de Brienne	Damietta taken 1219 (briefly)
Egypt	1248–1250	French	Louis IX	Damietta 1249 (briefly)
Tunisia	1270	France	Louis IX, Charles of Anjou	Carthage 1270
Egypt	1365	Venice, Cyprus	Pierre de Lusignan	Alexandria looted
Spain: Southern Castille	1212–1266	Reconquista Aragon, Castille	Alfonso VII, James I	Cordova, Seville Murcia retaken
Spain: Granada	1462–1492	Castille, Aragon	Ferdinand II	Gibraltar, Malaga, Granada Muslims expelled

How would one characterize Christian attitudes toward Muslims during the early years of Muslim expansion and the Crusade era?

As Islam expanded into the central Middle East and parts of the Byzantine Empire, Christians generally did not regard the Arabs as different than other invading groups. At first they referred to the invaders "ethnically" as Arabs, culturally and religiously as Agarenes (descendants of Hagar, Abraham's "slave" wife) and later Saracen (from the Greek *Sara kenos*, "Sarah's progeny," implying descent from Abraham's wife Sarah). During the Crusades, the name "Saracens" came to refer to their enemies more specifically as Muslims. In Spain and North Africa, Christians referred to Muslims as "Moors," and beginning with the era of the Crusades, the term "Turk" became more prominent and continued well in to late medieval and Renaissance times. During periods in which anti-Muslim fervor was especially intense, Muslims became the *Barbari* (barbarians/enemies). In general, Christians during late antiquity and early medieval times had virtually no clear notion of Islamic history and beliefs. Widespread views of the "enemy" were spread by literary works such as the *Chansons de Geste* ("Songs of Deeds"), popular poems, and works of epic adventure and romance in which Christian heroes dealt crushing blows to the foe. At a more refined level, many Christian scholars across the Mediterranean developed more sophisticated and, generally speaking, more accurate estimates of Islamic beliefs. On the whole, Christians regarded the areas under Muslim rule as outside the civilized world and as fields ripe for the harvest of conversion.

What are some further details about Islam's religious expansion in the Central Middle East?

Ninth-century Baghdad was a critical focal point in this respect, because of cultural and religious ferment in the still relatively new capital of the Abbasid dynasty. There were

What was the fate of medieval Christian pilgrims to the Holy Land?

Many Christians learned about Islam and Muslims by visiting Muslim lands on pilgrimage to holy sites. In an unusual, early ninth-century collaboration, Charlemagne and the Abbasid Caliph Harun ar-Rashid made arrangements for a hostel for the pilgrims in Jerusalem, which had been under Muslim control for nearly two centuries by this time. By the eleventh century, Muslim rulers allowed a fairly steady flow of Christian pilgrims, owing arguably to generally positive attitudes of Muslim rulers towards Christians. During the early period of the Crusades, some sources suggest it may have been difficult to differentiate between pilgrim and crusader. In the early thirteenth century, Francis of Assisi traveled to Damietta (Egypt) in hopes of converting the Ayyubid dynasty caliph. Earlier on, pilgrims generally did not expect to find anything of value in Islam or among the Muslim people, but after the thirteenth century, interest in Islam grew. From the fifteenth century on, European travelers' accounts about Muslims proliferated, and though understandably skewed by their negative preconceptions, many reports noted praiseworthy aspects of the religion and human qualities of its people.

conversions of Christians and Jews during this time period, for three main reasons: 1) fear of discrimination and even persecution; 2) relief from the *jizya*, or poll tax, levied on non-Muslims; and 3) enhancement of social standing within an Islamic society. The conversion rate was more rapid here than elsewhere generally in the Middle East. One estimate has it that the Muslim population in central Iraq grew from 18 percent in 800 to 50 percent in 882. This was not the result, however, of any discernible systematic missionary effort on the part of the Muslims.

What is known about early Muslim-Christian relationships in the Central Middle East?

Three documents of the period sum up Muslim-Christian relationships: a letter from Abd Allah ibn Ismail al-Hashimi (a Muslim) to Abd al-Masih ibn Ishaq al-Kindi (a Christian); al-Kindi's letter of response; and a treatise on Islam by Ali ibn Rabban al-Tabari, a convert from Christianity. All three documents operate on a theoretically elevated level, discussing the validity of theological issues such as the Trinity and Muhammad's prophethood. These documents show the widespread contact between Muslims and Christians, and reflect that, though there were radical Muslim groups that did not hesitate to use intimidation and even military threat to convert Christians, the majority of inter-religious encounters were peaceful and focused on a discussion of religious truths rather than violence.

How were relations among Christians and Arab Muslims in the Holy Lands before the Crusade era?

By the end of the tenth century, Palestine had different religious groups living within its borders. The relationship among these groups was marked by tolerance and interdependence, exemplified in the burgeoning, multivalent trade system. Communal celebrations were common and continued despite the Crusades. The demographic composition of Palestine changed with the arrival of Sunni Turks in 1065. These Turks harassed both pro-Fatimid Ismaili Muslims and their sympathizers (Jews, Christians). With the landscape shifted, the relationship between Muslims and Christians grew colder, though certainly not to the degree described in many European "reporters," most notably William of Tyre. The vituperative language used to describe Muslims in crusader memoirs was often hyperbolic. As the control of the Holy Land shifted from Muslim to Christian and back, distrust grew on both sides, and conversion and apostasy became huge issues for inhabitants of each faith. There was, however, little sign of forced conversions, and many times there were instances of an amalgamation of the cultures. Christian Franks adopted Muslim fashion and married Muslim women (who often converted to Christianity). Such "arabacized" Christians were regarded poorly by both Muslims and new European visitors; they were seen as half-Christians, an epithet from either a Christian or Muslim perspective. Muslims did hold Christian knights in high regard for their bravery and Christian monks for their piety, but held the everyday Frank living in Palestine in low esteem.

On the whole, the Crusades irreparably disrupted the peaceful coexistence of Muslims and Christians in the Holy Land.

What is known about Christian conversion to Islam and Christian-Muslim relations in medieval Spain?

From very early in Iberian Muslim history, Christianity was a "protected religion" under Muslim rulers. Historians are virtually unanimous that there was no early proselytizing or persecution of Christians by Muslims (the conversion rate during the eighth century was about 5 percent). An important ingredient in Christian–Muslim relations in eighth- and ninth-century Spain is known as the "adoptionist controversy," a proper understanding of which is useful here. "Adoptionism" in this instance refers to the notion that Jesus was the "adoptive" (not the *actual*) son of God. Some Christian leaders of the time attributed the prevalence of that notion in Spain to the influence of Muslim theology, with its belief that Jesus is neither divine nor the "actual" son of God. Pope Hadrian I believed that the controversy was a result of "too much association with the Jews and Muslims." Charlemagne, who had clashed with Muslims on a political and military level, opposed the controversy violently. He blamed it on the Muslims, and, in a letter to a Spanish Christian aristocrat, said that if the Spanish held to adoptionism, they would not receive "appropriate" help (i.e., military aid to fight the Muslims) from the Franks.

Does this view still prevail?

Historians now tend to argue that the low conversion rates during the early centuries of Muslim rule in Iberia militate against the view that Muslim influence exacerbated the wayward tendencies of "adoptionist" Spanish Christians; in other words, those Church authorities were reacting out of fear of Islam. During the eleventh century, the situation was in a way reversed: Islamic theology reflects a feeling of alienation and deep fear of Muslim apostasy and conversion to Christianity. These fears were provoked by the increased missionary work by the Cluniac monks in Spain and a degree of heteropraxy among Muslims. With the capture of Toledo in 1085, the Muslims were no longer invincible in Spain, and the Christian motivation for fighting was "no longer for the collection of tribute, but for the restoration of the land of St. Peter." Conflict thus became more explicitly religious and not purely political. When the Moroccan Almoravid Muslim dynasty filled the political vacuum in Spain in 1086, they won a decisive victory at Zallayah, provoking an all-out war by the Christians against Islam in the Iberian Peninsula and the East. The Christians wanted Muslims to be baptized, while the Muslims wanted King Alfonso VI to accept Islam. Christians had come to prefer war against the Muslims to dialogue with them.

How did North Africa become Islamized?

Muslim armies conquered the coastal regions of what are now Libya, Tunisia, Algeria, and Morocco during a long drive that ended with Umayyad troops crossing to Gibraltar in 711.

During the eighth century, much of that vast region remained in control of independent tribes of diverse ethnicity. Itinerant Kharijites managed to convert many Berbers (a major ethnic group) to their brand of "puritanical" Islam with its centripetal tendency to dissociate itself from central rule in Damascus and later Baghdad. But in 800, the first of many indigenous Muslim dynasties was founded by Ibrahim ibn al-Aghlab, after whom a line of hereditary governors were named "Aghlabids." Around 868 they declared "officially" their independence from the caliphate. They encountered their first serious competition with the rise of the Fatimid dynasty, whose founding figures traced their origins to the early Ismaili (aka Sevener) Shi'ites, hard-core opponents of

Ruins of a Fatimid castle in Ajdabiya, Libya. The Fatimid caliphate covered much of northern African and the Middle East, lasting from 909 to 1171 C.E.

Abbasid central rule in Baghdad. They were more politically activist than the Twelvers, who had effectively deferred hope of righteous rule until the Twelfth imam would emerge from Occultation (Concealment) as the *Mahdi*, Guided One, at the end of time. Convinced that there would always be an imam present and active in the world, the Fatimids (that is, "descendants of Fatima," Muhammad's daughter) pursued a vigorous missionary agenda of *da'wa* ("inviting" to Islam). Around 909, Ubayd Allah proclaimed himself the new imam, thus launching the Fatimid caliphate and beginning the conquest of what are now Algeria, Tunisia, Libya, and Egypt. In 969, the Fatimids founded the city of Cairo, from which they ruled the region until 1171, effectively cutting it off from the Abbasid caliphate.

How did the history of the central Arabicate Sphere unfold thereafter?

Among the numerous dynasties and political regimes that ruled throughout the Mediterranean and central and south Asia, several stand out. In Egypt, Saladin's Sunni Ayyubid dynasty (1171–1250) supplanted the Fatimids and was in turn overthrown by the Mamluk dynasty (1250–1517). The Mamluks presided over two and a half centuries of relative peace and prosperity throughout the central Middle East, ruling Egypt and Libya as well as much of "Greater Syria." They were patrons of the arts and architecture on a grand scale under whom Cairo, especially, grew into a worthy rival of any great Mediterranean city. The Ottoman Turks (1300–1921) succeeded the Mamluks as they expanded to conquer most of the former Byzantine empire and more. To the east, the Safavid dynasty (1501–1722) replaced the descendants of Genghis Khan, who had ruled Iraq and Iran for 250 years. Establishing Twelver Shi'i Islam as the official creed of the realm, the Safavids created splendid art and architecture in cities such as Isfahan.

THE PERSIANATE SPHERE

What is the Persianate sphere? And why not just call it "Persian"?

As the name suggests, at the core of this sphere are Persian language and ethnicity centered historically on the Iranian plateau. Its western reaches begin in eastern Iraq and stretch northward into the Caucasus, eastward across present-day Iran, through Afghanistan and parts of Pakistan, and north of there to cover much of Central Asia, overlapping historically with parts of the Turkic sphere (see below). Extremely diverse ethnically and linguistically, the western half of the sphere embraces ethnic groups such as Kurds, Baluchis, and Pashtuns. The eastern half of the sphere—most of South Asia— begins in eastern Pakistan and covers the northern two-thirds of India, much of Bangladesh, and Sri Lanka. In the "Indian subcontinent" Persianate culture blended with Hindu traditions of art, architecture, and literature, and the "classical Persian" language (already much influenced by Arabic) put its stamp on other Indo-European languages such as Sindhi, Punjabi, Gujarati, and Kashmiri. Urdu, now the "national language" of Pakistan and a tongue spoken by many Indian Muslims, is a rich amalgam of Indic, Persian, and some Turkic elements. The Persianate sphere is home to a rich religious diversity: Twelver Shi'ism, especially in the western half (over 90 percent of Iranians and over half of Iraqis, for example), Ismailis sprinkled through the eastern half, and smaller religious minorities such as the Bahais and Parsees (aka Zoroastrians). In addition, Sufi orders especially associated with the Persianate sphere include Chishtis and Suhrawardis as well as distinctive Shi'i orders like the Dhahabis. The term "Persianate" is used here because there are actually several "Persian" languages and because the sphere represents the results of centuries of linguistic and cultural *influence* that go well beyond lands now typically identified as "Persian."

How did Persia become Islamized?

When Arab Muslim forces moved into the Iranian plateau in the early seventh century, various Persian Empires had already ruled the region for over a millennium. The dominant languages belonged to the large "Indo-European" family of tongues, entirely different from the Semitic Arabic of the invaders. And the dominant religious tradition was Zoroastrianism, also about a thousand years old by then. Muslim armies brought down the last of the Sasanian rulers by 653 and continued to push eastward toward central and south Asia. Under the Umayyad and early Abbasid caliphates, Muslim administrations managed Persia through regional or provincial governors (*amir*, uh-MEER). By the mid-ninth century, governors of the always restive region began to proclaim themselves independent of Baghdad. From then on, Persia was ruled by a long succession of dynasties small and large. Most prominent were the Ilkhanids (thirteenth to fourteenth centuries) and the Timurids (fourteenth to fifteenth centuries), both tracing their ancestry to Genghis Khan and holding significant positions in Central Asia. Most of what is now the nation of Iran was unified by the region's first major Shi'ite dynasty, the Safavids, in the early sixteenth century, and Iran's dominant faith tradition has been more or less "officially" that of Twelver Shi'ism ever since.

How did Islam become important in South Asia?

Early conquests brought Islam to the region of Sind, in present-day Pakistan, by 711. Over the next several centuries a succession of Muslim dynasties made occasional advances into the Punjab in northwestern India. In 1191 the Ghurid dynasty captured Delhi and established the first major Muslim presence in the heart of India and the first of a succession of sultanates to hold sway in various regions of the subcontinent. The most important of those was that of Tughluq Shah (1320–1351), who managed to unite most of northern and central India from Delhi. For the next sixty years or so the Tughluquids shared power with several other dynasties that ruled to the south, while the kings of Bengal established their independent rule over a newly Islamized population. In 1526 Babur conquered Delhi and established the Islamic Mughal dynasty, whose rule would soon encompass most of the subcontinent.

What happened to the Mughal Empire?

The Mughal dynasty (1502–1757) established Islamic rule over much of south Asia, from Afghanistan across at least the northern two-thirds of India. Babur's grandson Akbar (r. 1556–1605) was the patron of major cultural and religious developments effected through a vast network of international relations. Akbar's son Jahangir and grandson Shah Jahan continued to rule in splendor. They constructed some of the world's finest architectural creations, including the Taj Mahal, in which Shah Jahan and his wife are buried. Akbar's great grandson Aurangzeb (1658–1707) reverted to a religiously intolerant rule and presided over the beginning of the end of Mughal glory.

How did the early Muslim conquerors of South Asia deal with the subject peoples? Did they insist on conversion to Islam?

When the first of the several waves of Muslim conquest arrived in 711 (about the same time Muslims crossed over to Gibraltar and began the conquest of Spain), General Muhammad ibn Qasim's forces allowed the populace to retain its ancient faith traditions. As Muslims entered predominantly Hindu lands, the military commander explicitly declared that their temples would enjoy the status of Christian churches, Jewish synagogues, and

The Taj Mahal is a seventeenth-century tomb constructed in Agra, India, by Mughal Muslim ruler Shah Jahan as a burial place for his favorite wife.

43

Zoroastrian fire temples already under Muslim law—that is, protected. Some three centuries later, Mahmud, Muslim ruler of Ghazna in present-day Afghanistan, conquered the region of Punjab. Even in the mid-eleventh century, Muslims remained a minority in the regions under Islamic administrations. Not until the early thirteenth century— that is, a full five hundred years after the initial Muslim conquests in the region—did the Muslim population in Northern India arrive at majority status, and this occurred primarily through natural growth rather than through forced conversion.

THE TURKIC SPHERE

How would one describe the "Turkic" sphere? And why not just call it Turkish?

As with all of our "spheres," the Turkic overlaps and intersects in fascinating ways with others, especially with the Persianate and Arabicate. In the former case, the contiguity of Central Asia, Turkic ancestral homeland, fostered a natural mingling of culture and ethnicities across Persia's northeastern boundaries; and toward their northwestern borders, Persians encountered Turkic peoples already present in the Caucasus (Khazars and Bulgars). Turkic elements entered the Arabicate sphere as early as the ninth century, originally as prisoners captured in military expeditions into Central Asia and brought back to the Central Middle East as "slave soldiers" who went on to establish themselves as independent dynasties (most notably the Mamluks). Sufi spirituality gradually replaced the traditions of Shamanism, Buddhism, and Manicheanism the Turkic peoples brought with them. As the Turkic peoples moved into Anatolia, they encountered Arabic culture in Iraq and adapted elements of Byzantine culture.

How extensive is the Turkic sphere today?

Today the Turkic sphere includes not only most of the Central Asian republics formerly under Soviet control as well as Anatolia, but parts of the Balkans to the west, and of western China to the east (especially in the province of Xinjiang). In addition, Turkic influence extended importantly into South Asia, since major Muslim rulers of late medieval India traced their legitimacy to descent from another major Central Asian source, the Mongols. The dominant law school is the Hanafi, and the Mevlevis, Naqshbandis, and Halvetis are among the most important Sufi orders. The term "Turkic" is used here because of the rich diversity of tribal and linguistic components, because the linguistic and cultural *influence* of the "Turks" is not limited to the use of the Turkish tongue, and because the sphere extends well beyond what is now called Turkey.

If Central Asia is the ancestral homeland of the Turkic peoples, how did Turks come to the Middle East?

A complex development started in the ninth century when Muslim Arab armies invading Central Asia began a policy of transporting young prisoners of Turkic origin back to

How did the nation-states of India, Pakistan, and Bangladesh come about?

After about the mid-eighteenth century, European colonialism began to make inroads into lands formerly under Islamic regimes. Not until the mid-twentieth century did major colonial powers begin to withdraw, ceding political control back to indigenous populations. One dramatic example of that relatively recent change is the independence of India from Britain and the partition of India that created the Muslim state of Pakistan (1948), itself divided in 1971 into Pakistan and Bangladesh. Pakistan and Bangladesh are almost entirely Muslim, while the Muslim population of India constitutes the world's largest Islamic minority. Collectively, the Indian subcontinent is home to over one quarter of the world's Muslims.

Baghdad and other major cities to serve as palace guards. Caliphs could easily make enemies even among family and friends and found it necessary to employ troops more capable of disinterested service. Thus was born a class of people within Islamic societies, the Turkish slave soldier. From time to time the Turkish guard would rise up and take temporary control of the reins in Baghdad. On several occasions promising members of the guard would work their way up through the ranks and even be appointed to high office in a provincial post. Some took the next logical step, declaring themselves independent rulers when the caliph back in Baghdad had too much on his mind to attend to the provinces.

How did the present-day state of Turkey become Turkish?

In the mid-eleventh century, a confederation of Central Asian Turkic tribes newly converted to Sunni Islam began to migrate westward, occupying the city of Baghdad in 1055. There they established the sultanate as a temporal institution parallel to the caliphate, which they had reduced largely to a position of spiritual leadership. Moving northward through Syria and into eastern Anatolia, the Saljuqid rulers launched campaigns northward against the eastern frontier of the Byzantine Empire in Anatolia. In 1071, the Turkic expeditionary force encountered a Byzantine army at Manzikert and won a decisive victory, after which a Byzantine call for help went out to Rome, resulting in the first Crusade in 1096. Under Sultan Alp Arslan (r. 1063–1072), the Turks continued their westward conquest and established their regional capital in Konya.

By the mid-twelfth century the Saljuqid tribe established its dominance under Sultan Kilij Arslan II (r. 1153–1192). Known as the Saljuqids of Rum (i.e., "eastern Rome"), they controlled central Anatolia until 1243 from Konya, amid continuing struggles for power with another Turkic group called the Danishmendids and the Byzantines. Konya became a Sufi center with a heavily Persian cultural substrate. Sufi orders facilitated the conversion of Greek and Armenian peoples to Islam.

Two important Sufi leaders were Haji Bektash, who synthesized Sunni and Shia beliefs, and Muslim and Christian practices; and Jalal ad-Din Rumi, known as a foundational figure of the so-called "Whirling Dervishes." Mongol forces migrating through the Middle East from Central Asia invaded the area in 1242–1243. Finally, in 1280, the Saljuqid dynasty was decisively overcome by the increasingly dominant Osmali Turkic tribe, which consolidated its power through a confederation of tribes that became the basis of the Ottoman Empire.

How did the Ottomans get started as an eastern Mediterranean power?

The early Ottoman "state" arose from one of the warrior states and was led by Ertugrul (d. c. 1280) and his son Osman (aka Othman; the namesake of the Ottoman Empire). Osman's confederation was the beginning of what would become the Ottoman Empire. Ottoman sultans generally conceived of themselves as supreme rulers of all Muslims, even if they did not claim the title of caliph. Expanding out of Anatolia in 1345, they crossed to Gallipoli (on the Dardanelles strait) and from there conquered Northern Greece, Macedonia, and Bulgaria. In 1389 they defeated a Serbian force at the Battle of Kosovo, largely securing their hold on the Balkans. (It was in June 1989, on the six hundredth anniversary of this battle, that Slobodan Milosevic declared his campaign for a "Greater Serbia" that would redress Ottoman oppression by defeating the Bosnian Muslims, regarded by Serbian nationalists as descendants of the Ottoman invaders.) In 1402, Mongol ruler Timur invaded Anatolia and temporarily slowed the Ottoman advance by making the Turks his vassals. After a brief hiatus, the Ottoman advance continued, posing a significant threat to eastern Europe. The Turks crushed a late-forming coalition of Crusaders in 1396 at Nicopolis and again in 1444 at Varna.

How did the Ottomans become an empire powerful enough to supplant the Byzantine Empire?

The Ottoman stranglehold on the remnant of Byzantium tightened steadily, and by 1449 the Ottomans had reached the Danube River further west. After a protracted siege of Constantinople, the Ottomans captured the city in 1453, renaming the Byzantine capital Istanbul. They proceeded to continue their takeover of what remained of formerly Byzantine lands. A rapid expansion was in part due to their support among the conquered Byzantine people whom they treated well, including their protection of the Greek Orthodox Church. At its height the Ottoman realm was one of the largest in history, stretching from the gates of Vienna, across the Balkans, from the Caucasus to the Yemen, and from Alexandria to Algeria. The Empire gave way to the Turkish Republic under Mustafa Kemal Atatürk in the 1920s.

What was the general course of conversion under the Ottomans?

By the fifteenth century, an estimated 90 percent of the population in Anatolia was Muslim—a measure of success due not only to conversion, but also to continued Muslim migration to the newly conquered areas. Other factors were the weakening of Anatolian

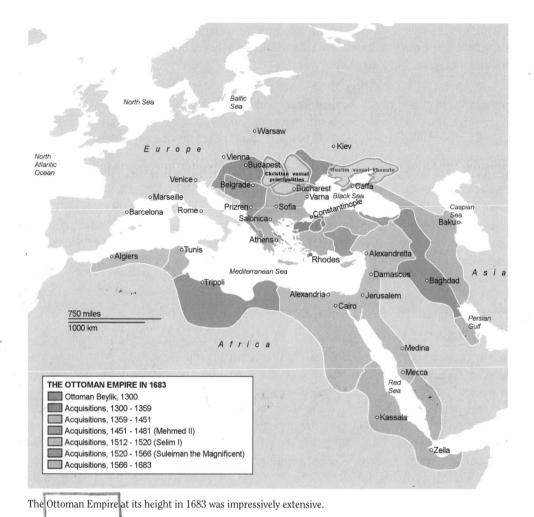

The Ottoman Empire at its height in 1683 was impressively extensive.

Christianity and the Greek Orthodox Church and concomitant growth of strong Muslim infrastructure of social and charitable institutions. In addition, many Christians regarded the Byzantine defeat at the hands of the Muslims as a divine punishment. By contrast, the Balkans remained mostly non-Muslim, with roughly 45 percent conversion, generally in urban areas. Muslim migration was far less important there than in Anatolia.

What happened to Christians under Saljuqid and Ottoman Rule from the eleventh to the sixteenth century?

Anatolia and the Balkans, among other regions ruled by the Saljuqids and Ottomans, employed tax tables to determine the number of Christians in a region, as well as the amount of taxes charged to Christians (particularly, if a *jizya*, or poll-tax, was in effect). The results of Muslim invasions, of what came to be known as Turkey, on Christian populations of the then-Byzantine realm are varied. In eleventh- to twelfth-century Anatolia, sixty-three Christian towns and villages were destroyed by invading Muslims, and the inhabitants were sold into slavery.

From the thirteenth through fifteenth centuries, twenty-five different Muslim tribal polities led to chaos, wars, and demographic migrations. An area that had four hundred bishoprics and thirty-five metropolitanates in time only had three bishoprics and seventeen metropolitanates (about 97 percent and 50 percent destroyed, respectively)—this according to tax tables used to estimate Christian survival rates. In times when the empire's central bureaucracy was in flux (new emperor, power struggle at the top), forced conversions were more prominent. The two empires (Saljuqid and Ottoman) developed a legal basis for making *dimmis* second-class citizens, mainly by disenfranchising their testimony in court. Apostasy from Islam was punishable by death, while conversion to Islam was rewarded. Finally, mixed marriages were more prevalent, because only a husband needed to be Muslim; thus, many women converted. In these ways, a one-way street for conversion from Christianity to Islam was created.

How did the Christian area called Armenia manage to survive as a distinct Christian enclave in the region?

When the Arabs first invaded Persia in the centuries following Muhammad, conversion of inhabitants to Islam had four levels. First, the upper layer of Persian society converted and intermarried with Arab magnates so as to save their hereditary rights. Second, partisans and craftsmen converted because the creed of Islam, which made no distinction between social classes, greatly appealed to them. Third, Christians and Jews were not discriminated against and were attracted to the religion for that reason. Finally, many people rejected the predominant religion of Zoroastrianism for various reasons, such as dislike for clergy and problems with the truths of the religion. Arab forces overtook the Transcaucasus and the land of the Jewish Khazars. When Arab forces in the northeastern province of Khurasan attacked the eastern border of Persia, nobility and townspeople again accepted the religion, so as to maintain their old privileges. The Armenians, who did not readily convert, nevertheless were, in this situation, valuable auxiliary troops. Various Khurasan chieftains and preachers tried to convert the Armenians somewhat forcefully. It is reported that one thousand converted, many of whom were noblemen who feigned conversion so that their lives would be spared, and who rescinded the apostasy when they were released. Intermarriage also factored into the conversion. Mostly though, the Armenians maintained their Armeno-Gregorian faith and maintained good relations with the Arabs through trade; all this despite the fact that Armenia itself was being ravaged by warfare. Armenia as a region suffered massive erosion as a result of battles and invasions, resulting ultimately in the great emigration, or *Sürgün*, of Armenians from their homeland. Largely because the Armenian people preserved their vernacular language and culture, they ensured the survival of their distinctive Christian identity, despite their ultimate separation from their original ancestral home.

How did the Ottomans expand into a major threat to Eastern Europe?

Mehmed II the Conqueror (r. 1444–1446, 1451–1481)—so named because of his defeat of Constantinople—laid the foundation for the Ottoman Empire. He began a long tradition of Ottoman codification of legal codes that incorporated separate categories for Muslim and non-Muslim subjects. It may be convenient to think of the sixteenth century as a period of expansion, the seventeenth as maintenance, and the eighteenth as the beginning of reversals in Ottoman fortunes. Under Mehmed's successors, especially Sulayman the Magnificent (r. 1520–1566), the Ottomans experienced dramatic growth and conquest of the central middle east. In 1516, the Ottomans conquered the Mamluks of Cairo, and their holdings in Syria-Palestine and took over northwestern Arabia. As custodians of the "two sanctuaries" (Mecca and Medina), the Sultans could claim symbolic leadership of Islamdom. Fierce naval competition with the Portuguese marked Ottoman efforts to control the Mediterranean. And on their eastern frontier, Iran was a major competitor. In response, Ottoman rulers sought to limit hitherto enormous Persian cul-

A memorial statue to Mehmed II the Conqueror stands in Istanbul (formerly Constantinople), Turkey.

tural impact by cutting ties in favor of Arabic cultural influence. On the western front, the Ottomans set their sights on Europe. By 1504, the Ottomans had crossed the Danube River, and by 1520, Belgrade and Hungary accepted Ottoman rule. In 1529, the Ottomans laid siege to Vienna but failed to take the city. In 1606, the Treaty of Zsitva Torok proclaimed Ottoman rule over Romania, Hungary, and Transylvania, with the condition of accepting the Habsburgs as equals. This effectively marked the limit of Ottoman expansion westward.

Didn't the Ottomans also become a Mediterranean power?

Ottoman naval strength was definitely a factor in late medieval and early modern European and North African history. Admiral Khayr ad-Din Barbarossa expanded the navy, took Algiers in 1529, and was given overall control of the fleet in 1533. Numerous battles ensued over control of the central Mediterranean, with Sicily and Tunisia major centers of struggle in 1534–1535. During the latter half of the sixteenth century, Ottoman naval forces seized Tripoli (1551), Malta (1565), and Cyprus (1570). An increasingly worried Catholic Europe successfully raised a naval coalition and defeated the Turks at the Battle of Lepanto in 1571. In 1580, European powers and the Ottomans declared a truce, and the resulting actual and symbolic borders between "Christian West" and "Muslim East" held until recent times.

What is the importance now of the Turkic republics that belonged to the former Soviet Union?

Several of the former Soviet republics have significant Muslim populations: Azerbaijan, Chechnya, and Dagestan in the Caucasus; and Kazakhstan, Turkmenistan, Kyrgyzstan, Uzbekistan, and Tajikistan (the "-(i)stan" suffix indicating the "place of" the people to whose name it is attached). There is a great deal of diversity among these republics, both ethnically and linguistically. The one nearly common link is a thread of Turkic an-

Did Turkic peoples remain significant in the Turkic ancestral homelands of Central Asia?

Turkic peoples have remained a major population in Central Asia over the centuries and are a significant presence in at least four of the five "-stans" of the region. The former Soviet-controlled regions are now the independent states of Kazakhstan, Turkmenistan, Uzbekistan, Kyrgyzstan, and Tajikistan. Taken as a whole, the predominantly Muslim region is sometimes referred to as "Western Turkistan," to distinguish it from the largely Muslim Chinese western provinces often called "Eastern Turkistan." As a result, Muslim areas of China fall within the Turkic Sphere.

cestry that runs through them all, with the exception of the Tajiks who are of Iranian descent and speak Persian. The Turkic connection has naturally made these republics a subject of intense interest to the Republic of Turkey, which regards them as natural economic and cultural allies.

Geographically the republics collectively represent a vast expanse; Kazakhstan, the largest, covers an area one-third as large as the "lower forty-eight" states; Uzbekistan is nearly the size of Spain; and Turkmenistan is as large as Missouri, Arkansas, and Oklahoma combined. Together their total Muslim population numbers nearly fifty million, with another ten million or so still living under the Russian Federation—the people of Chechnya and Dagestan in the Caucasus, for example. Soviet domination was very hard on the Muslims of these republics, imposing massive control and closing down hundreds of mosques and schools. During the Brezhnev years, Soviet agricultural policy nearly destroyed the Aral Sea, shrinking it from the world's fourth largest freshwater lake to less than half its original size. Central Asia's Muslims especially have had good reason to resent their former overlords and were a major force in compassing the end of the Soviet empire. From the time Stalin first cracked down on them to the end of Soviet rule, these Muslims managed to keep Islam alive through clandestine and risky illegal activities. Russia's concerted efforts to wipe out Soviet Islam may even have given some renewed energy to pass on the heritage to their children.

How did the Muslim Turkic minority in China originate?

According to ancient tradition, Islam came to China in the seventh century with Arab silk merchants. In the mid-eighth century an Abbasid caliph dispatched a regiment of Turkic soldiers to help the Chinese emperor put down the revolt of a mutinous officer. Remaining after the war, those soldiers formed the nucleus of inland Muslim communities. Over the next four centuries, the Muslim population grew very slowly in coastal and central regions. But in 1215 Genghis Khan's Mongols captured Beijing and eventually overthrew the Sung dynasty. Under the Yuan (Mongol) dynasty the Muslims enjoyed privileged status. Meanwhile, various segments of the population in the northwestern province of Xinjiang converted to Islam. After the Yuan dynasty fell to the Mingd (1368–1644), Muslim fortunes took a turn for the worse, and under the Manchu dynasty (1644–1911) Muslims endured several centuries of persecution. During Mao's Cultural Revolution, the Muslims suffered terribly again but have regained many important rights in the twenty-first century.

What are the basic facts about Islam in China? Are there any distinctively Chinese features of Islam there?

Approximately forty million citizens, perhaps more, of the People's Republic of China consider themselves Muslims. Fully ten different "nationalities" make up the total Muslim population, but about half the total belong to the Hui people. The Hui resemble the majority Han population in physical appearance and they speak Chinese (unlike the other Muslim minorities, several of whom speak Turkic languages). But the Hui think of themselves as a distinct people in that they disavow ancestor veneration, gambling, drinking, and eating pork. The term "Hui" is related to Chinese Muslims' traditional identification of themselves as ethnic "Uighurs." They consider themselves ethnically related to other Muslims who live to the west in Central Asia—all part of a great region known as Turkistan. Hui people speak a dialect of Turkic origin, and the Chinese province of Xinjiang is also known as "Eastern Turkistan." Many Chinese mosques are built in distinctively Chinese architectural styles. Their minarets are square rather than cylindrical and have the gracefully curved roofing associated with the pagoda.

THE SUB-SAHARAN AFRICAN SPHERE

What are the main characteristics of the Sub-Saharan (or Black) African Sphere?

Well over a dozen important nation-states, from the far west of Africa to the shores of the Red Sea and Indian Ocean, comprise the Sub-Saharan Black African sphere. Perhaps the most diverse of all the spheres, ethnically and linguistically as well as religiously, the sphere's west-east expanse is also impressive. In the northwest of the continent is the small but richly Islamic nation of Senegal, now most widely known for the cultural centrality of the Muridiyya Sufi order, a branch of the Qadiriyya unique to Senegal; and the Tijaniyya, a major African order. Further south, Mali is most famous for its major center of traditional Arabic scholarship in Timbuktu. Along with the Songhay and Kanem-Bornu empires, Mali was one of several "religious" polities begun from the eleventh century on.

Later developments included the Islamization of tribal communities identified by their dominant languages: the Fulani in Kano (Nigeria), the Hausa (from the fourteenth century), the Yoruba (from the sixteenth century), and the Bambara in upper Nigeria (from the seventeenth century). At the eastern limits of the sphere, where the African sphere overlaps significantly with the Arabicate, a major nation is Sudan, one of three geographically largest African states. Arabs conquered the Nubian and Funj in the fourteenth century, and Sufi missionaries converted much of the populace, making this a rare example of simultaneous Arabization and Islamization. Arabic remains the dominant main language here. In coastal states such as Somalia, Zanzibar, and Eritrea, by contrast, large numbers of people speak Swahili, a blend of Arabic and Persian on a foundation of Bantu origin. Though the vast majority of Muslims in the sphere are Sunni, more recent immigrants from the Indian subcontinent imported Shi'ism (especially Ismaili) to East Africa. Muslims make up a small minority of a score of other nations in central and south Africa, typically 4 percent or less of total populations.

How did Islam arrive and take root in Africa?

Muslims first arrived across North Africa during the early seventh century in connection with the earliest conquests of the Mediterranean coast of Africa. Beginning in about

638, the process of Islamization proceeded slowly, and the region's population, from Egypt westward to Morocco, was predominantly Muslim by around 1000. During the next seven centuries or so, from 1050 to 1750, Islam spread down the west coast of Africa, brought largely by Maghribi ("Where the sun sets," i.e., North Africa) merchants (who were mostly Berbers) and Sufis. Since these travelers were not chiefly interested in proselytizing as such, the brand of Islam they represented took root in ways that accommodated generously to the indigenous practices and beliefs of the so-called African Tribal/Traditional Religions (ATR). Both Muslim and Christian missionaries have often retroactively claimed credit for this form of Islamization and Christianization, but where either of those two faiths have gained ground, a major factor seems to have been ATR's affinity with the large cosmological frameworks of the two Abrahamic faiths. Those same itinerant Muslims brought Islam across the Sahara and down the east coast of Africa. At the same time, Muslim traders and exiled Muslims from southeast Asia and India populated Indian Ocean coasts from south Africa northward through Swahili-speaking areas like Kenya and Tanzania. In many regions, kings and other tribal leaders played significant roles in encouraging their people to accept Islam (or Christianity).

How has African Islam taken shape in more recent times?

Between 1750 and 1900, several militant and intolerant Muslim religious leaders established theocratic or jihadi regimes and managed to gain allegiance by replacing tribal bonds with allegiance to states regulated by Islamic law. Sudan and Nigeria saw noteworthy examples of such developments. Some influential teachers and holy men, supported by merchants and herdsmen, nurtured visions of reestablishing Islamic empires of legend that they had read about in Arabic historical sources. But the age of jihadists claiming the status of an exalted ruler such as a re-vitalized caliph, or as the expected *mahdi* (guided one with apocalyptic overtones), gave way under various forms of colonialist rule in the early twentieth century. Colonial powers introduced economic, technological, and religious influences that ironically contributed to the dissemination of Islam by undermining traditional social structures and patterns. Anti-Christian sentiment tended to hitch a ride on anti-colonial anger, and third-world Africans have often been more sympathetic to the plight of the Palestinians than to Israel. Identifying Christianity as the "white person's religion" and associating it with capitalism—often judged a dismal failure for Blacks and a prop to apartheid—many opted for Islam as a "third way." In addition, Islam's tolerance of polygamy was well-received in many regions for a time. Islam had also spread to many parts of the African continent well before Christianity: more portions of Black Africa have had a Muslim presence for a millennium than have seen continuous Christian presence for even a quarter of that time. Nowadays, Sub-saharan Africa is roughly forty percent Muslim, forty percent Christian, and twenty percent ATR—with a fair amount of syncretism. By far the majority of Muslims now live in the northern half of the continent, while in most central and southern nations Muslims typically account for four percent or less of the populations.

THE MALAY
(OR SOUTHEAST ASIAN) SPHERE

How would one describe the Malay or Southeast Asian sphere?

Farthest removed from the lands of Islam's origins, the Malay sphere comprises principally the nations of Malaysia and Indonesia, as well as the Muslim communities of the southern Philippines. In addition to being arguably more homogeneous ethnically than any of the other spheres, the manner of Islamization was also in general remarkably irenic. Islam began to arrive in the thirteenth century when Sufi missionaries went to Sumatra (the largest of Indonesia's several thousand islands) with merchants from India. Two centuries on, Islam arrived at neighboring Java, and about a century after that, Muslim rulers set up shop at Malacca (on the Malay peninsula) and at the Sumatran city of Acheh. Subsequent phases of Islamization, as well as a desire to expunge local practices of "folk" traditions, began with the growing importance of pilgrimage. Here a major influence was that some pilgrims stayed in Mecca and Medina to study formally and brought home more "traditional" interpretations of Islam's sacred sources. The Shafi'i school became the only significantly influential law school, and the spiritual tone of southeast Asian Islam was marked by major Sufi influence.

How did Islam enter the lands of Southeast Asia?

Sparse documentation makes it difficult to determine exactly when Islam took root in the Malay sphere, but there are indirect indicators. Hindu rulers of Sumatra had Muslim advisors as early as 1282, and ten years later, Marco Polo reported Muslim communities in North Sumatra. Celebrated Moroccan world traveler Ibn Battuta encountered established Muslim scholars there in 1345–1346. The presence of Islam on the Malay mainland around that time can be deduced because a deposed former ruler of Srivijaya named Iskandar went to Malacca and converted to Islam there. That city apparently became a base for the growth of Islam throughout the area, and by the late fifteenth century, Islam spread to interior territories. Moving to the east, the Moluccas became Muslim in 1498, and Islam had reached the Philippines by the early sixteenth century.

At what point did Muslims encounter European powers in Southeast Asia?

Around that same time, the age of colonialism arrived as the Portuguese asserted significant power in the Indian Ocean. In 1509 they took Goa, in India, and in 1511 conquered Malacca. Counterintuitively perhaps, Portuguese control in the region actually helped Islam spread, as Muslim scholars fled Malacca for Sumatra when the city fell to the Portuguese. Acheh emerged as a strong rival to Malacca, and Muslim sultanates, such as that of Johore (1512–1812), soon emerged on the Malay peninsula as well. Meanwhile, parts of the central Indonesian island of Java developed into a third center of Muslim power in the area. In search of pepper, the Dutch arrived in the southeastern region with naval firepower and took Batavia in 1619, Ceylon in 1640, and Malacca in 1641. The

Malaysian Muslims celebrate the birthday of the Prophet at Putrajaya Putra Mosque.

Dutch ousted both the Portuguese and regional Muslims, establishing themselves as the undisputed power through the seventeenth century. European control did not stifle Islam but instead facilitated its emergence as the main religion of the region.

Is it true that the "Islamization" of Southeast Asia occurred largely without conflict?

Much of the character of early Malay sphere Islam was influenced by major Sufi teachers, who were among the first scholars to translate Arabic sources and tradition into Malay. Their missionary approach was generally very adaptive and flexible. Hamza Fansuri (d. 1600) founded a branch of the Qadariya order, wrote commentaries in Malay, and taught the philosophy of Ibn al-Arabi. Abd as-Samad of Palembang (on Sumatra, 1779–1789) translated the works of the great eleventh-century theologian and Sufi al-Ghazali into Malay, thus introducing a reformist strain of Islam into the area. Still, the practice of Islam did not rule out celebration of indigenous non-Islamic observances. An eighteenth-century teacher named Tuanku Nan Tua led a religious revival attempting to eradicate local religious and social practices that did not conform to Islam; but his attempt at reform sparked a civil war. Nan Tua advocated pacifist reform while others in the movement were more militant, and the reform movement split.

Although many accepted Sharia and the reforms peacefully (especially the merchant communities), the local chieftains did not. When religious leaders asked the Dutch to intervene, the Dutch suppressed the reformers and took control. Malay Muslim leaders mounted an unsuccessful reprisal against Dutch rule. Meanwhile, a Javanese state had sought to combine Hindu and Muslim concepts of rule, but Islam was in fact just a façade for residual Hindu belief. The result was a Javanese society Islamic in name only, since for the villagers of Java, Islam remained chiefly a way to control spiritual forces in a cultural blend of Hindu, Muslim, and animist beliefs. A recently independent Indonesia is experiencing a wide range of new and ongoing attempts to "purify" Islam of such "un-Islamic" accretions.

How did colonialism and European imperialism play out in early modern times in relation to Southeast Asian Islam?

By the end of the eighteenth century, the Dutch commercial empire in Europe was undermined seriously by British competition, the French revolution, and the Napoleonic wars. But in the nineteenth century the Dutch revived as a territorial land-based empire in Southeast Asia. In 1871 and 1874, they annexed Acheh and abolished the sultanate. By 1911 they had complete control of the region and for the first time a single empire ruled over the entire "Indies," thus laying the foundation for Indonesia. The British were meanwhile extending their empire to Malaya (present-day Malaysia), which around 1819 witnessed an influx of Chinese and Indians in the area. From 1877 to 1889 the British consolidated their direct control in that part of mainland Southeast Asia. Muslim populations in the islands (especially Indonesia) grew apace, and the world's most populous Islamic nation gained its independence in the mid-twentieth century.

ISLAM AND EUROPE

Islam was once prominent in Spain. How did it become so important there?

Muslim armies crossed the straits of Gibraltar from North Africa in 711, and an important Arab-Islamic presence established itself in Spain within fifty years or so. After the fall of the Umayyad dynasty in Damascus, the incoming Abbasids sought to put an end to their Umayyad rivals by assassinating all of the family's princes. However, one managed to escape to Spain, where he established the Umayyad Emirate of Cordoba. Later it would grow to challenge Baghdad's authority as the Cordoba caliphate.

What was the overall religious and cultural situation in early Islamic Spain?

Spain's population had become "Latinized" over the preceding seven centuries or more. Jews who had lived in the Iberian peninsula since Roman times experienced considerable persecution under their Christian rulers and were among the first to taste the benefits of the Arab Muslim conquest: they were given their religious freedom, while the Christian population was allowed to retain its Roman institutional heritage as a basis for local order. For several centuries Cordoba would be a marvel of cultural splendor and interreligious harmony. On the whole, Cordoba was an outstanding example of how Jews, Christians, and Muslims could live together in peace under Muslim rule. As for larger political and cultural traditions, the Arabs drew heavily on their Middle Eastern roots. Educated Christians and Jews learned Arabic, and Middle Eastern taste in fashions and luxury items found ready acceptance. The over seven-hundred-year presence of Islam in Spain left a lasting influence on the Spanish language and the arts. The expression of enthusiastic approval "Ole!" comes from the Arabic *Wa'llahi*, ("By God!"), and dozens of Spanish words that begin with al-, such as *Alcazar* ("the castle") betray an Arabic influence.

In what other ways did Islam advance westward across the Mediterranean and into Europe?

The Byzantine empire ruled subjects harshly so many Christians welcomed Muslims and actually regarded the coming of Islam as a liberation. They preferred being *dhimmis* (protected minorities) to being under Byzantine rule. Eventually, many converted to Islam but for as many as four centuries, Muslims remained the minority in the Middle East generally. Christians were allowed their freedom in return for paying a "poll" tax. Jerusalem's citizens were mostly *dhimmis* for many generations. Further to the west, Muslim rule in Spain began in 711 and their advance toward central Europe was halted in 732 by Charles Martel at Poitiers. As a result, Muslims in the North of Spain no longer posed a significant threat to the portions of Europe then ruled by Charlemagne (crowned in 800). Minority populations of Muslims nonetheless trickled into parts of Switzerland and northern and southern Italy. Christians had largely lost con-

The Cordoba mosque, known to locals in Spain as Mezquita-Cathedral, is one of the oldest structures remaining from the age when Muslims ruled much of the Iberian Peninsula.

trol of the Mediterranean in the early ninth century after Sicily came under repeated Muslim invasions. In 831 the people of Palermo surrendered and in 966 Byzantines acknowledged Muslim rule there. That was short-lived, however, and by 1072 Sicily was back in Christian hands, but Muslims were allowed to remain. By the end of the Crusades, the Muslim presence in the central Mediterranean had largely vanished.

What is the meaning of the term *convivencia* and why is it applied to medieval Spain?

Convivencia is Spanish for "living together," and it refers to a period from the eighth to the fifteenth centuries because of the often romanticized notion that Christians and Jews lived together in peace under Muslim rule in the Iberian Peninsula. Some have referred to the "medieval" period in Spain as a Golden Age, and it is true that the early Middle Ages in Spain were in many ways a period of Muslim-Christian harmony. But these seven centuries witnessed more than enough difficulties, along with a genuinely remarkable cultural flourishing, during several periods within that long stretch of history in a land known as al-Andalus. In the area of juridical matters, Christians and Jews held the status of "protected minorities," or *dhimmis*—a status accorded to "peoples of the Book," that is, members of the Abrahamic faiths. All Jews and Christians were required to pay the *jizya*, or poll tax, in lieu of freedom from Muslim almsgiving requirements and military service. In exchange they were also guaranteed protection for their lives and possessions, freedom of livelihood, and religion. Christians and Jews were forbidden to proselytize among Muslims.

What are some examples of the benefits of *convivencia*?

In the realm of cultural affairs, many important connections occurred. Intermarriage was not unusual and Muslim rulers often married Christian women from the north of Spain. Many Spanish words have Arabic influences, words beginning with "al" and those associated with agriculture, crafts, and civil administration. Christian and Jewish architecture borrowed many formal and decorative conventions from Islamic buildings, such as the horseshoe arch, colored *voussoirs* (the periphery of arches), and stalactite-like features on vaulting called *muqarnas*. Perhaps most importantly, the city of Cordoba's intellectual life was rich with poetry, music, and science, offering educational opportunities that attracted members of all faiths from across Europe. This cross-pollination was essential in facilitating the transfer of much "Islamic" learning and scholarship to Europe by encouraging translation into Latin from Arabic. Living not far from the famous Muslim philosopher Ibn Rushd (Averroes) was a noted contemporary, the legendary Rabbi Maimonides. On the negative side, Jews and Muslims were often segregated in religious and ethnic ghettos called *juderias* and *morerias*, respectively; and slavery was very common in medieval Spain.

What was the *reconquista*?

Throughout much of the period in question, Christian rulers were engaged in the *reconquista*, attempting to "reconquer" the peninsula in the name of Christian monarchs, and this occasionally caused tension among those still under Muslim governance. With his fifty-seven campaigns, Caliph al-Mansur was very active militarily and often held captives in lengthy imprisonment. Under later Muslim sovereigns, Christian prisoners of war contributed to the Kutubiyya mosque in Marrakesh. On the other hand, victorious Christian rulers returned the favor, and Muslim prisoners of war helped build the pilgrimage center of Santiago de Compostela in the 1100s. Christianity's Fourth Lateran Council of 1215 addressed issues regarding Jews and Muslims, and included a number of harsh conditions for non-Christians enacted across much of Europe.

By the tenth century, the Iberian Peninsula was divided more or less in half, Christian kingdoms in the north and Muslims in the south. All sorts of curious social and religious changes followed. Muslim tolerance of Christians and Jews marked a high point in the tenth century, but many Christians converted, and the Arabized Christians were called Mozarabs (from an Arabic root meaning roughly "adopting Arab ways"). Shifts in religious allegiance were a cause of grave concern for both Muslims and Christians. A prominent Christian leader named Eulogius, archbishop of Cordoba, for example, raised alarms over what he perceived as dangerous signs of "Islamization." He lamented that Christians seemed to prefer Arabic to Latin. Christian women began veiling their faces, stopped eating pork, and appreciated Arabic culture, music, and poetry. With the decline of Cordoba, official toleration of Christians declined also: their houses had to be lower than those of Muslims, and they could not study the Quran, build new churches, or display crosses outdoors. Both Muslim and Christian attitudes hardened towards each other, and the conquering Christians persecuted and expelled Muslims from land they recaptured.

What are some examples of how Christian scholars thought of Islam and engaged their Muslim counterparts in the greater Mediterranean world of the Middle Ages?

Beginning as early as the late seventh century, Christian leaders and scholars of the central Middle East addressed seriously the phenomenon of Islam as a system of thought and belief. John of Damascus (c. 675–749) was one of the first Christians to devote himself to the formal study of Islam. His father and grandfather had both occupied high posts in the administration of the Umayyad dynasty in Damascus, though both remained Christian. John knew Arabic and had a solid understanding of fundamental Muslim texts and beliefs. In a major work, John discusses the "heresy" of Islam and calls the Prophet the Antichrist. But the mere fact that he took Islam seriously was enough to get him condemned by his fellow Christian authorities in 754 as "Saracen-minded." Subsequent generations of eastern Mediterranean Christian scholars became increasingly negative in their assessments of Islam, identifying Islam as the "Anti-Christ" and a harbinger of the apocalypse (and thus a tool of divine punishment of Christians for their infidelity), and inventing a lexicon of stunningly uncomplimentary epithets for Muhammad. During early medieval times, however, even as the Crusades were ramping up, some influential Christian scholars sought to present Islam more accurately. For the most part, they continued to regard Islam as a form of heresy—a step up from rank paganism. Peter the Venerable, the Abbot of Cluny (c. 1092–1156), asked Robert of Ketton to translate the Quran into Latin; Robert did so in 1143.

Christians in Europe during the fifteenth and sixteenth centuries often referred to Christendom's chief rival as "the infidel Turk." Why not "the infidel Arab"?

When a person like St. Ignatius Loyola (d. 1556), founder of the Society of Jesus, thought of what he could do for the Church of his day, toward the top of his list was the desire to convert "the Turk." He and many other devout Catholics would have liked nothing more than to make pilgrimage to the Holy Land, then in the hands of the Ottoman Empire. From the late-eleventh through the sixteenth centuries, that empire had gradually supplanted virtually all of what had been the Byzantine empire, a name given to a region that had continued to refer to itself as the Roman Empire until its demise in 1453. The story of how the people called Turks came to dominate nearly the whole of the Mediterranean world—and all of western Islamdom—is intriguing and a fine example of the dynamic quality of the history of Islam. But for sixteenth-century Europeans, Arabs were "ancient history" and no longer posed a serious threat of Mediterranean domination.

THE BROADER ISLAMIC
RELIGIOUS LANDSCAPE

Who are Sunni Muslims?

About eighty to eighty-five percent of the world's Muslims consider themselves Sunni. Their historic patrimony derives directly from the Prophet himself as institutionalized in the caliphate. Sunni tradition has been embodied in most of the regimes that have held political power from Morocco to Indonesia, since the early Middle Ages until early modern times. The ideal of the caliph, legitimate successor to Muhammad, as the spiritual as well as temporal ruler of all Muslims, has survived largely as a distant dream since the Mongols destroyed Baghdad in 1258. And since the last Ottoman sultan fell from power in the 1920s, virtually no Muslim ruler has been even nominally regarded as a universal ruler. Some Muslims still entertain the possibility of a resurgence of the caliphate, but that is definitely a minority view.

Who are Shi'i Muslims?

Various Shi'i communities have been identifiable since at least the eighth century. Among the principal features that distinguish Shi'i from Sunni tradition is the belief that a legitimate successor to leadership, called imam (ee-MAAM), must be designated by his predecessor and belong to the family of the Prophet. According to ancient Shi'i belief, Muhammad did designate his cousin Ali, but Abu Bakr, Umar, and Uthman managed to usurp power and prevent Ali from assuming his rightful place. Around the middle of the eighth century a split developed over who would be the seventh imam. One group continued to pledge its loyalty to a man named Ismail, who had just died, even though Ismail's father, the seventh imam Jafar, appointed a replacement when Ismail died. The faction that stayed with Ismail came to be called the Ismailis, or Seveners, since their line of *imams* ended then. There are now at least two major branches of Seveners, one of which looks to the Aga Khan as its spiritual leader. The larger group of Shi'ites in the eighth century believed the legitimate line of *imams* extended to a twelfth and ended when that imam went into concealment until his expected return at the end of time. Twelver Shi'ites are by far the majority community, constituting nearly all of Iran's and more than half of Iraq's people.

Who are the Bohras? Any connection with the Khojas? And where do the Nizari Ismailis fit in this picture?

Bohras belong to a community based largely in the Indian state of Gujarat with roots in medieval Ismaili Shia history. As early as the eleventh century, Ismaili converts had migrated from Egypt to India. During a schism within that community, many Ismailis then in India switched their allegiance to a Yemeni teaching authority. But that was only the beginning of a continuing history of division, for groups of Bohra Ismailis peeled off to form new sub-communities over the next several centuries. Now there are many groups, the largest being the Da'udis, Sulaymanis, Aliyahs, and Jafaris, mostly centered in India. Another important branch of the Ismaili community is known as Khojas (from a Persian word for teacher or exemplary figure, *khwajah*). They trace their origins to a fourteenth-century missionary among a community of Indian converts from Hinduism, Pir Sadr ad-Din. His legacy represents a fascinating chapter in the history of Muslim-Hindu relations in India. Khoja Ismailism's relationship to other Islamic communities and its complex internal development are especially significant. Some Khojas have historically identified themselves as Sunni Muslims, others as Twelver Shia, and still others as Nizari followers of the Aga Khan. In modern times, however, the majority of Khojas have come to identify themselves as Nizaris, altogether distinct from Twelver Shi'ism. Leaders of the global community have been known by the title Aga Khan since the late nineteenth century. Today Nizaris live in small community networks internationally, as do less numerous pockets of Ismailis.

Who are the Alawis?

In its original meaning, the term *Alawi* (or Alawite) referred to any Muslims with a special relationship to Muhammad's cousin and son-in-law Ali—in particular, members of any of a dozen or more communities otherwise known generically as the Shia. In current usage with respect to the Middle East, however, the term refers to a population descended specifically from a follower of the eleventh Shi'i imam (a spiritual guide of the "twelver" Shia who died in 873). That follower was Muhammad ibn Nusayr, who initially portrayed himself as a spokesperson of that imam, Hasan al-Askari. But when he went so far as to teach that Hasan was in fact divine, the imam renounced him. Ibn Nusayr nonetheless developed a following who lived mostly in the mountainous region crossing the borders of Turkey and Syria. In 1922, their status morphed into the Alawi community now associated with the ruling family of Syria, when the occupying French proclaimed a political entity called the Alawi Regime. Thus elevated to the status of a sort of proxy power over Syria under the French mandate, the Alawi community eventually became further politically empowered by joining in considerable numbers the Arab socialist Baath party that took control of the region in the 1940s.

Do the Alawis profess any distinctive beliefs?

In spite of their historical links to Shi'ism, with many still claiming to believe in Shi'i principles, the Alawis are theologically and religiously quite idiosyncratic—so much so that Sunni thinkers long ago labeled them "exaggerators." Like all Shia communities they observe the martyrdom of Husayn. Like "Twelver" Shia, they believe in an unbroken line of twelve *imams*, and like all Muslims they profess faith in one God. Some, however, still maintain that God has become incarnate seven times, the last being in the form of Ali himself. Needless to say, at this juncture Alawis and mainstream Muslims part company. Among other beliefs and practices, Alawis make unique theological associations between Husayn and Christ and celebrate various Christian feasts, with special attention to John the Baptist and Mary Magdalene; and some even celebrate Mass, but feature Ali as the divine illumination shone forth in the wine offered by Christ at the Last Supper. Some Alawis are still known by the name Nusayri.

Are the Druze people related to Islam in any way?

During the early eleventh century a ruler, al-Hakim (d. 1021), of the Fatimid dynasty—a type of Sevener Shi'ites—did not argue when his followers began to claim that he was divine. Among al-Hakim's supporters was a Turk named Darazi. Even after Darazi died and his former arch-rival claimed that he himself was the true spokesman of al-Hakim, the name of Darazi would live on in the word "Druze." Fatimid Ismaili doctrine had long

A group of Druze men from Majdal Shams, Israel, are seen in this photo from 2009. The number of Druze people worldwide exceeds one million, with the vast majority residing in the Middle East.

shown very esoteric tendencies in interpreting the role of its seven *imams*, and a similar esoterism remains a hallmark of Druze teaching. A collection of letters attributed to al-Hakim form the core sacred literature of the very closed and secretive communities, which now, for the most part, inhabit Lebanon, Syria, and the northern occupied West Bank of Palestine. Their esoteric teachings about al-Hakim, along with notions of reincarnation and other decidedly non-Islamic themes, leave them very much outside the fold of Islam.

While those of the Baha'i faith are said to have historical connections with Islam, is it true members don't consider themselves Muslims?

In mid-nineteenth century Persia, a faction called the Babis (followers of the Bab, "Gateway") broke away from Twelver Shi'ism. The Bab had prophesied the coming of a promised messiah-like figure, a role claimed by a man who called himself Baha' Allah and claimed the office of prophet. Upon his death in 1892, a follower took up the claim, as did others. According to mainstream Muslim belief, there can be no prophet after Muhammad, so Baha'is are considered non-Muslims.

What about the small community called the Ahmadiya—are they Muslims?

Around the time the Baha'i movement was getting started in Iran, a group formed around a Punjabi named Mirza Ghulam Ahmad (1835–1908), who claimed to be both the

63

Is Sufism considered a cult among Muslims?

Muslims have historically expressed a variety of opinions about the phenomenon known as Sufism. Those who have taken a dim view have generally fallen into two general groups. On the one hand, some have accused Sufis and their organizations of lax observance of Muslim law and tradition at best and outright antinomianism and heresy at worst. On the other hand, some have regarded Sufism as anti-intellectual and dismissive of the ancient Islamic regard for knowledge and learning. As for the first criticism, the historical record suggests that Sufism is not simply an idiosyncratic, aberrant sidetrack to "mainstream" Islamic tradition. Virtually all of the great Sufis who built the foundations of Sufi spirituality were explicitly aligned with one (or more) of the major law schools, and in no way did they play down the need for all Muslims to express their faith through the Five Pillars. Recent research clearly indicates that Sufism arose as a distinctive way of studying, interiorizing, and communicating that tradition that situated Sufis not as "spirit-filled radicals," but as "fierce upholders of the emerging moral and legal order." In other words, though many of the Sufi orders did indeed foster a distinct approach to community life, they were nothing like what contemporary Americans might identify as "cults."

Mahdi and Jesus's Second Coming. Around 1909 the Ahmadiyya (followers of Ahmad) split into two main factions. One faction claimed its founder was a prophet, thus meriting an official condemnation from Islamic authorities. The other Ahmadiyya faction insisted that Ahmad was only a religious reformer. Between half a million and a million members live in west Africa and Pakistan. Most Muslims today consider Baha'is and Ahmadiyyas non-Muslims.

INTERSECTION OF THEOLOGY AND POLITICS: A MAJOR HISTORICAL EXAMPLE

What is an example of the interaction between religion and politics during the Abbasid caliphate?

The late eighth-/early ninth-century Caliph Harun ar-Rashid (r. 786–809) and his two warring sons, al-Amin (r. 809–813) and al-Mamun (r. 813–833) stand out as seminal figures in the Abbasid history. Harun fostered a cosmopolitan atmosphere at court and an intellectual climate that welcomed novelty and exotic thinking. Most famous as a highly romanticized bon-vivant from *One Thousand and One Nights*, the Harun of the "historical" sources appears to have been another sort altogether. Later chroniclers make much of the ruler's religious devotion, and "traditionalist" interests prevailed in recasting the caliph as ascetically inclined and theologically mainstream. Out with the high-roller, in with the spiritual twin to the Prophet himself, a ruler easily moved to compassion and perfectly comfortable with taking advice from the religious scholars. These and other manifestations of religio-ideological spin are key elements of a traditionalist reconstruction of history that took place in the aftermath of the "inquisition" (*mihna*) sponsored by Harun's second successor, al-Mamun.

What was the outcome of the struggle between Harun's two sons as contenders for the title of caliph?

Harun's son al-Amin lost out to sibling al-Mamun, under whom especially the Abbasids vigorously supported the Mutazilite school of philosophical theologians, whose "theology-from-below" had the great political advantage of investing the caliph with enormous religious authority. By arguing that the Quran was created, rather than uncreated and co-eternal with God, the Mutazilites were theologically defending the divine unity while politically allowing the caliph, to whom God had entrusted the administration of all things created, final say in interpreting the Quran. Historical sources attempt to explain how the intemperate, impious, and politically inept al-Amin was an exception to the rule in the Abbasid line in order to justify his murder at the hands of his own brother. At the same time, a kind of hagiographic theme of "sympathy for al-Amin" persists in other accounts that suggests striking parallels between the murders of al-Amin two earlier caliphs, Uthman, the second of the Rightly Guided Caliphs, and the Umayyad al-Walid II, all of which are examples of religio-historiographical struggle around the enormity of regicide.

What was Caliph al-Mamun's role in the evolution of Islamic thought?

Abbasid Caliph al-Mamun's Mutazilite theology was a major point of contention in the history of Islamic political thought. He argued that caliphs are heirs to the prophets in that they possess knowledge based on reason that corroborates revelation. A defining characteristic of his caliphate was al-Mamun's concern for reconciling Muslim factions, but his critical mistake was using a form of "inquisition" to secure uniformity. The caliph's otherwise puzzling appointment of the eighth Shi'i imam, Ali ar-Rida, as heir apparent also arose out of his drive for unity. Perhaps as close to the classic "liberal" as one can find in medieval Islamic history, al-Mamun sought to smooth over divisions among the various schools and factions but ended up disastrously widening the gap between himself and an emerging and increasingly potent "proto-Sunni" consensus. Biographical sources on al-Mamun generally accepted his caliphate but rejected his claims to the imamate—in other words, even as early as the mid-ninth century, Muslim thinkers distinguished between civil and religious authority. They acknowledged al-Mamun as the legitimate political leader virtually by default and judged him as lacking the requisite knowledge to qualify as true spiritual leader (*imam*) and thus as authentic heir of the prophet.

In addition to murdering his brother, what other issues made al-Mamun controversial?

For all his acknowledged strengths and superior suitability for rule, al-Mamun had that nasty penchant for "heterodoxy," as judged by the traditionalists. Al-Mamun's popular association with liberal attitudes toward the seeking of wisdom parallels Harun's identification with romance and mystery. Far more important to some Abbasid historians was the danger he represented to traditionalist "theology from above," with its concern to subordinate the caliph's authority to that of God. But alongside that theme ran the virtually opposite view that al-Mamun was indeed not only worthy to be called "God's Shadow on Earth," but was the *mahdi* (Guided One), a messianic figure appearing in due course at the turn of a new Islamic century. According to that strand, the caliph was, at least as he approached death, the staunchest of Muslims.

What crisis reversed the religious and political directions of the Abbasid caliphate?

Two reigns after al-Mamun came the next major Abbasid, al-Mutawakkil (r. 847–61). His story is in a way a mirror-reverse of al-Mamun's: al-Mutawakkil began his reign by overturning al-Mamun's preference for the rationalist Mutazilites, but, according to the chronicles, he ended his life a moral and political failure as a murder victim—perhaps the chronicler's way of justifying the violent demise of yet another caliph. It was al-Mutawakkil who returned the caliphate's official Islamic ideology to that of the more conservative Traditionalists, especially as represented by renowned legal scholar Ahmad Ibn Hanbal (d. 855). Against the Mutazilites, the Traditionalists maintained that one must do theology "from above," beginning not with reason but with revelation, and they eschewed the notion that human beings can know definitively the mind of God, insisting instead upon divine transcendence and mystery.

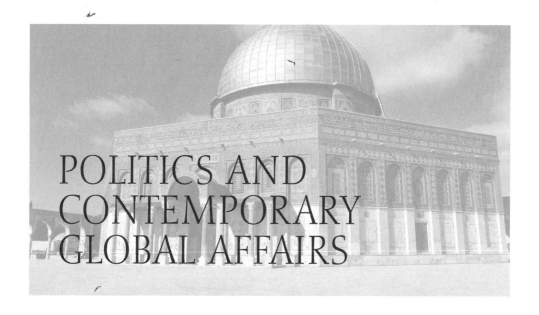

POLITICS AND CONTEMPORARY GLOBAL AFFAIRS

MUSLIM POPULATIONS TODAY

Is Islam the fastest growing religion in the world? Where are the largest concentrations of Muslim populations?

Among global religious communities, Islam does seem to show the fastest rate of growth, with Christianity running a close second. In total numbers, Christians still appear to outnumber the approximately 1.6 billion Muslims by perhaps five hundred million. The largest concentrations of Muslims by geographical region are in South Asia, with around a third of the world's total in Pakistan, India, and Bangladesh. Combining all the Muslims in the Middle East and Africa adds more than another third. And the populations of Indonesia, the nation with the largest number of Muslims, combined with those of the rest of East, Central, and Southeast Asia comprise roughly the final third.

Where do Muslims live today? What are their estimated numbers?

Islam is now a truly global religious tradition. Approximately 1.6 billion Muslims live worldwide, on every continent and in most countries. In very general terms, about a third of the total live in the Middle East and North Africa. Several major ethno-linguistic groups are represented there, including Arabs, Turks, Persians, and Berbers. Many people associate Islam with Arabs even though they are now a relatively small minority of the global population. Another third live in central and southern Asia, including the southern republics of the former Soviet Union, Western China, India, Pakistan, and Bangladesh. Pakistan is the most important modern example of a nation-state established as a Muslim land. Another third are in sub-Saharan Africa, Indonesia, and in smaller concentrations in several dozen other countries. Indonesia boasts the single largest national population of Muslims, approaching two hundred million. At over a hundred million, India is home

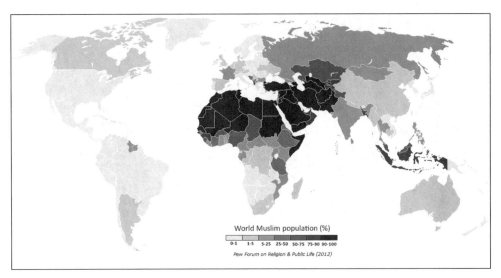

World Muslim population (%)

0-1 1-5 5-25 25-50 50-75 75-90 90-100

Pew Forum on Religion & Public Life (2012)

Followers of Islam are now present all over the world, numbering about 1.6 billion people as of 2014. This map indicates the percentage of people in each country who are Muslims.

to the world's largest minority Muslim population. Estimates as to American Muslims vary considerably, from three to eight million. It may also be helpful to think in terms of religio-cultural spheres, defined by key language groups, in which Islam has been a particularly important influence. The Arabicate sphere, for example, includes all those areas in which Arabic has been the dominant vehicle of Islamic expression, namely, the central Middle East, north Africa, and east Africa. The Persianate sphere consists of Iran, Afghanistan, and all of southern Asia. Within the Malayo-Polynesian sphere are Malaysia, Indonesia, and the Philippines. Central Asia, including western China, and present-day Turkey and the Balkans comprise the Turkic sphere. Last but not least is the sub-Saharan sphere, in which Nigeria and other west African nations are most significant.

In which countries do the largest majority Muslim populations live today?

Principal nations with majority Muslim populations include virtually all of the Middle Eastern and North African countries, plus a couple of sub-Saharan African states, such as Nigeria; Pakistan and Bangladesh; Malaysia and Indonesia; and the five Central Asian republics formerly belonging to the Soviet Union (Kazakhstan, Tajikistan, Kyrgyzstan, Uzbekistan, and Turkmenistan). Dozens of other nations include significant minority populations, with India's over one hundred million Muslims at the head of the list. Another important minority Muslim population that Westerners rarely hear about is that of the People's Republic of China.

Are most Muslims Arabs?

This is a widespread misperception. Arabs, the largest remaining population of Semitic ancestry, account for only about a fifth of the global Muslim population—a total roughly equivalent to the combined populations of Pakistan and Bangladesh alone. And within the Middle East, there are several other major ethnicities and language families. The two largest of these are Turks and Iranians—neither in any direct way related to Semitic peoples, and both using languages unrelated originally either to each other or to Arabic. In addition, significant sub-groups of Middle Eastern Muslims among Turkic peoples are, for example, Turkmen; and among Iranian peoples there are large numbers of Kurds as well as several major tribal groups living in present-day Iran.

What are some other major ethnic and cultural groups of Muslims in the World today?

Across North Africa one finds also Muslims who are ethnic Berbers and in sub-Saharan Africa dozens of tribal groups such as the Tuareg, Hausa, and Fulani. People of Indic background are by far the largest single group, if one considers a large number of ethnic subgroups together, totaling almost a third of the global Muslim population. Turkic descent accounts for the lineage of most of the citizens of Turkey as well as those of the former Soviet Central Asian republics and a region once called Eastern Turkestan that now makes up a large area of Western China—totaling about one-fifth. The people of both Iran and Afghanistan are largely of Indo-Aryan descent and are more closely related ethnically to the people of the Indian subcontinent than they are to their Arab or Turkic neighbors.

Tuareg Muslims, such as these men from Desert Timbuktu in Mali, are one of the many different ethnic and cultural groups that make up the Muslim community worldwide.

What are the most important languages in major Muslim populations?

As suggested in earlier questions about the "culture spheres," Muslims speak and write in dozens of major language groups. Arabic remains the chief Islamic language not only because so many Muslims speak it (over three hundred million), but because it is the language of the Quran and is thus associated with Islam's sacred origins. Multiple languages and dialects—Turkic, Indic (such as Urdu, Sindhi, and Gujarati) and Indo-European (such as Persian), Malayo-Polynesian, and African tongues—remain important spoken and literary languages and essential tools for careful study of Islam.

Do all Muslims belong to the same large religious group?

Asked whether they think of the global community of Islam as composed of various factions, most Muslims are likely to respond that all Muslims belong to the same universal *umma* (UM-mah, global community) or brother- and sisterhood of faith, and that any talk of sub-groups or sects is beside the point. All believe in the oneness of God, the prophetship of Muhammad, divine revelation in the Quran, the existence of angels, the ultimate accountability of all persons, and the Five Pillars—in short, all the fundamental items of belief and practice described earlier. But there are in fact various sub-communities within the larger *umma*, each with its unique histories and contributions to the larger history of Islam. Minority communities of Muslims have often had to contend with the same problems that have beset minorities always and everywhere, regardless of the composition of the majority in which they find themselves.

RADICAL POLITICALLY ACTIVIST AND RELIGIOUSLY IDEALIST FACTIONS

What are politically radical activists and religiously idealist factions?

In this context, "radical" refers to highly mission-oriented groups whose members subscribe to a hard-core exclusivist ideology and tend to be willing to use harsh or even "extremist" tactics to achieve their goals. The term "politically activist" describes an ideology focused on establishing and enforcing a comprehensive system of governance and social control. And, as the chapter on "Essential Beliefs" below will explain further, the phrase "religiously idealist" refers to factions whose interpretation of Muslim history calls for the systematic restoration of what they believe to be Prophetic "ideal"—to recreate as nearly as possible the overall environment they claim characterized the lifetime of Muhammad during the Medinan years (622–632).

What sort of Muslims are the "Taliban"?

A group originally of Pakistani and Afghan nationalities, mostly of Pashtun ethnicity, emerged during the 1980s during Afghanistan's struggle to fend off the Soviet Union's military invasion. Among the *mujahideen* (freedom fighters) engaged prominently in the struggle were a faction who called themselves *taliban* (a Persian plural meaning "seekers, students"). Most members of the faction consider a reclusive figure named *Mullah* Umar their foundational figure, but his role in the group's ongoing activities remains little understood. Taliban social policies are notoriously oppressive toward women especially, as manifest in their refusal to allow girls to be formally educated and public corporal punishment for women who violate their antiquated dress code. They seek to impose their own harsh interpretation of Sharia penal sanctions, including such barbaric practices as stoning for adultery and amputation of hands for theft.

What is the Muslim Brotherhood?

Hasan al-Banna (1906–1949), generally acknowledged as the founder of the Muslim Brotherhood (1927), was a well-educated man from a religiously conservative Egyptian family who believed that Muslims should be more active in promoting the broader societal implications of the Islamic faith. His theoretical works on "politicizing" Islam have been widely influential in the growth of a wide variety of contemporary activist Muslim organizations especially in the Middle East and North Africa. Politically activist organizations related to the Brotherhood include, for example, Hamas. Though the Brotherhood began and developed largely in Egypt, it has gained a political footing in other Middle East nations by running for office and having members elected to national assemblies. In countries such as Jordan, independent branches of the Brotherhood have arisen. More recently, the Brotherhood has exerted considerable influence in the after-

Protestors against the Muslim Brotherhood march in Cairo, Egypt, in 2013. The Brotherhood originated in Egypt.   71

math of early 2011 "revolutionary" events that resulted in the ouster of long-time dictator Husni Mubarak. Al-Banna himself did not advocate violent means, and his contemporary disciples generally strive to bring about their goal of integrating society under religious values—acknowledging religious pluralism and rights of non-Muslims—through political activism and reform. Some other organizations indirectly influenced by Brotherhood values have, however, embraced the use of violence as necessary for overthrowing non-Islamic rule. This includes such groups as al-Qaeda and its spinoffs, the Taliban, and a host of Islamic "jihadist" organizations based in various states from North Africa through the Middle East and into Central and South Asia.

Who are the Salafi Muslims and how influential are they?

Muslim religious scholars began using the term *salaf* over a millennium ago to refer to pious ancestors in faith. The term comes from an Arabic root meaning "to precede" and was for many years a general designation for early Muslims whose religious commitment made them exemplars for subsequent generations. About a century ago, prominent reformers Muhammad Abduh and Jalal ad-Din al-Afghani used the name *Salafiya* for their movement aimed at renewal of traditional values. More recently, the term has returned to more common usage in reference to a religio-cultural style or loosely organized school of thought that represents a decidedly "idealistic" interpretation of history. For contemporary Salafis, the concept of "reform" really means a return to, or recovery and renewal of, the values and practices they associate with the age of the Prophet and the Four Rightly Guided Caliphs (i.e., up to 661).

What is the current impact of the Salafis?

Salafi groups are reasserting their influence in many different political and cultural contexts, from the central Arab Middle East especially, but also well beyond. In places such as Egypt they have reinforced their influence by alliances with such politically organized and connected groups as the Muslim Brotherhood. Unfortunately, some Salafi groups have become increasingly prone to violent means in enforcing their more radical social and ethical norms. They are as hostile toward other self-described Muslims whom they declare destined for eternal damnation because they are guilty of all manner of "innovation" and heresy (that is, not truly Muslims at all), as they are to non-Muslims.

Who are the Wahhabi?

During the mid-late eighteenth century, a preacher and religious scholar named Muhammad ibn Abd al-Wahhab (1703–1792, wah-HAAB) mounted an attack on what he regarded as un-Islamic elements among Muslims of the Arabian Peninsula. He targeted Sufi groups in particular and called for the destruction of shrines dedicated to holy personages and often associated with Sufi organizations. He influenced Ibn Saud, "founder" of the Saudi dynasty, who in turn adopted the nascent Wahhabi ideology.

Among the more interesting features of the Wahhabi approach to religion and theology is its insistence on the principle of the scholar's responsibility for "independent investigation" (*ijtihad*, ij-ti-HAAD) and commensurate rejection of "unquestioning acceptance of tradition" (*taqlid*, tahk-LEED)—that is, simply swallowing whole what one has been told. Another is that Wahhabism claims as its theological forebear the redoubtable Ibn Taymiya—a brilliant, creative medieval thinker whose legacy has unfortunately been tarnished by uncritical (and unfair) association with more extreme forms of Wahhabi and Salafi elements.

Saudi public policy remains broadly influenced by the Wahhabi ideology, including an accelerated campaign to destroy historical sites (such as cemeteries and structures believed to date to Muhammad's time) judged to foster inappropriate devotion and distract from "pure monotheism." Wahhabi influence also characterizes the kingdom's practice of funding projects elsewhere that adhere to Wahhabi standards of piety—such as replacing ornately decorated classic mosque architecture in regions such as war-ravaged Bosnia with much simpler, less colorful structures.

What kinds of organizations call themselves Ansar?

The Arabic term *ansar* (ahn-SAAR) means "helpers" and takes its broader religious meaning from a segment of the early Muslim community in Medina (after the *Hijra*) who earned the name from their deliberate support and assistance for the Prophet in engaging various factions in Medina. Various organizations have adopted the term in their formal titles, beginning more recently in the nineteenth-century Mahdist movement in the Sudan. There the Ansar continued to function well into the twentieth century even after Sudan's independence in 1955. They were influential among tribal groups in Darfur (a large western region of the Sudan), and they supported the ongoing struggle against the central government in Khartoum. Still other groups far from Sudan have adopted the name more recently, as in one Ansar ash-Sharia (Partisans of Revealed Law), which rose as a faction in the post-Kaddafi Libyan revolution, and another based in Yemen. Both are extremist Salafi groups bent on eradicating "un-Islamic" beliefs and practices by violent means if necessary.

What are the factions called Hamas and Hizb Allah (Hezbollah)?

Hamas is an acronym for an Arabic expression meaning "Islamic Resistance Movement" (*harakat al-muqawamat al-is-lamiyya*). Originating, and still based, in the Palestinian region of Gaza, Hamas was in effect an activist offshoot of the Muslim Brotherhood. Not satisfied with the Brotherhood's relative passivity during the 1987 Palestinian *intifada* (in-ti-FAA-da, uprising), Hamas mobilized for the express pur-

A Hezbollah flag is draped on a wall behind a praying Lebanese woman sitting next to the grave of her family, victims of an Israeli bombardment.

pose of resisting Israeli occupation. It continues to refuse to acknowledge Israel's right to exist as a state and advocates engaging with Israel through military means. *Hezbollah*, the "Party of God," is in itself a generic title for a variety of factions in various regions that adopt the name to distinguish themselves from enemies of Muslim community labeled as "Parties of Satan" (*Hizb ash-Saytan*). Political parties by this name exist, for example, in Iran, Libya, Turkey, and Saudi Arabia. But by far the most publicized in recent events is the Lebanese Hezbollah, which arose to prominence during Lebanon's protracted civil war, and especially during the years after the suicide bombing of the U.S. Marine barracks in 1983. Whereas membership in Hamas is largely (if not exclusively) Sunni, Hezbollah's religious affiliation is Twelver Shi'i, with direct connections to Twelver Shi'i Iran. As such, the organization espouses the "political theology" of Iran's Islamic Revolution, according to which true "Islamic" governance centers on the "rule of the [Islamic] jurisprudent"—vested, in this instance, in the Ayatollah Khomeini and his current successor, Ali Khamenei.

Are there any other analogous "parties" or "factions" active today? Are they all politically oriented? Do any espouse explicit use of violent means of protest or political engagement?

There are in fact dozens of such organizations in the Middle East alone, and many more across the globe in nations and regions with predominantly Muslim populations. Various organizations dedicated to "reformist" movements, from Morocco to Indonesia, go by a variety of monikers: front (*jabha*, JAB-ha), progress/revival/reawakening (*nahda*, NAH-da), renewal (*tajdid*, taj-DEED) mission/proselytization (*dawa*, DA-wa), revolution (*thawr*), assembly or group or association (*jamaat*, ja-MAA-at, *jamiyyat*, jam-EE-yat), struggle (*jihad*—including "inward" as well as "outward"), and union (*ittihad*, it-tee-HAAD), to name only the more common designations. By far the majority of these organizations reject violent means except in genuine instances of self-defense, and the "platforms" of most are largely if not exclusively oriented to engagement in the political arena. That is not to say their engagement both individually and corporately does not include religious concerns and agendas—any more than one might encounter, for example, in contemporary American politics.

ISLAM AND VIOLENCE

One often hears the term "holy war" associated with certain groups who call themselves Muslims. Are their motives genuinely religious and are such groups representative of Muslims in general?

Muslims and non-Muslims alike have unfortunately been using the term "holy war" for generations. The expression is an inappropriate rendering of the Arabic term jihad (ji-HAAD), whose root meaning is "striving" or "struggle." What Muslims mean when they use the term to describe external military and political activities is something like "religiously justifiable struggle against injustice and oppression." In other words, in its classical meaning the term *jihad* is roughly analogous to Christian "just war theory." Most of the time the call for a *jihad* is 90 percent rhetoric, involving little or no serious reflection on what the tradition in its considerable depth and sophistication stipulates about criteria and conditions for waging a "just war." Political and economic considerations invariably intrude.

While the word jihad means "struggle" or "striving" toward a spiritual goal, the use of the word by radical Islamists has equated it with "Holy War."

Why is the expression "holy war" such a hot-button term?

Many non-Muslims express misgivings about what appears to be the Islamic idea of "holy war." They are often frankly afraid because they have formed the opinion that Islam is a violent religion. Many people have unfortunately and most unfairly come to expect that behind every episode of hostage-taking or large-scale terrorism there lurks a band of swarthy, bloodthirsty Arab or Iranian Muslims. Every time journalists use the term "jihad," either as part of a faction's name, or to describe the "holy war" a Muslim leader has allegedly called for, millions of listeners or readers have their worst fears confirmed. "There they go again!" one hears people say too often, citing such examples as Khomeini's death sentence on writer Salman Rushdie and Saddam Husayn's attempts during the Gulf War to galvanize Islamic support for a jihad against all infidels defiling sacred Arabian soil. In short, "holy war" is a term too often tossed around loosely, and questions in several chapters here will address specific aspects of the term and its implications.

Does Islamic tradition insist on specific limits to the use of violent means?

Questions abound concerning the conditions for religious sanctioning of violent means, which Islamic tradition shares with more than one other major religious tradition. There is no doubt that it is an important issue about which understanding several complex aspects is important. First, Muslims regard Muhammad as model; second, the actual aspirations of many millions of Muslims are for a life of peace; third, conditions governing authentic jihad are numerous and demanding; and finally, Americans and Europeans must try to appreciate the pain that the western domination of the Middle East and other parts of the world over the past century has caused in populations across the globe.

What is Muhammad's role in Muslim views about using violence?

Muhammad stands out as the prime exemplar of the ideal mode of fostering peaceful relations among interest groups and communities that are defined by overlapping or otherwise

75

conflicting claims. The story of the Prophet's replacing the Black Stone in the Kaba suggests, along with other traditional accounts, that Muhammad developed a public reputation very early as a trustworthy person and an effective negotiator. When envoys came south from Yathrib (later Medina) to offer Muhammad and the Muslim community a new home, part of what they wanted in return was that Muhammad act as arbitrator in various factional disputes then troubling their city. Tradition cites prominently Muhammad's diplomacy in forging treaties and alliances. It emphasizes especially Muhammad's preference for peaceful means and the centrality Muhammad accorded to the reconciliation of hearts.

Author Salman Rushdie was targeted for assassination because of his 1988 novel, *The Satanic Verses,* which many Muslims felt insulted the Prophet. Iran's Ayatollah Ruhollah Khomeini, issued a *fatwa* in 1989 to have Rushdie killed. The *fatwa* has since been rescinded.

Why is Muhammad's role in the unfolding of early Islamic history often portrayed so negatively in "western cultures"?

It is exceedingly difficult to see through the veil of dark images that has shrouded the picture of Muhammad in the thinking of many non-Muslims over the centuries. When non-Muslims read, for example, of Muhammad's decision to resort to fight the Jewish tribes of Medina, they are shocked. Unfortunate events like these seem to blind one to anything positive in the early history of Islam, and non-Muslims rarely (if ever) get the Muslim side of the story. At the opposite end of the spectrum, Muhammad remains for Muslims the paragon of gentleness and concern for the needs of people. One always needs to look for the truth somewhere in between the ideal of utter perfection most communities see in their foundational figures and the jaundiced view taken by people who for many reasons prefer to cling to negative assessments of "others."

Why is mutual understanding so hard to come by when it comes to such matters?

Part of the problem here is that there is sometimes a thin line between justifiable revolution and unlawful, treasonable action. How many colonial American preachers encouraged their congregations to support the "American revolution"? Whether in Northern Ireland or the Middle East, organizations like the IRA (Irish Republican Army) and Hamas have arisen to combat what they perceive as tyranny. Many of their members no doubt think of themselves as devout and sincerely religious. And many Irish-American Catholics and Arab-American Muslims who support these and other such causes financially no doubt regard their choice as highly ethical. But such support necessarily involves a terribly serious form

Does the media accurately portray the notion that many Muslims, with support from clerics, are involved in terrorist activities?

Suppose a non-Christian living outside of the United States had heard that most Americans identify their country as a Judeo-Christian nation. Suppose that the only reports about Christians were of sectarian violence emanating from Northern Ireland. Would the conclusion be that Christians prefer violence? If IRA bombings and murders alone did not persuade people of that, suppose there were credible reports that some Irish Catholic priests regularly gave their blessings to such activities. Suppose further that reports from that quarter were reinforced by occasional news of "Christian" bombings and assassinations at abortion clinics in the United States. And suppose that there were accounts of how racist groups such as the Ku Klux Klan or the Aryan Nation regularly cloaked their social views in biblical and other ostensibly religious teaching, and that organizations like them actively recruited with a message of hatred. Would that be enough to form an opinion that Christianity and violence somehow go together? Virtually everywhere, people have appealed to religion to justify actions and policies that most persons of good will would condemn as incompatible with their religious beliefs. Just because people claim to belong to a particular religious tradition does not mean that they fairly represent that tradition. It merely means that unscrupulous people can sometimes twist and manipulate religion for evil purposes.

of denial. It requires that one assert that no one on the "other side" is innocent, or at the very least, that it is sometimes acceptable to shed innocent blood to achieve a greater good.

How many different kinds of activist or extremist (i.e., violence-promoting) "jihadis" are there?

It is important to distinguish between two large categories of "jihadist" ideologies. For example, the "nationalist" type pursues strategy, objectives, and tactics limited in scope to a given political setting or nation-state. The Sunni organization based in Gaza and known as Hamas, for example, is focused sharply on the Palestinian cause; the Shi'ite and Iran-backed Hezbollah is centered in Lebanon and aims at what it regards as liberation from and destruction of the state of Israel; and the Taliban, with bases mostly in Pakistan currently, are intent on establishing Afghanistan as a Muslim state.

What about jihadism on a larger scale?

Some groups of "transnational" jihadis, such as al-Qaeda and related organizations, declare war on a more remote foe, typically identified as "the West"—especially the United States, with attention to its allies, Europe and Israel, as well as the non-Islamic governments of their own home countries. Transnational jihadists rally around what they claim are historical and ongoing Western-inspired offenses against, and systematic oppression of, Islam and Muslims. Just as the Iranian revolutionary ideologues have consistently condemned the United States as the Great Satan, transnational jihadis cast their struggle as a cosmic engagement between good and evil so intractable that only the most extreme forms of outward violence will affect any change. Anything short of constant warfare against this global enemy is collaboration and cowardice and refusal to engage in the struggle to reform Islam from the inner corruption that tempts Muslims to prefer comfort to warfare. Some preachers continue to invite martyrs for the cause, promising eternal rewards and support for their surviving families. Arguing that otherwise forbidden suicide is in this case "self-selected martyrdom," they engage in contorted exegesis of the Quran for the purpose of giving the highest justification to all-out warfare. Though the vast majority of Muslim religious scholars abhor their ideological distortions, the extremists call for the indiscriminate slaughter of whoever happens to be in the path of their cause.

What motivates some highly influential religious scholars to adopt such radical ideologies when the vast majority do not go to such extremes?

Recent social science research suggests that neither, say, poverty nor the views of their own teachers are to blame here, as many might suppose. Much more important are broader sociological factors, especially lack of support in their academic background and educational networks. People trained in religious studies who lack the "connections" needed to secure stable and respectable jobs as local *imams* or faculty members in major state institutions are most likely to drift toward the fringe. One reason is that established governments typically limit the spread of extremist groups by controlling the ideologies taught in those state-controlled institutions. The research shows that while only 2–3 percent of scholars whose networks helped them get the "good" jobs were ever inclined toward radical ideologies, over 50 percent of those who lacked influential "connections" and could not land state positions became radicalized. These individuals, disaffected and willing to engage in questionable interpretations of the tradition in order to get followers from outside the "system," are the teachers largely responsible for disseminating violent jihadist rationale.

Why was Ayatollah Khomeini so influential? Did he preach primarily military conflict with "the West"?

Ruhollah Musavi Khomeini (1902–1989) is certainly best known for his strident invectives against the "West," and especially against the United States. He was an accomplished orator and prolific writer and is widely regarded as the principle architect of the Iranian Revolution. Khomeini made his first public political declaration in the early 1940s, and he remained consistent in his views till his death. As for his views on jihad, Khomeini speaks of the traditional understanding of jihad or "struggle in the way of God" according to both its outward and inward aspects. The Greater Jihad, inner personal purification, is an absolute prerequisite for any outward attempts to establish justice and counter aggression. Without first establishing an interior conviction of this world's worthlessness in comparison to the ultimate worth of the next world, the Lesser Jihad remains just another way of serving this-worldly concerns. It is worth noting that Iraq, not Iran, was the aggressor in the nearly decade-long Iran-Iraq war, in which Saddam Husayn employed chemical weapons.

Are the twenty-first-century uprisings in predominantly Muslim lands across North Africa, through the Central Middle East, and into West and South Asia (Afghanistan and Pakistan) directly and uniquely a result of the religious tradition of Islam?

In many instances what outsiders see Muslims doing in other parts of the world is not very different from what outsiders would do in an instant if they were in Muslims' shoes. A primary difference, though, is that

The Ayatollah Ruhollah Musavi Khomeini (1902–1989) was the architect of the Iranian Revolution of 1979.

outsiders regard their own motives as political or economic while assuming that Muslims (outsiders seem unshakably convinced) are motivated by religion. The Afghan rebels have called their struggle against Russian military occupation a jihad, identifying themselves as *mujahidin*. Indeed the law of jihad does allow for military response to an invasion of one's territorial sovereignty. Numerous groups of Muslims who use the word "jihad" in their names genuinely believe their actions are justifiable and done precisely in defense, for they consider foreign presence in their part of the world invasive and unwelcome. What is most important to note here is this: on balance, Islamic tradition simply does not encourage, let alone recommend unreservedly, violent solutions to human problems.

Most Americans seem to be convinced that Muslim armies spread Islam largely by executing non-Muslims who refused to convert—is this accurate?

Quite the contrary. Early Muslim armies had established various forms of Islamic *government* from Spain to what is now Northern India by about one hundred years after Muhammad's death in 632. Over the next thousand years and more, when power changed hands across those lands and wherever Muslim regimes had been established subsequently, the new authorities battled against *Muslim* rulers and supporters of their regimes. Transfers of power from one dynasty have rarely (if ever) been orderly and peaceful, and it was mostly Muslims who suffered the consequences. Even accounting for a percentage of non-Muslims dying in Muslim invasions and subsequent periods of overt persecutions, the scores of times over twelve hundred years that Muslim dynasties and regimes supplanted other Muslim political entities would likely have accounted for significantly larger numbers of Muslim casualties than non-Muslim.

Did the Muslims pretty much invent "suicide bombing"?

This is not accurate. Here is some perspective on the unpleasant reality of suicide bombing: A careful study investigated the first forty-one such incidents taking place in the contemporary Middle East. The bombings occurred in Lebanon between 1982 and 1986. Researchers positively identified thirty-eight of the perpetrators and followed up with inquiries into their backgrounds, express motivations, and religious or ideological affiliations. Twenty-eight were avowedly secularist, communist, or members of leftist Arab organizations. Three were Christian, including a young woman who was a primary school teacher. Only seven of the thirty-eight were known to have espoused a distinctly Islamic religious ideology. It is also important that the first suicide bombings in recent times occurred not in the Middle East, but in Sri Lanka, and were perpetrated by members of the revolution Tamil Tigers, who were almost entirely of Hindu religious background.

A widespread belief is that in recent conflicts, non-Muslims have been the principal target of *jihadi* Muslims? Is this based on factual information?

In more recent times, Muslim extremists have killed far more Muslims than non-Muslims and continue to do so. Whether in the nearly ten-year Iran-Iraq war, in which an estimated half million or more died in hostilities, or through multiple counterinsurgencies in Iraq and Afghanistan, or the Sudan's attempted genocide of the Muslim (but ethnically "non-Arab") inhabitants of Darfur, or jihadi attempts to establish bases of operation in nations like Mali, or in the bloodbaths attending the revolt against Syrian president Bashar as-Asad, their victims have been almost entirely other Muslims. Even taking into consideration recent violence against Middle Eastern Christians, internal strife associated with the "Arab Spring," from North Africa to Egypt to Syria, is further evidence of the predominance of Muslim-on-Muslim violence. And in spite of the Prophet's injunctions against harming fellow believers, these factions have waved off any concern by arguing that their targets have forfeited the right to be called "true" Muslims because of alleged collaboration with the enemy or because they have clearly forsaken the true spirit of Muhammad.

ISLAM AND THE MESSAGE OF PEACE

If there are indeed "moderate" Muslims out there somewhere, why do they not loudly denounce any and all Muslim associations with violence?

As a matter of fact, and a seldom reported record, Muslim leaders have been denouncing and attempting to counteract claims of Islamic legitimacy by countless agitators for violence and supporters of groups like al-Qaeda since immediately after 9/11. Just as the data from international European police reporting have received virtually no press coverage, neither have the outcries of major Muslim groups and individual religious scholars throughout the past ten years simply have not been considered newsworthy because, some would argue, they do not support the dominant narrative about Islam and Muslims. For every *fatwa* calling for the destruction of "Zionists and Crusaders" (as in Usama bin Ladin's infamous 1998 declaration), there have been scores (perhaps even hundreds) of counter-*fatwas*.

Are there any examples of significant immediate Muslim denunciations of those events?

Perhaps more surprising for the vehemence of his denunciation was Shaykh Muhammad Husayn Fadlallah, spiritual leader of Lebanon's "islamist/jihadist" Shi'ite organization known as the Party of God (*Hizb Allah*). Saying that he was "horrified" by these "barbaric and un-Islamic" attacks, the *shaykh* condemned the misguided notion that any such act can be considered a form of laudable martyrdom. No suicide will be rewarded hereafter, because it is a crime; and no action that disregards the limitations placed on genuine *jihad* (as the 9/11 events did) is ever acceptable. Furthermore, he insisted that such acts in no way serve their intended purpose, and in fact work against the cause of Palestinians in particular and Muslims in general. "It is a horrible massacre on every level with no positive results for the basic causes of Islam." Fervent believers in Islam, the *shaykh* insisted, must adhere to the tradition's humane values; and though his own organization is opposed to the U.S. government and its policies, it does not blame the American people and cannot countenance the kind of action done on 9/11 for the purpose of retaliating against people who are not at fault for their administration's foreign policy. Nonetheless, there remains the vexing matter of Hezbollah's ongoing involvement in Middle Eastern violence.

Are there any distinctively Islamic approaches to the matter of international peace?

The vast majority of Muslims long for a world at peace. They sincerely believe that Islamic values seek to promote the possibility of such a world. Their tradition, they believe, stands not only for the absence of war, but for that positive state of safety, security, and freedom from anxiety that uniquely results from the condition of grateful surrender to God in faith (*islam, iman*). Those who get their entire picture of Muslims from media coverage of current events need to understand that they are getting a very limited perspective. Any Malaysian or Pakistani television viewer who relied on that medium to convey a sense of American values might very well develop a similarly truncated picture of Americans.

Have there been any modern and/or contemporary Muslim "pacifists"?

Quite a few, actually. Unfortunately news of violence-prone extremists invariably keeps such highly positive and idealistic organizations out of the news. Among earlier modern pacifist Muslim movements, Khuda Khidmatgar's organization of one hundred thousand Muslim Pathans, led by Abdul Ghaffar Khan, espoused a non-violent program of civil resistance and social reform under the British Raj during the twentieth century. In

Did any prominent Muslims denounce the atrocities of 9/11/2001 immediately after those events occurred?

Yes, there were many such denunciations, though the American press made virtually no mention of them. Two statements issued within forty-eight hours of the tragic events stand out especially, precisely because they were by individuals whose public positions might make many Americans think they would be prime examples of the *last* Muslims one might expect to make such statements. The first was from Shaykh Muhammad Sayyid al-Tantawi, the rector of Al-Azhar University in Cairo, the premier academic institution of traditional Sunni Islamic teaching. Shaykh Tantawi, a conservative cleric by any measure, delivered a weekly sermon in Cairo to an audience of thousands, insisting that God would punish all who attack innocent people. Such attacks, he argued, display only cowardice and stupidity and will result in their perpetrators facing a harsh judgment in the next life.

addition, numerous individual Muslim pacifists have contributed notably to non-violent activism. An Azhar-trained Syrian scholar named Jawdat Said is a good example. As early as the 1950s he condemned violence-prone organizations and movements as short-sighted and ultimately self-destructive. His public commitment inspired his sons to refuse compulsory service in the Syrian army, and they paid for their courage by being denied the right to graduate from the University of Damascus. Other prominent individuals who have spoken out in favor of Islamic non-violence include Iranian Ayatollah Mohammad ash-Shirazi, Saudi doctor Khalis Jalabi, Iraqi writer Khalid Kishtainy, and Indian scholar Asghar Ali Engineer. Most have preferred the more active term "civic jihad" to the passive-sounding "non-violence."

What about larger-scale, so-called "peace movements" that are more recent?

Again there have been more than a few such contemporary movements. Three stand out and exemplify their presence in various parts of the world. One takes its inspiration from twentieth-century Kurdish/Turkish thinker Said Nursi. His monumental Quran commentary the *Treatise (or Epistle) of Light* (*Risale-i Nur*) is the key text for the movement's nine million followers now spread across the globe. Another arises from the thought of contemporary Turkish scholar Fethullah Gülen and focuses on developing intercultural connections especially through engagement in education. Members of the organization tend to be highly educated professionals, including physicians, lawyers, and engineers, as well as academics spread across a broad range of disciplines. Another important movement is called the Asian Muslim Action Network (AMAN), whose presence impacts more than eighteen Asian nations through a host of social projects. None of these movements identifies itself explicitly with terms such as "peace-oriented," "non-

82

violent," or "pacifist." By calling themselves "Islamic" they intend to communicate an inherent concern and even active *drive* toward the peace that that name implies for the vast majority of Muslims. Among the more striking features of these developments are their truly international scope and diversity and the overwhelmingly positive impulse that has given rise to them.

Are there any examples of contemporary Sufi views of war and violence?

A Sri Lankan Sufi named Bawa Muhaiyaddeen (d. 1986), who lived much of his adult life in the United States, is known for his efforts to teach peace to Muslims and non-Muslims alike. His writing establishes a thoroughly positive and irenic tone, facing

Bawa Muhaiyaddeen was a Sufi *shaykh* from Sri Lanka who preached peace among Muslims and non-Muslims.

head on that most intractable of problems, the fate of Jerusalem. After a lengthy and eye-opening chronology of the city's changing fortunes over the centuries, the author appeals to world leaders to struggle against factionalism and enmity. Bawa bases his pacifist spirituality on the grounds of the rights of all to justice, on faith and the virtues of patience and trust in God, and on God as source of all peace. His treatment of Jihad in general likewise focuses entirely on the inward dimension, the "Greater Struggle" of self-conquest fought with the weapons of patience, gratitude, trust, and praise. In his writings, Bawa makes an idealistic distinction between the wars Muhammad fought and those that modern states wage against one another: the former served the spread of truth, the latter only promote mindless bloodshed. He treats the nasty business of outward warfare by referring to the strictures with which Islamic tradition has sought to limit the practice of justifiable conflict. He emphasizes how the Prophet prayed while others did battle, how he counseled lenience toward captives, and restraint.

What does Bawa Muhaiyaddeen think Islam's positive role should be?

In Bawa Muhaiyaddeen's strikingly non-triumphalistic view, Islam's task is to unify humanity in an inclusivist fashion. He thus considers virtually all scriptures as divine Word (including the Hindu Puranas and Zoroastrian Avesta). People must seek to view the world as God sees it rather than from partisan perspectives. He stands thus at the opposite end of the spectrum from, say, Sayyid Qutb and other recent "radicals," who have had enough of patience and long-suffering. But Bawa's efforts to build a community of peace-seekers near Philadelphia provides a wonderful example of one contemporary Muslim spirituality and will offer every reader much to ponder.

83

RELIGION AND POLITICS

Where, in general, do religion and political power come together?

Virtually every religious tradition has had to come to terms with its relationship to civil authority and power. As often as not, the relationship varies at least slightly from one political setting to another. Even in the United States many traditions have shifted their positions historically. Even the standard and seemingly straightforward principle of "separation of church and state" has been reinterpreted in various ways, with prominent religious figures seeking and winning national elected office as high as the U.S. Senate. The situation has historically been still more complex where political rulers have declared one religious tradition the "state creed." That has often meant hard times for members of faith communities that have not enjoyed official patronage and protection. Popular perception nowadays tends to label Islam as the tradition most likely to take political shape, as though no other has ever done so. But ample data from the history of religion suggests that questions the relationship of temporal to spiritual power have arisen for virtually every major tradition at some time or other.

Are there characteristically Muslim views about the convergence of religion and political power?

Muslims often describe their tradition as a "total way of life," a comprehensive approach that goes far beyond mere ritual observance or showing up at the mosque once a week. Some believe that such an all-encompassing teaching must ultimately be expressed in political terms, referring to early Muslim community life under the Prophet's leadership in Medina as the ideal. Throughout history Muslims have experimented with various models for balancing or integrating religious and civil authority. Some have worked well enough, allowing for freedom of religious practice and expression among members of religious minorities under Muslim rule. In fact, the historical record suggests that Muslims have been at least as successful as any other group at administering religiously sponsored regimes fairly and evenhandedly. Muslims in various parts of the world today continue to believe that an Islamic government represents the best hope of justice in a troubled world. But in a world where religious pluralism is increasingly evident, dividing humankind along religious lines seems a less than desirable option. The challenge now, as in the past, is to live by the Quranic dictum "There is no compulsion in religion."

Is it ever really useful to label conflicts as "religious wars"?

Wars are very seldom fought for purely religious reasons. Communities of faith often develop side-by-side in relative harmony. When problems arise, they are almost always initially political, economic, and social. Then, often enough, those who wish to keep the pot boiling invoke age-old religious differences as though they were the cause of every conflict. They remind their constituents that if they really want to be loyal, they will not rest until some ancient slight to the faith has been set right. Underneath it all is the awareness that wanting to destroy a people's will requires attacking the most powerful symbols of their identity, some of which are bound to be religious. So, for example, in Bosnia during the 1990s, a major thrust of Serb policy was to obliterate as completely as possible all visible signs of Muslim presence, destroying especially ancient mosques and libraries and leaving paved parking lots in their place. Numerous contemporary examples of significant conflict in predominantly Muslim lands feature Muslim-on-Muslim violence, even if the aggressors "dress up" their rhetoric to gather "religious" sympathy by insisting that the people they kill are in fact not "true" Muslims at all.

If Muslims all believe that Islam is not "just a religion" but a "total way of life," doesn't that imply perfect consonance of religious and civil/political spheres?

Americans often criticize Islam as inherently flawed because it allegedly refuses to distinguish between religious and civil spheres. On the contrary, there have historically been at least as many Islamically related regimes with separate administrative structures to deal with religious affairs as those that made no policy distinction between religious and civil spheres. This view also conveniently ignores centuries of European and American history. The critique might have some credibility except that those who voice it most loudly are the very people who increasingly insist that their own religious convictions are a legitimate standard of political action. A fine example of the melding of religious and civil spheres in America is the rhetoric of more than a few recent State of the Union addresses, in which a president hints that because of divine guidance, America is virtually infallible. But there are, and always have been, other far more spectacular examples of political ideology cloaked in the garb of religion.

How can one sum up the various models of administration and governance in Islamic history?

At various times in Islamic history different models of leadership have predominated. By far the single most important has been that of the caliphate. In that model, the succes-

---

Why do religious beliefs so often seem to be associated with intolerance?

Human beings dislike shades of gray. They prefer to convince themselves that they can keep truth and falsehood neatly separated. There is "us" and there is "them," and they know who has the truth. Stereotyping and demonizing are natural next steps. Not only are "they" wrong religiously, they are somehow not quite up to most people's standards of humanity and thus are to be pitied if not simply dismissed as irrelevant. Intolerance of religious diversity is a serious historical evil, a force that can easily be exploited by people of ill intent. And yet it costs so little to approach the massive fact of religious pluralism with an open mind.

sor to the Prophet, the caliph, has ideally served as both political and spiritual leader, Commander of the Army and of the Faithful. After its beginning in Medina and reestablishment for some eighty-nine years in Damascus, Baghdad was the caliphate's center for some five centuries; but the caliphate's authority did not go uncontested. Several rival caliphates laid claims, most notably in Cordoba and Cairo (under an Ismaili Shi'i dynasty called the Fatimids). In the mid-tenth century the caliphate suffered a severe abridgment when a Turkic dynasty overcame Baghdad and vested the caliph's temporal power in a new parallel institution called the sultanate. After the Mongols sacked Baghdad in 1258, various dynasties made largely symbolic attempts to prop up or otherwise revive the moribund institution. Nowadays the caliphate is a memory, though some still dream of its resurgence.

Have there been other movements based on other models?

Claimants to leadership of the imamate type arose from time to time. Mahdist movements (Sunni groups that focus on the return of a divinely "guided" person called the *Mahdi*) have been attempted with varying degrees of success until modern times. One abortive attempt at such a movement occurred as recently as 1979, around the beginning of the Iranian revolution and the storming of the American embassy in Tehran. At that time Sunni and Shi'i Muslims alike were observing the beginning of the fourteenth Islamic century. In Tehran Twelver Shi'ites relived the suffering of Husayn against the evil tyrant in their struggle against the evil Shah and the United States in regular observances that mark the beginning of every year, but take on renewed importance at the turn of a century. In Mecca a small Mahdist group, recalling the tradition that with each new century God would raise up for Islam a "renewer," took over the sanctuary of the Kaba and proclaimed a short-lived new age and paid with their lives for daring to violate the holy place.

There's been much talk concerning the fear of Islamic "invasion" of the West. Is the Muslim goal to restore the caliphate?

A small minority of extremists cherish the notion of a restored caliphate. But such a scenario presupposes several conditions that one looks for in vain in the history of Islamic political regimes. First, the caliphate of nostalgia is supposed to have been a truly global centralized rule in which the "commander of the faithful" exacted the fealty of Muslims everywhere. In fact, at no time during the history of the caliphate did it extend across the full expanse of territories in which Islam would eventually become a dominant presence or majority faith community. At its broadest extent, the caliphate, by any account a vast project, stretched from Spain to Northwest India. However, it never became established firmly in Iberia, and within half a century after the Abbasid dynasty had founded its new capital of Baghdad in 762, the fabric of the caliphate began to unravel from the edges. By the early ninth century, restive provinces broke off as practically independent amirates; by the mid-tenth century, a Shi'i faction had become the power behind the throne in Baghdad; a century later, the Seljuk Turks had virtually neutered the caliphate by establishing the sultanate as the de facto parallel institution with all the real power.

Were there "rival caliphates" elsewhere in Islamdom?

By the tenth and eleventh centuries, rival caliphates were well established in Spain and Egypt. In other words, the political map of Islamdom quickly took on the look of a crazy quilt, and the notion of a resurrected global Muslim rule is in reality a dream that has never come true as the people who fantasize about it might imagine. By the time the Ottoman dynasty incorporated the great middle swath of what had been the Byzantine Empire, even that great power included only part of North Africa and went no further east than Iraq. In addition, the kind of caliphate whose resurrection radical/puritanic/extremist groups envision, is not the extended dominion represented for several generations by the Umayyad and Abbasid dynasties. They look back instead to the pristine days of the Prophet and his four immediate successors in Medina, the Rightly Guided caliphs. They typically regard the subsequent dynastic regimes with their pretensions to royalty as betrayals of the Prophetic age. The problem here is that the Rightly Guided caliphs ruled a much reduced realm even at its greatest extent.

What other factors militate against a revived caliphate?

The idea of the caliphate presupposes the seamless integration—indeed, the simple identity of political and religious institutions. The historical reality is that the majority of the many political regimes under Islamic auspices across the globe over the course of more than a millennium actually represent a wide variety of blends and interrelationships of political and religious institutions. Take early modern Iran, for example. In 1500, Shi'i Islam was proclaimed the "state" creed by the ascendant Safavid dynasty. For most of the subsequent five hundred years, the royal and religious establishments each remained distinct. Religious officialdom played the role of a loyal opposition for the most part, and at no time did religious scholars mount a serious campaign to exercise actual political rule. Not until the Iranian Islamic Revolution in 1979 did Khomeini's radical reinterpretation of Iranian Shi'i traditions of political theology call for direct religious establishment control over political institutions.

Have rulers in states/regions with predominantly Muslim populations engaged or expressed overtly religious values to galvanize popular support?

No ruler wants to risk loss of authority by undercutting the religious legitimation upon which rule depends. But powerful religious figures and movements have often tugged at the allegiance of Muslims in many cultures, thus increasing the likelihood of divided loyalties among a ruler's subjects. Efforts to use such forces to advantage have often materialized in royal support for the institutions that serve the followers of charismatic religious leaders. From Morocco to Indonesia, enormous sums of money have gone into the endowment, building or renovation, and general financial support of

Given recent upheavals across the Arab Middle East and North Africa, especially the resurgence of al-Qaeda and related groups, what are the chances that those striving to resurrect the caliphate will threaten global stability and overrun the "Islamic World"?

Here, as always, historical perspective is essential. First, of the scores of *proclaimed* caliphates that various groups have announced over the past five hundred years, virtually none have attained greater than regional success and/or remained significantly influential for more than a generation or two. Second, in more recent memory and back as far as 1980, a group such as the Taliban proudly conferred on their leader, Mulla Omar, the name "Commander of the Faithful," a primary historical title of the caliph. No matter how loudly they shout their assumed prerogatives, the Taliban will likely remain a threat to regional stability in South Asia and not far beyond. Third, even though groups such as the "Islamic State in Iraq and the Levant/Syria" (ISIL/S) boldly advertise their establishment of a "caliphate" for which they claim sovereignty from the Mediterranean to Iran (with designs well beyond that, presumably), their recent alarming successes depend heavily on political and social factors that can still be reversed.

While "ISIL" might (like earlier temporarily successful attempts to reestablish a caliphate) manage to consolidate some territory and advertise its success in attempts to recruit young fighters, there are hundreds of millions of Muslims from Morocco to Malaysia who want nothing to do with such a development and who are horrified at ISIL's ideology and savagery. Finally, many major Muslim religious and legal scholars from the most respected and prestigious Islamic institutions have issued unmistakable denunciations of these extremists, their pretensions, and their methods as contrary to Islamic law's restrictions on the conduct of war and in no way representing Islam's deepest values. ISIL, they insist, has no right to use the term "Islamic" in its title.

holy places associated with holy persons. Some tomb-shrines have become the centers of entire towns. Those of Mulay Idris I (d. c. 793) on Mount Serhun near Fez, Morocco, and of Mulay Idris II (d. 828) in Fez are two such focal points. For centuries Moroccan governments have paid official attention to the maintenance of these holy sites, for devotion to these two Friends of God and descendants of Muhammad runs too deep among the people to ignore.

Are there other examples of rulers promoting religious values by promoting popular devotion and "shrines"?

Further to the east is an instructive example of a different sort of shrine associated with the legitimation of an Islamic ruling dynasty, the Timurid (referring to "descendants

Timur Lang, aka Tamerlane). In Iran and central Asia, rulers funded architectural projects as part of their programs of charitable works that would *demonstrate* their own genuine Islamic values. But this was not purely for show and often represents deep religious commitment on the part of these princely patrons. Ruling class figures were often genuinely attached to the teachings and legacy of venerable spiritual teachers. Timur Lang, for example, was so taken with the spirit of the already long-deceased Shaykh Ahmad Yasawi (d. 1166) that he undertook a major architectural project to honor the *shaykh*. In 1397 he built a glorious new tomb at the site of the original grave. Timur became personally involved in the project, even to stipulating the central dome's height of 126 feet. Highly visible near an oasis along a pilgrimage and caravan road, this splendid work was a statement of Timur's devotion as well as a monument to the *shaykh*.

Is such "devotion" not really a cover for political motives—more akin to currying favor among the wider population of believers?

Political motives do not necessarily rule out genuine devotion, though they may indeed cast a shadow of doubt on the sincerity of a ruler's claim of religious motivation. Many Ottoman Sultans well into modern times engaged in the renovation of shrines and tombs, with credible evidence of authentic piety. In fact, even during times when rulers have felt the need to officially suppress overt veneration of Friends of God and force devotees to go underground, those very authorities themselves may have continued to be devotees. For example, Jalal ad-Din Rumi's (d. 1273) tomb in Konya was originally built under a Saljuqid ruler, a predecessor dynasty to the Ottomans. But under Sulayman's rule, the tomb, already a popular place of pilgrimage for generations, was renovated and the facilities expanded. Now Rumi's final resting place provides a stunningly ironic example of the enormous power of such holy places.

Has this dynamic ever worked in reverse, with rulers trying to undermine popular devotion to a major religious figure?

When Mustafa Kemal Ataturk (d. 1938) officially proclaimed the secular Turkish Republic on October 29, 1923, he suppressed the Sufi orders because they represented too great a potential force for disruption in his experiment in governing a Muslim nation. Members of the Mevlevi tariqa were officially disbanded and no longer allowed to gather publicly. But the Turkish Ministry of Culture continues to subsidize

Mustafa Kemal Ataturk (d. 1938) founded the secular Turkish Republic after the fall of the Ottoman Empire.

89

Rumi's tomb as a "museum," and pilgrims continue to visit it as a shrine. A striking tribute to the enduring spirit of Rumi (and indirectly of scores of other holy persons) appears on a 5,000 Turkish lire currency note in use until inflation rendered it virtually worthless: one side depicts a sternly serious Ataturk in profile; the other, a benignly smiling Rumi next to the fluted green dome beneath which three dervishes whirl. On balance, political rulers throughout history and in many cultural and religious contexts have run a broad gamut of modes of expressing, cultivating, and, of course, manipulating religious beliefs for their own purposes.

Muhammad Reza Shah Pahlavi ruled Iran from 1941 until the Iranian Revolution of 1979. The Pahlavi shahs were considered by many Muslims to have been heavily influenced by the West and Russia.

Has Iran always been ruled by radical Shi'ite "clerics" like Khomeini and his successor, Khamenei?

Iran has been "officially" a Shi'i nation since around 1501—a relatively small portion of the Persian people's very long history, dating back as far as 2800 B.C.E. In the early sixteenth century, a Turkic dynasty with Sufi background, called the Safavids, came to power and declared Twelver Shi'ism the "state creed." For some 480 years, the religious establishment of scholars and specialists in Sharia functioned as a kind of loyal opposition in relation to the royal authorities. The Safavids were sandwiched between the two other "gunpowder empires"—the Ottomans and the Mughals, both Sunni dynasties. They engaged militarily with the Ottomans over several centuries, and some argue that by distracting the Ottomans in contests over territory the Safavids may well have prevented the Turks from conquering more of Europe. The Safavid dynasty weakened toward the end of the seventeenth century and suffered from an Afghan inter-regnum after a Pashtun invasion in 1722. After several decades of political instability, Iran was again stabilized by another Turkic dynasty, the Qajar, in 1794. From their new capital in Tehran, the Qajars ruled until overthrown by the Pahlavi family, an indigenous and short-lived Iranian dynasty.

How did Iran undergo such radical change after the mid-twentieth century?

Under the two Pahlavi shahs, Iran's foreign relations were marked by increasing influence by outsiders, especially Russia, Britain, and the United States. One notorious example of foreign interference was the CIA overthrow of Musaddiq's interruption in

The destruction of the sixteenth-century Bridge of Mostar in 1993 by Croatian forces was a symbol of major divisions between Serbs and Croats.

Pahlavi rule in 1953—an event that still colors Iran views of "the West." In 1963, an ayatollah named Ruhollah Khomeini spearheaded a popular attempt to overthrow the second Pahlavi shah and was exiled to Iraq. An inveterate firebrand, Khomeini continued to annoy Iraq's Baath rulers until Saddam Hussein banished him to France in the early 1970s, where he continued to agitate for the overthrow of the Shah of Iran. His Iranian Revolution succeeded in early 1979. The timing was powerfully symbolic, marking the very start of the Islamic lunar year 1400, and redolent of the ancient tradition that God would raise up a "renewer" at the outset of every (Islamic) century. Khomeini implemented what was a totally new political theology for modern Iran, centered as it was on the "Oversight of Religious Lawgiver," and seeking to foster a rare example of contemporary theocratic regime.

What, if any, is the religious connection with the late-twentieth-century strife among Muslims and Serbs and Croats in the former Yugoslavia?

Islam began to develop a significant presence in the Balkans with the Ottoman conquest of 1463. Christianity had already been deeply rooted among the Catholic Croats and Orthodox Serbs for many centuries. Conversion to Islam, while generally not coerced by the Ottomans, was definitely associated with foreign domination. Although the Croats and Serbs have by no means always been peaceful neighbors, there have been periods of still greater hostility between the Christians, who consider themselves the inheritors of the land, and the Muslims, who are often regarded as invaders. For many non-Muslim Bosnians, all things even remotely identifiable as Turkish represent the remnants of a historic scourge whose vestiges they would like to eliminate. Bosnian

Serbs, with the urging of the government of Serbia in Belgrade, have been engaged in the systematic eradication of virtually every visible reminder of the Ottoman presence that they associate with Islam. Scores of historic mosques, libraries, bridges, and other architectural treasures have been destroyed, all in an attempt to eradicate the identity of the Muslim people of Bosnia.

What has all the talk about "ethnic" cleansing got to do with religion?

The peoples of the Balkans are generally of Western Slavic stock, so the term "ethnic cleansing" is an inaccurate description of recent events in the republics of the former Yugoslavia. All of the inhabitants of the region given the national designation of Bosnia (comprised of an eastern section called Bosnia and a western called Herce-govina) speak a Slavic language often called Serbo-Croatian. While there are some differences in the ways Bosnian Croats, Serbs, and Muslims speak, the differences are analogous to those that distinguish British English from American English. Recent events in the Balkans have resulted largely from political decisions that have sought to aggravate divisions among people of various religious communities who had been learning to live together peacefully. As such, the religious distinctions are decidedly secondary, but a handy tool for demagogues whose success depends on their ability to promote divisiveness and hatred.

What is one example of a Christian power declaring war on Muslims for religious reasons?

In 1989, on the six hundredth anniversary of the Battle of Kosovo, Serbian leader Slobodan Milosevic launched his campaign for a Greater Serbia with a blood-curdling speech on the site of that historic conflict. He spoke of how Prince Lazar, who had died a glorious martyr's death defending his homeland against the Turks in 1389, was a Christ-figure and the Muslims were the Christ-killers. Milosevic then hinted that he was the new Prince Lazar whose mission was to reverse the score, and he soon launched a savage onslaught against the Muslims of Bosnia-Hercegovina, tearing apart a society in which Croatian Catholics, Serbian Orthodox, and Bosnian Muslims had lived in peace for many years. Even now, few careful observers of the Balkan conflict would identify religion as the true instigating factor, let alone claim that Christianity is inherently and irredeemably violent.

CONCERNS OF
TWENTY–FIRST CENTURY MUSLIMS

Is there an "Islamic economics"?

Beginning with the Quran, Islamic tradition has had specific concerns about economic transactions in relation to economic justice. Muhammad himself had been a businessman, working with the caravan trade owned by his first wife, Khadija. As in so many other matters, Muslims find an exemplar in the Medinan society of the Prophet's day. One issue the Quran addresses at least indirectly is that of considering money as "product" rather than as a simple means of exchange. In effect the Quran regards money as a measure of goods and services, not itself a basis for making more money.

Given the realities of contemporary economic life, can "Islamic economics" actually be workable these days?

Global banking and market systems are built on the concept that one can make money by loaning or investing it, without at the same time producing anything else. So how do Muslims manage? Many, of course, have simply been going along with the "system." But there has been increasing interest in new attempts to devise creative ways to make money work according to the principle that all parties to financial transactions—not just the borrower—must share equally in the risk as well as the profits. In other words, the focus of *all* parties is on the success of the project being funded rather than on the financial transaction. In addition, investors must screen their options carefully; the final criterion is not the promise of highest returns, but the certainty that the eventual product will be compatible with Islamic religious values (e.g., no stock in companies that produce weapons, alcohol, or pornography, or have gaming concerns). In that same spirit, Islamic banking provides for interest-free loans to the truly needy.

A Muslim woman shops at a vegetable stand in Delhi, India. Muslim values concerning economics are much less adversarial than in many Western cultures; the customer is considered a partner, not merely a consumer to be used.

What is the ultimate goal of Islamic values regarding economics?

Muslims engaged in implementing traditional Islamic values in today's global marketplace face a major challenge, but the goal is to ensure social equity and keep the profit-motive subordinate to a higher principle. This is Islam's major contribution to the evolution of "business ethics" in our time. Less adversarial than the financial arrangements most people have become accustomed to, the emphasis in Islamic banking is on cooperation, so that the customer is primarily a partner. Attempts to define "Islamic economics" as a discipline began in India during the 1930s and 1940s, not long before the creation of Pakistan.

A detail from a stained-glass window at the Saint-Julien cathedral in Sarthe, France, shows Adam and Eve's temptation in the Garden of Eden. Muslims and Christians share this and other stories from their holy books.

Where does this perspective fit on the spectrum of modern economic systems?

In theory, Islamic economics stands somewhere between capitalist free enterprise and socialist control: it seeks to maintain market forces, but within the limits of broad social consciousness. But there is as yet nothing like consensus on a coherent theory among Muslim economists. The Quran, for example, forbids *riba* (ree-BAA), a term generally understood to mean "taking interest," but economists do not agree precisely with what that means for today. In practice, developments are largely limited to the field of banking. The first modern Islamic bank was established in Dubai in 1975, but over the past twenty years or so, the experiment has grown dramatically. Magazines pitched to Muslims now include increasingly numerous ads for businesses that invite participation from people looking for sound investment opportunities that are also religiously acceptable (*halal*, ha-LAAL).

Are there Islamic websites?

Since the Internet has become such a handy way to communicate and advertise, naturally Muslims are finding ways to use it to good advantage. A cursory flip through the pages of almost any popular magazine published for a Muslim readership turns up dozens of interesting items. As expected, publishers and bookstores specializing in Islamic materials are among the most numerous advertisers. A close second are vendors of miscellaneous supplies of interest to Muslims, including clothing and jewelry with religious calligraphy; devotional materials such as prayer rugs, pictures of Mecca, and wall plaques with Quranic calligraphy; educational tools such as a "Pilgrimage to Mecca" board game; recorded versions of Quran recitation; and a growing array of software items to aid in the traditional religious sciences. Next come ads for special services such as arrangement of travel for pilgrimage, both the Hajj and the Umra (minor pilgrimage outside the formal season of Hajj) to Saudi Arabia, and programs in Islamic Studies at Islamic colleges. Muslim social service agencies seeking to raise funds for the care of orphans and the indigent are increasingly visible on the Internet as well. A type of advertising that seems to be generating increasing interest in this category of special services for Muslims consists of listings of financial options and banking and investment services that take into account the ethical concerns of those who believe Muslims ought to avoid the established institutions of mainstream capitalism if at all possible.

Are there any Quranic teachings that relate to contemporary understandings of the material world?

Beginning with the Quran, important Islamic texts and thinkers have addressed themselves to environmental issues. Take this text from the Quran for example: "Do they not see how each thing God has created, down to the very least, most humbly prostrates itself to God as its shadow revolves from the right and the left? To God all in heaven and on earth prostrates itself; from beasts to angels none withholds haughtily. In reverent fear of their transcendent Lord they do what they are bidden" (Quran 16:48–50). Unlike the Bible, the Quran contains no integrated narrative of creation, suggests that God would surely need no rest after his "work," and hints that a "day" might actually be a very long time. In both sources Adam is the first human being, but the Quran's descriptions of the material vary from dust to semen to water to a clot of blood. Though the Quran's

A view of the Old City of Jerusalem, Israel. The Church of the Holy Sepulchre is at the top, right. Jerusalem is considered a holy city by Christians, Jews, and Muslims alike.

Adam also knows the names of all creatures, the emphasis is on God's knowledge rather than Adam's. In the Quranic stories, human beings are not created in God's image, for that would compromise the divine transcendence.

How do the Bible and Quran differ with respect to the creation myth?

In general the Quran seems to place greater emphasis on God's sovereignty and power than does the biblical account. Whereas the Bible describes creation as a single original action, the Quran suggests that God is involved in creation as an ongoing activity, re-asserting His creative prerogative with the emergence of each new living being. In the Bible, God seems to commission the first people unreservedly to take charge of the earth. Islamic tradition also regards the creation as given to humans to use, but God seems to hesitate a bit in turning the operation over to Adam and Eve. God offered to Heaven, Earth, and the Mountains the "trust" of watching over creation. They declined out of fear, so God offered the Trust to humankind. Adam accepted, unjust and foolish as he was—and ungrateful in addition. When God informed his angels he was preparing to entrust creation to Adam as his representative (literally, caliph, vice regent), they warned the Creator that human beings would surely act wickedly. God assured the angels that the risk was worth taking. God reckoned it was a gamble worth taking for He had called forth from Adam's loins and assembled all of his yet unborn descendants and asked them, "Am I not your Lord?" They had responded as one and without hesitation, "Yes, we are witnesses to that!" (Quran 33:72, 2:30, 7:10, 172).

Can Muslims and Christians come together on matters of environmental stewardship?

Any discussion of religious attitudes toward the care and keeping of the planet is bound to run head-on into the unpleasant fact that virtually no major religious community can boast a very impressive record in implementing its stated values. Unfortunately, greed quickly swamps lofty but fragile ideals in its wake. However unrealistic it may seem to speak of a tradition's ideals without taking a hard look at how human beings have actually behaved, ideals do need to be restated. Muslims and Christians as communities need to get serious about understanding their *own* traditions' mandates about environmental concerns. Then there may be more solid ground on which to discuss *shared* responsibilities about confronting the global tendency to sacrifice the earth on the altar of the great god Profit.

ISLAM AND CONFLICT IN THE MIDDLE EAST

What is the role of "sacred place/space" in contemporary international affairs, especially in the Middle East?

Islamic tradition has expressed the most expansive sense of sacred place and has retained the strongest sense of traditional orientation to a sacred center. To the Arabian

Western Wall of the Jewish Temple, popularly known as the "Wailing Wall" because of its association with annual lamentation of the fast observed on the Ninth of Av over the destruction of the Temple. The lower courses of masonry are from King Herod's time, identifiable as Herodian by the trimmed outer margin of each stone. (Photo courtesy David Oughton).

cities of Mecca and Medina come pilgrims from all over the world to commemorate the central events in the prophetic missions of Abraham and Muhammad. When religionists decry the presence of non-Muslim military personnel on Arabian soil, they raise the unacceptable, if rather unlikely, prospect of an infidel invasion of the Holy Cities. To the Iraqi towns of Najaf and Karbala, Shi'ite pilgrims have come over the centuries to commemorate the deaths of Ali and his martyr-son Husayn. It was in part to liberate these two holy sites from Saddam Hussein that Khomeini persisted in the war with Iraq. Somewhere in Iraq even now, some Shi'ite *mullah* is surely exhorting his people to defend these sanctuaries of the martyrs from defilement by outsiders.

Why is the holy city of Jerusalem such a bone of contention in Middle Eastern politics?

Each of the three Abrahamic faiths revolves around a sacred story, a distinctive interpretation of history. At the center of every sacred story is at least one sacred place, which in turn carves out of the cosmos a space held to be inviolable and safe for believers, a sanctuary. For Jews, Jerusalem clearly focuses that sense of sacred place, and within Jerusalem it is the Western Wall (or Wailing Wall) that symbolizes Jewish identity above all. Here one can see and touch all that remains of the Solomonic and Herodian temples. Here one can lament the destruction of both temples and long for the raising of a new one. Unfortunately, time has made the situation agonizingly complex for Jews. The merest mention of rebuilding the temple evokes cries of outrage from the Muslim com-

97

munity, for on top of the temple mount there now stand the seventh-century shrine called the Dome of the Rock and the early eighth-century al-Aqsa mosque.

What do Muslims think is especially important and "Islamic" about Jerusalem?

For Muslims the place recalls the importance of Abraham and Solomon as prophets and adds a new layer of sacrality in the belief that this place was a way station in Muhammad's chief mystical experience, the Night Journey and Ascension. The Muslim holy places on the temple mount also bear an important historic relationship to Christianity. Inscriptions on the Dome of the Rock, as well as the Dome's axial relationship to the al-Aqsa's basilical hall (which, it appears, was laid out to parallel and outdo that of the Sepulcher with its dome and basilical hall), clearly suggest a statement of Muslim superiority over Christianity. Muslims count as their own, in addition, the mosque of the Ascension (of Jesus) on the Mount of Olives and the Mosque of Hebron that enshrines the cave of Machpelah, the tomb of Abraham and the patriarchs. Located as it is in an Arab town, the latter has been an important symbol for Palestinians.

What Middle Eastern sites are especially important to Christians?

For most Christians, the principal holy sites in the Middle East are of course the Church of the Nativity in Bethlehem, the Church of the Holy Sepulcher in Jerusalem, as well as several places in Nazareth. Perhaps no single place speaks more eloquently of the diversity of Christianity in the Middle East than the Holy Sepulcher. With its multiple side chapels representing various Christian communities, competing liturgical celebrations, and the olfactory dissonance that results from multiple flavors of incense, the Church of the Holy Sepulcher offers a virtual smorgasbord of the Christian tradition. It has been and remains an important symbol of Christian presence in Jerusalem. Christians have not always enjoyed free exercise of their rights in the Middle East, and access to the Sepulcher remains one symbolic anchor in their sense of identity. As a sacred city, Jerusalem is the single most important place in the Middle East. For Muslims, the Dome is a symbol of victory; for Jews, the Wall a symbol of loss; for Christians, the Sepulcher a symbol of victory through loss.

Is there a succinct summary to the history of the Israeli-Palestinian conflict?

Years ago a Palestinian uttered this story: Once upon a time, a camel and a scorpion happened upon each other on the banks of a river. As the camel prepared to swim across, the scorpion approached and asked for a ride. When the camel refused for fear the scorpion would take advantage of his kindness and sting him to death, the scorpion explained how foolish that would be, for then they would both die. The camel agreed and began to ferry his passenger across. Halfway over the scorpion stung the camel. With his last gasp the dromedary asked, "Why on earth did you sentence us both to death?" Said the scorpion as the two went under, "Welcome to the Middle East!" The Palestinian asked, "Who is the camel and who is the scorpion?"

A German ship, part of a North Atlantic Treaty Organization (NATO) force, docks at Istanbul. While one can't say that the West is unified against the East, many people often do see conflicts with Muslims under such generalized terms.

The conflict has deep historical roots but really began to assume its present proportions in 1917 when the Balfour Declaration established the British Mandate over Palestine and the Jewish population in the area saw steady increase for thirty years. In 1947 the UN partition plan allocated 56 percent of the land, including prize seacoast, to the Jews, who constituted about a third of the population. The partition proceeded rapidly and when Israel proclaimed statehood in 1948 the Arabs rebelled. Terror begot terror as the two sides confronted each other, but the Palestinians were steadily losing ground and being driven into exile as refugees. In 1956 the Suez crisis saw the last vestige of colonialism pitting the United States, Europe, and Israel against Egypt. Eleven years later Israel doubled its territory in the Six Day War. In 1973 the Arabs fought back and managed to regain some ground. It was not until 1978 that the Camp David Accord began to turn events around, very slowly. But in 1982 Israel invaded Lebanon all the way to Beirut, laying siege until the Palestine Liberation Organization (PLO) retreated. Israel has maintained a security zone south of Lebanon since then. Then in 1987 the Palestinian uprising known as the Intifada resulted in massive Israeli curtailments of human rights and ongoing retaliation and counter-retaliation by both Palestinian and Israeli interests.

What role has Islam to play currently in Middle Eastern affairs?

Islam has been a powerful symbolic factor in contemporary Middle Eastern affairs, from the formation of alliances against Israel to the current rhetoric of Palestinian organizations like Hamas and Islamic Jihad. But this intractable conflict is not and never has been a "religious" war—many Palestinians are Christian, for one thing, but the use of religious imagery has become inevitable in a land where nearly every stone has sacred associations for someone.

THE PERCEIVED CONFLICT BETWEEN "ISLAM AND THE WEST"

Is it true that Islam is the next major threat to "Western" civilization after the fall of communism?

At the risk of oversimplification in the other direction, one could say that, alas, every society needs its Evil Empire. When no obvious candidate fills the bill, society conjures one up in the vain hope that somehow it will make everyone feel better about themselves. During the past couple of decades there has been much talk about "resurgent Islam," fueled by such events as the Iranian Revolution, the Palestinian Intifada, and the ascendancy of the Afghan Taliban. Books with titles like *The Islamic Bomb: The Nuclear Threat to Israel and the Middle East* (1982) raised a specter of some sort of nuclear conspiracy, as though Islam represents a unitary political will intent on world domination. In fact, "Islam" is nothing quite like the various "-isms" one can realistically imagine bringing political and economic resources to bear on some global or even regional objective—capitalism, communism, colonialism, imperialism, or on a smaller scale, Zionism, for example.

Does it make sense to consider "the West" as some sort of unified force?

No. "The West" is not like a unified secularist bloc of political, economic, and cultural determination, set adamantly against the real or imagined religio-moral fervor of "the East." Still, it is much easier to construe the world as neatly defined opposing forces than to come to terms with the common humanity that underlies all differences. Muslims are on the whole just about as susceptible to these kinds of generalizations as non-Muslims, however, and are often equally responsible for perpetuating the sweeping dichotomy. It requires not only a scheme of enormous paranoid conspiratorial dimensions but also a presumption of practically cosmic evil intent to envision a world population of Muslims bent on Islamizing the globe. (It may help to keep in mind that many Christians pray fervently for the conversion of humanity to their creed.) In short, Islam as a religious tradition even at its most zealous for conversion is in no way a threat to world peace and order. On the contrary, it is as important a force for maintaining peace and order as any other tradition.

Does the concept of a "Clash of Civilizations" offer any real insight into the nature of these conflicts?

Perhaps the biggest flaw in the "Clash of Civilizations" paradigm is the way it glosses over the lack of unitary political will and socio-cultural cohesiveness in the Other Side: it seems to presuppose that such conflicts simply "happen" as a result of evil generated from across the great divide and that there is no question of responsibility on "our" side, except as the wronged party acting in self-defense. Purely evil intent toward "us" seems to be the hallmark of Clash-talk: "we" really have not done anything that warrants "their" evil acts and designs; we see no reason why we should re-examine our world view; we will not allow them to put us on the defensive—though we will, of course, defend ourselves; we're sorry "they" have pushed us into this conflict, but now we have no alternative but to respond in kind, and if that means destroying "them," so be it. At a certain point, it is simply assumed that a Law of Inexorability kicks in and that global conflict is as inevitable as—how about Armageddon, for example? One could argue that there was some credibility in the "Evil Empire" rhetoric of the Reagan era, to the extent that the principal protagonists, the USA and the USSR, fit that description to some degree. But the suggestion that either "Islam" or "the West" now represent integral forces—call them civilizations, call them socio-political-economic entities—is unhelpful, at best.

Is there any reliable data on terrorism in "the West" generally?

A significant but virtually unnoticed recent report of research on terrorist attacks perpetrated in Europe during 2006 puts the situation in a still more startling light. Europol tallied a total of 498 "terrorist attacks" during all of 2006. Of those attacks, ETA, the Basque separatist organization, was responsible for the highest tally (136), including the only fatal incident of the lot. Islamist groups perpetrated only one such attack, with reports of a total of two foiled Islamist plots filed by England and Denmark. More recently, the single most destructive terrorist attack in contemporary Europe was—most ironically—perpetrated by a Norwegian who claimed that his motive in slaughtering several young people and adults was to prevent the deleterious effects of the unfolding Islamic invasion of Europe. While there is always the potential for terrorist attacks by individuals identifying themselves as Muslims, the situation is far more complex than the typical media sound-bite can describe.

Some argue that Islam is incompatible with democracy. Is there any foundation for that view?

Two important assumptions contribute to this view. One is that the American "doctrine" of separation of Church and State remains perfectly intact and that American religion simply has not been a serious factor in U.S. political administrations. The other is that Muslims have everywhere and at all times regarded failure to meld the religious with the civil as fundamentally blasphemous. Several important ingredients in this perceived dichotomy deserve a closer look. One is the largely unchallenged conviction that, while it goes without saying that American presidents, important politicians, and celebrated preachers will describe major conflicts as just causes to be waged under the banner of divine approbation, every Islamic summons to jihad is just one more proof of the inherently bellicose nature of Muslims. Americans have a long history of regarding their nation's very reason for being as a "manifest destiny" to alter the course of human history, an incontrovertible mandate to implement the Creator's own justice on earth.

For all the talk of wanting to promote political self-determination throughout the world, U.S. administrations have long made it a policy to meddle in the affairs of duly elected regimes in Latin America. For all the talk of supporting freedom movements,

U.S. administrations have typically sided with repressive right-wing dictatorships to the south. Claiming that the absence of democratic institutions in many predominantly Muslim lands is somehow uniquely a result of Islam is like claiming the endless succession of failed democracies, one-party systems, murderous dictatorships, and countless "disappearances" and assassinations in Latin America is the fault of Catholicism.

ISLAM IN THE UNITED STATES

What are the origins of Islam in the United States?

Islam took root here much the same way Judaism and Christianity did, a non-native tradition imported with the expansion of Western Europe. What differs though is that the first Muslims to come to the New World did not do so voluntarily; they came as slaves. Many early slaves came from West Africa, and perhaps as many as 20 percent of African slaves brought during the eighteenth and nineteenth centuries were Muslim. Because they were slaves, these early Muslims had little chance to nurture the spread of their faith in any formal ways. That process would begin only in the late nineteenth century with an influx of mostly Arab Muslims from the Middle East. The period between the two world wars saw a second major migration; a third commenced just after World War II and continued for some twenty years. Unlike earlier immigrants, who had sought wealth that they could take back home later, those who came in subsequent waves were often fleeing political oppression. With requirements for entry to the United States stiffening in the mid-1960s, the most recent phase of immigration has included well-educated Muslims from a variety of countries, and notably from South Asia (India, Pakistan, and Bangladesh).

What has contributed to the continued growth of American Islam?

A second aspect of Islam's growth in America is its presence among African Americans. The story is one of fascinating sectarian developments especially over the past fifty years or so. Most readers will have heard of the "Black Muslims," and many non-Muslim Americans still think the term refers to those African Americans once associated with Elijah Muhammad. Actually, apart from members of prison populations among whom there are many converts to Islam, most Black American Muslims are now members of "mainstream" Muslim communities. The stories of these African

U.S. Congressman Keith Ellison represents the state of Minnesota. Not only is he the first African American to be elected for the office in Minnesota, he is the first Muslim to serve in Congress.

American Muslims offer great insight into how they adapted to their new life. One last small contingent of American Muslims is made up of indigenous, mostly female, white converts. Some become Muslim so as to share the faith of a spouse, but many women say they find Islam attractive because they believe it accorded women greater dignity than American society in general. A still smaller number of Americans consider themselves at least secondarily or incidentally Muslim by virtue of their belonging to "Sufi" groups, whose founders trace their spiritual lineages back to various mystical "orders." The terms "secondarily or incidentally" are used here because such groups often place greater emphasis on human unity than on exclusive membership in an Islamic faith community.

How has Islam been associated with the African American community?

Formal identification by African Americans with things at least nominally Islamic dates back to the early twentieth century, with Noble Drew Ali's founding of the Moorish American Science Temple. Remnants of the movement that began in Newark, New Jersey, can still be found here and there, its male members including the Turkish term for a nobleman, Bey, as part of their religious names. A much more important development began in Detroit, Michigan, during the 1930s. There a little-known character named W. D. Fard offered African Americans a way of identifying with their African roots: their ancestors had been Muslims and it was time to rediscover their heritage. When Elijah (Poole) Muhammad joined the group, "The Lost-Found Nation of Islam in the Wilderness of North America," Fard bestowed upon him the mantle of prophetic office. Elijah continued to develop a community called the Nation of Islam, or the Black Muslims. His original message had little in common with basic Islamic teachings and amounted to a form of reverse racism. Still the Nation of Islam offered the benefits of an enhanced sense of self-dignity and many positive community-building values.

How did the history of the Black Muslims and the Nation of Islam develop further?

Two prominent young followers of Elijah Muhammad were Malcolm X and Louis Farrakhan. Malcolm (Little) X tells in his autobiography how he discovered during his pilgrimage to Mecca that Elijah Muhammad's teachings of a kind of reverse racism were a lie. There he found that, contrary to Elijah's message of racial segregation and Black superiority over whites, everyone "snored in the same language." All human beings were brothers and sisters under God, and Malcolm re-

Malcolm X refuted the racist teachings of Nation of Islam leader Elijah Muhammad to embrace Islam after he took a pilgrimage to Mecca in 1964.

turned to try to counter-teach Elijah Muhammad's misinterpretations of Islam. Malcolm was assassinated in 1965, but ten years later, when Muhammad died, Elijah's son Wallace took over and continued to pursue the reform movement Malcolm X had begun. Wallace began the process of sweeping reforms with the intention of bringing the community into line doctrinally with mainstream Islam. That involved a frank repudiation of Elijah's most cherished views. Wallace sought to bring the Nation of Islam, newly named the World Community of Islam in the West, in line with mainstream Muslim teachings. Taking the religious name Warith Deen (close to the Arabic for "heir to the religion"), he would lead the community through a series of changes of name and identity over the next eight years. Its name was changed to the American Bilalian Community, and its newspaper called *Bilalian News*; tradition has it that the Prophet Muhammad chose as his *muezzin* an Abyssinian named Bilal, the first Black convert to Islam. Louis Farrakhan, on the other hand, chose to continue for some years the separatist doctrines of Elijah Muhammad and, with his approximately fifty thousand followers, retained the name Nation of Islam. The majority of African American Muslims no longer consider themselves a distinct religious society and have dropped such former names as World Community of Islam in the West and American Muslim Mission.

How has the growing Muslim presence been received in the United States?

Unfortunately, the growing presence of Islam in this country frightens many Americans. They have come to associate the very mention of Islam with strangeness and mystery and, alas, violence. The challenge now facing many American non-Muslims is that of understanding their Muslim neighbors as fellow citizens and brothers and sisters in the human race. The facts of religious and social change invite citizens to stretch their notions of who and what "belongs" where they live. Americans have generally been very good at rising to that challenge.

Several million Muslims now live in the United States—exact numbers are hard to come by, and estimates vary widely. The Islamic centers in Washington, D.C., and Perrysburg, Ohio, are but two of the more physically impressive institutions of their kind that have appeared on the American landscape over the past several decades. Such centers of Muslim identity now number between eight hundred and one thousand. Most are quite simple and ordinary in appearance, for they are merely converted residences, buildings that once housed small businesses, or even former Christian churches and schools. These places are increasingly becoming a concrete indication of the growth of Islam as an American religious tradition. At their present rate of growth, Muslims may in twenty-five years constitute the second largest faith community in the United States. Whatever the actual count, it is clear that Islam is no longer "over there somewhere."

What goes on in those Islamic centers?

The answer in general is simple: very much the same kinds of things that go on in churches and synagogues. Their primary function is that of mosque (Arabic *masjid*, literally place of prostration), though most manage to make room for a wide range of activities. As mosques they first need to provide for their members' ritual needs, including especially a place to perform the ablution before *salat*. But both because the development of secondary institutions needs time and financial resources, and because Islam has always adapted to its surroundings, American Muslim centers are used for everything from child care and religious education, to youth activities and pot-luck dinners, to public lectures and fund-raising appeals. Some of the older and better established centers include specific facilities for the broader range of activities. Perrysburg, for example, has a large room adjacent to the prayer hall for meetings and presentations, as well as a full kitchen and eating facility on the lower level for social gatherings. Plans call for a large expansion, including a separate educational wing and residential facility. Together these places of prayer and social gathering represent the collective aspirations of Muslims in America to establish a community of faith and values in which family and social solidarity can flourish.

Is there such a thing as "American Sufism"?

Some Sufi groups in the United States clearly understand themselves as Muslims and are careful to observe mainstream Islamic practices and religious law. Some so-called Sufi groups, who assemble to sing and dance as part of a religious ceremony, however, have become totally disconnected from Islam. They tend to define Sufism as a vaguely, but not necessarily, religious form of mysticism and ecstatic behavior that transcends all confessional boundaries. This kind of interpretation seems to arise from statements made by some of the greatest Sufi poets, some of whom raised more than a few eyebrows in their own time. However, when mystical poets such as Jalal ad-Din Rumi (d. 1274) and Fakhr ad-Din Iraqi (d. 1289) and others made statements apparently suggesting that true belief and love of God transport one beyond the confines of any one traditional community of faith, they did not intend for their listeners and readers to take them literally. They were not advocating antinomian behavior, but rather attempting to express the paradox of any authentic personal relationship to God. God, they reasoned, is bigger than all of one's petty divisions—including those that religious boundaries seem to create. In that sense no religious community is big enough to express the fullness of God, but the great Sufi teachers have never dispensed with the need for active participation in the life of the community of Muslims. Some Americans (and Europeans) associate themselves with an interpretation of Sufi mysticism that is expansive and flexible enough to allow them to pick and choose from various practices that may have no connection with the Five Pillars of Islam. For such groups, Sufism thus means a rather generic alternative, but not necessarily explicitly "religious"—let alone "Islamic"—approach to spirituality.

SACRED SOURCES AND THEIR INTERPRETATION

QURAN: GENERAL CONSIDERATIONS AND BACKGROUND

What is a sacred text or scripture?

Virtually all of the major faith traditions possess extensive sacred literatures. These sacred texts are commonly called scriptures—literally, writings. Some traditions revolve around a single scripture, a book composed over a relatively short period of time and perhaps associated with only a single human source; Islam's Quran is such a text. Others have generated their sacred writings in stages lasting many centuries, resulting in scriptures that are more like anthologies of smaller books bound together in a single larger volume; the Hebrew Scriptures, what many Christians call the Old Testament, is an example. Still other traditions revolve around the equivalent of whole libraries of sacred texts that came into being over as many as two millennia, as in the case of the greater Hinduism's vast patrimony. In addition to the primary sacred texts, many traditions have large collections of secondary texts, still considered essential but of just slightly lesser authority. Islam has its Sayings of Muhammad (Hadith), for example. In addition, the primary and secondary scriptures themselves often give rise to still further development of highly authoritative literature that takes the form of commentary on the scriptures. Rabbinical Judaism is enshrined in hundreds of volumes of this kind.

How many different kinds of scriptural writings are there in the major traditions?

Sacred literature has taken virtually every form imaginable. The most ancient texts in many traditions are poetic, hymns of praise, songs of thanksgiving for victory, or prayers of petition for favorable harvest. Early poetic texts are typically associated with liturgical rituals. Related to these are modified types of poetry adapted to specialized purposes **107** such as oracles or soothsaying or incantations meant to give power to the one who utters them. Wisdom sayings in the form of easy-to-remember proverbs are part of nearly every tradition. Narrative accounts in prose play several essential roles. One is to recount the deeds of the spiritual powers that brought the community into being (the "gods")—these are typically called "myth." Another is to preserve the history of the community or the biography of a foundational figure. Narratives also illustrate the central tenets of the tradition by way of vivid illustration, as in "just as our ancestor in faith … did when.…"

Prophetic texts can be either poetry or prose, but either way, their main purpose is not generally to foretell the future or predict as is commonly assumed. Prophets "speak on behalf of" an ultimate spiritual power and their focus is typically on the need for change here and now. Another important type of religious text is called "apocalyptic" (from a Greek term meaning "revelatory"). Apocalyptic literature often uses highly figurative language, describing in stunning detail events that the author has "seen" in visions or dreams and that will soon come to pass. Such dramatic texts are often taken as direct predictions of how the end of time will come about. Finally, many scriptures include rules or laws in the form of commands and prohibitions, but only a few sacred texts are entirely legal.

What is the correct spelling of Islam's sacred text: Koran, Coran, Qur'an, or Quran?

These variants all result from different conventions for "transliterating" Arabic. "Koran" was the most usual in English sources for many years (as was "Coran" in languages such as French, Spanish, Italian), largely because it seemed to represent the easiest pronunciation of the name. More recently, a concern for a more accurate transliteration of the original Arabic and a closer approximation of the way Arabs and most Muslims generally pronounce the name introduced "Quran." Finally, "Qur'an" represents an attempt at still greater accuracy, with a slight glottal stop between the r and a long double-*a* sounds indicated by the apostrophe.

What kind of book is the Quran?

Written in Arabic, the Quran is roughly the size of the New Testament. Unlike either the Hebrew or Greek testaments, however, the Quran unfolded over a relatively short period of time and its articulation is attributed to only one human being. Beginning in about 610 C.E., when he was about forty years old, Muhammad began to experience, in mostly auditory but occasionally visual form, what he would come to identify as divine revelations. Muhammad initially delivered the message orally, somewhat in the form of homiletical material. Not until more than two decades after the Prophet's death would a more or less definitive text be compiled and written. Tradition has divided the text into two main periods, the Meccan and Medinan, corresponding to the years before and after the *Hijra*, the move to Medina in 622 C.E. Scholars have more recently further divided the Meccan period into very early, early, middle, and late periods, on the basis of the form and content of the suras.

How big is the Quran and how is it organized?

The sacred scripture contains about sixty-two hundred verses and seventy-eight thousand words, roughly equivalent in length to the New Testament, arranged in 114 sections called *suras* (SU-rah). Muhammad's earliest revelations tend to be short, rhetorically potent utterances in an ancient form of rhymed prose used by pre-Islamic seers and soothsayers. Later suras tend to be lengthier and more prosaic and often take up more practical concerns. Suras are arranged in more or less descending order of length, so that many of the earlier sections are actually in the latter part of the book now. The heading of each sura contains the title, number of verses, and an indication as to whether it was revealed at Mecca or Medina. Interpreters consider it very important to place each text historically, for the "circumstances of the revelation" are critical in unwrapping its original meaning. Tradition has identified the suras, or portions of them, where it is clear that a single sura is actually a composite, as early, middle, or late Meccan (610–622), or Medinan (622–632). Muslims believe the Quran is the direct, literal word of God, communicated unfiltered and unmodified in any way by the Prophet.

How was the Quran compiled?

This is a complex, much-discussed, and too-little understood topic in contemporary scholarship. According to Muslim tradition, the text of the Quran was finalized only after the death of the Prophet Muhammad—to be specific, about twenty years after Muhammad's death under the Caliph Uthman. Though Muslim accounts conflict as to precisely who did establish the definitive text of the Quran, they agree that it was surely not Muhammad. Their denial of Muhammad's role in the collection of the scripture arose out of a growing conviction that the received text did not contain either literally all of the revelation originally given to Muhammad, or only those revelations that must still be considered as binding. Muslim scholars therefore came to explain the text's incompleteness on the ground that the collection occurred after Muhammad's death. Variant readings could then be attributed to the variant memories of the Companions of the Prophet who were said to have assembled to cooperate in finalizing the text. Scholars have typically accepted this narrative until relatively recently, but some (including a small number of Muslim scholars) have

Muslim scholars have begun exploring the Quran from historical and literary critical viewpoints.

109

begun to open the matter to further investigation, with some concluding that a "final" version of the Quran was basically produced by Muhammad himself.

Do Muslims study their scriptures critically?

Research in Quranic Studies enjoys arguably the longest history of any of the subfields of Islamic religious studies as a whole. Much of the earliest work was done by western scholars and was, not surprisingly, highly polemical in intent, often oriented toward subverting the credibility of Muhammad and, thus, the veracity of Islam in general by "proving" the Quran's abject dependence on biblical precedent. The field has made enormous strides since then, until today, it includes increasingly important and courageous work by Muslim scholars in historical and literary criticism of the sacred text. During the past decade or so, scholars of Islam's religious literary patrimony have made great strides both in applying sophisticated analytical tools to the material and in the still more daunting challenge of gaining interest and credibility among Muslims and non-Muslims alike. One of the key ingredients in the mix has been the growing and increasingly visible participation of Muslim scholars in this heady and fearsome enterprise. What's taken them so long to come forth, some might ask. It has often been tempting for non-Muslim critics to charge Islam with an inherent aversion to careful examination

What special qualities do religious believers generally attribute to their scriptures?

Four important attributes are literal and direct revelation, eternity, inerrancy, and inspiration. Some communities of faith regard their sacred texts as the literal, direct, unmediated divine word. Though that word has been delivered through a particular human being, tradition maintains that the messenger had no part in actually shaping the message. Naturally every scripture is communicated in some recognizable human language, a tongue in which the divine speaker chooses to be heard. Scriptures also unfold over time, sometimes evolving over relatively extended periods of history. Even so, some traditions teach that this sacred word is eternal, existing always in the divine mind and entering into the physical world of sound (and eventually writing) only at the moment the revealer deems proper. Another common teaching is that divine communication must surely be perfect in every detail since it comes from a perfect source. Insistence on this quality of "inerrancy" raises all sorts of practical problems for interpreters, who sometimes find themselves scrambling to explain away blatant inconsistencies in factual data such as chronology or geography. Some communities of faith acknowledge that individual persons functioned from the very outset as human "authors" of sacred texts. Here the quality of "inspiration" explains that the divine speaker remains the actual author who entrusts the communication to a human writer.

of the tradition's primary texts—as if Christians and Jews, for example, have universally and always been collectively comfortable putting their revelatory sources under the microscope. As a matter of perspective, it might be well to recall that Roman Catholics generally, and not a few Protestant communities, did not go gentle into the good night of "historical-critical method." Indeed, many Christians and Jews continue to denounce what they regard as a virtual sellout to the fleshpots of modernism.

What is an example of a particular occasion on which Muhammad received a revelation?

Over a period of twenty-three years or so, the divine interventions would come upon Muhammad in a variety of circumstances, often at times when he was struggling with a particular problem or issue. For example, for a while after the *Hijra*, the Muslims faced Jerusalem when they prayed, as did the local Jews. Apparently some friction caused a falling out with the Jewish community, causing Muhammad concern over the continued symbolic statement of the prayer orientation. Came the revelation, "We have seen you turning your face about toward the heavens. We shall now turn you toward a direction (*qibla*) that you will find satisfying. Turn your face toward the Mosque of the Sanctuary (site of the Ka'ba in Mecca); wherever you are, turn your faces toward it." (Quran 2:144) That verse sometimes serves as a decorative inscription over the *mihrab* (niche) in mosques.

MAJOR THEMES IN THE QURAN

What is the most important unifying theme in the Quran?

A good choice would be God's revelation through prophets, culminating in Muhammad. Muhammad himself was not initially comfortable with his prophetic call, with its awesome responsibility—and in this respect his story shares an important feature of the vocations of major biblical prophets, nearly all of whom were not eager to embrace the mission. As for Muhammad's initial experience, some of his earliest and most vocal critics dismissed his Quranic preaching as a mere repetition of "fables of the ancients," warmed-over tales of the prophets of old. That criticism and others like it only served to convince Muhammad of the need to recount still more insistently the history of God's revelation through His messengers. For the Prophet of Islam and countless Muslims since his time, the very thing that so many detractors have singled out as nullifying the force of the Quran has become one of the strongest of all arguments for the authenticity of its revelations. Muhammad proclaimed his acceptance of God's message to all previous prophets as the foundation of his own mission. "We believe in God and that which is revealed to us and that which is revealed to Abraham, and Ishmael, and Isaac, and Jacob, and the tribes, and that which Moses and Jesus received, and that which the Prophets received from their Lord. We make no distinction between any of them, and unto Him we have surrendered" (Quran 2:136).

How did those stories function in Muhammad's preaching?

Though the Quran was "sent down" piecemeal between 610 and 632, Muslims regard it as a single revelation that must be read as a whole. One of its unifying features is its teaching on the nature of revelation and the role of prophets as messengers. The message is initiated by God alone and mediated through prophets, without whom humanity would have very little chance of attaining to the Truth. Muhammad is the "Seal of the Prophets"; and although the Quran teaches Muslims to make no distinction among the messengers, it nevertheless states that some prophets have been exalted above others (e.g., 2:253, 17:55). God sends His prophets to teach people the Oneness of God, to bring the good tidings of belief, and to warn against the consequences of unbelief. Some, such as Moses and Jesus, have been "given a Book." As opposition to Muhammad's message increased, so did stories multiply of earlier prophets who had likewise met with unbelief and persecution.

Does the Quran develop an overall concept of prophetic revelation?

The Quran is not a systematic document and thus does not develop a coherent theory or system of prophetology; nor does it ordinarily recount the story of any one prophet all in one passage as a unified and continuous narrative. The lone exception in this respect is the story of Joseph (son of Jacob), which occupies all of Sura 12; and apart from a single passing reference, Joseph does not appear elsewhere in the scripture. Segments on the various prophets occur sporadically as part of Muhammad's homiletical material. Episodes and minor details from the stories of more important figures, such as Abraham, Moses, and Jesus, appear several times, each text retelling the tale either by adopting a slightly different point of emphasis or by adding variant minor details.

What are some differences between the biblical and the Quranic Abraham, and what is Abraham's place in wider religious lore?

Perhaps the most peculiar of all the biblical Abrahamic (Gn. 15:8–18) texts occurs in an intriguingly different version in Quran 2:260. In Genesis, Abraham asks God for a sign that he will indeed possess the land promised. God tells him to bring a heifer, a she-goat, a ram, a turtle dove, and a pigeon. Abraham then cut the animals—all but the birds—in two and separated the pieces. In the Quran, the prophet wants a sign that God has the power of life. Ibrahim is instructed to take four birds, cut them into pieces, and put a portion on various hills. He must then call to them, and they will fly together as proof of God's power. Islamic tradition also emphasizes key features of

Joseph, shown here in an illustration for Genesis in the Bible as he interprets the pharoah's dreams, is also featured in Sura 12 of the Quran.

Abraham as a spiritual model. Many Muslim mystical poets have delighted in transforming him into a paragon of mystical love. Ibrahim was a "sighful" man (*awwah*—the Persian expression for "sigh" is "heart-smoke") whose heart bubbled over when he thought of God. People said they could hear his heart "bubble" for miles, so intense was his longing. The Quran connects Ibrahim with Nimrod, unlike the Bible, which, in Genesis, mentions Nimrod only briefly and much earlier than Abraham (Gn. 10:8–10).

What is Nimrod's role in Islamic sources?

In Islamic lore, Nimrod functions as the Prophet's nemesis. Quran 21:68–70 alludes, without naming the evil king explicitly, to Ibrahim's conflict with the unbeliever. According to the important Islamic religious genre the Tales of the Prophets, Nimrod was to the child Ibrahim what Pharaoh would be to Moses and Herod to Jesus—a mortal enemy bent on the infant's destruction. Failing in his earlier attempts, Nimrod managed to capture Ibrahim and catapult him into a bonfire. But there in the flames, Gabriel appeared to transform them into a pleasant garden for the prophet.

How does Muslim tradition deal with the question of Abraham's "first-born son"? Is Isaac as important as he is for Jews and Christians?

A distinctively Islamic take on the Abraham story has to do with interpreting the tradition that God commanded the Prophet to sacrifice his "first-born son." By Islamic reckoning, Ishmael (Ismail in Arabic) merits that distinction, since he was indeed born before Isaac. The Quran does not specifically name the boy whom Ibrahim is prepared to sacrifice, but the tradition presumes, by this logic, that it was Ismail. Jewish and Christian traditions discount the son of Hagar as illegitimate and therefore not truly Abraham's son. The Tales of the Prophets devote considerably more attention than the Quran (11:72–78, 37:100–113, 51:24–34) to the individual birth stories of the two sons.

What are some of the key themes in early texts?

Five themes appear most often in the earliest suras. Evidently presuming belief in some deity on the part of their hearers, they emphasize God's creative power, providence, and guidance. There was at first no emphasis on belief in only one God. Second, they speak of accountability at judg-

In the Bible, it is Abraham's son Isaac whom God commands to be sacrificed, but in the Quran it is not clear which son it is. Islamic tradition, however, holds it to be Ishmael.

ment in a rather general way, without specific reference to particular reward or punishment as motivation for upright behavior. In view of these two, the suras suggest that the appropriate response for the individual is a combination of gratitude and worship. The former flows out of an inner recognition of one's total dependence on God expressed formally in prayer. Parallel social consequences are acknowledged in the need for generosity as expressed in giving to those in need and seeking a just distribution of wealth. Finally, the early message includes the theme of Muhammad's dawning awareness of his own prophetic mission and all that it would demand of him.

When did stories of the prophets begin to play an important role in the Quranic revelations?

During the middle Meccan period, both the tone and the content of the suras began to change. Stories first of indigenous Arabian and then of biblical prophets illustrated graphically the disastrous consequences attendant upon refusal to hear the prophetic message. Here one finds a growing insistence on monotheistic belief and forthright condemnation of idolatry. Toward the end of the Meccan period, emphasis on the rejection of past prophets grew apace with Muhammad's own experience of local opposition. During the Medinan period (622–632 C.E.), both the style and the content changed dramatically. Whereas the Meccan suras tended to be quite dramatic and poetic in tone, a form called rhymed prose (saj), the later message became more prose-like. Its content reflected the growing need to regulate the daily life of the expanding community of Muslims and the reality of increased contact with Christians and Jews (of whom several large tribes played a major part in the life of Medina).

How else do prophet stories link the Quran and the Bible?

Since the Islamic interpretation of history overlaps in significant ways with those of Judaism and Christianity, one should not be surprised to find that some material in the Quran parallels some biblical material. Some narrative treatments of various biblical patriarchs and kings, whom the Quran identifies as prophets and messengers, immediately recall aspects of biblical accounts. But there are also interesting variations in the stories. Adam and Eve's fall, for example, is connected with eating from a forbidden tree (or an ear of wheat in one version). Sprinkled throughout the scripture are references to Abraham's near-sacrifice of his son (whom Islamic tradition takes to be Ishmael rather than Isaac), and to Moses's mission to Pharaoh, David's musical gifts, Solomon's royal grandeur, and others.

Perhaps the single most important parallel is the story of Joseph. Sura 12 of the Quran retells the tale found in Genesis 39–50 with its own distinctive flavor and variations in detail. Only Joseph's story is told in its entirety, and all in a single sura dedicated entirely to it. Though many Jewish and Christian readers often conclude that Muhammad "borrowed" from the Bible, that is not necessarily the case. The way the Quran tells the stories, mostly in short excerpts and allusions, suggests that Muhammad's listeners must have already been familiar with at least the general drift of the narratives.

There are also some accounts of non-biblical prophetic figures, called Hud, Salih, and Shuayb, in some ways unique to the Arabian peninsula. It is important to note that Muslim tradition has discerned in both the Old and New Testaments references to the coming of Islam's prophet. God promised to raise up for Israel a prophet like Moses (Deuteronomy 18:18)—Muhammad. The prophet Isaiah sees two riders approaching, one on a donkey and the other on a camel: Jesus and Muhammad.

If Muhammad was not the only prophet, who were some of the other prophets and how do they fit into the Islamic scheme of things?

Jewish and Christian readers will already have some familiarity with the notion of prophets and prophetic mission. Since time immemorial, prophet-types have played a major role in the religious history of the Middle East. In the Hebrew Scriptures, prophets receive a mandate to speak on God's behalf. Their mission often requires that they stand up to the high and mighty, posing the divine challenge of justice for the powerless of the earth. The problem of how to discern true prophets from charlatans has exercised religious minds for millennia as well. In addition to the full-fledged prophets, lesser characters have also played a part. These include sages, oracles and soothsayers.

All of these religious types were familiar to many people in the Arabia of Muhammad's day. But as Muhammad would discover, the majority of the populace welcomed the advent of a prophet no more enthusiastically in the seventh century C.E. than they would have in the seventh century B.C.E. Islamic tradition numbers over two dozen figures sent to particular peoples, including David, Solomon, Noah, Jonah, as well as the Arabian figures Hud, Salih, and Shuayb. All of them are "prophets" (*nabi*, NA-bee, pl. *anbiya'*) commissioned to warn their people; some are also "messengers" (*rasul*, ra-SOOL, pl. *rusul*) to whom scriptures are revealed. All of the prophets and messengers experienced rejection at the hands of their people, and some were killed. In every instance, God dealt harshly with the people.

Were any individual prophets particularly important in Muhammad's experience?

Muhammad readily identified with several of the prophets especially with Abraham, the "Friend of the Merciful" (Khalil ar-Rahman) and Moses, "God's Conversant" (Kalim Allah). In Islamic tradition, Abraham was neither Jew nor Christian, but a hanif, a seeker after the one true God. As the Quran says:

> Truly Abraham was a model (lit. an *umma*), obedient to God, and a seeker (lit. hanif) who assigned no partner to God. He responded in gratitude to the bounty of the one who chose him and guided him to the Straight Path.... So We have revealed to you (Muhammad) that you should follow the believing ways (lit. *milla*) of Abraham the seeker.... (Quran 16:120–21, 123)

It was Abraham who had prayed that God would "send among them a messenger from their midst who will unfold to them your signs and teach them the Book and the wisdom" (Quran 2:129).

Is Moses as significant for Muslims as Abraham?

Moses's importance in the Quran is equal to that of Abraham. "We sent Moses with Our signs: 'Bring your people out from profound darkness into the light and make them mindful of the days of God.' Truly in that are signs for all who are long-suffering and grateful" (Quran 4:5). Quran 73:15 likens Muhammad especially to Moses. Islamic tradition likewise sees a reference to Muhammad in the words of Deuteronomy 18:18, in which God says to Moses, "I will raise up for them a prophet like you from among their kinsmen, and will put my words in his mouth; he shall tell them all that I command him." Curiously, one text of the Quran (7:155–157) has God speaking approvingly to Moses of "those who follow the apostle, the unlettered Prophet (i.e., Muhammad) whom they find written of (in their own) Torah and Gospel...."

What are some examples of how the Quran presents the stories of other important biblical "prophets"?

A look at the stories of two biblical figures regarded as prophets in the Islamic tradition offers important clues about how interpretation of their stories both changed and

This Christian image depicts Moses, whom Muslims consider as important as Abraham.

remained the same from one scripture to another. The biblical Job stars as the main figure in a book entirely dedicated to his story. In the Quran only a few brief allusions to Job suggest that he was a "servant of God" who suffered much in spite of being a just man. He confesses that God's justice is equal to God's infinite power and that both elude human comprehension. A model of deep religious understanding, Job is a prophet and hero of faith, ever turning to God in repentance, who ultimately finds peace in the presence of the Lord. Another figure who is the sole subject of his own biblical book is Jonah. Again, the Quran tells his story indirectly, through short references meant to serve as examples of essential religious values. As in the Bible, Jonah at first disobeys God and refuses to preach, but at length repents in the midst of his anger and self-pity. He realizes that God can offer the possibility of repentance and mercy to anyone He chooses. Jonah has to undergo a conversion to admit that even the people of Nineveh—a model of sinfulness in Jonah's eyes—deserved a second chance. As in the Gospels, the Quran ranks Jonah among the "great prophets." The Quran's piecemeal presentation of the stories of both Job and Jonah makes it clear that Muhammad's audiences were already familiar with the main outlines of already-ancient stories.

INTERPRETING THE SACRED SCRIPTURE

What do the terms "exegesis" and "hermeneutics" mean?

"Exegesis" derives from a pair of Greek words meaning "to draw out" (*ex*, meaning "out" *hegeomai*, meaning "to lead or draw"—also root of the word "hegemony"). It refers to the processes of reflection and study that allow for the interpretion of a text. "Hermeneutics" comes from the Greek word that means "principles or theories of interpretation" (*hermeneutike*). Whenever scholars probe a text—the U.S. Constitution, for example— they engage in exegesis that uses certain hermeneutical principles. A Supreme Court justice who prefers a more conservative approach, for example, might use a "strict constructionist" hermeneutics to interpret the Constitution. The idea is to implement the Constitution here and now without violating the spirit of the eighteenth-century document. One might think of hermeneutics as a set of lenses or filters—put them on and things will appear differently than through the naked eye. These filters bring out certain features of whatever is being viewed, but they also prevent seeing other features. That's the nature of all textual interpretation—it always starts from a particular point of view. The more clearly one is aware of the presuppositions brought to the text, the more honest the interpretation.

How have Muslim scholars interpreted stories of the prophets through the centuries?

Talented authors have discussed prophetic revelation from a wide variety of perspectives. During the second to fourth Islamic centuries (c. 750–1000), authors of "historical" texts were interested in situating the Islamic story of revelation in the broader context of "global" events as they knew them. Philosophers and theologians, too, began to formulate their distinctive views about this topic, central as it was/is to understanding how human beings can claim access to divine truths. And within a century or two later (especially 1100–1300), scholars with a more mystical and poetic bent also fashioned elaborate images to describe how through His prophets, God had continued to forge a loving bond with humankind and lavish His provident care on His servants.

How many different kinds of scriptural interpretation are there in the major traditions?

One of the most interesting—and volatile—areas in the study of religion has to do with the many ways the different religious traditions "read" their sacred texts. Virtually every tradition has developed a range of approaches, often applying several to the same text   117

What is "historical prophetology"?

The historical approach reads the Quran with an eye for the continuity and sequence of events that constitute a given prophet's personal history or "biography." Concerned with presenting a chronological narrative, this approach is largely interested in the story line and in gathering the myriad anecdotal details that render a story credible, engaging, and true-to-life, with a generous enough sprinkling of the fantastic to make it marvelous. Names, place-descriptions, personal relationships and encounters, genealogies, ages of the characters, and times and durations of events all form a concrete mundane context in which the supramundane becomes at once more plausible and more arresting. The prophet appears as a specific individual, an historical personage. Because of its interest in the concrete actions of a prophet, the historical approach implies a folkloristic or "midrashic" exegesis that freely fills in details that it takes to be in any way suggested by the Quranic text. Some works of this type gathered their information directly from earlier Quranic commentaries and rearranged it to fit a new framework. An example of folkloristic embellishment might be the inclusion of a conversation between a prophet and another character, not supplied in the Quran but which, given other details mentioned in the scripture, is quite imaginable.

to bring out its various "levels" of meaning. Every credible interpreter starts from a basic hermeneutical principle: to be true to the text, one must first know what kind of text it is. What was its original purpose? What is its point of view and what kind of information is it trying to communicate? Nobody reads the sports page looking for tasty recipes. The first concern is to determine what the text literally "says." But for any text to have a life expectancy greater than that of yesterday's sports page, it has to "mean" something beyond the bare facts. That's where religious interpreters begin to elaborate on the further significance of their sacred texts.

What is a concrete example of this exegetical issue?

Suppose that the "historical" meaning of a text is that "thus and so happened at a certain time and place." If that's all there is, the text is merely a museum piece. But religious exegesis looks deeper and draws out symbolic or allegorical meanings in which religious traditions find contemporary ethical implications. The dilemma in virtually all traditions is this: how to respect the historical reality of an ancient document while simultaneously explaining how its teachings are valid in every time and place. In more recent times, scholars working both within and outside of major religious traditions have begun to ask different kinds of questions about how best to interpret sacred texts. The so-called "historical-critical method" attempts to understand how a scripture can be both historically conditioned, and thus a product of a particular cultural context, and still claim substantial authority for all subsequent generations of believers.

How do Muslims in general interpret their sacred texts?

Discussion of the Quran is a regular activity in most mosques, usually in connection with the Friday congregational prayer (and in the United States also held on Sundays). One or more discussion leaders might present a text and then open the floor to comments and questions. The first concern is generally to establish the "circumstances of the revelation." What was the specific occasion on which this particular text was revealed to Muhammad? Was it revealed in connection with any unusual or momentous event? Was it a direct response to some question or predicament that had arisen in the early Muslim community? Contemporary Muslims can dip into an enormous reservoir of traditional scholarship for help in interpreting the Quran.

When and how did Islamic exegesis develop?

Exegetes began compiling detailed and extensive commentaries on the sacred scripture as early as the eighth century. They refined the tools of a specialty called *tafsir* (taf-SEER, "explanation, elaboration"). Dozens of multivolume works in Arabic (plus countless more in various other languages) of great antiquity and authority are still widely available from publishers of Islamic books, and many are now being translated into Western languages. Classical commentators and modern-day interpreters alike look first to the Hadith for help on obscure passages of the Quran, for Muhammad himself often responded to questions about specific texts. Careful study of Arabic grammar and a wide knowledge of other works of Arabic literature for purposes of comparison are also essential background for professional exegetes. In addition to elucidating the basic or literal meanings of a sacred text, Quran commentary can also probe into further levels of meaning. Muslim mystics especially have written allegorical or symbolic interpretations (called *ta'wil*, ta-WEEL) to uncover the deeper spiritual implications of the scripture.

How does the legal or juristic method work?

For all Muslims, Quran is at the very heart of all religious law, followed in short order by sayings attributed to Muhammad, called Hadith. It is the task of the legal scholar to search the text for the clearest, least ambiguous references to a given regulatory matter (from dietary law to family inheritance to criminal sanctions). What the jurist wants is to interpret the scripture so as to extend its applicability to present needs and circumstances, even if those were not obviously foremost at the time of the revelation. In other words, juristic exegesis is concerned chiefly with proper behavior across a broad spectrum, from the simplest daily acts (such as the motions performed during ritual prayer) to more ethically consequential problems typically associated with "criminal" law. See the chapter on "Authority, Law, and Ethics" for more detailed discussion.

What is distinctive about the more "theological" approach?

Ever since at least the late seventh/early eighth century, Muslims have been asking difficult questions about how the sacred text communicates the divine mystery. The im-

How many different approaches to scriptural interpretations have Muslims used in reading the Quran?

A wide variety of methods have allowed Muslims to explore the multiple facets of their revealed scripture. Bu the Quran itself makes a foundational observation as to the two principal ways human beings might understand its verses. "He it is who has revealed the Book to you. Some of its verses/signs are categorical in meaning. They are the mother (i.e., essence) of the Book. Others are open to interpretation (i.e., metaphorical or allegorical). Those whose hearts harbor ill-will pursue its metaphorical verses, in their desire for disharmony and esoteric interpretation (*ta'wil*). None but God knows the inner meaning" (Quran 3:7). That short text is remarkable in its succinct articulation of the central difficulty all scripture-based traditions must face. The text clearly comes down on the side of clarity and literal meaning. Unfortunately, it leaves unanswered the question as to why it contains the ambiguous at all. In general, it is useful to identify these varieties of exegetical (interpretative) method: legal or juristic, theological, distinctively Shi'ite, and mystical.

agery of God seated on the Throne has been at the center of much discussion in classical Islamic theology, for it raises the question of whether and to what degree one ought to interpret scripture literally. Taken literally, the text conjures up anthromorphic pictures of the deity: there is a Throne and God actually sits upon it, and so forth. Taken metaphorically, the text becomes a colorful reference to divine sovereignty and transcendence. Islamic tradition has on the whole considered the latter option a dangerous invitation to water down the meaning of the sacred text.

How would one describe the main differences of opinion on this kind of exegesis?

Two of the principal positions in the theological debate are those of a group called the Mutazilites and the school of a man named al-Ashari (d. 944). A fundamental tenet of the Mutazilites was that the Quran was not uncreated as the traditionalists argued, but created, and therefore subject to the critique of human reason. It sounds perhaps like so much hair splitting, but it had the import of Christian theological debate around the divinity and humanity of Jesus. Basing all their arguments on reason (doing theology from below, one could say), the Mutazilites believed that taking such texts as the Throne Verse literally made no sense at all; for the anthropomorphism thus entailed would bring God down to human scale. It was simply not rational to speak that way about the transcendent. In his classic Mutazilite commentary, al-Zamakhshari, a medieval Mutazilite scholar, says of the *kursi*, or footstool attached to the Throne: "It is no more than an image expressing God's greatness. In reality, there is neither *kursi*, and act of sitting, nor one who sits." The verse therefore uses a "fanciful image" to communicate the idea of God's extensive power, knowledge, and sovereignty.

Why did Ashari part company over the matter of interpretation?

Al-Ashari had been a member of the Mutazilites in his youth and became disaffected with their inability to rein in their own rational arguments. He countered that, on the contrary, what made no sense was any attempt to limit God in any direction whatsoever. He concluded that one simply ought not speculate about what God has in mind. If the Quran says God sits on a Throne, one must take the statement at face value and let it be. He quotes with utmost approval the Hadith of Muhammad, "The kursi is the place of the two feet (the footstool of God). It has a squeaking sound like that of a new saddle." His now famous methodological formula bila kayf ("without a how") sums up the notion that one simply ought not speculate on these things. Ashari's opinion has carried the day, for the most part, with its emphasis on divine mystery.

Why is there a distinctively "Shi'ite" approach? How is it different from "Sunni" interpretation?

Just as the jurists read scripture with any eye for regulatory items and the rationalist theologians focused on the Quran's "anthromorphisms," Shi'ite interpreters have been keen to focus on any text that might support the religious and political legitimacy of Muhammad's son-in-law Ali and his descendants. Shi'ite exegesis is therefore highly allegorical. Consider, for example, the Verse of Light:

> God is the Light of Heaven and Earth. Picture His light as a niche within which there is a lamp, and the lamp is within a glass. And it is as though the glass were a glittering star lit from a sacred olive tree neither of east nor west, whose oil would fairly radiate even without the touch of fire. Light upon light, and God guides to his light whom He will. (Quran 24:35)

One classic Shi'ite reading of it likens God's light to Muhammad, the niche to Muhammad's breast, the lamp to the knowledge of prophecy, the glass to Muhammad's prophetic knowledge passed along to Ali. That the tree is neither of east nor west means Ali was neither Jew nor Christian. Just as the tree nearly glowed even untouched by fire, so Ali would nearly utter the prophetic knowledge even if Muhammad had not passed it on. And the phrase "Light upon light" refers to the succession of one imam (spiritual descendent of Ali) from the previous imam.

What's unique about the "mystical" approach to exegesis?

Islamic mystics have read the sacred text for any hint of the possibility of an intimate relationship between human and divine. Traditionalists often found such talk at least slightly blasphemous, and rationalists regarded it as sentimental at best. But the rich mystical tradition has mined every reference to divine love and concern, every suggestion of divine immanence, discerning at least two levels of meaning in each tidbit. The outward meaning is apparent to most everyone; to arrive at the hidden meaning requires *ta'wil*, the very thing some would say the Quran counsels against (Quran 3:7 quoted above). Some examples of the Quranic phrases dearest to the mystics include the

Here's a classic example of how a major "mystic" handles the problem posed by anthropomorphic language in the Quran. In his reading of the Throne Verse, for example, the mystic Ibn Arabi considers the *kursi* to be the center of knowledge on the cosmic scale as is the human heart on the microcosmic level. He goes on to say that God does not tire of keeping all things in existence "because they have no existence without Him.... Rather the realm of the ideal form is His inner dimension and the realm of forms is His outer dimension. They have no existence except in Him. Nor are they other than He." Such statements, liable as they may seem to the charge of pantheistic monism, were the sort of utterances for which many a mystic ran afoul of more traditional thinkers.

following: "To God belong the East and the West; whereever you turn, there is the face of God" (2:115); "I am truly near: I answer the prayer of the petitioner who beseeches me. Therefore let them respond to me and have faith in me, that they might receive guidance" (2:186); "Everything on earth perishes; but the face of your Lord remains, majestic and most revered" (55:26–27). While the mystical tradition was not loathe to interpret such texts metaphorically, they did so without in any way deflating them of their mystery as the Mutazilite approach ran the risk of doing.

Are there any other texts of the Quran that give a sense of the power and inexhaustible grandeur Muslims experience in their scripture?

One such text emphasizes the infinitude of God's revelation, extending impossibly beyond creation's capacity: "If all the trees on earth were pens and all the oceans ink, with seven more seas besides, they would not suffice to record the words of God" (Quran 31:27, see also 18:109). Christian readers may be reminded of the text with which John's Gospel ends: "But there are so many other things which Jesus did; were every one of them to be written, I suppose that the world itself could not contain the books that would be written" (John 21:25). Another text is reminiscent of a theme associated with Mount Sinai. Sinai swooned when God gave Moses the Torah, and according to the mystics and rabbis, exploded into many pieces, each of which fell upon and blessed a part of the earth. "If we had sent this Quran down upon a mountain, you would have seen it crumble to pieces and humble itself for fear of God" (Quran 59:21).

Is fundamentalism the same as literal interpretation of a scripture?

Fundamentalism is an approach to religious teachings and values that emphasizes strict and direct reliance on a tradition's most ancient sources. That often means interpreting sacred texts quite literally, but even among fundamentalists extreme literalism remains the exception rather than the rule. Fundamentalist exegesis is found in many religious traditions. A major hermeneutical principle seems to be this: take the text literally, even if its literal meaning seems quite impossible in human terms, but interpret figuratively where a literal reading is clearly absurd. If the Book of Joshua says the sun stood still, take it as an actual divine intervention. But when Jesus says, "I am the Vine, you the branches," it should be obvious to all that he is using a figure of speech. Alas, such things are not always so obvious. In general a fundamentalist approach seeks to interpret a sacred text by means of the sacred text itself rather than appeal to the intervening history of interpretation that comprises the community's repository of tradition.

HADITH: TRADITIONS OF AND ABOUT MUHAMMAD

What is the relationship between scripture and "oral tradition" generally?

Numerous traditions preserve their teachings only in oral form or in ritual performance. Several dozen Native American and African traditions, for example, keep their heritages alive in the recitation of tribal storytellers and in the ritual reenactment of myth in the form of narrative dance. Some communities of believers have found it necessary to commit their heritage to writing in order to prevent it from being lost, given the advanced age of those entrusted with preserving it. Even then, the written version remains somehow less than the "real" tradition, and the ideal remains an oral and performative communication of the teaching, since committing it to writing was a last-ditch concession to the frailty of human memory. It is interesting to note that even in some of the religious traditions that boast the most voluminous sacred literatures, scripture began—and in some cases remained for many years—as oral communication. In many of those traditions the written text came to occupy a place of authority nearly equal to that of the recited text. In some traditions, reliance on "The Book" has rendered oral tradition virtually irrelevant.

What other early texts aside from the Quran are especially important for Muslims?

Second only to the Quran in both authority and antiquity is the large body of works containing sayings attributed to Muhammad, along with hundreds of anecdotes about him. This material is known collectively as Hadith (sayings or traditions, ha-DEETH). When Muhammad died, neither the scripture nor the Prophet's words and deeds had been formally committed to writing. And even long after the Quran had been carefully edited, Muslims hesitated to produce written versions of Muhammad's sayings. Custodians of these Prophetic Traditions kept them by heart, much as the earliest followers preserved the Quranic revelations. Not until over two centuries after Muhammad died did his community deem it necessary to gather and edit the Hadith. The impetus to do so came in part from legal scholars, who believed that the only way to interpret the spirit of the Quran faithfully in cases not explicitly treated in the scripture was to have a sound testimony of the Prophet's own views.

How did the "science of Hadith" develop?

Through much of the ninth century, Muslim religious scholars undertook the massive task of traveling widely and gathering and recording thousands of Hadiths from countless individuals known for their reliable memories. These scholars, often working independently and at some distance in time and space, then sifted through what they had gathered. Since the very existence of this treasure trove depended on its oral transmission from one generation to another, scholars looked first at the chains of transmission to see whether all individuals listed were trustworthy. If not, one likely could dismiss the Hadith itself as not entirely reliable. By the end of the ninth century, half a dozen authoritative collections, and many lesser ones as well, of Hadith were available, complete with scholarly evaluation as to the relative soundness of each saying and anecdote. Muslims traditionally consider the content of the Hadith to be divinely inspired, only expressed in Muhammad's own words, unlike the Quran, which is in God's own diction.

How do Muslims access this source of tradition?

At the top of the list of "authoritative" versions of the Hadith literature is a group of collections known generically as "The Six." Among those, the two generally acknowledged as the most important are the works of Bukhari (d. 870) and Muslim (d. 875—this is his "proper name"). Their collections are among the largest and most detailed and are generally arranged according to particular religious themes. But many important Ha-

What are the larger implications of the Hadith?

All Muslims agree on the primacy of the Quran as the source of revealed truth and on the importance of Hadith as the principal source of information about the example of the Prophet, the Sunna. Originally most Muslim scholars considered Sunna virtually coextensive with Hadith: all that one could know, or needed to know, about the Prophet's example, one could find in the collected sayings. Gradually the notion of Sunna expanded to include not only Muhammad's reported words and anecdotes about his deeds, but the actual living practice of a given community of believers. And that growing attitude was in turn based on a Hadith in which Muhammad is reported to have said, "My community will not agree on an error." It followed naturally that the community, striving in good faith to live out the Sunna of the Prophet, literally embodied a living Sunna that already presupposed an interpretation of Muhammad's example. In simple terms, the community strove to live as Muhammad surely would "if he were here now."

diths appear only in one or more of the other four major works, or in any of dozens of additional collections typically regarded as slightly less definitive.

What are some of the key themes in Hadith?

Hadiths take on many literary forms—e.g., a short quip in answer to a specific question, a dialogue between Prophet and community members, and detailed instructions for items mentioned in passing in the scripture. Large sections in the more thematically arranged collections are dedicated to traditions about faith, ritual purity, the "Five Pillars," marriage and divorce, the lofty moral qualities of Muhammad and his Companions, personal prayer, and the remembrance of God, and eschatological topics provide essential data for the study of theological themes. Quran and Hadith both function as sources of "inward" matters: prayers of all sorts, *du'a* (supplication or invocation), personal prayer and relationship with God, the nature of *tawhid* (belief and acknowledgment of monotheism), and *shukr* (thanksgiving). In addition the sacred texts provide guidance on more "outward" aspects of community life: *zakat* (almsgiving), understanding of the demands and limitations of external *jihad*, mercantile and fiscal concerns (from weights and measures to inheritance to compensation for services rendered), and a host of other actions in which a person engages the outside world.

What are some examples of typical Hadiths?

According to one famous Muslim (Abu Said al-Khudri), Muhammad said that Moses asked his Lord to teach him a way to be mindful of God to supplicate Him. God told him to say, "There is no god but God." He (Moses) replied that *all* God's servants said this, and that he wanted something particularly for himself. So God said, "Moses, if the seven heavens and their inhabitants apart from me and the seven earths were put on one side of a balance and the phrase 'There is no god but God' on the other, the saying 'There is no god but God' would outweigh the whole universe." Moses was satisfied with that explanation.

Another theme that appears in the Hadith literature is the meaning of Muhammad's *Hijra* —the community's "emigration" from Mecca to Medina. *Hijra* began to acquire important symbolic status fairly early in Islamic history. Two traditions from a popular anthology of Hadith offer some important clues as to why this occurred. In the first, one of the Companions asks Muhammad a series of questions about faith. He wants to know what are the "most excellent" aspects of certain Muslim beliefs and practices, and he asks specifically about the *Hijra*. Muhammad explains that its essential meaning is "abandoning what your Lord abhors." In other words, the Prophet is explaining the "spiritual" meaning of *Hijra*, because that "migration" had already clearly begun to mean something more than mere physical relocation. Elsewhere in that same anthology, a series of Hadiths apocalyptic in tone shed more light on this spiritual interpretation. In these sayings, Muhammad warns his people to prepare for the dissension and turmoil that will arise as time nears its end. That inevitable time of chaos and spiritual confusion will impose serious hardships and test every believer's commitment to religious observance. "The reward for engaging in worship during the turmoil," the Prophet explains, "will be like that for coming to me as emigrants (literally, 'making *hijra* to me')." In other words, those who remain steadfast when people all around seem to be abandoning values will reap the spiritual rewards of the very Muslims who made the original *Hijra* with Muhammad himself. The Prophet's emigration has thus become a kind of standard by which to measure religious merit.

Are there any other similarly "eschatological" themes in Hadith?

There are countless similar ethical-eschatological images that explain what believers will encounter at the end of days. One anecdotal saying of Muhammad has him telling his listeners how Death itself will be slaughtered, leaving the people of Paradise uninterrupted delight and the people of the Fire no hope for an end to their misery: Death is ushered in disguised as a black-and-white-spotted ram. Then a voice calls: "O People of Paradise!" And they crane their necks and look, and He (God Himself) says: "Do you recognize this (figure)?" They say: "Yes, that is Death." And each of them sees him. Then He calls: "O people of the Fire!" And they crane their necks and look, and He says: "Do you recognize this (figure)?" They say: "Yes, that is Death." And each of them sees him. Thereupon he is slaughtered. Then He says: "O people of Paradise! Eternity without death (is yours)! O people of the Fire, Eternity without death (is yours)."

What do the Hadiths say about human mortality?

A number of Hadiths are as much instructions on how to live as on how to die. "Die before you die," the Prophet advises; let preoccupation with self pass away now, so that when death comes you will have handed over already that which you fear most to lose. "As you live, so shall you die; and as you die, so shall you be raised up." Therefore, make your legacy good deeds, so that they will be your traveling companions on your journey after death. Some sayings about death are blatantly contradictory. Weep for the dead, do not weep for them; weep for only one day, weep for an extended period; the more you

What are some examples of "sacred Hadiths"?

A "Sacred Hadith," a tradition attributed to God rather than to Muhammad, says: "I was a hidden treasure and I desired to be known, so I created the world." Knowing God through that world renders all created beings naturally "muslim," for all nonhuman things by nature surrender to God. Sufi sources attribute similar sayings to God himself (Sacred Hadiths). For example: "I fulfill my servant's expectation of me" and "Though the heavens and the earth cannot contain me, there is ample room for me in the believer's heart." According to a Sacred Hadith, God told how he had divided the prayer "in two halves, between me and my servant." The first half contains the servant's praise and glorification of God. The second half, God explained, "is between me and my servant, and my servant shall have what he asks."

weep the more suffering the dead will feel from the pain of separation, weep to help them with your sympathy; and so forth. What is important here is simply that tradition attributes to the Prophet the complete range of responses to death and mortality.

QURAN AND HADITH IN ISLAMIC LIFE AND SPIRITUALITY

Traditional Muslims feel that only handwritten copies of the Quran are acceptable, so are there any printed versions that are used?

Because the Quran is considered the actual word of God, the way in which one reproduces it matters a great deal. Since very early in Islamic history, fine calligraphy has been an important dimension of the whole "experience" of the Quran for Muslims. An expert calligrapher who is commissioned to produce a copy of the sacred text does not merely sit down and dash it off as though it were just another job. Spiritual preparation is critical, for the act of writing the word of God is itself a devotional act. Inscribing the revealed writ must therefore be kept a human action so far as possible. It is true that Muslim publishers of editions of the Quran do not set the text in type the way, for example, a newspaper uses typesetting. However that does not necessarily mean that every copy of the Quran is actually handwritten. Use of lithography, a printing process by which a plate of a handwritten text is used to duplicate the page, has long been common practice.

What about using computer and other sophisticated software to study the sacred text; is that allowed?

In the age of computers, CD-ROMs, and the various multimedia devices available to students and devout persons, Muslims have worked to preserve a sense of the sacredness of the physical presence of the revealed text. One can now purchase at a very reasonable cost software packages that allow on-screen Quranic text together with recitation recorded by noted specialists. What appears on the screen is a reproduction of an originally handwritten page, now typically embellished with different colored "inks" and decorative touches. Many of these software packages include not only the Arabic text, but inter-

Traditionally, handwritten texts of the Quran are preferred by Muslims, but electronic versions are also available for study.

pretations of it in as many as half a dozen languages that can be displayed along with it, and some even provide selections from classical exegetical commentaries on the Quran. Programs like these also allow detailed searches of key terms, making the careful study of the Quran quite easy for those with computers.

Is the Quran as important in Islamic spirituality as the Bible is in Christian spirituality?

In some ways it is even more prominent in the spiritual practice of many Muslims. The Quran forms the core of all Islamic worship and devotional activity. As part of the daily ritual prayer, Muslims regularly recite the opening surah quoted earlier, as well as several other short pieces. An example is the very brief Sura 112 al-Ikhlas (Sincerity or Purity of Faith): "Proclaim: He is One God, God the besought of all; He does not beget; He is not begotten; and there is none like Him." This is unmistakably a reminder to Muslims that they are different from Christians with their belief in Father, Son, and Spirit. But perhaps just as important as the theological content is the sheer physical experience of reciting and/or hearing recitation of the Quran. The effect on listeners is often profound, for the mode of delivery combined with the extraordinarily earthy sound of Arabic make for an intensely moving experience. One commentator has likened the recitation to the Christian practice of Communion, in that in both instances, one has the Word on the tongue.

How does Quran recitation function in the lives of Muslims?

Quran recitation is also part of many religious occasions outside the five daily prayers. After a funeral, families of the deceased often hire a reciter to come and grace the time for condolence with appropriate scriptural texts. During the fasting month of Ramadan, Muslims make a special place for recitation. They commemorate the twenty-seventh of that lunar month as the "Night of Power," when Muhammad received the first revelation. In addition, the entire Quran is recited during the thirty nights of Ramadan. For that and other such "liturgical" purposes, the text of the scripture has been divided into thirty sections, each of which is further halved, and those halves further quartered, yielding a total of 240 divisions. One can easily keep track of how far one has to go during each period of recitation. There are further social dimensions as well. All across the Islamic world, the art of Quran recitation is highly prized. One can almost always tune to a radio station that broadcasts recitation and commentary all day. In some places, such as Malaysia and Indonesia and even on a smaller scale here in the United States, the art has become very competitive. National contests draw huge crowds to sports stadiums, and winners look forward to going to a grand final competition in Mecca. And in virtually any large Cairene mosque, for example, one can find people sitting alone and chanting their recitation quietly to themselves, or engaged in lively discussions about the text.

Why do some Muslims memorize the whole Quran?

On the level of individual devotion as well, the Quran functions prominently. Some Muslims still strive to memorize the entire book, all sixty-two hundred verses. Memorizing the

Recitation of the Quran is practiced everywhere in the Muslim world, in mosques, at special occasions, and in all varieties of social and religious contexts. Accomplished recitation is a skill that is much admired and celebrated.

text means having it in one's heart and "keeping" it there. Paralleling the memorization of the Quran is what has been called the Quranization of the memory. The phrase originally referred to the intensely scriptural way of thinking manifested by some of the great Muslim spiritual writers and mystical poets. But there are further implications as well. Especially throughout the Arabic speaking world, phrases from the Quran have become so much a part of ordinary speech, particularly among very traditional-minded Muslims, that many people no longer know where the sacred ends and the profane begins.

Where and in what context does the Bible allude to Muhammad?

Medieval Muslim theologians were intrigued by a text from the Gospel of John (14:16) in which Jesus promises to send "another paraclete" and have interpreted that text in a surprising manner. Speakers of Semitic languages such as Arabic become accustomed to finding basic meanings in consonantal roots of words that, when written, are without their vowels. Transferring that way of thinking to Greek, scholars reasoned that Christians had misread Jesus's term as *parakletos*, "Advocate or counselor," interpreted

129

by Christians as the Holy Spirit. A simple insertion of the correct vowels would yield *periklutos*, "the highly praised one," and thus a meaning more acceptable to Muslims. The name Muhammad in Arabic derives from the root HaMaDa, "to praise." When Arabic wants to intensify a root meaning, it doubles the middle consonant, hence HaM-MaDa, "to praise highly." In order to express the idea that a particular individual has been praised highly, Arabic forms a passive participle by adding the prefix "mu-" and producing the word muHaMMaD, the "highly praised one." What is most important to note in all this is the Muslim conviction that God sends a message to suit every circumstance perfectly. As the Quran says, "We (God) have sent no messenger except with the language of his people, that he might give them clarity. God allows to wander off whom He will, and He guides whom He will" (Quran 4:4).

How do Muslims experience their sacred scripture?

A fundamental belief is that the Quran is unique and inimitable—that is, that it would be impossible to duplicate without divine origination. The theological concept of "inimitability" (*i'jaz*, i-JAAZ) goes hand in hand with the notion that the Prophet was "un-lettered" (*ummi*)—a principle that emphasizes that the Prophet in no way "initiated" the scripture. Much as many Christians begin with the assumption that their sacred scripture presents an integrated, perfectly unified message, Muslims generally assume that the Quran presents no internal inconsistencies or contradictions. Anyone who detects such things is simply misreading the text. As a result the goal of theological exegesis and literary analysis aims to show how the varying suras fit together under this principle of unity. The Quran itself therefore represents the central prayer in the life of Islam as a whole and individual Muslims. Muslims typically encounter the scripture both as recited or spoken word, and as a visual or written word.

How do reciters perform their art? Is it a complicated process?

Professional specially trained reciters (called *qari* [KAA-ree]; pl. *qurra'* [kur-RAA]) are accomplished not only in the memorization of the whole sacred text, but in presenting the

How do people experience sacred scripture if they don't have a formal knowledge of Arabic?

Even people whose first language is not Arabic often memorize short texts in Arabic and experience public recitation of the sacred text on special ritual occasions. In addition, visual representations of the sacred word, both Quran and Hadith, remain an important point of contact, even for Muslims who do not know Arabic. Visual presentation of Hadiths, Quranic texts in calligraphic compositions (artistic writing), or epigraphy (inscriptions on buildings or objects such as Quran stands) are among the Islamic tradition's most treasured artistic works.

text in two technical forms of recitation. For less solemn, "ordinary" occasions, or when it is important to complete a set portion of the Quran in a limited period of time, reciters may employ the *tartil* (tar-TEEL, or "measured," *murattal* [mu-RAT-tal]) approach. Within a limited tonal range of four or five notes, the reciter proceeds through the text fairly expeditiously, rarely (if ever) pausing significantly or back-tracking to repeat sections. But for special occasions, reciters typically choose a much more elaborate and complex style called *tajwid* (taj-WEED, or "embellished," *mujawwad* [mu-JAW-wad]). Hallmarks of the style are a much broader tonal range, characterized by vocal flourishes called "arabesque"; more majestic pace further extended by frequent pauses and repetitions of phrases or even whole verses for emphasis; and a variety of vocal techniques designed to intensify the listening experience and foster a sense of *huzn* ("reflective sadness") in the listener.

ESSENTIAL BELIEFS

UNITY AND DIVERSITY IN A GLOBAL COMMUNITY OF FAITH

Many people—including more than a few Muslims—have the impression that Muslims are all alike in the way they approach their religion. Is this true?

Members of the same religious tradition seem to cherish the idea of unity in their ranks for positive reasons ("We all believe the same things"), even as outsiders often use similar observations for the purpose of dismissing others ("They're all alike"). Neither side is quite correct. From the earliest days there has been a variety of ways of understanding what it is to be a Muslim, even beyond the variations in "denomination" (Sunni/Shi'i) and legal methodology (the various "schools of law"). We can describe four "religio-cultural styles": the idealist, the traditionalist, the realist, and the personalist.

What is meant by the "idealist" interpretation of Islamic sources and history?

If one's only acquaintance with Muslims came via the news media, one might think all Muslims were "radical fundamentalists." Unfortunately, when non-Muslims hear the term "fundamentalist" so used, they often translate it as "lunatic fringe." "Revivalist" is useful in some contexts; and scholars have recently begun to use the terms "integralist" and "islamist" to describe this style. By whatever name, its general characteristics are a literalist reading of the Quran, whose absolute validity remains pure, universal, and unconditioned by historical circumstances. Often assumed to be rigidly traditional, this style has, ironically, often encouraged highly original and imaginative scriptural exegesis and virtually demands the exercise of independent investigation (*ijtihad*) in the elaboration of law. Politically activist, the approach seeks to recapture the spirit of the golden age of the Prophet and adapt it to contemporary needs, thereby establishing a society   133

The term "traditionalist" (other useful descriptors also include "conservative" or "normative") fairly describes the style that likely characterizes the vast majority of Muslims. Cautious and suspicious of all major change, this approach prefers to let stand the full record of Muslim history. Because it tends toward political passivity, it has generally preferred even leadership judged deficient by Islamic religious norms, to revolution and anarchy. Saudi Arabia and Jordan might be fair examples. Emphasis here is on the need to retain the full record of "Muslim history," all of which sheds light on the heritage and preservation of the broad "tradition."

purged of centuries of irrelevant medieval interpretation and of "western secularist" influences that have side-tracked Muslims from their original destiny. The term "idealist" is sometimes preferred because it describes the approach's selective interpretation of history and focus on an "ideal" period, effectively disowning the nearly fourteen centuries from Muhammad's age to the present, which is not unlike Protestant Christians devaluing "medieval, pre-Reformation" history or Mormons disregarding the centuries between St. Paul and the Prophet Joseph Smith. Movements such as the Wahhabi, the Taliban (literally, "Students") in Afghanistan, and the emergent Salafi in Egypt and various other regions are examples of this idealist approach.

Are there Muslims who approach changing times and needs from a more flexible perspective?

The "realist" (also sometimes called "acculturationist," "adaptationist," "rationalist," or "modernist") style favors fresh interpretation of Quran and Sunna in terms of changing needs and privileges reason as a key mode of inquiry and exegesis. As in other major faith traditions, this approach claims a minority of the global community. Like most Christians or Hindus, most Muslims gravitate to a more traditionalist approach. As for political issues, the realist approach takes a rather pragmatic view, recommending leadership models on the basis of utility rather than Islamic legitimacy. Adaptationists encourage the incorporation of non-Islamic contributions to world culture while at the same time raising Muslim consciousness about Islam's pioneering role in civilization. Twentieth-century Turkey might exemplify this style, as well as Tunisia (prior to more recent revolutionary events), which outlawed polygamy in 1957 in service of modernizing Islamic law.

What is the "personalist" approach to Islam?

The "personalist" (or "charismatic") style places the role of the inspired leader above all religious institutions, in fact if not in theory. Like the fundamentalist style, this approach also leans toward political activism and, if necessary, revolution to bring about its version of a just Islamic society. Contemporary Iran represents a good example of the style, especially under Khomeini. In the history of Muslim religious institutions one finds this approach represented particularly in Sufi religious orders. Those organizations originally developed around charismatic figures of legendary sanctity, called *shaykhs*, whose directives members accepted in blind obedience. The history of Christian religious orders offers numerous parallels.

CREED AND ISLAMIC TRADITION

What is a creed?

As a general concept, "creed" refers to the totality of what members of a religious tradition believe. As a technical term, creed means a formal statement that sums up the key points in a belief system. Creedal statements are typically short enough to memorize, but can be long enough to take two or three minutes to recite. Members of many religious traditions engage in ritual recitation of their creeds as a way of reaffirming their assent to core beliefs. Creedal statements are occasionally direct quotations from a scripture. More often than not they are a later development, refined by generations of reflection. More elaborate creedal formulas typically evolve only when diversity of views begins to divide a community of faith so that the majority feel a need to define themselves as a result of unacceptable tenets of an emerging minority. Some religious traditions see no need for creedal formulas.

Is there an Islamic creed?

One short, two-part statement sums up the essentials of Muslim belief. "I confess that there is no deity but God, and that Muhammad is the Messenger of God." In this "testimony" called the *Shahada* ("confession or witnessing, sha-HAA-da), Muslims affirm the two foundational elements from which all other beliefs and practices flow. First, they assert that only the one, transcendent, supreme being called Allah in Arabic can claim the full allegiance of humankind. Allah means literally "the deity," or what ordinary English usage calls God "with a capital G." Allah is therefore not a distinct name for God as such, but the primary designation for the Absolute, the deity above all other powers both spiritual and worldly. Affirming God's absolute oneness is called *tawhid* (taw-HEED). Second, Muslims attest that human beings know of this supreme being through the agency of prophets, the last of whom was Muhammad. This profession of faith is the first of the "Five Pillars" of Islam (along with almsgiving, daily ritual prayer, fasting during Ramadan [rah-ma-DAHN] and pilgrimage to Mecca, all of which will be discussed later in detail).

What are some of the further implications of the *Shahada*?

The fundamental profession of belief (*Shahada*) is a deceptively simple affirmation that "There is no deity but God and Muhammad is the Messenger of God." In this compact

135

two-part formula are hidden all the nuances of a faith that is, like all major religious traditions, immensely complex in the bigger picture. First it declares belief in the existence of a God who is a paradoxical amalgam of pure oneness and otherness, on the one hand, and continual and generous engagement with, and availability to, the created universe on the other. Second, the *Shahada* affirms the tradition's reliance on the veracity of the human means by which God has chosen to become known, namely, the succession of prophets of whom Muhammad is the last. Revelation through these exemplary messengers has, from the Islamic perspective, unfolded progressively over the millennia since Adam became God's first prophet.

How is the *Shahada* "deceptively simple"?

With the first half of the profession, "There is no deity but God," Muslims acknowledge the unity, uniqueness, and transcendence of God. This is about as pure and unvarnished a statement of religious focus as one can imagine, demanding of believers uncompromising discipline and vigilance over their affections and spiritual loyalties. It calls believers to the lifelong project of sensitivity to all the myriad subtle forms of idolatry to which human beings are susceptible. No one exemplifies dedication to that project better than the prophet Abraham, as in the Quran's account of how he severed his ties to home and family in search of a new direction in life. One night, the scripture says, Abraham beheld a star and said, "This is my Lord." But when the star soon disappeared, he confessed, "I love not things that set." When the moon rose, Abraham exclaimed, "This must be my Lord." But when it, too, set, he said, "Were not my Lord guiding me, I would surely be among the lost." And when he saw the sun come up, he said, "This must indeed be my Lord, for it is greater by far." But when the sun went down, Abraham addressed his father's people: "Far be it from me to set up partners with God as you do."

How does Abraham's experience in the story relate to "being a Muslim"?

In the following verse, the Quran has Abraham say the words all Muslims say at the start of the ritual prayer as they face Mecca: "I have turned my face toward Him who created heavens and earth (i.e., not to created nature itself), as a seeker after the One God, in grateful surrender (literally as a *hanif*, ha-NEEF, and a *muslim*), and I worship none but God" (Quran 6:76–79). Abraham could face the true center of life only after he had eliminated all that could compete for his attention. Abraham was reading what the Quran calls the "signs on the horizons" for what they reveal of God. Speaking of those who reject that self-discipline, the Quran says (God speaking):

> I will turn away from my signs those who walk proudly on earth. Though they see every sign, they will put no credence in them. Though they may see the way of uprightness they will not set out upon it. Should they see the errant way, that they will claim as theirs; for they denied and refused to attend to our signs (Quran 7:146).

How does this inform the meaning of the terms *islam* and *muslim?*

Here is the deepest meaning of the terms *islam* and *muslim*. The Arabic root S-L-M carries the connotation of being in that state of wholeness and balance that results from having all of one's relationships and priorities in order. That state is called *SaLaM* (related to the Hebrew *shalom*). Now when a person pursues that state in relation to God it means attributing to God and to no-one else what belongs to God, and that is the root meaning of *iSLaaM*. One who achieves that state of propriety in relation to God is a *muSLiM*, literally "one brings about a state of *SaLaaM*" by acknowledging that God alone, to follow up on the imagery of Abraham's story, "does not set."

What about the second half of the *Shahada*, the part about Muhammad?

"I confess that Muhammad is the Messenger of God" sums up all that Muslims believe about the need human beings have for guidance and about how God has provided that divine assistance through a succession of prophets. Muhammad is, of course, not the only messenger of God, but he is the last. In his definitive communication of God's word, Muslims see the corrective needed because of earlier misunderstandings and willful corruption of revelation delivered through previous prophets. Muhammad's message is not new. It reaffirms the truth of the original revelation brought by Moses, David, and Jesus. It differs from the earlier prophetic messages only in that God has chosen now to reveal the Word in Arabic. Islamic tradition names earlier Arabian prophets Hud, Salih, and Shuayb; but none of them brought a scriptural message and none was sent with a universal revelation. They were prophets (*nabi*), but not messengers (*rasul*, ra-SOOL).

Does the Quran mention any more specific statements of belief?

Various texts of the Quran elaborate slightly on the basic elements of the *Shahada*. One such statement is that "The Messenger believes in what has been revealed/sent down from his Lord, as do believers. Each of them believes in God, His angels, His scriptures, and His messengers" (2:285). A bit more expansively, another text runs: "O you who have faith, believe in God and His messenger, and the scripture that He revealed to His Messenger, and the scripture that He has previously revealed. Whoever does not believe in God, His angels, His scriptures,

Muslims believe in other prophets, such as Moses, but Muhammad is considered the last prophet and the first to receive an Arabic revelation.

137

His messengers, and the last day, is in extreme error" (4:135). In various places, the Quran effectively expands on the *Shahada*'s reference to prophetic revelation this way: "We believe in God, and what was revealed to us and to Abraham, Ismail, Isaac, Jacob, and the Tribes, and what was given to Moses and Jesus, and what was given to (all) the prophets from their Lord. We make no distinction among them" (2:136; also 3:84).

Does the Hadith literature offer further insights into creedal matters?

In the famous "Hadith of Gabriel," an unidentified young man approaches Muhammad, sits down before him, and begins to interrogate him about the fundamentals of the religion of Islam. Traditionally identified as Gabriel, the questioner asks the Prophet to explain the meaning of the terms *islam* (is-LAAM), *iman* (ee-MAAN), and *ihsan* (ih-SAAN). In the first category, Muhammad explains that "islam" encompasses the "Five Pillars" (affirmation that there is no deity but God and Muhammad is His Messenger, ritual prayer, alms, Ramadan fasting, and Pilgrimage). Faith (*iman*), the Prophet goes on, moves a step beyond the basic attitude of "surrender" (*islam*), and the Hadith describes the basic elements of its "content." To the five elements mentioned in the Quranic summaries (God, His Messengers, His books, His angels, and the Last Day), the Hadith adds explicitly a sixth element implicit in the concept of the Last Day, namely, the "measuring out." Muhammad then answers that *ihsan*, "doing what is beautiful," relates to an apocalyptic theme characterizing the end of time, called "the Hour," in which all things humankind will be definitively overturned. *Ihsan* accordingly has a strong ethical quality, reminding one to behave "as if God saw me, even if I do not see God."

Have Muslims formulated any longer, more detailed summaries of essentials of Islamic faith?

Muslim religious scholars between about 750 and 950 formulated a number of other, more detailed creedal statements, but none has been as widely known as the Nicene Creed among Christians or the "Thirteen Articles" among Jews. Those later Islamic creeds developed largely as correctives to theological positions that arose during Islam's early centuries, views that the creeds formally repudiated as unacceptable. Known technically by the term *aqida* (ahKEE-da, plural *aqa'id*, ah-KAA-id), which suggests a "binding" relationship, these documents are of widely varying lengths and diversity of content. Many of the earlier creeds read like detailed lists of responses to mistaken conceptions of basic tenets of the faith. Eventually these corrective summaries developed into more comprehensive theological treatises that discussed the full range of issues of faith in still greater detail, but always more for the purpose of clarifying rather than speculating or arguing for the sake of discussion as such. In general, these later creeds are in effect elaborations on the *Shahada*. However, one also finds elements of what could be called "development of doctrine," in the sense that divergent or sectarian views gave rise to the need to debate certain technical issues. A creed generally attributed to the great jurist Abu Hanifa, called the *Greater Fiqh* (deep understanding), exemplifies such a development, focusing as it does not explicitly on God or Muhammad, but on articulating distinctively Hanafi approaches to matters brought into dispute by sectarian positions advanced by Shi'ites and Kharijites, for example. The later creeds are usually statements of the doctrinal position of the various theological schools, orthodox and heretical, and are often the subject of many commentaries and glosses. Simpler *aqidas* can also take the form of children's catechism texts, framed as basic question-and-answer exercises.

What is an example of how one of these longer creedal statements explains specific points of controversy?

All of the ten "articles" of the *Greater Fiqh* respond to disputed questions, and since neither the transcendent oneness of God nor the prophetic mandate of Muhammad were among those, even these most foundational tenets receive no mention here. Here are the ten statements of this brief early creed, with a short explanation in parentheses:

1. We do not regard any person as unbeliever on the grounds of sinfulness, and we do not deny that such a person has faith. (Here the creed is responding explicitly to the Kharijites' very restrictive definition of "true Muslim," which rejected all serious sinners as unbelievers devoid of faith.)

2. We command the acceptable and condemn what is hateful. (This underscores Islam's inherent ethical activism and condemning the quietism of an early sect called the Jabriya. They argued that since God alone has the power to act, human beings are subject to moral compulsion (*jabr*) and one need not condemn behavior in which they have no free choice.)

3. What affects you could not have passed you by, and what passes you by could not have affected you. (One of the creed's more enigmatic assertions counters the belief of a sect called the Qadariya that human beings possess the capacity (*qadar*) to affect the events of their lives through primary agency and "free will." On the contrary, says the creed, God foreordains all things and everything occurs exactly so—there are no humanly devised alternatives, no "what ifs." Important political implications were among the key concerns behind the article: a ruler, for example, cannot be held solely responsible for an action or a policy that might otherwise betoken evil intent or corruption.)

4. We do not reject any of God's Messenger's Companions, nor do we give priority to any one of them. (Here and in article 5, the creed responds to controversies associated with important differences between Sunni and Shi'i interpretations of early Islamic history, concerning the question of legitimate succession to the Prophet.)

5. Concerning the matter of [the conflict between] Uthman and Ali, we defer to God who is aware of the inmost hidden meanings of things. (Again steering a neutral course on contested matters of community governance, the fifth article refers to the outcome of the first *fitna* (civil war) that arose between Uthman, third of the Rightly Guided Caliphs in Sunni reckoning, and Ali. The creed thereby seeks to avoid further dissension and recrimination as to guilt in the murder of Uthman, which many Sunni sources blamed on Ali's supporters.)

6. Understanding of religion is preferable to understanding in acquired learning and law. (In the final five articles, questions of religious knowledge and faith come to the fore. Article six gives insight into the priority of faith over expertise in religious and legal disciplines.)

7. Diversity of opinion [among religious scholars] is a sign of God's mercy to the community. (Some later theorists would clarify the assertion by insisting that this applied only to legal questions and not to doctrinal or theological issues.)

8. Anyone who accepts in faith all that one is expected to hold, but remains agnostic as to whether Jesus and Moses are among [God's] Messengers, is an unbeliever. (Commentators on the creed provide precious little insight as to why fashioners of the statement would have considered this a necessary addition.)

9. Anyone who asserts that he does not know if God is in the heavens or on the earth is an unbeliever. (Around the time of this creed, the notion that God abides neither in heaven nor on earth, but cannot be contained in any place, became a standard theological distinction. In fact, it may be that this article was meant as a critique of the "spiritualizing" tendency behind the notion of divine omnipresence.)

10. Anyone who asserts that he knows nothing of the suffering of the grave is a member of the Jahmiya sect who are bound for eternal punishment. (A small, little-understood faction, named after Jahm ibn Safwan (d. 746), held positions on the nature of the deity that were probably more influential [and controversial] than their eschatology. Traditional beliefs implicitly affirmed here include the notions that the newly interred deceased will be interrogated by two no-nonsense angels, Munkar and Nakir, and will experience a frightening sense of confinement.)

Muslims often use the expression *In sha' Allah*, which means (more or less) "God willing" or "If God wishes." Do they actually think their own choices are irrelevant?

A common misperception of Islamic tradition is that God exercises such minute and perfect control over all things that human actions have no bearing on the individual's ultimate destiny. When Muslims use the expression "God willing," they do not mean to suggest that human beings are mere marionettes dancing at the whim of the divine puppeteer. They are simply reminding themselves that God is ultimately in charge of everything, regardless of individual human preferences. True, the Quran often describes how God both guides and leads astray "whomever he chooses." But that does not suggest that God is capricious or spiteful, only that God is God and that lesser beings ought not to take God's sovereignty for granted even for a second. Equally often, the Quran reminds believers how God lays out his "signs" in creation and in the individual heart, adding "perhaps you will understand." Muslims believe in God's justice. The Quran insists that each person will be held accountable for his or her actions at judgment. But since God is just, Muslims conclude that human beings exercise a significant freedom of choice—otherwise accountability at the judgment would be a sham, a cruel hoax to which God hardly needs to resort. All in all, Muslim tradition seeks to maintain the delicate balance between belief in God's absolute power, and a limited, but more than adequate, human freedom to choose either good or evil.

But don't Muslims believe in predestination or fatalism?

It's a complicated question. On the one hand, many Muslims believe that an uncompromising form of predestination is a central tenet of Islamic theology. And it is true that even in the classic creedal formulations elaborated as far back as the eighth and ninth centuries, one finds cryptic expressions like "What hits you could not have missed you, and what misses you could not have hit you." Many people take that to mean that one's lot or destiny is set in stone from all eternity and the individual human being is powerless to alter that course. On the other hand, it is important to note the context in which such expressions originally occurred. One of the first theological issues to which Muslims addressed themselves arose in connection with political responsibility: is a leader fully responsible for his actions, and if so, should subjects rise up and overthrow a ruler who is behaving in ways not consistent with Islamic values? In the case of some of the early creeds, it seems clear that political considerations led some theorists to let some rulers off the hook ethically in the interest of avoiding social upheaval. Better to keep a reprehensible ruler than to risk chaos, they argued in effect. Majority opinion among Muslim thinkers has generally emphasized God's absolute power while paying less attention to what their statements implied about human beings. In other words, theological "anthropology" has largely left human beings in God's infinitely long shadow.

How do Quran and Hadith talk about self-determination?

Numerous texts in the Quran suggest that God never wrests effective power of self-determination from the individual. "We turn a person whichever way he/she wants to turn." "God does not change a people's state until they change what is within themselves" (Quran 8:53; see also 13:11). The scripture's insistence on the need to seek forgiveness unceasingly suggests the personal freedom to change. On balance, however, Muslim ethical thinking has always gotten around to confronting the issue of human responsibility. A saying attributed to Muhammad epitomizes the dilemma beautifully: "One who denies God's decree is an unbeliever, but one who claims never to have sinned is a liar." It expresses vividly the need to live with the paradoxical coexistence of God's absolute control over all affairs and the awareness that each human being remains responsible for every choice and cannot seek refuge in predestination by pleading, "God made me do it." Muhammad's saying "Trust in God but tie your camel" is not unlike a saying attributed to Ignatius Loyola: "Work as if everything depended on you, and pray as if everything depended on God." Both express something of the paradox attendant on believing in both the unfathomable mystery of God's omnipotence and human responsibility.

Are there important theological implications of all this?

Throughout Islamic history, but particularly in the early centuries, questions of the relationship between faith and works have been of political as well as theological import.

Is belief the same as faith in Islamic tradition?

Here is a useful distinction between belief and faith. Belief, understood either generally or as a reference to a particular tenet, refers to the content of a tradition's central teaching. When believers recite a creed, for example, they affirm that they share a certain set of beliefs. Faith is the act or process of relying on or assenting to realities that one might not be able to prove as easily as one might like. People talk about "acts" of faith and often describe faith as a "leap" into the unknown, or as a kind of fundamental trust. Not every belief or act of faith is necessarily religious. Beliefs of every description rule our daily lives—they're all the millions of things we take for granted, like gravity and sunrise. And no one could get past breakfast without a basic level of trust. Religious belief and faith can seem riskier, because their objects are often not subject to the validation of actual experience. But what finally distinguishes religious belief and faith from their more mundane counterparts is that religious believers are willing to live without conclusive proof indefinitely. Muslim religious scholars have discussed a variety of questions in this matter, such as whether faith can increase and decrease, how it relates to "good works," and whether an individual person has choices over what he or she has faith in.

Various opinions developed as to whether, and to what degree, a person known to have sinned could still be considered a Muslim. On one extreme, the Kharijites identified faith and works to such a degree that they virtually defined religious community as an assembly of the sinless. At the other end of the spectrum was the view that God's predetermination of events was so complete as to exonerate even blatant godlessness, with the important political implication that rulers could do as they pleased and revolution could not be justified. Majority opinion ended up somewhere closer to the middle. With respect to freedom of action, God creates all potential deeds, including evil ones, but leaves human beings the option as to which they will "appropriate" as their own. As for whether one's known choices render a person unfit to be called a Muslim, most would argue that the best position is to leave the ultimate judgment up to God.

Is there such a thing as heresy in Islamic tradition?

Muslim tradition recognizes varying degrees of deviation from pure faith or *iman* (ee-MAAN). Certain forms of departure from strict Quranic teaching and practices clearly identified as deriving from the Sunna of the Prophet have been labeled "innovation" (*bid'a*, BID-ah). Some things once considered innovations, such as attaching minarets to mosques, have long since become widely accepted. All but today's most traditionally minded Muslims give little consideration to this category. A daily danger for all human beings, one that Muslims seek to combat constantly, is called *shirk*, or associating partners with God. Any undue attention or attachment to that which is not God is thus a form of shirk, but while it is a natural tendency, it is not necessarily a permanent condition unless one chooses to make it so. A more serious problem, known technically as "deviation" (*ilhad*, il-HAAD), comes closer to what many understand by the term heresy. A *mulhid* is someone who deliberately strays from the broadly accepted tenets of the faith, introducing innovations to the extent that one can no longer readily recognize basic Islamic teachings in the new formulation. Farthest from adherence to true belief is the category of *kufr*, the kind of willful unbelief that leads to outright blasphemy.

How do Muslims feel when one of their members decides to leave the faith?

Departure from the community of believers has elicited a wide range of responses from families and society at large, depending on historical and cultural circumstances. Most of all, friends and relatives of an individual who has either simply slipped away from active involvement or made a deliberate choice to repudiate the Islamic tradition are eager to try to persuade the individual to reconsider. They will likely do whatever they can to support the individual in his or her dilemma. If they are unsuccessful, they will commend the individual to God's mercy and offer prayers on that person's behalf. Departure from a faith tradition is generally known as apostasy. Under certain social and political conditions, especially in regions where Muslims are in the majority and where the prevailing climate favors an emphasis on Islamic religious law, the response to apostasy may be more severe. This may include isolating the apostate from the religious community, or, in some cases, even declaring the individual worthy of death. Such extreme behavior is increasingly rare and is generally seen in the most traditional towns and villages, though now and then a more celebrated example makes news headlines.

Is there an Islamic fundamentalism?

Unfortunately, the term "fundamentalist" has become virtually synonymous with "Muslim" in contemporary American usage. This is unfortunate because, when applied to Muslims, "fundamentalist" has been simultaneously linked to terrorism. It is fair to say that most devout Muslims interpret their scriptures conservatively and quite literally, as do the vast majority of devout adherents to many traditions. Islamic fundamentalism is not inherently more likely to be expressed in extreme behavior than any other brand of fundamentalism. One can of course point to examples of such behavior in virtually every tradition—including the assassination of abortion providers by American Christians and the burning of Christian villagers by angry Hindu mobs in India. Extreme and violent behavior that claims religious justification invariably has a great deal to do with predominant political and social climates in particular places and times.

Do "outsiders" apply the term "fundamentalist" consistently to Muslims?

Non-Muslims often apply the epithet "fundamentalist" indiscriminately to widely diverse situations. For example, so-called militant fundamentalists in Algeria attempt to justify their activism on very different grounds than do, say, Shi'ite factions in southern Lebanon, the Palestinian organization called Hamas, the Taliban of Afghanistan and Pakistan, and the revolutionary government of Iran. On the other hand, Muslim-led states whose leaders are avowedly secularist in orientation are responsible for at least as much violence against their own people than avowedly "Islamist" states. In other words, while the term fundamentalism has value in describing some religious phenomena, it has become so imprecise as to be virtually useless as a way of describing Muslims. Recently a Palestinian Christian from Jerusalem said that the problem is not, and never has been, Muslim fundamentalism; it is rather the fundamentalism and intolerance of non–Middle Eastern Christian missionaries that has effectively driven wedges between Muslim and Christian Arabs. Surely there are intolerant and bigoted Muslims, who have their counterparts among Jews and Christians. Muslims have no monopoly on religious exclusivism. Religious violence likewise is not unique to Islam; nor does it constitute an essential characteristic of that religious tradition, while remaining merely an occasional, lamentable but forgivable lapse in others.

What does the term "doctrine" mean in general?

"Doctrine" in its general sense means "teaching" or "instruction" (from the Latin *doctrina*), both as an activity and as a collection of specific beliefs or principles. It is sometimes used in a non-religious sense, as in the geopolitical posture called the Monroe Doctrine (a warning that other governments who exert undue influence in the Americas should not be surprised if the United States pushes back). As a religious concept, doctrine means specifically all the individual teachings that a tradition identifies as essential.

Are "fundamentalism" and "literalism" synonymous?

One has to make several distinctions in the interest of simple fairness. First of all, fundamentalism is not necessarily the same as literalism in the interpretation of religious sources. Many people who consider themselves religiously engaged tend to be "fundamentalists" to the extent that they seek to live according to their traditions' "fundamental" values. Many religious persons, however, are quite sophisticated in their interpretation of the sources of their traditions. On the other hand, literalism remains a temptation for many, if only because it is the easiest approach to difficult questions, allowing one to abdicate personal responsibility for working through the ambiguities. In any case current conventional usage in describing religious phenomena continues to associate literalism and fundamentalism as though they were inseparable. Second, the vast majority of Muslims would say that people whose behavior slips over the edge into fanaticism have very definitely lost hold of the fundamentals of their faith. Most Christians, to broaden the point, would say that even though they do not approve of abortion on demand they abhor the extremism of those who attempt to justify violence in service of their cause. In short, most Muslims would likely agree that a life based on the fundamentals of Islam cannot embrace extremist behavior.

But why formulate a body of doctrine at all? Some traditions equate religious community with conformity of belief. Doctrine arises out of a desire to hold it all together and keep the tradition's inaugural insight as pure as possible. Doctrine is a measure of the role of authority in a religious tradition and provides a framework within which to pass along the content of the faith and to protect practices of ritual and worship from losing their distinctive character. So, in a general sense, there is definitely such a thing as "Muslim doctrine."

Is "dogma" synonymous with "doctrine"?

"Dogma" is a Greek work (from the verb *dokein*, to think or to seem good) meaning "belief" or "opinion." But in religious studies, dogma refers to a further specification of the category of doctrine. In some religious traditions, a teaching body or authority may deem it necessary under certain historical circumstances to clarify a particular doctrine. For example, suppose that the Buddhist monks in a certain region have gradually modified their interpretation of older ways of living the monastic life. Members of the larger Buddhist tradition might determine that they need to convene a "council" for the purpose of reaffirming and reinstating ancient practice. One can imagine other scenarios as well. When a tradition's core teachings come under attack, whether from within or without; or when changing times put undue pressure on traditional mores, those in leadership may decide corrective action is necessary. The result of the action is called dogma.

Are doctrine and dogma important to Muslims?

Islamic tradition centers on the relatively compact body of beliefs summed up in the *Shahada*. Straightforward affirmation of God's unity and transcendence, and divine communication through a succession of prophet-messengers, are the core of doctrine. Further basic elements that flow from these core doctrines include, especially, belief in God's use of angels as helpers and guides, resurrection of the body, personal accountability at judgment, and ultimate reward or punishment in heaven or hell in the next world. Since there is no central teaching authority, Muslims do not think in terms of official dogmatic formulations of their beliefs. Simplicity is the key. So long as one prefaces every act of faith with proper intention, one can be assured of pursuing the path God has revealed. In other words, Islamic tradition emphasizes orthopraxy over orthodoxy.

How do "doctrine" and "dogma" relate to creedal formulations?

It is essential to keep in mind that just as not all traditions possess specific creedal formulations, not all traditions have elaborated distinctive bodies of doctrine. Of those that do so, only some take the further more elaborate step of "defining" particular doctrines as dogma. In other words, non-creedal, non-theological traditions generally do not develop systems of beliefs that might function as "litmus test" indicators of a believer's compliance with mainstream views. As the creeds discussed above suggest, Muslim scholars have historically been very much concerned with clarifying key doctrines, but with "dogma" more secondarily, in that there is no single teaching authority.

GOD, REVELATION, AND PROPHETS

What does the term revelation mean? Is it uniquely Islamic?

Revelation means "drawing back the veil" that covers the deepest mysteries of life, thus disclosing their inner meaning. Religious traditions that explain their origins in terms of direct divine revelation generally teach that human beings are incapable of attaining ultimate truths on their own and therefore need a supernatural intervention to gain access to saving realities. This is especially true of the so-called Abrahamic traditions: Judaism, Christianity, and Islam.

How do these traditions differ with respect to their views of revelation?

Some sub-communities within the Abrahamic traditions are quite proprietary about their privileged and exclusive treasure, insisting that only a select few among the masses of humanity are chosen to benefit from the saving power of the divine self-disclosure. They emphasize to the highest degree the uniqueness of their elect status and seem little troubled by the notion that their convictions consign virtually the entire human race to damnation. Other sub-communities make more ample accommodation for the generality of humankind, leaving open some possibility that others not of the fold might still share in the revelation, however indirectly and secondarily. Some theologians talk of God's "special" revelation to their own traditions, with a broader or "general" revelation available to others. Alternatively they might talk of particular and universal revelation. These concessions presuppose that those outside the fold have missed out on the core revelation through no fault of their own and are in no way actively refusing to be illuminated by it. Revelation-based traditions typically envision the divine disclosure as mediated by a series of messengers called prophets, each sent

How do the Islamic sources describe the nature of the Prophet's experience of revelation?

According to both Quran and Hadith, Muhammad received revelations in a wide variety of circumstances. In some cases revelation is given in response to a particular question asked of the Prophet. In others, Muhammad is described as praying, preaching, eating, or even bathing. Muhammad is said to have experienced a variety of actual sensations when he received a revelation. He spoke of a sound like bees humming around his face, or a loud bell, the sound of which was physically painful. Sometimes he broke into a cold sweat or showed signs like those of a trance or seizure. All of the prophets are said to have experienced similar forms of revelation. What is most significant here is Muhammad's overwhelming sense of the divine presence at these moments.

to particular peoples to reaffirm various aspects of the original message at critical junctures of history.

What does the term revelation mean in Islamic tradition?

Islam's scripture, the Quran, consistently refers to itself as the word that God has "sent down" (*tanzil*, tan-ZEEL)) to humankind through Muhammad. That which is "sent down" represents a manifestation of truths that have existed from all eternity in the heavenly archetype of the Quran known as the "Mother of the Book." God reveals by communicating in a language understandable to the intended audience. Both the Quran and subsequent Muslim tradition describe the actual process of revelation by a technical term (*wahy*) that distinguishes prophetic revelation from the kinds of "inspiration" that animate holy persons and artists, for example. The prophetic intermediary "hears" the message, not with physical ears but with the ears of the spirit and heart. Some descriptions of revelation suggest a visionary dimension as well, as when the angel Gabriel or another mysterious unnamed presence appears.

What do traditions not focused on a "revelation" say about the source of religious truths?

Revealed traditions suggest that the truth is sent down from on high, so to speak, and "received" by specially chosen persons. That is sometimes called the "prophetic" model, a model distinctive of the Abrahamic faiths, but also of smaller traditions such as Zoroastrianism and the Baha'i faith. Other traditions have a rather different understanding of the process. From their perspective, eternal truth suffuses all things, filling the air with its creative sound and virtually bubbling up from the earth itself. Certain individuals specially endowed with unique sensitivities "discover," "hear," or "tune in" to this pervasive and timeless wisdom. The greater Hindu tradition exemplifies this understanding in various ways, teaching that the divine truth has been passed along since time immemorial by "seers" and "hearers." In China's major indigenous traditions, sages and rulers reflecting deeply on the signs all around them seek an awareness of the all-encompassing "mandate of heaven." Japan's Shinto tradition offers another variation on the theme, drawing on the ageless wellsprings of nature's wisdom for guidance in everyday life. As a general characterization, one could say that whereas the "prophetic" traditions understand revelation as a somewhat more restricted and privileged access to ultimate truths, the "wisdom" traditions regard the fundamental truths as more pervasive and available provided one is genuinely open to discovering them.

Do Muslims believe God reveals in ways other than the Quran and Muhammad's own sayings that expand on the scripture?

In addition to such scriptural texts as "If all the trees on the earth were pens, and all the oceans ink, and seven times that, they would not be able to record the words of God" (31:27; see also 18:109), Islamic tradition also sees important dimensions of divine dis-   147

According to the Quran, God reveals Himself in the written Word, in evidence as seen in His creations, and through signs. God also gives the "light" to prophets, who then help explain God's Word to the people.

closure in God's work as Creator, in nature broadly conceived, and in the individual human being. The Quran speaks of "signs" both on the "horizons" and within the "self" (Quran 41:53, 51:20–21). "Behold, in the heavens and the earth are signs for those who believe. And in your creation, and all the wild creatures He has scattered over the earth, are signs for a people of firm faith. And the alternation of night and day, and the sustenance that God sends down from the sky, to revive the earth after its death, and the shifting of the winds—these are signs for a people who understand.... Here is vision for humankind, guidance and mercy..." (Quran 45:3–5, 20).

So the created world itself is also "revelatory"?

Mention of God's handiwork occurs often in the Quran as the first, if not the foremost, locus of divine revelation. Anyone who sees the natural world in all its wonder with open eyes and an open heart will see there the unmistakable signs of the Creator. But the difference between God and creation is infinite; one discerns divinity through nature rather than precisely in nature. A "Sacred Hadith," a tradition attributed to God rather than to Muhammad, says: "I was a hidden treasure and I desired to be known, so I created the world." Knowing God through that world renders all created beings naturally "muslim," for all nonhuman things by nature surrender to God. As the Quran says, "Do you not see that it is God whom all in heaven and on earth, and the birds in formation, praise? Every being knows its proper prayer and praise" (Quran 24:41, with the word for

148

"prayer" being *salat*, the technical term for ritual prayer). Only human beings have to choose whether they will prefer self-centeredness and the illusion of control.

If God's "revelation" is available even to individuals, why are prophets needed?

God also reveals by means of "signs" within the individual person, but the tradition does not call God's disclosure in this instance "revelation." Instead, God casts into the heart a "light" that illuminates the individual's relationship to God. Scriptural verses such as "Wherever you turn, there is the face of God" (2:109) and: "We [God] are closer to the person than the jugular vein" (50:16) convey a sense of God's nearness. The same sentiment occurs in sayings of Muhammad, such as "Who knows oneself knows one's Lord," and in the Sacred Hadiths: "I fulfill my servant's expectations of Me" and "Though the heavens and the earth cannot contain Me, there is room for Me in the believer's heart." God sends prophets because human beings need them to access the "fullness" of divine disclosure.

What do Muslims mean by the term "Allah"?

Many non-Muslims have the impression that the term Allah refers to some despotic deity with a taste for violence and infidel blood. Perhaps that is because so many television and movie images of Muslim soldiers depict them screaming "Allahu Akbar" (God is supreme) as they attack or celebrate victory. How is it, many wonder, that they seem so readily to associate Allah with violence? In Arabic, the word Allah is simply a compound of *al-* (the definite article, "the") and *ilah* (god, deity). Joined together, they signify "God."

Do any non-Muslims use the term "Allah"? What are the inter-religious implications?

Nearly all Arabic speakers, including Iraqi Jews and Syrian Christians, refer to the supreme being as Allah. Most Jews and Christians are convinced their God is loving and kind, provident and generous, as well as thirsty for justice and equity. So are most Muslims. Of the "Ninety-Nine Most Beautiful Names" of God, the two by far most frequently invoked are "Gracious or Compassionate" and "Merciful." All but one of the Quran's 114 suras begin with the phrase "In the name of God, the Gracious and Merciful." One might say these two names are as important for Muslims

The Arabic word "Allah" is written on this heart-shaped bookmark.

as are the names Father, Son, and Holy Spirit heard in so many Christian invocations. Virtually every Muslim public speaker begins with that Quranic phrase and goes on to wish the audience the blessings and mercy of God.

What does the opening chapter of the Quran say about who Allah is?

The opening chapter of the Quran sets the tone of prayer for Muslims:

> In the Name of God, the Compassionate and Merciful: Praise to God, Lord of the Universe.
> The Compassionate, the Merciful,
> Master of the Day of Judgment.
> You alone do we serve; from you alone do we seek help.
> Lead us along the Straight Path,
> the path of those who experience the shower of your grace,
> not of those who have merited your anger
> or of those who have gone astray. (Quran 1:1–7)

Here one finds clues to several of the principal divine attributes. Compassion and mercy top the list and receive an emphatic second mention. In addition, God rules the "two worlds" (seen and unseen, i.e. the universe), takes account at Judgment, offers aid and grace, and manifests a wrathful side to those who prefer arrogant independence from the Origin of all things. Not one of the Ninety-Nine Names of God, on which Muslims meditate as they finger the thirty-three beads of the *tasbiha* (tas-BEEH-a), will sound a dissonant note in the ear of a Christian or Jew.

What does an awareness of the divine names do for Muslims?

All of the names conjure up divine attributes that Islamic tradition has divided into those that express God's beauty and approachability (*jamal*) and those that evoke the divine majesty and awe-inspiring power (*jalal*). These references to the two sides of God recall the theological distinction between immanence and transcendence. God is both near and accessible—closer even than the jugular vein, according to Quran 50:16—and infinitely beyond human experience and imagining. In the final analysis, many of the images Muslims have of God are very much like those Jews and Christians have, and they are gathered in the "Ninety-Nine Most Beautiful Names."

What are some distinctively Muslim emphases in their beliefs about God?

God is one, transcendent, and wholly unlike anything in ordinary human experience. But such a barebones description of ultimate reality leaves little for the human heart to grasp. Muslim tradition speaks of God most of all through the "Ninety-Nine Beautiful Names." "Compassionate" and "Merciful" are by far the most important of these. They occur in the phrase "In the name of God, the Compassionate, the Merciful," with which all but one of the suras of the Quran begin. Whatever devout Muslims do, they dedicate with that phrase.

God's names include about equally those that suggest divine power and majesty (*jalal*, ja-

LAAL) and those that speak of his beauty and infinite attractiveness (*jamal*, ja-MAAL). God both brings to life and causes to die, gives freely and calls all creation to account.

What is behind many non-Muslim misunderstandings of Muslim beliefs?

Non-Muslims often have the mistaken impression that the Islamic God is most of all a fearsome, even despotic, power before whom all must cower and cringe. To the contrary, while Muslims are ever aware of God's uncontested sovereignty and dominion over all things, they believe as well that, as the Quran teaches, God is closer to individual persons than even their jugular vein. Muslim tradition reminds believers that, in the end, God's mercy outweighs his anger. Scores of Hadiths describe this God of mercy in such beautiful and moving terms that any outsider who studies them can readily understand why so many Muslims find devotion to such a deity so compelling.

Why does the Islamic tradition make a distinction between God's "majesty" and God's "beauty"?

One of the essential "mysteries" of the divine reality is that God is purely "one" and yet is both utterly "transcendent" (that is, beyond all human imagining and understanding [majestic]) and "immanent" (that is, nearby, accessible, and even attractive [beautiful]). Islamic theologians use the term *tanzih* (tan-ZEEH, different from) to express God's transcendence, and the term *tashbih* (tash-BEEH, similar to) to talk about God's immanence. God's "Ninety-Nine Most Beautiful Names" describe the divine attributes, each suggesting either transcendence or immanence, majesty or beauty, approachability or distance. For example, names like "just" and "the one who causes death" emphasize *tanzih*, while others like "merciful" and "compassionate" emphasize *tashbih*.

How does Islamic tradition describe the "majestic" aspect of God?

Numerous verses of the Quran emphasize God's sovereignty and power. Two such texts come to mind. The first, called the "Throne Verse," appears as an inscription around the interior of domes in dozens of major mosques across the world:

> God—there is no deity but He; the Living, the Everlasting. Neither slumber nor sleep overcome Him. To Him belong all that heavens and earth encompass. Who can intercede with Him, except by his leave? He knows all that surrounds (created beings), while they can grasp nothing of what He knows, except as He chooses. His Throne stretches across heaven and earth; sovereignty over them tires him not, for He is the Exalted, the Magnificent. (Quran 2:255)

God is thus the beginning and end of all things, the Creator, the Sustainer, the Provider, the Lord of space and time. According to a saying of Muhammad (Hadith), the Throne Verse, like all the Quran, has existed eternally in the mind of God and was known to earlier prophets:

> Anas ibn Malik related that the Prophet said, "God revealed to Moses, Whoever continues to recite the Throne Verse after every prayer, on him will I bestow

151

more than that granted to those who are ever thankful. His reward shall be as great as that of prophets and that granted the righteous for their good deeds. I shall spread over him my right hand in mercy. Nothing would hinder him from entering Paradise...." Moses said, "My Lord, how can anyone hear this and not continue to observe it?" God said, "I grant this to no one except a prophet, a righteous person, a man I love...."

How does the tradition describe the more "immanent" and accessible side of God?

A second Quranic text, perhaps even more important as an architectural inscription than the "Throne Verse," offers a magnificently imaginative glimpse of the unimaginable. The "Verse of Light" provides another ingredient with its imagery of God's all-pervasive illumination—people cannot "see" God's Throne, but light is everywhere and thus represents the more "accessible" being of God, his *tashbih*—that is, connectedness with creation.

> God is the Light of Heaven and Earth. Picture His light as a niche within which there is a lamp, and the lamp is within a glass. And it is as though the glass were a glittering star lit from a sacred olive tree neither of east nor west, whose oil would fairly radiate even without the touch of fire. Light upon light, and God guides to his light whom He will. (Quran 24:35)

That text has inspired marvelous designs on prayer carpets and on the niches (*mihrab*, indicates orientation toward Mecca) of mosques all over the world. It recalls the symbolism of the revelatory cosmic tree, one that glows without being consumed and is so large it spans the universe (neither of east nor west)—not unlike the "Burning Bush" at which Moses heard the divine voice (Exodus, chapter 3). On the level of imagery, the text has functioned as a kind of summary, like the "Throne Verse," of divine qualities.

What's the meaning of that text's last line?

The last line brings to mind a question that has been significant in shaping Islamic intellectual history, namely, the matter of divine ordination of events or predestination. If God guides whom He will, then does He also *not* will to guide others? And if so, could those others truly be held responsible if they lose their way? The issue is complex. Suffice it to say for the moment that Islamic tradition has generally striven to strike a balance between God's unlimited power and the human person's limited freedom and commensurate accountability. It is useful to think of the apparent predilection for some form of divine predetermination as an analogy to the Biblical phenomenon of God's "hardening the heart" of Pharaoh and even some of the people of Israel.

What are the larger theological implications here?

The "Verse of Light" alludes to that crucial divine function of guidance, and that in turn harkens back to the image of journey. "Guide" is one of the ninety-nine names, and the Quran often speaks of God in that capacity. Just after the "Throne Verse," the scripture continues: "God is the Guardian of those who believe; He brings them forth from darkness into His light. Those who chose not to believe in their arrogance will be led from the light into darkness, there to become companions of the fire forever" (Quran 2:257). The irony, in view of the "Verse of Light," is striking. Those who rely on themselves cannot discover the authentic light, but come only to that fire that is darkness itself.

Ya Rasulullah
(messenger of God)

Written in Arabic calligraphy, this invocation (*dua*) says "O Messenger of God."

What is a prophet?

Especially important in the traditions of Middle Eastern origin, the prophet plays two indispensable roles. First, prophets are intermediaries in the divine communication to humankind. In the Abrahamic traditions, prophets speak on behalf of God, sometimes delivering a sacred scripture to the people to whom they are sent. In this capacity prophets appear often through history, whenever the divine revealer determines that the original message has been lost or become so diluted as to need restatement. In addition, prophets function as critics of the ethical and religious status quo. They confront the powerful with a mandate to establish justice for all their subjects. They challenge the wealthy to account for their responsibilities in societies where the gap between the haves and the have-nots grows ever wider. They remind ordinary folks of the need to render thanks to the divine source of life and giver of all gifts.

What's the difference between a prophet and a messenger according to Islamic teaching?

Central to Islamic tradition is the belief that God communicates ultimate truths through specially chosen persons called prophets. Without prophetic revelation, human beings would be forced to rely on intellect alone and thus could not arrive at the knowledge necessary to attain their final purpose. Every prophet (*nabi*, NA-bee) passes along the divine word to a particular people and inevitably meets with tremendous resistance, at least initially. Some of these prophets receive the further designation of "messenger" or "apostle" (*rasul*, ra-SOOL), "one who is sent." God sends but one messenger to a given people. Prophets specified as messengers include Noah, Lot, Ishmael, Moses, Shuayb, Hud, Salih, Jesus, and of course Muhammad. Prophets preach and warn their people, but messengers are also commissioned to lead a community of faith called an *umma*. Post-Quranic tradition also teaches that messengers function as lawgivers, whereas the other prophets do not. In short, one might say that all messengers are prophets, but not all prophets are messengers.

153

Is a reformer anything like a prophet?

Reformers can share important characteristics of prophets, such as their scathing critique of the status quo. But there are also notable differences. First, reformers appear in virtually every tradition, whereas prophets do not. Not all traditions teach that their sacred truths are delivered through intermediaries or spokespersons for the divine source. Second, reformers typically do not bring new revelations at all, nor do they claim an authority that simply abrogates all that has gone before them. Instead reformers try to awaken in their people an awareness that it is time to change, to renew, to recapture the original spirit that gave birth to the tradition. They do not necessarily advocate jettisoning the tradition's historical heritage to return to the sources, though that can be a feature in some fundamentalist reforms. Some reformers do, however, reevaluate religious teachings that they believe have become distorted or diluted and lay the ax to the root of institutions they believe have usurped unwarranted authority. The power of the papacy, for example, was a major target of Christianity's sixteenth-century reformers. There have been rare instances in which important religious figures functioned as reformers while they lived but were elevated after death to the status of prophets. In those cases it appears that some members of the reformer's tradition chose to break away from the parent tradition so dramatically that they required the added authority of prophethood to legitimate their claim to independence as a new religious entity. In the history of Islam, the notion of divinely sanctioned "renewers" is an ancient and important concept. According to a Hadith of Muhammad, God promised to raise up a renewer (*mujaddid*) at the outset of every *Islamic century*—that is, reckoning in lunar years, beginning in the solar year 622.

How does the Quranic view of Jesus differ from Christian tradition?

The Quran refers to Jesus as servant of God, spirit of God, and a word from God. God taught Jesus wisdom, gave him knowledge of the Torah, and strengthened him with the Holy Spirit (often associated with the angel Gabriel, the revealing angel). Among Jesus's special gifts were the power to raise the dead and heal the sick. Tradition says that Jesus ascended to either the second or the fourth heaven. A distinctive element in Muslim teaching about Jesus is the belief he was not actually crucified. Instead a look-alike took his place at the last minute (Quran 4:157), but another text mentions his death and resurrection (Quran 19:33).

Why are Jesus and Mary together important to Muslims?

Muslims revere Jesus (Arabic: Isa, EE-sa) as the second-last in a long line of prophets that culminated in Muhammad. They thus consider Jesus a man of lofty spiritual estate, but no more than a human being. Born of the Virgin Mary, Isa was a specially chosen instrument of divine revelation, but he was not the Son of God. Jesus appears in a total of fifteen suras of the Quran. Muslim texts call Jesus the *masih*, but the term does not carry the sense of expectation connoted by its nearest English equivalent, Messiah. He is "God's word," but not in the sense that Christians understand the term *logos*. Mary is mentioned more often by name in the Quran than in the Bible. The purely human nature of Jesus is not the only major issue on which Islamic tradition disagrees dramatically with the Christian view. Quran 4:157 states that though the Jews boasted they had killed Isa, they did not in fact do so. It was, rather, one who looked like Jesus who hung on the cross. Muslim tradition holds, nevertheless, that God did raise Jesus bodily into heaven in the Ascension. Since Isa did not die an earthly death, he did not experience resurrection. Isa has a significant place in the Quran. According to the Islamic sacred text, Mary became pregnant with Isa when the angel Gabriel appeared to her in human form to announce the news. Joseph plays no part in the Muslim story of Jesus. After the child was born, Mary brought him to her people. When even

While Jesus is certainly not considered the Son of God by Muslims, in the Quran he *is* considered to be a prophet and is honored by Muslims. In this photo, we see an icon of Jesus Christ found in the Hagia Sofia in Istanbul, Turkey.

they expressed doubt as to Mary's integrity, the infant spoke in her defense and lifted her opprobrium. One of the Quranic stories not found in the canonical Gospels is that the boy Isa formed a bird of clay in his hands, and when he breathed on it, it took flight—a story also told in a Christian apocryphal. Principal Quranic texts on Isa (and Mary) are: 3:37–48; 4:169–170; 5:76–79 and 109–117; 19:1–36; 21:91–92; 43:57–65; 57:26–27.

What non-scriptural Islamic sources speak of Jesus?

Hagiographical texts known collectively as Tales of the Prophets expand further a number of important themes. The Tales embellish the accounts of Isa's infancy and youth. They feature Isa as a wandering ascetic with the power to give and restore life. They also add to the number of his miracles and emphasize his sinlessness and the significance of his Ascension and second coming. Islam's mystical authors develop the figure of Isa in particularly colorful and imaginative ways. Isa is for many mystics the image of the near-perfect Sufi—near-perfect because he once carried a needle with him during his desert wanderings, thus falling short of absolute trust in God. But even when storms threatened, Isa refrained from seeking shelter, for he epitomized the homeless pilgrim. Still the Sufis celebrated Isa as the prophet who laughed heartily and often, by contrast with Yahya (John the Baptist), who had a penchant for weeping. Sufi poets delight in tales of Isa's ability to restore life through the incantation of a powerful name only a select few may utter. Though the Quran does not mention Lazarus (Azar) by name, Sufi writers picked up, from popular hagiography, the story of Isa's raising him from the dead. Finally, Sufis love to describe how Isa embodies their focus on mystical knowledge through his mastery of the "donkey" of the body, a symbol of ignorance.

Islam is called one of the "Abrahamic" faiths. Why is Abraham so important to Muslims?

Islam's sacred scripture, the Quran, makes numerous references to both biblical and extra-biblical stories about Abraham, whose Arabic name is Ibrahim. For Muslims, Ibrahim's status is that of a Prophet, a recipient of God's direct revelation. That he does not function as a patriarch in Islamic tradition is significant, for Ibrahim's primary theological role is not that of the father of a chosen nation, but that of the first "*muslim*"— the first human being to whom God revealed explicitly the call to be a seeker after divine unity and, therefore, the first to "surrender." The Arabic term *muslim* means "one who surrenders" to God and who thereby enacts the full meaning of the term *islam*.

ISLAMIC ESCHATOLOGICAL THEMES

What is eschatology? Are Islamic notions here similar to those of any other faiths?

"Eschatology" derives from two Greek words meaning the "study (*logos*) of the last things" (*eschata*). The so-called "four last things" include death, judgment, heaven, and hell and the study of them is often called "individual eschatology." In addition, "cosmic" eschatology encompasses religious teaching concerning how history and the world as we know it will come to an end. Although use of the term eschatology has been especially characteristic of the study of the Abrahamic traditions, it can also be useful in describing important aspects of belief in the religious traditions of Asian origin. Religious traditions of Middle Eastern origin have generally developed linear views of history whereby time is said to have a beginning, middle, and end, never again to be repeated. Their eschatologies explore the final and definitive transformations that will befall both individuals and the universe. Traditions of Asian origin tend to favor cyclical views of time. Although each cycle of time is unimaginably long, it is only part of a vast unending potentiality for further variations. As a result, though Asian traditions do talk of various realms of reward and punishment hereafter, they generally do not consider any of those realms to be a truly final destination for the individual. There is always the possibility of yet another existence and another outcome. Many traditions talk of an accountability after death, often describing it as a meeting between the individual soul and a judge or council charged with meting out just desserts. Islam and Christianity are very similar in their development of eschatological themes—in fact, the two traditions' concepts of death, resurrection, reward, and punishment in the hereafter are almost identical in their overall outlines, differing only in relatively smaller details.

What else do Muslims believe about the "last things"—death, judgment, heaven, hell?

Many features of Islamic eschatology will remind Christians of their own tradition's views of death, judgment, heaven, and hell. Nearly all of the Quran's many references to death refer at least indirectly to the omnipotence of the God who "brings to life" and "causes to die" (two of the ninety-nine names). One of the earliest references relates directly to the content of Muhammad's preaching and the refusal of his listeners to accept it: they have committed spiritual suicide. All unbelief amounts to inner death. Unbelievers scoff and insist they will suffer only the "first death" of the body when their predetermined span of life is done. Most of the relevant texts concern physical life and death in relation to God's power. As exhortatory devices in Muhammad's preaching, they remind that God's absolute dominion over life and death can give the believer unshakeable confidence. God's purposeful control over lifespan, as opposed to the arbitrary and despotic control the pre-Islamic Arabs had attributed to impersonal "Time" or "Fate," leaves the believer free to attend to life as it happens, in the conviction that life is not pure chance but part of a great design. God's providence gives the believer hope in the resurrection, for God will not suffer creation to come to naught.

Does anything like millennialism have a place in Islamic thinking?

Yes, so long as one understands "millennialism" broadly rather than as a precise reference to measures of a thousand years. Numerous Hadith, called Traditions of Discord, talk

The mythical giants Gog and Magog adorn this clock at the Royal Arcade in Melborne, Australia. In Arabic traditions, chaos is symbolized by these personages, bringing in the final chapter of history.

of various general features that mark a decidedly downward trend in human life. Honesty will be hard to find, fewer and fewer people will observe the religious law, and violence will rise. According to other ancient traditions, various explicit signs will herald the end of time itself. A resurgence of chaos symbolized by Gog and Magog will mark a radical turn for the worse, the beginning of the final chapter in the unraveling of history. A figure resembling the Prophet, called the *Mahdi* (Guided One), will usher in a temporary age of justice. Numerous individuals throughout the history of Islam have sought to gain political power by claiming to be the *Mahdi*, most recently in 1979, when armed bandits seized control of the sanctuary of the Ka'ba in Mecca. A one-eyed Antichrist figure (called the *Dajjal*, daj-JAAL) will supplant the *Mahdi*, luring people away through magic masquerading as miracle. Jesus will eventually return to battle the Antichrist, overthrowing that false prophet and paving the way for the Day of Judgment. Shi'ite tradition features its own distinctive type of millenarianism. According to the Shi'ite interpretation of history, Muhammad's spiritual authority was passed along through a series of descendants called *imams*. In the view of the "Twelvers," by far the majority of Shi'ites, the twelfth and last of these *imams* (also called the *Mahdi*) went into "greater concealment" in 940. This hidden imam did not die but has remained in a mysterious state from which he will return to establish full justice. In the meantime, the imam hears prayers and intercedes for believers. Although both the Quran and Hadith warn against attempting to calculate precisely the arrival of the "Hour" at which the world will come to an end, small groups of Muslims have tried to do just that through history.

Do Muslim creeds talk about these matters much? How about Muhammad's sayings?

Every major creedal statement formulated by the early theologians includes statements about death, and specifically about the "punishment of the tomb" and the angelic interrogators who question the deceased about their lives and deeds. Both features seem to arise from Hadith that suggest the dead retain their perceptive faculties. According to one Creed, body and soul are reunited in the tomb; infidels will surely suffer there, and believers who have sinned may also suffer. In any case, even the obedient believer will experience the "pressure" of the tomb. But, according to a Hadith, no punishment will be inflicted on a Muslim who dies on Friday, and the pressure will last only an hour. The Quran mentions neither the interrogating angels, Munkar and Nakir, nor the pressure and punishment of the grave. These traditional elements gradually became more detailed and embellished and have become, to some degree, articles of faith.

Some sayings about death are blatantly contradictory. Weep for the dead, do not weep for them; weep for only one day, weep for an extended period; the more you weep the more suffering the dead will feel from the pain of separation; weep to help them with your sympathy; and so forth. What is important here is simply that tradition attributes to the Prophet the complete range of responses to death and mortality. All will be held accountable for their deeds at Judgment. A number of Hadiths are as much instructions on how to live as on how to die. "Die before you die," the Prophet advises; let preoccupation with self pass away now, so that when death comes you will have handed over already that which you fear most to lose. "As you live, so shall you die; and as you die, so shall you be raised up." Therefore, leave your good deeds behind when you go and your good deeds will be your traveling companions on your journey after death.

How do the principal sources, Quran and Hadith, describe life after death?

After the resurrection of the body, everyone will experience either reward or punishment, heaven or hell. There is no Purgatory as such, but the passageway between this life and the next, called the *barzakh*, could be considered a loose parallel. In addition, some hold that a temporary stay in hell serves that function. The Hadith include many ethical-eschatological images. One anecdotal saying of Muhammad has him telling his listeners how death itself will be slaughtered, leaving the people of Paradise uninterrupted delight and the people of the Fire no hope for an end to their misery: Death is brought in the guise of a black-and-white-spotted ram. Then a caller calls: "O People of Paradise!" And they crane their necks and look, and He (God Himself) says: "Do you recognize this (figure)?" They say: "Yes, that is Death." And each of them sees him. Then He calls: "O people of the Fire!" And they crane their necks and look, and He says: "Do you recognize this (figure)?" They say: "Yes, that is Death." And each of them sees him. Thereupon he is slaughtered. Then He says: "O people of Paradise! Eternity without death (is yours)! O people of the Fire, Eternity without death (is yours)."

Many of the Meccans to whom Muhammad preached scoff at his teaching of the "second death" of eternal damnation. The Quran insists that in the Fire one neither lives nor dies; all who end up there will beg for death. The Quran's imagery of the double death is very similar to that of some Latin, Greek, and Syriac Patristic literature.

For those who have spent a life of faith and good works, eternal reward awaits. As in many other traditions, the scriptural imagery of paradise describes heaven as a realm of endless pleasures. Many Muslims understand the imagery in its widest sense to refer to a state of delight that results from being forever in God's presence.

What are these most distinctively Islamic notions of the afterlife, and how are they similar to Christian and Jewish conceptions?

Muslim eschatology has much in common with most Christian and some Jewish traditions about the afterlife. Death is not the end of life, but a transition to another level of existence. Muslims believe human beings are accountable for all of their free moral decisions. People are not held similarly responsible for actions with negative consequences but done under duress or in the absence of intent to do evil. Numerous texts of the Quran warn of the coming Day of Judgment, the Day of Resurrection, the Hour in which the true quality of everyone's deeds will be revealed. On the basis of that accounting, individuals will go across a narrow passage of no return called the *barzakh* (BAR-zakh) to one of several destinations.

A muslim graveyard in Kyrgyzstan. In Muslim eschatology, as with Christian and Jewish beliefs, death is not the end of life, but merely a transition.

What is the main Islamic metaphor for Paradise?

Paradise is called the Garden (*janna*, pronouned JAN-nah), a verdant place of repose and delight, an oasis for the just. Heaven is not so much literally a place as a state of being whose principal feature is the vision of God. Quranic texts refer to several different levels or degrees of heavenly reward. Hell, known as the Fire or Gehenna (*jahannam*, ja-HAN-nam), represents the state of refusal to acknowledge God's sovereignty. Some Muslim theologians have taught that hell is not necessarily a permanent state, since God can always forgive any sin except unrelenting denial of God's existence. Hell can thus function in a way similar to that of the state of purgatory in Christian tradition, though Islamic tradition does not have a separate term for that state of purification. Muslim tradition also hints at something like an intermediate state, perhaps similar to the Christian idea of limbo.

SPIRITUAL POWERS AND WONDERS

What does the term "miracle" mean generally?

A miracle is broadly defined as an apparent breach in the laws of nature that so defies rational explanation as to suggest the possibility of divine intervention. Miracles or the working of wonders figure prominently in the sacred texts and lore of most major religious traditions, but they do not necessarily serve the same purpose from one tradition to another. In some cases miracles are believed to provide incontrovertible proof of the truth of a particular revelation by establishing beyond doubt the power of the agent. Miracles are not just a fancy "extra" tossed in to entertain the masses, but an integral part of some systems of belief. Sometimes miracles occur in the context of a controversy by way of a dramatic settlement in favor of the miracle worker. One characteristic of miracles that does appear to be a feature in many traditions is that those who choose obstinately not to believe do not necessarily change their minds in the presence of a miracle. In fact, they simply do not see what the believers standing next to them see. That seems to suggest that, in some traditions at least, wonders are in the eye of the beholder, so that a witness must be predisposed to see a miracle. Some traditions regard miracles as gifts from a divine source to certain special persons, whether prophets or saints, designed to establish their spiritual credentials. A miracle can revolve around some symbolic action that, even apart from the apparently miraculous result, contains the central message.

Do Muslims believe in miracles? Are all "miracles" equal?

Three kinds of "miraculous" occurrences play important roles in Islamic tradition and the lives of countless Muslims. First, all of God's deeds visible in the created universe are known as divine "signs" (*ayat*, ah-YAAT), the fundamental evidence on which faith depends. Second, the Quran also describes numerous ways in which God works through His prophets. These "prophetic miracles" (*mujiza*, MU-ji-za) function as "proof" of the truthfulness of the message God communicates through His messengers. Third, a type of extraordinary manifestation of divine power worked through human beings is called the "saintly marvel" (*karama*, ka-RAA-ma). Exemplary figures called Friends of God are often said to manifest divine power and blessing through such deeds, ranging from curing illness to control over the forces of nature to unusual abilities such as instantaneous travel over impossibly large distances.

Does Islamic tradition attribute miraculous deeds to Muhammad?

Muhammad's early critics in Mecca sometimes taunted him for being so much like an ordinary human being: If he were really a prophet of God, surely he would entertain them with some sort of heavenly pyrotechnics. Muhammad regarded the Quran itself as his only miracle, a marvel of eloquence uttered by a man considered technically "unlettered." But the scripture does refer often to spectacular "signs" God brought about to vindicate earlier prophets. For example, Moses's staff became a dragon that devoured Pharaoh's magicians, and Moses's hand turned white with leprosy and was then restored to health (Quran 7:107–108). Within a generation or two of Muhammad's death, tradition had begun to attribute to the Prophet a number of extraordinary occurrences. He could fast for inordinately long periods, could see people behind him, heal various ailments, supply water where there was none, and stretch limited food sources as needed. Trees and stones saluted

Muhammad, a pillar in his house mourned that the Prophet no longer leaned on it when he preached, and the Prophet split the moon in two to confound his critics.

Are miracles attributed to anyone else?

Throughout the history of Islam, holy persons called "friends of God" have been famous for the ability to perform wondrous deeds. Many Muslims today regard accounts of such legend and lore of secondary importance. Classical Muslim theologians devised technical terms to distinguish between two levels of miracle. They called the works God did as proof of his prophets' truthfulness "evidentiary miracles" (*mu'jizat*, mu-ji-ZAAT), and those effected by Friends of God "marvels" (*karamat*, kar-aa-MAAT). Theologians further called attention to key differences between works of sorcery and wonders performed authentically under divine power.

What are angels? Do they have a role in very many traditions?

Angels and similar celestial beings appear in numerous traditions all over the world. The classic image of the angel, a winged ethereal body with human features and a pair of wings, may have originated in the Middle East. The ancient prophetic tradition called Zoroastrianism had a highly developed cosmology in which angel-like beings called *amesha spentas* were attendants at the heavenly court of Ahura Mazda. Even the early books of the Hebrew Bible mention heavenly emissaries who deliver divine messages to people. The name "angel" comes from the Greek word for messenger and got attached to the mysterious figures because of what appears to be their principal function. But angels play many other roles as well, including that of warrior, guardian and protector, heavenly councilor, winged mount, celestial guide, or escort, to name but a few. Angels play prominent roles in Christian and Islamic, as well as Biblical Jewish, lore and spirituality. On the whole they act as intermediaries between the realms of the divine and the human. Ancient Indian, especially Buddhist, tradition includes luminous beings called *apsaras*. Though not depicted as winged, these lovely beings usually float through the air in scenes decorating Buddhist temples all over Asia. They often function as dancers and musicians.

This manuscript painting from sometime during the Abbasid caliphate depicts the angel Israfil.

Do Muslims believe in angels?

Belief in angels is among the basic elements included in the extended creedal statements in the Quran that speak of

God's prophets, books, and the last day. Numerous Hadiths and charming traditional stories tell of the solicitous presence of countless angelic spirits, who are ready to attend the devout at every important moment and squire them through life's most trying challenges. Angels function in Islamic theology and tradition very much as they do in Christian thought: they represent an intermediary personal presence that embodies divine interest in the affairs of His creatures. They are beings of light and great intelligence who enjoy the presence of God and do the divine bidding throughout creation. Lofty as they are, even the first human being, Adam, knew something to which the angels were not privy, the divinely ordained names of all things created. To each person two guardian angels are assigned and there is much charming lore about the spiritual services these angels render. In addition there are innumerable anonymous angels who move among the levels of the heavenly realm and between heaven and earth. Other angels busy themselves ferrying blessings down to believers and bringing back to heaven word about the good things the believers are doing.

Are any specific angels of particular importance?

A small number of angels are mentioned in the Quran, and several occupy especially lofty standing. The four archangels include Gabriel, the most prominent. His role is that of delivering God's message to prophets. Michael's task is to supply sustenance to human bodies and knowledge to minds. The angel Israfil will sound the final trumpet at Judgment, but meanwhile is entrusted with ensouling bodies and relaying God's orders to Michael, archnemesis of Satan. To Azrael, the angel of death, falls the task of visiting each person whose time is at hand. In some important respects human beings stand above the angels. When God has Gabriel guide Muhammad through the seven heavens, Gabriel must part company with the Prophet as they approach the Throne of God, lest he be burnt to a crisp. Two famously brusque and businesslike angels called Munkar and Nakir have the unpleasant but necessary task of visiting each deceased person in the grave and administering a "final exam" about the content of the individual's beliefs.

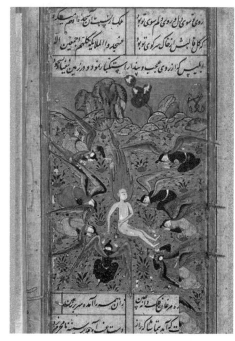

Do Muslims believe in the devil?

Within the larger category of jinn are many beings who were once angels. The principal diabolical figure is called Iblis (ib-LEES, from the Greek *diabolos*). God

A manuscript illustration of Qazwini's *Wonders of Creation* (c. 1370, Baghdad) depicts the angel Israfel.

ordered him to do homage to the newly created body of Adam, but Iblis refused, arguing that a creature of fire need not bow to one made of clay. God banished Iblis from Paradise and he became the personification of the choice for evil over good. It was Iblis who tempted Adam and Eve (Quran 2:35–39, 7:19–25, 20:120–121). Tradition also names the devil Shaytan (shay-TAHN) and often refers to many Satans, the lesser minions of Iblis who fan out to beset humanity with temptations of every kind. Some of Islam's mystics have focused on the story of Iblis's fall as an occasion for discussing the infinite mercy of God. As evil as the devil is, they argue, even Iblis still has hope of enjoying the transforming power of divine forgiveness at the end of time. The mystics are not suggesting that the devil is soft on sheer nastiness, only that no power in the universe can compare with God's mercy.

What are devils and demons? Are they all called Satan?

According to ancient Middle Eastern mythology, devils are angels gone bad. As with angels, the history of the development of devils is complex. A great deal has to do with the ways various traditions conceive of the supreme deity. In many there has been a need to name evil forces, since even if a tradition teaches that a supreme being has created all things including evil, it will not likely allow that the same being incites people to evil acts. The term devil typically refers to a single malevolent being of sufficient power that it may even appear to compete with the supreme being. The name Satan comes from a Hebrew root meaning "accuser" or "adversary" and first appears in the Book of Job. In the Abrahamic traditions, demons are generally lesser evil forces who act as Satan's minions. Satan sends his nasty foot soldiers out to tempt whom they may. Hindu myth tells numerous stories of immemorial struggles between gods and demons, originally distinguished not tidily as good and evil, but as clever and not so clever. Eventually the demons came to acquire the characteristics of malevolence and ability to deceive. Countless demonic forces inhabit Buddhist hells. They are capable of assuming virtually any human or animal form and appear in folk tales especially.

What is a jinn (or jinni)?

You've probably heard stories about the magical powers of "genies" who appear when someone rubs a magic lamp just right. The word "genie" comes from the Arabic word *jinni/jinn*, which refers to creatures of smokeless fire who inhabit a mysterious realm somewhere between the human and the divine. According to popular lore in Muhammad's time, the jinns would eavesdrop on the heavenly councils

In Arabic mythology, a *jinn* (or genie) is a creature of smokeless fire that inhabits a world between the divine and the human. They can help people but also create mischief.

and offer to divulge their secrets to a soothsayer (called a *kahin*, KAA-hin) who uttered the proper formula. Some of Muhammad's early critics charged that he was not a prophet but just another *majnun* (maj-NOON), one possessed by a jinn. To call someone majnun is to question the person's credibility as well as sanity. Countless jinns inhabit the world, some mischievous and some helpful and benevolent. King Solomon had the gift of "taming" the jinn and enlisting them for the construction of his majestic temple. Particularly troublesome are the frighteningly ugly jinns called *ghuls* (from which comes the word "ghoul"). For those who do not know how to handle them, jinns can make life unpleasant, but their powers are limited.

Are dreams and visions particularly important in Islamic tradition?

In the Quranic story of Joseph (Sura 12), Muslims find the paradigm of religious insight as represented by the ability to interpret dreams. Traditional Islamic sources further describe a wide range of religious and spiritual experiences, beginning of course with Muhammad's role in the unfolding revelation of the Quran. The Prophet "sees" mysterious visions as part of the divine communication. Later religious figures, especially noted spiritual guides and friends of God, have left numerous personal accounts of their dreams and interpretations of them. Muhammad himself is one of the presences they report meeting most often in dreams and visionary experiences. These reports tell of encountering various holy persons in addition to the Prophet, especially those who had in life been of particular significance to the dreamer or visionary. Sufis sometimes tell of meeting the mysterious Khizr, a figure included in many lists of prophets, who appears for the purpose of initiating the dreamer into the Sufi path through investiture with the "patched frock" (*khirqa*). Though the accounts sound as if they are reporting events as "real" as having breakfast, most are clearly talking about spiritual experiences that are well beyond the ordinary and thus are not subject to ordinary scrutiny.

Any link between dreams or visions and personifications of holiness and power?

Dreams and visions serve a number of important functions in religious traditions. Accounts of dreams and visions often describe an important figure's meeting with a still more important figure, including even the supreme being. The experience described is often that of the dreamer or visionary's receiving some special teaching or revelation. Dreams naturally tend to be more private, though famous religious figures have sometimes published extensive records of their dreaming states. Visions, on the other hand, occasionally become a rallying point for large numbers of believers. The visionary lets it be known that he or she has been privileged to encounter some important spiritual presence at a certain place or under certain circumstances. In some cases, the visionary claims assurance that further visions will occur on a timetable that has been revealed. Devotees may thereafter begin to gather in hopes of sharing the visions. For some people, the prospect of visionary experience assumes enormous importance, almost as though visions constitute the only credible form of religious experience. Visions and dreams can also function as vehicles of legitimation or induction of the subject into the ranks of some spiritual confraternity. These experiences amount to a kind of ultimate endorsement, with the dreamer or visionary now able to assert a higher level of authority on the basis of an exchange with some holy person.

FUNDAMENTALS OF FAITH AND ACTION

What are the "Five Pillars" of Islam? Are they a good summary of the basic beliefs and practices enjoined on all Muslims?

Virtually every summary of Islamic belief and practice begins with the notion of the "Five Pillars," a convenient device for remembering the basics so long as one keeps in mind that they represent minimum religious obligations and are thus only part of a much larger reality. Muslims practice adherence to these Five Pillars of Faith: 1) profession (*Shahada*, sha-HAA-da) of belief in Allah as the only God and Muhammad as his prophet; 2) ritual prayer (*salat*, sa-LAAT) five times daily—at dawn, at noon, in the af-

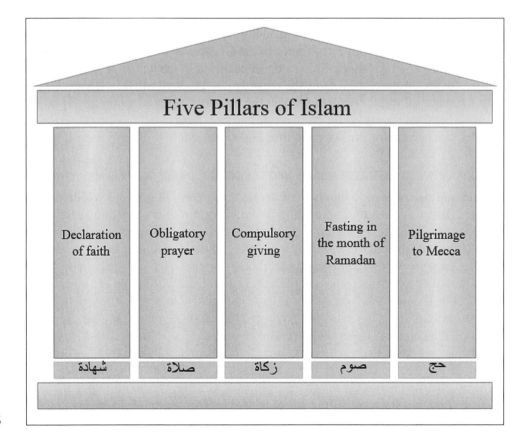

ternoon, in the evening, and at nightfall; 3) giving alms to the poor (*zakat*, za-KAAT); 4) fasting from dawn until dusk during the holy month of Ramadan (*sawm*); and 5) making the pilgrimage (*hajj*) to the holy city of Mecca at least once during their lifetime.

What does Islamic "ritual prayer" involve?

The second pillar is the observance of five brief but regular ritual prayer times that mark off sacred moments throughout each day, from early morning to late evening. One can perform the ritual prayer (*salat*) anywhere; the only spatial requirement is a physical orientation toward the Arabian city of Mecca, home of the ancient shrine of the Ka'ba. Water, a universal symbol of cleansing, provides the physical medium for Muslims as they wash before the five daily prayers. The tradition makes it clear that the purification is at least as much spiritual as it is bodily; if water is not available, one can use sand or even earth to wipe over the feet, forearms, and face. The requirements are thus far from literalistic. Purification functions primarily as an embodiment of the praying person's movement into a sacred time. If the profession of faith and ritual prayer call for daily, if not constant, awareness, the practice of the remaining three pillars, almsgiving, fasting, and pilgrimage, is more occasional.

How does the pillar of almsgiving function in Muslim life?

Islam's strong sense of social awareness recommends that Muslims be at all times as generous as possible to the needy through charitable gifts (called *sadaqa*). Almsgiving (*zakat*) strictly speaking resembles a tax with a more formal legal aspect in that tradition stipulates who is required to give *zakat* and from what kinds of resources. Again and again the Quran refers favorably to those "who perform the ritual prayer and provide alms," linking the two practices as though the one looked to the individual's spiritual welfare and the other to the larger community's external well-being. A central Muslim belief is that human beings do not own natural riches permanently; they are merely on loan. The same holds for other forms of wealth. Muslim tradition recommends that believers "give God a loan" and "spend in the way of God" as a way of caring for creation and sharing what they

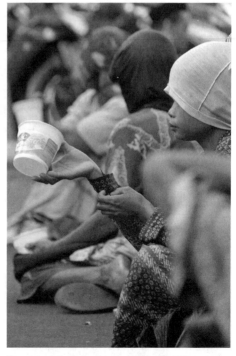

Beggars ask for help along a path leading to a mosque in Jakarta, Indonesia. Muslims believe that they should be generous to the needy whenever possible.

167

have received. The term *zakat* originally derives from a root that means "to purify one-self," in this case, of the delusion of ownership. God alone is substantially and eternally wealthy. The point of giving alms, like that of fasting, is to remind the donor of the source of all good gifts, rather than to give that warm feeling that comes from self-con-gratulation. In the Quran's words: "Give to kin, the poor and the traveler what they need; that is best for those who seek the face of God, and they will indeed fare well. What you give in the hope of profiting at the expense of people will gain you nothing in God's sight; what you give in the form of alms (lit. *zakat*) as you seek the face of God—that will produce abundant return" (Quran 30:38–39).

What does the practice of fasting entail?

Almost all religious traditions recommend fasting in some form or other, but Islamic practice retains a particularly rigorous version of the seasonal fast during the ninth lunar month of Ramadan (ra-ma-DAHN). Abstaining from food, drink, and sexual grat-ification from dawn to sunset every day (sometimes as long as eighteen hours or more when Ramadan falls in summertime) for thirty days breaks the ordinary pattern of life as a sharp reminder to focus on the more important dimensions of life. Refraining from ordinary recourse to creation's sustenance requires a discipline that is capable of re-

The *saei* (brisk walk) is performed by these Muslims as they travel seven times between Safa mount and Marwah mount in Mecca during Hajj.

minding the individual of a greater need that only God can fulfill. Not only from physical goods does one fast, but from a range of physical and spiritual evils as well, including envy and hatred, and lesser faults like complaining or cutting corners in one's work. Among the desired effects of the practice Muslims count a deepened compassion for people all too familiar with hunger, a heightened capacity to counter one's own baser tendencies, and a clearer sense of one's relationship to the Creator.

What about the practice of pilgrimage?

Of all the world's religious traditions, none has maintained so strong a sense of its members as a community on pilgrimage as has the Islamic tradition. Given good health and sufficient means, Muslims are enjoined to visit Mecca at least once in a lifetime during the sacred time of pilgrimage, the Hajj. Muslims are welcome to come to Mecca and Medina any time during the year, but fulfill formally the duty of Hajj only between the eighth and thirteenth days of the twelfth lunar month.

SYMBOLS, RITUALS, AND REGULAR OBSERVANCES

SIGNS AND SYMBOLS

What is the religious significance of the term "sign"?

In general terms a sign is any verbal or visual indicator that conveys some basic message. The capital letter P inside a circle, crossed out by a diagonal bar, has become a widely understood indicator for "No Parking." It conveys no further special message. In the language of religious studies, a sign is an object or an action that communicates some specific religious meaning. Members of a particular tradition grow up learning the language of their tradition's system of signs. Gestures and implements employed in ritual comprise one of the most common categories. A bow, a knee bent to touch the floor, a clap of the hands, a lighted candle, all can function as signs suggesting a certain mood or atmosphere. Objects and actions used this way do not necessarily carry complex meanings. Some objects and actions, however, do communicate more specialized and even arcane messages.

Where and how do religious traditions employ signs and symbols?

Everything from buildings to sacred books to substances like oil and incense play important roles in the everyday lives of religious practitioners. Primary ritual spaces are naturally the most prominent venues for the use of signs and symbols. Temples, synagogues, mosques, and shrines are often visual galleries filled with sensory input composed entirely of signs and symbols. Architectural style and structure incorporate forms characteristic of each tradition, including towers of various kinds, domes, courtyards, rooms for special functions, and gathering spaces designed to accommodate certain activities and groups of a certain size. Everything about a well-executed ritual space expresses the tradition's beliefs. In their homes, too, religious persons often use signs and symbols to remind themselves of their central spiritual values. Some go so far as to set up elaborate home shrines or altars at which to conduct their private devotions. In certain societies one can still readily identify members of some religious traditions by the signs and symbols they wear. For the majority of people who so identify themselves, signs and symbols of faith are at least as much a reminder to themselves of their faith commitment as they are a signal to others that they desire to hold certain things sacred.

What is the religious significance of the term "symbol"?

A symbol is an object or act that represents some reality other than itself. Most religious traditions use symbols to remind believers of the central realities of the faith, sometimes because that reality is considered too sacred to depict and sometimes because it is simply easier to use the shorthand of symbolism. Symbolism can be economical in many ways since it can pack a great deal of meaning into a small, often inexpensive, item. Visual symbols are called an "aniconic" form of expression when they use a non-representational image to refer to a sacred personage. So, for example, the fish symbolizes Christ and the empty throne or riderless horse represent the Buddha.

What does the crescent moon and star symbol mean to Muslims?

A crescent moon embracing a single star adorns the flags of a number of modern nation-states with majority Muslim populations. The sign is almost certainly not of Arab origin, and the Ottoman Turks may have appropriated the symbolism from Byzantium. At first, the symbol appeared on the flags of lands formerly under Ottoman rule, but other states with no historical connection to the Ottoman empire have also adopted the imagery. Popular understanding of the symbol usually identifies the crescent moon as the essential indicator of the beginning of Ramadan, the ninth lunar month. More generally still, the symbol reminds some of the lunar cycles that regulate Islam's religious calendar. Appearing frequently at the top of domes and minarets, the symbol has become a generic reminder of Islam, much the way the cross has for Christianity and the six-pointed star for Judaism.

What is the meaning of the hand symbol some Muslims use?

Silhouettes of a five-fingered open hand appear often as a motif in jewelry and on staffs that function as standards in some Shi'i religious rituals. Called "the five," the symbol reminds devotees of the five prin-

The crescent moon and star adorn a mosque in Malaysia Mosque in Singapore, the *Masjid* Sultan.

cipal members of the Prophet's family: Muhammad, Fatima, Ali, Hasan, and Husayn. Many Shi'ite mosques display the hand as a finial on both domes and minarets in mosques of classical design. Sometimes the hand was hoisted atop a staff as a battle standard, emblazoned with prayers to Ali on the fingers and the names of all twelve *imams* encircling the palm. As a symbol used by Muslims in various parts of the world by Muslims of various communities, the hand functions as a talismanic magical device, a symbol of control or power associated with Muhammad's daughter Fatima.

Have relics ever been important for Muslims?

Popular Islamic spirituality in many parts of the world has included devotional practices associated with the tombs of holy persons. People visit the shrines of the friends of God in hopes of gaining blessings and other favors as a result of saintly intercession. Many of these shrines hold items the saint is believed to have owned, such as headgear, a symbolic frock called the *khirqa*, walking staff, begging bowl, prayer beads, or symbolic weapon. Devotees who come to the shrines sometimes receive an object, such as a simple head wrapping or other token, that has been in contact with the holy person's tomb. Several objects have been similarly associated with Muhammad. Since the thirteenth century, Turkish Muslims believed they owned the so-called mantle of the Prophet, a green robe now in the possession of the Topkapi Museum in Istanbul. People there and in many other countries still recite a traditional poem called the Burda (mantle poem) during the observance of Muhammad's birthday, but the mantle itself has never been the focus of devotional practice as have the relics of many friends of God.

Reliquaries believed to hold remnants of the Prophet's beard represent a different kind of remembrance of Muhammad, something actually once part of his physical person. Two of the best known of these are a small cask in Konya, Turkey, in the mosque that houses the tomb of Rumi, and in the Dome of the Rock in Jerusalem. Sacred footprints

function in Islamic tradition, as in many others as well, like relics. Pilgrims to Mecca pray at the "Station of Abraham" just opposite the door of the Ka'ba—a small glass and gold-colored cupola covers a small stone said to contain footprints God caused Abraham to leave in the softened stone as a proof of his prophethood. Tradition says that as Muhammad rose heavenward on his Ascension, he left still-visible prints in the large stone beneath the Dome of the Rock. Muhammad's footprints became the inspiration for several types of visual symbolism still popular in North Africa, for example. Footprints of Ali have likewise been at the

Many Muslim men grow beards as a remembrance of the Prophet.

devotional center of a number of shrines.

Do Muslims make use of anything like religious "souvenirs" as reminders of important experiences?

Muslims with sufficient means do travel for religious purposes, including not only international travel to Arabia for the Hajj proper or the "lesser pilgrimage" (Umra), but regionally for indigenous cultural events or visitation to sites associated with exemplary figures (Friends of God). Sometimes they will bring back specific items that function, in fact, as souvenirs of the journey's experience. A good example is that pilgrims on Hajj or Umra often return with small decorative plastic jugs containing water of Zamzam, the ancient spring in the Ka'ba believed to have miraculously bubbled forth when Hagar searched frantically for water for herself and her baby Ismail. Many Muslim families also have household mementoes of home, if they have emigrated abroad, or symbols of individual figures—such as images of Shi'i *imams*—or theological themes—such as the Ninety-Nine Names of God.

What other sorts of signs or symbols do Muslims use at home?

Many Muslim families decorate their homes with wall hangings and other small objects with religious significance. Popular items include cloth or paper panels showing beautifully written texts of the Quran. Pictures of Mecca, Medina, Jerusalem, or of other important mosques or shrines are quite common. Some families prominently display a copy of the Quran, often kept in a case or wrapping, on a book-stand or on the mantel. Shi'ite households frequently have pictures of Ali, his two sons Hasan and Husayn, and sometimes also of other *imams* or their burial places. Muslim households will not own or display a picture of Muhammad or any of the other prophets.

Ritual times and seasons often call for religious ornament. Some families put the Quran center-stage during Ramadan, for example. In addition, many Muslim families with ties to ancestral homelands carry on culturally linked traditions which, although not explicitly of "Islamic" origin, nonetheless employ Islamic religious symbolism. So, for example, Iranian Americans often observe the spring festival of Nawruz (New [year's] Day), reckoned according to an ancient Persian solar calendar. A central group of symbols is known as the *Haft Seen*, or the "Seven Objects whose names begin with S (Seen),ʺ often blending a variety of symbols associated with Iran's pre-Islamic history as well. Along with nature symbols such as a mirror, herbs, and eggs, the Quran is almost always prominently displayed, thus "islamizing" the overall symbolic package.

Is number, letter, color, or animal symbolism important in Islamic tradition?

These and other types of related symbolism abound. The following examples provide only a hint of the variety of symbolism. Every letter in the Arabic language has a numerical value. A common use of number symbolism involves totaling up the numerical value of all the letters in a particular phrase and then using the number as a reminder of the phrase. For example, Muslims often repeat the phrase "In the name of God, the Compassionate, the Merciful." It is called the *basmallah*, after the sound of the first three words, *Bi 'smi 'Llahi* (*'r-Rahmani 'r-Rahim*). The numerical value of all the letters in the phrase is 786, and the symbol appears often, in a sort of sunburst design, in pictures of holy places such as the Ka'ba. Letter symbolism is especially prominent in classical religious poetry in languages like Persian, Urdu, and Turkish. Poets love to play on meanings suggested by the shapes of the Arabic letters.

As for colors, green has come to be known as the color of the prophets, and of Muhammad in particular. Animal symbols, too, have been widespread in many cultures. Muhammad's cousin and son-in-law, Ali, was known as the "Lion of God" because of his courage. Shi'i artists in particular often included images of a lion when they wanted to suggest the spiritual presence of the first imam, Ali.

What signs or symbols distinguish Muslim ritual or religious specialists?

There is no *ordained* Muslim clergy as such, but a category of specialists, known as religious scholars, sometimes wear distinctive garb. Style and color generally depend on variant traditions in the country of origin. Many religious scholars from many lands prefer the *fez* wrapped in the white cloth (signifying that the wearer has made Hajj). Some, from the Sudan for example, wear a white turban. Shi'ite *mullahs* and higher ranking scholars in Iran and Iraq often wear a black turban that identifies them as *Sayyids*, descendants of Muhammad through his daughter Fatima and her husband, Ali. Other Iranian Shi'ite clergy generally wear white turbans. Size, color, number of turbans, and so forth, allow a practiced eye to distinguish national and sectarian connections. Members of Sufi orders often wear special clothing, particularly during their prayer gatherings. Various organizations have unique headgear, sometimes using colors or varied ways of wrapping the basic cap with windings to indicate rank or status within the order.

Are there any signs or symbols that might identify an individual as a Muslim?

Muslim men and women sometimes wear items or styles of clothing that clearly set them apart from non-Muslims. Men arriving at the local mosque on a Friday afternoon will often wear long flowing gowns and small knit or other fabric caps that cover most of the head, in honor of Muhammad's practice of covering his head during prayer. Men of southern Asian origin (India, Pakistan, Bangladesh) sometimes wear a kind of boat-shaped cap commonly worn back home. In some parts of the world, men who have made the Hajj signify their status as hajjis by wearing a burgundy fez wrapped in a white cloth. The rimless fez became popular because it was practical for use during prostration in prayer, allowing easy contact of the forehead with the ground. More than likely the women attending a mosque will be wearing some form of head covering and an ankle-length dress or tunic with slacks.

What are some of the personal reasons behind choice of symbolic items like clothing?

In many instances the choice of distinctive garb is related to an individual's personal devotion and desire to symbolize his or her commitment to Islamic religious and social values. Most items of clothing are best understood as traditional rather than inherently religious, since they carry no explicit and uniquely Islamic symbolism. However, many Muslim women and men wear various items of jewelry bearing Islamic symbols. Most common are rings, pendants, and bracelets containing religious words or phrases in Arabic. Some show a star within a crescent moon, a symbol some interpret as a reference to the astronomical signs that mark the onset of the month of Ramadan. Favorite texts include the word Allah, phrases such as *In sha'a 'Llah* (God Willing), the *Shahada*, names of Muhammad, and the four Rightly Guided Caliphs (Abu Bakr, Umar, Uthman, and Ali). Muslim designers produce a wide range of religious adornment and market them through an increasing number of suppliers and boutiques that advertise in Muslim publications worldwide.

Are Muslim women required to veil their faces?

Use of the veil depends a great deal on cultural custom. The Quran does not explicitly require that women cover their faces. It calls for modest dress, but some have interpreted one ambiguous text—"they should draw their veils over their bosoms ..." (Quran 24:31)—to mean that the head covering should continue down over the upper body. In some cultures, Muslim women wear various forms of facial covering, whether drawn across the lower face from side to side, or covering the head completely like a small tent. Those coverings also vary in texture from a fine gauze to a fairly heavy weave with slits cut at eye level. The majority of women who wear some form of distinctive clothing, technically known as *hijab* (hi-JAAB, veiling or covering), opt for a head scarf down to the mid-forehead so that it covers all the hair. Some wear a flowing gown (*jilbab*, jil-BAAB) that extends to the ankles; some a face veil (*niqab*, ni-KAAB) that leaves only the eyes exposed; still others the *burqa* (BUR-ka) a tent-like garment the covers all but the feet. Note that the emphasis is on modesty rather than on some specific style of covering.

There are a variety of ways Muslim women cover themselves, including the *niqab* shown here. More common is the *hijab*, a scarf covering the head and neck but not the face.

Muslim immigrants to Europe or the United States from the Middle East or southern Asia might choose to continue wearing styles common in their homelands. Where prevailing social norms allow greater latitude in choice of dress, Muslim women often report that they opt for fuller covering for two reasons: They seek an explicit symbolic connection with Islamic practice and they choose to make a statement of personal freedom from the general exploitation of women that they often experience in society at large.

Do Muslims mark their sacred spaces with any distinctive signs and symbols?

One is likely to notice two distinctive features about a nearby mosque. Attached to, or alongside, the building is a tower called a minaret. Originally designed to provide maximum broadcast of the call to prayer, the minaret eventually became a visual symbol of Islamic presence. Most structures designed as mosques feature a dome of some sort, typically spanning the central interior space called the prayer hall. Many synagogues and Eastern Christian churches also use central domes but generally do not have towers that one might mistake for minarets. Atop some minarets and domes is a finial in the shape of a crescent moon encircling a single star.

Some communities choose to have their mosques reflect architecturally a particular national or regional heritage. They might hire, for example, an Egyptian architect to

The Sultan Ahmet mosque in Istanbul is a fine example of typical Ottoman imperial mosque construction. Note the two minarets flanking the building (this mosque has six minarets total).

design in a neo-classical Egyptian style, as with the national mosque in Washington, D.C. Or they might choose to incorporate into the design some visual allusion to a particularly important mosque, the way the new Islamic Center of Cleveland aligns a large central and a smaller secondary dome, recalling the Dome of the Rock and Al-Aqsa mosque in Jerusalem. Interior decorations typically feature elegant calligraphic texts, either painted or carved in marble or other stone, of the names Allah and Muhammad, and of the *Shahada* and Basmallah ("In the name of God ..."), and possibly of any number of the Ninety-Nine Beautiful Names of God. Calligraphic decoration often appears around the drum of the dome and around the niche on the wall facing Mecca. Prayer rugs or carpeting sometimes show niche designs like that of the *mihrab* (mih-RAAB, niche). And somewhere in the mosque there will more than likely be a large picture of the sanctuary of the Ka'ba in Mecca, and possibly also of the Prophet's mosque in Medina.

ORDINARY RITUAL PRACTICES

One often hears Muslims characterized as "ritualistic." Is such a pejorative term fair?

People who are seriously engaged in their own religious traditions frequently regard the religious practices of others as mechanical and rote. Every tradition—even the so-called "non-liturgical" ones—has its rituals, but some are more elaborate than others. Other people's rituals inevitably strike outsiders as strange, simply because religious ritual is among the more obvious features that distinguish insiders from outsiders. And religious ritual is highly vulnerable to caricature: Catholics are the ones who watch a priest go through a bunch of strange motions and say strange words; Muslims are the ones who bob up and down facing Mecca; Hindus are the ones who offer food to statues with lots of arms.... Many people have a hard time de-mystifying the actions they associate with the religious practice of others, but it is important to keep in mind that there is a reason for all of it, and that ritual endures because it works in some important way.

What keeps rituals meaningful for Muslims?

Any ritual can become a matter of habit, just a question of going through the motions. And if religious people aren't mindful, any ritual can be reduced to a crude form of magic: do it precisely and it will produce the desired effect, almost as if one could twist God's arm by offering the right flavor of incense. Muslims are no more likely than non-Muslims to take the deeper meaning of their rituals for granted. In fact, Islamic tradition deals with the problem very directly, teaching that a deliberate awareness of intention (*niyyat*) must precede the performance of every act of worship. Apart from explicit attentiveness to their purpose, deeds of piety have no religious meaning. At a still deeper level, one needs the enduring habit of "presence of the heart" in order to approach each individual act of devotion with the mental and spiritual focus required to articulate the intention.

Muslims perform the Islamic religious rite ceremony of ablution at a mosque prior to ritual prayer.

What is an example of "extenuating circumstances" concerning Islamic ritual obligations?

A good example of the Islamic tradition's sense of the meaning underlying the externals of ritual is the requirement of ritual purification prior to performing the ritual prayer. Ordinarily worshippers have access to water with which to cleanse face, hands, arms, and feet. But if at prayer time water is not available to a traveler, for example, he or she may use sand or even dust. This alternative provision suggests a non-literal understanding of purification as a change of mind and heart. In addition, the term *masjid*, usually translated as mosque, means "place of prostration," and that can be any place so designated by a deliberate appropriation of the space for spiritual purposes. Intention and purification prepare the worshipper to move temporarily into another way of being by stepping out of the ordinary rhythms of daily life into sacred time and space. For attentive Muslims, the five daily moments of ritual prayer become a way of sanctifying time. The orientation toward Mecca, whether one is praying in the mosque or elsewhere, with or without a prayer rug, is a way of sanctifying place, creating a sacred space. Ultimately it is not the external action that counts, but the quality of the relationship between worshipper and worshipped that the action expresses.

What is the difference between a custom and a ritual?

Custom includes the whole range of activities that people in a particular time and cultural setting become so used to doing that they rarely examine their reasons for acting   179 that way. Custom is "the way we've always done" things. It includes everything from social expectations and etiquette to the specific kinds of food people serve for special occasions. "Common law" is a type of customary social norm, including practices that have been in use so long that they have assumed legal status and authority. Custom operates at various levels, from that of a society at large to that of the local community and family. Rituals are typically part of the larger category of custom, but ritual practices tend to follow a rigid sequence in the interest of insuring that the action is "correct." For example, it is customary in certain cultures for participants in a wedding to wear certain kinds of clothes. But wedding rituals often mandate certain specific actions in a set order, even when the principal participants opt for non-customary fashions.

Is almsgiving technically a custom or a ritual? How does the practice of almsgiving express Muslims' sense of community?

Zakat (za-KAAT), almsgiving, is one of the Five Pillars. Unlike the other four pillars, almsgiving is not so clearly associated with sacred times or places and can be practiced whenever and wherever needed and possible. So it is in an interesting way a blend of custom and ritual, but not clearly either one or the other: custom in that it's simply something one does out of concern for others in need, but ritual in that it is prescribed religiously. It requires all financially stable Muslims to contribute varying amounts, depending on the type of goods being taxed. For example, it comes to 10 percent of agricultural produce in general, but 2.5 percent of a person's savings or profits over and above what one needs to live. There are many ways of calculating the matter these days.

What is the underlying religious motivation for almsgiving?

What is most important to understand about religious almsgiving is that for Muslims it is an institutionalized form of social concern. Muslim authorities see to the distribution of the funds among the neediest, both at home and abroad. The United Arab Emirates, for example, might earmark charitable funds for building an airstrip for the delivery of desperately needed supplies to the Albanian Muslim refugees from Kosovo. Devout Muslims are encouraged to give far beyond the minimum *zakat* as well. At the end of the month-long fast of Ramadan, many give generously to the *zakat al-fitr*, or alms for the breaking of the fast. Those and all other voluntary charitable donations are called *sadaqa* (SA-dak-ah, "righteousness, uprightness"), for through these signs of social concern individual Muslims gain blessing and forgiveness. A related practice among Shi'i Muslims is the *khums*, or "fifth." The tax was originally the custom of providing the Prophet a portion of the military spoils, but some Shi'ite religious authorities have collected it from their constituencies up to modern times as an offering for the Twelfth imam expected to return at the end of time.

What is the purpose of religious rituals?

Religious rituals function primarily to help believers establish relationships of presence, imagination, or memory with some spiritual reality. There is naturally some overlapping among these three goals of ritual. Some rituals effect or mediate a connection between participants and a divine or spiritual presence. The relationship established allows believers to access powers beyond the ordinary human condition. An important feature here and in other types of ritual as well is the kind of emotion or feeling, such as dread or longing or joy, the situation fosters in the participants. Other rituals engage the imagination and intellect primarily, allowing participants to enter into another level of experience through meditation or contemplation, for example. Still other rituals help believers connect in memory (and sometimes grief as well) with persons now departed or with past formative spiritual experiences they want to recall.

What makes important religious practices "rituals" and insures that they "work"?

In addition to the various primary ritual functions are a host of lesser or secondary ritual acts that help participants establish a proper ritual setting and insure that the actions are maximally efficacious. Setting means all those ingredients of space, time, and feeling that make a ritual "work." Many rituals of course occur in spaces already set up for the purpose. But in some instances separate preparatory rituals are used to mark the boundaries of a ritual sacred space. That can include sub-rituals such as procession, circumambulation, or purification ceremonies. Other sub-rituals establish the boundaries of sacred time. Ringing bells, pounding drums, or calls to prayer mark the opening and closing of a ritual. Still other lesser rituals enhance a particular feeling or mood by appealing to the senses. Use of incense burners is an example of a widespread practice. Finally, some traditions assure continuity and purity of ritual practice through the use of precise instructions on how to perform a ritual exactly. These instructions are often called "rubrics," because they are sometimes printed in red (Latin *ruber*) to distinguish directions from the actual text of the ritual. Muslims take great care to see that they perform all ordinary and special ritual actions according to Prophetic tradition and example, from hand positions during *salat* to specific invocatory prayers said during the Hajj.

How and where do members of local Muslim communities come together?

When small local communities of Muslims begin to form in new locations, they typically begin by meeting in each others' homes for social and religious purposes. As their numbers grow, they need to look for a space large enough to accommodate them. In many American cities, for example, Muslims have acquired everything from former storefront buildings to former Christian churches. There they will remain until further growth and financial success permit more ambitious options, such as acquiring a piece of property, having it zoned properly, and building a dedicated facility. Whatever the venue in which they gather for prayer, Muslims call that place a *masjid*, a "place of prostration." The word "mosque" is rooted in the medieval Spanish pronunciation of *masjid*. Technically one needs no specific place for the prostration of ritual prayer—every place is a mosque, so long as one hallows the space and orients it toward Mecca. But community growth and the requirement of coming together on Fridays for a congregational prayer have made the institution known as the "mosque" a common sight all over the world,

181

and increasingly in the United States as well—there are now more than a thousand mosques across the country. Most mosque communities eventually develop a full complement of governing, advisory, and functional committees, with emphasis on a fairly egalitarian form of governance.

What activities do Muslims typically do in and around the mosque?

Throughout history and in many parts of the world, mosques have stood at the center of an enormous range of activities. In Egypt, Turkey, Iran, and India, for example, mosque complexes have combined educational facilities of various levels, libraries, medical schools and hospitals, social service facilities, funerary facilities, and religious residences. Many of the monumental complexes depended on the sort of equally monumental royal patronage that is rare these days. But plans for somewhat less ambitious projects are afoot now in various parts of the United States. As local communities grow, mosque complexes will become increasingly visible. Meeting and social spaces are just the first of many needs beyond the basic requirement of a place for communal ritual prayer.

Do Sunni and Shi'i Muslims worship in separate mosques?

That depends on a host of other social and political circumstances. In many places where Muslims are a small minority of the regional population, there are very few mosques.

In many mosques around the world, teaching has become part of the regular activities. Mosques also typically offer funeral services, as well as other social functions.

182

Most of them serve Muslims from all over the world without inquiring as to whether new members are Sunni or Shi'i. Shi'i Muslims who attend a predominantly Sunni mosque may discover that some themes they were accustomed to hearing in sermons, for example, are no longer so prominent. In some areas of countries like the United States, where there are growing numbers of immigrant and indigenous Muslims—people with ties to Iran or Iraq—for example, there might be sufficient numbers to begin plans for a Shi'i mosque. The motivation for doing so more than likely will have a great deal to do with ties to a country of origin as well as a desire for a kind of spirituality more in keeping with distinctively Shi'ite interpretations of history and emphasis on the redemptive suffering of the *imams*.

What is the Muslim "call to prayer"? Is it similar to "church bells"?

In the earliest days of Muslim expansion outward from Arabia, the call to prayer distinguished Muslim congregational practice from that of Christians with their church bells and from the Jewish use of a clapper-like device. The call to prayer is recited in a form of something like chanting whose canons have become virtually universal. In its basic outline, the call (*adhan*, ad-HAAN) includes the following phrases, typically repeated, practiced with some variation depending on one's "law school": "God is Supreme"; "I confess that there is no god but God"; "I confess that Muhammad is the Messenger of God"; "Rise to ritual prayer"; "Rise to success"; "God is supreme." After the congregation has assembled inside the mosque, the muezzin (the one who makes the *adhan*) intones a shorter version of the call, to indicate that the *salat* is beginning.

Is there a standard Islamic group liturgical worship?

Islamic ritual prayer, performed five times daily, is called *salat* (from a root that means to make holy). Whenever Muslims gather they perform the ritual prayer together. That applies not only to the prescribed Friday midday congregational prayer but to any of the set times at which two or more Muslims come together any day of the week, whether in the mosque or elsewhere. As with all Muslim ritual practice, worshipers preface this prayer with the clearly stated intention (*niyya*, NEE-yah), saying, "I intend to pray the dawn (for example) salat." From two to four cycles of standing, bowing to place hands on knees (*ruku'*, ru-KOO), sitting on the heels (*jalsa*, JAL-sah), stretching forward toward

Speakers mounted to a minaret broadcast the call to prayer five times a day.

183

Ancient Muslim tradition identified Friday as the most important day of the week for signature Islamic religious observances. One reason, historically speaking, is that the choice makes a clear distinction between Christian sanctification of Sunday as "the Lord's Day" and the Jewish hallowing of Saturday as the "Sabbath," a day completely devoted to prayer, reflection, and cessation of ordinary labors. Friday is not necessarily a "day of rest" for all Muslims, but in traditional societies many ordinary activities are set aside during times of ritual prayer. This is particularly true of the mid-day prayer, when believers are enjoined to attend *salat* at the local mosque, during which the imam is expected to deliver some sort of a religiously inspirational message or sermon (*khutba*, "address").

prostration (*sajda*, SAJ-dah) to place hands flat on the floor at shoulder width, and touching the forehead to the floor make up the fundamental Salat ritual. The number of cycles (*rak'a*, RAK-ah) depends on which prescribed prayer one is performing.

How does preaching function in Muslim ritual?

Preaching plays an important role in various ritual settings. First and foremost is its use in the context of the five daily ritual prayers (*salat*). Members of the congregation sit on the floor while the preacher stands near the niche (*mihrab*) or ascends a few steps of a pulpit called the *minbar* (MIN-bar). In larger, more established mosques, the imam generally delivers the sermon on Fridays at the early afternoon congregational prayer. But either the imam or some other adult might also offer some reflections at other times when smaller groups gather for *salat*. But the most important form of "liturgical oratory" (*khutba*, "address") occurs at the mid-day prayer on Friday, a time at which attendance during ordinary weeks is at its highest. Over the centuries, Muslim authors have generated a considerable "literature of the pulpit" (*adab al-minbar*) that acts as a record of famous sermons and a repository of material from which preachers can draw. In addition, noted preachers may be called upon to speak on special occasions, such as the birthday or death anniversary of a celebrated holy person, a Friend of God, a member of Muhammad's family, or one of the Companions. Such events often draw crowds to the Friend's tomb or to a place associated with his or her life. Here the sermons often include narrative and interpretation of stories of the past, reminding people of God's blessings, and aim at "instilling reverential fear that softens the heart."

What are some common themes of a Friday sermons? How are they structured?

Speakers have a wide range of appropriate topics from which to choose. High on the list are ethical concerns such as social and ethical responsibility, the need for parents to take an active part in their children's education, economic justice, and speaking out in public venues about problems that need attention from concerned citizens. Speakers might also choose any of scores of devotional themes, such as cultivating one's relationship with God or the need to set aside time for personal reading and reflection on the Quran, and the need to attend to personal spiritual transformation following an experience of liminality such as Muslims' experience on Pilgrimage (*Hajj*) to Mecca. Preachers often tailor their sermons to a specific religious season, especially during Ramadan and pilgrimage season. Encouragement during the month-long fast is always helpful and welcome. Scripture naturally plays a major part in sermons, and preachers generally cite Hadiths along with Quranic texts to illustrate their themes. Sermons vary in length from five or ten minutes to perhaps a half hour for special occasions. These formal sermons are typically divided into four sections, following an ancient classical model: a brief introduction recalling some theme and perhaps citing texts of the Quran and Hadith is followed by the body of the address. Here the preacher typically calls the congregation to be mindful of the need for a change of mind and heart and repentance for failings and follows with a short reprise of the theme. He then concludes with short supplications and formulaic texts with Quranic overtones.

What kinds of rituals do Muslims engage in privately or individually?

Since one can perform the five daily ritual prayers anywhere, most Muslims generally pray the *salat* alone or in small groups. In mosques everywhere, individual Muslims pray privately outside the regular ritual prayer times as well. But Muslims also engage in a variety of other private devotions. Some are associated with local or regional custom, others practiced across the globe. Private recitation of the sacred scripture is foremost among the universal customs. Muslims who read Arabic but who are not formally trained in the refinements of performative recitation often sit alone and recite in a low voice. Meditative reading of the text in any language can nourish the spiritual life. Another popular devotion involves a prayerful consideration of the "Ninety-Nine Beautiful Names" of God. Many Muslims use the *tasbiha*, a set of either thirty-three or ninety-nine beads, to keep count. (These are the so-called "worry beads" people all over the world like to fidget with even when not praying.) Islamic traditions of spirituality also offer a vast array of devotional literature, from hagiography (lives of prophets and holy persons) to prayers recommended for daily use to refined religious poetry suitable for praying.

Do Muslims follow specific dietary customs or rituals?

Muslim dietary practice is similar in many ways to Jewish traditions known as *kashrut*, or keeping kosher. Certain foods are forbidden altogether, except in direst need. These include intoxicating beverages, pork, blood, foods prepared or cooked with pork fat (some would include, for example, doughnuts and other fried breads), and animals that eat mainly carrion (i.e., scavengers). If non-Muslims invite Muslim friends for a celebration with a meal, it is important that they give due consideration to what they will serve. Muslims do not require the separation of meats from dairy products as do Orthodox Jews, but hosts should avoid pork of any kind if at all possible. Meat of certain animals is acceptable only when the animal has been ritually slaughtered.

As with Jewish culture, devout Muslims follow certain dietary practices that ban some foods, such as pork, blood, alcohol, and foods cooked in pork fat.

What are some essential features of food-related rituals and customs?

As in every Muslim ritual, one begins by declaring the "intention" to perform the action religiously. After pronouncing the first part of the *basmallah* (In the name of God—leaving off the names Compassionate and Merciful) and the *takbir* (tak-BEER, that is, saying "Allahu akbar," "God is supreme"), the butcher severs the jugular and windpipe with a single blade stroke. The idea is to drain as much of the blood as possible, for it symbolizes the life force. By custom, Muslims in various places consider certain foods traditional for festal occasions, such as the meal that breaks the daily fast of Ramadan and the celebration that marks the end of that month. Many of these customs are inspired by Muhammad's own practice. For example, he is said to have broken his daily fast with a glass of water and a few dates before taking a meal, so Muslims generally try to do likewise.

Do Muslims engage in any specific purification rituals?

Prior to each act of ritual prayer Muslims perform a brief purification called *wudu'* (wu-DOO). Worshipers perform each of the following cleansing motions three times: rinse hands and wrists, rinse out the mouth, then the nostrils likewise, rinse the whole face, arms up to the elbows, whole head and neck, and finally toes and feet up to the ankles. Mosques today typically provide separate facilities in which men and women can perform the ablution. Older mosques often have fountains or taps running along an exterior wall, with small benches or stools for worshipers to sit on.

Is water the only "medium" of purification?

They usually use tap water, but under peculiar circumstances even sand or earth is acceptable, in which case it is called *tayammum* (ta-YAM-mum). Clearly the idea is to prepare oneself symbolically to enter a state of mindfulness. In addition to this cleansing, Muslims also regard a more thorough bathing (called *ghusl*) essential to restore the state of ritual purity after sexual intercourse, seminal discharge, or the menstrual cycle. *Ghusl* includes the motions of the ablution just described, but encompasses the entire body as well. The intent of these rituals is to put the individual in a state of maximum attentiveness to and spiritual worthiness for entering into the presence of God.

What is a ritual object or implement?

Ritual objects include a large number of items both symbolic and practical that are the essential devices of religious practice. They may be as outwardly pedestrian as containers for the raw materials of religious offering—rice, salt, wine, bread—or the utensils needed to move those materials around. These tools often have no major symbolic meaning but are largely utilitarian, though they are generally regarded as sacred because of the context and are not to be used for non-ritual purposes. Many other ritual objects are more symbolic than practical in function. Every tradition has its symbols for the ultimate spiritual reality, for the various kinds of benefits and blessings believers seek from that reality, and for the gifts devotees bring as offerings. Among the most common are images or icons, books or scrolls of sacred text, lamps, musical instruments, weapons, special vestments, or garb for officiants and sometimes participants.

What kinds of ritual objects figure in Muslim worship and prayer?

By far the most important ritual object is the Quran. Since Muslims regard the sacred book as the very word of God, they try to treat the physical object with the greatest respect. Some mosques own ancient and beautifully wrought Qurans, often in multiple volumes, that are used only for special occasions. The more ancient the mosque, the more likely it will also have specially crafted podiums on which to place the Quran, and possibly also storage containers. Both stand and box often feature carefully chosen inscriptions from the Quran and Hadith that remind devotees of the divine origin and power of the sacred word. One of the most important among the relatively few other items that have been a regular part of Muslim devotions is the classic prayer rug. Displaying a central shape that recalls the *mihrab* on the Mecca-ward wall of the mosque, high quality prayer rugs often use geometric and floral design inspired by the Quran's "Verse of Light": "God is the light of the heavens and the earth. His light is like a niche in which is a lamp within a glass like a shining star kindled from a sacred olive tree neither of east nor west whose oil would nearly glow even if no fire touched it" (Quran 24:35). Inspired by the same verse, beautifully enameled glass lamps were once raised to a fine art and hung by the dozens in the great mosques of the Middle East. The shimmering light cast through their multicolored Quranic inscriptions and arabesque designs would have been similar to that cast through Europe's stained glass windows.

What is a votive offering? Is this in common use among Muslims?

Votive offerings are directly associated with the making of vows (from the Latin *votum*, something promised or "vowed") in connection with requests for special favors. When religious believers visit a special holy place, they often write their needs on some object and leave the object within the sacred precincts. They vow to perform certain devotional or charitable acts if the deity will grant their heartfelt request. Votive offerings include any of hundreds of ways in which people symbolize their willingness to repay the divine favor. Among the more common devotional acts are those associated with visiting holy places or making pilgrimage. The devotee promises, for example, to approach the place on his or her knees from a certain point, or to make a certain number of prostrations before a particular sacred image. One of the most widespread

Prayer rugs like this one from Turkey are among the few items that have been a regular part of Muslim devotions.

of votive practices is the lighting of small candles after making an offering to the holy place. In some instances the use of candles has become dissociated from making vows in the truest sense of that term, so that lighting a wick often merely symbolizes or accompanies a request for divine help. Larger places of worship in many traditions provide appropriate votive offerings for sale in small shops attached to the church, temple, or shrine. For a fee, considered part of the offering, devotees receive an object such as a small statue of a holy person associated with the place, a devotional card, or even a tiny replica of the holy place itself or some part thereof. For example, adherents of Shinto often hang miniature torii gates on racks designed to receive hundreds of them. Here again, ordinary Muslim ritual typically makes no use of votive items, though countless Muslims do use such things as part of devotional pilgrimage or visitation (*ziyara*, zee-YAA-ra) to shrine-like places associated with famous exemplary holy figures.

Are music and dance important in Islamic religious ritual?

Muslims do not incorporate either music or dance into their primary religious rituals, and they use no musical instruments as part of communal worship. Though Muslims do not as a group sing hymns or other types of vocal prayer set to music, a type of tonal recitation is very much a part of Islamic religious life. A "call to prayer" (*adhan*) broadcast from the minaret (at least in areas where Muslims are the majority population) announces each of the five daily times for salat. The *muezzin* (mu-EZ-zin) makes the call using a form of chanting that can strike the ear as very musical, even though it has no melody such as is generally associated with songs.

Where does Quran recitation fit in this picture?

Formal "recitation" of the Quran is perhaps the closest approximation to music in regular Muslim ritual. Specially trained reciters, who typically have memorized the entire Quran, chant texts of the scripture using either of two styles of presentation. The simpler form is called "measured" and is sung with a recurring pattern of only four or five notes. A more ornate form, called "embellished," uses a much wider tonal range, proceeds much more slowly, and punctuates the text with dramatic silences. Such recitation can be part of any religious observance in any venue. Outside of primary ritual contexts, Muslims all over the world have set religious themes and sentiments to music in countless local and regional styles and languages. Muslim musicians and singers across the globe are now producing devotional music for mass-market consumption. From Morocco to Indonesia, tapes and CDs filled with contemporary musical interpretations of classical texts and prayers are becoming increasingly popular. Dancing often accompanies popular musical performances, especially those associated with the feasts of local holy persons.

Do Muslims sing hymns or incorporate music into ritual?

Strictly speaking, Quran recitation is a type of music, but to Muslim ears it is something else altogether—a celestial sound in a category all by itself. Muslims do not engage in individual or communal singing at their formal ritual prayer sessions. Earthier music is an integral part of all cultures, however, and those in which Islam has played a dominant role are no exception. There is definitely such a thing as religious music, sometimes used for devotional purposes and sometimes as a more broadly entertaining medium. Devotional music is often, but not solely, associated with the paraliturgical rituals popular religious confraternities often associated with mystical devotion. Virtually all the Sufi orders have their distinctive musical ritual sessions called *sama* ("audition" or "listening"), in spite of the fact that theologians and jurists have often condemned the practice as unduly distracting and sensual. That is a testimony to music's acknowledged power over human emotions, which in turn is the principal reason why Muslims continue to be enthralled by well-performed songs that develop popular religious themes, such as the wonders and virtues of the Prophet Muhammad.

Is dance important in religious ritual generally?

Sacred dance is one of the oldest forms of religious ritual known. Many liturgical traditions have developed out of classical religious dance, which often arose in turn as a medium in which to reenact central mythic narratives. Dance can assume various forms, from performance by ritual specialists alone, to visual display by a highly trained and

Whirling Dervishes perform a spinning dance, a traditional ritual dance symbolizing the revolution of the planets around the sun.

richly decked-out troupe, to whole congregations performing relatively simple repetitive movements. Here is where the use of ritual costume sometimes extends beyond the clergy or central ritual specialists. Some traditions, such as Shinto and other indigenous communities of faith, use dance at various levels of sacrality.

Special rites might occur at or near the holiest part of a place of worship, while dance of a more entertaining and less esoteric sort might be available on separate small stages elsewhere on the grounds. Most sacred are reenactments of central mythic stories. More popular performances often teach some moral point humorously. Musical accompaniment to religious ritual takes many forms and is generally more widespread than dance. Religious traditions run the gamut, from those that use no instrumental or vocal music at all to those whose rituals are almost entirely musical. Some traditions favor very arcane music, played on ancient instruments, to establish a mood of solemnity by creating the kind of sounds one would hear only in a particular ritual setting. This kind of music can be difficult to listen to, but its purpose is to mark the occasion as genuinely out of the ordinary. Others use music designed to encourage maximum participation rather than to establish distance. The latter typically develops extensive hymnographies.

How about dance in Muslim ritual?

Muslims do not incorporate "liturgical dance" into their formal ritual prayer in the mosque, but there are settings in which dance is important. The so-called Whirling

Dervishes, members of the Mevlevi order named after Mevlana ("our master") Jalal ad-Din Rumi, are perhaps the best known of such groups. Their communal prayer rituals involve a highly symbolic dance in which the members spin or "whirl" not only around their own axes but around the shaykh who stands in the middle. The imagery is that of the planets revolving around the sun, eternally seeking their source. Accompanying Mevlevi ritual dancing is an ensemble made up of reed flutes called *neys*, backed up by various kinds of plucked and bowed strings and percussions.

SACRED TIME

What is sacred time?

Most traditions attach special meanings to history as a whole, to specific moments in the lifetime of an individual, and to various times in the ordinary cycles of days, months, and years. Ordinary time in human experience is inextricably linked to change, that most troublesome of all realities. Religious traditions offer a partial remedy to the perplexities of change in the notion that reliving or reenacting events of cosmic significance offers a brief respite, an opportunity to stop time or perhaps step out of ordinary time for a moment. From the perspective of a tradition's ritual life, sacred time is the time of ritual encounter with the divine. But in addition, religious believers also seek to hallow decisive life experiences with rites of passage.

What is a religious calendar?

Since anchoring sacredness in time is so fundamental, most religious traditions have developed ways of keeping precise track of their distinctive ways of hallowing the days and years. Religious (sometimes called "liturgical"—see below) calendars establish a definitive pattern of moments meant to recall specific events in the life of a divine or foundational figure. Each year thus becomes a replay of the sacred person's life in miniature. An annual calendar can also symbolically recapitulate the whole expanse of a tradition's sacred history by laying out essential events in sequence on a time line. With every year, then, the community celebrates a renewal in faith, confident that each new cycle brings with it sufficient spiritual aid to carry on. The religious calendar functions as a kind of map of time that highlights certain seasons. Even the times in between the high festivities thus take on special meanings as periods of waiting or expectation. In traditions whose view of time is linear, the religious calendar seems to have a forward motion, rising to a peak and moving toward a symbolic end of history. For traditions with a more cyclic understanding of history, the calendar year remains but one more in an endless series of cycles, with its own high and low points built in and celebrated as feasts or religious holidays.

How many different kinds of religious calendar are there?

All calendars naturally have intimate connections to some sort of astronomical calculation but there are various ways of determining the particulars. There are solar and lunar calendars, seasonal and non-seasonal. Seasonal calendars are generally solar, anchored in the movements of the sun. Each major observance falls each year during the same part of the agricultural cycle in a given region. Some festivities are associated with planting, others with harvest, still others with the fallow season of winter. Such calendars often place special emphasis on the winter and summer solstices (respectively the shortest and longest days of the year) and on the vernal and autumnal equinoxes (the days in spring and fall when daylight and nighttime hours are equal).

Lunar calendars can be either seasonal or non-seasonal. That depends on whether and how the system intercalates days or months to compensate for the fact that the lunar year rotates backwards against the solar. Each lunar year begins approximately eleven days earlier each solar year. If day one of a lunar calendar corresponds with day one of this year's solar calendar, next year the lunar calendar will commence on the equivalent of December 20 or 21. A lunar calendar that intercalates an extra month every couple of solar years can both maintain its observance of the shorter lunar months and keep each festivity connected to the appropriate part of the agricultural cycle.

Non-seasonal calendars, generally lunar, do not compensate for the discrepancy between the religious year and the agricultural seasons. As a result, major annual observances rotate backwards against the solar calendar about every thirty-three years.

What kind of religious calendar do Muslims observe?

Muslims follow a lunar calendar whose twelve months add up to 354 days. In a cycle of thirty lunar years, eleven are leap years, with one day added to the last month. During Muhammad's time the lunar months were associated with seasons (*Ramadan*, ra-ma-
DAAN, means "extreme heat," *Rabi'* "rainy season," and *Jumada* "dry season," for example). As in the Jewish calendar, the pre-Islamic year maintained its connection with agricultural cycles and seasons by the intercalation of a whole month in certain years. Since the practice of intercalation ended around Muhammad's time, the Islamic lunar year rotates backwards eleven days each year in relation to the Gregorian solar year. If Ramadan, for example, begins on January 12 this year, next year it will begin on January 1, and so on. Certain practical results of this backward rotation are worth noting because of the way timing can affect religious practice. When Ramadan (the ninth month) occurs in the dead of winter, when days are shortest, the fast from sunrise to sunset is less arduous

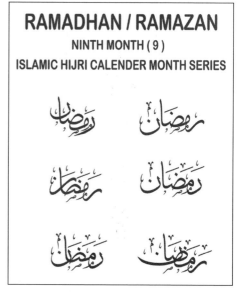

RAMADHAN / RAMAZAN
NINTH MONTH (9)
ISLAMIC HIJRI CALENDER MONTH SERIES

The word "Ramadan" is written here in six variations of calligraphy.

than when Ramadan falls during the height of summer. Pilgrimage to Mecca can also be more strenuous when the season of Hajj (in the twelfth month) occurs during the hottest season. Muslims the world over therefore must learn to work with two different systems of marking special times. Muslims begin their count of years with the *Hijra* of 622. Approximately every thirty-three years the beginnings of the Islamic lunar and Gregorian solar years roughly coincide.

Major Muslim Observances, with names of the Islamic Lunar Months

1 Muharram	Islamic New Year
10 Muharram	Day of Ashura (i.e. "tenth" day). For Sunni Muslims, day of recommended fast (parallel to Jewish Day of Atonement originally). For Shia Muslims, the martyrdom of Husayn ibn Ali, the grandson of Muhammad, and his followers in 680 C.E.
12 Rabi al-Awal	Birthday of the Prophet observed by many Sunni Muslims
17 Rabi al-Awal	Birthday of the Prophet observed by Twelver Shia Muslims
13 Rajab	Birthday of Ali ibn Abi Talib
27 Rajab	Muhammad's Night Journey and Ascension
15 Sha'ban	Middle of Sha'ban, or Night of Forgiveness, and the birthday of Muhammad al-*Mahdi*, Twelfth Shia imam
1 Ramadan	Beginning of month-long fast
21 Ramadan	Martyrdom of Ali ibn Abi Talib
27 Ramadan	Initial "descent/revelation of the Quran," observed on 17 Ramadan in Indonesia and Malaysia, also known as the "Night of Power"
1 Shawwal	Feast of the Breaking of the Fast, closing Ramadan—one of the two greatest festal days
8–13 Dhu al-Hijjah	Season of official Hajj to Mecca
10 Dhu al-Hijjah	Feast of Sacrifice during Hajj season, recalling God's command that Abraham sacrifice his son (Ismail)—second of the two greatest festal days
18 Dhu al-Hijjah	Feast of Ghadir Khumm, Shia observance of the Prophet's designation of Ali as his "caliph"

What is the connection between regular observances and sacred history?

A fascinating variant in the ways different traditions arrange their calendars is how they determine the beginning of their reckoning of religious time or sacred history. Here are some of the variants. Sacred history can begin with the creation itself (Judaism), with the birth of a foundational figure (Christianity), with some major political event or era (India and Japan), or with some signal event in the early history of the community (Islam). Some traditions regard the primordial event as a kind of midpoint in all of human history, a fullness of time. Others, especially those with cyclical notions of time, place considerably less emphasis on any particular event. For Muslims, the all-important time-marker is the *Hijra* in 622, as well as (secondarily) events in the life of the Prophet and his family—such as the "Night of Power" associated with the initial revelation of the Quran.

SACRED SPACE

What does geography have to do with religion?

A separate sub-discipline of religious studies called the Geography of Religion investigates how and why religious communities start and spread as they do. Geographers of religion don't just provide detailed maps that illustrate spatially where the world's major religious groups are and what percentages of a regional population belong to what tradition. They also study how people attach religious meanings to the physical circumstances in which they live and move. Practically every religious tradition has its "sacred geography." Cartographers devise a number of different kinds of maps—physical, political, meteorological.

Sacred geography results in what might be called spiritual maps. These spiritual maps exist first in the minds of religious believers and reflect the distinctive perspective of their traditions, but how various religious traditions map their world can also be plotted on paper. Places that are especially sacred to a particular community of faith provide believers with a unique kind of orientation to the larger world. In many instances a special place functions as a spiritual "center" of the universe, so that everything revolves around it. Many traditions eventually develop networks of holy places. Their holiness can derive from their association with events in the life of some sacred person, from the belief that some special event occurred there, or simply from the perception that a natural feature such as a tree or mountain or spring possess unusual spiritual power. What is most important to keep in mind is that physical settings matter a great deal and that religious traditions "claim" pieces of this earth as sacred to themselves. Sometimes claims overlap and that can cause problems.

What is sacred space?

Many religious rituals call for a particular physical setting for their proper and effective performance. Nearly every major religious tradition has developed primary ritual sites dedicated in varying degrees to their chief rituals. Mosques, temples, shrines, synagogues, and churches provide the most important communal sacred spaces. But the degree to which the primary ritual sites are dedicated and restricted to specific ritual actions varies. Some ritual spaces are in effect multipurpose facilities, and some traditions' rituals simply require no special kind of space. But when local communities of most traditions have grown enough to have bank accounts, plans for dedicated facilities are rarely far behind. Individuals and families in some traditions (such as Hinduism, Buddhism, and Shinto) also perform sacred rituals at home. In those instances believers often establish a small corner of the house as a sacred space or shrine. Believers perform some rituals (such as Islamic daily prayer) wherever they happen to be. They simply make that place sacred for the duration of the ritual action by intending it to be so. At the other end of the space spectrum are the holy places associated with particular geographical locations such as holy cities and pilgrimage goals. Some traditions establish perimeters around those places, marking them off as sacred and inviolable, sometimes limiting access to believers only.

A Muslim prays inside Ortakoy Mosque in Istanbul. When it comes to what is considered "sacred space," some rituals can be performed anywhere, while others, such as pilgrimage sites, are reserved for certain practices only.

What is a holy city and how do cities become holy?

Dozens of cities, towns, and villages across the globe have become especially sacred. Some places actually start off sacred. People acknowledge a place as the site of a unique revelatory event (often called a theophany, or divine manifestation). Some decide to settle around the sacred site. Since holiness is often associated with natural features conducive to human habitation (springs, rivers, fertile soil), settlements can develop and expand. Other sacred places begin unremarkably as centers of population and acquire their sacredness later, often because a holy person has lived there.

Whatever the genesis of a city's sacred character, people often come to believe that the place has always been holy. Over a period of centuries, a holy city may take on more and more religious associations, so that eventually believers regard it as the place where virtually everything of religious significance has happened. The holy city thus becomes a spiritual world unto itself. In a similar way, if believers perceive their holy city not only as the place where it all began but the place where it will all come to an end, the city also becomes a microcosm of history. All power and even time itself comes into focus in this one place, this center of the universe. Though it may seem an affront to logic, this kind of symbolic religious cosmology sometimes finds room for more than one "center." In other words, some traditions claim several sacred cities, often ranked hierarchically, but all uniquely sacred. It has its own logic: wherever believers gather, for whatever reason, there is the meeting place of heaven and earth.

195

What does one typically find at a mosque?

Approaching almost any purpose-built mosque, you would first see a slender tower called a minaret—perhaps even two, or in the case of especially large foundations, four or six. Many still function to announce the call to prayer, but most now sport loudspeakers for that purpose; and in the United States, minarets function as a visual symbol only. Most mosques also feature some sort of dome over the prayer hall, perhaps visible from some distance. In warmer climates, from Morocco to Indonesia, one would enter an open courtyard with a central fountain for ritual ablution. Where winter intrudes regularly, ablution facilities are generally interior. Entering the prayer facility, one would notice carpeting decorated with some sort of geometric device suggesting placement of rows of worshippers laterally facing the *qibla* (Mecca-ward) wall. In the center of that wall would be the *mihrab*, a small apsidal structure, to the right of which stands a *minbar* or pulpit-like set of steps. More lavishly decorated mosques would ornament especially the *mihrab* and interior of the dome, and in "classic" structures built long ago with royal patronage, visitors would be dazzled by the richness of the ornament covering virtually the entire interior space.

SEASONAL, FUNCTIONAL, AND COMMEMORATIVE OBSERVANCES

Does the beginning of the Muslim year have any particular significance?

During the first ten days of the month of Muharram, Muslims reflect on a variety of spiritual themes. During Muhammad's time the community observed a one-day fast on the tenth of the month ('Ashura, aa-SHOO-rah), possibly paralleling the Jewish practice of fasting on the tenth of Tishri, generally known as Yom Kippur. Though the major fast was formally shifted to Ramadan, Muslims still observe this day, some with fasting and prayer. Like many holy days, 'Ashura has become associated with ancient events of great significance. 'Ashura marks the day on which Noah left the ark. Many "Stories of the Prophets" that include accounts of the messenger's infancy frequently include the detail that he was born on the tenth of Muharram, making special note that it was a Friday. Visitors to Mecca can enter the Ka'ba itself (not just the sanctuary around it) on this day alone. Looking at the bigger picture, a Hadith says that at the beginning of each new century (on the lunar Islamic calendar), God will raise up for the Muslim community a "renewer" who will call all believers to a fuller participation in the faith.

Are there any distinctively Shi'i ritual observances of 'Ashura?

The first ten days of the year are typically more important for Shi'i Muslims than for Sunnis. Some readers may recall the day in 1979 when Iranian students took over the U.S. embassy in Tehran. Though news coverage neglected to mention this, it occurred with symbolic significance on the First of Muharram in the year 1400 after the *Hijra*.

Undoubtedly the single most important communal Muslim observance of death and its ultimate significance occurs in the Shi'ite commemoration of the martyrdom of Husayn, who died at the Iraqi site of Karbala in 680 while confronting the evil Caliph Yazid. Beginning on the first day of the first lunar month, Muharram, Shi'ites participate vicariously in Husayn's redemptive suffering and death. A ten-day observance includes various penances, self-flagellation, and processions of mourning, and culminates (at least in more traditional areas) in the "passion play" (*taziya*, ta-ZEE-ya) of Karbala. Scenes in the elaborate drama vary with locality but always inculcate aspects of the paradigmatic sufferings of earlier prophets such as Abraham, Noah, and Moses. In the finale the actors play out Husayn's tragic death; grandfather Muhammad persuades Husayn not only to forgive, but to intercede on behalf of, his murderers. This dramatic reenactment celebrates the importance of "redemptive suffering" and death. Sunni Muslims place far less significance on Husayn's death, but veneration of saints and small pilgrimages (*ziyara*, zee-YAA-ra) to their tombs are still common in many places.

Procession of Shi'a Muslims carrying a model of the tomb of the proto-martyr Husayn in a commemoration of his death as they observe 'Ashura (the tenth day of the first lunar month) in Rawalpindi, Pakistan (*photo courtesy David Edwards*).

What is the importance of the month of Ramadan?

During pre-Islamic times the month called Ramadan ("high summer") was religiously significant as a time during which the Arab tribes observed a truce from all hostilities. Of all the months, the Quran mentions only Ramadan by name, identifying it as the month during which the scripture was revealed. Scripture suggests that the initial divine revelation is the reason for the practice of fasting throughout the month. Ramadan, the ninth lunar month of the Islamic calendar, begins with the sighting of the new moon on the last night of the eighth month. Each day, from dawn until sunset, Muslims are enjoined to fast from all food and liquid, as well as from sexual activity and other forms of sensual pleasure. Fasting also means refraining from negative attitudes and complaining and developing a sense of solidarity with those who suffer from want all year long. After Muslims break the fast with some water and dates, they eat a meal before retiring. Before dawn they may have another meal, but limit other forms of celebration during the en-

Two girls hold ornate lanterns as part of a festive custom—but not a religious tradition—that has become associated with Ramadan.

tire month. Special prayers are scheduled in mosques, along with the recitation of one of thirty "sections" of the Quran, completing the entire sacred text over the thirty nights.

Do any specific key religious "events" fall during Ramadan?

A number of important dates fall during Ramadan. Most important is the "Night of Power," one of the odd-numbered nights among the last ten, usually observed on the twenty-seventh. Muslims believe that God's initial revelation to Muhammad makes this the holiest time of the entire year. Other important times during Ramadan include the birthday of the martyr Husayn (6th); death of Muhammad's first wife, Khadija (10th); the Battle of Badr (a key event in 625, the 17th); the retaking of Mecca in 630 (19th); the deaths of Ali and of the eighth Shi'i imam, Ali Reza (21st); and Ali's birthday (22nd). Where Muslims are in the majority or a very sizable minority, the rhythm of life slows dramatically during Ramadan. At the sighting of the next new moon, all rejoice in the Feast of Fastbreaking, 'Id al-Fitr.

What is Hajj and when do Muslims make pilgrimage to Mecca and how does it commence?

Hajj season begins in the second week of the twelfth lunar month. The journey is required of all Muslims with sufficient health and financial resources, assuming also that making the Hajj would not require them to shirk serious family responsibilities at home.

Pilgrims inaugurate the elaborate experience officially on the seventh day of the twelfth lunar month with preparation and symbolic entry into the sacred space and time of the Hajj (shower, ritual purification, donning the *ihram* garment), followed by initial circumambulation of the Ka'ba and engaging in the ordinary times of daily *salat*. As pilgrims enter a "forbidden zone" that encircles Mecca (called the *haram*), they put on the plain white wraps called the *ihram* (ih-RAAM). The garb marks a transition to sacred space and time and reminds pilgrims of their simple equality before God. Precise ritual activities depend both on variations within the four Sunni law schools and on whether or not pilgrims intend to combine Hajj with *'Umra* (lesser pilgrimage).

What are some other details about the particular rituals in which pilgrims participate on the days of Hajj season?

On the first day they usually circumambulate the Ka'ba seven times, pray at the Station of Abraham, pray two cycles of prostrations, and drink from the spring of Zamzam. Day two (eighth of Hajj month) brings a walking journey to Mina (outside Mecca) before dawn, with a further walk to the plain of Arafat the next day for formal prayers at the Mount of Mercy (where Abraham prayed and where Muhammad preached his "farewell sermon"). After sunset on day three (ninth Hajj), pilgrims head back toward Mecca, stopping for prayers in Muzdalifa (between Arafat and Mina) and to gather seventy pebbles. They depart Muzdalifa early on day four for Mina, where they stone a pillar symbolizing Satan, get a haircut symbolizing change of spiritual state, celebrate the Feast of Sacrifice (*'Id al-Adha*) with its ritual animal slaughter, remove the *ihram*, and shower. Later that same day they return to Mecca for circumambulation of the Ka'ba and the "running" (*say*) between the hills Safa and Marwa, recalling Hagar's frantic search for water. Day five (eleventh of Hajj month) brings a return to Mina for a full cycle of *salat* prayers and to throw their remaining pebbles at three pillars. After overnighting in Mina, pilgrims return to Mecca for a final circumambulation of the Ka'ba and evening ritual prayer. It's a very full schedule and particularly demanding during the hottest times of the year.

Do Muslims ever visit their holy cities outside of the formal pilgrimage season?

Hajj, or major pilgrimage, fulfills a religious duty only in connection with the formal season. But travelers to the holy city can perform the *Umra* or lesser pilgrimage any time of year. Umra is a strictly devotional activity, optional but highly recommended. Rituals include a much scaled-down version of important Hajj activities. To be more precise, Umra is actually a component of Hajj that can be performed separately. Pilgrims enter into the state of ritual consecration by donning the same seamless white cloth worn for Hajj, before entering the sacred zone surrounding Mecca. They proceed to the Ka'ba, circumambulate it seven times, perform two cycles of ritual prayer, take a drink from the well of Zamzam, and walk rapidly seven times between the small hillocks called Marwa and Safa. They conclude the lesser pilgrimage by clipping a lock of hair or shaving the head, symbolizing the spiritual change desired as a result of the pilgrimage. As at Hajj time, many pilgrims add a visit to the Prophet's Mosque in Medina, but that is a separate devotional activity.

Are any occasions associated with Muhammad especially important?

Since medieval times Muslims in many countries have celebrated Muhammad's birthday, *Mawlid an-Nabi*, on the twelfth of Rabi'i. Street parties and grand banquets often provide opportunity for prayers and speeches. A very popular part of the festivities is the recitation of a poem by the thirteenth-century Egyptian poet Busiri, the *Burda* ("Mantle," BURdah). Translated into Swahili and a number of other languages, the poem sings the Prophet's praises in truly cosmic terms, attributing to his birth all manner of marvels and blessings. In some places, where festivities are minimized or forbidden altogether, even the Prophet's birthday is a kind of national holiday. On the twenty-seventh of Rajab, Muslims recall the Night Journey and Ascension (*Laylat al-Isra wa-'l-Mi'raj*). According to traditional accounts, the Prophet experienced this timeless mystical moment sometime during the years just before the *Hijra*. A major feature of the celebrations is the retelling of any of several narratives that follow Gabriel and Muhammad through the heavens, including descriptions of his meetings and conversations with the other major prophets, each associated with one of the seven celestial levels. During the course of his journey Muhammad received instructions about instituting the five daily ritual prayers.

Are there any other forms of religious pilgrimage?

Ziyara (zee-YAA-rah, meaning "visitation") is a form of minor pilgrimage still popular all over the world, with a few regional exceptions such as the Arabian peninsula. Devout Muslims travel to the tombs of holy persons to receive *baraka* (blessing/power, BA-ra-ka), by association with the saint's power and holiness. Elaborate shrine complexes have grown up around some of these sacred sites. Since the nineteenth century especially, Muslim authorities in Saudi Arabia have sought to stamp out the practice because they have deemed the veneration of miracle-working saints a threat to pure monotheism. Ironically, Saudi Arabia remains the home of the prime example of *ziyara*. Each year millions of pilgrims to Mecca make a trip north to Medina to visit the mosque in which Muhammad, his daughter Fatima, and the first caliph, Abu Bakr, are buried. Sunni Muslims from Morocco to Malaysia continue to visit secondary holy places, most of which are graves of Sufi *shaykhs*. Shi'i Muslims also visit sites connected with similar friends of God, but their devotional travel revolves more around a number of distinctively Shi'ite holy places. They are the tombs of the *imams*, spiritual and biological descendants of Muhammad through his daughter Fatima. Most of the *imams'* shrines are in Iran, with its overwhelmingly Shi'i population, and southern Iraq, where most of that country's slight majority of Shi'ites live.

Do Muslims celebrate events in connection with any other religious figures?

Popular practice in many places still includes annual commemorations of birthdays and death anniversaries of various important holy persons and friends of God. Birthday celebrations of members of the Prophet's family, such as Sayyida Zaynab, remain popular in places like Egypt. Lasting for up to seven days, the festivities are like sprawling street parties. Crowds grow daily, as does the intensity of the celebration. Vendors sell food and souvenirs and Quran reciters fill the air with sacred sounds from their booths up and down the streets. Mosques within the central area of celebration can be packed to overflowing. Birthdays of famous friends of God frequently include recitation of classic poems extolling the saints' spiritual achievements and glorious intimacy with God. Anniversaries of the death of God's friends are also important in many regions, especially those further to the east. Since holy persons are fully united with God at death, the occasions are sometimes referred to as the saint's Wedding Day (*'Urs*, OORS). On the 6th of Rajab many Indian Muslims (and members of other faiths as well) observe the *'Urs* of Mu'in ad-Din Chishti, founder of a famous Sufi order, at his tomb in the city of Ajmer.

What are some of the other religious days Muslims observe?

On the fifteenth day of Sha'ban many Muslims, especially in south Asia, observe the Night of Forgiveness (*Laylat al-Bara'a*, ba-RAA-ah). Popular belief says that the names of all persons are written on the leaves of a great cosmic tree. On the evening of the 14th, the tree shakes and loses some of its leaves. Those whose leaves fall are destined to die during the coming year. According to a Hadith, God comes down to the lowest heaven that night and asks if anyone seeks forgiveness. That is the moment for all to wipe the slate clean, since no one knows whether his or her leaf has fallen. Celebrations of many holy persons, often centering around the individual's tomb, vary according to region. In addition to birthday (*mawlid*) and death anniversary (*'urs*) celebrations, Muslims in various places observe seasonal times (*mawsim*) with festivities connected to agricultural or other natural cycles. One such celebration is that of Nabi Musa (Prophet Moses), observed around his alleged tomb-shrine near Jericho. Its timing coincides roughly with the Orthodox Christian Holy Week, featuring elaborate processions that begin in Jerusalem.

Do Muslims use ritual sacrifice?

Muslims mark the high point of the annual season of Hajj, which runs from the eighth to the thirteenth day of the ninth lunar month, with the Feast of the Sacrifice. Also called "The Great Feast," the rituals on the tenth of the month include the slaughtering of an animal in memory of God providing a ram for Abraham to sacrifice in lieu of his son Ishmael. Sheep, goats, oxen or cows, and camels are traditional sacrificial animals. The person performing the sacrifice dedicates the animals to God and mentions the names of those partaking of the fruits of the sacrifice. Muslims all over the world observe the Feast of Sacrifice with prescribed activities. Food ritually sacrificed is usually prepared in large quantities, so that as those present for the festivities share in the feast, the abundance can be distributed to those in need. Animals ritually slaughtered during Hajj season are not sold for profit. In some parts of the world, Muslims still sacrifice a sheep in connection with an optional birth ritual. When a child is seven days old, some families shave the baby's head, a practice dating to Muhammad's time.

RITES OF PASSAGE

What is a rite of passage?

In the life of every individual, certain times naturally stand out as particularly significant. Birth, the transition from childhood to adulthood (or puberty), the assumption of a new state in life (as in a marriage), and death are especially critical times. Religious traditions generally acknowledge these and other formative experiences by developing rituals designed to help people cope with the changes they bring. Sheer difficulty and challenge can sometimes be the distinguishing features of important moments or phases of a life. Confusion, sense of loss and grief, even overwhelming joy or feelings of limitless possibility can be cause for recourse to the comfort and direction rites of passage can afford. Rituals of this kind help believers by allowing them to step out of ordinary time and space for a while to regain their bearings. They can then return to "real life" feeling renewed, spiritually refreshed, and strengthened for the challenges ahead.

How do Muslims celebrate birth?

A recommended but optional ceremony called the 'Aqiqa (a-KEE-kah) occurs when a baby is seven days old. In the home or in a part of the mosque outside the prayer hall, parents name their child and clip a lock of hair. Tradition suggests that parents give at least the hair's weight in silver as a charitable donation. In some places it remains customary to perform ritual animal sacrifice and distribute food to the needy. Parents can formally name their child at this time, often choosing from among the names of religiously important men and women. Sometimes also the baby's father will whisper the call to prayer (adhan, a-THAAN) in the infant's right ear and the invitation to begin the prayer (iqama, i-QAA-mah) in the left. Some

When a baby is born, Muslims give the child a name and clip a lock of hair. In some cultures the hair is weighed and the parents give that weight in silver to a charity.

Muslims choose to practice a rite of circumcision on infant boys, though some prefer to postpone the practice until puberty. Depending on circumstances, some kind of reception may follow the rituals.

Are there distinctive forms of Islamic initiation ritual?

Teenagers can be welcomed formally into the adult community of believers with a simple ceremony during which the young man or woman pronounces the *Shahada* before two male or eight female witnesses. Sometimes the occasion is combined with a regular congregational prayer service on Friday afternoon, but the ritual can also take place in the home. The young Muslims so initiated may also recite various prayers in Arabic as part of the ceremony. There is ordinarily no reception following the ritual. As a rite of passage, the ritual itself is roughly parallel to the Jewish *bar* and *bat mitzvah*.

What are the Islamic rituals of marriage? Do Muslims favor "arranged" marriages?

In the United States, Muslim nuptials (*nikah*, ni-KAAH) can occur in the prayer hall of the local mosque in a separate ceremony not connected with the regular ritual prayer. In other places, weddings typically occur in homes or in the presence of a Muslim judge (*qadi*, KAA-dee). The imam of the mosque, or the judge, presides over the ceremony and may offer religious reflections on the sacredness of the marriage contract. In some countries elaborate processions and house-warming ceremonies are part of the festivities. As in many other traditions, two witnesses attest to the agreement. Written documentation includes both mosque records and the usual license required by civil law. A reception called a *walima* (wa-LEE-mah) follows weddings nearly everywhere. In some countries the bridal dowry remains an essential item in the social contract between families. Many Muslim families continue to prefer marriages in which the parents do the initial negotiating. They present their favored prospect to their son or daughter, but in most situations the young people have the option of declining. Many Muslims regard open dating as undesirable and believe the arranged relationship is healthier and more acceptable morally. Some parents will even take out ads, especially on behalf of a daughter, in the "personal" sections of Muslim publications, seeking interested parties who are well-educated and religiously committed.

For many Muslims, arranged marriages are still the preferred way to match men and women in matrimony.

How do Muslims deal ritually with death and mourning?

Before a burial, mourners gather in a mosque, in front of the deceased person's house, or in a specially constructed enclosure to pronounce the *takbir* ("God is Supreme," Allahu akbar) four times, interspersed with longer devotional prayers calling down blessings on the deceased and on all present. Although the *takbir* is part of all Muslim prayer and begins the call to prayer itself, its prominence in the funeral rite is such that saying the *takbir* is equivalent to saying "this person (or thing in other contexts) is dead to me," that is, "I have surrendered this to God." All attention falls on God's grandeur so that nothing else can distract. In most places Muslims retain the ancient custom of burying the unembalmed body before sundown on the day of death. Family members generally prepare the body with purification rituals similar to those used prior to prayer or to remove some ritual impurity. Sometimes mourners will say special prayers in the mosque after the regular ritual prayer, with or without the body.

Are there any distinctive themes addressed in Muslim bereavement practices?

Loneliness is among the most feared sufferings of the tomb. Prayers popular throughout the Islamic world make this very evident. The idea that the spirit returns to the body in the grave serves to heighten the apprehension that the deceased will experience a terrible solitude and acute pain of separation. A final graveside prayer from Egypt says:

> O God, Companion of every lonely one, Present One who are never a stranger, Near One when others are far, be the Companion O God of our loneliness and his (the deceased) loneliness, have mercy on our strangeness and his strangeness, and whiten his page (i.e., forgive sin) and forgive us and forgive him and forgive the one who stood over his grave to say: "There is no god but God, and Muhammad is the Messenger of God."

Many believe that after the burial they may apply the merit of their prayers toward the mitigation of the grave's terrors.

Are there any distinctive features in American contexts?

In the United States, Muslim obsequies often occur in funeral homes, always with a closed casket. There the imam of the mosque leads mourners in prayer and may also deliver a brief eulogy. American funerals often do not occur immediately after death as in some other countries. At the cemetery, mourners gather around the grave and offer burial prayers called *janaza* (ja-NAA-zah). Muslims do not practice cremation. Bodies are buried in such a way that if turned onto their right side, they would be facing Mecca. Following burial, mourners generally gather to express condolences either at the family home or in a space set aside specially for the purpose. Some families arrange to have a Quran reciter present or else play recorded recitation for silent reflection.

Do these traditions have deep historical associations?

Shortly after Muhammad's death, his successor, Abu Bakr, is reported to have addressed the crowd keeping vigil outside the house in Medina: "If you worship Muhammad, know that he is dead; if you worship God, know that he lives forever." According to conflicting Hadiths, Muhammad both encouraged and forbade Muslims to visit his tomb. Most pilgrims to Mecca opt for the positive tradition and go to pray at the Prophet's grave. A popular belief that salvation is assured to anyone who dies at or en route to the pilgrimage goal is no doubt enhanced by the inclusion of Muhammad's tomb among the customary sites of the pilgrim's circuit. Most Muslims will die without having the opportunity to visit Muhammad's grave, but few will lack the blessing of a symbolic presence of the Prophet at theirs.

The following prayer that Muhammad is said to have offered at the funerals of early Muslims is still in use, as are many others like it:

> O God, forgive the living among us and those of us who have died; those present and those absent; the small and the great among us; our women and our men. O God, make alive with grateful surrender [lit. islam] whomever among us you cause to remain alive; and cause to die in the faith whichever of us you cause to die. O God, do not keep from us the reward awaiting the deceased, and do not make life hard for us with this passing.

Are there any related rituals outside of mourning the death of an individual?

In many parts of the Islamic world, the fifteenth day of the eighth lunar month, Shaban, calls for special reflection on human mortality and remembrance of the dead. According-

Muslims believe that the deceased experience the suffering of loneliness and separation in the grave; mourners pray that the departed will be spared this experience.

ing to tradition, the tree of life is shaken on the eve of that day. On the leaves are written the names of the living, and all whose leaves fall in the shaking will die during the next year. Of course, no one alive knows whose leaves have fallen; so many people take the occasion to offer prayers like this Shi'ite petition: "Have mercy on me on the day when I come before you alone, my gaze turned towards you, my deeds tied round my neck, all creatures dissociating themselves from me, yes even my father and my mother and those for whom I toiled and strove. Then if you do not show me mercy who will have mercy upon me?... Who will teach my tongue to speak when I am alone with my deeds, and am asked concerning those things that you know better than I?"

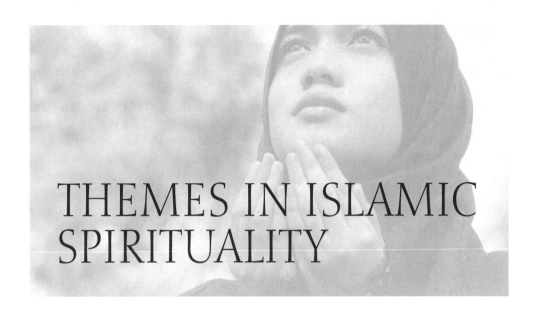

THEMES IN ISLAMIC SPIRITUALITY

SPIRITUALITY AND THEOLOGICAL ANTHROPOLOGY

What does the term spirituality mean?

A workable definition of spirituality goes something like this: it is the experiential dimension of a religious tradition, including all aspects of how believers engage in the personal quest for ultimate reality. Theologies and creeds communicate the content of a tradition; myths and rituals describe how believers ought to externalize those beliefs in action; religious ethics suggests norms by which to evaluate one's behavior. Spirituality presupposes all that and goes deeper. Spirituality is about what all those things have to do with the relationship between a believer, both as an individual and as a member of a community of faith, and the source and final goal of human existence. Every tradition offers a rich menu of help for understanding how that central relationship unfolds through one's entire life. In many traditions, the types of personalities and powers described in the following section are an integral part of spirituality. But beyond these personalities and powers, religious persons express their spiritualities in the whole range of manifestations that this book covers, from literature to architecture, from the minutest details of ritual to the largest institutions and structures of authority.

"Spirituality" is a widely and often loosely used term; what does it mean with respect to Islam?

Emphasizing the experiential and relational aspects of religion, the study of spirituality focuses on how the tradition assists its members to discover and cultivate their inmost selves, and to embark on a lifelong journey toward their ultimate end. Unlike the study of theology, that of spirituality allows one to take fuller account of affective and devotional themes, while de-emphasizing doctrinal and other more technical issues. Islamic spirituality includes a wide range of themes. Beginning, as always, with the Quran and traditions of Muhammad, Muslims have developed ways of reading and interpreting the sacred sources with an eye for references to God's nearness. In addition, Muslim writers, poets, and artists across the world have evolved dozens of literary and visual forms by which to express their experience of God's presence in everything from communal ritual prayer to glorying in a sunset to the tragedy of heartbreaking loss. Muslims can draw upon a rich repository of spiritual models as well, stories of men and women whose achievements mark them as especially favored by God. Through books, pictures, and performance, their example continues to inspire, challenge, and entertain Muslims in search of greater depth to their faith.

How does spirituality relate to community?

Since an integral part of Muslim identity is the sense of belonging to a society of believers, the study of Islamic spirituality must also take into account the various ways Muslims have fostered community through their development of institutions such as mosques, schools, social services, and religious confraternities. Beyond the kind of basic religious education that Muslims have traditionally passed along to their children, spiritual theologians and other "specialists" have also developed sophisticated principles and finely tuned techniques both for assisting seekers toward more advanced progress along the spiritual path, and for analyzing that progress. Finally, perhaps the most difficult and subtle materials are the records of personal experience—autobiographies, diaries, and ecstatic utterances—left by some of Islam's most colorful and enigmatic mystical characters.

What is religious or theological anthropology and what core questions does it ask?

Virtually all religious traditions develop in considerable detail their views of what it means to be a human being. A couple of especially important themes stand out. First there are questions about the origin and makeup of the human person. Stories of human beginnings muse over whether they should be ascribed to direct creation, a freak happenstance, or a long process of evolution. What constitutes "a person"? Is a person spirit as well as body? What happens when the body dies—is that all there is? Or does something of the individual survive death?

Do psychological models figure in "religious anthropology"?

Some traditions have elaborated amazingly detailed psychological analyses of the human person. Two very broad types of religious psychology stand out. First there

Exploring one's spirituality involves emphasizing the experiential and how traditions can help Muslims improve their inmost selves.

are those that see at the core of each individual an eternal, indestructible faculty or element called "soul" or "true self." Sometimes called "substantialist" psychologies, these approaches describe in great detail the capabilities and needs of the spiritual self. In answer to the question "What happens to the soul after death?" two general views predominate. One holds that each individual passes through this world only once. At death the soul moves on to another level, undergoing a variety of new experiences, never to return. The other is based on the concept that an unimaginable but still limited number of "selves" are continuously embodied in various forms in this world. At death, each living being's soul is recycled, eventually becoming re-embodied in some other life form. This is called reincarnation or metempsychosis. An enormous percentage of human beings alive now are heavily influenced by this view. The second important type of religious psychology, represented especially by classical Buddhist thought, denies that there is a substantial self or soul at the core of the person. Individuality itself is a construct held together by the "glue" of inappropriate craving, desire so powerful that it can perpetuate the cycle of rebirth and suffering through faulty thinking.

What other important aspects of "religious anthropology" are there?

Another important anthropological theme is what some would call religious ethics. Here crucial questions of human relationships arise. As for the human-divine relationship, are human beings slaves? Puppets? Beggars? Heirs of a wealthy parent? Ambassadors of the deity to those unfortunate "outsiders"? The notion of grace is important in this context. How much help do humans need and get from the supreme being, and what shape does that help take?

As for how human beings relate to one another, religious traditions offer a range of explanations. People are siblings estranged and in need of reconciliation, natural enemies who can hope only for an uneasy truce, perhaps even neutral entities dodging one another like so many billiard balls. The intractable problem of human suffering occasions a similar range of explanations: suffering is humankind's just dessert, the outcome of mindless fate, the sadistic entertainment of evil cosmic powers, or perhaps a tough-love form of pedagogy designed to set human beings on the road to reform. What moral options are available as solutions—means to salvation, in other words? Everything from altruistic service of others to the pursuit of enlightened self-interest, from quiet contemplation to extroverted worship, and from active cultivation of good deeds to hopeful resignation in the face of a foreordained outcome.

What are some of the key themes in traditional Islamic understandings of what it means to be a human being?

Islam's spiritual anthropology takes into account four aspects of the human person: the individual's psycho-spiritual makeup and struggle for self-knowledge and discipline; the universal human need of guidance in various forms; the individual's relationship to God; and the social dimensions of personhood. Muslim authors, beginning over a millennium ago and often with "Sufi" connections, have elaborated detailed and sophisticated typologies of spiritual development. Most individuals need the assistance of wise, experienced supervision as they embark on the difficult path to refining those inner capabilities and persevering in their spiritual quest. Known as the "Science of Hearts," the ancient tradition of spiritual tutelage assists seekers in identifying the ways God calls them through manifold movements of spirit, as well as in balancing inner growth with their responsibilities and relationships with fellow travelers.

How do classic Islamic sources describe what it means to be "authentically human"?

Over a thousand years ago, Abu Said al-Kharraz (d. c. 900) wrote the *Book of Authenticity*, one of the earliest works of Islamic spiritual pedagogy. Structured around the literary conceit of a dialogue in which the author puts questions to an anonymous teacher, the work explores a series of "stations" and "states" that mark the seeker's progress along the path of spiritual questing. The "teacher" describes for his pupil how one can identify the authentic experience of, for example, penitence, asceticism, trust in God, and longing for God. Kharraz seems to be using the key term *sidq* (authenticity) in two slightly different ways. First, learning how to discern authenticity in one's inner experience is the overall purpose of the dialogue. Second, Kharraz introduces the topic by explaining that there are three principles with which to identify authenticity. Those three hallmarks are sincerity (*ikhlas*), patience (*sabr*, the virtue so central to the story of Joseph), and veracity or truthfulness (*sidq*).

How did Kharraz structure his analysis and assistance for seekers?

He begins by anchoring his reflections solidly in the Quran: Sincerity is the first [principle], as in the following scriptural texts: "Therefore serve God in sincere devotion; does God not deserve sincere devotion?" (Quran 39:2–3). "So call upon God in sincere devotion" (40:14); "Say: I am surely commanded to serve God in sincere devotion" (39:11); "Say: God I serve with my sincere devotion" (39:14); "And mention Moses in the Book: he was a sincere man and a messenger and prophet" (19:51). Then comes truthfulness (*sidq*): "O you who believe, fear God and be among those who are *truthful*" (9:119); "If they were *true* to God it would be better for them" (47:21); "[Among believers are] people who have been *true* to what they have covenanted with God" (33:23); "And mention Ismail in the Book, for he was *true* to the covenant" (19:54); and [speaking of a covenant with Noah, Abraham, Moses, and Jesus] "that He might ask the *truthful* ones about their authenticity" (33:8). As for the quality of patience, Kharraz cites: "O you who believe, be patient and vie [with one another] in *patience*" (3:200); "And if you are *patient*, it is best for those who are patient; so be patient, and your patience is only from (lit. in) God" (16:126–27); "Patiently await your Lord's judgment, for you are in Our sight" (52:48); "And give good news to those who are patient" (2:155).

Kharraz explains how his three richly connotative key qualities/virtues apply to [i.e., are essential characteristics of] all actions. Without them no action is complete; acts that depart from them are vitiated and partial. Similarly, none of these three principles is integral without the other two; if one is missing, the other two are of no avail. Sincerity is incomplete unless there is truthfulness in it and patience accompanying it. Patience is incomplete if it does not encompass truthfulness and sincerity. And truthfulness is incomplete unless it has patience over it and sincerity in it.

What is an example of this classic spiritual master's "voice"—to give a sense of how he actually communicated about such subtle themes?

Here's an excerpt from Kharraz, to offer a sense of his "pedagogical" style:

> Now the beginning of [all] actions is sincerity. You are required to believe in God and to know, confirm, and testify that there is no god but God alone, and he has no partner; and that he is the "first and the last, the manifest and the concealed," the creator, the fashioner, the shaper, the sustainer, the giver of life and death unto whom "matters return"; that Muhammad is his servant and messenger who brings truth from the Truth; that there are truly prophets entrusted with a message and of eminent counsel; and that the Garden is a reality, as are the resurrection and the return to God Most High, who "forgives whom he will and chastises whom he will."

Kharraz sums up:

> Let that be your unswerving and unstinting conviction expressed with your tongue while your heart rests in agreement with what you have assented to and confirmed. In that way no doubt will assail you concerning what has come to you from God on his Prophet's tongue, may God bless him and give him peace, in all that he has mentioned from his Lord, exalted and glorified.

How did Kharraz deal with the problem of "shame"? How can it be beneficial?

Kharraz uses the framework of a "dialogue" between student and master to discuss the difficult but essential experience of "shame"—that is, admission of one's failings:

> I asked: And what rouses shame? He said: Three aspects: the unceasing beneficence of God Most High toward you in spite of your lack of gratitude and your continuing sinfulness and excesses. Second, that you are aware that you will be in God's sight, exalted and glorified, in your final dwelling [literally, the place of overturning and being buried, i.e., the grave]. And third, mindfulness that you will stand before God, exalted and glorified, and that he will interrogate you about the small and the great.

> I asked: And what redoubles shame and strengthens it? He replied: Fear of God, exalted and glorified, when the passing movement of passion descends upon the heart and the heart is terrified and desolate, for it knows that God most high sees what is in it. Thus the shame [in the presence of] God is established, and if it continues in that vein, the shame increases and strengthens.

> I asked: And what is it that gives birth to shame? He said: Anxiety that God most high will turn away from one in disgust and displeasure with one's deeds.

211

How does Islamic tradition describe the underlying makeup of the human "self"?

A classic model of the human psyche situates the human heart at the center of the struggle, a sort of tug of war between spirit and ego. The Arabic word for heart, *qalb*, comes from a root that suggests the ability to turn in various directions or even rotate. From one side, the ego or baser self (*nafs*, from a root one of whose meanings is "to cast an evil eye") offers its narcissistic blandishments, hoping the heart will incline in its direction. From the other side, spirit (*ruh*) counters temptations to self-centeredness and heedlessness with a message of openness and complete trust in God. Conversion is thus the heart's "turnabout" from alienation to relationship. Sometimes the wayward ego is associated with, or reinforced by, the temptations of Satan and his minions. The Fall of Adam does not result in an inherited "original sin"; human sinfulness arises from an innate tendency to forgetfulness exacerbated by a certain laziness.

I said: And what takes over the heart of one who is in shame before his Lord? He explained: The sublimity of the gaze of the one who sees him, so that he is in dread of God, exalted and glorified, and feels shame because before Him....

I said: How is shame diminished? He said: By foregoing self-examination and piety.

I asked: And what are the spiritual states of one who experiences shame? He said: Enduring humility, unceasing self-effacement, a head bowed down, control of the glance, gazing at the heavens only rarely, and dulling [the edge of] the tongue against excessive talking....

What are some key aspects of the human-divine relationship?

The individual's relationship to God is perhaps best characterized by a pair of polar concepts. On the one hand, God is the Sovereign, the Lord of the Universe, the Master, as in the famous Verse of the Throne:

God—there is no deity but He; the Living, the Everlasting. Neither slumber nor sleep overcomes Him. To Him belong all that the heavens and earth can encompass. Who can intercede with Him, except by His leave? He knows all that surrounds [created beings], while they can grasp nothing of what He knows, except as He chooses. His Throne stretches across heaven and earth; sovereignty over them tires Him not, for He is the Exalted, the Magnificent. (Quran 2:255)

On the other hand, God is the Compassionate and the Merciful, the source of life who is "closer to you than your jugular vein," as the Quran puts it (50:15). God makes

His presence known both within and without through innumerable "signs" illuminated by God's own light. "We (God) will show you Our signs on the horizons and within your very selves, that perhaps you will understand," says the Quran (51:20–21; see also 41:53). Everything in creation is revelatory, as is every inner movement of the spirit, provided the individual is open to the divine illumination that alone can show those signs for what they really are. And "Wherever you turn, you see the face of God."

Do other Islamic sources offer further helpful insights into the divine-human relationship?

The Hadith literature enshrines countless intimations of God's nearness and accessibility to His servants. Two famous "Sacred Hadiths" (*Hadith Qudsi*, sayings traditionally attributed to God as cited by the Prophet), recorded in the authoritative collections of ninth-century scholars named Muslim and Bukhari, do just that. One is known as the Hadith of Supererogatory acts (*Hadith an-Nawafil*): "My servant draws near to me with works of devotion until I demonstrate my love for him. When I love a servant, I the Lord am the ear with which he hears, the eye with which he sees, the tongue by which he speaks, and the hand by which he grasps" (Bukhari).

The other Hadith has to do with the connection between awareness or recollection of God and the experience of God's presence. God says: "When my servant remembers me in his heart, I remember my servant in My heart. When he remembers me in company with others, I remember him in an even better company. When my servant draws near to me a hand's breadth, I draw near an arm's length. When he approaches me an arm's length, I approach the space of outstretched arms. When my servant comes toward me walking, I go toward him running. And if my servant brings to me sins the size of the earth itself, my forgiveness will more than cover them" (Muslim).

SPIRITUAL VALUES
AND EVERYDAY LIFE EXPERIENCE

How does Islamic tradition describe the role of "struggle" in human experience?

If for Buddhists, to live is above all to confront the reality of suffering, for Muslims to live is first to *struggle*, to strive all out—to engage in *jihad* at all times and on various levels. Unfortunately Muslims and non-Muslims alike have effectively reduced the term *jihad* to only one of its many meanings, that of armed struggle. That very misleading and inadequate expression "holy war" has gotten stuck in ordinary parlance as the only equivalent to *jihad*. Use of force in response to certain types of oppression is indeed not only countenanced in the Islamic tradition, as in many other religious traditions, but is considered a responsibility in the face of manifest injustice.

Muslims are heirs to a range of highly nuanced views as to how best to mount the good struggle across the full spectrum of life's challenges. In one Hadith, a questioner asks Muhammad what the best jihad is, and the Prophet replies, "It is to speak a word of justice in the hearing of a tyrant." *Jihad* means struggle for justice in every facet of life. In addition, ancient tradition has applied the term to the inner striving of the spiritual life, the disciplined encounter with one's own baser tendencies and self-centeredness. According to a saying attributed to Muhammad, this inner striving is called the "Greater *Jihad*." One does not prevail easily in this inward struggle, for as Muhammad put it, "your greatest enemy (the *nafs*) is between your two sides." An example is available in the lives of the Prophets and Friends of God (personifications of holiness similar to saints), whose deeds live on in a vigorous tradition of written and oral hagiography. In addition, a tradition of spiritual direction founded on a sophisticated and subtle "science of hearts" has deep roots. Spiritual guidance includes a broad range of psycho-spiritual models, representing various "schools" of spirituality over the centuries, as well as important practices such as prayer, retreat, and certain forms of spiritual discipline.

What is an ascetic?

An ascetic is a person who engages in demanding "exercise" (from the Greek *askesis*) in the interest of spiritual progress. One of the ascetic's chief goals is freedom from the encumbrances of material existence. Various forms of self-denial and increased attentiveness to inner movements of spirit are therefore at the heart of ascetical practice. Fasting, the use of the simplest possible clothing and other material needs, and the cultivation of solitude are common themes in ascetical discipline. In many religious traditions ascetics are known for their observance of silence for long periods. Ascetics vigorously pursue detachment from all that is not conducive to realizing one's nothingness in the face of ultimate reality.

Is there such a thing as Islamic asceticism?

Although the tradition does not feature the notion of "self-denial" quite the way some Christian traditions do, the concept of "struggle" or "striving" is multifaceted. One Hadith tells how a young man told Muhammad how desperately he wanted to join his fellow Muslims in defending the faith. Muhammad asked whether the young man's parents were growing old. When he said they were, the Prophet told the youth to consider taking care of them as his jihad. Jihad includes even the smallest and apparently least significant action, so long as it represents genuine effort and every struggle and sacrifice made "in the

A jihad ("struggle" or "exertion") doesn't necessarily have to involve huge tasks; it can mean something that seems relatively mundane, such as taking care of one's mother. The Prophet entreated people to do such tasks "in the way of God."

way of God." Thus, expressing the truth, exhorting others to act justly, discouraging injustice, and sacrificing one's own resources and even one's life, if necessary, are part of meritorious struggle.

What are the most religiously important modes of the expression of "struggle" for Muslims?

Muslim tradition speaks of jihad of the pen, of the tongue, of the mind, and of the sword. Above all, jihad means personal and communal discipline. All of the good things God bestows on an individual are to be enjoyed to the full as reminders of the divine generosity. Self-denial does have its place, however. The fast of Ramadan, the provision of alms, and attention to daily ritual prayer are all very demanding practices, but they are means rather than ends in themselves. Their ultimate purpose is to help believers keep things in perspective: every good thing comes from God and returns to God. Spiritual practice is meant to keep that reality ever before the believer.

Are ascetics really "mainstream" figures in most religious traditions?

These spiritual athletes often appear to others to be going to unhealthy extremes—and in relation to widespread societal norms of ordinary behavior, they are indeed sometimes extremists. Some ascetics are best known for such practices as sitting atop pillars for long periods, staring at a blank wall for years, or lowering themselves head-first into the depths of a well. But there is another important way of understanding asceticism. Every human being who works hard at living a good life practices asceticism at some level. The ordinary disciplines of dealing with life's predictable setbacks, of treating others with consistent kindness, and of shouldering all of one's responsibilities are forms of asceticism. Most religious people must make the most of the ordinary opportunities, allowing their traditions' "professional" ascetics to remind them occasionally of the need to look deeper in the quest for spiritual freedom.

What is a martyr?

The word "martyr" comes from a Greek word that means "witness." Some traditions have made a special place for believers so committed to their faith that they have been willing to die, either in its active spread and defense or as a way of protesting forced conversion or apostasy. Most people will likely associate martyrdom with Christianity and Islam. But there are numerous and astonishing examples of unconditional witnessing to religious beliefs and values from a host of traditions. Some examples involve self-immolation by fire or voluntary starvation. Many great religious leaders have engaged in fasting as protest even to the ultimate price. Whether they die in battle or in protest, all martyrs give witness to values they believe are more important than life itself.

Are some "martyrs" simply extremists or violent people?

Some individuals acclaimed as "martyrs" are indeed not truly representative of the essential values of Islam or any other major faith tradition. They are not authentic wit-

215

Martyr's Hill in Pristina, Kosovo, is the last resting place of thousands of innocent civilians who died in the 1998 Kosovo conflict.

nesses for faith but are acting out serious personal problems and merely calling attention to themselves. And in some instances, social pressure is the operative force, making it impossible for certain people not to participate. That too can result in a grotesque distortion of the ideal of committed witnessing. Real martyrs don't necessarily *want* to die, much less are they possessed by a mania for death. It is also useful to note that the term "martyr" commonly appears in non-religious contexts. For example, in the lobby of FBI headquarters in Washington, D.C., a "wall of remembrance" pays tribute to those who have "died as martyrs in service" to their nation.

Has the concept of martyrdom been significant generally in Islamic history and tradition?

Muslims in many different societies and cultures have identified as "martyrs" (*shahid*, sha-HEED) countless individuals who have died as victims of injustice or in defense of faith or nation. Surely the best known examples of such acknowledgments are also in many ways the most misleading and non-representative of the spiritual and religious values most dear to Muslims. Rhetoric espoused by such extremist groups as al-Qaeda, with its promise of "seventy virgins" as a reward for "martyrs," grotesquely distorts ancient Islamic beliefs. Their rhetoric glorifies both indiscriminate slaughter and suicide (unambiguously condemned in Islamic tradition) by claiming the violence against others is defensive and calling suicide "self-selected martyrdom." Much more in line with ancient tradition are cultural practices such as honoring as martyrs the many Afghan *mujahideen* who died in the protracted struggle during the 1980s to drive out Soviet army forces that had invaded their country.

Who are some of the most important martyrs in Islamic history?

Since earliest times Muslim sources have referred to those who gave their lives for the cause of Islam as martyrs. Shi'i tradition has held martyrs in especially high regard. Beginning with Muhammad's grandson Husayn, killed with his small band of fighters resisting the tyranny of the Umayyads in 680 C.E., the *imams* have been the focus of a central belief in redemptive suffering. In this case the blood of the martyr not only assures the martyr's place in heaven but becomes a source of grace for all believers. When the Ayatollah Khomeini returned to Iran from his exile in France in 1979, he made his first major address in a cemetery called the Paradise of Martyrs, associating the revolutionary struggle of twentieth-century Shi'i Iranians with that of the proto-martyr Husayn. Placing such value on martyrdom does not imply that Shi'ites or other Muslims are eager to die. It means that some Muslims, like believers in several other traditions, value their faith and are willing to give their lives for it.

What is the source of the apparent claim that every person who dies a "martyr" in jihad will have seventy-two virgins awaiting in Paradise?

The Quran itself mentions nothing of the sort, referring only to the presence of houris (dark-eyed maidens, perhaps) in the "Gardens" of reward and including no reference to martyrdom in that context. Only two Hadiths (sayings of Muhammad), each found in only one of the "Six" authoritative collections of Hadiths (those of Tirmidhi and Ibn Majah), seem to refer to this claim. One of the traditions places seventy-two houris among the "eighty thousand servants" (not seventy-two for each) residing in the "lowest heaven" and makes no mention of martyrs there (Ibn Majah); and martyrs are typically said to reside in a loftier heaven.

This version is the most quoted: "The martyr has six distinctions in the view of God: he will be forgiven from the start, be shown his resting place in Paradise, be protected from the torment of the tomb, be secured from the greatest terror, have a crown of dignity put on his head, of which one ruby will be better than the world and all that is in it, be married to seventy-two wives among the houris and be given to intercede for seventy of his relatives" (Tirmidhi). Note that this Hadith says nothing about precisely what constitutes "martyrdom," while equally ancient and much better-attested traditions condemn all forms of suicide unequivocally. Both traditions are attested by only one transmitting source and are thereby judged by most scholars to be well below the maximum level of authenticity and credibility. Attestation of a saying by so few authoritative sources, and its correspondingly low authenticity rating, are among the criteria that undercut the credibility of a saying attributed to Muhammad. In other words, the text almost automatically cited in news reports as clear motivation is not only flimsily attested, according to the well-known judgments of ancient Muslim scholars, but does not in fact say precisely, let alone clearly, what popular reporting (both Muslim as well as non-Muslim) claims it says.

Do Muslims believe that God "tests" people?

Life's ordinary difficulties are God's way of testing and strengthening people, a form of ongoing discipline. There have, of course, been various ascetical movements of a more pronounced type from time to time during Islamic history. And the history of Sufism in particular evidences several remarkable examples of the institutionalization of ascetical practice, but they represent a small portion of Islamic society at any given time. A text from the Quran sums up a number of the central themes in Islamic spirituality and relates them, in the last verse, to this question of spiritual discipline: "Uprightness is not a question of turning your faces to the *qibla* of East or West. Uprightness means rather believing in God and in the final day, and in the angels and the Book and the prophets. It means sharing your wealth, dear as it is to you (some would translate this phrase "out of love for Him"), with kinfolk, orphans, the poor, the traveler (lit. son of the road), those who come asking, and for setting slaves free. It means performing the ritual prayer (*salat*), giving alms (*zakat*), living up to one's solemn word, and bearing up under the most intense hardship and in dire straits" (Quran 2:177).

What is the traditional Muslim understanding of the reality of "suffering"?

Muslims are about as susceptible as the rest of us to the nagging suspicion that more than ordinary human suffering, especially on a vast scale as in natural disasters, results from the deity's displeasure at humankind's waywardness and stubbornness. But on the whole, two theological views of suffering are most important to an appreciation of Islamic spirituality overall. One is that suffering is, like all ordinary aspects of human experience, full of signs that, if read rightly, point back to the Creator of all things. Suffering is part of one's human condition, a powerful and persistent reminder that one is not God. Islamic tradition teaches that one need never ask for suffering, for everyone will get whatever difficulty in life God has in mind for them, and in any case there is always more than enough of it to go around. But that does not mean one should not pray for the best, and in fact one ought rather to be bold in asking for the opposite of suffering. A charming story tells how Muhammad went to visit a young man he had heard was not feeling well. Turns out the man had been fasting so severely that he had wasted away till he was no bigger than a twig. Muhammad immediately asked him what he had been praying for. He replied that he had been asking God to give him hardship in this life as a way of ensuring better things in the next. Muhammad said, "Instead, ask for good both in this life and in the next," since this life will include an ample share of hardship.

Are there any distinctively Shi'i understandings of suffering?

An important aspect of suffering as interpreted by Muslims is the view most characteristic of the Shia community, namely, that the suffering of God's elect—the prophets and the immediate descendants of Muhammad—is redemptive and integral to the interces-

What is meant by the term "suffering of the grave"?

A distinctively Islamic perspective on the topic has to do with the notion of the "suffering of the grave," evidently based on a saying of Muhammad that suggests that the deceased retain their perceptive faculties. Tradition has it that even those who have lived an upright life will experience some sense of constriction and loneliness in the grave, while those who die as unrepentant sinners begin to taste their deserved punishment more keenly immediately upon interment. And suffering in the form of punishment in hellfire awaits those who steadfastly refuse God's mercy. Part of the punishment of the tomb arises when two angels, Munkar and Nakir, interrogate the deceased as to the state of his or her belief, asking specific questions about creedal tenets. Mourners can help to alleviate the experience of suffering by praying for the departed at the grave and exhorting him or her not to be intimidated by the angels, for they are also just creatures.

sory capacity of the holy ones. Here we have a fully developed theology of history and a rather elaborate soteriology. Shi'i tradition holds that all the prophets suffered at the hands of the unbelieving people to whom God sent them. More importantly, the successors to the last prophet, the descendants of Muhammad in the line of Ali, paid the ultimate price of martyrdom. Beginning with Ali's son Husayn, who was slaughtered along with numerous members of his family in 680 at Karbala (in southern Iraq), the *imams* all died as martyrs and became redemptive intercessors for their people.

In the moving scenes of traditional Shi'i passion plays, one martyr after another is so gracious as to ask forgiveness even for those who treated them most savagely. The plays, called *taziya* (literally "consolation"), are reenacted during the first ten days (called *ashura*) of the first lunar month, Muharram, as part of elaborate commemorations of Husayn's martyrdom. These observances are generally the occasion for evening news images of processions of Shi'i mourners in the Middle East, drawing blood by self-flagellation as they identify with the suffering prophets and *imams*. It was no accident that the takeover of the American embassy in Tehran in 1979 coincided with the beginning of the *ashura* activities; public rhetoric identified the Iranian people with a beleaguered Husayn oppressed by the tyrant Shah and his American lackeys. The imagery of redemptive suffering remains a potent force.

What additional aids to one's spiritual life does Islamic tradition offer?

Every "traveler" needs signs along the way and light by which to make them out for what they are, and help for the journey begins with the sacred scripture. In several texts of the Quran, God speaks of showing "signs on the horizons" and "within their/your very selves" (Quran 41:53, 51:20–21). In addition the sacred text refers to itself as made up of "signs" or *ayat* (aah-YAAT, plural of *aya*), a word that has therefore come to mean "verses" as well.

219

Hence the scripture is itself one large series of signs. Problem: left to themselves, human beings are incapable of reading those signs adequately. Solution: The scripture explains in several lovely passages that God is himself the light of the heavens and the earth; that the fundamental mission of every prophet is to bring his people from darkness into light; and that the Quran stands as a light illuminating itself in its progressive unfolding.

What are the foundations and basic ingredients of the "science of hearts"?

Many centuries back, perceptive Muslim authors concluded that, almost without exception, spiritual seekers need objective assistance to persevere on the path toward God—just as all human beings require prophets to reveal God's overall design for them. These specialists in "spirituality" developed a set of criteria and qualifications of an authentic spiritual guide, or *shaykh*. Among these attributes they list: privileged access to God's mercy, a heart purified of all knowledge not of human origin, forbearance, generosity, compassion, selflessness, contentment with one's lot in life, tranquility, courage, and a presence worthy of reverence—all in addition to the less demanding qualities expected of all believers. Requisite special attributes of the *seeker*, on the other hand, include repentance, patience, willingness to engage in the "greater jihad" against one's baser tendencies, sincerity, willingness to suffer reproach even when undeserved, even temperament, surrender to the *shaykh* "as though a corpse in the hands of a corpse washer," and total abandonment to God.

Given suitable candidates for both guide and seeker, what's the process of guidance about?

The goal of the Science of Hearts is to help the seeker assess his/her inner needs and name God's way of dealing with the unique individual. Its overarching concern is that the seeker

What is meant by content and affective tone?

Content—i.e., the "message" an individual receives spiritually—can range from promises of ease or comfort, as in Satanic whisperings, to temptation, with promises of pleasures, honor, fame, wealth, and vengeance from the lower self. By contrast, divine intimations identify themselves by their consonance with the revealed Law, as well as many individuals' fierce resistance to them. Affective tone is illusive and harder to pinpoint, since more intense emotional responses tend to be associated with more fleeting movements that may disguise themselves as originating in God rather than in human effort. As a seeker progresses in self-awareness, he/she moves from the more enduring "stations" of the "purgative" stage in which personal effort and striving (*mujahada*) predominate, through the more fleeting "states" of the "illuminative" stage of contemplative vision (*mukashafa*). Ultimately, the goal, achieved by few, is the "unitive" stage generally attained by people many traditions call mystics.

understand humanity's absolute need of God and God's perfect willingness to fill that need and supply all needed "provisions" for the inner journey. The seeker accesses those provisions via a process of discernment that produces a heightened awareness of the source, duration, content, and affective tone of the "movements of soul" that constitute the inward life. First, one must sort out whether the movement originates with the "world," Satan, a good angel, the spirit, reason, God, or the "lower self" (*nafs*). Second, one notes whether these inner movements are momentary and occur in rapid succession or perdure, and whether they cause either agitation or exert a more subtle influence. Movements that originate in God tend to stay but momentarily and require keen attentiveness. By contrast, Satanic insinuations (for example) assault, withdraw, and renew the attack. Notions that arise from the lower self tend to linger, as the *nafs* rationalizes and procrastinates.

SPIRITUAL MODELS AND EXEMPLARS

What is a religious exemplar?

Individuals who embody to the highest degree a religious tradition's spiritual ideals function in a variety of ways. Some traditions, such as Sunni Islam and various Christian denominations, emphasize the importance of each individual's direct relationship with the supreme being. They teach that no human being has the power or authority to act as mediator for anyone else. But the need for help in achieving the highest spiritual aspirations seems to run so deep that examples of "saintly" characters appear during some periods in the histories of virtually every religious tradition. The ability to perform miracles is a major feature in some traditions.

Healing is perhaps the most common claim, but miracles can include everything from finding small lost objects to raising the dead. Saints in some traditions turn out to be more powerful and active after death than during their lives, with devotees showering them with requests generation after generation. According to some traditions, such as Roman Catholicism, individuals reputed for their holiness in life must have their worthiness to be formally declared saints by having certified miracles attributed to them after death. Healings comprise the bulk of these wonders needed to bring about the saint's "canonization." Special "cults" (in the sense not of exclusive religious organizations, but of people who "cultivate" a particular devotion) of certain saints have developed in some communities. Believers sometimes claim a particular holy person as their "patron" saint, associating him or her with a particular place and with specific types of miracles. But saints can also develop a more universal following and have devotees wherever members of a particular tradition are to be found.

How does the Prophet Muhammad provide a spiritual "model" for Muslims?

The Prophet's example is never far from the consciousness of the average Muslim. Beyond the myriad particular details of Muhammad's ordinary behavior that survive in the speech and actions of twentieth-century Muslims, one can point to an overarching theme in his life that continues to provide Muslims with a larger spiritual structure and frame of reference. Muhammad was a wayfarer, a journeyer along what the Quran calls the Straight Path. Two clusters of metaphors offer a way to understand the uniquely Islamic mode of religious sojourning. The first cluster surrounds the image of Muhammad as exemplary wayfarer and the need for Muslims to follow in his footsteps. Three specific journeys in the Prophet's life stand out as especially significant and paradigmatic for Muslims. The first (not chronologically, but in terms of its foundational implications for the Muslim community) is that of the *Hijra* or Emigration from Mecca to Medina in 622 C.E. That journey marks the official beginning of Muslim history; but in addition it has become a metaphor for a fundamental requirement of all Muslims in their relationship to the world around them. They must be willing to "leave home" symbolically; to hear God's call to establish a community of justice in an unjust world; to risk, as Abraham did long before Muhammad, the censure of a culture of unbelief in the interest of a community of faith and trust in God.

Does Muhammad play a role in Islamic spirituality, and is it anything like Jesus's role in Christian spirituality?

Since Muslims regard Muhammad as no more than a human being, while Christians believe Jesus is divine, the two figures naturally occupy very different positions in the spiritualities of their respective traditions. That is not to suggest, however, that Muhammad occupies a *lesser* place for Muslims—just different from a theological perspective. Muhammad's first role is that of a teacher and model. In addition to serving as the foremost conduit of revelation, the Prophet is the prime exemplar for virtually every facet of the life of piety and virtue. He models spiritual values of fatherly and spousal devotion, of justice and fairness, and of responsible and selfless leadership. The other prophets share some of Muhammad's limelight in this respect, since they too brought revelation and were collectively humanity's proudest boast.

How important is the Prophet on a more personal spiritual level?

Muhammad has also functioned for many Muslims as a focus of intense popular devotion. As the creature who enjoys the most intimate relationship with God, Muhammad elicits extraordinary outpourings of affection from Muslims the world over. Even in countries that officially consider festivities in honor of the Prophet's birthday as extravagant or theologically unwarranted, devout Muslims invariably express their feelings for Muhammad quite effusively. Many people implore Muhammad's intercession with God for the fulfillment of a variety of needs. Some even ask the Prophet directly to bestow on them his spiritual power and blessing (*baraka*, BA-ra-ka).

How do Muhammad's own spiritual journeys function as models for Muslims?

Very near the end of his life, Muhammad made a pilgrimage or *Hajj* to Mecca from Medina. From a religio-political perspective, it was a statement of control over the already ancient holy site. As for its symbolic spiritual implications, his pilgrimage was a return to a sacred center long before hallowed by the presence of Abraham. Ever since, Muslims have followed Muhammad's pilgrim steps, not only in a literal journey to Mecca but as life-long sojourners and seekers after the divine center. In addition, many Muslims look—from an awe-struck distance, to be sure—to an early mystical experience in Muhammad's life. Tradition has it that God carried him by night from the "mosque of the sanctuary" in Mecca to the "farther mosque" in Jerusalem, whence Muhammad ascended to the throne of God and was shown the various regions of the heavens and underworld. The first segment is called the Night Journey (*Isra*, is-RAA), the second the Ascension (*Mir'aj*, mi-RAAJ). Though no Muslim would presume to lay claim to Muhammad's exalted prerogatives, the Prophet's mystical journey has nevertheless remained an important paradigm of the spiritual life.

Is there such a thing as a Muslim saint?

In addition to sages and prophets, widespread Muslim tradition holds in high regard other individuals singled out for particularly intimate relationships with God. They are called friends of God (*Awliya*, aw-lee-YAA, singular *wali*) and are generally analogous to what Christians and others mean when they refer to "saints." A major difference is that friends of God are popularly acclaimed as such rather than formally declared by an in-

Are there religious heroes in Islam? How are they different from saints?

Every culture has its heroes and heroines. Sometimes these pillars of strength and unusual ability represent largely "secular" or natural virtues. But in many instances heroes and heroines whose life stories and legends are not explicitly religious in origin gradually take on religious associations. One typical pattern is that a local heroic figure rises to prominence on a larger scale and becomes a sort of "national" hero. A religious tradition formerly unknown in the region moves in, perhaps arriving on the wake of military conquest and newly established political power, and eventually becomes the dominant religious influence in the area. Heroes and heroines who had formerly been characters in folk or royal epic tales begin to rub shoulders with the saints and other prominent religious personalities imported by the now-dominant religious tradition. Before long (in the grand scheme of things, at least—but still generations or even centuries), the local or national heroes begin to acquire the characteristics and virtues of their religious counterparts. They may never rise to the status of "saints," but they definitely qualify for the title of religious hero. Here is a useful distinction. Wonders attributed to a saint typically speak loudly of divine power. A religious hero's spectacular deeds, on the other hand, typically reflect a sort of natural perfection now understood as part of a divine dispensation even if not a direct result of divine intervention.

stitutional procedure. Muslims from Muhammad's own generation are among the earliest individuals called Friends of God, some so designated because of their devotion to the Prophet. Subsequent generations of Muslims have acclaimed friends of God virtually everywhere right on down to modern times, with the notable exception of Saudi Arabia and other Gulf states. There and in a few other places, modern reformers have sought to purge Islamic practice of devotional customs judged inauthentic expressions of Islam and distortions of core teachings. They have argued that beseeching friends of God for miracles is simply unnecessary, since no human being can mediate between the individual believer and his or her God. Virtually everywhere else, from Morocco's *marabouts* to Indonesia's distinctive *wali songo* (Nine Friends of God), devotion to holy persons has been an important element in the spiritual life of hundreds of millions.

What distinguishes Friends of God from Prophets?

Friends of God are considered distinct from prophets in several important ways. First, prophets are entrusted explicitly with revealed messages and sent to specific peoples—though in Muhammad's case, the message is directed to all peoples. Second, major prophets such as Moses, David, Jesus, and Muhammad also brought specific scriptures, whereas Friends have no connection with sacred texts. Third, the modalities through which God manifests divine power are very different for prophets and Friends of God. Even though both are capable of manifesting God's power in extraordinary deeds, Islamic tradition makes a crucial distinction. Marvels of divine power granted through prophets are known as "evidentiary miracles" (*mujizat*) effected to establish the veracity of the prophet's claim, whereas saintly miracles are called "wonders" (*karamat*, ka-RAA-maat). Friends of God are very important in popular piety, though in many places Muslim authorities have been mounting massive education campaigns in an attempt to purge the vestiges of what they consider un-Islamic superstition that, at best, dilutes the message of the prophets.

Who are some of the most important Friends of God?

Friends of God are represented in every land and culture in which Islam has been a formative presence, whether or not the region is now predominantly Muslim. And the renown of these figures can range from local (popular in a given city or even village), to regional (a small country or portion of a larger one), to trans-regional (extending across national boundaries, as in the Indian Sub-continent), to global. A good example of a local Friend is a thirteenth-century woman named Sayyida Manoubiya, who remains popular among women of rural Tunisia. Regional Friends include figures like Indonesian "national" Friend Yusuf of Makasar. Some Friends, such as the mystic and poet Jalal ad-Din Rumi, claim multinational and cultural followings—Afghans claim him because he was born in the north of that nation; Iranians claim him because he wrote largely in Persian; Turks claim him because he lived most of his life on Turkish soil; and South Asians claim him because Persian was for centuries a major language of learning and culture in India and Pakistan, and Rumi's poetry has remained popular there. A

The mystic and poet Jalal ad-Din Rumi is buried in Konya, Turkey, at the Mevlana museum.

small coterie of Friends have developed more global followings long before modern times, so one can find Abd al-Qadir Jilani stained glass hangings in North Africa and graphic novels and coloring books in Indonesia. Contemporary mass communication has arguably brought Rumi also into that circle.

What sort of spiritual role models does Islamic tradition offer to young women?

Islamic tradition is rich with stories of exemplary individuals. As in Christian and other traditions, men far outnumber women, but there are many prominent Muslim women who model faith and virtue. Foremost among them is Fatima, daughter of Muhammad and his first wife, Khadija, who died when Fatima was quite young. Fatima is best known as the wife of Ali and mother of Husayn and Hasan, the first two Shi'i martyr-*imams*. Hadith accounts do not gloss over the difficult times Fatima experienced with her husband, with Muhammad himself acting as arbiter in their disputes. But she fought against Abu Bakr (the first caliph, by Sunni reckoning) for Ali's right to succeed Muhammad. More recently, several Muslim scholars, male and female, have interpreted Fatima as the paradigm of the liberated woman as exemplified by her independent thinking and courage in adversity. In traditional and popular sources, however, Fatima appears as the utterly devoted wife. Stories about Fatima have been told in many languages and cultural settings throughout the history of Islam. As one might expect, some features of her life and experience remain fairly constant whenever and wherever Muslims have recounted her life. But Fatima also takes on the characteristics of every culture that preserves her memory. In other words, she is a model held up for the emulation of Muslim women of every age; but her image is also shaped by the values of each society in that she becomes a reflection of a society's prevalent image of the "ideal" woman. The Fatima of Swahili epic poetry is rather different from the Fatima of Persian Shi'i literature or North African popular lore. One can observe the same sort of cultural reinterpretation in stories of the Virgin Mary, for example: Christians may discern a very similar message underlying all her claimed apparitions, but the Lady of Guadalupe is different from the Lady of Medjugorje in ways that go beyond clothing style.

Do Muslims revere any persons as especially gifted with wisdom?

In Islamic tradition, as in Jewish and Christian tradition, King Solomon (Sulayman) is the paradigm of wisdom. Solomon's sagacity enabled him to communicate with creatures of every kind, so that his sovereignty encompassed all of creation. Another figure from pre-Islamic history known for his wisdom is Luqman. Some traditions include him among the ranks of the prophets, but he is best understood as a prince among Muslim sages. According to the Quran, one chapter of which bears his name, Luqman was

A depiction of King Solomon meeting the Queen of Sheba on one of the door panels to the Florence Baptistery. As with Christian and Jewish tradition, Solomon is honored by Muslims for his wisdom.

a teacher and coiner of proverbs. "Walk at a moderate pace and speak in measured tones," he advises, "for the most annoying of voices is that of the jackass" (Quran 31:19). Islamic lore describes Luqman in ways that recall the Greek sage Aesop.

Wisdom did not cease with the passing of the ancients. Muslims have continued to discern in teachers, scholars, and spiritual guides the embodiment of a practical insight that goes far beyond mere intellectual understanding. God has entrusted certain individuals with the gift of wisdom, the ability to penetrate the veils of life's mystery, and to untangle the snarl of daily experience. Perhaps the most unusual personality in this general category is Khidr. The name means "Green One," suggesting that this character originated as a generic mythic or folkloric fertility figure. Some scholars connect Khidr with the Gilgamesh epic's sage Utnapishtim, who had survived the Flood. Gilgamesh searches for Utnapishtim in hopes that the sage will guide him to a plant that will provide him with the secret of immortality. Islamic lore attributes to Khidr arcane knowledge of the whereabouts of the Fountain of Life. Some accounts of his discovery of the Fountain pair him with Ilyas, since Elijah is another of the few who (along with Jesus and Idris) have attained immortality. Even as Jews often leave a chair and a glass for Elijah on ritual occasions, some Muslims greet the unseen Khidr because they know he is there somewhere.

Khidr is kind of a peculiar, even confusing figure. How did such a strange character find his way into Muslim religious lore?

Khidr's mysteriousness is deepened by the fact that he is one of only three significant figures not specifically identified in the Quran to whom later tradition has attached names. The others are Alexander the Great, associated with the Quranic Dhu'l-Qarnayn—"The One with Two Horns"—and Joshua, who is said to be the anonymous servant of Moses in the Quranic story now connected with Khidr. An intriguing narrative in Quran 18:61–83 tells how Musa (Moses) and his servant (Joshua) head off in search of the Confluence of the Two Seas (which some interpreters take as a symbol of the juncture between the seen and unseen worlds). The two have brought along a fish to eat, but when Moses looks away momentarily, the fish comes to life and swims away. This they take as a sign that they must retrace their steps, for they have apparently gone too far unawares. Turning back, they meet the figure whom God describes as "one to whom we gave mercy from ourselves and to whom we taught a knowledge from our presence" (Quran 18:64). Recognizing this person as a guide, Moses asks to follow him. The guide hesitates, insisting that Moses will be too impatient with the guide's actions. Moses promises to hold his peace on pain of being left to journey on alone. As they proceed, Khidr performs three actions that Moses deems morally untenable: he scuttles a ship, murders a boy, and rebuilds a wall for people of questionable character. At each juncture, Moses criticizes Khidr's actions. Finally, Khidr has had enough; he agrees to explain himself, but then Moses is on his own. He sunk the ship because he knew an evil king was planning to do great harm with it; he killed the youth to prevent his parents from having to grieve his inevitable rebelliousness; and he rebuilt the wall so that the owner's orphaned children would eventually be able to inherit the treasure their father had buried beneath it for them.

So is Khidr a prophet or a Friend of God?

Khidr is in a way a "bridge" figure, representing qualities of both prophet and Friend of God. Exegetes often explain the story by associating Moses with outward knowledge and Khidr with the inward, esoteric knowledge that comes uniquely from the divine presence. Some argue that Khidr must have been a prophet, for Moses would surely not have followed a figure of lesser stature than himself. Special knowledge is without a doubt Khidr's decisive attribute. It is on this account that he assumes a life of his own beyond his scriptural relationship with Moses. Since he represents esoteric, mystical knowledge, Khidr is of great importance in the history of Sufism. Sufi exegetes and poets transform Khidr into the master of the mystery to which all seekers must surrender them-

The Quranic figure known as Khidr may have originally emerged from folkloric tradition to become a character associated with Moses. Khidr possesses special, inward knowledge afforded him by the divine presence.

selves in their quest for guidance on the Path. Spiritual aspirants must be willing to endure his apparently draconian authority in view of higher meanings. For Sufis, Khidr functions as the spirit- *shaykh* who appears in dreams and visions to invest seekers with the patched frock of spiritual poverty that is the mark of all duly initiated. He is the symbol of the spiritual "sap"—the Water of Life—that greens all things in its upward movement through creation. As one who reads hearts and sees with the very eyes of God, Khidr is the epitome of the spiritual guide. Serious seekers must be willing to set out on the very ship (the body) that Khidr has scuttled, as a token of authentic spiritual poverty.

PRAYER AND MYSTICISM

How does ritual prayer function in Islamic spiritual traditions generally?

Perhaps the most widely known feature of Islamic practice is the daily ritual prayer oriented toward Mecca, the symbol of sacred centrality on earth. Non-Muslims are often duly impressed with the idea that Muslims will stop whatever they are doing when the proper times arrive, to devote the next ten to fifteen minutes to hallowing their otherwise ordinary times and spaces. Naturally there are practical problems, particularly in non-Muslim societies; and even under optimal conditions, Muslims do not all engage in each ritual prayer any more than "all Catholics go to Mass on Sunday." What is important about the Islamic ritual practice is precisely that it represents one of the few examples of a regular sacralization of time and space recommended to masses of ordinary folk and not just to professionally religious types. Only the stricter observances in Judaism, apart from Islam, have maintained an absolute sacred geographical orientation (Jews facing Jerusalem, Muslims toward Mecca) along with regular daily times for ordinary prayer.

What are the essential ingredients of daily ritual prayer?

Ritual prayer involves first of all the critical expression of intention, without which the prayer is empty. Symbolic purification with water, if available, or even with dust or gravel if no water can be had, immediately precedes the ritual. There follows a series of cycles, each of which begins with standing and placing hands on the knees, moves to both a kneeling posture in which one sits back on the heels and to prostrations in which one's forehead touches the floor, returns to the sitting position, and ends with standing. The number of cycles varies from two to four, depending on the day and time; various phrases, such as "God hears those who praise Him," and verses from the Quran are the "text" of the prostration cycles. On Friday at noon prayer, the ideal situation finds people gathered in the mosque, where two cycles of prayer are combined with a homiletical address from the mosque's imam.

Certain postures done in a particular order must be executed during ritual prayer, and Muslims must pray with sincere intention or else the gestures are meaningless. (Photo courtesy David Oughton).

Do Muslims engage in other forms of prayer besides the *salat*?

Alongside the practice of the five daily ritual prayers, offered in concert with millions of others, the Islamic tradition recommends a variety of private devotional or "free" prayer, usually called by the generic term *dua*, or supplication. The best prayer is any that Muhammad first pronounced. Even the angels took their cue from the Prophet. A favorite prayer of Muhammad's was one he recommended Muslims pray on their pilgrim way to Mecca:

> O God, indeed you know and see where I stand and hear what I say. You know me inside and out; nothing of me is hidden from you. And I am the lowly, needy one who seeks your aid and sanctuary, aware of my sinfulness in shame and confusion. I make my request of you as one who is poor; as a humbled sinner I make my plea; fearful in my blindness I call out to you, head bowed before you, eyes pouring out tears to you, body grown thin for you, face in the dust at your feet. O God, as I cry out to you, do not disappoint me; but be kind and compassionate to me, you who are beyond any that can be petitioned, most generous of any that give, most merciful of those who show mercy (a reference to Quran 12). Praise to God, Lord of the universe.

Are there other examples of favorite prayers of Muhammad himself?

Muhammad himself left a number of prayers that have remained popular, such as this request, reminiscent of the Lord's Prayer, that God heal a sick member of his community: "God Our Lord, you who are in the heavens, may your name be sanctified. Yours is the command in the heavens and on earth. As your mercy is in the heavens, so let your mercy be on earth. Forgive our sins and failures. You are the Lord of those who seek to do good. Upon this illness send down mercy from your mercy and healing from your healing."

Here is a prayer Muhammad is said to have prayed for himself: "O God, guide me among those you have guided, and sustain me among those you have sustained. Make me your intimate friend among those you have made your intimate friends. Bless me in what you have given me." And this gem of simplicity and directness: "O God, create light in my heart, and light in my eye, and light in my hearing, and light on my right, and light on my left, light above me, light below me, light in front of me, light behind me. Create light for me: on my tongue, light; in my muscles, light; in my flesh, light; in my hair, light; in my body, light; in my soul, light. Make light grow for me. O God, grant me light!"

Are there examples of "personal" or "individual" prayer in the Quran?

Islam also has a rich treasury of personal prayer from which individuals may choose when words of their own do not come easily to the tongue. Naturally some of the earliest examples of favorite prayers are attributed to Muhammad himself; but there are some with even more ancient origins, namely those ascribed to prophets like Abraham and Moses in the Quran. Moses prays as God sends him to face Pharaoh:

> Lord, expand the core of my being; make easy the discharge of your command to me; loosen my tongue that the people might understand what I say; give me

Aaron, my brother, as a helper from among my people. Affirm in him my strength by making him my co-worker, so that we may give you great glory and be mindful of you in all things. Indeed you are ever watchful over us. (Quran 20:25–35)

Do we have examples of prayers of some of the early Muslim mystics?

Some of the most vivid and evocative prayers have come from the great mystics, such as Junayd (d. 910) of Baghdad. He addresses God: "I have come to realize that you are in my inmost being, and I have conversed with you intimately. We are in a way, then, united, but in a way we are quite separated. Even if your sublime grandeur has kept you inaccessible to my eye's glance, still, loving ecstasy has caused me to feel your touch within me."

The martyr-mystic al-Hallaj (d. 922) describes his awareness of God as he reads the "signs within the self." "O God, the sun neither rises nor sets but that your love is one with my breathing. Never have I sat in conversation, but that it was you who spoke to me from among those seated round. Never have I been mindful of you, either in sadness or rejoicing, but that you were there in my heart amidst my inmost whisperings. Never have I decided on a drink of water in my thirst, but that I saw your image in the cup." Elsewhere Hallaj says God is so close as to "flow between my heart and its sheath as tears flow between eye and eyelid."

Have any early women mystics left samples of personal prayer?

A number of Islam's women mystics, too, have left us samples of their favorite prayers. After the night ritual prayer was over, Rabia al-Adawiya (d. 801) liked to pray: "Eyes are heavy with sleep, unaware of their forgetfulness. And still Rabia the sinner abides in your presence in the hope that you might look on her with a gaze that will keep sleep from diminishing her service of you. By your power and majesty, may I not slacken in serving you either night or day until I meet you (in death)." A younger contemporary named Zahra prayed: "You whose powers are without limit, you the munificent and eternal, make the eyes of my heart rejoice in the gardens of your power. Join my anxious care to your tender largesse, O gracious one. In your majesty and splendor take me away from the paths of those who only make a show of power, O compassionate one. Make me a servant and a seeker, and be, O light of my heart and ultimate desire, my Friend."

What is a mystic?

A mystic is one who has special insight into the deepest of spiritual mysteries. Mystics often report first-hand, direct experience of realities far beyond the ordinary. There are some apparent similarities in the accounts of mystics across traditions. In a number of traditions, there are two principal types of mystical experience. One is a highly personal encounter between the human subject and the divine reality, in which there is no permanent loss of individuality. This type is sometimes called "theistic" or "dualistic" mysticism. Another describes the mystic as utterly absorbed, annihilated, lost in a largely

Jalal ad-Din Muhammad Rumi (1207–1273) was a Persian mystic and poet who believed that music, poetry, and dance could help a person connect with God.

impersonal cosmic reality. "Monistic" is the name often used to describe this second type. There are equally telling differences from one tradition to another, and it is misleading to conclude that all religious traditions come together in mysticism. Especially in instances of theistic mysticism, the subject invariably describes the object of the experience in terms distinctive of his or her tradition. For example, Christians encounter Christ and Mary, Muslims receive guidance from Muhammad, and Hindus merge in loving union with Shiva. There are surely points of important crossover in the mysticisms of the various traditions. Still the differences remain and need to be acknowledged.

How have some of the most famous mystical poets prayed?

Dozens of superb mystical poets have left a vast legacy of personal prayer in their writings. They address God with a candid reserve and a bold humility as they fashion striking metaphors of the divine-human relationship. One brief sample from the man whose followers came to be known as the "Whirling Dervishes" will have to suffice here. Jalal ad-Din Rumi (d. 1273) wrote some sixty thousand lines of Persian poetry, just over half in the form of short lyric pieces in which the lover addresses the Beloved. Here is one that captures a vivid sense of the poet's insight into the ultimate paradox.

> You who attract lovers like sugar,
> lead my soul on gently, if lead me you would.
> Death at your hand is sweet and pleasant,
> for you give vision to one who would see.
> Eagerly I await your inevitable magic,
> for it is mostly at magic-time that you lead me on.
> Unanswerable in your speech, you deal out grief-dispelling grief.
> You who scatter, fan us like sparks, lead us on.
> Your every word is a rebuff—let them roll like a torrent!
> You who have set sword at liberty, be my shield. (Divan-i Shams 3019)

What if no words come or seem appropriate?

Sometimes one cannot find the appropriate words for prayer; perhaps no words at all come trippingly to the tongue. In moments like that, heart's desire and mind's intent more than make up for whatever else seems lacking. The thirteenth-century mystical poet Rumi tells a marvelous tale about a pious Muslim who made haste one Friday toward the mosque. Muhammad was leading the community in the congregational prayer that day, and the man was particularly eager to be there with them. Arriving at the mosque, he found a crowd leaving early. When he asked the people why, they replied that he was simply too late, for Muhammad had just dismissed them with a blessing. At that the man heaved such a sigh of frustrated longing that his heart smoked ("sigh" is "heart-smoke" in Persian). One of those just leaving the mosque noticed the sigh and was so taken by it that he said, "I will trade you all of my formal prayer for that one sigh of yours." The latecomer agreed to the swap. Later that evening, as the man who accepted the sigh went off to sleep, a voice assured him, "You have bought the water of life and healing. To honor your choice, I accept the ritual prayer of all my people."

What if it feels like God does not answer prayer?

Rumi tells another story about a man who prayed devoutly, keeping vigil late into the night. Once when he began to tire and weaken in his resolve to persevere, Satan saw his chance and planted a suggestion in his weary soul. "For all your calling out 'O God,' have you ever once heard God reply, 'Here I am'?" The man had to admit he had never detected even a faint whisper in reply. God took note of all this and sent a messenger to the praying man. All of the fear and love the man had poured into his invocation, the messenger assured him, were already God's gift, unrequested and unrealized. "Beneath every 'O Lord' of yours lies many a 'Here I am' from me." No one seeks God but that God has first planted the desire to seek; the answer is prior to the question. In prayer as in so many other dimensions of the spiritual life, Abraham sets the example. Rumi notes that where there is no sighing, there is no ecstasy; and Abraham was the "sighful man" par excellence. When the patriarch prayed, his personal commitment and intensity caused his heart to bubble. You could hear Abraham praying for miles.

What is Sufism?

Sufism is a complex spiritual, devotional, intellectual, and institutional movement that traces its origins to Islam's earliest generations. The term Sufism has come to refer to the Islamic mystical tradition, but more broadly, it represents a potent tradition of Muslim knowledge and practice (in-

A Sufi man at a market in Isfahan, Iran. Sufism is a mystical tradition whose members belong to Sufi organizations in virtually every predominantly Muslim land.

cluding various forms of meditation and symbolic movement) designed to foster the individual's nearness to God.

How, in general, do Sufi sources describe the origins of Sufism?

Sufis universally trace their traditions to none other than the Prophet Muhammad via an often elaborate genealogy ("family tree," called a *silsila*) populated by Friends of God (similar to Christian saints). As early as the time of Muhammad, assorted individuals in such diverse cities as Medina, Damascus, and Baghdad developed reputations for exceptional and distinctive piety. Among the first generations of Muslims, Sufis were ascetics, spiritual athletes who strove to detach themselves from whatever distracted them from worshiping God. Garments of rough wool symbolized their desire for a simple life. Some of course considered them merely eccentric, and others felt these people were going against a Hadith that seemed to rule out such "monk-like" practices (though there are other Hadiths in which Muhammad is reported to speak highly of certain forms of asceticism.) The term Sufi came to be applied to some of those individuals, perhaps in connection with their wearing rough garments of wool (*suf* in Arabic). Out of the early ascetical movement, which arose partly as a protest against the increasingly regal style of the Umayyad caliphs, grew the beginnings of mysticism. Over the next century or so, informal circles had begun to cluster around men and women known for their sanctity. Around the end of the eighth century, a woman named Rabia appeared in Baghdad; she would become the first great mystical poet who dared speak of her loving relationship with God. A few, like Hallaj (d. 922), would die for their presumptuousness, accused of blasphemy and fatally misinterpreted, thus sharing the fate of mystics in many traditions. Within a century, more such poets appeared, speakers of Persian as well as of Arabic, all over the central Middle East. Gradually small groups of seekers began to cluster around these and other holy persons.

How did Sufism take on institutional dimensions?

Groups at first small enough to meet and even take shelter in the homes of the *shaykhs* and *shaykhas* (female spiritual guides) eventually outgrew those accommodations. Thus were initiated the first Sufi architectural designs intended to provide for all the formal and functional needs of the orders: residential, ritual, and social, including libraries and soup kitchens. These are called variously *zawiya, khanqah, tekkiye*. The earliest informal circles were the roots of what would later develop into formally constituted religious orders. Many such foundations eventually included a funerary function, beginning as the burial places of founders and later serving as cemeteries for subsequent *shaykhs* and administrators of the orders. The first of these was long traditionally attributed to the famous and still widely popular *shaykh* Abd al-Qadir al-Jilani (d. 1166), though historical research dates the earliest orders to the late tenth and early eleventh centuries in Iran. The term *tariqa,* or "personal spiritual path," originally used to describe the individual's search for God, came to refer to the formal orders. Each seeker thus became an aspirant, an initiate, and an adept within a particular Tariqa. As in the Christian tradition, many of the orders grew and spread rapidly, some splitting into sub-orders and establishing their own variant of the original founder's charism.

What role did the Sufi orders play in the spread of Islam?

Itinerant Sufis have historically been an essential link in the spread of Islam in many parts of the world. To what degree these Muslim travelers journeyed with explicit intent to spread the faith is difficult to determine, but it seems very clear that such "missionaries" had a significant impact in large regions from Africa to Southeast Asia. Often traveling with Muslim merchants, Sufi preachers generally brought an accommodating approach to introducing the faith in new cultural contexts. In places like Malaysia and Indonesia, for example, they did not insist on anything like the scorched earth eradication of pre-Islamic practices associated with some missionary protocols. Sufi preachers generally preferred a less jarring pedagogical approach that built on the beliefs and practices of the indigenous people. In many regions, various Sufi organizations ("orders," or *tariqas*) also gradually expanded the institutional reach of Sufism by establishing centers around the burial places of leaders credited with bringing Islam to these newly Islamized lands. Muslim reformers have in more recent times sought to counteract what they regard as Sufi permissiveness in this regard, by purging Islam of the "folk" beliefs and practices that they consider corrupt and idolatrous. In any case, Sufi "missionaries" have represented a generally non-violent mode of proselytization and Islamization that presents an important and largely ignored counter-narrative to more prevalent characterizations of Islam as uniformly spread "by the sword." In some parts of the world, such as the Central Asian republics that made up the southern tier of the former Soviet Union, Sufi orders have been responsible in large part for the very survival of Islam through very difficult times.

What kinds of specific practices are associated with Sufi spirituality?

Sufi traditions developed a number of spiritual disciplines and exercises designed to aid the traveler in keeping to the Path. As Muhammad needed the guidance of Gabriel on his passage to the Unseen World, so does every individual require some assistance in interpreting the signs within the self. One

Sufis played a big role in the spread of Islam, often traveling with other Muslims and explaining the faith in ways that people from other cultures could accept and understand.

of the signature practices that developed in distinctive ways within the various Sufi orders is the gathering of seekers for a prayer service known as *dhikr* ("recollection, remembrance") or *sama* ("audition"). These often complex and extended rituals typically involve recitation of the Quran, chanting of mantra-like words and phrases in Arabic, and dancing. In Cairo, for example, during festivities honoring holy personages such as members of the Prophet's family, one can find groups of people engaging in ritual dancing and chanting.

What role does Muhammad play in Islamic mystical traditions?

Muslim mystics have often interpreted Muhammad as the model for their spiritual quest. His experience of the Night Journey and Ascension became the touchstone against which some have evaluated their own experiences. Some Sufis have considered Muhammad as the ultimate *shaykh*, the celestial spiritual guide who appears in dreams to initiate individuals into the Sufi Order by conferring upon them the symbolic patched frock. The more speculative mystics have even pictured Muhammad as a cosmic being, the Perfect Person whose spiritual presence suffuses all of creation. At this end of the theological spectrum, which majority theological opinion generally regards as at least "innovation" if not outright heresy, Muhammad bears some similarity to the cosmic Christ of Ephesians.

FORGIVENESS, HOPE, COMMUNITY, AND SERVICE

Is forgiveness an important theme in Islamic spirituality?

Along with the divine names "Compassionate" (*rahman*, rah-MAAN) and "Merciful" (*rahim*, ra-HEEM), the names "Forgiver" (*ghafur*, gha-FOOR), "Forgiving" (*ghaffar*, ghaf-FAAR), "Oft-turning" or "Relenting" (*tawwab*, taw-WAAB), and "Pardoning" (*afuw*, A-fuw) are among the most used in prayer and frequently discussed by Muslim spiritual writers. A Sacred Hadith says that God descends to the lowest heaven during the third watch of each night and calls out, "Is there anyone who seeks my forgiveness, that I might forgive?" According to a Hadith, Muhammad said, "My heart is clouded until I have sought God's forgiveness seventy times day and night." Dozens of other sayings like these about both God and Muhammad appear in large sections of the great collections of Hadith dedicated to traditions about forgiveness and repentance. The term for "seeking forgiveness" from God (*istighfar*, is-tigh-FAAR) has the root meaning of asking that God "cover over" or "render ineffective" one's evil actions. The term for repentance (*tawba*) means "turning around." The Islamic sources convey a vivid sense of God's infinite patience and of the need for human beings to learn, after the example of Muhammad, to embody forbearance in their daily lives.

What motivates a believing Muslim to repent?

Ideally one's repentance arises not out of fear of a God who will exact vengeance of the sinner, a divine despot who wields the threat of eternal damnation. Fear of hell might help

A son asks his father for forgiveness during the Eid ul-Fitri, the final day of Ramadan, and a national holiday in Indonesia. Practicing forgiveness is an important part of the Islamic faith.

"jump-start" individuals who are particularly heedless, but in the long run the desired motive is the simple conviction that, as the Muslim saying goes, "God's mercy outweighs his wrath." Awareness of God's tender mercies is also a natural corrective for scrupulosity, for God taxes no soul beyond its limit and requires only that each person sincerely seek to rid his or her life of false gods, whatever shape they may take. Forgiveness is as important in human relations as in the individual's relationship with God. The Quran teaches often that one should dispense with grudges as soon as possible, insisting that even in divorce the separating partners must seek to forgive each other (2:237). Those who refuse to forgive and be reconciled with others can hardly expect that God will deal gently with them in the final accounting. A saying of Muhammad sums it all up: "If anyone continually asks pardon, God will show that person a way out of every difficulty and respite from every anxiety, with sustenance from where he least expected it."

What does "forgiveness" really mean to the individual given God's absolute control?

It would appear, at first, that if God determines all human affairs, the individual has no freedom. He or she cannot therefore be held accountable, and forgiveness, it seems, becomes meaningless. Muslim theologians have always been concerned most of all with preserving God's absolute unity, power, and transcendence from even the slightest hint of dilution. As a result, their statements about God sometimes strike non-Muslims as extreme; they seem to describe a cold despotic deity before whom human beings can only 237 cower. But the strong statements of the theologians are far more about who God is than about what human beings are not. For example, if all power and initiative belongs to God, the logical conclusion is that human beings are left with no freedom and no responsibility. From that apparently inexorable logic arises the popular conception that Muslims are entirely fatalistic. That is not quite the case. The Quran's insistence on moral accountability, the certainty of ultimate reward or punishment, and God's refusal to interfere in the details of the choices people make all clearly point to a significant measure of human freedom.

Where does the virtue of "hope" fit in the traditional Islamic scheme of things?

As in the title of the classic one-act play, so in Islamic tradition, hope is "a thing with feathers," and it follows directly from the possibility of forgiveness. One of Islam's most influential pastoral theologians, Abu Hamid al-Ghazali (d. 1111), likens fear and hope to the two wings of a bird: if either is missing or injured, the bird cannot fly. Nearly every major classic work of Islamic spiritual theology pairs hope with fear, for according to an ancient axiom, things are known by their opposites. In other words, one who knows no fear cannot truly hope. The pair work together theologically in a most intriguing fashion.

Does the tradition warn against complacency in one's relationship to God?

God is *God*, and human beings who wax nonchalant in His presence do so at their peril. One of the Quran's many descriptions of God calls Him "the best of those who scheme." References to the divine "ruse" (*makr*) are not meant to suggest that God is simply capricious and likes to trifle with His creatures, but to make it clear that God is beyond human grasp and full of surprises. Even if God says, as He does to Muhammad and Gabriel in a famous Hadith, "Have no fear, you are secure," no sane person will abandon fear entirely. Only in the context of such a healthy fear, of one's own sinfulness and God's right to be God, can one experience authentic hope in God's mercy and forgiveness.

How does Islamic tradition describe God's availability to the individual in this context?

A "Sacred Hadith," an extra-Quranic saying attributed to God rather than to Muhammad, sums up the situation beautifully. Leading naturally into the subject of prayer, God speaks:

> If anyone comes to me a hand's breadth, I will approach by an arm's length. If anyone comes to me an arm's length, I will come forward the space of outstretched arms. If anyone comes to me walking, I will come running. And if someone brings me sins the size of earth itself, my forgiveness will be more than their equal.

In images of such an available God, a God whose mercy ultimately outweighs His wrath, Muslims find great cause for hope.

How does Islamic tradition describe the social aspects of personhood—what does "community" mean?

Two important aspects of the understanding of "community" are essential here. First, traditional sources (beginning with the Quran) speak of global human community, of whatever religious affiliation. "Humankind were once a single community," says the Quran (2:213), but disagreement grew rampant because of self-centered stubbornness, and divisions multiplied. God could have kept that from happening, of course, but preferred to test humanity in this way. In an interesting twist, the Quran then turns disunity to advantage, issuing a challenge to humankind: "Therefore vie with one another in good deeds, for God is the final goal for all of you, and it is he who will clarify for you those things about which you now argue" (Quran 5:48; see also 2:148 and 23:61). Second, Muslims use the concept of *umma* to describe the global community of *Muslims*. As in other faith traditions generally, the sense of solidarity with fellow believers tends to take precedence. But the tradition calls on Muslims also to remain aware of the larger reality of the whole human race under God.

How does the concept of "service" figure in all of this?

No notion captures the Muslim view of humanity's fundamental character more aptly than that of servanthood. Every human being is essentially an *abd allah*, a "servant of God." Service is God's due. Strictly speaking, only God has "rights," one of which is the absolute right to the servanthood of His creation. Islamic law divides all human acts into two broad categories: *ibadat* (ee-baa-DAAT), or deeds of worshipfulness that are all that is expected of human beings in their relationship to God; and *muamalat* (mu-AA-ma-LAAT), deeds of reciprocity that include all aspects of societal and interpersonal relations. Service of God means primarily deeds of the heart, of course; but tradition measures those in relation to the fulfillment of ordinary religious duties and observances as in the Five Pillars. Everything else is privilege, except insofar as God confers rights on His creatures by virtue of their affinity with God. Human rights are therefore entirely relative in the bigger picture. But within that context, Islamic tradition insists that human beings do have certain God-given rights. Conscientious and responsible service is an acknowledgement of the dignity and destiny of the individual person.

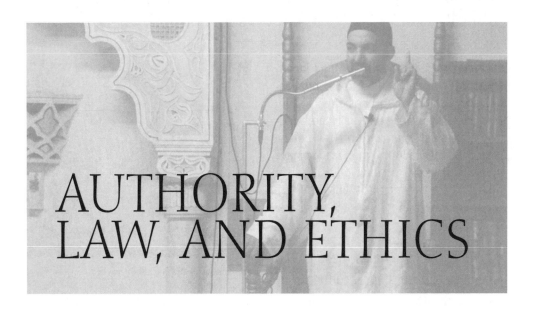

AUTHORITY, LAW, AND ETHICS

AUTHORITY ROLES AND STRUCTURES OF LEADERSHIP

What role does authority play in religious traditions generally?

At its best, religious authority provides needed guidance for individuals and functions as a moral compass for the community. It also serves as a community's backbone and a powerfully cohesive force. At its worst, religious authority, like any other kind, can be abusive and manipulative, playing on members' guilt and lack of confidence in their own sense of justice. Major religious traditions have developed a wide variety of authority structures. Some have highly centralized administrative systems, as in Roman Catholicism, the Church of Jesus Christ of Latter-day Saints (Mormons), and the main branch of Shi'i Islam. The chain of command begins with God and descends through various levels of scholars, specialists, and bureaucrats. Those at the upper levels make decisions on large questions and those down the line communicate the decisions to the people and implement them. Structures of this sort can tend toward either a monarchy or oligarchy, depending on the relative dominance of the person and office at the top. The hallmark of centralized structures is that they strive to elicit conformity from all members. At the other extreme are traditions in which authority is entirely local, centered in the village (as in tribal traditions or village Hinduism) or in the individual community place of worship or gathering (such as in churches of the Society of Friends, aka the Quakers).

What kinds of structures come between the largely centralized and mostly autonomous?

Many traditions fall somewhere in between these two extremes. They have no direct line of authority from top to bottom, but local communities can be affiliated by conventions or conferences, for example. Many Japanese Shinto shrines belong to national associations. Baptist churches often belong to national "conventions" that meet regularly to decide organization-wide policy. American Muslim community leaders have formed a national council of *imams*. In most of these cases and dozens of others like them, the majority of decisions are made locally.

An imam leads the faithful in prayer.

What does the term *imam* mean in general as applied to local contexts?

In Arabic, the word *imam* (ee-MAAM) means "one who is in front." Three distinct meanings are attached to the term. First, and most commonly, imam refers to the individual who leads the ritual prayer in the local mosque. Any mature adult can fulfill the role, and members of local communities frequently share this responsibility. Women may lead prayer and preach to groups of women only. Once local communities become large enough to have the necessary funds, they typically hire a religious scholar to serve as full-time spiritual leader with the more official title of imam (with a capital I).

How does the imam function in this instance?

An imam's overall function is roughly similar to that of the pastor of a parish church. In addition to leading the main occasions of ritual prayer, the imam instructs young people planning to marry, visits sick members of the congregation, performs funeral services, may serve as chaplain to prisoners or to some branch of the armed services as a military officer, and acts as overall administrator of the foundation. In many cases that may include oversight of a school. To assist him in his work, the community often hires secretaries, directors of education and other services, and teachers, if the mosque sponsors a school. Some *imams* in this country also engage in inter-religious activities. Even in larger congregations, other male members of the community will take turns leading the ritual prayer on days when the imam cannot be at the mosque during prayer time.

What about as a more honorific or theologically rooted title in broader settings?

Important spiritual and intellectual leaders throughout Islamic history have gained the title imam in recognition of their prominence and accomplishments—such as the medieval teacher imam al-Ghazali, globally revered even today. In those instances the title is honorary rather than functional. In addition, the term imam refers to the individuals whom the various Shi'i communities regard as spiritual descendants of Muhammad. This narrowest and most theologically technical of the various meanings is applied and interpreted in different ways by the major Shi'ite groups (Twelvers, Seveners, and Fivers). Most recently Twelver Shi'ites of Iran and Iraq bestowed the title on the Ayatollah Khomeini in a way that suggested a blend of the second and third meanings explained here.

Many Christian and Jewish communities have some sort of specially educated and even ordained clergy or officialdom entrusted with teaching and governing. Do Muslims have anything similar?

Islam has no ordained clergy as such, though some individuals do pursue special training in religious studies and law for the purpose of scholarship and local leadership in their communities. Those studies emphasize a thorough familiarity with the Quran in its original language, Arabic, with the extensive tradition of scriptural exegesis (*tafsir*) and the literature enshrining the sayings of Muhammad, and with the religious law of one of the dominant methodological schools. Larger mosques often hire an imam with special training in law or religious studies generally; but such local specialists are not ordained as such. In smaller, less-established congregations, various members of the community may take their turns in the role, chosen from among the upright and competent members of the local community to lead the prayer and to preach the Friday sermon.

How do Muslim communities find and attract *imams* to local mosques?

In the United States and Canada, many communities have sought out their *imams* from among religious scholars known to their members or individuals whose availability for service comes to be known through the "grapevine" or through ads in Islamic publications. Among the most important qualifications of an imam are fluency in both English and Arabic; solid grounding in the religious sciences of Quran and Hadith and *fiqh*; knowing the Quran by heart and developed skills in recitation; and some administrative and teaching experience. Congregations still sometimes bring in an imam from overseas, since some regard the quality of formal education in religious sciences available in places like Cairo and Saudi Arabia as highly desirable in an imam.

What are some of the main varieties of Islamic religious officials or specialists?

Islamic religious specialists are a large general class of people called *ulama* (oo-la-MAA), meaning "those who possess knowledge" (*'ilm*). An *'alim* (AA-lim, commonly used singular of *ulama*) is an individual who has done extensive study of the Quran, *tafsir* (exegetical commentary), and Hadith, for starters. Some become specialists in Quran recitation. One who memorizes the entire text and learns to "recite" it in an elaborate and demanding style called *tajwid* (taj-WEED, "embellished, excellent") is called a *qari* (KAAH-ree, "professional Quran reciter"). Some religious scholars further specialize in religious jurisprudence (*fiqh*, "understanding"). Such a scholar is called a *faqih* (fa-KEEH), "one who understands deeply," because he applies his intellect to plumb the depths of the fundamental religious sources in an effort to apply their principles to daily life. Some religious scholars routinely engage in the categorization of various acts according to their relative legal and moral acceptability. In that capacity the scholar is   243 called a *mufti* (MUF-tee), "one who issues a legal advisory called a *fatwa*" (FAT-wah). Specialists in the religious sciences often carry the honorific title of *shaykh*, "elder," a term that was reserved for tribal leaders during pre-Islamic times. Spiritual guides of the various Sufi organizations called "orders" or "paths" (*tariqa*, ta-REE-kah) also generally bear the title of *shaykh* or its Persian equivalent, *pir* (PEER).

How much variety is there in the ways religious communities in general structure their internal administrations?

Structure and organization generally relate directly to the role and shape of authority within a religious tradition. Some traditions develop various levels of organization such as denominations and sects, for example, representing a variety of structures along a spectrum from rigidly hierarchical to egalitarian. Hierarchically oriented traditions (such as Roman and English Catholicism, Twelver Shi'i Islam, or the Mormons) often feature a pyramid of power capped by a single figure who often holds enormous moral and juridical authority. Just below that leader there is sometimes a rank or two of administrators who hold jurisdiction over specified territories within the tradition's geographic expanse. In some cases those top administrators may form a deliberative body or council that advises the leader in matters of tradition-wide importance. On the next rung or two down toward the base of the pyramid there will typically be ranks of administrative and pastoral offices charged with the daily affairs of the smallest community units where most members gather. Smaller religious traditions enjoy the practical luxury of opting for more egalitarian structures with fewer administrative offices.

Whether large or small, all traditions have to deal with the practicalities of how their administrations are chosen. In some hierarchical structures the top official is elected by the members of the highest deliberative body, whose members in turn are appointees of the head. In others, such as Shi'i Islam, the process by which both the head and those next in rank are chosen is more a matter of public acclaim. In still other traditions with prominent official classification, such as temple Hinduism and Shinto, the priesthood is often associated with family and heredity and is typically entered for life.

In the most egalitarian communities, all administrators are chosen democratically, serving either for set terms of office or indefinitely at the pleasure of the local community.

Are there distinctly hierarchical structures in any branch of Islam?

Sunni Muslims constitute the vast majority of Islam's global membership. Since the generation that succeeded Muhammad, the dominant ideal of governance has been that a leader should be first among equals. Centuries of caliphal splendor might persuade a student of history that a type of monarchy was the preferred form of Islamic governance. In practice many of the most powerful Muslim rulers over the centuries have at least tried to call the shots religiously as well as politically. Nevertheless, Sunni Islam has never evolved quite the kind of hierarchical structure found, for example, in Roman Catholicism. Muslim authority structures in various countries and regions often take the form of

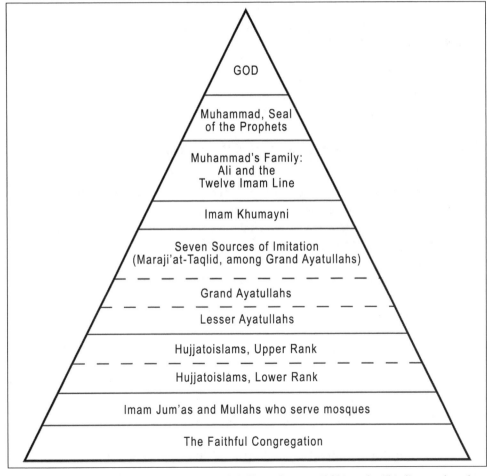

Imami Shi'ism has evolved a centralized structure in the form of a pyramidal hierarchy. This diagram shows how the different levels of authority are organized in the Islamic Republic of Iran.

councils of religious or legal scholars, or of *imams*. In practice, jurisdiction in matters of religious law and discipline is limited generally to the confines of modern nation-states.

Following a very different model, the largest branch of Shi'i Islam, Twelver or Imami Shi'ism, has evolved a much more centralized authority structure. As a result of the Iranian revolution of 1979, the Ayatollah Khomeini and his followers sought to replace a monarchy with a theocracy. They established a pyramidal hierarchy of religious authority with Khomeini at the top. He was the most influential of a number of leading ayatollahs (Sign of God) and won the title *imam* by virtue of his dominance. Below him was a cluster of "grand ayatollahs" and a larger group of lesser ayatollahs. Just beneath them were two ranks of religious scholars with the title *Hujjatolislam* (Proof of Islam), and finally the several thousand *Mullahs* (from a word that means roughly "master, reverend") who staffed the country's mosques.

What is the general meaning of the term "ayatollah"?

"Ayatollah" is Arabic for "Sign of God," an honorific title conferred on leading Shi'ite religious scholars, especially in Iran and Iraq. In traditional Shi'ite circles, accomplished scholars can attain the rank of ayatollah by popular acclaim and through the acknowledgment of their peers. Among those of that rank, "Of those, in turn, a group of seven have traditionally been singled out as "Sources of Imitation" and are thereby acknowledged as the most influential teachers among Shi'ite Muslims.

What are some other roles and functions of the ayatollah in traditional Shi'i Muslim society?

A bit of history will help here. Three terms most commonly associated with Islamic religious officialdom everywhere are these: *ulama*, a general category that refers to all "learned" in religious matters; *faqih*, referring more specifically to those who exercise the formal function of *fiqh*, jurisprudence; and *mujtahid*, a title given to the most eminent of the *ulama* who have proven themselves fit to exercise *ijtihad*, independent investigation into and articulation of religious law. The Shi'i doctrine of the Greater Concealment of the Twelfth imam required the establishment of an authority structure capable of interpreting (fallibly) the mind of the absent (infallible) imam. Hence, the exalted office of the *mujtahid*. Under the Safavid dynasty (1501–1722), *mujtahids* were few in number. Over the decades the religious institution witnessed a sort of honorific inflation, so that there are at present various ranks within the category of *mujtahid*, including two levels of *hujjatolislam*, "proof of Islam" and two grades of *ayatullah*, "sign of God," accorded by virtue of ability, constituency, etc. Readers who have followed events in the Middle East over the past decade have seen these terms often in the press.

Are ayatollahs further distinguished and given special titles and roles?

Some are accorded the title Grand Ayatollah; and among those, several at any one time might be acknowledged as "sources of imitation" (*marja-i taqlid*, mar-JAA-i taq-LEED).

Prior to the Iranian revolution, for example, Khomeini was reckoned as one of seven chief "sources of imitation." The period since the beginning of the Pahlavi dynasty (1925–1979) has witnessed a dramatic "repoliticization" of Iranian Shi'ism. That came to a head when Ruhollah Khomeini returned to Iran to proclaim the end of the Pahlavi dynasty and the beginning of the Islamic Republic of Iran. Khomeini thus became the supreme lawgiver whose authority could not be questioned, for he represented the spiritual descendants of Muhammad, the *imams*. His interpretation of Shi'ite political theology marked a major departure from the classical doctrine, according to which the religious scholars generally functioned outside of political structures, exercising often the rights of a kind of loyal opposition. The end of the Iran-Iraq war and Khomeini's death in 1989 brought new challenges to the young revolutionary nation: questions of succession, the preservation of administrative structures in the absence of the charismatic leader, and accommodation to the world outside.

METHODS AND PROCEDURES IN SACRED LAW (SHARIA)

What is the shape and purpose of religious law in general?

In its most basic form, religious law consists of whatever strictures and sanctions a tradition's sacred texts call for. Many traditions that have not developed centralized authority structures strive for the simplicity of this kind of normative scriptural orientation. Some of these, such as the greater Hindu tradition, for example, eventually include in the general category of "sacred text" a variety of documents of a distinctly legal character. A large number of other religious communities develop the equivalent of charters, constitutions, or by-laws to which they can appeal for clarification in the event that the scriptural text either does not address a particular issue at all or offers only ambiguous answers. Some, such as Islam, Judaism, and Roman Catholicism, have developed elaborate systems of religious law. This has often resulted in tension between the community's internal law and the civil law of the surrounding society. Resolution of the tension depends a great deal on the relationship of the religious authority structure to the local and regional political regime at any given time.

Where does the concept of customary law fit in this picture?

Custom, the long-standing practice of local communities even prior to the coming of a particular religious tradition, inevitably has a significant impact on the religious law of most traditions. Over the long haul, religious law may "sanctify" certain local practices not specifically mentioned in the sacred text at all. For example, in some cultures Muslim women cover their faces. And though the Quran does not explicitly call for that, many Muslims will insist that it is a religious requirement. Sometimes local custom simply replaces older, even scripturally based, practices. Roman Catholic women in the

The Quran contains some explicit regulations regarding matters of personal and social morality as well as ritual practice, but in general the Muslim scripture does not function as a legislative handbook. Very early in Islamic history, local communities faced issues about which the book rendered no explicit opinion or ruling. Then, as now, the community's most pressing challenge was how to interpret the sacred text so as to preserve its spirit and still respond to changing needs. In the earliest years, especially during the Medina period, Muhammad himself functioned as the "lawgiver" and arbiter of all significant disputes.

United States once covered their heads in church, following a specific scriptural text. Custom has changed that.

What happened to this guiding "tradition" after the Prophet's death?

While Muhammad lived, problematical issues could be decided by the Prophet's responses and clarifications. Not long after his death, what had begun as a rather informal process of preserving Muhammad's utterances in the living memory of Muslims evolved into a more formal process. To prevent the loss of Prophetic tradition, scholars went in search of Hadith (sayings or traditions) across the world. Collecting massive numbers of them, they sifted through the material, attempting to sort out the authentic from the spurious. By the end of the ninth century, Muhammad's words and deeds had been institutionalized into a number of written collections, six of which have been considered especially authoritative. These collections of Hadith came to form the second major source upon which scholars would base their decisions on the shape of Muslim life.

How did the community continue to preserve the "example" of Muhammad?

All Muslims agree on the primacy of the Quran as the source of revealed truth and on the importance of Hadith as the principal source of information about the example of the Prophet, the Sunna. Originally most Muslim scholars considered Sunna virtually coextensive with Hadith: all that one could know, or needed to know, about the Prophet's example, one could find in the collected sayings. Gradually the notion of Sunna expanded to include not only Muhammad's reported words and anecdotes about his deeds, but the actual living practice of a given community of believers. And that growing attitude was in turn based on a Hadith in which Muhammad is reported to have said, "My community will not agree on an error." It followed naturally that the community, striving in good faith to live out the Sunna of the Prophet, literally embodied a living Sunna that already presupposed an interpretation of Muhammad's example. In simple terms, the community strove to live as Muhammad surely would "if he were here now."

248

How did this shift to the "exemplary community" alter the process of implementing the Sharia in changing circumstances?

With this expanding notion of Sunna, from the example of Muhammad himself to the "lived behavior" of a community acting in good faith, a third source of religious law, after Quran and Hadith, began; namely, the consensus or agreed practice of the faithful. Eventually consensus, called *ijma* (ij-MAA), became a technical tool for extending the applicability of the revealed law. If a question arose upon which neither Quran nor Hadith made any specific statement, one could seek the solution in the actual practice of the community. The idea is not terribly unlike the classical Roman Catholic notion of *sensus fidelium*, the "conviction of the faithful." It is a grass-roots elaboration of how religious persons live out their commitments.

How did Islamic religious law evolve?

As the young community grew and established itself in Medina, it became increasingly necessary for Muhammad to address countless questions of order and acceptable practice. Some of the later texts of the Quran deal with specific issues, such as how to pray, what foods and activities to avoid, and how to observe basic social relationships. After Muhammad died and the Arab armies expanded into new territories and encountered new cultures and religious communities, the Muslims had to confront countless problems previously unknown: How would they deal with issues that neither the Quran nor the Hadith addressed? Local Muslim leaders often had to improvise, exercising their best personal judgment and acting as they believed Muhammad would have done. They strove to perpetuate the Prophet's example, his *sunna*. But authorities and leading scholars in Medina, and later in other cities, looked for ways to standardize the procedure of extending the application of Quran and Hadith to changing circumstances. They gradually agreed that one could solve problems not treated directly in Quran and Hadith by appealing to the "actual practice" of the local community or to the "consensus" (*ijma'*, ij-MAA) of legal scholars. But since some questions were too new for any consensus to have developed, scholars agreed that one could apply a form of "reasoning by analogy" (*qiyas*, kee-YAAS) that followed strict rules so as to keep the process as free of personal whim as possible. Leading legal scholars in different cities devised slightly different formulas for using the four "roots" of the law (Quran, Hadith, Consensus, and Analogical Reasoning), some allowing greater latitude in appealing to the third and fourth roots. Four legal methodologies dominant among Sunni Muslims came to be called the "schools" (*madhhabs*), while several other distinctively Shi'i schools eventually developed as well.

What is the "division of labor" in this system of religious law?

Some legal specialists rise to greater prominence because of their erudition, earning the title *mujtahid* (MUJ-ta-hid, "one who exercises independent investigation" of the sacred sources). In Sunni tradition, the "door of independent investigation" closed by the year 900, making further bold scholarship of this level unnecessary. According to

249

that classical view, the founders of the four major Sunni schools of legal theory were the last *mujtahids*. But in Shi'i tradition, the highest ranking ayatollahs continue to exercise the authority of *mujtahids*. In both traditions, it is up to scholars to offer rulings on controversial or contemporary issues. If a new ethical and legal question arises—a question of artificial life support or some other thorny bio-medical matter, for example—a legal scholar would search the relevant sources to determine whether the Quran or Hadith might shed light on the precise issue at hand. If the scholar found only vague parallels that offer insufficient evidence to make a firm ruling on the new problem, he would then study further to see whether in the actual practice of Muslim communities there was an approach that might solve the problem. If the problem is too new to have any kind of useful history, the scholar might appeal to reasoning by analogy, looking for a "link" between ancient sources and practice and the new problem. Ancient sources may say nothing about artificial life support, but they have much to say about the nature of human life and about human authority to intervene.

What is an example of how all this works in practice?

Suppose that an issue arose upon which neither the Quran nor Hadith nor actual practice could shed definitive light. What then? In the earliest days of the Islamic expansion, the religious judges (*qadi*) appointed to oversee the ordinary affairs of communities in newly conquered territory were accorded considerable latitude in the exercise of "individual judgment" (*ra'y*). Many scholars were concerned that the practice was too fluid and easy prey to the unbridled use of personal opinion. As a result, the more informal process of *ra'y* was gradually forged into the more rigorous and tightly controlled tool of reasoning called analogy (*qiyas*), somewhat like what lawyers today call "argument from precedent." A rough example might be crack cocaine. Neither Quran nor Hadith specifically mention such a thing, and since it has never before surfaced in the local community, one can find no "living Sunna" about the matter. One can then, as a last resort, appeal to analogy. Crack cocaine impairs one's rational faculties. Both Quran and Hadith make it clear that intoxicants are forbidden. In addition, the practice of the local

---

What's a *fatwa*?

On the basis of his research, the scholar might issue a legal advisory called a *fatwa*. In that statement he would indicate which of five ethico-legal categories the proposed course of action (say, disconnecting life support in a particular case) belonged: forbidden, discouraged, neutral, recommended, or required. Acting upon the advisory, the parties to the case might then choose to bring the matter before a religious judge called a *qadi* (KAA-dee, himself authorized as a *mufti*) to adjudicate the matter. The outcome of all this study and interpretation is called *Shari'a* (sha-REE-ah), the divinely revealed law or way of life prescribed for all Muslims.

community has steadfastly refused to allow such destructive behavior. One can therefore conclude, on the basis of the "link" between an unknown and a known, that revealed law condemns the use of crack cocaine. Taken together, Quran, Sunna—as enshrined both in the Hadith and the community—consensus, and analogical reasoning came to be called the four roots of religious law.

Do all Muslims interpret the law in exactly the same way?

Evidence of some variation in legal method dates back to the late seventh century. The community as a whole began elaborating various interpretative principles and procedures. Schools of legal methodology came into being, each with its own peculiar emphasis on one or another aspect of juristic thinking. As the initially all–Arab Muslim community came into contact with an ever wider range of ethnic groups and cultural settings, the need to be able to address new problems grew. Since each culture and ethnic group the Muslims met already had its own legal and religious history, the Muslims had to find ways to put their stamp on the conquered territory without destroying what they found there. They thus had to learn how to incorporate the "customary" law of the place, extending the umbrella of their own system so as to allow the conquered peoples some latitude of practice.

How did traditional loyalties and changing cultural contexts influence variety and flexibility of legal method?

As one might expect, a city like Medina, whose people considered themselves custodians of the original legacy of Muhammad, would naturally tend toward a more cautious and conservative approach. Meanwhile in territories such as Syria and Iraq, the conquering Muslim armies had been posted as a matter of policy away from the major existing cities, in newly founded garrison towns. Eventually such sites grew into cities of importance in their own right. In Iraq, for example, there were Basra and Kufa; across Egypt and North Africa, there was Fustat near modern day Cairo and Qayrawan in Tunisia. Located as they were in areas more culturally and ethnically diverse than the Arabian Peninsula, these cities frequently—though not always—fostered more innovative and flexible approaches to religious issues.

When and how did the system become further diversified?

By the end of the ninth century, about the time the major authoritative written collections of Hadith had come into being, several distinctive schools of jurisprudence had formed. Four Sunni schools remain active today. Each traces its origins back to a founding figure. Abu Hanifa (d. 767 c.e.) lived and worked in the Iraqi town of Kufa. His school or *madhhab* ("way of proceeding," MADH-hab), the Hanafi or Hanafite, developed a somewhat greater tolerance for the use of analogy than the other schools. Today the Hanafi is the dominant school in Turkey, India, and Pakistan. At the other end of the spectrum stands the school named after Ibn Hanbal (d. 855). A major figure in the religious and intellectual life of ninth-century Baghdad, Ibn Hanbal debated with the Mutazilites over their elevation of reason to a position above divine revelation. The harder the Mutazilites pushed, the harder Ibn Hanbal pushed back, so that the two sides grew further and further apart. Over the next century or so, the more conservative and traditional approach of Ibn Hanbal became the order of the day. Hanbali influence in modern times is limited to the Arabian Peninsula, where it has virtually no competition from other *madhhabs*.

If the Hanafi and Hanbali schools represent ends of the methodological spectrum, what's in between?

Between the Hanafi and Hanbali schools stand the Shafii, named after Shafii (d. c. 819), and the Maliki, founded by Malik ibn Anas (d. 795). Though there are no hard and fast distinctions in the ways they differ from the other schools—and the history of Islamic legal decisions is full of unexpected surprises—the Maliki may be a bit more conservative than the Shafii in some respects. The former functions largely in Southeast Asia and parts of Egypt, the latter mostly in North Africa. On the whole, Islamic jurisprudence seeks to strike a balance between individual and community, in terms of needs, rights and responsibilities, and legislative authority.

What is a good summation of the range of opinions and interpretations possible in Islamic law?

As in every system of religious law, Muslim jurists and their rulings have historically balanced a variety of "tensions" built into the decision-making process. First, the relationship between Revelation and Reason: Here the key question is how to address issues not explicitly and obviously addressed in the sacred sources without in effect setting up

Are there separate Shi'i legal schools?

The name "Jafari" is often used to refer to several distinct schools within the various Shi'i communities, after Jafar as-Sadiq, whom the vast majority of Shia recognize as the legitimate Sixth imam. Shi'i legal scholars developed at least several major law schools, of which one currently dominates the scene in Iran. That school, called the Usuli (based on "principles") or Mujtahidi, emphasizes the requirement for every Muslim to subscribe to the teaching of a particular living *mujtahid*, a legal scholar authorized to exercise independent legal investigation, called *ijtihad*. Whereas, at least in theory, Sunni legal tradition has claimed that the "door of *ijtihad* "swung closed around 900 C.E., Shi'i jurisprudence has consistently taught the need of ongoing elaboration and reinterpretation. Two other schools, now "dormant" and of lesser import today, are called the Shaykhi and the Akhbari.

some human agent as an independent lawgiver who acts on the notion that even *God* is bound to be "reasonable." Second, the "big picture" of the evolution of Islamic law evidences a tension between the *ideal* of global Muslim unity and the *reality* of diversity—cultural, political, linguistic, for starters. Muhammad himself referred to the fact of divergence of opinion even amid the most unified of human communities.

Ideally, Sharia is a comprehensive system meant to establish an ideal society; realistically, the judgments of Muslim jurisprudence are part of larger social and cultural complexities. But the Prophet called difference of opinion a "mercy," and an ancient Arabic proverb says that one who does not understand diversity inherent in jurisprudence (*fiqh*) "has not caught its scent." A third spectrum is that between authoritarianism and liberality in rendering legal judgment. Scholars have discussed at length how free a jurist might be from the expectation of abiding by "traditional judgment" (*taqlid*, tak-LEED, uncritical acceptance on the authority of others) in formulating, on the one hand, a "true" legal judgment and, on the other hand, how much emphasis to place on the theological concept of "divine tolerance" (*ibaha*, ee-BAA-ha) in matters not explicitly treated in earlier legal decisions. Finally, Muslim jurists have had to balance the desire for stability with the fact of continual change in human experience.

"Divine" law is by definition "eternally valid," but applying it as such presents major problems in a changing world. When change is clearly needed, therefore, Islamic law has evolved a variety of principles of adaptation designed to soften the harsh edge of law too rigidly enforced. An excellent example is the principle of "public welfare" or "common good," which seeks to avoid harm to the larger community in the process of meting out punishments to individual members of the community.

Is there a central teaching authority for Muslims?

No single individual or institution has universal authority over the global Islamic community. For Sunni Muslims the nearest approximation to centralized teaching authorities are religiously affiliated educational institutions in Egypt and Saudi Arabia, venerable and influential for very different reasons. Cairo's al-Azhar, founded in 972 by the Isma'ili (Sevener Shi'ite) Fatimid dynasty, has worn the mantle of religious prestige and authoritative conservatism since it was converted by Saladin and his dynasty (after 1171) for the task of defending the cause of Sunni Islam. In Saudi Arabia, educational institutions of Mecca and Medina have come to share in al-Azhar's prestige in modern times. Young men seeking careers in religious studies come from all over the world, looking forward to returning home with credentials from these institutions.

In current practice, do jurists claim that their rulings are "universally binding"?

Nowadays, a senior jurist somewhere might on very rare occasions issue a legal advisory (*fatwa*) claiming universal force, so that every Muslim ought to abide by it. The Ayatollah Khomeini, for example, delivered an order that writer Salman Rushdie should receive the death penalty for blasphemy, and Usama bin Ladin called for a jihad against the

253

Shaikh Ali Gomaa (center), the Grand Mufti of Egypt, meets with Rev. Dr. Bishop Mouneer Hanna, Head of the Anglican Church in the Middle East and North Africa (left) and Foreign Office Minister Alistair Burt in London, England. A grand mufti is the most senior religious authority in a given country.

United States. But rare claims of that sort do not have the binding authority of a centralized institution like the papacy. In various parts of the world, religious scholars join together for consultative purposes. In the United States, for example, a council of *imams* holds regular gatherings to discuss practical and pastoral problems that arise in local communities. Elsewhere, muftis in a given region sometimes submit their decisions to the further judgment of a "grand *mufti*," who exercises jurisdiction in religious matters.

What are some examples of how religious scholars have responded to problematic events of recent times?

A total of 170 specialists from over thirty-five countries participated in the International Islamic Conference in Amman, the Hashemite Kingdom of Jordan, under the title "True Islam and Its Role in Modern Society." The conference convened July 4–6, 2005—shortly (and purely by coincidence) before the horrific public transportation bombings in London. They were building on the legal advisories (*fatwas*) issued by a host of respected legal scholars including the Grand imam Shaykh of Cairo's al-Azhar, Iraqi Grand Ayatollah Sayyid Ali al-Sistani, the Grand Mufti of Egypt, major Shi'i clerics of both Shi'i law schools, the Grand Mufti of the Sultanate of Oman, the Islamic Fiqh Academy in the Kingdom of Saudi Arabia, the Turkish Council for Religious Affairs, the Grand Mufti of the Hashemite Kingdom of Jordan and members of Jordan's National Fatwa Committee, and the eminent Egyptian Shaykh Dr. Yusuf al-Qaradawi. The conference took its cue from the opening remarks of Jordan's King Abdullah II bin al-Hussein about the need to deliberate as a unified conference even though they represented diverse groups of Muslims. Just beneath the surface was the desire to address the problem of the proliferation of non-authoritative *fatwas*, and they did so in the larger context of a perceived disunity among Muslims.

What was the first matter of concern that formed the basis of these scholars' conclusions?

Their first concern was to address the unacceptable tendency to be critical of other Muslims who belonged to "other" legal schools. They affirmed that anyone who belongs to *any* of the legal schools—whether the four Sunni Schools of Jurisprudence (Hanafi, Maliki, Shafii, and Hanbali), the Jafari (Twelver Shi'i) School of Jurispru-

Ayatollah Hosein Nuri-Hamadani is a leading conservative Shi'ite cleric in Iran. Ayatollahs are at the top of the hierarchy of Shi'ite religious authority.

dence, the Zaydi School of Jurisprudence, the Ibadi School of Jurisprudence, or the Zahiri School of Jurisprudence—is to be acknowledged as a Muslim. In other words, they rejected any claim that any such person be called an *apostate* and affirmed that all such individuals' lives, honor, and property are inviolable. In addition, they held unassailable the theological views of adherents to the Ashari creed, Sufis, and true Salafis—all three groups that have historically been targets of harsh judgment. Finally, all those who believe in Allah and His Messenger and the pillars of faith, respect the pillars of Islam, and do not deny any necessary article of religion are worthy of calling themselves Muslims.

Why did they find it so necessary to begin with this affirmation of unity?

Because these scholars wanted to make clear that the various schools of thought are united by more common values than they are divided by technical or methodological details, to emphasize that the position their deliberations led to were unanimous. They affirmed that all eight schools of jurisprudence agree on all basic Islamic principles: belief in Allah the Mighty and Sublime, the One and the Unique, whose revealed word is the Quran; and that Muhammad is a Prophet and Messenger unto all mankind. All are in agreement about the Five Pillars of Islam: the "two testaments of faith" (*shahadatayn*, sha-HAA-da-TAYN), the ritual prayer (*salat*), almsgiving (*zakat*), fasting the month of Ramadan (*sawm*), and the Hajj to the "Sacred House." All are also in agreement about the foundations of belief: belief in Allah, His Angels, His Scriptures, His Messengers, and in the Day of Judgment, in Divine providence—good and evil. They noted that any disagreement among religious scholars pertains only to the "branches of religion" (*furu*) and not the principles and fundamentals (*usul*), and that any such disagreement is in fact a sign of divine mercy.

Was this an attempt at moving toward a centralized authority?

Not exactly, in that the conference acknowledged the *de facto* multiplicity of "schools"; but it was an expression of concern that Muslims express solidarity in the essential matter of religious law. The scholars underscored that all schools adhere to the same legal and ethical principles, a single methodology, when issuing *fatwas*, and insisted that no one may issue a *fatwa* without the requisite personal qualifications that each school of jurisprudence defines. No one may issue a *fatwa* without adhering to the methodology of the schools of jurisprudence. No one may claim to do absolute *Ijtihad* and create a new school of jurisprudence or to issue unacceptable *fatwas* that take Muslims out of the principles and certainties of the Sharia and what has been established in respect of its Schools of Jurisprudence. Here they clearly intended a critique of the unfounded claims to juristic authority of none other than Usama bin Ladin.

How did the conference frame its central message and conclusions?

The conference leaders prominently noted their deliberations on the "Night of Power" (traditionally the night on which Muhammad received his initial Quranic revelation), and that they had sought maximum fairness, moderation, mutual forgiveness, compassion, and engaging in dialogue with others, and called upon Muslims to disavow all discord and outside interference between them. In acknowledgement of the Palestinian struggle, they recommended exerting all possible efforts for the protection of the Al-Aqsa Mosque in Jerusalem against the dangers and encroachments it is exposed to. This can only be done through putting an end to occupation and through the liberation of holy places. Through their admittedly rare united front as representatives of "genuine" Islam, they sought to deal a blow to advocates of terror, by agreeing on what they considered sound theological reasons for rejecting calls to violence by the likes of bin Ladin, whom they condemned as superficial and un-Islamic, not least of all because such people so often target Muslims as readily as non-Muslims by *proclaiming* them unbelievers. Hence the need to reaffirm that nobody who accepts Islam's basic beliefs should be denied the label of Muslim. So doing, the scholars sought to disenfranchise and counteract the shrill voices who condemn outright anyone who disagrees with them. While these schools' leaders will never concur on everything, they recognized each other's authority in their respective communities and resolved to deny authority to anybody who purports to be a scholar but lacks the training.

What was the greatest service these scholars performed for Muslims and non-Muslims?

They attempted, for the first time in centuries, to restore mutual respect among Muslims of divergent and often highly critical opinions. Their call for unity was also aimed at trying to bring peace to Iraq, where Sunni Muslim insurgents were attacking their fellow Muslims because they regarded Shia as weak Muslims at best and heretics at worst. They also made clear that Usama bin Laden's 1998 *fatwa* condemning to death all "Crusaders and Zionists" was invalid and totally unacceptable. That document cited the Quranic verse "slay the pagans wherever you find them, seize them, beleaguer them, lie in wait for them with every stratagem" as mandate to attack Westerners and Jews. The scholars implicitly argued that this and similar verses were revealed when Muhammad had been ambushed by enemies after signing a treaty.

FUNDAMENTAL ETHICAL PRINCIPLES

The phrase "Judeo-Christian ethic" has become a common American expression. Is there an "Islamic ethic," and if so how does it compare with the "Judeo-Christian ethic"?

People who seek to live out the Judeo-Christian ethic are actually espousing a Judeo-Christian-Islamic ethic. Christians and Jews are often shocked when it is suggested that Islam's basic ethical teachings are entirely consistent with those of Judaism and Christianity. Their surprise, it turns out, usually arises out of the unfair association of Muslims with violence in news reports on the Middle East. Of course, the *theologies* behind them are both different and distinctive, but the practical ramifications are entirely compatible. To begin with, Islam, like virtually every major religious tradition, has its version of the "Golden Rule," enshrined in a saying of Muhammad: "None among you is a believer until he wishes for his brothers what he wishes for himself." But as in Judaism and Christianity, the fundamental requirements are far more demanding than that. Islamic tradition does not have a "decalogue" as such, but it most definitely demands all of that and more as its "ethical minimum." In fact, the moral injunction to "command the good and forbid the evil" goes a step further than the saying familiar to most Christians, "do good and avoid evil."

Is there anything in Islamic tradition similar to the Judeo-Christian "Ten Commandments"?

Quran 17:23–39 offers a similar "list" whose main points can be summed up like this:
1. Worship only the One True God.
2. Treat your father and mother kindly and respectfully.
3. Give generously to family, the poor, and travelers.
4. Do not kill your children in hopes of avoiding poverty.
5. Do not commit adultery.
6. Do not kill.
7. Honor all promises and commitments.

257

One of the most important things for all good Muslims to do is to remember God every day of one's life. A happier life comes with keeping God's present in everything one does.

8. Treat all with honesty.
9. Be mindful that you will be called to account for your choices and deeds.
10. Avoid pride and hypocrisy.

Many Muslim commentators on the sacred text have noted that these principles are congruent with other ethical traditions and represent a kind of ethical minimum.

Is there an Islamic concept of sin?

Islam's teachings on sin and final accountability are highly developed. The essential sin is that of forgetfulness of God, the heedlessness that can gradually stifle the voice of conscience until it becomes but a "distant call" (Quran 41:44). Forgetfulness of God leads directly to forgetfulness of one's inmost self. Remembrance of God (*dhikr*) affects personal integration and balances the tension between power and powerlessness, hope and despair, knowledge and ignorance, and freedom and determinism. Prospects for the individual in Islam are thoroughly positive so long as one grants the need for reverent awe in God's presence, so long as one acknowledges that God's mercy will overcome his wrath. God will burden no person beyond his or her capacity to persevere.

What about the concept of "original sin" and consequent need for "redemption"?

Islam rejects the notions of hereditary original sin and redemption because human beings are directly responsible. Adam and Eve sinned, but humankind has not inherited their guilt. No human action makes the slightest personal difference to God; the moral quality of each individual's choices turns on their ultimate benefit to the human race. It is not God, therefore, but the individual who decides his or her own final destiny. Those who make their choices in this life in isolation from the needs of the human community as a whole will fashion their own hell hereafter. Those who delude themselves into thinking their choices have created mountains will see them reduced to a particle of sand. One of the terms the Quran frequently uses to describe greed, selfishness, and sinfulness generally is "going nowhere fast" (*dalal*, da-LAAL, aimlessness, wandering in error).

What are some traditional criminal sanctions in Islamic law?

Within the sphere of penal law, death is warranted for apostasy and for highway robbery; amputation of the hand for theft; death by stoning for sexual relations outside of marriage when the offender is married and one hundred lashes if the offender is unmarried; and eighty lashes for the drinking of an intoxicant or for an unproved accusation of unchastity. Civil offenses against the person—homicide, for example, or assault—are punishable by retaliation, with the offender subjected to the same treatment as the victim. In such civil cases, only the victim or his family has the right to prosecute since the crime is not considered to be against the state. Often, the victim will choose monetary compensation (*diya*, "blood money") in place of retaliation. Few predominantly Muslim societies today enact the traditional penalties as originally enjoined.

Is it accurate that Islam is "fatalistic" in nature and that "predestination" is a key concept for Muslims?

Many people, Muslim and non-Muslim alike, tend toward this general characterization of the Islamic ethical tradition, but the situation is much more complex and nuanced. An ancient proverb captures the dilemma: Anyone who denies that God is all-powerful is an unbeliever, but anyone who denies being a sinner is a liar. This deceptively simple statement combines two logically incompatible religious truths in a stark contrast. Yes, basic Islamic teaching (like fundamental Christian and Jewish teaching) insists that God is omnipotent, and by implication, completely free to act as God wishes. Logically speaking this leaves no power or freedom of action for human beings. But the saying does not stop there. It insists that no human being can argue that he or she is therefore "off the hook" ethically because "God made me do" whatever evil he or she has done. In other words, every Muslim must find a way to reconcile two large but seemingly contradictory truths in order to be a genuine person of faith and moral responsibility.

The result is that one believes that *ultimate* power and freedom belong only to God, but that, at the same time, human beings are given sufficient freedom of choice to remain accountable for their actions. To believe otherwise would be to imply that God is a tyrant, predetermining every aspect of human action and still reserving the right to punish humans with hellfire (or to reward them with heaven, for that matter) even when they had *no choice* in the matter. And Muslims refuse to attribute such caprice and unfairness to a merciful God.

BIOMEDICAL AND REPRODUCTIVE ETHICS AND LEGAL ISSUES

What general issues concerning abortion distinguish the four major Sunni "schools of law"?

The Quran (23:12–14) speaks of a four-stage physical development of the fetus in the womb. These stages were elaborated, according to several Hadiths, by the Companion Ibn Masud in the following way: First the semen is gathered in the womb for forty days before becoming a "clot of blood." Forty days later it becomes a "clump of flesh." Finally, after another forty days, bones and other recognizably "human" features develop, and the soul is implanted. From this "raw data" Muslim jurists have developed a wide range of legal prescriptions. There is general agreement that after ensoulment at 120 days, abortion is forbidden. For representatives of the Hanafi school, abortion before 120 days is typically condoned, though some require the existence of a compelling "justification." The Hanbali school is somewhat more restrictive. While some jurists of this school have ruled as the Hanafi, most Hanbali jurists permit abortion only before the forty-day mark, when the contents of the womb are recognized no longer as semen, but as a forming (if not yet formed) human being. The Maliki school is the most restrictive, where debate centers on whether abortion is permitted at all after coitus or if it is allowed until forty days. Shafii opinion is the most diverse on this issue. Members of this school can be found taking all of the above positions.

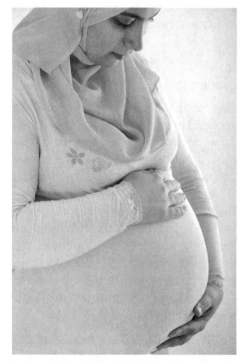

In Sunni "schools of law" it is believed than ensoulment of a fetus occurs at 120 days after conception. Therefore, in some cases, abortion before 120 days may be allowed.

What other specific critical issues about abortion are of concern to Muslims?

Besides the questions of "if" and "when" an abortion is allowed is the determination of the nature of the situation itself. Jurists typically do not regard the abortion of even an ensouled fetus as equivalent to the murder of a live-born child, and abortion is considered preferable when it will save the mother's life. In the most extreme cases, therapeutic abortions may be allowed after ensoulment in order to protect the mother's life and health, employing the principle that one should choose the lesser of two evils. In such a case established tradition holds that the mother's life takes priority over that of even a fully developed fetus, since the mother has responsibilities and obligations not yet incurred by a fetus. In a case where testing reveals defects in the fetus, a physician may not disclose them or act upon them except in so far as they threaten the mother's life.

For the majority of jurists, who forbid early, "pre-ensouled" abortions, the severity of what they view as an offense is typically thought to increase with each successive stage of fetal development as this is understood from the Hadith above—that is, as the fetus becomes "more human," its abortion becomes a more serious sin. For only a handful of jurists does abortion ever approach the opprobrium of murder, and then only when it occurs late enough in pregnancy for the fetus to be considered viable (typically around six months gestation).

But there are other concerns besides the bourgeoning life of the fetus that drive Muslim legal opinions on this matter. Some rule against early abortion in consideration of the parents or the community. Abortion, motivated (as it so often is) by fear that the child could not be cared for properly, is considered a manifestation of faithlessness in God's provision and is condemned on those grounds. Other jurists find that abortion for the sake of convenience or a desire to avoid responsibility is a betrayal of the Muslim faith community, which has an interest in growing its numbers. In an interesting example of interreligious convergence, at a recent world conference in Cairo, this issue became unexpected common ground uniting Muslims with representatives from the Vatican.

What do Muslims generally think about birth control?

Islamic tradition has nearly always considered some form of birth control acceptable under certain specific circumstances. *Coitus interruptus*, for example, so long as both parties agree to its use, is permissible, especially in view of concerns over anticipated financial problems in caring for a larger family. In more recent times concern over population growth has raised awareness, except in very rural areas, of the need for family planning. But many traditionalist teachers condemn any form of birth control because it invites promiscuity and, indirectly when it fails, increases demands for abortion.

What about other ethical questions concerning human reproduction, such as *in vitro* fertilization and surrogate motherhood or fatherhood?

In vitro fertilization with subsequent insertion of the ovum in the biological mother's uterus is considered an acceptable medical solution to a problem such as blockage of the fallopian tubes. On the topic of surrogate motherhood, Islamic law considers the placing of a man's sperm in the womb of a woman other than his wife the equivalent of adultery even if the sperm is placed there by a medical procedure. (Minority opinion now allows that medical implantation removes the stigma of adultery but that the procedure is still unacceptable because of the separation of parental responsibilities and the implications for inheritance legislation.) In addition, such an arrangement might also involve sexual abuse of the husband of the woman who has agreed to bear the child, since while his wife is pregnant with someone else's child, her husband's right to conceive with her is denied. Even in a case where a fertilized ovum is inserted in the womb of a surrogate mother, Islamic law considers the woman who actually gives birth to the child its legal mother, so that those who contributed the procreative material have no legal claim. Therefore, a child thus born is considered illegitimate. In short, Islamic law disallows any version of surrogate parenting and considers all contracts for such agreements invalid. Any attempt to transfer parenthood of a child brought to birth by an outside party is regarded as selling a human being, a serious offense. Two of the problems around surrogacy are the implications for adoption and the child's right to know his or her parentage.

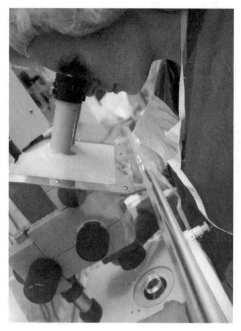

While *in vitro* fertilization has become an accepted medical procedure among Muslims, surrogate parentage is still considered adultery and is forbidden.

Do Muslims have explicit teachings about other problems in medical ethics?

Since there is no central teaching body or authority for the world's Muslims, there is no single "official" position on these matters to which all are expected to adhere. Nevertheless, contemporary Muslim religious scholars are addressing the thorny issues raised with technological and scientific change as it relates to health and mortality. As they address the problems these scholars are engaging in the Islamic analogy to Christian "moral theology" or "theological ethics," attempting to interpret the sources of the tradition in light of contemporary experience—and vice versa. And the practical outcome is religious law. Muslim religious law recognizes a spectrum of five categories used to characterize human acts. At the opposite ends of the spectrum are acts considered either "required" or "forbidden"; squarely in the middle are those considered moral and legally neutral; and to either side of those indifferent acts are those labeled either "recommended" or "disapproved."

How much, if any, unanimity exists among scholars in deciding such questions?

Not all religious scholars will necessarily arrive at the same conclusion as to the categories in which all questionable acts belong, since both Sunni and Shi'i Muslims recognize several variations in legal methodology. What is important here is that moral decisions are highly nuanced. Still more important is the fundamental notion that the human body is not merely a highly sophisticated machine that functions according to a set of mechanical and chemical laws, but a vessel of the spirit that has its own needs in addition to its spiritual function. The prime ethical responsibility of both the individual person and those involved in health care is to base all decisions on an assessment that balances both the rights accorded a human body in Islamic law (rights to food and shelter, for example) and the ultimate purpose of the body.

What about "gender reassignment surgery"?

It comes as a considerable surprise to many to hear that contemporary Iran leads Muslim countries by a huge margin in the legal provision of gender reassignment surgery. Given Iranian officials' much-publicized condemnation of, for example, homosexuality, many people simply assume that anything even remotely related to sexual identity would be equally taboo. On the contrary, Iranian Shi'ite theologians have ruled that individuals medically judged to be genuinely suffering from trans-sexuality and other serious gender identification problems have a religious and legal right to seek to rectify the situation surgically. As early as 1963, Ayatollah Khomeini declared in a *fatwa* that there was no theological impediment to gender reassignment, and his successor Ali Khamenei reaffirmed the earlier position. As a result, Muslims from many lands have made their way to Iran for the surgery.

In this age of AIDS, Muslims are surely affected as deeply by its scourge as others. Are there distinctively Islamic approaches to the problem?

In some regional populations in central Africa with heavy concentrations of Muslims, incidence of AIDS has been tragically high, but Muslims everywhere are and will continue to be affected by the AIDS crisis. Like their non-Muslim brothers and sisters, Muslims too have to continually summon up reserves of compassion and struggle against the temptation to be judgmental toward persons with AIDS. Like some Christians, some Muslims are inclined to interpret the incidence of the disease as divine punishment for immoral behavior. But since it is clear that AIDS does not respect many boundaries, Muslims face the challenge of helping to turn the tide of a major threat to the societies in which they live, wherever they may be. The majority opinion among religiously engaged Muslims is simply this: sexual promiscuity and the use of illegal drugs, the kinds of voluntary behavior often responsible for the spread of AIDS, are unacceptable and Muslims have a duty to counsel against them. People who are aware that individuals they know have engaged in high-risk activities have a responsibility to recommend screening. In short, the majority Muslim view concerning AIDS calls for compassion, understanding, and prayer along with active social concern wherever that is clearly warranted.

FAMILY LAW AND ETHICAL ISSUES

Can Muslims get divorced? Do they have to go through the same legal procedures as other Americans if they live here?

Islamic tradition has always recognized and allowed for divorce under certain specific circumstances, although according to tradition, God considers divorce the most hateful of all licit acts. Husband and wife can divorce by mutual consent, a relatively simple procedure. A wife can also initiate a divorce proceeding for cause, including a variety of marital "defects," among which are impotence, apostasy, and insanity. A husband can divorce his wife by means of a triple repudiation in a process that ordinarily takes several months. He must wait three menstrual periods to ascertain that his wife is not pregnant, pronouncing the repudiation each month. If she is pregnant, he must wait for a period after the child is born. The couple can reconcile if the husband does not complete the three repudiations. In some countries, authorities have sought to build in further safeguards for women by situating the practice firmly within a juridical context. Syrian law discourages easy repudiation by requiring husbands to continue to provide support to

Divorce is allowed among Muslims under certain circumstances—such as apostasy, insanity, and impotence—and if husband and wife both consent. A husband must wait for his wife to go through three menstrual cycles to make sure she is not pregnant before the divorce can proceed.

a wife for at least a year after divorce. Muslims who live in the United States must also abide by civil law in obtaining a legal divorce.

Do Muslims ever marry outside their faith? How do they deal with "mixed marriages"?

After his first wife died, Muhammad himself married Christian and Jewish women. At least one important Quranic text addresses the issue and allows the Prophet the liberty to do so (5:5). Some of the women became Muslims, some did not. Many historians consider Muhammad's practice the exception rather than the rule, justifiable in the interest of social reconstruction and establishing necessary "political" alliances. From later Islamic history as well come significant examples of prominent Muslim rulers marrying non-Muslim women, including Hindus and others clearly not included among the "People of the Book." Majority opinion among the classic legal schools holds that, though it is a less than ideal situation, Muslim men may marry non-Muslim women, but Muslim women may not marry non-Muslim men.

Does polygamy have ancient roots in Muslim tradition?

The practice of polygamy—or more precisely, polygyny, marriage to "many women"—in the Middle East predates Islam by many centuries, with several major Biblical figures (Abraham, David, Solomon) among the most celebrated polygynists. With Islam came a systematic regulation on the practice in the Arabian peninsula. The Quran states fairly unambiguously that a man may marry up to four wives, so long as he can treat them all equally both materially and emotionally (4:3): "Marry women of your choice, two, three, or four; but if you are concerned that you may not be able to treat them justly, then only one...." Special Quranic dispensation allowed Muhammad to exceed that limit by reason of his responsibilities as leader of an increasingly complex social entity. Early practice of polygyny had the social advantage of providing a place of refuge for unattached women who would find it virtually impossible to survive on their own. Times of war were especially perilous for the wives and children of men who had gone off to do battle. Muhammad himself and a number of his Companions are said to have married widows under such circumstances.

Do Muslims practice polygyny widely today?

In recent times, polygyny has been either outlawed or tightly controlled in many Muslim nations. One of the arguments against it has been that although in complex contemporary societies a man might manage material equality, emotional and psychological equity is no longer possible. Even in the Quran one finds the suggestion that beyond the material realm, such equal treatment is very difficult in practice: "You will not be able to treat the wives with equality, however much you desire that. Do not turn away entirely, leaving her in suspense" (Quran 4:129). For any number of reasons, the vast majority of Muslims simply assume that monogamy is the only feasible marriage practice. Polygyny is now strictly regulated in a number of Muslim countries, so that few men would actually be able to meet the legal requirements. Some modern Muslims, such as Muhammad Abduh (1849–1905), have argued that Muslims can no longer consider polygyny an option, interpreting the Quran's warning verse (4:129 cited above) as a virtual prohibition. Various surveys of Muslim women suggest that they are almost unanimous in stating a preference for monogamy.

Does Islam condone "honor killings"? Or is this more of a culture-validated phenomenon?

Some years ago a criminal defense attorney sought an "expert witness" for a case in which his client, a Muslim immigrant from the Middle East, was charged with murder in the death of his daughter. There was no dispute as to whether the defendant (and his wife, the victim's mother) had killed the young woman: the parents admitted they had killed the girl because she refused to cut off an unacceptable relationship with a non-Muslim male. In fact, a wire-tapped phone recording actually captured the gruesome event after the daughter frantically called for help. The attorney wanted the potential "expert" to testify that the defendant could indeed claim mitigating circumstances on the grounds that this killing would not even have been prosecuted in his land of origin, because such honor killings were not only acceptable but demanded in order to maintain the integrity of the family. The Islamic studies specialist declined to do so for the simple reason that nothing in Islam's sacred sources or, in mainstream modern legal opinion, sanctioned any such "honor killing." In other words, though there may be "cultural" support for such horrific actions in various regions, Islamic religious values in no way sanction them. For comparative purposes it is useful to note two seldom appreciated facts. First, even in the United States, many people of "Judeo-Christian" background "look the other way" in many thousands of such "intimate crimes" every year; and second, "honor killings" continue to occur in countless religious and cultural settings across the world, and perpetrators of these crimes who call themselves Muslims are by no means alone in claiming religious/cultural forbearance of such atrocities.

HUMAN RIGHTS AND SOCIAL JUSTICE

Does Islamic tradition enshrine concerns about human rights?

Closely related to the Islamic concern for economic justice is the desire not to let the rights of the individual become swallowed up by those of society as a whole. It seeks a balance between the rampant individualism many Muslims associate with capitalist cultures and the stifling of individual initiative frequently identified with totalitarian systems. Muslims think of Islam as the last bastion of genuine egalitarianism under God. Like non-Muslims, Muslims have had a hard time translating ideals into realities. They trace the origin of "human rights" issues in their tradition back to Muhammad.

In what ancient sources do Muslims find insight about human rights?

Two early documents form the basic charter. Shortly after the *Hijra*, Muhammad promulgated what came to be known as the "Constitution of Medina," in which he set out the principal terms governing the relationships of Muslims to one another and to the non-Muslim groups in the region. Equally fundamental are several of the stipulations of Muhammad's "Farewell Sermon," delivered in 632 C.E. during his final pilgrimage to Mecca. That document contains basic statements about important social relationships. This sample gives a sense of its tone: "Your lives and property are sacred and inviolable among one another.... (You) have rights over your wives and your wives have rights over you. Treat your wives with kindness and love.... The aristocracy of yore is trampled under my feet. The Arab has no superiority over the non-Arab and the non-Arab has no superiority over the Arab. All are children of Adam and Adam was made of earth.... Know that all Muslims are brothers unto one another. You are one brotherhood. Nothing that belongs to another is lawful to his brother, unless freely given. Guard yourselves against committing injustice...."

Muslim writers often situate human rights within the context of "God's Rights." God has the right to, but no need of, human beings' faith, acceptance of divine guidance, obedience, and worship. The Quran makes the very direct statement that "There is no compulsion in religion" (Quran 2:256). Many Muslims take that to mean that all persons are free to respond to God's signs as they please. Islamic history is full of examples of what Islamic historian Marshall Hodgson called the triumph of the universalistic spirit, in which Muslims and non-Muslims lived together in harmony. At times, however, the spirit of "communalism" has dominated, with disastrous consequences.

Are there any contemporary parallels to the ancient sources mentioned above?

The "Universal Islamic Declaration of Human Rights," promulgated in 1981 by an Islamic Council, a non-authoritative body made up of invited members from a number

How do Muslims address questions of human rights today?

Various modern reforms have seen dramatic change in a number of nations with strong Muslim majorities, usually in connection with developments in constitutional forms of government. But there have generally been trade-offs. For example, the modern Turkish republic superseded the Ottoman Empire in the 1920s and proclaimed a range of human rights unsupported previously; but the republic also suppressed the religious freedom of Muslims who posed a threat to its secularizing program. The Iranian revolutionary constitution also proclaimed its support of economic, social, and cultural rights, but put severe limits on political and civil rights.

of Middle Eastern and south Asian Muslim countries, represents one of the fullest recent articulations of Islamic values on the subject. The document affirms a "commitment to uphold the following inviolable and inalienable human rights that we consider are enjoined by Islam"—right to life; right to freedom; right to equality and prohibition against impermissible discrimination; right to justice; right to fair trial; right to protection against abuse of power; right to protection against torture; right to protection of honor and reputation; right to asylum; rights of minorities; right and obligation to participate in the conduct and management of public affairs; right to freedom of belief, thought, and speech; right to freedom of religion; right to free association; economic order; right to protection of property; status and dignity of workers; right to social security; right to found a family and related matters; rights of married women; right to education; right of privacy; and right to freedom of movement and residence. In 1990, the Organization of the Islamic Conference, whose membership includes representatives of virtually all the nations with majority Muslim populations, put forth a charter of rights; but it differs from the International Bill of Human Rights in that the Islamic charter continues to subsume all rights under the controlling authority of religious law, or sharia.

While it's essential for Muslims to trace all key values back to the Quran and Muhammad, how do Muslims put these values into action?

Concerned Muslims in our time have focused considerable attention on questions of human rights. As is the case with human rights organizations all over the world, those that have formed within the greater Islamic community often have lacked the political clout needed to bring about effective change in governmental policy. Evidence of violations apparently sanctioned at the highest levels in certain nations whose populations are predominantly Muslim has prompted some outside observers to criticize Muslims for failing to safeguard basic human rights. The charge is misdirected. Critics would argue that where Muslims are "in control," and preach the unity of religious and civil spheres, they have no excuse for not implementing Islam's loftiest values in their societies. Such criticism might be right on the mark but for a pair of unpleasant realities. First, when ostensibly religious ideals are explicitly incorporated into political programs they often get pushed aside by more pressing pragmatic concerns, even as government spokespersons continue to employ religious rhetoric. In short, Muslims, like others, don't always live up to their stated ideals. Second, religious ideals that are so appropriated are often quite selective, do not represent the tradition's full scope, and thus fail to take account of conflicting claims. Islamic ideals in this respect are extremely high and, like all such challenging aspirations, very difficult to put into practice.

What is a recent specific example of attention to Islamic values?

A few decades ago, Pakistan hosted the International Islamic Seminar on the Application of the Revealed Law. In a statement obviously meant to refute a number of charges, the seminar declared: "…the Islamic code of life lays down not only moral, but social, economic, political, cultural and educational norms and rules based on the principles of equality, brotherhood and justice…. The Islamic code is designed to create a just and free society in which every individual enjoys equal rights and equal opportunities regardless of rank, birth, caste, color, or creed."

What are some examples of how the Quran talks about social justice?

Numerous texts in the Quran make it clear that at the heart of the original message stands the challenge of fostering genuine community, on a foundation of justice and integrity that goes well beyond deeds of piety and devotion.

> [Moral u]prightness is not a question of turning your faces to the *qibla* of East or West [i.e., facing Mecca in ritual prayer]. [Moral u]prightness means rather believing in God and in the final day, and in the angels and the Book and the prophets. It means sharing your wealth, dear as it is to you [some would translate this phrase "out of love for Him"], with kinfolk, orphans, the poor, the traveler [lit. son of the road], those who come asking, and for setting slaves free. It means performing the ritual prayer [*salat*], giving alms [*zakat*], living up to one's solemn word, and bearing up under the most intense hardship and in dire straits. (Quran 2:177)

In its ideals, Islam has always been a highly service-oriented tradition informed by a keen sense of social responsibility.

Do the ancient sources generally focus on questions of economic justice?

Among the earliest and most insistent themes in the Quran is the call to establish economic justice and to attend to the needs of society's marginalized and disadvantaged. Life was especially hard in seventh-century Mecca for orphans and widows, as well as for the poor. Growth of the local trading economy made it possible for members of privileged clans and families, and even for some individuals, to amass large fortunes at the expense of others. Observing with alarm the growing gap between the haves and the have-nots, Muhammad delivered a challenging response in the form of Quranic pronouncements and gave further views on matters of social justice in the Hadith. Countless Hadiths likewise speak of the need for social awareness and action. Muhammad tells, for example, of a man who made his living by loaning money to others. The man used to say to the fellow who worked for him, "When you come upon a man who has fallen on hard times, go easy on him, and perhaps God will go easy on us." Muhammad then observed, "And when that employer came to meet God, God went easy on him."

What are Muslims enjoined to do in response to manifest social injustice?

The spectrum of social justice and ethical service to one's fellow human beings runs a considerable gamut, all the way from daily courtesies to the "steep ascent." One's intention in service is, as always, critical to the moral and spiritual quality of an act, as in this scriptural text: "Do you see the person in denial of the (future) judgment? That is the one who drives away the orphan and does not contribute to feeding the poor. Woe betide those who perform the ritual while remaining oblivious to the (meaning of the) prayer; they want only to be seen, but refuse ordinary acts of kindness" (Quran 107:1–7). Another scriptural text reinforces the point as it enjoins Muslims to: "Give to kin, the poor and the traveler what they need; that is best for those who seek the face of God, and they will indeed fare well. What you give in the hope of profiting at the expense of people will gain you nothing in God's sight…" (Quran 30:38–39). More advanced moral demands of the life of service the Quran calls the "steep ascent": "Ah, what will make clear to you what the steep ascent is—It is to free a slave, and to feed in time of hunger an orphan near of kin, or some poor wretch in misery, and to be among those who believe and exhort one another to perseverance and encourage each other to compassion" (Quran 90:12–17). Both sacred sources are full of recommendations that amount to the "works of mercy" that are part of the Christian tradition. All in all, the Muslim tradition issues a demanding call for attention to issues of social morality.

LAW, ETHICS, VIOLENCE, AND WARFARE

Is jihad a legal concept for Muslims?

As a legal obligation, the responsibility to engage in jihad is considered a "duty of a sufficient number" (*fard kifaya*) of Muslims, as distinguished from an "individual duty" (*fard ayn*) incumbent on *every* Muslim. By contrast, for example, the obligation to "seek knowledge" is an *individual* duty, requiring all Muslims to pursue learning diligently and in every way possible. Jihad, on the other hand, is a specifically limited duty to be engaged within a range of precisely defined parameters. Islamic criteria governing the call for, and actually engaging in, a jihad against an outward enemy are as stringent as Christianity's terms for waging a "just war."

What are the essential criteria in classical and modern "just war" theory?

Ethicists in various traditions have for centuries discussed questions of religiously legitimate use of large-scale violence. Their efforts have focused on three aspects of this large and complex matter: justification for a) declaring war (*jus ad bellum*), b) specific methods used in the conduct of war (*jus in bello*), and c) matters pertaining to just resolution of hostilities and treatment of the conquered (*jus post bellum*). Principal criteria for each of these dimensions are as follows: To "declare war," there must be a just cause (defense against aggression, human rights…); legitimate authority (e.g., the

United Nations); right intent (peace, not vengeance or conquest); likely success (actually achievable objectives); violence as a last resort (after diplomacy, etc.); and proportionality (results not more evil than the target of the violence). Second, the "conduct of war" must be based on a combination of proportionality (minimum force required), and discrimination (targeting only actual combatants). Finally, contemporary scholars have begun to discuss in detail a dimension not found in most pre-modern theory, namely, "postwar justice," including again just cause (finalizing as much as possible the original purpose for declaring war); reconciliation (among warring and aggrieved parties); punishment (including accountability and restitution); and restoration (including reestablishing conditions for as normal a life as possible, all things considered).

What are some fundamental Islamic criteria for declaring jihad?

As in other religious and cultural contexts, Islamic law also establishes criteria under which "just jihad" can be contemplated and declared formally. Muslim specialists differ as widely as do Christian theologians as to the circumstances under which one can claim to have met those criteria. In addition, one must distinguish between popular sentiment and the core of a faith tradition. Under prescribed circumstances jihad can include offensive military action where the free practice of Islam is under threat of constraint. Many scholars in recent times have held that one cannot justify an offensive jihad unless Muslims are being persecuted religiously. Even then, therefore, it is a type of defensive action. Military jihad has always been subject to strict criteria and is in many ways parallel to the Christian notion of "just war." Criteria in classical sources include the following: warriors must be believers (though some jurists disagree, and Muhammad was flexible), adult, and male (except in surprise attack or indirect support roles); and they must be of sound mind and body, free, economically independent, and acting with parental support and good intentions. Jihad must be declared by an authoritative leader following an offer of terms of peace. Warriors must spare non-combatants unless they are clearly helping enemy cause. Very few, if any, recent calls for jihad have actually satisfied the necessary criteria.

Under what conditions can actually waging jihad be considered "just"?

Most Muslims are as unfamiliar with the classic conditions for jihad as their Christian counterparts are with their tradition's criteria for a "just war." According to Muslim tradition, for example, no action can be justified as authentic jihad if any of the following conditions apply: killing non-combatants, prisoners of war, or diplomatic personnel; use of poisonous weapons (beginning with poison-tipped arrows and swords, for example) or inhumane means to kill; atrocities in conquered lands, including mutilation of persons and animals, and wanton despoliation of natural resources; and the sexual abuse of captive women.

271

Does Muslim tradition use the term jihad in other contexts?

Muslim sources beyond the specifically "legal" tradition also speak of various non-violent forms of jihad. One can battle injustice and evil through jihad of the pen or the tongue, for example. When someone asked Muhammad what the greatest jihad was, the Prophet replied that it was to speak a word of truth in the ear of a tyrant. An important theme in Islamic spirituality has been called the "Greater Jihad," as distinct from all the various forms of exterior, lesser jihads. Warriors of the spirit must take up the sword of self-knowledge against the fiercest enemy of all, their own inner tendencies to evil and idolatry.

Is there any specific historical data useful in clarifying questions about jihad?

Islamic tradition dating from the earliest military encounters between the Muslims of Medina and other groups includes numerous guidelines on these and other such issues. Legislation of peacetime relations likewise lays down specific obligations in the conduct of international trade, the use of slaves, the conclusion of treaties, diplomatic protection, recognition of sovereignty, and the right to asylum. All of that, however, has not prevented horrors from being perpetrated in the very name of Islam, to the great sorrow of many millions of Muslims. Nothing can excuse those who engage in such atrocities, whatever their express motivation or avowed religious affiliation.

Is there a parallel to jihad in other religious traditions?

Jihad actually refers to any justifiable struggle against aggression, oppression, and injustice. For many Americans, the term conjures up images of crazed young men brandishing bloody scimitars and screaming "Allahu Akbar" as they wade into the ranks of some infidel foe. Jihad remains, nevertheless, a potent and valid concept in the history of religious thought and has in practice often approximated what Christians refer to as "just war." Jihad has indeed been exploited. More than a few Middle Eastern leaders who care not at all for genuine religious values have soiled the escutcheon of jihad in the very act of bestirring their constituents to rally around it. This means it is wise to look beyond the appearances to the authentic call of conscience that has made the concept of jihad a genuine religious value. When a Middle Eastern voice makes a call to jihad, there must be an attempt to understand what evil the call targets, rather than immediately discrediting the caller as just another Muslim fanatic. Both Christian and Islamic traditions sanction recourse to violent means to rectify blatant injustice. But authentic mainstream teaching in both allows such action only in sheer desperation, only as a last resort, after pursuing every conceivable alternative. Nevertheless, both traditions encourage peaceful resolution to all conflicts. Islam, like Christianity, teaches in the strongest terms that terrorism is simply wrong. Nothing whatever in mainstream Islamic tradition and teaching defends any activity generally recognized as terrorism.

Does it present an irreconcilable conflict if Muslims in the U.S. military are ordered to do battle against fellow Muslims in Iraq or Afghanistan, for example?

One of the leading scholars involved in the Jordan conference (mentioned above), Yusuf al-Qaradawi, was asked to give a *fatwa* on precisely this issue shortly after the 9/11 terrorist attacks. Muhammad Abdur-Rashid was the senior Muslim chaplain in the American Armed forces, which at the time numbered some fifteen thousand. He wrote to Shaykh Qaradawi for his legal ruling on the permissibility of Muslim military personnel within the U.S. armed

Egyptian Shaykh Dr. Yusuf al-Qaradawi was asked to give a *fatwa* on the 9/11 attacks. He responded by asserting that Muslims must condemn the killing of innocent, non-combatants.

forces to participate in the war operations and its related efforts in Afghanistan and in other predominantly Muslim countries. The Shaykh replied on September 27, 2001. He framed the *fatwa* by listing the petitioner's description of the requisite military goals that gave his troops pause: 1) Retaliation against those "who are thought to have participated" in planning and financing the suicide operations on September 11, against civilian and military targets in New York and Washington (he then detailed the consequences of these operations). 2) Eliminating the elements that use Afghanistan and elsewhere as safe haven, as well as deterring the governments that harbor them, sanction them, or allow them the opportunity for military training in order to achieve their goals around the world. 3) Restoring the veneration and respect to the United States as a sole superpower in the world. Abdur-Rashid concluded by explaining that if the troops refused to participate in fighting, they would have no choice but to resign, which might also entail other consequences; and he asked if such duties were religiously permissible and, if not, might the conscientious objectors request transfer to serve in capacities other than direct combat.

How did the Shaykh formulate his *fatwa*?

He began in the traditional manner by framing the dilemma and immediately suggesting the direction of his legal judgment: "Praise be to God and peace and blessing be upon the messengers of God. We say: This question presents a very complicated issue and a highly sensitive situation for our Muslim brothers and sisters serving in the American army as well as other armies that face similar situations. *All Muslims ought to be united against all those who terrorize the innocents, and those who permit the killing of non-combatants without a justifiable reason.* Islam has declared the spilling of blood and the destruction of property as absolute prohibitions until the Day of Judgment. God said (in the Quran):

273

Because of that We ordained unto the Children of Israel that if anyone killed a human being—unless it be in punishment for murder or for spreading mischief on earth— it would be as though he killed all of humanity; whereas, if anyone saved a life, it would be as though he saved the life of all humanity. And indeed, there came to them Our messengers with clear signs (proofs and evidences), even then after that, many of them continued to commit mischief on earth. (5:32)

He stated clearly that anyone who

... violates these pointed Islamic texts is an offender deserving of the appropriate punishment according to their offence and according to its consequences for destruction and mischief. It is incumbent upon our military brothers in the American armed forces to *make this stand and its religious reasoning well known to all their superiors, as well as to their peers, and to voice it and not to be silent. Conveying this is part of the true nature of the Islamic teachings that have often been distorted or smeared by the media.* [author's italics]

Did the Shaykh deal at all with the problem of terrorist acts that put the U.S. Muslim troops in their dilemma?

Shaykh Qaradawi addressed the issue directly: Under Islamic Sharia, the terrorist acts of 9/11/2001 are considered the crime of *Hiraba* (waging war against society), and he quoted from the Quran's vivid description of the punishment that would be prescribed for the terrorists, including that they are condemned to Hell (Quran 5: 33–34). The text concludes with this proviso: "Except for those who (having fled away and then) came back with repentance before they fall into your power; (in that case) know that God is Oft-Forgiving, Most Merciful." He insisted that the perpetrators of the terrorism, "as well as those who aid and abet them through incitement, financing or other support," be dealt with legally and punished appropriately. He hoped this would act as a deterrent to others like them who easily slay the lives of innocents, destroy properties, and terrorize people. Hence, it is a duty on Muslims to participate in this effort with all possible means, in accordance with God's (Most High) saying: "And help one another in virtue and righteousness, but do not help one another in sin and transgression" (5:2).

Does the *fatwa* raise any other related matters?

After expressing the concern that only the clearly and manifestly guilty be so dealt with, Qaradawi added that since these Muslim soldiers were citizens and members of a regular army, they must follow orders lest they cast doubt on their allegiance and loyalty and incur loss of privileges of citizenship. He wrote: "The Muslim (soldier) must perform his duty in this fight despite the feeling of uneasiness of 'fighting without discriminating.' His intention (*niyyat*) must be to fight for enjoining of the truth and defeating falsehood. It is to prevent aggression on the innocents, or to apprehend the perpetrators and bring them to justice." A soldier must not be deterred by concern for "what other consequences of the fighting that might result in his personal discomfort, since he alone can neither control it nor prevent it. Furthermore, all deeds are accounted (by God) according to the intentions. God (the Most High) does not burden any soul except what it can bear. In addition, Muslim jurists have ruled that what a Muslim cannot control he cannot be held accountable for, as God (the Most High) says: "And keep your duty to God as much as you can" (64:16). The Prophet (prayer and peace be upon him) said: "When I ask of you to do something, do it as much as you can." The Muslim here is a part of a whole, if he absconds, his departure will result in a greater harm, not only for him but also for the Muslim community in his country—and here there are many millions of them. Moreover, even if fighting causes him discomfort spiritually or psychologically, this personal hardship must be endured for the greater public good, as the jurisprudential (*fiqhi*) rule states."

What about the petitioner's question concerning the possibility that Muslim military personnel might serve behind the lines in logistical support rather than in combat?

Qaradawi insisted that such an accommodation should be sought only if the results would in no way imperil the Muslim soldiers' fellow military personnel or any other American Muslim citizens. Most of all, he indicated, let them avoid at all cost raising doubts about their allegiance or loyalty, or any option that might risk false accusations as to their loyalty or patriotism, or harm their future career possibilities. He concluded:

> To sum up, it is acceptable—God willing—for the Muslim American military personnel to partake in the fighting in the upcoming battles, against whomever, their country decides, has perpetrated terrorism against them. Keeping in mind to have the proper intention as explained earlier, so no doubts would be cast about their loyalty to their country, or to prevent harm to befall them as might be expected. This is in accordance with the Islamic jurisprudence rules which state that necessities dictate exceptions, as well as the rule that says one may endure a small harm to avoid a much greater harm.

What is another recent example of a prominent internationally known Muslim scholar issuing a *fatwa* against terrorism?

As the previous example suggests, since immediately after the horrors of 9/11/2001, Muslim religious scholars have been publishing legal advisories known as *fatwas* denouncing the actions of al-Qaeda and other organizations that claim religious legitimacy for their use of the tactics of indiscriminate mass violence. Such public denunciations have, for a variety of reasons, almost never been reported in European or American news media. But here are some principles by which one of the more recent, and most detailed, *fatwas* distinguishes between legitimate *jihad* and religiously indefensible uses of violence.

London-based Pakistani Shaykh Tahir al-Qadri argues, first, that Islamic teaching forbids the indiscriminate torturing or killing of Muslims or non-Muslims, even in the conduct of legitimate warfare. He then assembles extensive evidence from Islamic history and major sources condemning the forcing of Islamic beliefs on non-Muslims, the destruction of non-Muslim places of worship, and rebellion by Muslims against legitimate Muslim government administration. In considerable detail, the *shaykh* addresses forthrightly the historical reality that people identifying themselves as Muslims have indeed rationalized numerous violations of all of these explicit prohibitions. He identifies the seventh-century Khawarij (seceeders) as the earliest such movement: they rebelled against Ali (the fourth Rightly Guided Caliph) and condemned Ali and all who continued to support him as infidels and proclaimed that all such people should be eliminated. The *shaykh* describes in detail how the Khawarij, and other groups like them through history, have portrayed themselves as the champions of "true" Islam and attempted to persuade the public of the religious righteousness of their cause and methods, all the while distorting the tradition to arrive at their conclusions; and they have recruited and brainwashed adolescents to do their dirty work. Qadri concludes with evidence of Muhammad's own condemnation of such people as "the dogs of hell," and calls on the global Muslim community to fulfill their historical obligation of struggling (i.e., engaging in *jihad*) to eliminate the scourge of the modern-day Khawarij.

Is it true that Muhammad both preached and engaged in military campaigns? Were these actions offensive, and did they amount to "holy war"?

The Prophet did engage in conflict against both non-Muslim enemies of the young Muslim community and to neutralize internal dissension, but the term "holy war" applies only in the first instance—and then only in the case of action "waged to propagate the combatants' religion." Historical data from the early *Sira* (prophet's biography) literature on the subjects of the "raids" (*ghazwa*) in which Muhammad himself took part, and the "expeditions" (*sariya*) sent off by but not necessarily accompanied by the Prophet provide important information on the topic. The vast majority of the first type (eighteen of twenty-seven raids) involved preaching but not military combat, and the remaining nine fighting events were defensive. None of the events in question here truly qualify as "holy wars," but represent other forms of *jihad* for the purposes of preaching Islam, negotiating pacts of nonaggression with the tribes, or engaging in defensive actions. There is an essential distinction between combat joined to spread a religious belief system and fighting for broader socio-political goals. No verse in the Quran permits combat aimed at converting others to Islam, but only for the purpose of removing conditions adverse to Muslim practice of Islam without constraint—including the peaceful preaching of Islam. Thus, response to aggression alone—not any difference in creed on the part of the "other"—justifies resorting to war. A major problem in the interpretation of these matters is that one faction's defense is another's offense—and that's without even a hint of "preemptive" warfare to confuse things further.

Is it true that the Quran is the most violence-filled scripture ever?

A major problem here is that the application of different sets of exegetical criteria to other people's scriptures than to one's own is an ancient and growing problem. Christ-

Are there major differences between "outsider" and "insider" interpretations of the meaning of *jihad* and use of violent means as Islamically legitimate?

There is indeed a gaping chasm between "outsider" and "insider" readings of *jihad*, an abyss that continues to widen as old stereotypes based on uncritical repetition of flimsy past scholarship are perpetuated. A large problem currently is the result of a Muslim minority that continues to hold a view that they attribute to the legal scholar Shafii, eponym of one of the four extant Sunni law schools: they claim that he understood jihad as offensive war against non-Muslims that is justifiable—indeed mandated—because of their rejection of Islam or refusal to submit to the Islamic state. That minority view is, not surprisingly, represented in extremist groups such as al-Qaeda and the Taliban. But the vast majority of Muslims, today and historically, have espoused the views of the other three law schools limiting *jihad* to defensive ends. Here one has also to include the uncounted millions in regions under Shafii law who are not the least disposed toward violence, regardless of views advanced by the venerable jurist twelve hundred years ago.

ian preachers commonly trot out a handful of verses from the Quran that, taken at face value, enjoin violence against members of other communities—not a word about context, of course. They invariably insist that Jesus was a man of peace, and leave the issue there. If they were to read the Bible, both testaments, with the same spectacles with which they had scanned the Muslim scripture, they would find that, verse for verse, the Bible is far more violent than the Quran—in terms of both descriptive and prescriptive violence. The Gospels have their share of violent parables, and the plot of the Book of Revelation is not G rated. The Torah recommends that the parents of an incorrigible son take him to the edge of town so that their fellow citizens can stone him to death. Ah, but the difference, the rejoinder goes, is that Muslims still enact their violent texts, whereas Jews and Christians do not. In a major newspaper recently, one evangelical missionary condemned Muslims as praying only to make points with God, implying, of course that Christians uniformly draw their spiritual practices from wellsprings of the purest motivation.

What is the most widely accepted belief about suicide? How is suicide different from "self-selected martyrdom"?

Classic sources universally condemn all manner of deliberately ending one's own life, for whatever reason. Most of those sources make it crystal clear that individuals who choose suicide as a way out will be punished severely in the next life. Unfortunately, terrorist methods over the past couple of decades have increasingly resorted to the use of "suicide bombers" to take vengeance on people identified by the perpetrators as enemies of

Islam. Most such perpetrators have chosen to distort the ancient and unambiguous prohibition of suicide by re-labeling such self-destructive behavior "self-selected martyrdom," arguing that God not only forgives such conduct but indeed rewards it for its unselfish defense of Islam against infidels.

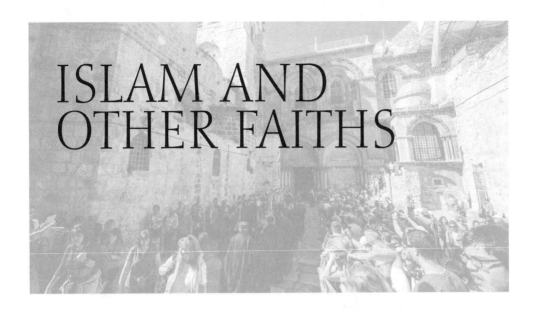

ISLAM AND OTHER FAITHS

SIMILARITIES AMONG FAITHS

How does the Quran explain the de facto diversity of communities of religious belief?

One of the many intriguing facets of the Quran is that it often addresses the problem of diversity and the roots of religious disparity, explaining all of this as part of the divine plan for humankind. The Quran addresses the issue of pluralism directly. Several texts address God's plan in creating the world in all its human variety:

> Humankind were once a single community. God sent prophets with news and warnings, and through them revealed the Book in truth that He might judge between people when they disagreed with one another. But, after the clear indicators had come to them, it was only out of self-centered stubbornness that they differed among themselves. God guided those who believed to the truth over which they argued, for God guides to the Straight Path whom He will. (Quran 2:213)

How does the Quran explain the ultimate purpose of human diversity?

The scripture makes very intriguing remarks in this respect, beginning with gender and social diversity: "O humankind! We created you male and female, and we made you into peoples and tribes that you *might learn to know* one another. Indeed God considers the noblest among you those of most reverent awe (of God)" (Quran 49:13; see also 30:22, 14:4). More specifically several texts speak of diversity in the context of plural communities of faith. God could have made humankind all of one group, but instead left the human race composed of many segments in order to *test* and *challenge* human beings to work things out with each other. Frequent references to "vying with one another in good deeds" set the tone of all human, and especially religious, relationships. "We have

Several passages in the Quran speak of the importance of diversity in the community as a test from God to see how well human beings can work together.

made for each among you a revealed road (*shira*, related to term *sharia*) and a way to travel. Had God wished, he would have made you a single community; but (God wished) to test you according to what he has given each of you. Therefore vie with one another in good deeds, for God is the final goal for all of you, and it is he who will clarify for you those things about which you now argue" (Quran 5:48; see also 2:148 and 23:61).

Does Muslim tradition teach Islam's affinities with other specific faiths?

According to the Quran, Muslims have a special relationship to certain other religious communities. Especially in post-*Hijra* texts, the Quran speaks of Muslims as having much in common with the "Peoples of the Book." The term originally referred to Jews and Christians and eventually expanded to include other communities as well. These groups were known as *dhimmis*, or protected communities. And the notion that "there is no compulsion in religious matters" (*din*, Quran 2:256) is surely a central concept in Islamic views of relations with other traditions. But there is no doubt that the ultimate goal is a return to the pristine unity in which all creation worships God together. There is also no doubt that non-Muslims living in largely Muslim nations have sometimes confronted odious restrictions in religious practice. The realities of inter-religious relations have not always been cordial, and much difficult work needs to be done on this matter all over the world. When it comes to acceptance of diversity, all human beings have a hard time moving from theory to practice.

Do Muslims, Christians, and Jews worship the "same God"?

"Allah" is an Arabic term that derives from a combination of the definite article ("the") al-, with ilah, an ancient Arabic term for "deity." "Allah" therefore means "the [only] deity," and that's what Christians and Jews generally mean by the word "God." Islamic tradition describes God further by means of the "Ninety-Nine Most Beautiful Names." Among these names are Merciful, Compassionate, All-Hearing, All-Seeing, All-Knowing, Oft-Returning, Just Judge, Giver of Life, Bringer of Death, Victorious, Beneficent, and Guide. Muslims traditionally meditate on these names as they ply their "rosary" beads. Christians and Jews will find nothing in the list that is in any way incompatible with their own fundamental beliefs.

What are some examples of specific, shared conceptions of God?

Like Christians and Jews, Muslims believe God created the universe from nothing and has communicated through a series of prophets. Allah is intimately involved in the events of human history, which ends for each individual with death, resurrection, judgment, and either reward in Heaven or punishment in Hell. As for the ultimate fate of the human race collectively, Muslim tradition holds that history will end with a cosmic conflict in which the Messiah will play a role in subduing a figure very similar to the "Anti-Christ." From the Jewish perspective, the Ninety-Nine Names describe the God of the Hebrew Scriptures almost perfectly. From the Christian perspective, two essential aspects of God are conspicuously missing from the Islamic list of divine attributes: the notions that God has become flesh in the Incarnation and consequent Divinity of Jesus, and that God is both One and a Trinity of Father, Son, and Holy Spirit. Is the "God" of

---

Who are the "People of the Book"?

Judaism, Christianity, and Islam come together in Islamic thought under the metaphor of Peoples of the Book. The idea is that God has given revelations through prophets, in the form of scriptures, to more than one community of believers over the millennia. According to the Quran, Muslims have a special relationship to these religious communities. Especially in post- Hijra texts, the Quran speaks of Muslims as having much in common with the "Peoples of the Book." The term originally referred to Jews and Christians and eventually expanded to include other communities as well, such as Zoroastrians (now commonly called Parsees). The ultimate goal is a return to the pristine unity in which all creation worships God together.

Jews and Christians and the "Allah" of Muslims the same supreme being? It is reasonable to say, at least, that they are so remarkably similar that members of the three faiths have ample reason for considering themselves siblings as "children of Abraham."

What "images of God" do Christians and Jews share with Muslims?

Most Jews and Christians are convinced their "own" supreme being is loving and kind, provident and generous, as well as thirsty for justice and equity. So are most Muslims. Of the "Ninety-Nine Most Beautiful Names" of God, the two by far most frequently invoked are "Gracious or Compassionate" and "Merciful." All but one of the Quran's 114 *suras* (chapters) begins with the phrase, "In the name of God, the Gracious and Merciful." One might say these two names are as important for Muslims as are the names Father, Son, and Holy Spirit heard in so many Christian invocations. Virtually every Muslim public speaker begins with that Quranic phrase and goes on to wish the audience the blessings and mercy of God.

The opening chapter of the Quran sets the tone of Muslim spiritual life and includes themes very similar to those of the Christian "Lord's Prayer":

> In the Name of God, the Compassionate and Merciful: Praise to God, Lord of the Universe.
> The Compassionate, the Merciful,
> Master of the Day of Judgment.
> You alone do we serve; from you alone do we seek help.
> Lead us along the Straight Path,
> the path of those who experience the shower of your grace,
> not of those who have merited your anger
> or of those who have gone astray. (Quran 1:1–7)

The text features several of the principal divine attributes. Compassion and mercy top the list and receive an emphatic second mention. In addition, God rules the "two worlds" (seen and unseen, i.e., the universe), takes account at Judgment, offers aid and grace, and manifests a wrathful side to those who prefer arrogant independence from the origin of all things. At the center of the prayer, the Muslim asks for guidance on the Straight Path, a path laid out and marked as the way of divine graciousness.

Are Islam's "Ninety-Nine Most Beautiful Names" of God truly compatible with Christian and Jewish conceptions of God?

None of the "Ninety-Nine Most Beautiful Names of God," on which Muslims meditate as they finger the thirty-three beads of the rosary, will sound a dissonant note in the ear of Christian or Jew. All of those names conjure up images of God. Islamic tradition has divided the names into those that express an awareness of God's beauty and approachability (*jamal*) and those that evoke a sense of the divine majesty and awe-inspiring power (*jalal*). These references to the two sides of God recall the theological distinction between immanence and transcendence. God is both near and accessible—closer even than the jugular vein, according to Quran 50:16—and infinitely beyond human experience and imagining. Rudolf Otto's classic definition of the "holy" can further clarify the matter. The great German thinker calls the "sacred" or "holy" "the mystery both terrifying and fascinating." "Mystery" refers to irreducible, unanalyzable meaning, before which one can only stand silent. Still, paradoxically, one who experiences mystery cannot but be filled simultaneously with intimations of both irresistible attractiveness and sheer dread. One thinks, for example, of Moses's curiosity at the sight of the burning bush and of his terror at finding himself in the presence of the Living God. He is riveted between the desire to flee and wanting to stay forever. The Quranic rendition of the story darkens the already dramatic scene with a nighttime setting.

Muslims, like Catholics, use rosary beads to meditate. In the case of Muslims, the strand has ninety-nine beads relating to the "Ninety-Nine Most Beautiful Names of God."

Why is Jesus an important person to Muslims?

Referred to in Arabic as Isa (EE-sa), Jesus appears often in the Quran, in a total of ninety-three verses scattered among fifteen suras. Jesus is the second-last of the prophets, a messenger sent to humankind with the "Gospel" (*injil*, in-JEEL). The Muslim scripture recounts several events in the life of Jesus that appear in the New Testament, but with significant differences. In addition one finds in the Quran echoes of stories that appear in what Christians call apocryphal literature. A number of "signs" attest to his prophetic mission: as a youth he fashions a bird of clay and breathes life into it; he later cures a leper and a man born blind; he raises the dead by God's leave; and causes a table spread with a feast to descend from heaven for his apostles.

Is there an Islamic Christology?

Strictly speaking there is and can be no Islamic "Christology" since Jesus is not the "Christ" in Muslim thought. But one could speak of an Islamic "Jesus-ology." Several of Jesus's Quranic titles are important. The Quran refers to him eleven times as *masih* (ma-SEEH) but "messiah" here does not have the theological import that it has in Christian thought. The title "Servant of God," on the other hand, has important theological implications. It suggests that Jesus was no more than a creature, a human being, explicitly ruling out from the Muslim perspective the more expansive meanings Christians have attached to the "suffering servant" imagery of the Hebrew Scriptures. The Quran speaks of

283

a "Word of God" coming to Jesus, and some Muslim scholars have interpreted that to mean Jesus was the Word in that he spoke for God, or that he was "a" word because he embodied the "good news."

Does Mary also have a place in Islamic tradition?

Mary occupies a very important position in Muslim sacred history. She is, first of all, the mother of a prophet and thus worthy of high honor in keeping with the role God chose for her. Sura (19) of the Quran is named after Mary and she is mentioned more often by name in the Muslim scripture than in the Christian scripture. Sura 19 and other Quranic texts include a number of parallels to scenes recorded in Biblical texts, but almost always with very interesting differences. No other woman is mentioned by name in the Quran. Mary's own birth is miraculous and Zachary looks after her in her youth. A "spirit of God" in human form, whom later tradition identifies as Gabriel, visits Mary and "breathes" the Word into her garment and she hastens to "a remote place" for shame at her unmarried pregnancy. There she gives birth while clinging to a palm tree for support. As she shakes the tree in labor, it showers her with fresh ripe dates. Invited to eat her fill, she chooses to fast and to keep silence through the day, a "fast of silence" that later Muslim mystical poets would interpret as her call to think of nothing but God. When relatives accuse her unjustly, Mary's infant son speaks up in her defense. The principal difference between Muslim and Christian views is that since Islam does not consider Jesus divine, Mary is not the Mother of God.

A stained-glass window in the Notre Dame Cathedral depicts Jesus. Jesus appears in the Quran and is considered the penultimate prophet.

How does Islamic teaching position Mary in the larger picture of tradition?

Popular lore ranks Mary among the "four most beautiful" women God created. Called the "best of the world's women," the four also include Asiya, martyred wife of the Pharaoh of Moses's time; Muhammad's first wife, Khadija; and Fatima, the daughter of Muhammad and Khadija. There are a number of interesting parallels between Mary and the roles of other women in popular Islamic piety. Like Asiya, who "adopted" the infant Moses, Mary was the mother of a prophet. Sunni tradition accords Fatima special status partly because of her mourning for the loss of her father; in Shi'i tradition, especially, her grief at the loss of her martyred sons makes Fatima, like Mary, the "Lady of Sorrow." Tradition regards Mary and Jesus as the only two human beings born without the "touch of Satan" that makes newborn infants cry. Mainstream tradition has denied Mary and all other women the status of prophethood; but it is worth noting that at least one historically important religious scholar, Ibn Hazm of Cordoba (d. 1064), held that Mary did indeed receive the revealed message that makes one a prophet (*nabi*), even though she did not receive the full status of "messenger" (*rasul*) accorded to a number of prophets. Joseph does not appear in the Quran, but traditional lore includes him along with most of the scenes in which Joseph participates in the New Testament.

What other areas of faith and spirituality might offer common ground for Christians and Muslims?

The general notion of how one defines religious devotion or "righteousness" is a good starting place. The Quran's "verse of righteousness" (2:177) says:

> Righteousness does not consist in whether you face east or west (in prayer). The righteous person is the one who believes in God and the Last Day, in the angels and the Book and the prophets; who, though he loves it dearly, gives his wealth away to his kinfolk, to orphans, to the destitute, to the traveler in need and to beggars, and for the redemption of captives; who attends to his prayers and renders the (religiously stipulated) alms.

In addition numerous prayers express themes that are mutually important to both Muslims and Christians. Moving beyond the fundamentals of the Opening Sura of the Quran (above), some of Muhammad's own favorite supplications are also reminiscent of the Lord's Prayer, as in this plea for God's healing of an early Muslim:

> God Our Lord, who are in the heavens, may your name be sanctified. Yours is the Command in the heavens and on earth. As your Mercy is in the heavens, so let your Mercy be on earth. Forgive our sins and failures. You are the Lord of those who seek to do good. Upon this illness send down mercy from your Mercy and healing from your Healing.

Have important later sources and authors contributed similar themes?

Hallaj (d. 922, hal-LAAJ), a famous Baghdadi who suffered a martyr's death, was one of Islam's most revered mystics and earliest Arabic religious poets. His thoughts and prayers survive in a small body of striking poetry, such as this description of how he, like none other than St. Ignatius Loyola, "found God in all things":

> O God, the sun neither rises nor sets
> > but that your love is one with my breathing.
> Never have I sat in conversation
> > but that it was You who spoke to me from among those seated round.
> Never have I been mindful of you, whether in sadness or joy,
> > but that You were there in my heart amidst my inmost whisperings.
> Never have I sought a drink of water in my thirst,
> > but that I saw Your image in the cup.

285

Sanai (d. 1131, sa-NAW-ee) was a Persian-writing mystical poet, from what is now Afghanistan, whose most important work is a lengthy didactic poem called "The Garden of Ultimate Reality." It begins, as do virtually all works of its kind, with a lovely invocation to the God of all creation. Sanai emphasizes the divine transcendence and grandeur, adding a note of supplication at the end of a song of praise.

> O you who nourish the soul and ornament the visible world,
> And you who grant wisdom and are indulgent with those who lack it;
> Creator and sustainer of space and of time,
> Custodian and provider of dweller and dwelling;
> All is of your making, dwelling and dweller,
> All is within your compass, time and space.
> Fire and air, water and earth,
> All are mysteriously within the scope of your power.
> All that is between your Throne and this earth
> Are but a fraction of your handiwork;
> Inspirited intelligence acts as your swift herald,
> Every living tongue that moves in every mouth
> Has but one purpose: to give you praise.
> Your sublime and exalted names
> Evidence your beneficence and grace and kindness.
> Every one of them outstrips throne and globe and dominion;
> They are a thousand plus one and a hundred less one.
> But to those who are outside the spiritual sanctuary,
> The names are veiled.
> O Lord, in your largesse and mercy
> Allow this heart and soul a glimpse of your name!

OVERLAPPING CLAIMS TO SACRED REAL ESTATE

What significance does the "Temple Mount" in Jerusalem have for Muslims? And why don't Muslims want Jews to rebuild their temple?

The merest mention of rebuilding the temple evokes cries of outrage from the Muslim community, for on top of what Jews call the Temple Mount there now stands the seventh-century shrine called the Dome of the Rock and the early eighth-century al-Aqsa mosque. For Muslims, who refer to the area as the Noble Sanctuary, the place recalls the importance of Abraham and Solomon as prophets and adds a new layer of sacredness in the belief that this place was a way station in Muhammad's chief mystical experience, the Night Journey and Ascension.

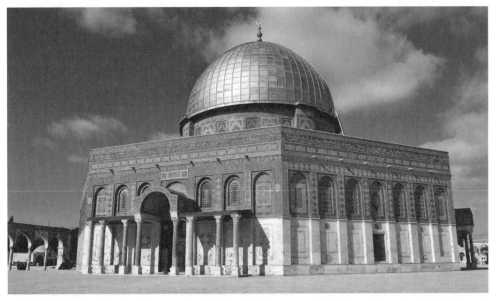

The Dome of the Rock in Jerusalem contains what is said to be a remnant of Solomon's temple, which is the rock from which the Prophet ascended in the Mi'raj. Jews also hold it as the holy place that is a spiritual junction between Heaven and Earth.

Are there any significant Muslim-Christian connections associated with the monumental Muslim structures in the Old City of Jerusalem?

Muslim Holy Places on the "Temple Mount" bear an important symbolic historic relationship to Christianity as well as to Judaism. It is no mere coincidence that the dimensions of the main dome of the Holy Sepulcher and those of the Dome of the Rock are within inches of each other: the dome of the Church of the Holy Sepulcher is 20.90m in diameter and 21.05m in elevation (height), while the Dome of the Rock measures 20.20m in diameter and 20.48m in elevation. In addition, just as the *original* church of the Holy Sepulcher (built by Constantine) consisted of a free-standing domed structure over the "aedicule" ("little building") of the Resurrection linked to a basilical hall by a columned courtyard, so the free-standing Dome of the Rock is axially aligned to a basilical hall (the al-Aqsa mosque) across an open courtyard. The similarities suggest a clear intent to compete visually with the Sepulcher complex. Finally, major inscriptions inside and on the exterior of the Dome of the Rock, with their clearly anti-Incarnational and anti-Trinitarian theological references, further suggest a Muslim attempt to make a statement of victory over Christianity.

Are there any reliable historical accounts of the very earliest contacts between Muslims and Christians in the Middle East? What were they like?

When the Muslim armies took the city of Jerusalem in 636, largely a peaceful transfer of power, a remarkable exchange is said to have taken place at the Holy Sepulcher. Ac- 287 cording to ancient accounts, the Muslim general presented himself to the Byzantine Patriarch Sophronius to receive his surrender of the city peacefully. The Patriarch agreed that he would do so, but only to the Caliph himself. But since the second Muslim Caliph, Umar (r.634–644), had not accompanied the military expedition, the general agreed to send for him. When Umar arrived from the long journey, he went to the Holy Sepulcher to meet Sophronius. The Patriarch cordially invited Umar in to the sacred place to pray, knowing that the new Muslim ruler's faith held Jesus in the highest esteem. Umar was grateful for the invitation, but declined: he did not want his actions to be interpreted as claiming a Christian holy place in the name of Islam. So instead, he and his retinue prayed in a space just across from the church, a spot now marked by a small building known as the mosque of Umar.

How has the Holy Sepulcher in Jerusalem played a historical role in Christian-Muslim relations?

As far back as the Middle Ages, Muslims have had an important and highly symbolic, but little appreciated, relationship to the Holy Sepulcher. It is no secret that various Christian denominations—Catholics, Greek Orthodox, Copts, and Armenians, for starters—have claimed symbolic "ownership" over various revered sites in the "Holy Land" for many centuries. Intra-Christian relations in the matter of custody and oversight of these shrines have not always been amicable, to say the least. In hopes of taking some of the

The entrance to the Church of the Holy Sepulchre in Jerusalem.

What is the "official" Vatican position on Jerusalem?

Papal interest in Jerusalem and the Holy Places revolves around the need to address the sources of tensions resident Christians face there. Among those sources are long-standing Christian-Muslim prejudices, divisiveness among the various Christian groups (especially evident in disputes over custody of holy places), the alarming rate of Christian emigration, and the Israeli government's official attitude toward non-Jewish communities. Vatican solutions to such problems highlight the need to make Jerusalem an internationally protected city and to guarantee the religious and civil rights of Jerusalem's Arabs. The Vatican has expressed consistent and increasing appreciation for the broader significance of Jerusalem and its place in the global perspective of the Abrahamic traditions. Meanwhile, the future of Christian presence in Jerusalem remains increasingly uncertain and the issue will test the Vatican's skill as a transnational actor. The Vatican considers the Holy City a microcosm of the multifaceted conflicts that plague the Middle East and has occasionally shaded from neutrality over toward the Palestinians, a minority of whom are Catholics, to express its solidarity with the oppressed and disenfranchised. That attitude has been a theme in the Vatican's pragmatic diplomacy.

resulting embarrassment of day-to-day management out of the hands of squabbling Christians, Christian leaders agreed centuries ago to entrust the key of the Holy Sepulcher to two respected Muslim families whose roots in Jerusalem go back as far as a thousand years. Until a few years ago, the Joudeh family guarded the key every night, while a member of the Nusseibeh family picked it up each morning, opened the Church, and locked it at night before returning the key to the first family. Because of the addition of a second exit for safety reasons in 1999, that arrangement came to an end. But it was a powerful symbol for some eight centuries that Christians preferred to entrust such an important role to Muslims rather than to other Christians.

Why do Jews, Christians, and Muslims all claim parts of Israel/Palestine as "Holy Land"?

Palestine lies in southwest Asia at the eastern end of the Mediterranean Sea. It is the Holy Land of Jews, since it was here that Moses led the Israelites after he led them out of slavery in Egypt and where they subsequently established their homeland; of Christians, since it is where Jesus Christ was born, lived, and died; and of Muslims, since the Arab people conquered Palestine in the seventh century and, except for a brief period during the Crusades, it was ruled by various Muslim dynasties until 1516 (when it became part of the Ottoman Empire). Palestine, which covers an area of just over 10,000 square miles, is roughly the size of Maryland.

The Mount of Olives (named after the olive grove that once existed there) is the site of a three-thousand-year-old Jewish cemetery. It is also a sacred place for Christians and Muslims, who built the Mosque (Chapel) of Ascension there.

Palestine's capital, Jerusalem, is also claimed as a holy city by all three religions. Jews call it the City of David (or the City of the Great King) since it was made the capital of the ancient kingdom of Israel around 1000 B.C.E. Christians regard it as holy since Jesus traveled with his disciples to Jerusalem to observe the Passover. It is the site of the Last Supper, and just outside the city, at Golgotha, Jesus was crucified (c. 30). Muslim Arabs captured the city in 638 (just after Muhammad's death), and, like the rest of Palestine, it has a long history of Muslim Arab rule. Jerusalem, which is now part of the modern state of Israel, is home to numerous synagogues, churches, and mosques. It also has been the site of numerous religious conflicts throughout history.

Besides the Western Wall, what are some examples of multiple claims to sacred sites?

Muslims count as their own, in addition, the mosque of the Ascension (of Jesus) on the Mount of Olives and the Mosque of Hebron that enshrines the cave of Machpelah, the tomb of Abraham and the patriarchs. Located as it is in an Arab town, the latter has been an important symbol for Palestinians. For most Christians, the principal holy sites in the Middle East are of course the Church of the Nativity in Bethlehem, the Church of the Holy Sepulcher in Jerusalem, as well as several places in Nazareth. But perhaps no single place speaks more eloquently of the diversity of Christianity in the Middle East than the Holy Sepulcher. With its multiple side chapels representing various Christian communities, competing liturgical celebrations, and the olfactory dissonance that results from multiple flavors of incense, the Church of the Holy Sepulcher offers a virtual smorgasbord of the Christian tradition. It has been and remains an important symbol of Christian presence in Jerusalem. Christian have not always enjoyed free exercise of their rights in the Middle East, and access to the Sepulcher remains one symbolic anchor in their sense of identity. In summary: As a sacred city, Jerusalem is the single most important place in the Middle East. For Muslims, the Dome is a symbol of victory; for Jews, the Wall a symbol of loss; for Christians, the Sepulcher a symbol of victory through loss.

Western sources frequently describe the Crusades as a totally justifiable, even heroic, quest to liberate the Holy Land from the infidels, while other accounts are less than flattering to the Crusaders. How can one sort this out?

Recent research has begun to change the views of European and American scholars about the Crusades by shedding new light on Islamic sources and revealing more about Christian motives and methods. As is so often the case with major military campaigns, the call to liberate the Holy Land served as a major distraction from problems at home. Popes and kings alike through the Middle Ages had ample reason to turn the minds of their constituents abroad. Crusade preaching developed into a major medieval theme to which the most persuasive of ecclesiastical orators bent their talents, promising indulgences and forgiveness of sin as well as the blessings of setting foot on sacred soil. Hope of adventure and material, as well as spiritual reward, was sufficient motive for thousands of warriors. From the Christian side, therefore, the Crusades were both pilgrimage and an honorable way for a young man to spend the forseeable future.

What, if anything, did the Crusades have to do with Islam—and how do Muslims interpret them?

From the Muslim side, the Crusades represented an unjustifiable declaration of all-out war on a part of the world they had ruled, even-handedly they believed, for over four hundred years. When the Muslims took Jerusalem from the weakened Byzantines in 636, they soon began to beautify the holy city. In view of the connection they saw in Muhammad's Night Journey and Ascension, they considered Jerusalem as much their Holy City as anyone else's; and they had welcomed Jewish and Christian pilgrims. Viewed from the great Muslim capitals of Cairo and Baghdad, however, the Crusades were not an overwhelming threat, with the exception of the initial success of the Latin Kingdom of Jerusalem (1099–1189) that resulted from the first Crusade. As result of this relative insulation from the Crusades, relatively few Muslim sources describe the events firsthand.

What about the historical Christian perspective on the Crusades?

From the side of countless Orthodox and Middle Eastern Christians, the Crusades were perhaps the greatest disaster of all. Latin troops began the Fourth Crusade by visiting apocalyptic horrors on the Christians of Constantinople during the Easter Triduum of

In this magazine illustration from Paris, France, published in 1844, Peter the Hermit is depicted preaching to the masses as to why they should fight in the First Crusade.

1204. For the various smaller ancient Christian communities of the Levant, the Crusades disrupted what had for the most part settled into a reasonably peaceful status quo under Muslim rule, causing massive reprisals. That culminated in the fall of Acre to Muslim forces in 1291, an event that betokened a serious blow to Christian presence in, and hopes for control of, the Middle East.

INTER–RELIGIOUS ENCOUNTERS

Do religious differences always result in broader social/political/cultural conflict?

Concerns over religious cohesiveness and identity vary with social and political circumstances. For example, in the former Yugoslavia, Croatian Catholics, Serbian Orthodox Christians, and Muslims managed a remarkably peaceful coexistence. When political disintegration followed the death of Marshal Tito, divisions along religious lines began to assume greater importance. That was not a direct result of differences in religious beliefs, but because age-old social divisions had occurred along the lines of communities of faith centuries earlier. With the loss of political cohesiveness came the convenient demonizing of "the others" and subsequent "ethnic cleansing." Most Bosnians, for example, had made little noise about their Muslim identity until they found themselves with little else to call their own. Serb propaganda warned of the imminent danger of a theocratic, fundamentalist Islamic state in their midst—the farthest thing from the minds of most Bosnian Muslims. Ironically, the loss of political standing has left the Muslims little choice but to reassert their religious distinctiveness. In the United States, concern over the danger of assimilation has likewise been associated with social factors. When Roman Catholics were still a small minority and subject to discrimination in several areas, they sought to maintain not only their Catholic distinctiveness but their nation of origin identities as well. American Jewish communities run the gamut from highly distinctive orthodox and conservative to highly assimilated. New Muslim communities are now facing the same issues in a story yet to unfold here.

What is an example of Christian-Muslim dialogue in the early centuries of encounter between the two faiths?

A fascinating text records a dialogue, initiated evidently by the Muslim side, that purportedly occurred in early ninth-century Jerusalem (c. 820). A monk named Abraham of Tiberias accepts the invitation of the Muslim *amir* (governor of Jerusalem) to participate, along with several other Muslim, Jewish, and Christian discussants, in the presence of the Patriarch of Jerusalem. This is a setting that might well amaze readers new to the study of late antique Middle Eastern Christian history. What the text presents is no mere informal gathering of casually interested parties, but a rather high level "official" discussion of all the major theological topics one might expect in such a venue: Trinity, Incarnation, Scriptural revelation, Cross and Resurrection of Jesus, etc. The Abraham of this dialogue represents the first generation of Arab Christian theologians alongside the other more famous apologists. Abraham's views represent an apologetic, ecumenical theology in mission, distinct from other patrologies and theologies, for it is heir to the Syriac, Greek, and Coptic traditions alike. Abraham's dialogue offers the reader a sample of a theology that arose in the Melkite faith, evolved in a Syriac context, and is here expressed in Arabic. It seems fairly certain that the dialogue actually transpired pretty much as described, although there are clearly some literary embellishments in the document.

What does "syncretism" mean?

Syncretism is from a Greek root meaning "mixed together" and refers in general to the blending of doctrinal and ritual elements from two or more religious traditions to form a new tradition or sub-tradition. When two or more traditions co-exist in a cultural context, they invariably rub elbows and influence each other religiously to some extent. Though the main traditions typically retain their characteristic features, there are often pockets or areas in a region in which elements of the larger traditions coalesce to shape

ISLAM AND OTHER FAITHS

293

a recognizably new system of belief. The Druze communities of the Middle East, combining Islamic and Christian themes, and India's Sikh tradition, blending Hindu and Islamic elements, are examples. Syncretism can also describe to some extent the fact of change within major traditions themselves when over many centuries they develop in such a way that, say, a modern form of the tradition looks very different from much earlier stages. The histories of the greater Hindu and Buddhist traditions exemplify this type. Tibetan Buddhism, to be more specific, represents a remarkable blend of elements from indigenous Tibetan Bon shamanism, Tantric Hinduism, and Buddhism.

How well did the early Muslims get along with the Jews and Christians living in Arabia during Muhammad's time?

Christians lived in various parts of the Arabian Peninsula and its environs during Muhammad's time. To the northwest the Arab tribe called the Ghassanids, the Byzantine "buffer state" against the Sasanian dynasty of Persia during Muhammad's earliest years, was Christian. To the southwest, in the Yemen, also were small Christian kingdoms. And just to the west of the Yemen, across the Red Sea, was the Abyssinian Christian kingdom of the Negus who gave asylum to a small group of Muhammad's community in the year 615. In the city of Medina there was a significant Jewish presence as well, in three influential Jewish tribes. Muhammad's clashes with them as he shaped the new Muslim polity were, to say the least, a very grim chapter in the story of Islam's beginnings. In short, religious diversity was part of the scene in which Islam grew up, and Muslim relations with the Christians were in general much less problematic than with the Jews.

Have Muslims traditionally sent out missionaries to convert others?

Islam has been a missionary tradition since its earliest days. Muhammad's preaching eventually gathered a community of Meccans, which in turn grew dramatically after migrating to Medina in the *Hijra*. Muslims believe in spreading the word whenever possible. Proselytizing is called "inviting" (*da'wa*, DA'wah) others to join the community of Islam. Many regard it as a basic religious duty, second only to their fulfillment of the Five Pillars. Despite perceptions to the contrary, Islam has spread far more often through peaceful means than

Converting to Islam is a simple matter of acknowledging God's transcendent unity and accepting Muhammad as his Prophet.

through the sword. Among the earliest dedicated missionaries were Sufis who traveled with Muslim merchants along the trade routes to establish communities all over Asia and Africa. Some larger mission-oriented organizations have developed and moved into new territory with local or governmental sponsorship in a home country, but Muslim missionary societies are generally fewer and smaller than their Christian counterparts.

What does one do to convert to Islam?

Converting to Islam is a relatively simple matter. Interested individuals have typically already done some basic study of the tradition, but no prescribed course of religious education is required or expected. Naturally, most Muslims believe that the more converts know about the tradition and its history, the more likely it is to make an informed decision. Before entering into the brief ceremony that renders a candidate officially Muslim, the convert performs the major purification ritual called *ghusl*. Formal assent to the tenets of Islam entails a simple repetition of the *Shahada* before any two adult male witnesses.

HISTORICAL MUSLIM ATTITUDES TOWARD CHRISTIANS AND VICE VERSA

Are there any biblical criteria that might offer Christians ways of thinking about positive connections between Islam and Christianity?

Paul's Letter to the Galatians (5:22), as well as other sources, talks of "Fruits of the Holy Spirit." Muslims, too, experience and manifest these gifts: love, joy, patience, peace, kindness, goodness, faithfulness, gentleness, and self-control. Second, Christians speak of the Spiritual and Corporal works of mercy. And when Muslims engage with religious motives in such deeds as feeding the hungry, visiting the sick, and burying the dead, they share in the very same values Christians express through these and other expressions of kindness and compassion. Third, Christians talk of the "Cardinal" and "Theological Virtues": prudence, fortitude, temperance, justice; and faith, hope, and love, respectively. Muslims, too, manifest these virtues in their everyday lives. Fourth, Matthew's Gospel (chapter 13) enshrines images of the "kingdom of God" in parables and suggests that these images are accessible to a wide range of persons. In addition, Matthew (25:31–46) details criteria for judging who will inherit the kingdom, including: feeding the hungry, giving drink to the thirsty, welcoming the stranger, clothing the naked, and visiting the sick and imprisoned. Muslims too emphasize the centrality of such care and concern as essential to their religious responsibilities. Finally, the "Eight Beatitudes" (Matthew 5) speak to many more religious values that define the personal lives of countless Muslims: blessed are the poor in spirit, for theirs is the kingdom; those who mourn will be comforted; the meek, who will inherit the earth; who hunger and thirst for justice, and shall be satisfied; the merciful, who will obtain mercy; the pure in heart, who will see God; the peacemakers, who will be called children of God; who are persecuted for justice's sake, for theirs is the kingdom of heaven.

Do we have evidence of how Christians responded to early Muslim conquests of the Central Middle East?

Christian theologians living in formerly Byzantine lands in the ninth and tenth centuries crafted a technical language with which to respond to the religion of their Muslim governing class, specifically to show how Muslim analysis of the divine attributes was inconsistent and rationally questionable. Muslim theologians, beginning in the tenth century, responded with polemics aimed not at Christian teaching as a whole, but at demonstrating the irrationality of the doctrines of Trinity and Incarnation, all in service of defending their own construction of God's absolute and perfect transcendent unity. In addition, Christians also expressed their views of the situation in the more accessible and "popular" literary genre of hagiography, particularly the stories of Christian martyrs. Authors writing in Arabic tended to prefer what one could call an "apologetics of affinity" that emphasized comity and irenic relations between Christians and their Muslim rulers. By contrast, those who wrote in Greek—and whose works were less likely to be read by Muslims—tended to articulate an "apologetics of difference," emphasizing disparities in religion and the difficulty of living under alien rule.

How did medieval Western (European) Christians view Islam in general?

Some Christians had actual personal encounters with Muslims (away from the battlefield), and some spent years working in Muslim lands and dedicated themselves to learning Arabic and first-hand study of key texts such as Quran and Hadith. Not likely by mere happenstance, it was those who knew Muslims (e.g., Ramon Llull, Burchard of Strasbourg, and Riccoldo da Monte Croce) who inclined toward more positive views of Islam. In most instances, however, venomous diatribes by the likes of Peter the Venerable (of Cluniac reform fame), Thomas Aquinas, and others emitted in abundance from a climate in which fear of an impending Muslim threat was the air so many medieval Christians

St. Thomas Aquinas, like virtually all major medieval European Christian thinkers, regarded Islam as a threat to Europe.

breathed. Quite negative approaches characterized the "Saracen" nemesis variously as pagan idolaters or heretics (the latter allowing at least some form of original connection with the Christian family). They indicted the arch-Saracen, Muhammad, as a charlatan or magician at best; diabolically possessed, criminally debauched, or pathologically violent at worst. Whether as an instrument of divine retribution for Christian infidelities or an embodiment of sheer evil, Islam symbolized a potentially apocalyptic force only the faithless or the fool could face with equanimity. By way of exception, Saladin, the Muslim hero of the anti-Crusade, merited surprising praise, not as a Muslim but as a paragon of knightly virtue and fair-mindedness.

What is an example of some more recent explicitly Christian perspectives on Islam?

The Catholic Second Vatican Council's 1965 watershed document "In Our Age" (*Nostra Aetate*) proclaimed that the church "rejects nothing that is true and holy" in the other great faith traditions. The document did not articulate precisely and in detail "what is true and holy in Islam" in so many words, but it did offer some limited but important clues: "The church regards Muslims with esteem. They adore the one God, living and subsisting in Himself, merciful and all-powerful, the Creator of heaven and earth, who has spoken to humans; they take pains to submit wholeheartedly to His inscrutable decrees, just as Abraham, with whom the faith of Islam is linking itself, submitted to God.... They value the moral life and worship God especially through prayer, almsgiving, and fasting. Since in the course of centuries not a few quarrels have arisen between Christians and Muslims, this sacred Synod urges all to forget the past, work sincerely for mutual understanding and ... promote together for the benefit of humankind social justice and moral welfare as well as peace and freedom."

Does that Christian statement provide any further insight into larger theological themes Islam shares with Christianity?

"In our Age" lists several large themes. First, Islamic monotheism focuses on one transcendent deity who not only creates all things, but has a unique relationship to humanity. Second, Prophetic revelation becomes accessible to humankind through the preaching of the prophets, and then via sacred scriptures. Third, a mutual concern for religiously founded ethics and social justice means that Muslims and Christians share fundamental responsibility for caring for others as well as for creation in all its dimensions. Surprisingly, Vatican II did not mention the very strong Muslim-Christian theological link of eschatology—belief in the "last things" (death, judgment, resurrection of the body, heaven/hell). Though there are some details in which Islamic "cosmology" (the structure of the spiritual universe) differs from Christian views, the essentials of mortality and moral accountability before God are similar in many striking ways. Not surprisingly, the council document made no mention at all of Muhammad. The reason? Christians believe that the "finality" of God's revelation in Jesus Christ rules out any subsequent claims to the "finality" Muslims claim for Muhammad's message and mission.

What do Islam's sacred sources say explicitly about religion in general?

Beginning with the Quran, Islamic tradition possesses a well-articulated attitude toward other faith communities. No other world religious scripture of the Quran's antiquity contains such a clearly articulated approach to this matter. It employs several terms to denote the various dimensions of human religious life. Most importantly, the term *din* (deen) broadly refers to religiosity. As a fundamental impulse that God infuses into every person, *din* has always been one and the same. It implies the basic attitude of grateful surrender in a generic sense. That original unity of human religious response ramified into different groups for a variety of reasons (see e.g. Quran 2:213, 23:51–4). Even though God sent new messengers to correct the deviations that occurred through history, many people chose not to accept the corrective and kept to the old ways.

What do Islam's sacred sources say about religious groups or faith communities as such?

The Quran uses the term *milla* (MIL-la) to refer to specific religious communities that arose as a result of those deviations. Abraham, for example, was the leader of a *milla*. At various times in Islamic history, most notably during the Ottoman dynasty, the so-called "millet system" had granted internal autonomy to individual religious groups. The key term for the overall Muslim religious entity was (and remains) the *umma*, the community of believers under the tutelage of Islamic religious officialdom. While the laws of the *umma* pertained generally to the whole population, specific rules pertaining to the religious practice of the various non-Muslim communities were allowed to take precedence. For example, the central Muslim authorities respected the dietary and ritual needs of each *milla*. The overriding principle in this model is that God has allowed humankind to become religiously diverse precisely as a test, to see how well they can work out their differences, and an impetus to a beneficial moral competition.

How do Muslims view Islam's "message" in relation to those of other religious traditions?

According to the Quran, the revelation delivered through Muhammad is not new, but a continuation and reaffirmation of the divine message given to all the earlier prophets acknowledged in the Jewish and Christian traditions. If prior generations of Jews and Christians had not misinterpreted or even willfully corrupted the message, subsequent corrective revelations would have been unnecessary. In other words, Muslims regard Islam's relationship to the earlier Abrahamic faiths somewhat similar to the way Christians regard their tradition's relationship to Judaism. The later revelation completes, fulfills, corrects, or abrogates the earlier one. As mentioned above, Islamic tradition regards the "Peoples of the Book" as especially close kin. It also presents a sort of "hierarchy" of kinship among them, as well as among communities beyond that grouping. The Quran suggests that Muslims should consider Christians perhaps somewhat closer than Jews, even though there are far larger theological differences between Islam and

Christianity than between Islam and Judaism. The concept of "Peoples of the Book" also came to include other minority religious communities of the Middle East, such as the Zoroastrians. In general, Muslims are inclined to regard members of other traditions, such as Hindus and Buddhists, for example, as considerably further removed from the possibility of salvation. But views of that sort naturally vary somewhat from region to region, as for example, in India, where Muslims and Hindus often live side by side.

With significant populations of Christians living in various parts of the Middle East, have any Christian groups weighed in on issues of Middle East justice and Muslim-Christian relations?

Numerous Christian churches continue to express concern over conflicts that increasingly affect adversely the lives of Middle Eastern Christians. One example is Catholic Christian approaches to these difficulties. Beginning with the withdrawal of the charge of Christocide long ago leveled at Jews by Christians, Catholic concerns expressed in words and deeds have been considerable in relation to three of the major actors in the current Middle East scene: the Israelis, the Palestinians, and indigenous Christian minorities. Three large issues are noteworthy: responses to the Israeli-Palestinian dispute, perceptions of the Catholic Church's responsibilities with respect to Jerusalem and the Holy Places, and concrete initiatives in the wake of Lebanon's fifteen-year civil war (1975–1990). The Catholic Church has consistently sought to exercise its moral suasion to provide humanitarian relief and to implore the intervention of outside powers in ending the carnage.

What is an example of the kind of misunderstanding that drives wedges between Muslims and Christians?

In 2006, Pope Benedict gave a speech at Regensburg University, where he had once taught. He referred to the comments of a fourteenth-century Byzantine ruler to the effect that the teachings of Muhammad were backward and violent. Muslims in various nations staged angry demonstrations calling for a repudiation of Benedict's comments. Although the pope sought to clarify his remarks by saying that he was merely citing the opinion of a medieval Christian figure and did not subscribe to his views, many people continued to believe that the pope should never have included such a negative assessment of Islam without

Pope Benedict XVI, who was pope from 2005 to 2013, drew considerable ire from the Muslim community when he gave a speech at Regensburg University implying that Islam was a violent faith.

clearly dissociating himself from it. Several weeks after the speech, the pope visited Turkey and expressed a desire to smooth over any misunderstanding. Many Turkish Muslims were cautiously optimistic and were pleasantly surprised at what actually happened: the pope visited the Sultan Ahmet mosque in Istanbul (near the great Byzantine cathedral of Hagia Sophia) with the minister of religion and culture, and he silently bowed in a moment of reflection under the great dome of the mosque. Many Turks who watched the event on TV responded very positively to the pope's simple gesture of respect and reverence. Within weeks of the Regensburg address, some three dozen Muslim scholars reached out in a letter to the Vatican seeking reconciliation. No direct response was forthcoming from the Vatican at that time, and press coverage virtually disregarded the Muslim voices.

What are some examples of Muslims taking the initiative to resolve Muslim-Christian misunderstanding?

In 2007, something truly remarkable in Muslim-Christian relations happened, and yet few Americans were aware of it. A total of 138 Muslim religious scholars from over twenty countries signed an open letter to Pope Benedict and to some two dozen leaders of Orthodox and Protestant churches. Overwhelmingly conciliatory and non-polemical, the document simply lays out evidence from the Bible and Quran that all three Abrahamic faiths share a common focus on the "two great commandments," love of God and love of one's neighbor as oneself. But this most noteworthy development has been almost totally ignored. It received virtually no electronic media coverage and was consigned to back-page blurbs of major newspapers. Had the letter been a venomous diatribe against Christianity and the leaders of the many churches, it would almost certainly have grabbed banner coverage.

MOVING FORWARD
TO MUTUAL UNDERSTANDING

What do the terms "ecumenism" and "inter-religious dialogue" mean?

Ecumenism includes all the ways in which members of the many Christian churches and denominations have sought to come together in dialogue for mutual understanding. It does not necessarily envision any eventual unification, though that has happened in some instances. Inter-religious dialogue refers to the wider arena of direct attempts by members and administrations of the larger faith traditions to come together in hopes of deeper appreciation of their common interests as well as of the issues that divide them. So for example, there are Muslim-Christian, Buddhist-Christian, and other organizations for dialogue. Attempts at inter-religious dialogue are gradually developing independent institutions, such as the Elijah School in Jerusalem, which focuses on the notion that all the world's traditions have great treasures of wisdom to share with each other. Many people fear dialogue because they think it implies the eventual loss of diversity. People being what we are, there is little danger of that. Pluralism is a screamingly obvious fact of life. Mutual understanding is no longer a luxury but an absolute prerequisite for peace in the world.

It's common to refer to Judaism, Christianity, and Islam as the Abrahamic Faiths, but how realistic is the expectation of real cooperation among the three these days?

The potential of such a notion for fostering a sense of unity and mutual understanding is balanced by its potential, paradoxically, for divisiveness. In every "sibling relationship" there is the potential for "sibling rivalry." On the positive side, the classical Islamic understanding of the familial connection represents perhaps the only well-developed position on inter-religious relations one can find in any primary scripture. Islam possesses a mechanism for understanding its relationship to Judaism and Christianity, but the converse is not the case.

On the negative side, the same classical doctrine just as naturally fosters the conviction that adherence to Islam brings with it an inherent, even automatic, knowledge of the essential message of Christianity. Jews and Christians have, over the centuries, progressively lost touch with the essence of their revelations. The result is that Muslims know Christianity better than Christians, for Christians have suffered an alienation from their truest religious selves. "True Christianity" in its original, uncorrupted form, was identical to the fundamental teachings of Islam.

Even though members of the same "family" don't always get along, one would think that religious communities that all trace their lineage back to Abraham could find at least a little to agree on. Paradoxically, the potential of family membership for fostering a sense of unity and mutual understanding is balanced off by its potential for divisiveness. Every family struggles with problems of sibling rivalry. On the one hand, the clas-

What's the underlying difficulty of the "sibling relationship" between Abrahamic faiths?

Two major problems in positing or presuming a familial relationship are first, that, as in all families, the relationship is not chosen but seen as a fact of life; and second, that as in all families, there are skeletons in the closet. One can respond to the first either by agreeing to work with the actual situation, by deciding to make the best of an unpleasant situation, or by acting out one's resentment of it. All three modes of responding to the problem of an unasked-for familial relationship involve communication. Acting out or other forms of passive aggressive behavior are notoriously difficult to combat, as most any counselor or therapist will explain, because their inherent designs for sabotage occur together with an avowed desire to cooperate.

Islam, Judaism, and Christianity are all Abrahamic faiths with much in common.

sical Islamic understanding of the familial connection represents a highly developed position on inter-religious relations. Islam's scripture articulates its relationship to the scriptures of Judaism and Christianity in a way that the scriptures of the earlier traditions could not have done.

What is the story about King Solomon and the Queen of Sheba that is a metaphor for the skeletons in the closet among Abrahamic faiths?

Classic Islamic tradition provides perceptive insights on this problem. A brilliant thirteenth-century Persian poet named Nizami reflected on it in his splendid mystical epic, the *Seven Portraits*. Once upon a time, King Solomon married the Queen of Sheba. Together they had a child who was ill from birth. As the child grew, its health became more worrisome to the parents so that they feared for its life. They earnestly besought God to heal the languishing tot and vowed they would willingly do anything God asked of them to bring about their hearts' desire. Came the divine message: reveal to one another your deepest secret and your child will begin to recover forthwith.

Bilqis, queen of Sheba, searched her soul and admitted to Solomon that she still harbored resentment over one thing Solomon had done to her. Solomon had once tricked her into lifting the hem of her skirt by requiring her to walk across a floor so glossy she would think it was covered with water. The King had heard the queen walked on cloven hooves and wanted to find out discreetly if the rumor were true. Still, Bilqis confessed, she yearned to trick Solomon back for his perfidy. Solomon for his part admitted that, wealthy and powerful as he was, and as far-reaching as was his sovereignty—now including even the lands of Sheba as well as all the animal kingdoms—he nevertheless wanted more. Yes, he was indeed greedy and not quite content with the extent of his dominion. The moment the royal couple had brought their dark secrets into the light, their child began to heal.

If "clearing the air" is really important, where do Muslims and Christians have to start?

What is abundantly clear is that Muslims and Christians each have tucked away some embarrassing little secrets about their feelings toward the other; but it is equally clear that each hides them far less effectively than imagined. The destructive energies of these thinly veiled real feelings, fears, and suspicions inevitably manifest themselves, taking shape indirectly in social and cultural institutions. As people entrusted with the care and nurturance of the race and the planet, Muslims and Christians can see—if they are honest—what family systems therapists often discern in troubled marriages: bad communication hurts posterity, and the wounds of one generation are incarnated in the next.

Are there any anecdotes from ancient Muslim tradition that offer insights into the subject of "inter-religious" relations?

A charming story illustrates the ideal of inter-religious openness the Islamic tradition holds up to its members. Abraham, the paragon of hospitality, was in the habit of postponing his breakfast each day until some hungry wayfarer should happen by his house. He would then invite the stranger in to share his table. One day an old man came along. As the two were about to refresh themselves, Abraham began to pronounce a blessing. When he noted that the old man's lips formed the words of another prayer, that of a Zoroastrian, Abraham became incensed and drove the stranger away—how could he offer hospitality to a Fire Worshipper? God was displeased, and reprimanded Abraham, saying, "I have given this man life and food for a hundred years. Could you not give him hospitality for one day, even if he does homage to fire?" Abraham immediately went after the old man and brought him back to his home. Abraham, already known as the paragon of hospitality, thus becomes also the model of openness to religious diversity. Even to the "Friend of the Merciful" (*Khalil ar-Rahman*) that virtue apparently did not come naturally.

What is a major historical example of relations between ruling Muslims and members of communities not included among the "Peoples of the Book"?

Under the greatest of the Indian Muslim dynasties, the Mughals, the most powerful of the rulers, Emperor Akbar (r. 1556–1605), had an unusually open policy toward religious pluralism. He instituted a practice of having open debate and discussion at the palace, inviting religious scholars and representatives of all the faiths represented in his realm, which included over half of the Indian subcontinent. He even funded the construction of lavish Hindu temples, and Catholic Jesuit missionaries from Europe were honored guests at court. Things began to change somewhat under his immediate successors, who regarded Akbar as much too religiously accommodating. His son Jahangir remained generally quite tolerant of existing institutions and practices of other faiths, as did his grandson, Shah Jahan, builder of the Taj Mahal. But neither went so far as to fund non-Muslim places of worship. Akbar's great grandson, Aurangzeb, however, opted for a much less open attitude, going so far as to destroy non-Muslim places of worship.

Do Muslims have rituals similar to Christian baptism, Jewish bar and bat mitzvah, or circumcision?

All religious traditions seek to offer their members assistance in getting through important or difficult experiences in life by means of "rites of passage." These practices vary to some degree from one culture to another, but there is generally a common core in the rituals. Baptism and bar/bat mitzvah observances are examples of initiatory rites, celebrations of a young person's formal religious welcoming into the community.

Islam also has its initiatory rites. On the seventh day after birth, a child's hair is shaved and parents give its weight in currency to the poor. At that time a father might whisper the *adhan* or call to prayer into the child's right ear and the *iqama* (the invitation to begin prayer that is announced once worshippers gather in the mosque) into the left ear. Formal naming occurs in this context as well, with preference given to names traditionally associated with outstanding Muslims, beginning of course with Muhammad.

Muslims also practice a rite of circumcision, but age and ritual circumstances vary regionally. In some places it is a puberty rite; in others, infants are circumcised. Feast days of Friends of God are often favorite occasions for the circumcision of older individuals especially. Their initiation is thereby associated with the *baraka*, blessing and grace, bestowed in connection with the powerful presence of the saint.

What about fasting as a common ritual practice among the Abrahamic faiths?

Fasting is another important ritual link among the three traditions. Jews recognize a number of day-long fasts through the year, the most important being Yom Kippur (Day of Atonement) and the Ninth of Av (mourning for the destruction of the Temple) on which participants fast from sunset to sunset. Other occasions commemorate tragic events in Jewish history or preparatory rites, such as the day immediately preceding festive Purim or Passover. Christians traditionally think of the forty days of Lent as a time of fasting, but the observance is generally marked by partial rather than complete fasting through the day and in recent times has become somewhat relaxed in its demands. The Muslim fast through the thirty days of Ramadan extends across a shorter period, but calls on participants to fast altogether from dawn to sunset. The three traditions recommend fasting for a variety of similar reasons, but Judaism is unique in its observance of specific occasions of historic tragedy.

A Muslim family fasts during Ramadan. Fasting reminds people that there are others in the world less fortunate than they are.

What do people talk about in Christian-Muslim dialogue groups?

Such gatherings generally welcome Christians and Muslims of all perspectives, emphasize the need to understand the other party as that party wishes to be understood, and describe the other's beliefs as he or she would express them. These groups seek both to listen and to inform, to pass along to their co-religionists the fruits of their dialogue, to focus on human dignity, and to promote educational endeavors designed to break down stereotypes. Proselytizing has no place in the dialogue group. Possible themes for dialogue include a search for common ground in matters of belief (scriptures, the role of prophets, major images of God, the place of Muhammad and Jesus, and Mary the Mother of Jesus) and responses to questions of environment, family life, education, neighborhood, and works of mercy.

What might Muslims and Christians in dialogue discuss profitably about the life of religious seekers together on earth?

Muslims and Christians can agree with Robert Frost's line, "Earth's the right place for loving"; but with the following line, "I can't imagine where it is likely to go better," they would beg to differ. Both could most definitely imagine where it *was* likely to go better. Life in this world is not an end in itself, but merely a way station on a journey across a much broader terrain. From a Muslim perspective, life on earth is a time for remembering, for nostalgia, for longing to return to one's origin. But on the Christian side, the centrality of the Incarnation brings the "way back to that origin" down to earth. For Muslims, the problem that Incarnation poses is that it appears to compromise the Divine Unity and transcendence. Still, the two sides can share a strong conviction of the paradox of divine availability.

Muslims believe God is closer than the jugular vein, that everywhere one looks one can see the face of God, that the heart of the believer is like a pen between the two fingers of the Merciful. As for the Christian concept of the Trinity, Muslims believe it is a form of polytheism and unnecessarily overloads the image of God with superfluous structures and complications—even contradiction. On the other hand, Muslims can agree that it is appropriate to describe God as having many names. There the two sides can find an important point of contact.

And how do Muslims view the Christian belief in the "Holy Spirit"?

Muslims might see the Spirit's role and function reflected in a number of the "Ninety-Nine Most Beautiful Names" of God. In fact, together Christians and Muslims could very well pray a litany made up of a blend of Christian invocations of the Spirit and Muslim Divine Names. Together they might, for example, invoke God as the Comforter, the Gracious and Merciful, the Source of Peace, the Subtle and Aware. "O Gatherer," they might pray together, "bring us together; O Light, illumine our world; O Long-Awaiting, wait for us when we tarry...."

Is there a larger underlying theological theme implied here that is of mutual concern to Muslims and Christians?

Deep in both traditions is the symbolism of humankind on pilgrimage back to God along the "road" of Creation. Christians and Muslims can agree on Creation's potential for making known its Creator, and that God's purpose in Creation is to communicate the divine goodness. Both agree that Creation's ultimate purpose is to glorify God and to reveal that glory indirectly to humankind, thereby to lead humanity back to its source. They agree that God is the final cause, the ultimate purpose, of all creation, and that human beings have a difficult time getting the idea.

A Christian stained glass window depicts the Holy Spirit in the form of a dove. Muslims speak of a Holy Spirit, but in reference to the Angel Gabriel.

Christians and Muslims do, to be sure, have slightly different notions as to how God helps people get the idea and follow the true path to their goal. For Christians, the solution is redemption from an otherwise impossible predicament. God becomes part of the world and of humanity to show the way by an exemplary share in the human condition. For Muslims, the solution to the dilemma takes the form of God's sending prophets, beginning with Adam and proceeding through history down to and culminating in Muhammad. Prophets are the trail-blazing pilgrims uniquely equipped to help humankind see the revelatory signs of which creation is composed.

How do the two traditions address the shared human problem of keeping to the path back to God?

For Christians the obstacle to staying on the road is that unpleasant condition resulting from the sin of Adam. Islamic tradition does not attribute any such dramatic change in the human condition to human choice. In Muslim tradition, human beings are born blind to the virtually numberless revelatory signs God has arrayed before them. In what amounts to a variation on the Biblical theme of God's hardening of the heart, the Creator drops a veil of forgetfulness and heedlessness over human vision, so that they cannot see clearly. Heedlessness is the divinely ordained equivalent to the "happy fault," in that it maintains the world in existence as it is, and thus paradoxically preserves it as the theater of the ongoing revelation of God's attributes. Into this world of forgetfulness, however, God sends along a select few who know the whole truth. These are the prophets. The process of pilgrimage in the light of prophetic revelation gradually polishes that rust of heedlessness from the mirror of the heart, so that the pilgrim can see there at least a reflection of God's beauty in creation. Heart thus becomes a microcosm of creation, according to the sacred saying: "Heaven and Earth cannot contain Me; but in the heart of the believer there is ample room." And here is where Jesus fits in the Islamic worldview. Known as Mary's Son, Jesus models almost-perfect trust in God. His breath could bring the dead to life; though his cousin John was a serious character, Jesus loved to laugh. Both traditions affirm Mary's role in the divine plan—to the extent of being the mother, by God's intervention, of a great prophet. Mary is one of the few individuals after whom an entire chapter of the Quran has been named, and she is one of the four "perfect" women.

What are some of the chief lessons learned in dialogue groups?

Perhaps the most fundamental lesson is an appreciation of doctrinal similarities and differences. Once participants come to know each other better, what may have begun as a kind of technical catechism-like exchange can become a more personal reflection on how each person has internalized the basic beliefs. Included here, but perhaps approachable at a more advanced stage, is that very delicate matter of acknowledging built-in theological positions that can prejudice or even sabotage dialogue: in particular, the Christian view of its revelation as final, and the classic Muslim view that the once pure message at the heart of Christianity and Judaism became corrupt and in need of definitive restatement.

A second major lesson concerns the matter of honesty about personal attitudes over the long haul in dialogue. Here one finds acknowledgement of the importance of simply meeting one another in breaking down stereotypes, of the need for patience and persistence, of letting go the desire to see the other change, of willingness to risk putting one's fears on the table, and of a willingness to be misunderstood and be told one does not understand. All such matters demand a considerable level of personal security, maturity, and freedom, since they touch on issues potentially very threatening.

What about lessons relating to cultural sensitivities?

A number of important lessons fit under the heading of cultural sensitivities. Although it is virtually impossible ultimately to separate religious concerns neatly from geo-political concerns, Muslim-Christian dialogue requires some ability to distinguish truly American issues that bear directly on the interaction of the participants, from international "fallout." Obviously, American involvement in the Middle East and elsewhere—for example—is hardly negligible; but participants need to be aware of how such issues can drive wedges between American participants. A related lesson concerns the need for sensitivity to social concerns, including an awareness of dietary restrictions and ritual needs. Social occasions should include alternatives to pork and to non-alcoholic beverages. During the month of Ramadan, non-Muslims might be especially sensitive about whether they will serve refreshments during daylight hours, when fasting Muslims would not be able to share the food. Ritual needs are a second major category. Gatherings should take into account daily Muslim times of ritual prayer, allowing for Muslims who wish to pray to do so. Christian dialogue partners and planners ought to familiarize themselves with the current year's religious calendar and be aware of when the sacred observances and festivities of the Muslim lunar schedule will fall. For American Christians, such concerns have often been removed from active consideration by a taken-for-granted calendar and menu of readily available grocery items.

What are some models for inter-religious dialogue and their various advantages and disadvantages?

Two broad "levels" of possible dialogue come to mind—formal and informal. Of the more formal sort, two models stand out. First there is interaction between "official" representatives of the traditions on a local level, priest or minister and imam. The advantage is that both partners exercise leadership roles and can bring the message home to the parish church and mosque. There are two disadvantages. One is that levels of religious education and intellectual sophistication may vary greatly and lead to frustrated expectations concerning the quality and tone of the exchange. In addition, where a Catholic is involved, a priest may regard himself as speaking in some way for the whole church, whereas the imam plays no such official role in Islam. The challenge in this model is that of persuading prospective partners that the discussion is not about winning and losing, or even scoring points, but about increasing mutual understanding.

What are some "informal" kinds of dialogue?

Parent-to-parent dialogue raises interesting possibilities. A more pastoral kind of conversation has already begun all over the country, wherever Muslims and Christians discover that their children attend the same schools, for instance. Common concerns over values in education can lead to further and more personal sharing of faith, of the experience of God's action in the world, and of diverse ways of celebrating religious convictions. Such conversation can occur, for example, as a result of memberships in school or neighborhood organizations. They have the advantage of bringing people together with a common project that demands cooperation and mutual respect. On the other hand, people may not have the time to allow their conversations to move beyond more immediate issues, may be embarrassed to ask questions about the other's beliefs, or may be afraid to admit their ignorance. The challenge here is to persuade people that mutual understanding of religious values is just as important to the future of their neighborhoods and schools as getting the sidewalk fixed or making sure the cafeteria serves healthy food.

Is explicitly "inter-religious education" an important ingredient here?

Educational input, such as through high school and college courses of various kinds, can be an excellent way of introducing students to each other's faiths and cultural backgrounds. A major advantage is that younger students especially have a natural curiosity about their peers from other backgrounds. A disadvantage is that it may be difficult for some students to admit that they have not kept in touch with their faith communities. Sometimes poorly informed partners in conversation can actually reinforce stereotypes about their own traditions. The challenge therefore is to foster genuine openness and get around the implicit threat of differences between cultures and belief systems.

CULTURE AND RELIGION

INCULTURATION AND ISLAMIZATION

Why bring in the topic of "culture"? Aren't "religion" and "faith" unique and distinct aspects of human life, uncorrupted by cultural or political influences?

It is tempting to imagine that there is such a thing as "pure" religion and "unalloyed" faith. But the challenging reality is that, though they may try, human beings cannot simply disentangle religion from culture. Every facet of human interpretation of sacred texts or expression of religious values is shaped and colored by the cultural, ethnic, and political dimensions of one's lives. So powerful and pervasive are the multiple aspects of culture that they frequently trump even the more positive effects of religion.

How does religion relate, for example, to gender as a cultural feature?

Take the much-publicized matter of what some Muslims identify as mandatory clothing restrictions for women. A large majority of people who insist that Muslim women are religiously required to dress in some specific variety of "covering" also insist that such requirements are clearly and explicitly mandated by the Quran. In fact, however, the sacred scripture makes only the rather generic demand that women "modestly cover their charms/attractiveness," without providing any kind of sartorial specifics. That does not deter Muslims from dozens of cultural backgrounds from assuring all inquirers that *their* women's religiously mandated couture is a direct response to revelation. Here's the problem: a cursory search on the Web turns up not only a list of at least half a dozen strikingly different types (each providing coverage of varying parts and percentages of the female body), but an even greater profusion of fashion styles, designs, and colors, not to mention preferred optional accessories. Even in this fairly obvious example of disparity between culturally accepted norms and less-than-accurate assumptions about divinely revealed norms, culture invariably wins out.

What are some ways of understanding how Islam has interacted with the cultures in which it has taken root? Where does the one begin and the other end?

Social scientists and theologians have recently been using the term "inculturation" to describe how religious traditions interact with their various cultural contexts. First of all, it is important to understand the circumstances under which a religious community has begun to grow in a new cultural setting. The relationship of the tradition to political and military power, and of majority to minority status, are primary variables. Second, it is helpful to talk in terms of the complementary dynamics of Islamization and indigenization.

Islamization means the process by which the religious tradition called Islam becomes a decisive factor within a culture or ethnic group or region. Indigenization means the process by which a culture, ethnic group, or region confers its distinctive colors and textures on Islam. The shape of "Islamdom" as both unified and diverse is a function of these two processes operating at different rates in different settings.

What are some important historical Islamic examples of these dynamics?

When early Muslims brought Islam into Iraq and Persia, they were in political control; but they initially made a deliberate decision to disrupt the life of the subject peoples as little as possible. As Muslims gradually became the majority, Islam became the dominant religious culture of the Middle East. Even those minority Christian communities that struggled to maintain their uniqueness came increasingly to take on cultural features originally imported by the immigrating Muslims: they learned to speak Arabic and translated their own religious concepts into Arabic, and they gradually adapted to their minority status. In other words, even non-Muslim communities in the Middle East have been Islamized to some degree.

At the same time the way Muslims have expressed their Islam in different settings has invariably been modified at least slightly by local tradition. Even within the Middle East one finds subtle and interesting variations from one region to another—not in the basic Muslim beliefs, but in the pattern of activities readily identified as "Islamic." In Egypt, for example, intense devotion to "Friends of God," including visitation at their tombs and exuberant celebrations of their feasts, is central to the piety of millions. A few hundred miles to the east, in Saudi Arabia, the dominant view is that such practices are entirely un-Islamic and perhaps even heretical. In other words, it is clear that Islam adapts to cultures in which it takes root.

What about circumstances in which Muslims find themselves socially and religiously in the minority?

In the United States, for example, the growing Muslim community faces critical and complex questions about how and to what degree they should adapt to American culture. Since the American Muslim community is made up of people from a dozen or more national and racial backgrounds, they already face the challenge of internal cultural accommodation if they are to be unified among themselves. In some areas this has led to distinct ethnic enclaves: in St. Louis, for example, there are now at least forty thousand Bosnian Americans, and the Detroit area is home to a very sizeable Arab population. But in addition, one finds a broad range of views about, for example, how "American" Islam ought to become. Meanwhile, slowly and almost imperceptibly, the presence of Muslims and their religious needs and values has begun to change the way many Americans think and act.

What is another recent example of the kinds of problems that can arise from the intersection among religion, culture, ethnicity, and politics?

A useful example is the sad history that unfolded in Bosnia-Herzegovina during the late 1980s and early 1990s, some aspects of which earlier questions have addressed. Prior to the outbreak of armed conflict in predominantly Catholic Croatia just to the north, Muslims, Catholics, and Serbian Orthodox inhabitants of Bosnia-Herzegovina had coexisted peacefully for generations. They lived in the same neighborhoods, intermarried, and were godparents for the children of members of the other faiths. Bosnia's Muslims were in no way seen as religiously intolerant, let alone bent on aggressive proselytization. Most in fact identified themselves primarily as citizens of the former Yugoslavia. As the hostilities widened and intensified, "ethnic cleansing" became the order of the day, and Bosnian Muslims found themselves under attack not only for their perceived religious (radical Islamic) and cultural (i.e. Turkish-leaning) allegiances, but for their presumed national/political disloyalty as Bosnians. With the proclamation of a drive toward a "greater Serbia," Bosnian Muslims became increasingly the target of a campaign of disinformation and fear-mongering: these neighbors of yours are in fact enemies hiding in your midst, hatching sinister plots to impose Sharia law on everyone and convert all to Islam or kill those who refuse to change. Ironically, and tragically, hundreds of thousands of Muslims who had previously been not the least bit inclined to religious clannishness (let alone intolerance) now found their cultural, ethnic, national, *and* religious identities under fire and suddenly found that being Muslim was pretty much the only identity to which they could cling.

Does language have a particular symbolic or liturgical value? And do Muslims pray in any particular language?

Arabic is the liturgical language of Islam. All formal prayers and Quran recitation are in Arabic. Most non-Arabic speaking Muslims learn at least some texts of the scripture by heart in Arabic, along with a dozen or so other short texts that are recited regularly during ritual prayer as well as in personal devotions. Scriptural texts include, for example, Sura 1, called The Opening, a lovely prayer reminiscent of the Christian Lord's Prayer; and Sura 112, an affirmation of God's absolute oneness. In addition to the *Shahada*, shorter phrases used during ritual prayer include *Allahu akbar* (God is Supreme), *Al-hamdu li-'llahi* (Praise be to God), and *Sami'a 'llahu li-man yusabbihhu* (God listens to one who praises him). Other Arabic phrases in common use all over the world include *In*

313

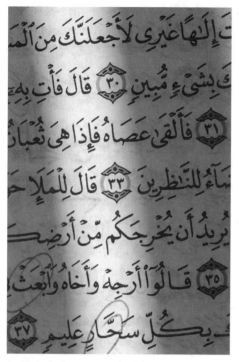

Arabic is the language in which formal prayers are made, and it is the language of the Quran.

sha'a 'Llah (God willing), *Wa 'Llahu a'lam* (God knows best), and *La hawla wa la quwwata illa bi 'Llah* (In God alone is power and strength). During the midday congregational prayer on Friday, the prayer leader gives an address, sometimes called a sermon. The preacher often prefaces the sermon with a series of divine praises in Arabic and then delivers the address in the local vernacular. Preachers occasionally deliver the entire address in Arabic and then provide a translation. Arabic is so important because it is the language of the Quran and of the Prophet, whose very sound carries great symbolic associations even for Muslims who do not speak it.

Do Muslim communities run private schools for their children?

A tradition of Islamic religious education began many centuries ago. Younger children attended a Quran school called a *kuttab* (kut-TAAB). They might progress to more advanced studies in Hadith and eventually to the equivalent of modern-day higher education provided in institutions called *madrasas*. Students in a *madrasa* (ma-DRA-sah) pursue a curriculum built around the teaching of one of the legal methodologies, *madhhabs* (MADH-hab), and eventually receive credentials, a kind of license, as professional religious scholars. Many mosques in the United States are continuing that tradition by establishing primary and, increasingly, secondary schools in which religious education is prominent. Along with the regular course of studies required by state and local accreditation authorities, children study basic Quranic Arabic and related Islamic topics such as religious history and ritual practice. Students who attend public or other schools may attend weekend religious education sessions at the local mosque.

What means do Muslim communities use to engage society at large?

In addition to the various forms of charitable giving, an important traditional device within Islamic law has had an enormous impact on life in many Islamic communities throughout history. A *waqf* is a religious endowment by which a donor can stipulate that his or her funds be used for a particular project in perpetuity, or as long as the funds last. All over the Middle East and southern Asia, for example, scores of these dedicated trust funds established centuries ago remain in force, administered by members of particular families or by government officials entrusted with a specific mandate for the oversight of the endowments. Many endowments historically have been funded by royalty, but a significant number are supported by the generosity of other wealthy individuals or even collectives of many devout individuals. Trusts remain an important matter today, and many Muslims are devising other ways in which concerned fellow believers can contribute to endowments supporting important communal projects.

Are there any organizations or institutions that have their own distinctive structures of leadership within any of the branches of Islam?

Beginning in early medieval times, groups of Muslims throughout the Middle East coalesced informally around individuals reputed for their holiness. At first the groups typically gathered at the home of the *shaykh* (or *shaykha*, since some were women) to pray and listen to the teacher's reflections on sacred texts and topics. As they grew, these groups often found they needed larger spaces in which to meet. Some members also felt the need for a more permanent form of membership. As years went on and the central holy persons aged and died, the question of succession in leadership also arose. Eventually these groups became more highly organized and established formal courses of training. Their rules or charters often reflected highly structured membership with various ranks and offices. And they developed distinctive types of buildings combining prayer and devotional space, residences for the administrators and ordinary members, and often social services facilities as well. These organizations came to be called *Tariqas* (ta-REE-kas), analogous in some ways to the religious orders so important in Christian, Buddhist, and other traditions.

GENDER, FAMILY, ETHNICITY

Why are gender issues important in understanding religion?

Gender roles are significant everywhere on planet earth, both religiously and socially. A common pattern is that gender roles deeply rooted in local custom gradually acquire religious justification. As a result of the added weight of sacred authority, social change can become considerably more traumatic and threatening. Gender roles both social and religious have a great deal to do with the exercise of power. Religious rhetoric invariably canonizes the social status quo in the interest of greater stability, arguing that time-honored gender-based divisions of labor are no less than divinely ordained. To tamper with the balance in quest of gender equality is to court disaster, traditionalists argue. Face the fact that men and women are different by divine design, and that implies different roles both in religious practice and in society at large. Sweeping change is never easy. When it seems to imply major shifts in the exercise of religious authority, it can be excruciating. Dramatic realignments are afoot now all over the world, yielding slow improvements in the social standing of women and children. Those changes will inevitably manifest themselves in the social structures of religious communities everywhere. Fifty years hence scholars will be adding important new chapters to the history of religion, chapters in which women's roles will be much more evident.

What gender-related issues are important for Muslims?

Muslim tradition places great emphasis on understanding and facilitating social relations according to gender-appropriate roles and religiously acceptable behavior. In some societies, women are excluded from certain occupations, but in most instances those are cultural rather than explicitly religious norms. For example, American Muslim women participate in a wider range of professions than do their sisters in some other countries. Non-Muslim American professional women may experience the same kinds of occupational limitations as their Muslim counterparts. All societies and cultures have their gender biases, and religious sanction and justification often become inextricably intertwined with them, largely because religious argument can be a useful element in social control. Gender-related restrictions by which many devout Muslims abide are largely family matters arising from the belief that God has ordained certain tasks to men and certain others to women. Gender and sex differences are real, they observe, and part of a larger plan. Traditional family life calls for a division of labor and a clear understanding of individual and collective priorities. Non-Muslims sometimes conclude that Muslim women who choose to observe a dress code are oppressed. Talk to the Muslim women, many of whom are successful physicians, lawyers, and engineers, and one gets a different perspective.

Westerners sometimes confuse differences between how men and women are treated in Arab and other primarily Islamic societies as based on religious beliefs when, actually, they often have to do with local cultures.

What is this "honor killing" that is associated with the Middle East and especially Arab Muslims? Is this an "Islamic" phenomenon?

Nothing whatsoever about "honor killing" is inherently—let alone uniquely—"Islamic," Arab, or Middle Eastern. Such horrific acts generally involve a parent, husband, or brother acting impulsively to remove perceived "shame" inflicted on a family or clan by a wayward daughter, sister, or wife. Some perpetrators stop short of murder, satisfied with tactics designed to make the wayward female suffer physically and psychologically and render her a pariah. In many cultures around the globe, segments of societies with deep traditional roots have countenanced even extreme measures aimed at restoring "honor." Some of those cultures have predominantly Muslim populations.

An example of one such setting has authorities struggling with distressingly meager success against honor killings. Recent social efforts in Pakistan's Sindh province have shown that such events are directly linked to ancient tribal systems with high levels of illiteracy. Estimates of killings in Sindh range widely from as low as a thousand to as many as ten thousand a year during the first decade of the twenty-first century. Honor killing has long been denounced by Muslim legal scholars and is explicitly condemned in Pakistan's constitution and federal law. The chief problems with enforcing the laws are that, at best, many police officers lump such killings in the same category as all other cases of homicide; at worst, they are personally sympathetic to the practice themselves. Given the resulting social climate of fear, witnesses frequently recant or refuse to appear in court. This combination of poor policing and a weak, often corrupt, legal system in some areas militates against effective protection for women.

How can one be sure that Islamic religious tradition itself is not "the problem" here?

Consider, for example, a parallel—and even larger-scale—socio-legal problem in Pakistan's enormous neighbor to the east. Of India's total population of about 1.2 billion, nearly a billion are Hindu. Among them are a beleaguered sub-group of millions of widows (some estimate as many as forty million or more currently), some of whose families continue to believe that ancient tradition requires honorable women to throw themselves on their husband's funeral pyre. In recent generations, more widows have refused to do so, and some have suffered the Indian equivalent of honor killings. Those who survive attempts to be rid of them are left to fend for themselves, leaving home with no resources and bearing the stigma of the unmarriageable.

The ancient Hindu city of Vrindavan, sanctified by its association with the life story of the deity Krishna, has lately become the last refuge of many thousands of destitute widows who flock there in hopes of finding any place at all to live and whatever scraps of food they can beg. Countless among them have died alone and with no one to provide the dignified death rites of cremation, their bodies dismembered by local authorities and dumped into the Jumna river. Only in relatively recent years have significant efforts been advanced to serve these discarded women, whose fate the vast majority of believing Hindus grieve and deplore. One could cite similar socio-cultural atrocities occurring on a   317 large scale across the globe: human trafficking for sexual and labor purposes has now reached pandemic proportions, including across the "West," whose populations are overwhelmingly non-Muslim and non-Hindu. The point is simply this: in all these contexts, such brutal injustices as honor killing and human trafficking continue unabated not because of Islam or Hinduism or Christianity, but in spite of those religious traditions.

Why do some people, such as the Taliban, not want girls to get an education?

An unfortunate feature of some extreme religious ideologies, among non-Muslims as well as Muslims, is the desire to keep women and girls under control and under wraps. The expressed motivation and justification is invariably cloaked in the language of an ancient divine dispensation in which females were subordinated to males. And beneath that motivation is the "theo-

Malala Yousafzai (1997–) became a champion for female education after she was shot in her native Pakistan by members of the Taliban who tried to prevent her and other girls from attending school. Yousafzai received the Nobel Peace Prize in 2014.

logical" assumption that the original divine message was meant to be interpreted as universally valid in its original terms and literal meanings forever and in all contexts. That assumption is in turn bolstered by the additional conviction that control and suppression are the only ways to insure the integrity of the family and society as a whole, because women represent a threat to good order by reason of their inherent ability to tempt, manipulate, and deceive men if allowed to do so. In short, societies under the control of such truly benighted influences are determined to prevent young girls from becoming educated lest they discover there are other life options. The Taliban represent only one of many such warped social systems, and the result is only marginally "religious"—the oppression of women is a global injustice suffered within social systems dominated by every imaginable ideology, religious or secular.

Saudi women are not allowed to drive cars, and the Taliban in Afghanistan has forbidden women to work outside the home. Is there some official prohibition on women having a public place in society?

In many societies across the world, Muslim women occupy a wide variety of positions in business and the professions, from banking and engineering to health care and social

A Saudi woman drives in defiance of local laws preventing women from operating a vehicle.

services. There are also areas in which those who hold political power continue to exercise rigid social control by severely limiting the options available to women, invariably claiming Quranic sanction for their policies. In some cases the practices that now appear to outsiders as backward and oppressive arose as a reaction to colonialism as a way of protecting Muslim women from countless ill effects of the unwanted intrusion and as a way of keeping families intact. But what about the strong evidence that many Muslim women do not enjoy social equality with men? How much of that is "Islamic"? It is virtually impossible to separate religious sanction from deeply ingrained cultural values. But it is highly instructive to observe the wide variation of the status of women from one culture to another.

It seems so easy to associate Islam with gender (and other types of) inequity these days—is that justified?

It is helpful to keep in mind that even in the most "liberated" societies it is not always perfectly clear what constitutes genuine freedom. Many Muslims—men and women—sincerely believe that what passes for freedom and gender equality in some cultural settings is far more demeaning than what they perceive in their own systems as responsible and necessary protective measures. In many traditional societies, including some with predominantly Islamic populations, women have not enjoyed equal educational opportunities for the simple reason that their female gender roles as traditionally understood

319

neither required nor allowed time for education. This is changing, slowly in most places but rather dramatically in a few, and it will in time become clearer to Muslim and non-Muslim observers alike that a world of educated women is not only compatible with Islam but virtually demanded by Islam's core emphasis on human dignity.

What about female circumcision? Is it widely practiced? And does it have anything really to do with Islamic teaching?

Female circumcision, or clitoridectomy, is still practiced in some societies, and some of those are predominantly Muslim. But the practice is not originally or inherently Islamic and is best understood in cultural rather than religious terms. The Quran does not mention clitoridectomy at all, and the Hadith mentions it rather briefly by way of ruling out any but the most minimal form of it. Islamic law sources list the practice as recommended, rather than required, but for reasons of custom rather than religion. In many societies, "custom" includes the belief that clitoridectomy is necessary to protect a young woman's virginity, virtue, fertility, and marriageability. Because the practice represents such a clear attempt at social control, a number of contemporary feminist writers, both Muslim and non-Muslim, have targeted clitoridectomy and all other forms of female genital mutilation as inhumane and both morally and religiously indefensible. Some countries with large Muslim populations have officially outlawed the practice, while in others, including the religiously conservative Saudi Arabia, custom has ruled it out more informally.

Are there distinctively Islamic family values?

Traditional Muslim views on family emphasize the understanding of clear roles for husband and father, wife and mother, and children. Family means different things from one society and culture to another, but it is reasonably safe to say that in most societies where Muslims constitute majorities or large minorities people think of family as extended rather than nuclear. As Muslim populations grow in Europe and the Americas over the next several generations, it will be very interesting to see to what extent Muslim families are influenced by the dominant understanding of a nuclear family.

What does the Quran say about family life?

One of the earliest Quranic correctives to a serious problem in pre-Islamic family custom is its condemnation of burying alive unwanted children, especially girls. The scripture also accorded women a number of clear rights and responsibilities not previously acknowledged in Arabian custom. In addition to limiting the number of wives allowed to one man, the Quran secured many improvements in the lot of women. It stipulates that a wife is entitled to personal ownership of money and goods—the dower went directly to her rather than to her male guardian as was previously the practice; to terminate a marriage under certain circumstances; and to a set portion of inheritance. Scripture does not unequivocally mandate veiling and seclusion, but it does allow a woman to retain her name and guarantees her privacy. In some respects Islam as a religious and ethical code established men and women on a remarkably equal footing.

What about women's roles in family life?

By tradition and custom, women have almost universally stood at the center of the Muslim family. In addition Muslim law includes extensive development of family issues such as inheritance, divorce, and child custody. For example, women generally get custody of younger children, but after puberty children usually stay with the father on the assumption that he will be better able to provide for their increasing financial needs. On the whole, the husband clearly has the greater legal advantage, in spite of efforts by reformers in the twenty-first century to find a balance. Opposition to change in the law of personal status has often gone hand in hand with resistance to residual colonialism and a desire not to accommodate too readily to influences perceived as "Western."

Women are traditionally the center of any Muslim family, but in legal matters concerning marriage, the law often favors husbands.

Does Islam require women to wear face veils or not?

Nowhere does the Quran specify that women are to wear veils on their faces. It merely stipulates that women dress modestly at all times. However, in some societies female modesty has been judged to include covering the face to varying degrees, all the way to using a semi-see-through covering that doesn't even include openings for the eyes. In very traditional areas all over the Middle East and North Africa, for example, one is still likely to see veiled women. But in places like Indonesia, Malaysia, and the United States, some Muslim women wear full-length robes and head scarves when they are in public or when any but women friends or their closest male relatives visit them in their homes. Many non-Muslims look disapprovingly on Muslim women who choose to "cover" themselves, regarding them as reactionary or hyper-conservative. Like most groups, Muslims would rather be judged by their character than by external appearances.

Why does the matter of women's attire seem to attract so much controversy?

It is important to appreciate how Muslims understand the primary intent of traditional norms about such things as modest clothing, for both men and women: respect for the human dignity of each person. Many Muslims think some contemporary societies, including American society, show little respect for women. So much advertising makes it clear that women's bodies are either the commodity for sale or the chief enticement in marketing another product. It is hardly surprising that some Muslims seek support in their religious tradition for a more humane and dignified treatment of women.

321

Do women have a place in the Islamic view of human rights?

An area of Islamic human rights that non-Muslims have often cited in recent times as problematical is the place of women in society. Outsiders frequently fault Islam for failing to secure the kind of social equality that would allow women to pursue careers outside the home. As a prime example, some critics point to the recent arrest of a number of Saudi women who violated a ban on driving automobiles. But if "Islam" is the operative value system in this instance, one must ask why in so many other predominantly Muslim countries all over the world most women do not wear veils and are free to drive cars. In nearby Jordan, numbers of women now study in *Shari'a* schools once open only to men. Actual practices in relation to these and other similar social issues are clearly too complex and variegated to be explained by reference to Islamic religious injunctions, especially those that seem to be country- or region-specific.

Is it reasonable or fair to judge all cultures and societies by a single set of standards?

One has to keep a number of factors in mind when presuming to judge other cultural and religious systems. First, no humanly devised social structure is perfectly just, and that includes those that claim divine sanction. Second, all cultures and societies have their unchallenged assumptions and are subject to a certain amount of upheaval when those assumptions are challenged. Third, one cannot simply impose one's own preferences on another culture. Cultural differences come about as close to an absolute value as anything in human experience and add a richness and diversity to life on earth. One should not therefore simply transplant into other cultural settings everything that Americans think is essential to a free and just society. Finally, though there may be a fine line between certain unquestioned practices in a given society and violations of human rights, outside observers have the duty to look for that line and not simply assume those under scrutiny have crossed it.

Do Muslims practice polygamy?

Long before the beginnings of Islam, plural marriage was a fairly common practice. A number of the biblical patriarchs and kings had several wives. Wealthier men of the pre-Islamic Arab tribes apparently engaged in polygamy, marrying as many wives as their wealth would allow. A major concern seems to have been that, in the inhospitable environs of that desert world, women not attached to families had little hope of survival. As cities like Mecca developed, the practice survived in somewhat modified form. But according to a text of the Quran, polygamy in the early Muslim community was to be limited. A man could marry up to four women, provided he could treat all of his wives with complete equity, both materially and emotionally. In modern times a number of national governments in the Middle East have outlawed the practice, arguing that modern social and economic conditions have made perfectly fair treatment all but impossible. Even where local laws allow polygamy, relatively few men marry more than one woman, and those who marry four are a very small minority.

It's easy to get the impression that Muslim women have a much harder time than non-Muslim American women being recognized as independent and capable. Why is that impression so prevalent?

Possibly because of reports about the fate of so many women in Afghanistan after the takeover by the Taliban revolutionaries; or media images of Middle Eastern, especially Iranian, women covered from head to toe apparently participating in anti-American or anti-Western demonstrations. Whatever the reason, the oppression of women is in no way a distinctively, let alone uniquely, Islamic issue. While it is undoubtedly true that Muslims have often used religion to control social behavior in various contexts, Muslims are not alone in this action. The roots of the clearly subordinate social status of women evidenced in numerous societies today—including, some would argue, American—go much deeper and are much more ancient than Islam or any other system of religious values.

What's the underlying problem in understanding whether these situations are truly "religious" in origin?

A basic problem has always been how to interpret an ancient scripture in modern times. The Quran's teachings about women were enormously progressive in their original historical context. Women's legal and financial rights saw dramatic advances over pre-Islamic social norms. Since Muslims generally understand the Quran to be eternally valid and universally applicable, the desire to implement Quranic teachings here and now is perfectly understandable. The hypothetical question of whether a twentieth-century revelation would be identical with a seventh century revelation, or call for similar advances over current social values, always stirs interesting discussion. Traditional Islamic values include a very clear picture of gender roles, especially within the family. But the predominant *traditional* view is that in order to maintain family order, the husband and father has the final say in matters of dispute and has the authority to discipline when necessary.

Are racial and ethnic issues a significant factor in religion and among Muslims?

Race is just as formative an element in the history of religion as gender. When religious traditions expand beyond their regions of origin, they must adapt to new cultural, racial, and ethnic circumstances. If political power accompanies the tradition's expansion, the social balances in the new territory will very likely call for change in the expanding tradition as well as in the lives of the local populations. What one might call "religious colonialism" often goes hand in hand with cultural hegemony. When a religious tradition is heavily identified with a racial or ethnic group, converts to the tradition may find themselves still second-class citizens. Within the greater American Christian tradition, for example, black churches formed because of de facto segregation, even though in theory all Christians enjoy equality in the sight of God. Muslims, like members of countless other faiths, strive to remain open toward all their brothers and sisters in religion (and outside). But no one has yet found a way to stamp out prejudices at all times and in all circumstances, no matter how well motivated. Once again, culture plays an important role, and

323

human beings tend to be more comfortable with, and therefore gravitate toward, the company of others they can identify as "their" folks. Sometimes ethnicity, nationality, and other such considerations come into play, despite the best of intentions.

CHRISTIAN–MUSLIM CULTURAL CONFLICT IN HISTORY AND LITERATURE

What did some of the premier medieval Christian religious scholars think of Islam and Muhammad?

Thomas Aquinas (1225–1274) took two distinctly different approaches to Islam as he knew it. On the one hand, he did not mince words in his chief polemical work against Islam. In his *Summa Contra Gentiles* (*Against the Non-Christians*), Aquinas attacked in detail what he regarded as doctrinally flawed beliefs and practices, beginning with a denunciation of the Muslim conception of Muhammad as the "final" conduit of prophetic revelation. On the other hand, Aquinas makes it clear that he takes seriously the views of major Muslim scholars on a number of central theological positions. Take, for example, the large topic of prophecy and prophetic revelation: in his section on the theme in his magisterial *Summa of Theology*, roughly two-thirds of his material relates either directly or indirectly to the earlier speculations of Muslims (such as Ibn Sina, Ibn Rushd, and Ghazali) and Jews (especially Maimonides). Quantitatively speaking, more than half of Aquinas's texts on the subject find correspondences in Islamic and Rabbinic literature. Two centuries later, German theologian/philosopher Nicholas of Cusa (1401–1464) took Islam even more seriously, engaging in a thorough and detailed study of the Quran. Yes, he did so ultimately in order to refute the Muslim scripture; but along the way he also found many themes of common concern to Christians and Muslims. During the Reformation, two major thinkers were less amenable to Islam. Martin Luther (1483–1546) saw Turks as a punishment from God and regarded Muslims as devil-worshippers and their prophet as an abomination. John Calvin (1509–1564) drew comparisons, surprisingly, between Muslims and the Catholic "Papists," whom he considered the dregs of Christendom.

Theologian and priest Martin Luther regarded Muslims as devil-worshippers sent as a punishment from God.

What sorts of opinions of Islam and Muslims do we find in medieval Christian popular literature?

Popular European literature generally depicted Muslims as pagans and expressed deep revulsion for Muhammad. Islam was an entirely unacceptable religion without a hint of authentic spiritual values. A problem for Christians was the perceived role of force in the spread of the faith, and popular culture portrayed Muslims as inherently and uniquely given to terror. Widespread stories exaggerated horrific details, at best, and were frequently invented whole cloth. Hildebert's vernacular *History of Muhammad* was the most widely read work dealing with Islam and responsible for the broad currency of countless negative stories about the Prophet. In 1258 Alexandre du Pont wrote a widely influential French *Romance of Muhammad*, which portrayed the prophet as an imposter who tricked his followers into believing him. His story replicated all the popular fictions of the time about Muhammad. The French epic genre known as *Chansons de Geste* appeared from the eleventh to the fourteenth centuries in three main cycles of songs, the oldest and most famous being the *Song of Roland*. The third cycle takes place in the East after the Christians captured Jerusalem in 1099. A general characteristic of this genre is a grossly inaccurate portrayal of Islam as the worship of multiple gods, of whom the most powerful was "Mahomet" or "Mahon." In a still further distortion, some works claim that Muslims worship a trinity of gods—Mahomet (Mahon), Tervagent (Tervagan), and Apollin—in places of worship called "sinagogues."

Are there dominant cultural stereotypes in Christian popular literature?

These popular works describe "Saracens" in most unflattering terms, as enormous horned ink-black monsters sporting huge noses, ears, eyes like coals, and fearsome teeth. Some sources also occasionally allowed that some Muslims were good-hearted enough, but, alas, to be pitied because they had no hope of salvation. Some Christian sources admitted that Muslim soldiers were courageous and chivalrous, especially during the second Crusade. A surprising motif in some medieval European romances in the chansons depicts a Frankish knight falling in love with a Muslim princess while her father holds him hostage. Beautiful, virtuous, and worthy of love, she works valiantly to free her Christian beloved and converts before a physical relationship could begin. A curious feature is that the chansons tend to cast Muslims in a thoroughly negative light when the relationship portrayed was described as Christian-Muslim, but more kindly when characterizing the relationship as Frank-Arab.

What are some examples of the divergent perspectives of Muslim and Christian authors writing on the "other"?

Rashid ad-Din (1247–1318) was a major Persian Muslim scholar who wrote a history of the Franks, and it was through this work that many Muslims learned about Christian history and society. Although Muslims generally take an interest in Christian societies, they were concerned with the Christian religion itself. Scholars and polemicists penned   325

As with their Christian counterparts, most Muslims had no knowledge about Christianity and no interest in it either. They viewed Christians as barbarians. For instance, with the presumption that all of Islamdom was united (at least in theory) by a single sacred tongue, Arabic, Muslim sources often assumed that because Europeans spoke many different languages, they must surely be an inferior civilization. Medieval Muslim sources referred to the Byzantine Empire as "Rome" (Rum), as the Byzantines themselves did. The few reports about Christian lands that filtered into Middle East societies were generally from the western parts of the Muslim world (in the twelfth to fourteenth century)—the Maghrib (North Africa) and Andalusia. Those sources typically categorized both the Franks and the Africans as barbarians and, not surprisingly, expressed disdain for European culture.

many works designed to refute Christianity. These were based largely on the Quran and often were not as persuasive as their authors would have liked. For their part, Christians wrote works condemning Islam on the basis of Biblical texts alone. The more deeply Islam encroached on formerly Christian territories, the more inter-religious debate was generated. Ali ibn Rabban al-Tabari (d. 855), a Nestorian Christian convert to Islam, wrote a refutation of Christianity arguing the need for Muslims to equip themselves to counter Christian narratives by detecting their inherent rational flaws. After the Abbasid Caliph al-Mamun (r. 813–833) opened the Baghdad "House of Wisdom" library and center for inter-religious philosophical and theological study and debate in 830, many Greek and Syriac texts began to be translated into Arabic. This promoted the introduction of Aristotelian logic into religious argument formerly based entirely on sacred scripture (on all sides). Among the major critics of these developments in subsequent centuries was the redoubtable Taqi al-Din Ibn Taymiya (1263–1328) of Damascus, who wrote a thousand-page book to refute a work by a Christian. There is actually good news here: he took the work of that Christian very seriously rather than merely dismissing it outright.

Some say that Muslims and Christians have such a hard time understanding each other because the Islamic world never experienced an "Enlightenment." Is that true?

A classic Islamic story provides some initial context. Once upon a time an itinerant grammarian came to a body of water and enlisted the services of a boatman to ferry him across. Attempting to strike up a conversation on his favorite topic, the grammarian asked the boatman, "Do you know the science of grammar?" The humble boatman thought for a moment and responded rather disappointedly that he did not. A while later a gathering storm threatened to capsize the small vessel. Said the boatman to the grammarian, "Do you know the science of swimming?" The two both had their abilities, their special interests; but they had a hard time meeting because they were looking at life through very different lenses and beginning from very different assumptions about what is most important. A key question here is: enlightened compared to what? Point of view depends a great deal on what one regards as critical at any given moment in history. Many European and American non-Muslims have gotten into the habit of looking at the world through the filters of Enlightenment values. The view has become so accepted that some are convinced that any other view must be either naive or just plain wrong. Viewed from that perspective, Islam appears to some as the last holdout against the Enlightenment's appreciation of critical intelligence. Islam thus represents for some a refusal to view the world rationally and critically. For many Muslims, on the other hand, the Renaissance is virtually synonymous with presumptuous anthropocentrism and the Enlightenment with the arrogant denial of the ultimately divine causality of all events.

What's the problem here from the Muslim perspective?

A major symbolic issue for many Muslims is the pervasive feeling that the tendency of Euro-American non-Muslims to apply the Renaissance-Enlightenment yardstick to Islamic history and culture and find it wanting is just another example of "Western" cultural imperialism. They resent the implication that Muslims are somehow genetically medieval and need to be "fixed" by an injection of critical thinking. The more outsiders insist that Muslims need to shed traditional notions such as the classical ideal of the unity of civil and religious spheres, the more Muslims ask why. Revolutionary changes in worldview, what some have called paradigm shifts, have indeed been afoot among Muslims of our time. As is always the case with dramatic change, however, wide acceptance happens very gradually: neither the Renaissance nor the Enlightenment caught on overnight. Christians can likewise look to the Islamic world's rich history of humanistic insight, and to its record of achievement in literature and the arts, for key connections as well as for sources of misunderstanding.

What's a useful way to think about these cultural misunderstandings?

There are pros and cons. For the sake of argument, call the positive dimension the Renaissance connection, and the negative dimension the Reformation reaction. Non-Muslim Euro-Americans often find it difficult to appreciate the classical Islamic insistence on the unity of religious and civil spheres. On the other hand, there is common ground in the coalescence of poetry and piety and of architecture and aspiration that has characterized so much high culture all over Islamdom. With that awareness comes the possibility of mutual appreciation of shared values that both transcend and undergird our respective confessional convictions.

There is also a negative side to the renaissance connection. In sixteenth-century Europe (and perhaps now again in the United States?) a reaction to Renaissance values gave rise to the Reformation. Within the Islamic world, too, an analogous change has been in progress. In a revivalist mode, Muslims too can draw a line between their tradition's own deepest humanistic sensibilities and human rights in our crowded pluralistic world, on the one hand, and their sense of the priority of divine justice and God's rights on the other. Practical political consequences aside, such a change bodes ill for Christian-Muslim relations, for the Christian doctrine of the Incarnation, already a major stumbling block on the level of theology, now loses its potential for fruitful connection on the cultural level. Christianity's sense that the Incarnation confers religious validation on all things human suddenly finds itself orphaned in the face of a religious tradition in which the human dimension seems to evaporate in the face of the demands of divine legitimation.

How does the issue of "historical-critical thinking" enter into this debate?

Only diehard believers in a trickle-down theory of Enlightenment Thinking would argue, against enormous evidence to the contrary, that Christian and Jewish Americans generally apply "historical-critical" principles to their understanding of their sacred texts. Literalism is alive and well among rank-and-file Christians, not only in "the Third World," but in "the West" as well. Manifestations of the oft-vaunted liberating effects of Renaissance and Enlightenment in current American popular attitudes to religion and politics remain as scarce as Irish Lutherans. Those enumerating the fatal flaws of once-born/unenlightened "Islamic Civilization" do not seem to notice that neither China nor Japan have had the benefit of either Renaissance or Enlightenment, and yet they would never dream of attributing China's communism to something inherently Chinese or Japan's World War II atrocities to a radical Japanese-ness. For comparison's sake, consider the much-troubled history of Catholic Latin American states: many of the very dictators who entertained Catholic hierarchical figures and who obligingly baptized, married, and buried generations of their families from grand Renaissance edifices were often directly responsible for countless "disappeared" people and massive attempts to wipe out indigenous populations. Why no outcry about the moral bankruptcy of Roman Catholicism? Why, then, blame perceived cultural backwardness and major social problems elsewhere on the religion of Islam?

CULTURAL DIFFERENCES AND CONTEMPORARY MUSLIM–CHRISTIAN MISUNDERSTANDING

Some critics see Islam as an uncivilized, backward, or "desert" religion. Is this a fair or accurate characterization?

Step back to the year 1000—when London and Paris were still little more than country towns, and unruly mobs roved the streets of Rome—and imagine travelling across the

Mediterranean world from east to west, beginning in Baghdad, where an array of splendid world-class cities existed. Though India and China, along with Central and South America, boasted many of the world's finest cities, virtually the only non-Muslim city in the greater Mediterranean world worth a second look at the time was Constantinople.

Baghdad was founded in 762 as the new capital of the Abbasid dynasty. The caliph designed it as a perfect circle with the palace and its mosque at the center, its surrounding walls reserving places for representatives of virtually every segment of society within Islamdom. Obviously an idealized structure, the original design did not last long because of rapid expansion. Still, in the mid-eleventh century, Baghdad was an important center of learning and culture. By 1100 the city boasted some of the premier intellectual institutions in the world. Further to the west was the city of Cairo, founded in 969 by a Sevener Shi'i dynasty called the Fatimids. A century into its history Cairo was booming, a center of trade, culture, and learning. There in 972 the al-Azhar mosque was founded, the forerunner of what would become one of the world's oldest institutions of higher learning. Portions of the fortified wall of the old Fatimid city of Cairo still stand in testimony to its medieval glory.

Were there advanced "Islamic" cities in the Mediterranean West?

Moving further west one finds a number of important urban centers, from Qayrawan in present-day Tunisia, to Fez in Morocco. Founded as a garrison city in 670, Qayrawan grew into one of several important North African centers of learning. Fez originated about a century later and, along with Marrakesh (founded 1070), was at or near the center of several Moroccan Arab and Berber dynasties over the subsequent six centuries. Arguably the most splendid city in Western Europe in the year 1000 was the Andalusian jewel called Cordoba. Founded in early Roman times, it passed from the Romans to the Vandals to the Byzantines and back to the Visigoths. With the Muslim occupation of Cordoba in 711, what had been a minor lackluster town began its steady four-century rise to prominence. Some of the great monuments of Islamic Cordoba remain a major

What were major cities east of Baghdad like?

Many other less well known urban centers continued as cultural beacons when the great capitals of Europe had reached their medieval and renaissance primes. Cities like Shiraz and Isfahan in present-day Iran were architecturally resplendent and home to remarkable literary figures from the twelfth through sixteenth centuries. Further to the east, in Central Asia, were cosmopolitan cities like Herat, Samarkand, and Bukhara. Still farther and to the south, in present-day Pakistan and India, artists, architects, musicians, religious scholars, and scientists found homes and appreciative patrons in Lahore, Delhi, Hyderabad, and a host of other royal haunts.

attraction to travelers. As the scene of remarkable symbiosis of the three Abrahamic faiths for several hundred years, a "convivencia" of Judaism, Christianity, and Islam, two of Cordoba's most famous citizens were Ibn Rushd (aka Averroes, d. 1198) and Maimonides (d. 1204).

How does all of this relate to Islamic and Christian notions of how "religion" and "culture" overlap?

Both Christianity and Islam have long histories of wrestling with their relationships to culture and learning. Many Christians oddly enough seem to have been taken in by the stereotyped notion that Islam is anti-intellectual, while many Muslims have seen Christians as easy prey to secularism. Neither view takes account of the actual role of culture in the histories of either tradition. It is a complex matter. Islam's tradition of highly developed cultural and educational strengths goes back to the Prophet's reputation for concerning with learning: Seek knowledge even as far as China; the scholar's ink is holier than the blood of martyrs; a single scholar is harder on Satan than a thousand ascetics. (Also, however: a handful of luck is sometimes more useful than six camel loads of books.)

What about the "Islam vs. the West" dichotomy?

The notion entertained by many Muslims that "the West" is somehow inherently inimical to the practice of Islam or any genuine religious values misses the point. Wherever Muslims live, whether in Pakistan, the Middle East, Indonesia, or the United States, they must make some sort of accommodation to cultural forces. Christians can feel a great deal of sympathy with the words of the Hadith, "Islam came into the world a stranger and will go out a stranger." In this country, at least, Muslims and Christians have a great deal to say to each other about maintaining their values in the face of enormous cultural pressures to the contrary.

The ultimate *authentically* Renaissance/humanistic contribution to Muslim-Christian relations would be perhaps a greater understanding of our mutual xenophobias. Why do we have such terrible difficulty accepting otherness?

Both traditions possess the tools for critical assessment of culture, and they need to be shared. Both Muslims and Christians have struggled with issues of Renaissance and Enlightenment, sought reform and counter-reform, and sought to critique the critique of Reason. Both know what it is like to seek intellectual integrity not in utter license, but within the context of a faith in a revealed truth. With respect to mutual quests for truth, finally, Muslims and Christians are both subject to a certain hypocrisy so long as they are not vigilant against that hypocrisy. Muhammad had noticed that a Companion named Hudhayfa ibn al-Yaman seemed to have special insight into hypocrisy, so he designated Hudhayfa as the community's expert on hypocrisy and its telltale signs. One day a Muslim approached Hudhayfa and expressed this concern: "I am afraid I am becoming a hypocrite." "Don't worry," Hudhayfa replied. "Hypocrites are not afraid of hypocrisy."

There is a lot of damning criticism leveled at Muhammad by non-Muslims, dismissing him as a terrorist and a pedophile and using a host of other such horrific epithets. How much of this is simply bigotry?

Muhammad-bashing has enjoyed a long history among Christians. As always, the logic of bigotry involves the use of double standards. Those who know they are right invariably apply criteria to the "others" that they would never apply to themselves. One influential Christian preacher recently called Muhammad a demon-possessed pedophile because he was a polygamist and one of his wives was a child. Applying double standards, he conveniently glossed over the flaws of a number of major Biblical and Christian figures. A man many Christians revere as Saint Augustine was betrothed to a child by his mother, now revered as St. Monica. In addition, the Book of Genesis says twice that the patriarch Abraham lied, saying that his wife (who had suggested he have a child by his concubine Hagar) was really his sister; today he would likely be called a child abuser because he was prepared to slaughter his young son. Solomon, acknowledged in scripture as a world-class philanderer with multiple wives and scores of concubines, nonetheless remains a paragon of wisdom for Christians and Jews. Another prominent Christian leader condemned Muhammad as a "terrorist and a violent man," but would surely have bristled at the suggestion that King David was an astonishingly violent man who was dominated by his passions and deserves to be condemned outright. He would likely also explain away the clear biblical "fact" that even Moses was a murderer by noting that God forgave Moses for his failing. The New Testament also declares openly that Saint Paul participated in the stoning death of St. Stephen and by his own admission persecuted new Christians violently for years prior to his own conversion, yet Christians revere him as one of the essential contributors to sacred scripture. One noted televangelist assured his viewers that the problem is that "we haven't read the Quran," for if we had we would see clearly Islam's sanctioning of violence. He has evidently not read the Bible either, or he would have seen that Moses was a murderer and that Jesus said, "I have come not to bring peace, but the sword."

What about Muhammad's campaigns against the Jews of Medina?

A commonly expressed argument for the essential link between Islam and violence is that Muhammad ruthlessly attacked the Jewish tribes in Medina with the clear purpose of wiping them out. Muslims traditionally understand that the Jewish tribes forced Muhammad to take action because of their duplicity, publicly welcoming him and promising their support, while privately seeking to undermine his efforts to lead Medinan society. However one interprets these episodes, they are indeed a dark chapter in the story of Muhammad's life and the genesis of the Islamic community. More importantly, there are parallels in other traditions, most notably the Biblical mandate to the Israelites to conquer all peoples inhabiting the Promised Land at the time of the Exodus. But in the biblical accounts, duplicity is not a criterion. The inhabitants of the land have no options. God not only gives the invaders power over the earlier inhabitants, but in fact mandates "total war" on them so that no living thing is left alive. The command to destroy the indigenous peoples of the Promised Land is unconditional and presupposes only that the enemy has no right to be there except perhaps in the capacity of slaves and concubines (See e.g. Dt. 20:10–18).

Aren't there important shared concerns that can provide common cultural grounds on which Muslims and Christians can stand together?

A set of issues on which Muslims and Christians have more to say to each other than members of either tradition might suspect has to do with the relationships between religion and the visual arts. Here Renaissance and Enlightenment questions converge; here the classic characterizations of Christianity as iconic and Islam as aniconic come into question and force us to rethink our understandings of how the two traditions are similar and how different with respect to the realities to which their modes of visual expression have sought to orient believers.

Muslims and non-Muslims confront each other in 2009 at Park 51 in New York City, where a Muslim community center was in the works close to where terrorists had brought down the World Trade Center. In 2014, plans were revised and the center will instead contain a museum and prayer space.

In 2009 there was considerable turmoil connected with plans of the New York City Muslim community to build a community center a couple of blocks from the site of the former World Trade Center—aka, Ground Zero of the 9/11 attack. What was the problem with that?

In the most recent metamorphosis of American popular attitudes toward Islam and Muslims, the concrete reality of "the mosque" has taken on heightened symbolic importance. Talk of plans to include a prayer space (i.e., mosque) in a future Muslim community center near the site of the World Trade Center has focused the concerns of many Americans across the country not only on plans for new mosques, but on the suddenly more ominous presence of long-established Muslim places of worship in local communities. Amid all the shouting, virtually no one has asked publicly why there has been no outrage about the prayer space dedicated shortly after 9/11 in the Pentagon itself, on the very spot where nearly two hundred government employees lost their lives that day. Though the chapel is not dedicated as a "mosque" as such, it is available to Muslims as well as to Christians, Jews, and members of other faiths. In fact, when Muslims gather there, that space becomes a *masjid* (mosque), from an Arabic term that means simply "place of prayerful prostration." Surely an extension of the current antirational discourse must raise a hue and cry for the Pentagon to bar Muslims from gathering there to hatch their Sharia-soaked plots, if not to shut the chapel down entirely?

Is there any truth to the idea that the "Ground Zero mosque" is really part of a stealth takeover of Christian symbolism?

Another element recently highlighted in some popular discourse on the Ground Zero controversy is the belief that Islam and Muslims are once again trying to engineer a symbolic supersession over Christendom by building on someone else's hallowed ground. Those who want their constituents to be outraged that Islam is up to its old tricks—this time on American soil—point to medieval Cordoba (the center was to be called Cordoba House), Spain, as a historic example of Muslims "turning a cathedral into one of the world's biggest mosques." The historical reality is that such architectural appropriation is an age-old feature of dueling sacred spaces. Christians, Muslims, Hindus, and others have regularly made such symbolic statements of their political ascendancies. In the sweep of history, the real estate of worship sites has regularly changed hands, back and forth, thousands of times across the world. When Christian armies claimed Latin America for Catholicism, the missionaries in attendance regularly proclaimed that local cathedrals and churches would henceforth stand atop hundreds of pre-Columbian pyramid-temples.

Isn't it true that there are plenty of historical examples of Muslim appropriation of sites holy to other faiths?

Yes, indeed, when Muslims conquered southern Spain, they built a mosque where there had once stood an Arian Visigothic church, which in turn had been built on the ruins of a Roman temple. And by the early sixteenth century, that mosque had sprouted a cathedral, complete with flying buttresses. Around 1500, Muslim conquerors of northern India erected a mosque on a site claimed by Hindus as the birthplace of the deity Rama. Then in 1992, Hindu mobs descended on that nearly five-hundred-year-old mosque and dismantled it stone by stone—nearly a century and a half after the last Muslim ruler had disappeared from the scene at the hands of the British (who, by the by, treated their Hindu subjects far more brutally than the earlier Muslim overlords had). The recent Ground Zero controversy, however, is in no way another example of such appropriation. Another more typical historical pattern offers a much more apposite parallel. The history of Muslim inculturation in the United States has often witnessed a much more peaceful and not at all triumphalistic exchange: many early mosques did indeed nestle into buildings originally designed as churches, but only when abandoned storefronts were not readily available, and when the local Christian communities were no longer interested in using them further for their own purposes and thus "deconsecrated" them. A Muslim prayer space near Ground Zero does not take over the space of another tradition; it makes its own contribution to this sacred landscape.

Are the distorted media images of Muslims and people of Middle Eastern origin one of the last "acceptable" public stereotypes in American society?

Executives and creative directors in the entertainment (and news) industry bear an enormous responsibility. So much of what people believe about others has to do with the images of those "others" that they see from day to day. Those who produce mass entertainment in whatever medium face a considerable challenge in their choice as to what is appropriate in their portrayal of persons as well as in their development of story lines. Mass media play an important educational role in society and therefore cannot be allowed to equate profits with propriety. But how does one decide what is "proper" in entertainment imagery? Unfortunately a simple "golden rule"—portray others only as you would like to see yourself portrayed—is not adequate here, because producers of mass media entertainment also have some responsibility to seek accuracy. But there is a fine line between the legitimate desire for historical accuracy and the unfair characterization of groups of human beings. Proportion, frequency, and intensity in the use of certain images are critical here. The villains and plots of the top-grossing "action-adventure" films of the past ten or twenty years or so have created the powerful impression that Muslims or Arabs are ignorant, violent, and untrustworthy.

Why don't people just lighten up with this concern for "political correctness"? Why all the hypersensitivity?

Social propriety has a great deal to do with cultural context. Arabs, Persians, Turks, and Pakistanis, to name only a few of the major ethnic groups whose members are mostly Muslim, are as richly endowed with a sense of humor as members of any other ethnic groups. They laugh at themselves as readily as any American Christians or Jews might laugh at Steve Martin or Woody Allen. Popular soap-opera-like movies in Cairo, for example, caricature Arab bad guys mercilessly. They might even have the villains use sarcastic distortions of religious expressions such as "I seek refuge in God from the wrath of God!" And people howl at the barbs without a second thought. Transplant such caricatures into another cultural context, however, and the effect is very different. Movie images are particularly influential in shaping children's views of Muslims and people of Middle Eastern and Asian ancestry. That includes movies like Disney's *Aladdin* and *Kazaam*. In both cases the villains are unmistakably identified, sometimes rather subtly, with trappings most viewers would associate at least vaguely with Islam. But aren't the heroes and heroines similarly identified? In some cases, yes; but in these instances, that positive identification is far outweighed by the reinforcement of negative connotations of "Muslim" and "Arab" already prevalent in our society.

How has bigotry toward Arabs and other largely Muslim ethnic groups been apparent in American culture in recent times?

"Yoooo-hooo, Mistah Ayyyraaab!" called Bugs Bunny from a large bank of TV sets in the store. Seems the globe-trotting carrot eater was on adventure in the "Sierra Desert" when he once again encountered his ancient nemesis, Yosemite Sam. No sooner had the narrator introduced him as "the stupidest person on earth" than Sam appeared in traditional Arab garb doing what stupid people everywhere are wont to do: getting duped into bouncing himself off the wall of a desert bastion, ever the hapless loser. That scene happened in a department store at 10 o'clock on a Saturday morning, some years ago; but it might have been any Saturday morning in countless dens and living rooms across America. Millions of children still grow up primed to chuckle at what one writer calls the last acceptable ethnic joke. Elsewhere in the same department store, and in middle-American toy chests, one might also find an angry doll named "Nomad," heavily armed and clearly identifiable as a Palestinian. Not quite so funny. The good news is that there has been some improvement in this arena, except that films and video games continue to favor "Middle Eastern" and "Islamic" types as villains, arguing that they are simply after "realistic" portrayal of world affairs. Far more alarming, though, are the countless documented instances of singling out individuals precisely as Muslims and excluding them from gatherings advertised as "free and open to the public," or worse still, apprehending and accusing individuals on criminal charges because they "look Muslim."

KNOWLEDGE, SCHOLARSHIP, AND THE ISLAMIC HUMANITIES

LEARNING AND THE ISLAMIC SENSE OF HISTORY

Is "knowledge" considered a matter of religious importance in Islamic tradition?

Muslims have always regarded the quest for knowledge as an essential foundation of their religious tradition. Many sayings about knowledge are attributed to Muhammad, but one in particular stands out: "Seek knowledge (*'ilm*), even [if you have to go] as far as China." Religious scholars have long considered this sound evidence that the quest for learning is not merely helpful and useful for "some" people, but a religious duty for *all* Muslims. There are, of course, different *types* of knowledge, and some subjects or disciplines are required not for all but for a "sufficient number" (somewhat like a quorum) of Muslims to serve the needs of all. Such specialized learning includes more technical subjects, such as religious law, traditionally covered by professional religious scholars. But it is incumbent on all to strive at all times to banish ignorance through the effort of serious study. Some authors also distinguish between acquired, traditional, or discursive knowledge (*'ilm*) and a more subtle kind of experiential, infused, or even "mystical" knowledge (*ma'rifa*), entirely a gift of God and unavailable through ordinary human effort. But in general, one of the most important realms of "religious learning" recommended to all is a good understanding of the role of prophets in divine revelation and God's ongoing dealings with humankind throughout history.

What is meant by "Islamic humanities"?

The expression is just a way of suggesting distinctive ways in which Muslim thinkers, literary figures, and scholars of all kinds have developed rich treasures of thought and culture across the full range of subjects and means of expression generally associated with

337

Education is a high priority in the minds of most Muslims, including education for girls.

the Humanities. That includes history, philosophy, theology, and *belles lettres* of every description: prose and poetry; epic, lyric, and didactic works; theoretical treatises, practical ethics, and essays; and in dozens of languages across the length and breadth of the globe from Africa to Central and South Asia to Indonesia and beyond. The Humanities also include architecture, the visual arts, and related topics to be discussed in the next chapter. Muslims have traditionally addressed all of the very same human concerns confronting people everywhere and throughout history, but—like all others whose worldviews are shaped by their own cultural and religious traditions—they do so from distinctively "Islamic" perspectives.

How have Muslim scholars traditionally approached and described these core concerns?

Muslim specialists in a number of disciplines in the Humanities began well over a millennium ago to study the theme of divine revelation through prophets from several different perspectives. For example, an important genre known as the "universal history" situates the stories of Islam's prophets in the context of global history, thus providing insight into how Muslims have understood their traditions in relation to other major religions and cultures. Sometimes commissioned by the princely class, the histories sought to bolster the reputations of their patrons as cosmopolitan rulers. They include stories and characters from a whole range of religious traditions—not always presented in an entirely favorable light, to be sure, but nevertheless acknowledged as part of the known world. These figures include Buddha, Confucius, and various religious heroes; assorted Greek philosophers; and major folk and royal heroes. As works of literature their intended public was likely to be smaller than those to which "tales" (*qisas*) and "narrative accounts" (*hikaya*) forms appealed, but perhaps broader than those for which the biographical dictionary types were intended. At a time when historical works being produced in Europe tended to be more limited in scope, the wide-ranging interest of these Muslim historians is remarkable.

Who are some of the most important scholars who produced such works?

Among the earliest examples are the Arabic histories of Yaqubi (d. 897), Tabari (d. 923), and Masudi (d. 956). Their accounts of the great religious figures, especially of the prophets from Adam to Jesus, have much in common with those of, for example, the *Tales of the Prophets*. Several historiographers of the fifteenth and sixteenth centuries agreed that historical accounts of the prophets comprise one of the authentic branches of history. Some historians occasionally went back to the beginning of the Creation. One of the chief benefits of studying history is the data it yields about the prophets and their way of behaving that can offer perspective on the relation of life in this world to the afterlife.

Have classical Islamic historians given special attention to the role of prophets in history?

Two of the most important writers who restricted themselves to the lives of the prophets after giving an account of the Creation were Thalabi (d. 1036) and Kisai (fl. c. 1200). In the preface to his *Tales of the Prophets*, Thalabi ennumerates five aspects of God's wisdom in revealing to Muhammad the prophetic stories. Four hundred years later the historian's historian Sakhawi would reiterate those same five features as an epitome of the meaning and function of prophetic histories. These stories, he argues, prove that the "unlettered" Muhammad was the recipient of an authentic revelation; they both encourage imitation of the heroic prophets and caution against the behavior of the unbelievers; they demonstrate how specially favored Muhammad's people were by contrast with earlier peoples who had suffered far more severely; they educate; and they bring to mind noble prophetic deeds, hold out the hope of reward for the righteous, and show that good deeds live on for the edification of posterity.

Do all "classical" Islamic historical sources emphasize religious themes so pointedly?

The tone and attitude of both Thalabi and Kisai are set in high relief by contrast with those of Miskawayh (d. 1030), who assiduously avoided any mention either of the pre-Islamic prophets or of the specifically religious history of Muhammad. Describing his methods and motives, Miskawayh wrote: "I am beginning with reporting the historical information about the time after the Deluge, because the information about events before it can be little trusted, and also because that information is in no way useful for accomplishing the professed purpose of the work (namely, to mention experiences that could serve as examples). For the very same reason, we did not undertake to report the miracles and their political achievements, because the people of our time can gain experience for the tasks they will face in the future only from human behavior that is unconnected with anything miraculous." Miskawayh was one of a number of major authorities who brought a more critical, perhaps even skeptical, approach to the study of history.

ISLAM AND PHILOSOPHY

Is there a distinctly philosophical approach to understanding divine revelation?

One of the most original results of the Muslim encounter with Greek thought beginning in the ninth century was the evolution of a philosophical approach to prophetic revelation. Prophetic epistemology and the role of the prophet as lawgiver were the philosophers' paramount concerns. Their noetic-political perspective came to regard the prophet as an elite sub-type of humanity endowed with special powers: prophet is as prophet knows, and, on the basis of that higher knowledge, as prophet governs. Although the philosophers never used the Quran as a prophetological sourcebook in the same way that, for example, the mystics and historians did, the philosophers were generally careful to try to reconcile their conclusions with the sacred text—or at least to demonstrate that their conclusions did not constitute an unacceptable departure from revealed truth.

Has philosophy continued to be of interest to Muslim scholars in recent times?

One twentieth-century Muslim scholar describes the background of the philosophical theory of prophetic revelation as follows: Islamic metaphysics managed to address itself point by point to all the major tenets of religious doctrine, but it never quite made a perfect match of the two. A serious question therefore arose. Either there was a double truth, one apprehended by philosophy, the other by religion, or the truth was unitary but appeared now in rational, and again in a metaphorical, imaginative form. The first alternative, that of two truths, did not seem possible rationally and so the philosophers decided to pursue the latter line of thought. Religious truth is but rational truth, but instead of being expressed in nakedly rational formulas, it manifested itself in imaginative symbols—a fact that was responsible for its widespread acceptance by, and effectiveness among, the masses. An important theme in such philosophical works involves understanding the political resonances and implications of prophecy and the affinity between divinely revealed and humanly devised law.

Who are some of the major philosophical figures who wrote on this large subject?

Al-Farabi, Ibn Sina (Avicenna), and Ibn Rushd (Averroes) are key figures. All three begin with at least a minimal acknowledgement that Muhammad had come proclaiming a Divinely revealed universal law. Of the three, however, only Ibn Rushd preserved intact the notion of God's "sending down" the revelation; the two earlier thinkers reduced the revealing angel to the agent intellect. As the originator of the "psychological" explanation of prophecy, al-Farabi (870–950) identified the imagination as the seat of prophecy. The faculty of imagination takes the impressions made upon it as a result of the activity of sense perception and either connect those images with each other or separate them from each other so as to produce either true or false representations of past sense experiences within the soul. Imagination is thus the bridge between perception and reason. During sleep every individual's imagination can engage by "imitation" in activity that is independent of sense perception; but, for a select few, the gift of prophecy makes the fullness of imaginative activity possible even in the waking state. In the latter case the imagination becomes "connected" with the higher faculty of reason, allowing the prophet to acquire the highest type of knowledge. Nevertheless the prophet is not quite the equal of the philosopher in the attainment of knowledge's upper reaches.

Why is Ibn Sina (Avicenna) important?

Ibn Sina (980–1037) gives Divinely Revealed Law preeminence, equating the ideal person with the prophet rather than with the philosopher (as some earlier Muslim philosophers had done). He elevated the prophetic intellect to a level of its own, from which knowledge flows into the imagination, where symbols are formed. Of the exalted status of the prophet, Ibn Sina says, "If one combines with justice speculative wisdom, he is indeed the happy man. And whoever, in addition to this, wins the prophetic qualities, becomes almost a human god. Worship of him, after worship of God, becomes almost allowed. He is indeed the world's earthly master and God's deputy in it."

Why was Ibn Rushd (Averroes) important?

Ibn Rushd (1126–1198) was an exact contemporary of the great Jewish rabbi Maimonides (d. 1204)—in fact, the two grew up just across town from each other in the traditional Jewish and Muslim quarters in the magnificent city of Cordoba, Spain. Ibn Rushd defended most successfully the necessity of the Divinely Revealed Law as the only law capable of securing happiness for all humankind. He insisted that the Divine Will can be known only through prophecy, but he denied Farabi's claim that every ideal ruler must also possess the gift of prophecy. Every prophet may be called a philosopher, but not every philosopher

A statue of Avicenna (980–1037), a major intellectual figure from Central Asia.

may be called a prophet, for Muhammad was the Seal of the Prophets. Even though his adherence to orthodoxy prevented Ibn Rushd from holding that a prophet might arise after Muhammad, his political realism led him to concede that a post-prophetic law-giver might indeed appear. Still he insisted that it was the reception of a Divine Law, not the performance of miracles, that constituted proof of prophethood. That Divine Law is a gift given to all people through their prophets, while philosophy remains the province of a select few.

ISLAM AND THEOLOGY

What is a good "working definition" of theology?

Theology is talk or thinking (*logos*) about God (*theos*). A wide variety of religious traditions naturally engage in some kinds of theology understood in this general sense. Myth at its best is a type of "narrative theology," reflections on the nature of the supreme reality that give rise to story and reenactment of myth in ritual. Some traditions develop the formal discipline of theology much more fully. In those traditions, theology generally does three things. First, it involves a systematic reflection on the basic data, including scripture and/or the teachings of a foundational figure. Theologians sort out and organize the major themes, commenting on the original sources with a view to highlighting main ideas about the ultimate reality (or God), humanity, and the material world. In so doing, they effectively help earlier generations of believers to shape the community's "master narrative," the guiding account by which believers begin to make sense of their lives. (For Jews, it is the story of God's delivering his people from slavery and bringing them to a promised land; for Christians, it is the life, death, and resurrection of Jesus in which they see victory over suffering and death, for example.) Second, theologians begin to formulate a distinctive way of talking about the tradition's central teachings. At this stage theological language begins to become more technical and idiosyncratic. Theology is now using a set of symbols that require some specialized training in the particular tradition to appreciate what the theologians are saying. Finally, theologians articulate those distinctive symbols into a unique system of thought.

Is it true that Muslims "don't do theology"?

This is a common misconception—even among many Muslims. It's connected with the widespread impression that Christians are more concerned with "orthodoxy" (correct belief), whereas Muslims and Jews are more concerned with "orthopraxy" (correct behavior). This, too, is a bit of an oversimplification. All three traditions agree that there is a basic minimum of "creedal" affirmations expected of all believers. While it is generally true that Christian creedal statements tend to be more detailed than either Jewish or Muslim professions of faith, it is also true that Islamic religious thought has long included schools of scholars who are in fact concerned with how and why Muslims articulate their beliefs as they do. That's fundamental to the discipline called theo-logy (God-talk), and a critical ingredient is the study of whether and how divine disclosure (revelation) is related to human understanding and access to truth (reason), and how to reconcile conflicts when revelation and reason seem to lead to different conclusions. Yes, it is true that Muslim specialists in religious law have always outnumbered experts in theology, but theological scholarship has nonetheless played an important role in Islamic intellectual history.

What are some of the key methodological approaches with which Muslim scholars have practiced the craft of theology?

There are two principal Muslim approaches to the study of theology. One method builds on a foundation of the "rational sciences," including the skill of building arguments from rational proofs (*kalam*, ka-LAAM) and sometimes syllogistic logic (*mantiq*). Their purpose is to shore up essential beliefs with rational proof. Some of these scholars also allow use of an interpretive tool called "metaphorical interpretation" (*ta'wil*, ta-WEEL) to interpret sacred texts that appear to imply a conflict between reason and revelation. Such an apparent contradiction might be, for example, the gap between the fundamental principle (found in many religious traditions) that God is "perfectly other" than anything created on the one hand, and the Quran's references to God's "face," "hand," and "sitting on a throne" on the other hand. Some scholars engage the question of how and to what degree one can interpret these "metaphors"; other scholars have more cautiously declined to ask questions, preferring to argue that the scripture's use of these terms simply cannot be explained. They call this deferral to God's perfect knowledge of all mysteries (like this one) "entrusting" (*tafwid*, taf-WEED) the problem to divine wisdom.

As for the second major approach to theological questions, more "traditional" scholars prefer not to employ overtly rational methods at all. Some of these do embrace the concept of "entrusting" imponderables to God, while the most theologically conservative reject even that tool in favor of as strictly literal a reading of the foundational texts as possible. A peculiar paradox is that scholars of this last persuasion, whether Islamic or Christian, invariably end up making occasional "stealth" concessions to "reasoned" interpretation.

Does Islam have theologians like Augustine and Thomas Aquinas and the other great Christian thinkers?

Interest in theological questions developed very early in Islamic history. Though it is true that the interest arose out of concerns more practical than theoretical, the questions early Muslim theologians addressed nevertheless have genuinely theological implications. The oft-repeated criticism that classical and medieval Muslim religious writers were limited to a defensive rehashing of the same old questions, unable to break free of the trammels of traditionalism, is on the whole no more true of the great Muslim thinkers than of their European Christian counterparts. One needs always to consider the tenor of the age in question. As Christian tradition owes a great deal to its great teachers, such as Augustine and Aquinas, Islamic tradition also rests on the massive achievements of its outstanding intellectual figures. A closer look at figures like al-Ghazali, Ibn al-Arabi, and Ibn Taymiyya, for example, three figures every bit as important for Muslim thought as Augustine, Aquinas, and Luther for Christian thought, reveals a great deal of creating thinking.

Who was al-Ghazali?

Abu Hamid al-Ghazali (d. 1111) was born in northeastern Iran in the mid-eleventh century. Showing signs of serious intellectual ability at a very young age, he enjoyed the benefits of the best education available. His reputation for learning spread quickly and the prime minister of the Saljuqid Sultan in Baghdad invited Ghazali to head his new "flagship" *madrasa*. After some years of considerable success teaching religious studies, Ghazali had a sort of midlife crisis that left him experiencing considerable doubt and confusion. In a short autobiography, often compared with Augustine's *Confessions*, he describes how he embarked on a spiritual journey that led him to refocus his life. One important result was his manual of pastoral theology called *The Revitalization of the Religious Disciplines*, an itinerary of spiritual wisdom in forty sections that stretch from repentance to intimate knowledge of God.

Who was Ibn Arabi?

Ibn Arabi (d. 1240) was born in the southern Iberian city of Murcia and was educated in Seville. In his twenties and thirties, he travelled in North Africa to study with spiritual teachers, and at thirty-five headed for Mecca. There he began his *Meccan Revelations*, an encyclopedic and highly original systematic treatise of spiritual theology. Ibn Arabi's very creative thinking naturally stirred considerable controversy among his fellow Muslims and does so still. Virtually every serious religious author since his time has either embraced him or condemned him as an innovator, but almost no one has been able to ignore him. One critical element in his thinking about how one can describe God's perfect transcendent unity is his fine and often misunderstood distinction between the "Unity of Witnessing," the notion that a human being is capable only of "confess-

Ibn Arabi (d. 1240) was the author of *Meccan Revelations*, an encyclopedic and highly original systematic treatise of spiritual theology often viewed as controversial.

ing" God's unity, and the "Unity of Being," the belief that some spiritually advanced individuals can experience *actual union* with God.

Why is Ibn Taymiyya important?

Taqi ad-Din Ibn Taymiyya (d. 1328) was a noted jurist and theologian and a reformer of sorts. Like Ibn Arabi, he generated his share of controversy, but for very different reasons; he was among those who condemned Ibn Arabi. During a career spent largely in Damascus and Cairo, he sought to integrate tradition, reason, and free will in a theological synthesis, much of which he composed while in prison for views political authorities found unacceptable. Because of his posthumous association with the Wahhabi movement that supplied modern Saudi Arabia with its very strict religious ideology, Ibn Taymiyya has been unfairly written off as reactionary. He was in fact a gifted man who took his theology seriously enough to suffer for it and whose influence and originality have yet to be fully appreciated.

Which of these theologians enjoys the broadest popularity today?

Abu Hamid al-Ghazali's (d. 1111) works cover a wide range of theological, philosophical, and spiritual themes. Some have compared him to Christianity's Augustine, citing rough similarities between Augustine's *Confessions* and Ghazali's intriguing quasi-autobiographical account of his personal spiritual quest. One could also argue that Ghazali's influence on Islamic tradition equaled that of Thomas Aquinas on Christian thought. Ghazali produced one of the most influential and perhaps also the most systematic treatment of the spiritual quest. He organized his multivolume *Revitalization of the Religious Disciplines* into four large sections consisting of ten "books" each. Structuring the whole work along the lines of a juridical treatise, he begins with the fundamentals required of those just embarking on the journey, external comportment in relation to God.

Part Two treats external obligations in relation to other people. After ending the second section with a book on the Prophet as ultimate human exemplar, Ghazali moves from action to virtue and addresses the more difficult task of inward disposition required for the reformation of character. Finally, drawing on such earlier masters as Muhasibi and Abu Talib, he leads the traveler up the steep slope to the pinnacle of mystical experience, ecstatic love of God. Ghazali's work integrates mystical theology into the larger framework of pastoral theology, embracing the spiritual needs of the broadest possible spectrum of Muslim faithful.

Many Christians seem to think that "the Muslim God" is inclined toward despotic control over His creatures—especially people. Is this a misunderstanding?

In a word, yes. Such misconceptions often arise from misinterpreting certain conceptions of God in the faiths of others. One fascinating Muslim image of God that is both highly instructive and easily misinterpreted is that of the divine ruse. One occasionally hears non-

Muslims characterize Islam's God as wily or tricky, as though God delighted in cruel hoaxes. Not so. The Quran refers to God as "best of those who devise schemes" (See, e.g., Quran 3:47, 8:30, 13:42, 27:51) to indicate that no human being can know the mind of God. Al-Ghazali, one of Islam's greatest pastoral theologians, develops the idea further. Partially because of its shock value, Ghazali sees in the divine stratagem (*makr*) the ultimate reminder that human beings are better off not trying to second guess their creator.

Ghazali tells the story of how once when Gabriel was with Muhammad, the two acknowledged to each other that they felt stark terror in the presence of God. God then spoke to them to reassure them; they need not be afraid, for He had made them secure. Should they indeed be unafraid? Muhammad wondered; had not God Himself told them not to tremble? Gabriel cautioned that they ought not banish their fear too casually, regardless of the apparent meaning of God's words; they were, after all, in the presence of God. There, only a fool would know no dread. This arresting image is meant to emphasize God's utter transcendence of human imagining. A human being who thinks he or she has God down to a pattern has wandered from the Straight Path into the realm of presumptuousness. Let no one imagine that God is so boring as to be predictable.

How have Muslim theologians addressed the core theological questions in general?

Muslim theologians have been interested most of all in preserving the mysterious and inexplicable character of God's communication to His people. For them the prophet is to be regarded primarily as instrumental in the plan of God, the pen with which the Divine Calligrapher writes. Because their apologetic approach evolved as a way of dialoging with the philosophers, the theologians employed much of the technical jargon of the philosophers. They gave their attention most of all to two issues: prophetic epistemology, which they believed the philosophers had overintellectualized and overhumanized, and evidentiary miracles as necessary proof of prophetic authenticity, which they felt the philosophers had devalued and underemphasized. Whereas many proponents of rationalism held that the Quran, God's speech, could not be regarded as an attribute of God and must therefore be created in time, the theologians staunchly defended a doctrine of the Quran as God's eternal, uncreated speech.

Who were some of the earliest Muslims to synthesize the discipline of theology?

The first Muslim thinker to forge a convincing synthesis of the logical methods of the philosophers with the doctrinal concerns of the theologians was Ash'ari (c. 873–935), himself a convert to orthodoxy from the rationalist Mutazilite school. One of Ash'ari's most prominent followers, Baqillani (d. 1013), authored a treatise on miracles and magic and the vast difference between the two phenomena. His work is in many ways characteristic of an important aspect of theological prophetology. Baqillani discusses prophetic evidentiary miracles from every conceivable angle, distinguishing them from all manner of "unusual" happenings and focusing on the necessity of miracles as a legitimation of the law-giving mission of the prophets. In connection with their interest in miracles and their desire to defend God's primary causality, Baqillani and his fellow Ash'arites espoused a doctrine of atomism.

TRADITIONALISM, REFORMERS, LIBERATION THEOLOGY

Who was Ahmad Ibn Hanbal and why was he important in the evolution of Islamic law and traditionalist theology?

Traditionalist religious scholar and jurist Ahmad ibn Hanbal (d. 855) figured prominently from the reign of al-Mamun through that of al-Mutawakkil, but his role changed dramatically from that of thorn-in-the-side to theological patron saint. Perhaps more than any other single figure, Ibn Hanbal stands out as the leader of the emerging Sunni traditionalist view, vindicated by al-Mutawakkil after years of persecution under the Inquisition. Prolonged suffering for his deeply held convictions gave Ibn Hanbal much of his credibility. There is a delicious irony in his story: a hagiographical tradition that sometimes labelled Ibn Hanbal a Sufi and Friend of God (roughly equivalent to "saint") would eventually make of him a patron of the early modern Wahhabi movement now best known for its often violent rejection of Sufism and the cult of Friends of God.

Has the notion of "religious reform" been important historically for Muslims? Have there been any modern or contemporary "reform" movements or major individual "reformers"?

According to a tradition attributed to Muhammad himself, God promised to raise up a "renewer" (*mujaddid*) who calls people to a fresh awareness of their faith. Muslim tradition has identified a succession of important historical renewers who appear at the outset of each new Islamic century—that is, every one hundred lunar years, beginning in the solar year 622, the "official" origin of the Islamic *umma* in the *Hijra*. Many important religious figures have been identified as such a renewer, often different individuals recognized as such by different constituencies in cultural and religious contexts at the same time. Precisely how their followers understood how these renewers were meant to function has varied considerably—from reinforcing ancient values to waking people up to the need for adaptation to hitherto unknown forces. As indicated in other questions in this chapter, various groups have also claimed legitimacy and authority to reform Islamic thought and practice, first in their region and, in time, globally. Such reform-minded movements typically focus on rooting out residual pre-Islamic elements of faith or practice or more recent un-Islamic accretions. One such development in Indonesia is the Muhammadiya movement, which claims some thirty million Sunni Muslims. Concern for heightened awareness of Islam's ethical demands and the desire to educate Indonesians to discern the difference between pre-Islamic traditions, such as animism and a blend of residual Hindu and Buddhist elements, and authentic Islamic teaching are hallmarks of the movement.

In modern times, too, a number of major reformers have taken on the daunting task of inciting their fellow religionists to adapt their ancient faith heritage to changing circumstances. Like reformers in any tradition, these Muslim pioneers have often met with resistance to the changes they proposed. Muhammad Abduh (1849–1905), for example, worked to promote reason as nearly equal with revelation as a source of knowledge. His suggestion that some elements of the Quran were not of divine origin caused considerable stir. Abduh, nevertheless, served as Grand Mufti of Egypt and was a leading influence at the al-Azhar University, a flagship institution of Islamic traditionalism.

Who was Muhammad Abduh and what impact did he have on "reform" movements?

Sometimes called one of the progenitors of Islamic "modernism," Muhammad Abduh (1849–1905) was a major Egyptian religious scholar who emphasized the importance of accommodating "Western" scientific and technological methods as perfectly compatible with Islamic teaching. At the core of his argument was the conviction that the God-given faculty of reason is a legitimate and even necessary concomitant to divine revelation and no threat to genuine faith and religious knowledge. A fine example of the "realist" approach to the interpretation of sacred sources and Islamic religious history, modernism argues that Muslims can and must learn from all facets of their historical and cultural heritages. More radical Muslims, however, counter that modernists have lost touch with the uniqueness of Islamic identity by too readily surrendering to, and assimilating with, all things "Western."

Egyptian mufti and Islamic reformer Muhammad Abduh (1849–1905) fostered the concept of Islamic "modernism."

Who are the Deobandis?

Founders of a reformist school in the town of Deoband, not far from Delhi, launched their program in 1867 to improve education of Muslims in the basic disciplines of religious studies. A number of famous Indian Muslim scholars taught at Deoband during the later nineteenth and early twentieth centuries. Many were affiliated with the Chishti and Naqshbandi Sufi orders, but their brand of Sufism sought to wean popular spiritual practice of what they believed represented non-Islamic ac-

348

What is the Tablighi Jamaat?

A twentieth-century South Asian "reform" movement called "The Organization for Calling (others) to Fulfillment" (Tab-LEEGH-ee Jam-AA-at) takes its name from its missionary focus of "inviting" non-Muslims to Islam. Beginning in northern pre-Partition India, it drew much of its foundational spirituality from such influential Indian Naqshbandi Sufis as Shah Wali Allah and Ahmad Sirhindi. A major impetus in its founding and growth was a perceived need to counteract increasing hostility to Muslims from proselytization by several powerful Hindu organizations, which claimed as their main mission reclaiming former Hindus who had been lured away to Islam. Tablighi missionaries sought to improve Muslims' fundamental knowledge of basic beliefs and practices, while also recommending the Sufi meditative/contemplative ritual practice of *dhikr* (DHI-kr), recollection or remembrance of God. The latter is a distinctive feature characteristic of very few "reform" movements, most of which have tended to be bent on eradicating any vestige of Sufi spirituality. Today members of Tablighi Jamaat number well into the millions and are found across the globe. Their annual conference in Pakistan may in fact attract the largest assemblage of Muslims other than Pilgrimage to Mecca.

cretions, such as veneration and intercessory prayer at the tombs of famous holy men and women. By the year 1900, Deobandi schools had arisen across India and eventually numbered nearly nine thousand education institutions from the most basic to the equivalent of college and even graduate studies. In the past century or so, some Deobandis have joined forces with the Tablighi Jamaat.

What is the importance of the movement called "Revival of the Religious Scholars"?

A major Indonesian development called the "Revival [or Awakening] of the Religious Scholars" (*nahdat al-ulama*) coalesced in part to counteract the Muhammadiyah movement, which the Revival's founders regarded as unacceptably "modernist" in tone and ideology. Some claim that the Revival movement is one of the largest such developments anywhere (perhaps more than thirty million). Founded in 1926, the movement has fostered important educational institutions centered on the pesantren schools, whose curriculum emphasizes traditional study of Quran and Hadith. The movement's stated purposes include cementing links between the religious scholars and the Sunni law schools, founding and funding *madrasas* to propagate "orthodox" teachings and root out un-Islamic beliefs and practices, and social outreach for the marginalized. Unlike other reform movements, such as the Wahhabi, the Revival has not waged all-out ideological war against Sufi organizations and associated forms of "popular" spirituality, such as reverence (not worship) for exemplary figures like Abd al-Qadir al-Jilani, a major personality in the history of Sufism.

Does Islam have anything similar to the "Liberation Theology" movement in Christianity?

Most Christians have heard the term "Liberation Theology," a movement aimed at lightening the oppression of the poor in the light of a Gospel whose message is interpreted as essentially Good News for the poor. Beginning in the 1960s a number of Latin American Catholic thinkers began articulating a political theology geared to transforming society by enfranchising the poor. Not surprisingly, the results have met with decidedly mixed reviews, critics dismissing it as warmed-over Marxism and supporters hailing it as a fresh insight into the heart of the Gospel message. In recent times Muslims, too, have sought to devise religiously supported social theories focusing on throwing off the yoke of oppression that some regard as the legacy of modern colonial domination over much of the Muslim world. Perhaps the most obvious view both groups would agree on is that theology always has political and social implications and that in modern times, at least, the masses of the poor suffer from the identification of mainstream religious thinking with the privileged members of society. In the view of some Muslim activists, the latter are colonialists and their Muslim collaborators.

Ironically, while Catholics tend to characterize the liberation theology deriving from their tradition as left wing and liberal, those movements among Muslims that are at least roughly parallel are almost always characterized (even by many Muslims) as right wing and reactionary. Muslim thinkers do with the Quran and sayings of Muhammad what Catholic liberationists do with their sources: search them for indications of divine sanction for social concern. Naturally there are numerous differences behind these and other apparent similarities and significant variations among Muslim liberationists as well. But it is important to understand that at least some of the contemporary movements within the Islamic world are motivated by convictions not unlike those of Catholic liberationists.

What are some good examples of Muslim liberation theologians?

Several Muslim "liberationists" were very well aware of the work of Christian counterparts but put a distinctive stamp on the subject. A major thinker associated with the Iranian revolution, Ali Shariati, has written extensively along these lines. Even some of the Muslim groups that have of late become notorious for their terrorist activities, such as Hamas and the Muslim Brotherhood, have strong and legitimate social action missions, establishing a range of medical and educational services for the poor. In whatever form, liberation movements are rarely tidy and domestic, calling as they inevitably do for a destabilizing of the status quo. Muslim or Christian, these movements are indeed radical in the rethinking of values and the reordering of society they demand.

Sayyid Qutb (1909–1966) of Egypt is another good example of an influential liberation theorist. His thought has become the ideological backbone of the Muslim Brotherhood, founded in 1929 by an Egyptian named Hasan al-Banna (1906–1949). Just around the time Latin American liberation theology was developing, coincidentally, Sayyid Qutb was emerging as a martyr for the cause as a result of his lengthy imprisonment and execution for conspiracy. He argued forcefully on religious grounds for the need to provide educational and economic opportunity for all, and his thought lives on in several of the contemporary Middle Eastern movements.

ISLAMIC HUMANITIES AND INTER-CULTURAL CONNECTIONS

American college textbooks commonly dismiss "the Arabian philosophers" as Aristotle's free ride to Europe via North Africa. Is that an accurate picture?

Philosophy courses were pretty typical in passing over a philosophical tradition that is not only deep and broad in its own right, but practically essential for a serious understanding of medieval Christian thinking. First of all, only a couple of the many significant philosophers and philosophical theologians who have called themselves Muslims were Arabs, and none actually hailed from Arabia itself. Most were of Persian or Turkic or other ethnic background. Medieval Islamic philosophers did indeed play a major role in communicating some of Aristotle's critical insights to European Christian intellectuals, but that is not their sole claim to our attention. More importantly, Muslim intellectuals have produced a vast body of philosophical literature that deserves to be taken seriously in its own right.

Muslim philosophical thinking began in the ninth century and continued to develop themes with important religious implications well into the seventeenth. One such theme was the nature revelation vis-a-vis reason. Theorizing about such a theologically sensitive subject naturally put some philosophers squarely in the crosshairs of religious officialdom's big guns. The most famous of these bold individuals were Ibn Sina (aka Avicenna, d. 1037), from what is now the former Soviet Central Asian republic of Uzbekistan; Ibn Rushd (aka Averroes, d. 1198), from Cordoba, a contemporary and fellow townsman of the great Jewish thinker Maimonides (d. 1204); and the Persian founder of the "Illuminationist" school, Shihab ad-Din Suhrawardi, who was executed in 1191 for thinking too boldly.

What is truly astounding about the greatest of these thinkers is that they were such multidimensional personalities and talents. Astonishingly learned, they often combined expertise in math, various physical sciences, and medicine, as well as in law—Ibn Rushd, for example, was from a famous family of judges in Cordoba. Their reputations are richly deserved and their creativity appreciated.

Many people seem to accuse Islam of being "anti-intellectual"—is that a fair characterization?

It's an unfounded stereotype for a variety of reasons. First of all, Muslim educational institutions do have a long and distinguished history, and in some cases they bear some similarity to those that developed in Europe during the "High Middle Ages." Much Islamic religious education remained relatively informal. "Circles" gathered on the floor around teaching *shaykhs* who sat on "chairs" in mosques, but curriculum remained largely unstructured and limited to Quran and Hadith, until the late tenth century. The first major institutional development occurred with the founding in 970 of the mosque called al-Azhar ("The Resplendent One"). At the heart of their new capital, the Fatimid dynasty began organized teaching at that mosque about 978. Since the Fatimids were an Isma'ili dynasty, the "curriculum" focused on religious issues from a Shi'i perspective and that continued for nearly two hundred years.

Meanwhile, further east, the Saljuqid Turks took Baghdad in 1055 and began to develop a type of educational institution that revolutionized higher learning in the religious sciences, the *madrasa*. Originally designed for instruction in religious law (*fiqh*), the *madrasa* spread as an instrument for promulgating Sunni teaching in areas where Shi'i thought was strong. Gradually the *madrasa* developed broad-based religious studies curricula. Usually supported entirely by extensive charitable endowments (called *waqfs*), the great *madrasas* grew to encompass not only instructional facilities but residential quarters for faculty and students, libraries, liturgical space, and even social service wings housing hospitals and hostels.

If it's accurate to say that the first university anywhere appeared in Cairo long before the rise of the great European universities, did its founding lead to further developments?

In 1171 Salah ad-Din (Saladin) brought down the Fatimids and established his Ayyubid dynasty in Cairo. Salah ad-Din and his successors transformed al-Azhar into a Sunni institution, and it became but one of many important *madrasas* in Cairo and across the Middle East and North Africa. Al-Azhar may indeed qualify as the "first university" in the Mediterranean world, but it developed in ways sufficiently different from the European "university" that one can't trace the analogy much beyond superficial similarities. Here are some common organizational themes: division of the "college" into departments by subject matter (Quran and exegesis, law, theology); academic "ranks" within those departments (*shaykhs* or "masters" who held the equivalent of "endowed chairs," professors, and assistant professors, with larger departments providing also "teaching assistants"); course of instruction equivalent to "degree programs" leading to "licenses" roughly analogous to a diploma.

Muslim educational institutions share an important but little appreciated feature with those of Euro-American origin: they are slow to change. But inherent conservatism is not the same as anti-intellectualism. Al-Azhar has gradually become a modern university with a broad curriculum in the arts and sciences, but its image is still largely that of a guardian of Islamic tradition against the onslaught of secularism. Though it has never had anything like the magisterial authority that the Vatican has exercised among Catholics, al-Azhar has played a similar symbolic role among Muslims. Meanwhile, in the

Founded in 970 C.E., Al-Azhar University in Cairo is one of the world's oldest educational institutions and an important center for Arabic literature and Islamic learning.

United States, a desire to preserve and pass on Islamic religious tradition has led to the growth of Muslim private education that offers interesting parallels with traditional Catholic parochial schooling.

Some say that Islam is incompatible with "reason." Is that a fair assertion?

An old and persistent, but seriously flawed, argument to that effect goes like this:

1. Muslims have historically been uniquely inclined toward the use of violence in the name of God.

2. Such a tendency obviously runs contrary to reason, for God Himself is inherently reasonable.

3. Unfortunately for Muslims, the theology of famed eleventh-century Iberian religious scholar Ibn Hazm clearly represents a form of "voluntarism"—according to which God has the freedom to declare good or evil whatever God chooses to so declare, thus suggesting that Muslims apparently believe in a God who is not subject to the strictures of reason.

4. Therefore, Ibn Hazm and fellow proponents of this "theology from above" that absolves God from being bound by the dictates of reason, are in effect according God the freedom to act like a capricious tyrant, who can command as "good," even grotesque, violence—ironically, not unlike the God of the Old Testament.

353

5. And, the argument concludes, the unbridled *irrationality* of Ibn Hazm represents mainstream Islamic religious thought much the way the *rationality* of Aquinas and Augustine represents mainstream Christian thought.

Unfortunately, this argument replays rather uncritically another ancient misrepresentation that is piled high with difficulty. Yes, Ibn Hazm's theology can fairly be characterized as "voluntaristic," and yes, taken to extremes, this voluntarism can be exploited as a defense of virtually any form of behavior espoused by a despotic deity. The central problem here is that Ibn Hazm in no way represents mainstream Islamic theology.

What's behind the misunderstanding of the broad historical reality of Islamic theological thinking?

The scenario long accepted as "conventional wisdom"—even among Islamic studies not specializing in systematic theology (*kalam*, ka-LAAM)—is that the whole story is summed up in the ninth-century conflict between the "rationalist" Mutazili theologians who had caliphal support in Baghdad and the "traditionalist" school represented by renowned jurist Ahmad ibn Hanbal. When a new caliph took the throne in 847, the scenario runs, he disenfranchised the rationalists and sprung their arch enemy Ibn Hanbal from the prison in which the Mutazili had confined him for his refusal to affirm the created nature of the Quran—a little like a Christian denying the humanity of Jesus.

How did those early theologians work out these conflicting concerns? Was this a definitive turning point in Islamic thought?

For a few generations the traditionalists held forth in Baghdad, until the early tenth century when an ex-Mutazili theologian named Ashari decided it was time to propose a synthesis between the rationalist and traditionalist approaches. As he tells the story, his conversion from "pure" rationalism resulted from a dream in which he was confronted with the dilemma of ethically and religiously unacceptable results of taking reason to its theological extremes. Though Ashari's solution still favored a heavy emphasis on absolute Divine freedom, notable Asharite theologians such as Abu Hamid al-Ghazali and Fakhr ad-Din ar-Razi (and their disciples) insisted that one could still count on God's behaving "reasonably." Divine despotism, after all, would only make a mockery of the need for both theology and law, both representing works to which the great Asharites were clearly dedicated. Meanwhile, the "officially" marginalized Mutazili approach was systematically adopted and developed by especially the Twelver Shi'i over the next several centuries. It is not incidental that, from a Sunni perspective, this unfolding affinity with Shi'i thought merely pounded another nail into the coffin of the Mutazili school. Here the conventionally accepted scenario ends, for all practical purposes.

Why has this skewed narrative about Islamic theology persisted?

Unfortunately, for lack of in-depth scholarship needed to fill out the story, that account has gone largely unchallenged until fairly recently. The missing piece, one that is gradually stretching our knowledge of the full spectrum of Islamic theological options, is the place of a theological school that developed contemporaneously with the Ashari school, but many miles to the northeast. In Central Asia, Maturidi's (d. 944) school offered an option still more amenable to overtly rational inquiry than the Ashari. And while the Ashari school became allied with the relatively conservative Shafi'i school of religious law, the Maturidi school was growing increasingly entwined with the methodologically more expansive Hanafi law school.

So, in spite of the more "conservative" tenor of medieval Islamic thought, does the label "irrational" still not tell the whole story?

This "missing chapter" in the way the story has typically been told is extremely important as a corrective to the misrepresentation of Islam as "irrational." First, the Hanafi school of religious law and its theological twin the Maturidi school became increasingly associated with non-Arab Muslim populations. It was eventually adopted almost exclusively by the Turkic peoples of Central Asia and was carried westward with the Turkic migrations that eventuated in the Turkification of what was then Anatolia. They became the fulcrum of the religious institutions of the longest-lived and largest early modern Islamic political entity, the Ottoman Empire. Meanwhile, the same pair became the theoretical backbone of the second largest and second longest-lived political entity in Islamic history, the Mughal Empire. Eventual Mughal domination of all of South Asia planted Hanafi-Maturidi thought from Afghanistan through all of northern India, including what became Pakistan and Bangladesh, a region now home to nearly half a billion Muslims.

Why hasn't this broader understanding of Islam's inherent "rationality" been generally acknowledged?

Unfortunately, essential chapters in the still unfolding story of Islamic thought are only lately coming to light as a result of careful scholarship. It is reasonable to suggest that Islamic religious thought spans a broad spectrum historically, including, moving from right to left: Ibn Hazm and the Zahiri ("externalist") law school (defunct since the early middle ages) on the far right; Ibn Taymiya's theology, filtered through the Wahhabi school, in league with the Hanbali law school; the Ashari-Shafii connection; the Maturidi-Hanafi alliance that grew out of the early Murjia theological persuasion, with its assertion that since only God knows the ultimate disposition of any one's soul, no human being has the authority to judge their current religious status; the various Mutazili-influenced Shi'i theological/legal schools; and the Mutazili tradition, furthest to the "left," which has in recent times resurfaced in the views of so-called Muslim Modernists. In short, it is unfair and inaccurate to characterize Islamic religious thought as monolithic and hopelessly mired in the kind of theistic subjectivism that reduced God to an amoral tyrant.

Together, the Ottoman and Mughal domains secured the prominence of this combination of theological and legal institutions across well over half the global population of Muslims. A natural question in this context might be: if the more theologically/legally "liberal" schools established a dominant presence in Central and South Asia long ago, how is it that Pakistan and Afghanistan have become hothouses for extremist ideologies? One important reason is the increasing recent influence of Wahhabi/Hanbali outreach efforts through *madrasas* and social programs extensively funded with Arab (especially Saudi) oil money.

MYSTICAL THEOLOGY AND INTER–RELIGIOUS CONNECTIONS

What's distinctive about how the mystics have talked about prophetic revelation?

Jalal ad-Din Rumi represents the finest and most original achievements in a tradition of mystical poetry that began with Hallaj (d. 922), developed through Sanai (d. 1131), Attar (d. 1220), and Ibn al-Farid (d. 1235), and continued down to Muhammad Iqbal (d. 1938). The mystical poets generally read the Quran looking neither precisely for story line, nor for "mainstream" modes of expression (though they frequently quote the Quran), nor for very esoteric and abstract etymological associations. The mystics fill their poetry with original and richly evocative imagery. They are adept at playing on words as they strive to enhance the Quran's already vivid word-pictures. Poetic imagination is in fact, if not in theory, the principal means by which the mystical poets transport the reader to an understanding of prophetic revelation, an understanding that transcends even intellectual perplexity. Bewilderment is not an impasse. It is the beginning of true mystical knowledge.

For the mystics the prophet is the paradigm of the relationship between creature and Creator. The prophet is neither merely an historical figure nor merely a personification of some divine attribute or of some other abstract quality, though these features do occasionally emerge from the poetry. A prophet is an exemplar, a person whose life-story can exert a living influence on the life of the observant believer. Story lines are indeed important for the mystics, but they are more interested in the patterns of value and behavior beneath the specifics of the prophet's biography. The poets therefore fashion allegories and fables. They tell stories of human and animal characters who embody prophetic virtues and who are clearly types of the prophet. Occasionally they also use stories in which the prophets themselves symbolize someone or something else, that is, in which the prophets themselves are "types" of humanity.

What are some more details about Jalal ad-Din Rumi and his contributions?

Jalal ad-Din Rumi (d. 1273) was a most remarkable man best known for his enormous contributions to the world of mystical poetry, but he was a brilliant man with wide-ranging interests and a deep knowledge of Islamic intellectual history. He knew and appreciated the accomplishments of the towering figures who had founded the major religious law schools, as well as the pioneers in other branches of the religious humanities, especially literature, theology, and philosophy. But he took a critical view of the Muslim philosophers he had studied in his youth and thought they had taken a wrong turn. From Rumi's perspective, philosophers like Ibn Sina and al-Farabi simply let reason get away with murder, and love was the victim. Rumi preferred to use poetic metaphor and allegory to express the inexpressible.

How does a mystic like Rumi use metaphors to teach?

A key thematic image in Jalal ad-Din Rumi's prophetology is that of the Royal Falcon. It is by no means the only image he employs, but it is so fully developed in several passages and recurs so frequently in fleeting allusions that scarcely any other image can compete with the Royal Falcon for the prophetological limelight. Rumi makes it clear that the Falcon does not refer either to a single specific prophet or only to actual prophets. His rationale in creating the image is to present a standard of life that is truly that of all the prophets, but which is also a touchstone for all believers.

Rumi relates in two segments how the king's favorite falcon flew from the palace into the custody of an old hag (a symbol of the world with all its false promises). She clipped the bird's wings and talons and tried to feed it a stew to which the falcon was not accustomed. When the bird refused to eat, the angry woman poured the boiling broth on the bird's crown. Meanwhile, the king's anxious search brought him at length to the old woman's tent. His Majesty's tears sharpened the falcon's own anguish at separation from the king. Immediately after this first segment of the story Rumi tells of the adversity that Moses, Noah, and Muhammad had suffered at the hands of their enemies.

In the second segment the poet makes an association between the eye of the falcon, weeping both from the pain of the boiling broth and from longing for the king, and the eye of Muhammad, which "turned not aside" on the night when Muhammad journeyed through the heavens in his Ascension: the prophet is not distracted from the vision of God. Then the falcon speaks and likens himself to the pre-Islamic Arabian prophet Salih, who had endured such pain among the unbelieving people of Thamud.

What is another example of Rumi's mastery of the allegorical fable as a teaching tool?

Like many "classic" storytellers, Rumi was a master of the "frame tale"—a genre in which the storyteller begins one story, begins another, and then completes the "sandwich." Before proceeding to develop a variation on this first falcon story, Rumi spins a related allegory. A certain king had two slaves, one true and the other false. As the king grew to esteem the true slave more highly, the royal courtiers became more and more envious, even as unbelievers have always envied their prophets. Within that context, the poet returns to his first theme and sets his "new" story of the falcon who, momentarily blinded by destiny, fell among owls. Fearful that the falcon had come to take over their homeland, the owls attacked. Said the falcon: "I have no desire to remain here; I am leaving and will return to the King of Kings. Do not be undone in your concern, Owls, for I will not settle down here. I will return to my home. You consider this ruin a viable dwelling place; but for me it is to the forearm of the king that I must return." The owls persisted in their suspicion that the falcon was a crafty deceiver, and they mocked his talk of returning to the king. The falcon explained in reply that even though he was indeed not the king's equal, he would gladly experience loss of self (mystical annihilation) for His Majesty's sake.

Does Rumi develop this allegorical theme further?

Rumi later recapitulates his theme in a story entitled "The cause of a bird's flying and feeding with a bird that is not of its own kind." How is it that a royal falcon should descend from the vault of heaven to the level of the low-born owl? Part of the prophet's mission is to sow unity where there is chronic discord, even as Muhammad had defused the tensions among the rival factions in Medina. Rumi then recounts a story of the prophet Solomon, who understood the speech of the birds and who had often served as arbitrator among them. Addressing his readers on behalf of all the prophets, the poet writes: "Listen all you wrangling birds, be attentive like the falcon to the King's falcon-drum...." [And the birds reply:] "We birds are blind and oblivious, for we have never recognized that Solomon. We, like the owls, have been hostile to the falcons and now find ourselves left behind in this ruin."

Rumi then explains the behavior of the birds: when the falcon descends among the owls they often mistake the royal bird for a crow (*zagh* in Persian), the owl's natural enemy, because the falcon brings a message that upsets the birds. In reality the falcon is one who lives ever in the presence of the king and whose gaze, like that of Muhammad on his mystical journey to the Throne, "turned not aside" [*ma zagh* in Arabic, quoting here the text of the Quran, which alludes to Muhammad's Ascension; *ma zagh* also means "not a crow," thus neatly rounding off Rumi's imagery]. Finally, Rumi also often alludes to the Royal Falcon in his shorter, lyric poetry. His entire prophetology is summed up in this one verse: "Nothing can deter the falcon from forgetting its prey to return to the King, once it hears from drum and drumstick the call, 'Come back.'"

AESTHETICS, LITERATURE, AND THE VISUAL AND SPATIAL ARTS

AESTHETICS, FAITH, AND CREATIVITY

Does a sense of beauty and aesthetics have a place in Islamic religious beliefs and cultural values?

Islamic faith tradition has a strong aesthetic sensibility integral to its fundamental concepts. The religious value "Making a beautiful life" is itself a response to the divine beauty (*jamal*, ja-MAAL) revealed through a purely altruistic impulse on God's part—as in the Sacred Hadith, "I was a hidden treasure and I desired to be known, so I created the universe." The divine beauty is revealed in what the Quran calls "signs" on three levels: on the horizons—that is, all of creation; within the self—that is, in every movement of spirit, every impulse determined through the science of hearts to be at least arguably of divine origin, however indirectly; and within the sacred text—whose "verses" are themselves the signs (*ayat*, a-YAAT). This notion of multilevel revelation is similar to the medieval Christian concept of "reading" the three "books" of revelation—the book of Creation, the book of the soul, and the book of Scripture. But in order to "read" the signs, which rarely if ever present themselves in a simple, obvious form, one needs the capacity and daring to surrender oneself to metaphor and similitude—acknowledging one of the Quran's own most frequently used idioms.

How have Muslims distinguished between religious expression resulting from "revelation" as opposed to "inspiration" or human creativity?

As with so many facets of the cultural expression of religious values, the relationship between literary inspiration and divine revelation has never been easy for Muslims to define precisely. Muhammad's detractors accused him of being a "mere poet," and yet subsequent tradition has pointed to the scripture's unmatched eloquence as one sign of

Creativity is the imaginative response to the divine initiative manifest in signs all around and within us. According to a Hadith, "God is beautiful and loves beauty"—so it follows naturally that love of God is intimately bound to the quest for the deepest beauty. The Islamic tradition therefore balances off its call to be attentive to beauty with a beauty-alert. Because God's own beauty coexists with the divine majesty (*jalal*, ja-LAAL), we are well advised not to be too comfortable in the presence of beauty and its myriad signs. As the poet Rilke says, and as countless Muslim poets have said in other words, "Beauty is only the first touch of terror we can still bear, and it awes us so much because it so coolly disdains to destroy us." And that brings a return to the beginning of the cycle: *islam*, surrender in gratitude, and *iman* (ee-MAAN), the search for ever deeper understanding of ways to read the signs, and a higher capacity for *ihsan* (ih-SAAN)—responding to the beautiful with at least a pale reflection of the divine loveliness.

its divine origin, developing the notion of the "inimitability of the Quran" as a theological principle. Scripture is therefore in a sense God's literary creation, infinitely above any human creation. But there remains an undeniable if problematic link between divine articulateness in a human tongue and the human need to express divinely inspired longings in the same language.

How does the term "Islamic" apply to works of Muslims in the arts and architecture?

Several decades back, a very influential historian of Islamic civilization, Marshall Hodgson, defined a set of terms that will be useful in this context. He began by identifying "Islam" as the religious tradition whose sources are the Quran, the Hadith (sayings attributed to Muhammad), and related exegetical concerns, and whose further elaboration encompasses a host of religious institutions and themes, including *Shari'a* law with its ritual and ethical prescriptions as well as mystical and hagiographical traditions. He then proposed the term "Islamdom" as a way of referring to the network of social, historical, and cultural contexts in which Islam has been, and continues to be, a dominant influence. Finally, Hodgson coined the adjective "Islamicate" to refer to the myriad cultural products of individuals and groups living within the various orbits of Islamdom, including, for example, poetry, literary criticism, historiography, and political theory—as well as architecture and the visual arts.

How does one know when the product of human creativity is truly "religious"?

Another set of distinctions is useful here. "Religious" applies to works of art and architecture whose *themes* are explicitly "Islamic," and "sacred" applies to religious works whose *function* is central to the practice of the religious tradition of Islam. So, combining the two sets of distinctions, one might call Islamic any product of explicitly religious concern and action whose function is explicitly religious. On the other hand, the term "Islamicate" better describes works of literature and art produced within societies deeply shaped by the presence of Islam, but whose function is not explicitly sacred and whose content is not clearly religious. In short: within the global social phenomenon of Islamdom, the religious tradition called Islam has generated explicitly religious artifacts worthy of the adjective "Islamic" but has in addition informed a wider range of cultural products fairly described as "Islamicate."

This page showing eastern Kufic script is an example of a sacred text that also exemplifies artistic calligraphy.

How do the arts relate to the larger "community of believers"?

There are many "functional" connections between artistic creativity and religious community. At the level of the smaller arts, such as calligraphy and "arts of the book," Muslim artists and craftsmen began early on to devise ways to beautify the Quran—the word of God. Many other lovely objects beautified with calligraphy-related motifs followed and have become popular in Muslim homes everywhere. As such, the arts of decoration and ornament in any setting are reminders of God, who is "beautiful and loves beauty." Secondly, Muslims, like members of all faith traditions, require communal spaces for a range of purposes. Beginning very early in Islamic history, the spatial arts developed in response to those needs. First came mosques, then *madrasas*, then a host of smaller practical structures—such as Qur'an and Hadith schools—as well as social service facilities such as public kitchens, fountains to provide water, libraries, hospitals, and medical schools. Many of the larger dynasties developed monumental complexes that combined several of these functions, all in service of Muslim community needs.

Art and architecture are expensive. How have Muslim communities funded such activities?

Throughout history and across the globe, "patronage" has been essential to all refined, advanced creative endeavor. No people can give expression to their core values without developing financial institutions to supply needed funding. And Muslim cultures began long ago to devise multiple modes of "patronage." An essential type of support, dating back well over a thousand years, is the so-called "pious endowment" (*waqf*), with a necessary legal apparatus attached to assure that the donor's intentions are carried out.

Waqfs have historically been used to endow thousands of immense religious and social institutions, stipulating everything from the design, building, and maintenance of monumental complexes down to the minutest details of the remuneration of staff and provision of housing for students. Virtually all of the dozens of "dynasties" have patronized cultural developments, generally in proportion to their size and wealth. Their support has gone not only to monumental works of architecture and urban planning, but also to arts far less expensive but equally essential to all civilized societies, such as literature, painting, and a host of "decorative" arts such as metal, wood, and ceramic creations.

What organizations have historically been among the larger sources of patronage?

Among the most extraordinary of dynastic patrons, the Mamluks (1250–1517) and Ottomans (1300–1921) dominated in the central Middle Eastern arena; the Ilkhanids (1256–1385), Timurids (late 1300s–early 1500s), and Safavids (1501–1722) in Iran and Central Asia; and the Mughals (c. 1500–1757) in South Asia. Though the documentary evidence of these developments hardly makes riveting reading in itself, *waqf* documentation nevertheless tells an amazing story of immense commitment and creativity across a global civilization, a story of how a blend of religious, legal, and social values reflected the inspiration of the Quran and ancient tradition in rich material cultures. But in addition, there have been countless examples of "middle class" patronage in many Muslim societies, and in some instances these have been related to organizations not unlike European guilds.

Have the arts played an important role politically?

As is so often the case, people in power hold the purse strings and do not hesitate to spend those resources. Art, especially on a monumental scale, can effectively convey a leader's message of authority and publicize his piety. Funerary architecture has often functioned as a way of showing the power and glory of dynasty. Rulers have frequently established works dedicated to public service—mosques, libraries, schools, hospitals, among many types—as tokens of their religious sincerity and bid for salvation in the next life. Historical documents related to such efforts offer insights into the religious motivations of some important rulers, as well as the religious milieu of their time. As always, human motivation can be complex, and even when such efforts are associated with political aspiration, they are not therefore necessarily unreligious and without spiritual merit.

What is known about the "intentions" of artists in the various media—any insight into how they thought about being explicitly *Muslim* artists?

Muslim artists and architects have spoken eloquently and evocatively, if sometimes also enigmatically, through their works. With respect to architecture and the visual arts, unfortunately they have left precious little textual documentation as to either their methods or their intentions regarding, say, explicitly "symbolic" dimensions of their work. Balanced interpretation of their visual legacy requires first of all a careful assessment of the monuments and objects themselves, including analysis of material, structure, style,

The graceful architecture of the Great Mosque of Cordoba in Spain is an inspiring example of Islamic art that is both beautiful and functional.

and inscriptions. But these creations must also be related to their broader religious, cultural, and social contexts. In the absence of specific conceptual background provided by the creators themselves about, for example, the use of symbolism, the greatest challenge of contextual interpretation is that of relating the visual material to the thought-world of the artists and builders without claiming to read their minds. Although some residual ambiguity as to the original meanings of a monument or work of art may be inevitable, this overview gives at least a hint as to how the major aesthetic dimensions of the visual arts can suggest Islamic purposes and values. Massive urban complexes and miniature masterpieces alike reveal something of the essential beliefs and convictions of Muslims and evoke intriguing images of the societies in which they were produced. Fortunately, literary artists have much more often reflected on their purposes and motivations, especially in the "forewords" or "prefaces" of their larger poetic or prose compositions.

What are some specific examples of how aesthetic values play out in Islamic cultures?

Like other cultural traditions in the arts, Muslim artists have typically sought to express various levels of "harmony" in their work: sensual; psychological; ethical; theological; even at times mystical. Classic sources have suggested that, for example, calligraphy can reach and attain all five levels, for it is a reflection of the "perfect hand" of God, the "divine calligrapher." As for the question of whether and to what degree Muslim artists

363

have developed and employed explicitly intended forms of "visual symbolism," there are varying scholarly views. Some Muslim scholars have held that one can discern in the "Islamic" arts expressions of the principle of *tawhid*.

On the more "minimalist" side of this view is the suggestion that abstract geometric *shapes* in the design of both small objects and of large spatial creations hints at the infinity of the Creator—here, all symbolism is *implicit*. Some take the more "maximalist" view that there is *explicit* (rather than merely abstract) symbolism in such things as the use of specific colors and the choice of sacred texts used in decorating ritual places—and here, symbolism is *explicit*. So, for example, archetypal shapes such as square and circle represent earth and heaven, respectively. Somewhere between maximalist and minimalist views is one that takes a more multilayered approach to architectural symbolism, distinguishing among functional, connotative, and literal symbols. For example, the four minarets of the Sulaymaniye Mosque in Istanbul symbolize the four "rightly guided caliphs" and the fact that Sultan Sulayman was the fourth to rule after the fall of Constantinople; while the ten galleries on the minarets (three each on one pair, two each on the other) represent Sulayman's position as the tenth Ottoman Sultan since the founding of the dynasty. Literal symbolism in this view refers to the verbal associations contained in the inscriptions chosen to adorn the space, such as references from the Quran that imply an identification of the space as a reflection of Paradise.

VARIETIES OF ISLAMIC LITERATURE: PROSE

Muslims consider the Quran both the epitome of Arabic literature and a work that transcends the ordinary canons of literary excellence. What role does literature play in Islamic tradition?

It is helpful first to draw a general distinction among several different kinds of Islamic religious literature. Works of a more technical type include a wide range of materials from exegetical and legal texts to theological tracts. These are typically of rather limited interest among the general public and of greater concern to specialists. Instructional and inspirational types of literature run the gamut from hagiography that enshrines the life stories of countless prophets and Friends of God to more specialized instruction in negotiating the upward path of the spiritual quest. Each of these literary types with its various genres developed its own canons of excellence over the centuries, but in general none of them crosses over into the realm of literature as a "fine art," or belles lettres.

Within the broad category of devotional literature, there is a different situation. A great deal of the literature of piety is made up of collections of prayers and accounts of spiritual experience, such as diaries and dream journals. But it is especially in the various genres of religious poetry that Islamic literature becomes a highly refined art form.

Building on a rich tradition of Arabic lyric poetry, early Arab Muslim poets translated favored pre-Islamic metaphors of the quest for a lost love into expressions of the believer's thirst for God. The great lyricists who wrote in Persian and Turkish, especially, but eventually in a host of other regional languages, developed a breathtaking array of evocative imagery with which to allude to the ineffable relationship between seeker and Sought, lover and Beloved.

What kinds of written sources have major spiritual teachers left as a record of their experience and insight?

Several types of literature preserve the classic teaching of major spiritual guides, typically called *shaykhs* or *pirs* (elders) from across a wide spectrum of cultures and languages of origin. First, there are extensive collections of letters written in response to the actual inquiries of spiritual seekers or advisees concerning specific questions or challenges they encounter in their daily lives. These include all the same kinds of perplexities sincere people of virtually every religious tradition find themselves confronting, from matters of livelihood, family life, personal relationships, ethical dilemmas, and even political advice in questions of how a religious person ought to understand his or her duties to duly constituted civil authority. Dozens of major figures through the centuries have left such valuable documents.

More subtle analysis of a seeker's inner spiritual experience may also be addressed in letters, but such matters are often the subject of two additional types of literature. One of these is the collected and edited sayings of a teacher given in response to assembled followers' specific questions. These gatherings are typically of members of important Sufi or-

What literary forms might be more accessible to a wider public?

A popular pedagogical device is a question-and-answer model, sometimes cast as a student-teacher dialogue; some such works record actual exchanges, but more typically they are constructed as a literary conceit. Works of this type can function as do-it-yourself books for seekers of the greater truth, but more often they presume the ongoing assistance of an actual living preceptor. Essential themes include training in the demanding art of spiritual discernment, or the "science of hearts." This involves developing a sensitivity to becoming aware of the immediate sources of a spiritual movement (is it from God? or from a more nefarious source?). One also needs to attend to an interior movement's duration and understand whether it results from the seeker's own initiative or arises from God's intervention. An important theme and emphasis in understanding how this literature functions is that the spiritual guide is not the seeker's *friend* in the common sense of that term, but rather an objective observer who can advise the seeker with what may need to be a "tough love" approach.

ders, and the resulting texts written down by scribes represent a crucial record of the institutional life of the order in question. Another form is the usually longer and more comprehensive "treatise" addressed to a more limited and more "spiritually advanced" readership. Though a significant number of *shaykhs* have also composed these written works, they are fewer than either collected letters or editions of "group teaching sessions."

What are some specific examples of teachers who have communicated in literature to assist those who seek their guidance?

A rich body of works of "spiritual guidance" makes up an important genre of Islamic religious literature. Written in a dozen major languages beginning in medieval times, such works typically originated either as edited collections of the sayings of a teacher delivered orally to his or her students, or as literary creations from the outset. Often organized around metaphors of spiritual journey (e.g., Ansari's *One Hundred Fields* and *Resting Place of the Wayfarers*), the literature teaches readers how to read subtle "allusions" or "hints" (*isharat*) needed to stay on the correct "path." This genre of literature tends to be addressed to more advanced seekers and couched in more esoteric language.

What other sorts of spiritually pedagogical literature has been important?

Beginning as early as the ninth century, individuals acknowledged for their spiritual authority composed prose works designed to assist "seekers" to find their way along the "path." Tomes with names like *The Book of Light Flashes*, *The Sustenance of Hearts*, and *The Revelation of Things Veiled* were influential across the Middle East, and even as far as Spain to the west and India to the east. Over several centuries, these Muslim teachers developed a remarkably consistent "technical" vocabulary to help seekers analyze and gain insight into their inner lives. Pedagogical tools focused on elucidating the subtleties of "conventional usages" (*istilihat*) and clarification of ambiguous terms (*bayan al-mushkilat*) in this expanding lexicon of spiritual analysis. Taken together, the best of these remarkably insightful works constructed a subtle system designed to help dedicated people to understand the most elusive aspects of their personal religious experience.

What kind of literature is the principal source for information on holy persons?

A large and very important type of literature called "hagiography" (from the Greek terms for "writings about holy persons," *hagie graphe*) forms an important source in nearly every major religious tradition. Hagiography as a traditional literary genre is quite different from the more familiar modern forms of history and biography. As with sacred scriptures, it is essential to know what kind of document a work of hagiography is. That means reading with different lenses than are appropriate for more contemporary forms of communication. In general, hagiographical writing underscores the amazing and often downright miraculous elements in the life story of an important holy person. More often than not, special signs attend the birth of the individual, who goes on to have an extraordinary childhood. The spiritually precocious youngster often seems to move directly into a religious maturity characterized by feats of towering personal endurance and asceticism. Alternatively, a holy person may spend many years wallowing in immorality and ignorance of the religious tradition's truth, then go through an astounding conversion. Many traditions have produced whole libraries of hagiography that include women's stories, but usually in notably smaller numbers than men's.

What are some of the different kinds of Islamic hagiography?

Life stories of various categories of human exemplars have taken several important literary forms. First, the literary genre known as *Tales of the Prophets* typically takes the form of an anthology of fairly brief stories of individual prophets, beginning with Adam and proceeding through Jesus, sometimes including a life of Muhammad as its culmination. Following a similar model are *Tales of the Friends of God*, containing from dozens to hundreds of short bio-sketches. Such collections of lives of the prophets and other holy persons emphasize how they live in a world ordered to a divine plan, and the stories function as an accessible form of cultural and religious ideals. Another important genre is the individual life story, the model for which was the original and most famous *sira* of Muhammad himself. Many Muslim authors have used the single-life narrative for both individual prophets other than Muhammad and for famous Sufis and other Friends of God, the latter including prominently a genre dedicated to the marvelous deeds of the subject.

Are these kinds of works mostly antiquarian curiosities for scholars only, or are they still available and read by "ordinary" educated Muslims?

Here's an example of how books like these remain highly sought after for many millions of Muslims and how amazingly accessible they are to the average person. An educated Iranian-American recently visited her family in Tehran and went in search of a pair of medieval "classics" of Islamic hagiography. She was looking specifically for Farid ad-Din Attar's (d. 1221) *Remembrances of the Friends of God*, and *Warm Breezes of Intimacy* by Jami (d. 1492). She discovered the Attar book in the fifteenth printing of a 1981 critical edition. This was not just a run-of-the-mill version, but something only highly educated individuals would look for. It was a beautifully produced, six-hundred-page hardback for which she had paid the equivalent of nine dollars. Those qualities alone make her find surprising on several counts. But still more amazing is that she found the volume not at one of the dozen or so bookstores across from Tehran University (where one would expect to find such an edition), but in a non-academic bookstore in a large suburban mall! When asked whether he also had a copy of the Jami book in stock, the merchant apologized profusely and said that he had just sold out of a similar (critical) edition of that work. Were one to inquire at a national chain bookstore in a local mall for the latest printing of the most recent critical edition of the works of, say, Thomas Aquinas or John of the Cross *in their original languages*, one would surely be met with a blank stare. The willingness of major Middle East publishing houses to continue printing works of this kind is a subtle but revealing measure of how important and widespread such books remain for educated Muslims today.

What is "wisdom literature"?

Wisdom literature refers to texts that reflect specifically on what it is to be human, focusing on appropriate conduct as defined by a particular religious tradition. These texts can take the form either of short memorable proverbial sayings or fuller treatises in prose or poetry or combinations thereof. In Jewish tradition, wisdom literature is associated largely with such books of the Bible as Proverbs, Wisdom, Ecclesiastes, and Job, and with the person of King Solomon in particular. Muslims consider their own scripture as the source of wisdom as well. An important wisdom figure named Luqman (sometimes likened to Aesop, "author" of the most famous classical "Fables") appears prominently in the Quran; but as a genre Islamic wisdom, literature is mostly non-scriptural.

Have Muslims developed wisdom literature?

Muslim authors have developed especially two types of wisdom literature. A more "formal" type, generally referred to as the "Mirror for Princes," applies canons of ideal behavior to political contexts. Here very bold authors pull no punches in the advice they give to sovereigns of all kinds of Muslim regimes, in works such as *Treatise on Government* (*Siyasatnama*) by the celebrated Abbasid prime minister Nizam al-Mulk; Ghazali's *Book of Counsel for Kings* (*Nasihat al-muluk*); and the anonymous Persian work *The Sea of Precious Virtues* (*Bahr al-fawa'id*).

Have Muslim authors penned spiritual autobiographies?

Nothing captivates the imagination like stories of personal experience. More than that, accounts of the wonders and adventures of a celebrated personality can assume mythic proportions; the subject of such a story becomes larger than life and functions as an in-

---

Works of advice to princes sound fairly elitist— anything that provides wisdom for ordinary folk?

Muslims writing in many different languages have penned more "popular" works for a broader readership. Rather than offering rulers advice on how to govern justly and in the spirit of the Quran, these works offer a kind of "lay spirituality" whose principles authors present in two kinds of literature. First, proverb-like aphorisms culled from the writings and addresses of major teachers and compiled according to themes recall biblical books such as Proverbs and the Wisdom of Solomon. Second, talented and witty authors like the much-loved thirteenth-century Sadi of Shiraz (in Iran) crafted very thoughtful works combining prose, poetry, anecdote, and reflection. In addition, a literary form mentioned briefly above, the "aphorism" (called *hikam*, plural of the word for wisdom, *hikma*) represents the most compact form of "wisdom literature," and is a kind of Islamic religious adaptation of the ancient genre called the "proverb."

spiration and goal to be emulated. That is one reason why the tales of Islam's religious heroes have played such an important role as exemplars for millions of Muslims. The hagiographical tales of prophets and Friends of God described earlier emphasize how God works through the intermediacy of human beings but seldom reveal much of the heart and soul of the heroic figure. Several other kinds of literature, however, break the surface of external action and marvelous deeds. These experiential narratives speak not of the heroic figure's instrumental role, but of the individual's personal relationship to the goal of the journey, God. First-person accounts of spiritual journey, often modeled on that of Muhammad, offer a glimpse of a more intensely personal realm, penetrating to the very marrow of what it is to be, from a religious perspective, truly human.

VARIETIES OF ISLAMIC LITERATURE: POETRY

What are some important kinds of poetry through which Muslims have expressed their religious beliefs and values?

Though poetry did not hold a high place in Muslim society during Muhammad's lifetime or for first- and second-generation Muslims, poets came into their own and flourished under the Umayyad dynasty (661–750) among dissenting groups like the Shia and Khawarij, who fashioned poetic forms as a vehicle of protest. During the Abbasid caliphate, a new religious focus on asceticism, discipline, and withdrawal from the world emerged in new forms of poetry. Simple, more "popular" varieties of Arabic poems became associated with mystics such as Rabia al-Adawiya (d. 801) and Hallaj (d. 922). By the twelfth and thirteenth centuries, Persian had become an important poetic language, and poets had fashioned a repertoire of beautiful metaphors, analogies for God, and the divine-human relationship expressed as the human lover's longing for the divine beloved and lover. Metaphorical imagery of God as the wine and the human lover intoxicated by it raised eyebrows but remained current among Sufi communities. Didactic poetry tended to be longer and more narrative in form; lyric poetry was typically shorter and more emotive. Today Muslims in countless societies continue to revel in the works of their "own" poets, classical and contemporary, who continue to express deep religious sentiments in scores of languages.

What is an example of how "allegory" can communicate important understandings of the "spiritual journey/quest" in the lives of Muslims?

A marvelous tale by the Persian poet Farid ad-Din Attar (d. 1220), entitled *The Conference of the Birds*, admirably illustrates the concept of spiritual life as a pilgrimage. Once upon a time, all the birds of the world assembled to discuss their place in creation. They decided that they, no less than the other animal kingdoms, ought to have a king. In their

369

quest for the feathered monarch, however, they would need an experienced guide. Fortunately one of their number, the crested Hoopoe, had served the prophet Solomon as his ambassador to the Queen of Sheba. The Hoopoe volunteered his services. In his inaugural address, he announced that the birds indeed already had a king who dwelt in a mysterious and mountainous land many days distant. Already experienced in the demands of life in the Unseen World, the Hoopoe warned that the journey would be arduous.

One after another the birds stood up to express their misgivings and offer excuses for staying at home. To each in turn, the Hoopoe responded with a further elaboration of the importance of the journey and the magnificent prospect of meeting the King, the Simurgh. "We are but the King's shadow on earth," he went on; and though none of us is truly fit to gaze on the King's beauty directly, "by his abounding grace he has given us a mirror to reflect himself, and this mirror is the heart. Look into your heart and there you will see his image."

Seven perilous valleys must the birds traverse. Quest, Love, Understanding, Detachment, acknowledgement of God's Unity, Bewilderment, and, at last, Poverty and Death to Self lay before all willing to go forth. By the end survivors numbered only thirty birds (*si* = thirty, *murgh* = bird in Persian). After the bedraggled flock had waited for what seemed an eternity at the door of the King's palace, a chamberlain emerged to advise them to turn back, for they could never hope to endure the King's glorious presence. The birds insisted on their steadfast desire. At length the servant opened the door and ushered them in. As he vanished from their sight he pulled back a hundred veils. With that, "the sun of majesty sent forth its rays, and in the reflection of each other's faces these thirty birds of the outer world contemplated the face of the Simurgh of the inner world."

Do Muslims today still connect culturally with more "classical" modes of "poetic" expression?

Classic works of religious lyric poetry remain popular among Muslims everywhere. In many parts of the world devotional poems supply both the text and inspiration for musical entertainment. Moviegoers who saw *Dead Man Walking* experienced something of the cross-cultural power of a prominent exponent of an Urdu form of singing called *qawwali* by the intensely engaging Nusrat Fateh Ali Khan, one of Pakistan's most popular entertainers. Didactic religious poetry, too, retains its popularity for countless Muslims. In Iran, for instance, taxi riders are likely to get a cabbie who expresses sincere delight if his fare drops the slightest hint of interest in a great Persian religious poet who died in the thirteenth century. Chances are good that the driver will even recite a great medieval mystical lyric that he knows by heart. In the United States, some Muslims welcomed a small group into their home to read in Persian the Spiritual Couplets by the great thirteenth-century mystic Jalal ad-Din Rumi, the man perhaps most famous as the original "whirling dervish." Islamic religious poetry is alive and well and continues to play an important role in the lives of Muslims everywhere.

THE "SMALLER" VISUAL ARTS

Is it true that many Quran manuscripts are elaborately decorated—and if so, what's the source of this practice?

Islamic tradition shares the deep-seated Jewish concern over "graven images" and has never developed a tradition of religious sculpture. Even so, Muslim artists have developed a number of spectacular two-dimensional expressions of religious themes and images. Calligraphy, illumination, and illustration are the three most important. Since there was no extensive tradition of written Arabic literature, and the Quran itself was all originally delivered orally, calligraphers gradually refined a system of writing Arabic designed to insure maximum accuracy in reading and handing on the sacred text. But it was not long before talented calligraphers moved beyond the more immediately utilitarian concerns and began to create ways of beautifying manuscripts of the Quran. As they invented new and more attractive calligraphic styles, they started experimenting with decorative panels of floral and geometric patterns both as frontispieces and as visual interludes between chapters of the Quran. To those designs they soon added text, integrating calligraphy into the geometric and vegetal creations. Panels between chapters came to include the name of the sura, the number of verses contained, and the sacred text's place of origin (either Mecca or Medina). These forms of illumination offer excellent examples of "arabesque," infinitely repeatable patterning.

Do Muslims make religious use of figural images? Under what circumstances?

Human and animal imagery do not, it is true, function within the context of ritual space and liturgical prayer and one can thus safely claim their function is not "sacred." But to conclude that they are not "religious" is misleading, akin to insisting that Durer images of the Evangelists or Fathers of the Western Church are not religious when they do not appear within a church or as Bible illustrations; or that Books of Hours are not religious because they also contain "secular" images, such as the labors of the months. Some scholars suggest that when such images do appear they are decidedly subordinate to the overall program of ornamentation, whereas in fact many Muslim artists have used such imagery as a sophisticated visual exegesis of historical and mystical texts and as an important tool for religious education. In other words, these images matter religiously and not just aesthetically. Muslims have used figural imagery for decidedly religious purposes, and they continue to do so. They are not mere visual luxury for the elites of the past or eye-candy for contemporary children who read the scores of illustrated books available in countless mosque bookstores.

What are some important dimensions of the interplay between religion and material or visual culture in Islamic tradition?

Throughout the complex global history of Islamdom, in its numerous political, religious, and cultural incarnations, Muslims have fashioned countless ways of expressing

371

What is meant by the distinction between "image" and "likeness," and how does it help to understand visual arts produced by Muslims?

Many people, including many Muslims, believe that the ancient Islamic tradition unconditionally bans the use of *all* depictions of living beings, other than vegetable forms. The historical record tells a very different story. In fact, according to an account in the earliest "biography" of Muhammad, the Prophet made a very telling comment about the images of Jesus and Mary found in the Ka'ba. He was asked whether the image should be destroyed; let it be, he replied, no harm will come of it. Through the centuries, many Muslim artists have crafted "images," even of important human beings. But a careful look at the vast majority of these images makes it very clear that the artists did not intend to produce a "likeness"— that is, a realistic "portrait" designed to truly "represent" a specific individual. The critical religious principle here is the need to avoid producing an image that 1) seems to coopt God's sole creative prerogative, and/or 2) poses a danger of "idolatry" by providing an object of *worship*.

What this means in practice is that the widely held conception that Muslims don't use figural art of any kind, or that, at the very least, Muslim artists never depict human beings, is not quite accurate. It is more accurate to say that Muslims never attempt to depict God visually, do not use representational art in cultic settings at all (i.e., in a mosque), rarely depict Muhammad (there are many historical examples, however), and sometimes look askance at the depiction of other religiously significant figures. A cursory glance at the children's religious education books available in many mosque bookstores should be enough to dispel the general misconception about a total ban on images—they're full of illustrative drawings. And in many parts of the Islamic world, one can easily find comic and coloring books featuring famous figures from Islamic history and religious lore. The critical issue is that one not use figural imagery in an attempt either to "play God" by attempting to imitate what only God can do, or to give visual expression to what is by definition inexpressible, namely God's unity and transcendence.

their beliefs and values in arresting and original ways. Core Islamic values have everywhere been communicated in ways distinctive of regional and local cultures and ethnicities. What most underlies all that diversity of expression particularized in specific geographical areas are a fundamental human need for community; an aesthetic sense of taste and style; and practical ways of supporting creativity economically and politically.

Is it true that Muslims never depict human or animal figures?

Readers browsing the pages of virtually any publication designed for Muslims may be surprised at the number of illustrations featuring human and animal figures. Shelves of mosque bookstores are filled with books, especially those designed for children, similarly illustrated. Still, the notion persists, among Muslims and non-Muslims alike, that "Muslims don't do pictures." What most people popularly perceive as a blanket prohibition of images actually applies only to ritual settings. In other words, figural or representational imagery will not be found in a mosque. Islamic and Jewish tradition share the concern that inherent in representational visual imagery, especially of the three-dimensional sort (sculpture), is the risk of idolatry.

Muslim artists throughout the ages and across the globe have produced a great deal of figural art, even including images of prophets and other holy persons. But their images are so clearly abstract and non-realistic that they can scarcely be taken as the artist's attempt to usurp God's creative power. For purposes of education and entertainment,

A 1237 manuscript illustration by Wasiti incorporates human and animal forms.

two-dimensional images generally have been perfectly acceptable. In fact, even the prohibition on three-dimensional imagery is far from absolute, except in the context of worship. For example, Muslim children play with dolls.

Devout Muslims express a preference for educationally suitable imagery that exemplifies virtue and ethical values. Under the heading "Move Over Barbie!" one company markets a doll called Razanne, dressed in white head-and-shoulder covering (the *hijab*) and green full-length gown (*jilbab*). The *hijab* is removable so that little girls can learn about donning the proper covering. Razanne's clothes are decoratively trimmed, but she wears no makeup.

How have Muslim artists gotten around the strictures against producing "images" in any key *religious* context?

Illustration of manuscripts goes a major step beyond illumination and does not occur in manuscripts of the Quran. Many important religious and historical texts in a dozen major languages have appeared in lavishly executed manuscripts over the centuries. Persia, Turkey, and India have produced the best and the most numerous of these, with relatively few coming from the Arab world. Perhaps the single most important genre of illustrated manuscript from the perspective of religious studies has been that of mystical poetry created between the twelfth and sixteenth centuries. Second in importance are illustrated versions of hagiographical texts, stories of the prophets and Friends of God (similar to what Christians call saints).

What do Islam's ancient sources provide by way of specific guidance about this matter?

Sources of Islamic tradition, from the Quran to the Hadith to subsequent interpretations by eminent religious scholars, present a wide spectrum of positions. Those who do not insist on a complete ban generally discuss any (or all) of four key overlapping criteria. First, the context in which the image occurs: In one Hadith, Muhammad's wife Aisha describes a curtain depicting a bird that hung in their front room. When someone raised a question, the Prophet instructed his wife to "put it somewhere else" because it reminded him of "the [non-spiritual] world." Even some strictly conservative Muslim authorities conclude that if images were forbidden altogether, Muhammad would have ordered it destroyed and it would never have hung *anywhere* in the house to begin with.

Second, its function—the ways people *use*, or are *likely* to use it: Images are strictly prohibited for ritual uses but are acceptable for pedagogical purposes. Such images must be only two-dimensional (cast no shadow) and can include a wide range of teaching tools and mundane devices such as calendars and passports. However, there are also traditions that suggest that Muhammad allowed both a wife and daughter to keep their dolls, on the grounds that they were merely play things.

Third, the intent of the one who produced the image: An early biography of Muhammad describes how, when he went to cleanse the Ka'ba in 630, he ordered destroyed images of Abraham and Ishmael holding arrows of divination, because no prophet would use such devices. But he protected images of Jesus and Mary because their content was consonant with Muslim faith and presented no danger of being worshipped.

Sounds like there are various ways of interpreting the sources—is there any other consideration than can help clarify the matter?

An interesting factor in all of this is that one must also consider potential unintended consequences that might follow from the production and use of images. Here are some specific examples. One classical legal scholar argued that early tradition had forbidden images (or even abstract decoration) on clothing purely out of fear that a community only recently converted from idolatry might revert. But once monotheism had become better established, he argued, Muslims were allowed to ornament "items of trade" without danger to their faith. Muslims who gravitate toward a broad condemnation of images often find cause for their position in reports of Muhammad's warning that anyone who creates a picture of a *person* will suffer eternal punishment at the hands of their "creations" after God breathes a soul into them. But many also acknowledge that the Prophet then added that, if people insist on creating images, "let them paint trees and other inanimate things."

Were any important historical texts ever illustrated? How do their images function?

Though works of this genre are not primarily religious in intent, the form is a part of a continuum of important sources. One scholar suggests that the illustrations of religious themes in classical Iranian manuscripts of historical works do not serve a religious purpose at all. Instead, he argues they serve the more purely political function of connecting the dynasty that supplied the patronage with their dynastic past, thus supporting the regime's enduring, deeply rooted authority and legitimacy. Some have argued that the religious figures' lack of any distinguishing visual apparatus, such as haloes or flaming nimbus or facial veil, suggests that the authors, painters, and patrons regarded them from a purely secular point of view. That argument fails to convince, in view of the practice of a number of clearly religious works in which none of the key faces are veiled; or of several illustrated universal histories in which even evil characters receive haloes.

Are there any illustrated texts that do depict Muhammad or other prophets? What for?

A number of important illustrated universal histories do contain illustrations of stories from Muhammad's life. Choice of scenes to be illustrated in any given manuscript opens a window into the life and values of the painters and their patrons. In some cases the artists give visual emphasis to occurrences that rate barely a passing mention in the text. What was of marginal significance to the author has taken on increased importance to a later generation of Muslims. For example, a Shi'i patron might wish to emphasize elements of Muslim history that support the Shi'i interpretation of Muhammad's

375

choice of his successor to leadership of the community. Whatever the emphasis in a particular work's visual interpretation, each one provides a glimpse of some aspect of Islamic spirituality's multidimensional sense of story as the arena in which God deals with humanity through the agency of paradigmatic figures.

Where do such texts fit in the larger literary and religious context?

Stories of prophets and other exemplary figures are indeed part of a larger picture, and a political entity might naturally hope to seek legitimacy within an Islamic setting by associating itself with such figures. That does not, however, simply evacuate the stories of all religious significance. A story told with a view to making history come alive and to making important historical associations can also serve to reinforce the broadly religious significance of history. Many images of important illustrated manuscripts likely played an educational role for the very rulers who commissioned

A sixteenth-century artwork from a Turkish biography of the Prophet illustrates Muhammad with attendees and the angels Gabriel, Michael, Israfil, and Azrail.

them, but who had converted to Islam in the very recent past and had no previous background in the lore of the ancient tradition. Not unlike medieval stained glass windows, the images may have supplied the patrons with basic reminders of the essential elements of the Quran's fundamental narratives and religious figures.

Is there any similarity between Muslim and Christian art?

Virtually identical stucco decor in churches and mosques, the ubiquity of illuminated sacred text in both traditions, the dematerialization of nature so evident in Muslim miniatures and Christian icons alike, all point to art as the trans-creedal coin of the realm in regions where Muslims and Christians have coexisted. Beneath the religio-aesthetic concerns shared across the whole spectrum of traditions lies a stylistic osmosis that has actually given birth to an amalgam of Islamic-Christian art. Muslim artists subsumed the arts previously shared by the Christian cities of Rome, Constantinople, Alexandria, Antioch, and Jerusalem, continuing the tradition of denaturalized images of a "non-composite" world—as richly presented in monuments like Jerusalem's Dome of the Rock and Cordoba's Great Mosque. And under Muslim rule in the eastern Mediterranean, the symbiosis continued in reverse, as Christians reabsorbed literary and visual themes developed by Muslim artists. As often happens, cultures and religious traditions meet each other in the visual arts even when conflicts at the political level conspire to divide them.

ISLAMIC RELIGIOUS ARCHITECTURE

Is religious architecture required by Islamic tradition? How did the architectural function of the mosque evolve?

Although the Arabic word for mosque, *masjid*, means simply "place of prostration" and denotes no particular structure, Muslims have devoted enormous attention to creating architectural contexts in which to pray. The first mosque structure of any significance was Muhammad's house in Medina, equipped with a large open air courtyard. Within a few generations, Arab and Persian architects had begun to devise distinctive combinations of covered and uncovered space suited to Muslim ritual needs. The space generally included a covered prayer hall, an open courtyard surrounded by a covered arcade one or two aisles wide, and a minaret from which to make the call to prayer at the five specified daily times. Early mosques were relatively simple with little exterior ornamentation. Designers gradually added small domes to accentuate the roofline of the prayer hall, and as the mosque assumed a higher profile within the city scape, monumental decorative facades and portals displayed a beautiful face to the public. A number of the early mosques, such as those in Cordoba and Damascus, arose on the sites of earlier Christian churches, which in turn rested on the ruins of still earlier Roman temples.

Were early Muslim architects influenced at all by surrounding cultures?

At the center of the former Byzantine Empire, Turkish architects experimented with the hemispheric dome and half-dome as basic elements of design. With Hagia Sophia as their model, they achieved extraordinary expanses of space in their prayer halls. To accentuate both the prayer hall and the courtyard, which is typically about equal in area with the covered space, they experimented with the placement of two or more thin, graceful minarets. In Persia, the courtyard became the central unit of composition, with as many as four inward-facing facades covered in multicolored ceramic tile mosaic emphasizing the interiority favored in Persian architecture. Large, slightly bulbous tiled domes crown the prayer hall entered through one of the four inward-facing facades. Tile facing was the preferred method of enhancing the baked brick that supplied the only readily available building stock. Further east monumental architecture developed still greater material and stylistic refinement.

Architects "on loan" from Persian courts integrated the best elements of Iranian design with the finer construction materials India had to offer—red sandstone and white marble. The results were the great mosques of the capital cities of Lahore and Delhi and perhaps the most famous funerary monument of all time, the Taj Mahal in Agra.

From Cordoba to Kuala Lumpur and beyond, the legacy of Islamic religious architecture embraces scores of masterworks in a half dozen major styles that communicate so much about the tradition that words cannot express.

What are some basic architectural functions other than that of the mosque?

In addition to the principal ritual function supplied by the mosque, architectural developments responded to a host of other functional needs throughout Islamic history. In addition to mosques, a variety of other architectural forms and functions became the focus of considerable creativity. By the mid-eleventh century, institutions of higher learning, or *madrasas*, came into their own as architecturally significant works, whether as free-standing structures or as integral components in larger mosque complexes. Classic design, whatever the dominant regional style, included a central courtyard with residential and instructional facilities built into surrounding covered structures. Major free-standing *madrasas* also often incorporated a prayer hall and sometimes the mausoleum of the patron or founder and his/her family.

Funerary structures also became an important focus of architectural creativity, despite Muhammad's warnings against the temptation to aggrandize any mere mortal's final resting place. Finally, many of the larger Sufi brotherhoods eventually developed distinctive forms of residential/ritual complexes as symbols of their prominence and influence. The wealthier brotherhoods sometimes designed and built extensive and ar-

The Bukhara Registan Shir-dar *madrasa* in Uzbekistan is an example of Persian/Central Asian style architecture of an institution of higher religious learning.

chitecturally distinctive foundations, often with financial assistance of royal patrons seeking spiritual merit. Tomb-shrines have been particularly important in the histories and legacies of many Sufi orders, and major institutions have developed around a founder's grave.

What are some of the principal functional aspects of the mosque?

After Muhammad's death, Muslim forces began to introduce Islam into surrounding areas, establishing garrison cities at Basra and Kufa in Iraq, at Fustat (near present-day Cairo), at Qayrawan (in present-day Tunisia), and other newly conquered territories. Early mosques in areas of expansion assumed the form of the hypostyle basilical hall, with the apse adapted into what would become the prime symbol of the orientation to Mecca, the *mihrab* (prayer niche). Architects gradually added visual embellishments, such as a small dome over the niche and later a similar dome at the opposite end of the central aisle (or nave). Though the prayer hall was the principal covered space of the early mosques, an uncovered space of equal or greater size surrounded by a covered portico became a standard compositional element in the ritual space. In time, another functional/symbolic element became a regular feature of mosque architecture—the minaret, a galleried tower from which the muezzin intoned the call to prayer (*adhan*) five times daily.

Did distinctive architectural forms or styles develop?

Between the tenth and fifteenth centuries, Muslim architects from Spain to Indonesia adapted various construction and decorative materials, compositional elements, and design plus aesthetic considerations. The long-term result was the evolution of half a dozen major architectural styles characteristic of Spain and North Africa (hypostyle prayer hall, square single-stage minarets); Syria and Egypt (hypostyle halls early on, more prominent monumental-domed prayer halls in stone and marble, multistaged and shaped elaborately carved minarets); Turkey (central-domed prayer halls in gray granite, multidomed courtyard porticoes, slender cylindrical conical-topped minarets with up to three balconies); Iran and Central Asia (domed prayer halls, arcade-enclosed courtyards with iwan-façade side halls, baked brick structures with elaborate tile decoration, cylindrical single-balcony minarets); and India and southeast Asia (forms similar to Iranian, but using marble and sandstone building materials, and multicolored decorative mosaics).

If Muslims simply do not use representational imagery in sacred settings, does that mean that mosques are totally unadorned?

Quite the contrary. Mosques in all the many cultural and stylistic variations mentioned earlier display an extraordinary repertoire of ornament. In Persian, Central Asian, and South Asian traditions, mosques are often as varied and colorful exteriorly as on the inside. There, combinations of three major types of arabesque—floral, geometric, and calligraphic—appear in astonishingly creative combinations, whether in tile mosaic or more expensive techniques that inlay semi-precious stones and minerals into materials such as white marble or red sandstone. In most of the eastern Mediterranean regions (Turkey and the Arab lands of the Middle East), where many types of stone are available for construction, the look is very different. Here outward appearances, while less flashy than further east, feature elegant and costly stone carving and inlaid polychrome marble, for example. Inside, however, Middle Eastern mosques can be dazzling for color and design.

What is an example of a supreme architectural achievement in a major mosque?

On the brow of a gentle hill overlooking the main road into the ancient Turkish city of Edirne sits one of the most elegant creations of religious architecture anywhere on earth. This crowning work in the long career of the great architect Sinan was commissioned by Selim II, son of Sulayman the Magnificent, in whose service the architect had spent most of his life. Sinan had spent his early career as an army builder, specializing in battlements and bridges. When Sinan visited Hagia Sophia, after being summoned to work for the Sultan on loftier projects, he vowed that he would one day outdo that spectacular mosque—some 102 feet in diameter and 180 feet in height. During his long career, Sinan experimented with variations on the theme of the central domed structure, with half-domes used to give the main dome greater elevation. He expanded Hagia Sophia's two half-dome design to four; experimented with central domes without semi-domes; and did several structures based not on the square (as at Hagia Sophia), but on the hexagon and the octagon—resting a central dome on six and eight piers respectively. At the Selimiye in Edirne, Sinan's last major work, he achieved part of his wish: the dome is several feet wider in diameter than that of Hagia Sophia, but still forty feet shy in height.

Churches sometimes use stained glass to teach Christian tradition. What is an example of how architects have communicated Muslim tradition without the use of representational imagery?

A careful look at the Selimiye mosque in Edirne reveals a great deal of information. The mosque's abundant aniconic ornament, as well as specific inscriptions from Quran and Hadith throughout the building, reveals a remarkable story of unmistakable historically rooted theological purpose. Selim funded the monumental project with spoils from the conquest of Cyprus in 1572 and began the mosque a year after a disastrous loss to a Catholic military alliance at Lepanto (1571). The Sultan's choice of texts emphasizes his polemical mood, as in the anti-Trinitarian Quranic verses of Sura 112 rarely chosen for the center of a mosque dome. Surrounding that, around the dome, is a rhyming litany of eight of the ninety-nine names of God chosen for their resonance in the wake of losing a major sea battle: "O Light of Lights! O Omniscient One who knows what is in all hearts! O Resuscitator of those left lifeless in the Sea! O Eternal, remaining despite the rush of ages! O you who are All-sufficing for every need! O Healer of all hearts! O Merciful One who acts not in haste! O Generous One who gives unstintingly!"

In addition to the usual Ottoman penchant for including the "eight revered names"—Allah, Muhammad, Abu Bakr, Umar, Uthman, Ali, Hasan, and Husayn—on the arches between the eight columns upholding the dome, the designers chose verses for

The Selimye mosque in Edirne, Turkey was the great architect Sinan's last major work. While its dome is wider, the building stands forty feet shorter than the Hagia Sophia.

four of the half-domes fanning out from the main dome, a text on ritual prayer and "recollection of God" (from Surat al-Juma 62:9–10). The latter is a clear nod to the prominence of Sufi orders in the Ottoman realm and a turn to a more lenient and humanistic interpretation of Islam than under Sulayman. On the *qibla* wall (facing Mecca) is a selection of texts summing up main themes of divine revelation from the first three chapters of Quran; and on the "back" wall (opposite the *qibla*) is a very rarely used Hadith on the necessity of congregational Friday prayers. Around the *mihrab* set into a recessed alcove on the *qibla* wall, the designer has placed Sura 1, the *Shahada*, and a brief text from Sura 2:285–286 that is in effect a brief commentary on Sura 1. Also prominent, and a bit unusual in a mosque, are eschatological texts that stress the role of a merciful God and supreme ruler at Judgment, imploring God's guidance and reprieve from eternal punishment—in marked contrast to Selim's father's grand imperial mosque in Istanbul, whose major theme emphasizes God's promises of reward to obedient worshippers.

But why would a powerful ruler be so public about his repentance?

Selim is known to have believed that his forces were vanquished at Lepanto as a divine retribution for his personal sins, and he had an apocalyptic sense that Lepanto was a sign of an impending Final Judgment. The foundational text on the entry portal makes all this explicit: Selim, Sultan of Sultans, built the mosque for his own salvation, in hopes of securing a similar dwelling in paradise. Selim (known as "The Sot") had led a hedonistic life and in his latter years sought spiritual guidance from a *shaykh* of the Halveti Sufi order. And the message continues in the royal loge, available only to the Sultan's family overlooking the prayer hall. There the designers placed yet another very unusual scriptural text for a mosque setting, one that asks forgiveness on the day of judgment for "one who brings a pure heart" (*salim*, the Sultan's own name, to which he knows he has not done justice). In the loge, just above his "private" *mihrab*, is the Quranic text: "My Lord, grant me wisdom and unite me with the righteous, and place me among the inheritors of the Garden of Delight." In addition to the profuse textual ornament, floral arabesque suffuses the interior, a feature the architect wrote he hoped would evoke thoughts of a Paradise Garden, even as the flowing script of the texts would remind viewers of the rivers of paradise.

Appendix A

MAJOR MUSLIM DYNASTIES

Name	Dates of Rule	Capital(s)	Major Figure(s)	Max. Extent
Umayyad	661–750	Damascus	Abd al-Malik ibn Marwan, Umar II	Northern Iberia to Indus River
Abbasid	750–1258	Baghdad (founded)	Harun ar-Rashid, Mamun	North Africa to Central Asia
Umayyad/Spain	756–1031	Cordoba	Abd ar-Rahman III	Southern Iberia
Fatimid	969–1171	Cairo (founded)	Al-Hakim	Egypt, N. Af., Greater Syria, Hijaz
Ayyubid	1171–1250	Cairo	Salah ad-Din (Saladin)	Egypt, Greater Syria
Mamluk	1250–1517	Cairo	Baybars, Qayt Bay	Egypt, Greater Syria, Hijaz
Saljuqid/Eastern	1055–1157	Khurasan (various) Baghdad, Isfahan	Tughril Beg, Alp-Arslan, Malikshah	Persia, Central ME
Saljuqid/Turkey	1077–1307	Konya	Qilij Arslan II	Eastern Anatolia
Ottoman	1300–1922	Bursa, Istanbul	Mehmet II (the Conqueror) Sulayman I (the Magnificent)	Anatolia, CME, Hijaz, N.Af., Balkans
Mongol/Ilkhanid	1258–1370	Baghdad, Tabriz	Uljaytu Khan	W. Persia, CME
Timurid	1370–1506	Samarkand	Timur Lang	W. Persia, CA
Safavid	1500–1722	Tabriz, Isfahan	Shah Abbas	Persia
Mughal	1501–1757	Lahore, Delhi	Emperor Akbar, Shah Jahan	South Asia (Pakistan, N. India)

Appendix B

MAJOR CULTURAL CENTERS

Baghdad, Iraq: Abbasids' new capital, host to centuries of architecture, higher learning

Cairo, Egypt: Fatimid dynasty founded as new capital, flourishing patronage of architecture for two centuries; still considered center of traditional Muslim theology and law

Cordova, Spain: Ancient Iberian Roman town, capital of Andalusian Umayyads, wonderful urban planning, architecture

Delhi, India: north-central Indian capital of early Muslim dynasties in South Asia, home to many famous poets and mystics, shrines of Friends of God, manuscript libraries

Fez, Morocco: ancient Moroccan religious city, home to spectacular Moorish architecture and shrines serving as goal to pilgrim devotees of several major Friends of God

Herat, Afghanistan: now in northwest Afghanistan, once host to many major late-medieval literary figures and art-of-the-book (miniature) painters, as well as important Sufis

Isfahan, Iran: major medieval city of southwestern Iran, capital of Safavid dynasty, exquisite royal city with numerous gloriously tiled mosques, palaces, *madrasas*

Istanbul, Turkey: now Turkey's largest city, originally first capital of Byzantium, Ottoman stronghold for over four centuries; treasure house of spectacular architecture, art, and manuscript libraries

Jogjakarta, Indonesia: classic Indonesian city in the center of the island of Java, in world's largest Muslim nation

Lahore, Pakistan: capital of several major dynasties, now cultural hub of Pakistan

Qayrawan, Tunisia: Early center of learning and architecture in what is now Tunisia

Samarkand, Uzbekistan: now in Uzbekistan, once capital of Tamerlane's dynasty, superb Central Asian architecture

Timbuktu, Mali: in West African nation of Mali, ancient center of learning, custodian of major libraries of priceless medieval manuscripts

Appendix C

MAJOR SCHOOLS OF RELIGIOUS LAW

Name	Eponym/ founder	Denomination/ Interpretive style/Principle of adaptability	Main Theological Affinity	Regions of Dominance
Hanafi	Abu Hanifa (d. 767), Kufa (Iraq)	Sunni/Realist/ "equity" to soften harsh rulings	Mostly Maturidi	Turkey, Balkans, Iraq, Central & South Asia, Caucasus
Maliki	Malik ibn Anas (d. 795)	Sunni/Traditionalist/ "continuity"— presumption that prior conditions endure	Mostly Ashari	N. and W. Africa, Kuwait, UAE, parts of Persian Gulf, S. Egypt; (formerly Iberia)
Shafii	Ahmad ibn Idris ash-Shafii (d. 820)	Sunni/Traditionalist/as above + "public interest" privileging common good	Mostly Ashari	S. Egypt; Jordan, Palestine; Kurdistan; parts of Arabian Penin., Somalia; majority of SE Asia
Hanbali	Ahmad ibn Hanbal (d. 855)	Sunni/Idealist/"Gov't. by Sharia" = authority to govern by revealed law	Hanbali Traditional/ "textualist"	Arabian Peninsula; areas w. heavy Salafi influence
Zahiri	Dawud (d. 884)	Sunni/Idealist—"literalist" bent, emph. on "outer, apparent" (*zahir*) meaning	Ibn Hazm, Traditional	Once Iberia, now dormant
Usuli	(Anon.)	Shii/Personalist/independent investigation (*ijtihad* of scholar)	Twelver Shii	Iran, Iraq, other areas of Twelver population
Akhbari	(Anon.)	Shii/Personalist/ reliance on "reports/Hadith"—*akhbar*	Twelver Shii	Bahrain; Minor influence in CME

Appendix D

TEN COMMANDMENTS AND ISLAMIC PARALLELS

		Text
Bible:	Exodus 20:2-3	I am the Lord your God, you shall have no other deities before me.
Quran:	41:79, and many others	There is no deity but God.
Bible:	Ex. 20:4	You shall make no graven image (of anything in heave, earth, or under the earth).
Quran:	42:11, 112:7	There is none/nothing similar to Him.
Bible:	Ex. 20:7	You shall not take the name of the Lord your God in vain
Quran:	2:224	Do not use the name of God as justification for your oaths.
Bible:	Ex. 20:8	Remember to keep holy (sanctify) the Sabbath.
Quran:	62:9	When you hear the call to Friday prayer, hasten to the remembrance of God and cease from your daily labors.
Bible:	Ex. 20:12	Honor your father and your mother.
Quran:	4:36	Be gracious to your parents if they grow old during your life. Speak not contemptuously of them or reject them; speak to them with honor.
Bible:	Ex. 20:13	You shall not kill.
Quran:	5:32	Killing a single person is tantamount to killing all of humankind.
Bible:	Ex. 20:14	You shall not commit adultery.
Quran:	17:32	Avoid even the hint of adultery, for it is abhorrent and will lead to worse evils.
Bible:	Ex. 20: 15	You shall not steal.
Quran:	5:38-39	Cut off the hands of the thief, male or female; but those who repent of their crime and amend their lives will receive God's merciful forgiveness.
Bible:	Ex. 20:16	You shall not bear false witness against your neighbor.
Quran:	2:283, 24:7	Those who lie are in effect cursing God. Do not conceal (true) testimony.
Bible:	Ex. 20:17	You shall not covet (your neighbor's house or wife or possessions).
Quran:	4:36	Do (only) good to your parents, kin, and neighbors.

Appendix E

MAJOR (SUNNI) SUFI ORDERS

Name	Eponym or Founder	Place of Origin/ Distinguishing Features	Major Figures	Principal Regions of Influence
Qadiriya	Abd al-Qadir al-Jilani (d. 1166)	Baghdad, one of earliest, most widespread orders	Abd al-Haqq of Delhi, Dara Shikoh	N. Africa, Central ME, Central & South Asia
Mevleviya, "Whirling Dervishes"	Jalal ad-Din Rumi (d. 1274)	Central Anatolia (Turkey), "whirling" ritual	Sultan Walad (Rumi's son), Yunus Emre (poet)	Turkey, Balkans, Central ME, C. Asia
Naqshbandiya	Baha ad-Din Naqshband (d. 1389), of Bukhara	Central Asia, second widest spread, ritual of "visualizing" *shaykh* in meditation	Khwaja Ahrar, Jami (poet), Ahmad Sirhindi	Central Asia, S. and SE Asia, Turkey, Balkans, Persia
Chishtiya	Muin ad-Din Chishti (d. 1236) Ajmer	Central India, vocal dhikr, breath control concern for poor	Nizam ad-Din Awliya, Ganj-i Shakar, Gisu Daraz, Hujwiri	S. Asia, most influential of Indian orders
Suhrawardiya	Abu Najib as-Suhra-wardi (d. 1168)	Baghdad, founder wrote very early "rule" for Sufi seekers	Abu Hafs Umar as-Suhrawardi, Baha ad-Din Zakariya, Fakhr ad-Din Iraqi	Central ME, S. and SE Asia
Shadhiliya	Abu al-Hasan ash-Shadhili (d. 1258)	North Africa, emphasized "lay" spirituality/lifestyle	Abu al-Abbas Mursi, Ibn Ata Allah, Ibn Abbad of Ronda	N. Africa, parts of E. and Sub-Saharan Africa
Tijaniya	Ahmad at-Tijani (d. 1815)	Tlemcen (Algeria), major resistance to French colonialism	Umar ibn Said Tall, Al-Hajj Malik Si	N and W Africa, Egypt, E Africa

Name	Eponym or Founder	Place of Origin/ Distinguishing Features	Major Figures	Principal Regions of Influence
Muridiya	Amadu Bamba Mbacke (d. 1927)	Senegal W. Africa in 1883; powerful vs. French colonialism	Ibrahim Fall	W & Sub-Saharan Africa
Sanusiya	Muhammad ibn Ali as-Sanusi (d. 1859)	Mecca (founder from Fez, Morocco); center in Libya, anti-colonialist activism	Sayyid Ahmad Sanusi	N & Sub-Saharan Africa

Appendix F

RELIGIOUS TEXTS ON VIOLENCE QUIZ

Religious texts, if not read within the proper textual and historical contexts, are easily distorted and manipulated. See if you can identify the sources of these scriptural texts.

A = Old Testament; B = New Testament; C = Qur'an

1. I will make my arrows drunk with blood, and my sword shall devour flesh; and that with the blood of the slain and of the captives, from the beginning of revenges upon the enemy.

2. Kill them wherever you catch them.... War is prescribed for you, though it be hateful to you ... it is nevertheless a good thing.

3. And when the Lord your God delivers them before you and you defeat them, destroy them utterly. Make no covenant with them and show no favor to them.

4. I say to you that to everyone who has, more shall be given, but from the one who does not have, even what he does have shall be taken away. As for my enemies who do not want me to reign over them, bring them here and kill them in my presence.

5. When you approach a city to fight it, offer it terms of peace. If it agrees to make peace with you and opens to you, all the people found in it shall become your forced labor and shall become your forced labor and shall serve you. However, if it does not make peace with you, but makes war against you, besiege it. [After defeating it,] kill all the men in it. Take as booty only the women, children, animals, and all that is in the city, all its spoils.... Do not leave alive anything that breathes.

6. ... then fight and slay the Pagans wherever you find them. Seize them, besiege them, and lie in wait for them.

7. Kill every male among the little ones, and kill every woman who has known man intimately. But spare for yourselves all virgin maidens.

8. Do not think that I have come to send peace on Earth. I did not come to send peace, but a sword. I am sent to set a man against his father, a daughter against her mother, and a daughter-in-law against her mother-in-law.

9. (One who has a rebellious son, a glutton and a drunkard, who continually disobeys, should take him to the city gates with the elders of the city,) then all of the men of the city will stone him to death; so you will purge the evil in your midst.... 389

10. When you face the unbelievers coming in battle array, do not turn your backs on them. Anyone who does so will incur God's wrath and end up in the Fire.

Answers: 1. (A; Dt 34–42) 2. (C; Q 2:191, 195) 3. (A; Dt 7:1–2) 4. (B; Lk 19:26–27) 5. (A; Dt 20:10–17) 6. (C; Q 9:5) 7. (B; Num 31:17–18) 8. (B; Mt 10:34–35) 9. (A; Dt 21:18–21) 10. (C; Q 8:18)

Further Reading

Abdel Haleem, M. A. S., trans. *The Qur'an*. Oxford: Oxford University Press, 2008.

Ahmed, Akbar. *Journey into America: The Challenge of Islam*. Washington, DC: Brookings Institution 2010.

Afsaruddin, Asma. *The First Muslims: History and Memory*. Oxford: Oneworld, 2008.

Ali, Kecia. *Sexual Ethics and Islam: Feminist Reflections on Qur'an, Hadith and Jurisprudence*. Oxford: Oneworld, 2006.

Amanat, Abbas, and Frank Griffel, eds. *Shari'a: Islamic Law in the Contemporary Context*. Palo Alto, CA: Stanford University Press, 2009.

Berg, Herbert. *Elijah Muhammad and Islam*. New York: New York University, 2009.

Bonner, Michael. *Jihad in Islamic History: Doctrines and Practice*. Princeton: Princeton University Press, 2008.

Bonney, Richard. *Jihad from Qur'an to bin Laden*. New York: Palgrave Macmillan, 2004.

Bowen, John R. *A New Anthropology of Islam*. Cambridge: Cambridge University Press, 2012.

Brockopp, Jonathan, ed. *Islamic Ethics of Life: Abortion, War, and Euthanasia*. Columbia: South Carolina University Press, 2002.

Campo, Juan Eduardo. *Encyclopedia of Islam*. New York: Facts On File, 2009.

Cook, Michael, ed. *The New Cambridge History of Islam*. Cambridge; New York: Cambridge University Press, 2010.

Crone, Patricia. *God's Rule—Government and Islam: Six Centuries of Medieval Islamic Political Thought*. New York: Columbia University Press, 2005.

Dallal, Ahmad S. *Islam, Science, and the Challenge of History*. New Haven: Yale University Press, 2010.

Denny, Frederick Mathewson. *An Introduction to Islam*. Upper Saddle River, NJ: Pearson Prentice Hall, 2011.

Donner, Fred. *Muhammad and the Believers: At the Origins of Islam*. Cambridge: Harvard University Press, 2010.

Elias, Jamal, J. ed. *Key Themes for the Study of Islam*. Oxford: Oneworld, 2010.

Elias, Jamal J. *Aisha's Cushion: Religious Art, Perception, and Practice in Islam*. Cambridge: Harvard University Press, 2012.

Ernst, Carl W. *How to Read the Qur'an: A New Guide, with Select Translations*. Chapel Hill: North Carolina University Press, 2011.

Esposito, John L. *Islam: The Straight Path*. New York: Oxford University Press, 2011.

Green, Nile. *Sufism: A Global History*. Malden, MA: Wiley-Blackwell, 2012.

Hafez, Sherine. *An Islam of Her Own: Reconsidering Religion and Secularism in Women's Islamic Movements*. New York: New York University Press, 2011.

Hallaq, Wael B. *An Introduction to Islamic Law*. Cambridge: Cambridge University Press, 2009.

Halverson, Jeffry R. *Theology and Creed in Sunni Islam: The Muslim Brotherhood, Ash'arism, and Political Sunnism*. New York: Palgrave Macmillan, 2010.

Hirji, Zulfikar, ed. *Diversity and Pluralism in Islam: Historical and Contemporary Discourses amongst Muslims*. London; New York: I.B. Tauris Publishers/Institute of Ismaili Studies, 2010.

Juergensmeyer, Mark. *Global Rebellion: Religious Challenges to the Secular State, from Christian Militias to al Qaeda*. Berkeley: University of California Press, 2009.

Kamali, Mohammad Hashim. *Shari'ah Law: An Introduction*. Oxford: Oneworld, 2008.

Kamrava, Mehran, ed. *Innovation in Islam: Traditions and Contributions*. Berkeley: University of California Press, 2011.

Katz, Marion Holmes. *Prayer in Islamic Thought and Practice*. Cambridge: Cambridge University Press, 2013.

Kennedy, Hugh. *When Baghdad Ruled the Muslim World: The Rise and Fall of Islam's Greatest Dynasty*. Cambridge, MA: Da Capo, 2004.

Lowney, Chris. *A Vanished World: Medieval Spain's Golden Age of Enlightenment*. New York: Free Press, 2005.

Mattson, Ingrid. *The Story of the Qur'an: Its History and Place in Muslim Life*. Malden, MA: Blackwell, 2008.

Menocal, Maria Rosa. *The Ornament of the World: How Muslims, Jews and Christians Created a Culture of Tolerance in Medieval Spain*. New York: Little, Brown, 2002.

Michel, Thomas F. *A Christian View of Islam: Essays on Dialogue*. Maryknoll, NY: Orbis, 2010.

Murata, Sachiko, and William C. Chittick. *The Vision of Islam*. St. Paul: Paragon, 1994.

Nasr, Vali. *The Shia Revival: How Conflicts within Islam Will Shape the Future*. New York: Norton, 2007.

Ramadan, Tariq. *In the Footsteps of the Prophet: Lessons from the Life of Muhammad*. Oxford: Oxford University Press, 2009.

Rasmussen, Anne. *Women, the Recited Qur'an, and Islamic Music in Indonesia*. Berkeley: University of California Press, 2010.

Renard, John. *Friends of God: Islamic Images of Piety, Commitment and Servanthood*. Berkeley: University of California Press, 2008.

Renard, John, ed. and trans. *Tales of God's Friends: Islamic Hagiography in Translation*. Berkeley: University of California Press, 2009.

Renard, John. *Islam and Christianity: Theological Themes in Comparative Perspective*. Berkeley: University of California Press, 2011.

Sachedina, Abdulaziz A. *Islam and the Challenge of Human Rights*. Oxford and New York: Oxford University Press, 2009.

Sachedina, Abdulaziz A. *Islamic Biomedical Ethics: Principles and Application*. Oxford: Oxford University Press, 2011.

Safi, Omid. *Memories of Muhammad: Why the Prophet Matters*. San Francisco: HarperOne, 2009.

Sells, Michael A., *Approaching the Qur'an: The Early Revelation*. 2nd ed. Ashland, OR: White Cloud, 2007.

Shepard, William E. *Introducing Islam*. London; New York: Routledge, 2009.

Smith, Jane I. *Islam in America*. New York: Columbia University Press, 2010.

Sonn, Tamara. *Islam: A Brief History*. Chichester, West Sussex, UK, and Malden, MA: Wiley-Blackwell, 2010.

Volpi, Frédáric. *Political Islam Observed: Disciplinary Perspectives*. New York: Columbia University Press, 2010.

Woodward, Mark R. *Java, Indonesia and Islam*. Dordrecht, Germany, and New York: Springer Verlag, 2011.

Wright, Elaine. *Islam: Faith, Art, Culture*. New York: Scala, 2009.

Yilmaz, Hakan, and Çagla E. Aykaç, eds. *Perceptions of Islam in Europe: Culture, Identity and the Muslim "Other"*. London: Tauris Academic Studies, 2010.

Glossary

[Pronunciation aids—"dh" pronounced like "th" in "this"; uppercase = syllable emphasized; *internal* glottal stops included in pronunciation guides indicated as follows: ' = *ayn* (hard stop); ' = *hamza* (soft stop, as at beginning of "honor." Use of a slash / indicates plural after singular.]

abaya (aBAYa)—Loose ankle-length robe, typically black and common in Arabia and North Africa, worn either with or without face-covering *niqab*.

abd—Servant [of God], all human beings of good faith.

Abd Allah—Male name, "Servant of God."

adhan (aDHAAN)—The call to prayer before each *salat*.

Ahl al-Bayt—Members of the Family of the Prophet Muhammad, esp. Shii groups.

Ahl al-Kitab—The People of the Book or Earlier Revelations, that is, Jews and Christians; later also included Zoroastrians.

akhira (AAkhira)—The afterlife, the world to come.

alim/ulama (AAlim/ulaMAA)—"Knowledgeable one," scholar in religious disciplines.

Andalus, al-—Andalusia, traditional Muslim name for Spain.

ansar (anSAAR)—"Helpers," early converts to Islam among the citizens of Madina, "assisted" Muhammad and the *muhajirun* in 622 C.E.

aqida (aKEEda)—Creedal summary.

aqiqa (aKEEka)—"Cutting," rite of passage for seven day old child.

asbab an-nuzul (asBAAB an-nuZOOL)—The occasions of revelation that record the contexts in which portions of the Quran were revealed.

Ashura Day (AAshooraa)—The "tenth" day of Muharram (first lunar month), observance of Husayn's martyrdom for Shia, and for Sunnis.

Ayatollah—"Sign of God," top rank of religious scholars in Twelver Shi'a Islam.

aya(t) (AAya/AAyAAT)—"Verse" of the Quran; a "sign" of God in the created world; also signs as in marvels, miracles.

Azhar, Al- (AZhar)—An important center of learning in Cairo, founded over a thousand years ago. Today it is the best known institution of Muslim higher learning worldwide.

Baraka (BAraka)—"Blessing," the spiritual power coming from God through the Prophet or a *wali*.

baqa (baKAA)—"Surviving," Sufi term for abiding in God.

barzakh (BARzakh)—Life in the grave in a state of timeless awareness.

basmala—Contraction of the Arabic phrase *Bismi 'llahi ar-Rahman ar-Rahim.* "In the name of God, the Merciful, the Compassionate."

batini (BAAtinee)—Esoteric or hidden dimensions to the interpretation of the Quran.

baya (BAY'a)—The bond of allegiance made by a murid to a *shaykh*.

bida (BID'a)—Doctrinal innovation.

bila kayf (biLAA kayf)—"Without [asking] how"; Asharite theological axiom symbolizing caution about attempts to penetrate the inscrutable mystery of God's designs.

Bohras—A branch of the Sevener or Ismaili Shia Muslims.

burqa (BOORka)—Total uni-body covering with grill-like panel for eyes.

Buraq (buRAAK)—Name of a winged human-headed quadruped (name from root associated with "lightning") assigned to convey Muhammad on his Night Journey (*isra*) from Makka to Jerusalem and Ascension (*mir'aj*) to the Throne of God.

Caliph (KAYliff)—From *Khalifa,* "successor," title of individual acknowledged as universal leader of Muslims, beginning with Muhammad's immediate successor.

chador (chawDOR)—Traditional Iranian women's garment, single angle-length wrap for top/back of head and body, no face covering.

dai (DAA'ee)—Someone who "invites" to membership in Islam, generically "preacher," often used of Ismaili Shii missionaries.

daif (da'EEF)—"Weak," classification of Hadiths of lesser reliability because of a weak "link" in their chains of transmission.

Dajjal (dajJAAL)—The Great Impostor who will lead the forces of evil at the end of time.

dawa (DA'wa)—"Inviting" others to convert to Islam, hence also apologetics, missionary preaching.

dervish—From Persian *dar-vish* (darVEESH, door-seeker, i.e. mendicant), generic label of many Sufis.

dhikr (DHIKr)—Recollection, remembrance, either individual or in communal ritual by the same name in Sufi communities, involving Quran recitation, para-liturgical dance.

dhimmi (DHIMmee)—Literally "the protected people," member of protected religious minority, including especially Jews and Christians under Muslim rule.

Dua (du'AA)—(Call, appeal, invocation) private, "free" devotional prayer of supplication.

Eid (EED)—"Feast," referring to two major observances, *Eid al-Fitr* (Feast of Fast-breaking ending Ramadan) and *Eid al-Adha* (Feast of Sacrifice during the days of Hajj).

fana (faNAA)—Sufi term for dying to self but being alive in God.

faqih (faKEEH)—Jurist, someone who studies and interprets *fiqh*.

faqir (faKEER)—"Poor," both materially or spiritually, but especially the latter in reference to the simple poverty of Sufi dependence on God alone.

fard—"Requirement," legal category applied to specific compulsory deeds.

fard ayn—"Specific requirement," "individual duty" (i.e., required of each and every individual).

fard kifaya (Fard kiFAAya)—"Duty of a sufficiency" (i.e., not required of all, so that a "sufficient" portion of the global community can fulfill the duty on behalf of all).

farq/firaq—"Division" (same root as *furqan* below), referring to sub-groups within the Muslim Community, hence sect or faction.

fatwa (FATwa)—A legal advisory issued by a specialist called a *mufti*, offering guidance as to the legal status of a proposed course of action.

fiqh (FIKH)—"Penetrating understanding," in-depth study of the sources of tradition for the purpose of developing positive law, applied jurisprudence.

fitra (FITra)—Original disposition, in-born true faith with which every child begins life.

Furqan (furKAAN)—Decisive judgment or "criterion," one of the names of the Quran.

Ghadir Khum—An oasis where Shiites believe Muhammad "designated" his son-in-law (and cousin) Ali as his legitimate successor.

ghayba (GHAYba)—"Concealment" or occultation, a state into which the Twelfth Shiite Imam entered, first the "lesser," during which his representatives were his contact with believers, then the "greater," which continues today.

ghusl—Major ritual ablution required to cleanse from specific defilements by total immersion and washing.

hadd—"Limit," a specific determination in penal law, most mentioned in the Quran.

Hadith (haDEETH)—"Tradition, Sayings" of Muhammad, second in authority only to the Quran.

Hadith qudsi (haDEETH kudSEE)—"Sacred sayings" attributed to God, in which the Prophet "quotes" God, but clearly distinguished from God's words in the Quran.

hafiz (HAAfiz)—"One who keeps custody," one who has memorized the Quran.

Hajj—(Major) Pilgrimage to Mecca during the pilgrimage month, twelfth of the lunar year.

hal/ahwal (ahWAAL)—"State," key term in Sufi psychology denoting a stage on the spiritual path purely a divine gift that is fleeting.

halal (haLAAL)—Acceptable, not forbidden, whether referring to an action or some specific item to be used, such as certain foods.

al-hamdu li 'llah—"Praise (or thanks) to God," common response to the question "how are you" (i.e., fine, thank God).

hanif (haNEEF)—Seeker after the one God; sometimes used to refer to great religious figures prior to Islam, especially Abraham.

haram (haRAAM)—Explicitly forbidden, whether an act or association or use of unacceptable objects (such as food or drink).

haram (HAram)—"Forbidden area," i.e. sanctuary as in Kaba enclosure in Mecca.

hasan (HAsan)—"Good, excellent," technically a classification of Hadiths as authentic, reliable.

hijab (hiJAAB)—"Veiling," generic term for "covering" in women's garments, not including face covering generally.

Hijra (HIJra)—Muhammad's "emigration" from Mecca to Medina in 622 C.E., marking the beginning of Islamic history; also a religious metaphor referring to the willingness to "leave home" for one's faith.

Huda (HOOda)—The Guidance, name given to the Quran.

hulul (huLOOL)—Indwelling, embodiment.

ibada (eeBAAda)—"Servanthood," worshipfulness, i.e. all manner of actions symbolizing one's relationship with God.

iftar (ifTAAR)—Breaking the daily fast during Ramadan with a light meal after dusk.

ihram (ihRAAM)—Related to *haram* (above), the male pilgrim garb (a wrap of two white sheets) symbolizing entry into a state "forbidden" to outsiders or those not spiritually prepared.

ihsan (ihSAAN)—"Making [one's life] good/beautiful," by living at all times as if God sees, even if one does not see God.

Ijma (ijMAA')—"Consensus" of the community (more recently of scholar-specialists) with regard to the implementation of the revealed law, Sharia.

Ijtihad (ijtiHAAD)—Exerting oneself (struggling) in the interpretation of Islamic legal sources, independent investigation.

ilham (ilHAAM)—(Divine) inspiration, a concept especially important in Sufi thought.

imam/(a) (eeMAAM/a)—"Leader," spiritual descendant of Muhammad (Shiite); imamate, authoritative religious leadership. Also an honorific given to especially renowned scholars, and a functional title of local prayer leaders in mosques.

iman (eeMAAN)—Faith, especially understanding the "content" of belief, essential to making one's surrender (*islam*) spiritually effective.

Injil (inJEEL)—Variant on the Greek *eu-angelion*, Good News or Gospel, the scripture revealed to the Prophet Jesus.

Insha'a'llah (in SHAA'allAAh)—"God willing," common interjection in ordinary Muslim conversational speech, emphasizing that nothing happens without God's involvement.

iqamat as-salat (iKAAmat as-saLAAT)—Announcement by the *muezzin* inside the prayer (after the *adhan*) that *salat* is about to "commence."

irja (irJAA)—"Postponement" of judgment on the status of a sinner, since only God knows that.

ishara (ishAAra)—"Spiritual allusion," a level of interpretation or exegesis associated particularly with Sufism.

Islam (isLAAM)—"Grateful surrender," as manifest initially at least in one's adherence to tradition and the Five Pillars; eventually characterizing perfect balance in all of one's relationships.

Ismailis (ismaa'EElis)—A minority of Shiites also called Seveners, who parted ways with the Twelvers over the authentic Seventh Imam.

isnad (isNAAD)—A "chain" of individuals who have transmitted a saying or anecdote related to the Prophet, critical to evaluating a Hadith's reliability and authenticity.

isra (isRAA)—"Night journey" in which God "conveyed His servant" Muhammad from the "mosque of the sanctuary" in Mecca to the "Farther Mosque" (al-Aqsa) in Jerusalem.

Ithna Ashari—"Twelver," majority group of Shiites, whose theology of history counts Twelve Imams, the last of whom remains in "Greater Occultation."

jabr/jabriya (JABr/jabREEya)—Divine determinism/school that holds this view.

Jafari (JA'faree)—School; generic title for the Twelver law school, named after the sixth Imam, Jafar as-Sadiq (more specific divisions carry other names as well).

Jahannam (jaHANnam)—Related etymologically to the biblical name "gehenna"; along with "the Fire," a name for Hell.

Janna (JANna)—"Garden," most common name for Paradise.

Jibril (jiBREEL)—Arabic for Gabriel, the revealing archangel.

jihad (jiHAAD)—"Exertion, struggle" including various tactics designed to instill discipline and fight injustice. Can be either outward (lesser struggle, including religiously sanctioned warfare) or inward (greater struggle, combat against one's baser tendencies).

jilbab (jilBAAB)—Ankle-length loose cloak, leaving head, face and hands visible; many women also wear head-scarf.

jinn—Creatures of smokeless fire (aka "genies"), ranging from helpful to harmless to morally problematic.

jizya (JIZya)—A "poll tax" levied historically (but no longer, as a rule) on Christians and Jews.

juz—"Part," referring to one-thirtieth of the Quran, broken into liturgically functional segments.

Kaba (KA'ba)—The "cube-shaped" structure in the center of Mecca, variously said to have been built by Adam and rebuilt by Abraham and son Ismail, the earthly focus of prayer.

kalam (kaLAAM)—Literally "speech"; short for *ilm al-kalam*, dialectical or philosophical theology.

karama/t (kaRAAma/aat)—"Marvel, wonder," an extraordinary deed performed by a Friend of God as distinct from the "miracles" attributed to prophets.

khanaqah (KHANaka)—Residential institution serving itinerant Sufis traveling to study with a renowned master.

khums—A "fifth" as a measure of amount of one's income expected as charitable donation of Shiites.

khutba (KHUTba)—An "address" or sermon delivered in mosques on Friday at the early afternnoon *salat*.

kiswa (KISwa)—The extravagantly embroidered "veil" covering the Kaba, cut up and given as mementoes of Hajj and renewed each year.

kufr—"Covering over" the truth, i.e. denying religious tradition; hence, an unbeliever is a "truth concealer" (*kafir*, KAAfir).

Kursi (kurSEE)—Footstool of a throne related to the "throne" of God.

Laylat al-Qadr (LAYlat al-kadr)—The "Night of Power" (or Divine Destiny), toward the end of Ramadan, on which Muslims commemorate the initial revelation of the Quran.

madhhab (MADHhab)—"Way of proceeding," as in a school of Islamic jurisprudence or legal methodology Sunnis recognize four of these, one now predominant among Shiites.

madrasa (madRAsa)—College of religious studies, esp. *fiqh*.

Mahdi (MAHdee)—The "Guided One" whom all Muslims believe will appear at the end of time—for Sunnis, he will join Jesus in battle against the Dajjal; for Twelver Shiites, it is a title of the Hidden Twelfth Imam who will reappear.

majdhub (majDHOOB)—"One who is drawn" toward God, as opposed to one to requires a more laborious progress in the spiritual path; the *majdhub* is thus considered to enjoy a closer relationship to God.

maqam/at (maKAAM/AAT)—"Station," marking various points on the Sufi path, attainable to some extent by personal effort and may endure for some time.

matn—The "body" or actual "quoted text" of a Hadith, as distinct from the chain of transmitters called the *isnad*.

mawlid (MAWlid)—"Birthday" observance, of the Prophet or of many Friends of God.

Mecca—City in west-central Arabia along an ancient north-south caravan route, where Muhammad was born and Islam began.

Medina—Arabian caravan city some two-hundred and fifty miles north of Mecca, where the Muslim community first became a majority, and which served as the first "capital" after the Prophet's death.

mihrab (mihRAAB)—A small apsidal structure or niche built into the *qibla* (Mecca-facing) wall in a mosque; often one of the more elaborately decorated features of the mosque, along with the dome.

milla/milal (MILla/MILal)—(Religion, sect) a Quranic term that refers to various religious traditions; used especially of those that trace their lineage back to Abraham.

minbar (MINbar)—"Pulpit-like" structure, with a staircase accessing an elevated usually to the right of the *mihrab* from which the *khutba* is delivered.

Minaret—A tall, slender tower attached to a mosque from which the call to prayer emanates.

Mir'aj (mi'RAAJ)—"Ascension" of Muhammad into Heaven; metaphor for spiritual journey.

miswak (misWAAK)—Tooth-stick made of soft, absorbent wood used by Muhammad for dental hygiene, and thus recommended to all Muslims.

muadhdhin (mu'ADHDHin)—"One who causes to hear," i.e., who announces the time of prayer; commonly spelled and pronounced with the simpler form, muezzin.

mubah (muBAAH)—A legally neutral act that is neither required nor forbidden, neither recommended not discouraged.

mudaraba (muDAAraba)—Economics term for installment purchase.

Mufti (MUFtee)—Legal specialist with the authority to issue *fatwas*.

muhajirun (muHAAjiROON)—Those who "made the *Hijra* (with Muhammad)" and were the earliest Muslims to reside in Mecca, in 622.

Muharram (muHARram)—The first Muslim lunar month, with first ten days recalling the suffering and martyrdom of Imam Husayn (for Shiites), as well as functioning as a period during which Muhammad recommended fasting for all in commemoration of God's granting Moses victory over Pharaoh.

Mujahidin (muJAAhiDEEN)—Persons who partake in *jihad*, whether physical or spiritual.

Mujtahid (MUJtahid)—"One with authority to engage in independent investigation," i.e. a legal scholar capable of *ijtihad*

murid (murREED)—"Aspirant," one who "desires" spiritual quest under the tutelate of a spiritual guide called a *murshid* or *shaykh*.

murjia (murJEE'a)—Early theological school emphasizing *irja*, "postponement" of judgment about the religious status of others.

musharaka (muSHAAraka)—Economics term for equity sharing.

muta (MUT'a)—"Temporary marriage" practiced (historically and occasionally now) only by Shiites.

mutakallim/-un (mutaKALLim/-oon)—One who engages in kalam.

mutazila (mu'TAzila)—Early *mutakallimun* who emphasized role of reason.

nabi (NAbee)—A Prophet, normally one not sent with a Book but who comes to reinforce an earlier revelation.

nafs—"Self" (usually the "lower self") or "soul" more generally.

nasheed (naSHEED)—A song in praise of the Prophet Muhammad.

nihla/nihal (NIHla/NIhal)—Sectarian movement, term used by early Muslim historians of religion to refer to various Muslim and non-Muslim groups.

nikah (niKAAH)—Marriage and its rituals.

niqab (niKAAB)—Full-face covering with eye-slit (as distinct from grill as in *burqa*), separate from body-covering robe (such as *abaya*).

niyya (NEEya)—Requisite intention without which no religious action is meaningful, allowing full "presence of the heart."

Nizaris—A sub-sect of Ismailis who regard the Aga Khan as the Living Imam.

qada (kaDAA)—Immutable and inexorable divine decree.

qadar (KAdar)—Predetermination, God's perfect control of human acts and destiny.

qadi (KAAdee)—A "judge," a legal official who functions much like a magistrate, handling all kinds of ordinary judicial matters.

qadr/qadariya (kadaREEya)—Human moral agency/school that emphasizes individual ethical capacity, responsibility.

Qari (KAAree)—"Reciter" or one who "makes Quran," especially one who has memorized the scripture and has studied both the simpler and more elaborate modes of recitation.

qibla (KIBla)—The direction to be faced in formal prayer (*salat*), toward the Ka'ba in Mecca.

qiyas (keeYAAS)—Analogical reasoning or reasoning from precedent, the "fourth root of the law," after Quran, Hadith, and Consensus.

Quran (kur'AAN)—"Recitation," the scripture sent down to Muhammad, 610–632 C.E., which the Prophet originally delivered in a purely oral form.

qurban (kurBAAN)—"Dedicated," that is, set aside for specific ritual purposes, as with meat of the sacrificial animals slaughtered during at Eid al-Adha in order to feed the poor.

qurbani (kurBAAnee)—Money offered during Hajj to provide an animal to be slaughtered for the poor as *qurban*.

raka (RAK'a)—"Cycle" of prostration, prayer, and other physical gestures during *salat*, with varying numbers of cycles prescribed for the different daily time slots.

Ramadan—Ninth Muslim lunar month most are expected to fast from dawn to dusk (absent circumstances that make fasting unhealthful). Though the name originally referred to "blazing summer heat," adoption of a lunar calendar meant that the month rotates backwards eleven days a year against the solar calendar, so that it occurs in all seasons.

Rashidun (RAAshiDOOn)—"Rightly Guided" in reference to the first four "Caliphs" whom Sunnis credit as the first legitimate successors to Muhammad.

rasul (raSOOL)—"Messenger" or "apostle"—one "sent" and who brings a revealed scripture (unlike the majority of "prophets").

ray (RA'y)—"Opinion" or individual judgment exercised by specially trained scholars in interpreting scripture and tradition, but not recognized by all schools of thought/law.

riba (reBAA)—Economic exploitation, giving or taking interest.

ribat (reeBAAT)—A sufi residential spiritual center, originally meant outpost for defense of borders.

ridda (RIDda)—Literally "apostasy," but specifically referring to the rebellion of some Arab clans after the death of Muhammad.

sabr—Virtue of patience essential in spiritual life.

sadaqa (SAdaka)—Bearing one another's burdens, the principle of charity.

safa (saFAA)—A possible root for the word "Sufi," connoting purification.

sahih (SAAlih)—In Hadith studies, a sound Hadith without defects.

Saj (SAJ)—The literary form of many Quranic suras; rhymed prose.

as-salam(u) alaykum (as-saLAAMu aLAYkoom)—Traditional Muslim greeting—May you come ever more completely into the state of islam; more commonly, "Peace be with you."

salat (saLAAT)—Ritual prayer five times daily.

salat al-asr (saLAAT al-Asr)—Late afternoon ritual prayer.

salat al-fajr (saLAAT al-FAjr)—Ritual prayer before sunrise.

salat al-isha (saLAAT al-'iSHAA)—The night prayer.

salat al-janaza (saLAAT al-jaNAAza)—Ritual prayer specifically for funerals.

salat al-juma (saLAAT al-JUM'a)—"Congregational" ritual prayer, that is, Friday early afternoon.

salat al-maghrib (saLAAT al-MAGHrib)—Prayer just after sunset.

salat az-zuhr (saLAAT az-ZUHr)—Ritual after the sun's zenith.

sama (saMAA)—"Audition, hearing," ritual involving music, especially in Sufi paraliturgical rituals.

sawm—Ritual fasting, especially during the month of Ramadan.

say (SA'yee)—Running between two hills in Makka, a rite during the Hajj.

sayyid (SAYyid)—Honorific reserved to direct descendants of Muhammad through his grandson Husayn.

Shahada (shaHAAda)—"Testimony, witness"; essential "creed"; "I confess that there is no deity but God, and that Muhammad is the Messenger of God."

Sharia (shaREE'a)—Literally the "main road," hence all that God ordains for believers, including but not limited to formal religious "law."

sharif (shaREEF)—Honorific title denoting descendants of Muhammad through his grandson Hasan.

shawq—"Desire," longing for the presence of God.

Shaykh/a—"Elder" (male/female), sometimes refers to a religious scholar, sometimes to a Sufi spiritual teacher and master.

Shaytan (shayTAAN)—Arabic version of "Satan," a fallen jinn; Iblis.

Shia (SHEE'a)—The minority group among Muslims (ten percent of the total) who hold that leaders (Imams) must come from the Ahl al-Bayt, i.e. the Family of the Prophet.

shirk—Setting up partners or associates with God; idolatry.

shukr—Thankfulness, gratitude.

sifat (siFAAT)—Qualities, especially divine attributes.

silsila (SILsila)—"Chain," Sufi spiritual genealogy that traces one's spiritual guide back to the Prophet.

sira (SEEra)—Muhammad's "life story" or biography.

Subhan Allah (subHAAN allAAH)—God be praised.

suf (SOOF)—"Wool," most likely the root of the word "sufi."

Sufism—Complex phenomenon often associated with "mystical dimension of Islam," but also including major literary, organizational, and ritual features developed by members of "orders."

Sunna (SUNna)—Exemplary behavior, patterned on the life and conduct of Muhammad as transmitted largely in the Hadith.

sunna—Reference to the legal status of a recommended way of acting.

Sunni—The largest grouping among Muslims, approximately ninety percent of the total.

sura (SOOra)—Equivalent to a "chapter" among the 114 such units in the Quran.

tafsir (tafSEER)—Exegetical commentary written on the Quran.

tafsir bi 'r-ray (tafSEER bi'r-RA'y)—Exegesis based on rational judgment or individual opinion.

tafsir bi 'l-mathur (tafSEER bi'l-ma'THOOR)—Exegesis commentary based on the Hadith of Muhammad.

Taghut (taaGHOOT)—Transgression, hubris, tyranny; transgressing the boundaries of one's humanity.

tahrif/tabdil/taghyir (tahREEF, tabDEEL, taghYEER)—Corruption/substitution/alteration (of a non-Muslim scripture by non-Muslims).

tajsim (tajSEEM)—"Ascribing a body" (*jism*) [to God], type of extreme anthropomorphism.

talaq (TAlak)—Divorce by verbal triple repudiation by the husband.

tanzil (tanZEEL)—Literally, "the sending down," used to describe the revelation of a Book.

tanzih (tanZEEH)—Considering God beyond any anthropomorphic conceptions.

taqlid (takLEED)—Acceptance of a theological or legal position purely on another's authority.

taqwa (TAKwaa)—Reverential fear of God, God-wariness.

tarawih (taRAAweeh)—Communal nightly prayers during Ramadan, including recitation of a "thirtieth" of the Quran.

tariqa (taREEka)—A sufi order, "Path" or "road," relatively amorphous organization, or the structures and practices of these groups, or their leadership; term for Sufism in general.

tarwiz (tarWEEZ)—A portion of the Quran written on parchment contained in a leather pouch and worn by a Muslim.

tashbih (tashBEEH)—"Likening" or "comparing" God to some known quality, anthropomorphism.

tasawwuf (taSAWwuf)—Sufism, based on root related to *suf*, "wool."

tasbih (tasBEEH)—Set of prayer beads used by Muslims, with full set of 99, but smaller sets of 33 also common, on which to related to the 99 Names of God.

tatil (ta'TEEL)—Denial of divine attributes.

tawaf (taWAAF)—Circumambulation of the Kaba seven times as part of the rites of the Hajj.

tawakkul (taWAKkul)—Perfect trust (in God), one of the stations on the Sufi path.

tawatur (taWAAtur)—Broad dispersion, usually referring to the spread of a Hadith, dissemination, breadth of diffusion—an essential criterion among standards of authenticity applied in Hadith scholarship.

tawba (TAWba)—"Turning," hence repentance, usually one of the very first stations on the Sufi path.

tawhid (tawHEED)—Assertion and affirmation of God's oneness and transcendence

Tawrat (tawRAAT)—Torah or scripture revealed to the Prophet Moses.

tekke (TEKkyeh)—Sufi residential spiritual center.

Ulama (oolaMAA)—Class of persons who are "learned" in religious matters, religious scholars.

Umayyads (ooMAYyads)—The first dynasty of Sunni Islam, based in Damascus from 661 to 750 C.E.

Umma—The global community of Muslims.

ummi—"Unlettered" or "without book learning," the state of Muhammad before the Quran was revealed to him.

Umra (OOMra)—(Lesser) Pilgrimage to Mecca, often performed outside of formal Pilgrimage month.

usul al-fiqh (ooSOOL al-fikh)—Principles of jurisprudence.

wahy (WAHy)—The technical term used for revelation.

wajib (WAAjib)—A compulsory act, legal requirement.

wakil (waKEEL)—One of four representatives to whom the Twelfth Imam communicated during his "Lesser Concealment."

wali/awliya (WAlee/awleeYA)—"Patron" in reference to God; "protégée" in reference to human beings close to God; often rendered Friend of God.

waqf—A charitable trust, traditionally an foundational endowment in perpetuity to fund an institution (such as a *madrasa*), its staffing, and upkeep.

wudu (wuDOO)—The ritual ablution that must be made before formal prayer or handling the Quran.

zandaqa/zindiq (ZANdaka/zinDEEK)—Free-thinking, religious views considered treasonous/one so accused.

Zabur (zaBOOR)—Psalms, the scripture revealed to the Prophet David.

zahiri (ZAAhiree)—The literalist school of Quranic commentary.

zakat (zaKAAT)—Purification of wealth by passing on two and a half percent of surplus wealth each year to those in need.

zakat al-fitr (zaKAAT al-FIRr)—A payment to those in need before the celebration of Eid al-Fitr; the cost of one meal per person in the household.

Zamzam (ZAMzam)—The spring in Makka that was miraculously provided by God for Ismail and Hagar.

Zaydis (ZAYdees)—The Fivers among the Shia, who recognized a different Fifth Imam to the majority.

zawiya (ZAAweeya)—"Corner," Sufi residence originally; expanded to mean larger facility for Sufi activities.

ziyara (zeeYAAra)—(Visitation) Smaller scale local or regional pilgrimages to the tombs of saints or Imams.

zuhd—Asceticism, self-discipline, particularly in Sufi literature.

Timeline

Note: All dates are C.E.

Year	Event
c. 550–610	Regional conflict between Byzantine and Sasanian Empires via Arab client tribes
c. 570	Birth of Muhammad
605	Birth of Fatimah (to Khadija and Muhammad), wife of Ali ibn Abi Talib, spiritual matriarch of all of Muhammad's descendants
c. 610	Muhammad receives first revelation in a Mt. Hira cave near Mecca
613	Declaration at Mount Safa inviting the general public to Islam
614	Persecution of the Muslims by the Quraysh
615–16	Muslims emigrate to Abyssinia, seek shelter of Christian Negus
617	Quraysh boycott of the Hashimite clan and Muhammad
619	Boycott lifted. Deaths of Prophet's uncle Abu Talib and wife Khadija
c. 610–22	Muhammad preaches, Meccan period of Quranic revelations
621	Traditional dating of Muhammad's "Night Journey" and "Ascension"
622	*Hijra* —Muhammad and followers flee to Medina, Year 1 in Islamic calendar (AH, Year of the *Hijra*)
622	Constitution of Medina, first "Islamic state"
624	Muslims victorious against Quraysh at Battle of Badr, expel Jewish Banu Qaynuqa from Medina
625	Quraysh defeat Muslims at Uhud; Banu Nadir Jews expelled from Medina
626	Battle of the Ditch; killing and enslavement of Banu Qurayza
628	Treaty of Hudaybiyya with Meccans; Battle of Khaybar; Muhammad sends letters to various regional heads of state
630	Muslims capture Mecca, cleanse Kaba of idols; pilgrimage rites Islamized, tribes of Arabia vow allegiance to Muhammad
632	Farewell pilgrimage to Mecca, death of Muhammad not long thereafter. Abu Bakr chosen as caliph, not recognized by all (Sunni/Shii divide)
632–661	Period of the four "Rightly Guided Caliphs," first successors to Muhammad
632–33	Wars of *ridda* (apostasy) restore allegiance to Islam

633	Muslim conquests begin outside of Arabian Peninsula
633–42	Muslim armies take parts of Arabian coasts, the Fertile Crescent (Egypt, Syria, Palestine, Mesopotamia), North African coast, parts of Persian and Byzantine Empires
634	Death of Abu Bakr, Umar ibn al-Khattab becomes second caliph
637	Conquest of Syria, Jerusalem
642–44	Conquest of Egypt, parts of Persia. Assassination of Umar, succeeded by Uthman ibn Affan
656	Uthman killed, succeeded by Ali ibn Abi Talib as fourth caliph. Battle of the Camel, beginning of series of "civil wars"
657	Ali moves capital from Medina to Kufa (garrison city in Iraq). Battle of Siffin, "Kharijites" split with Ali
660	Ali recaptures Hijaz and Yemen from Muawiya, who declares himself caliph at Damascus.
661	Ali assassinated by Kharijites
661–750	Period of the Umayyad Dynasty, capital at Damascus, major expansion as far as Spain and India; gradual development of Shii Islam following death of Ali
669	Hasan ibn Ali, the second Shii imam, dies of poisoning; brother Husayn ibn Ali becomes Imam
670	Conquest of Algeria and Morocco
680	Death of Shii martyr Husayn at Karbala in Iraq
680	Death of Muawiya, succeeded by Yazid I
684	Abd Allah ibn Zubayr in Mecca declares himself counter-caliph to Marwan in Damascus.
685–705	Reign of Umayyad Caliph Abd al-Malik, builds Dome of the Rock, Jerusalem
686	Al-Mukhtar rises as rebel caliph at Kufa
692	Mecca falls to Umayyads, Ibn Zubayr dies; Abdul Malik now sole caliph
late 600s	Ruling classes in East and West Africa convert to Islam
705–15	Conquest of Spain, Sind, Central Asia
711	Arab armies cross Gibraltar into Spain led by Tariq ibn Ziyad, take Transoxiana (Central Asia) under Qutayba ibn Muslim
712	Advance into Sind to the Indus River led by Muhammad ibn Qasim
728	Death of Hasan al-Basri, famous early ascetic
717–18	Second unsuccessful siege of Constantinople
732	Empire reaches its furthest western extent, stopped at Battle of Tours
747	Revolt of Abu Muslim in Khurasan erodes Umayyad power to brink of collapse
750	Abu al-Abbas becomes first Abbasid caliph in Iraq
750–900	Formation of the four major Sunni schools of religious law, major developments in Quranic exegetical sciences, canonization of the Hadith literature
750–1258	Period of the Abbasid Dynasty, capital at Baghdad, gradual breakdown into regional political entities from Spain to India

756	Abd ar-Rahman founds Umayyad Dynasty in Cordoba, Spain
762	Baghdad (Madinat as-Salam, "city of peace") newly founded capital of the Abbasid empire, near former Sasanian capital of Ctesiphon
765	Death of Sixth Imam, Jafar, yields split among Shiites between "accommodationist" Imami (Twelvers) and Ismailis (Seveners) who continue active resistance to Abbasid Caliphate
767	Death of jurist Abu Hanifa
786–809	Reign of Harun ar-Rashid, key figure of *The Thousand and One Nights*
795	Death of jurist Malik ibn Anas
800	Musa al-Kazim, seventh Shii Imam, is poisoned in prison of Harun ar-Rashid, succeeded by Ali ar-Rida
801	Death of Rabia of Basra, first mystic, most prominent early woman associated with Sufism
mid–800s	Written collections of Hadith (sayings of the Prophet) compiled; Muslims extend rule to Sicily
813–33	Reign of Mamun, after conquering brother Amin in civil war; theological controversy; Quran created or uncreated and eternal; founds center for translation of texts from Greek to Arabic in Baghdad
818	Ali ar-Rida dies in Mashhad, Muhammad at-Taqi becomes 9th Imam
820	Death of jurist Shafii
827	Ali al-Hadi, the 10th Shia Imam is born; Mamun declares the Mutazili creed as the state creed, enforced by the inquisitorial *Mihna* courts, which imprisoned traditionalists like Ahmad ibn Hanbal; beginning of the Muslim conquest of Sicily
833	Death of Caliph Mamun, succeeded by al-Mutasim
835	Muhammad at-Taqi is poisoned, Ali al-Hadi becomes 10th Shii Imam
836	al-Mutasim moves the capital to Samarra, palace-city north of Baghdad
849	Maliki school of law dominant in Spain and North Africa
850	Al-Mutawakkil restores traditionalist school to authority, jails Mutazilite leaders
852	Death of Abd ar-Rahman II of Spain; accession of Muhammad I
855	Death of jurist Ahmad ibn Hanbal
857	death of Muhasibi, major early theorist of Sufi psychology
860	Ahmad the Samanid sets up dynasty in Transoxiana ("across the Oxus," Central Asia)
861	Murder of the Abbasid Caliph al-Mutawakkil; accession of al-Muntasir and beginning of the "Anarchy at Samarra"; death of Dhu 'n-Nun of Egypt, famous early Sufi
866	Abbasid Civil War continues internal dissension
868	Ali al-Hadi is poisoned, succeeded by Hasan al-Askari as 11th Imam, and Muhammad al-Mahdi, the last Imam-to-be is born
869	Ahmad ibn Tulun, of Turkic ethnicity, founds Tulunid dynasty in Egypt claiming freedom from Baghdad.
874	11th Imam, Hasan al-Askari, dies of poison; Muhammad al-Mahdi becomes Imam,

but does not rule—enters Lesser Occultation, does not die

899	Death of Abu Said al-Kharraz, early Sufi theorist, ethicist, teacher
909	First Fatimid caliph in Tunisia
910	Death of Junayd, dean of Sufis of Baghdad
922	Execution of Hallaj, acknowledged by Sufis as first martyr-mystic
928	Umayyad Abd ar-Rahman III declares himself caliph in Cordoba
934	Deposition of the Abbasid Caliph al-Qahir; accession of ar-Radi. Death of the Fatimid Caliph Ubaydullah
935	Death of major theologian in Baghdad Ashari, "founder" of Asharite school
940	Muhammad al-Mahdi, the twelfth imam, enters Greater Occultation, expected to return at end of time and usher in age of justice
944	Death of major Central Asian theologian Maturidi, in Samarkand (Uzbekistan)
945	Muizz al-Dawla captures power in Baghdad and establishes the Twelver Buwayhid dynasty in Iraq—Shiite "power behind the throne"
961	Turkish mamluk Alptigin founds the rule of the Ghazanavids in Afghanistan
961	Death of the Umayyad Caliph Abd-ar-Rahman III in Spain; accession of al-Hakam II
969	Fatimids gain power in Egypt and attack Palestine, Syria, and Arabia, found Cairo
969–1171	Regime of Fatimids in central Middle East
976	In Spain, death of the Umayyad Caliph al-Hakam II, accession of Hisham II
c. 990	Deaths of major Sufi "theorists" Abu Nasr as-Sarraj (d. 988), Kalabadhi (d. c. 994), Abu Talib al-Makki (d. 996)
1000–50	Reconquista restores more of Spain to Christians, Sicily falls to the Normans, Crusader kingdoms are briefly established in Palestine and Syria
1019	Conquest of the Punjab by Mahmud of Ghazni
1020	Buwayhid Sultan overthrown by Musharaf ad-Dawla, Death of the Fatimid Caliph al-Hakim in Cairo, accession of Ali az-Zahir
1021	Hamza ibn Ali, dissenting from Fatimid Ismaili teaching, forms basis of esoteric Druze faith; Fatimids lose grip on North Africa
1024	In Spain, assassination of Abd ar-Rahman IV
1025	Death of Abd al-Jabbar, major Mutazilite systematic theologian
1037	Death of Avicenna (Ibn Sina), Persian physician and Aristotelian philosopher
1031	Umayyad caliphate in Cordoba defeated by the Christian Reconquista
1040	Battle of Dandanqan, the Saljuqid Turks defeat the Ghazanavids. Almoravids rise in North Africa
1055	Saljuqid Turks take Baghdad, found Sultanate, rendering "caliph" largely powerless figurehead
1058	Death of Mawardi, influential early political theorist
1063	Death of the Saljuqid Sultan Tughrul Bey, accession of Alp Arslan who leads Turkic march north-westward

1064	Death of Ibn Hazm of Cordoba, important theologian
1071	Battle of Manzikert, eastern Anatolia, Saljuqids capture Byzantine emperor
1077	Saljuqids found Sultanate of Rum in Konya, Turkey
1082	Almoravids conquer Algeria
1086	Almoravids defeat Christian force in Spain
1090	Ismaili leader Hasan as-Sabbah takes Alamut in the Persian mountains, home of the "Assassins"
1096	First crusade called by Pope Urban II
1099	Crusaders capture Jerusalem, rule "Latin Kingdom" until 1189
1100–1400	Growth and spread of major Sufi brotherhoods from Iberia to Indonesia
1111	Death of major theologian and Sufi author Ghazali
1116	Death of the Rum (Anatolia) Saljuqid Sultan Malik Shah
1118	Death of the Saljuqid Sultan Muhammad; death of Abbasid Caliph al-Mustazhir, accession of al-Mustarshid. In Spain the Christians capture Zaragoza.
1147	In the Maghrib, Almoravids overthrown by the Almohads under Abd al-Mumin; Second Crusade led by Louis VII
1148	Crusader siege of Damascus repulsed by Muslim defenders
1166	Death of Abd al-Qadir al-Jilani, early influence on institutionalization of Sufi communal life
1171	Death of the Fatimid Caliph Al-Adid, bringing end of Fatimid dynasty
1171–1250	Saladin's Ayyubid dynasty rules much of Middle East from Cairo
1174	Saladin annexes Syria
1176	Death of the Saljuqid Sultan Arslan Shah, accession of Tughril III
1179	Death of the Abbasid Caliph al-Mustadi, accession of an-Nasir. Ghurid Shahab ad-Din captures Peshawar (now in Pakistan)
1185	Death of the Almohad caliph Yusuf I, accession of Yaqub in Iberia
1186	Ghurids overthrow the Ghaznavid dynasty in the Punjab
1187	Saladin recaptures Jerusalem from the Christians
1189–1290	Third crusade, followed by a century of Muslim responses to subsequent major Crusades, leaving Muslims in control of most of the central Middle East
1193	Death of Saladin; accession of Ayyubid Sultan Al-Aziz Uthman
1194	Occupation of Delhi by Muslims. End of the Saljuqid rule further west
1198	Death of Ibn Rushd (Averroes), famed Iberian-born philosopher (from Cordoba)
1199	Death of Almohad Caliph Yaqub. Conquest of Northern India and Bengal by the Ghurids
1200s	Assassins wiped out by the Mongols; Delhi rulers take title of Sultan
1221	Genghis Khan and the Mongols enter Persia
1202	Death of the Ghurid Sultan Ghiyath ad-Din; accession of Mahmud the Ghurid
1206	Qutb ad-Din Aybak crowned ruler in Lahore
1210	Assassination of the Ghurid Sultan Mahmud; death of Qutb ad-Din Aybak, acces-

sion of Aram Shah in India

1210–1526	Delhi Sultanates, powerful Muslim presence in India
1211	End of the Ghurid rule, their territories annexed by the Khawarazm Shahs
1212	Christians defeat Almohads at Battle of Las Navas de Tolosa in Spain, Almohad Sultan Muhammad an-Nasir escapes to Morocco
1213	Almohad Sultan Muhammad an-Nasir dies, son Yusuf II news Almohad Caliph
1216	Marinids, under Abd al-Haqq, occupy northeastern part of Morocco; Almohads fall to Marinids at Battle of Nakur
1217	Marinids suffer defeat in the battle fought on the banks of the Sibu River; Abdul Haq is killed and the Marinids evacuate Morocco
1218	Death of the Ayyubid ruler Al-Adil I, accession of Al-Kamil; the Marinids return to Morocco under their leader Othman and occupy Fez
1221	Death of Farid ad-Din Attar, major Persian Sufi literary figure
1223	Death of the Almohad ruler Yusuf II, Almohad Caliph, accession of Abdul-Wahid I, Almohad Caliph; in Spain a brother of Yusuf II, Almohad Caliph declares his independence and assumes the title of Al-Adil
1225	Death of the Abbasid Caliph An-Nasir, accession of Az-Zahir
1228	Death of major Hanbali theologian Ibn Taymiyya, Damascus
1229	Ayyubid Sultan Al-Kamil restores Jerusalem to the Christians via peace treaty with Frederick II
1230	End of the Khwarazm-shah Empire in Central Asia
1235	Death of Ibn al-Farid of Egypt, premier Arabic Sufi mystical poet
1240	Death of Ibn Arabi, famed Iberian-born Sufi mystic and theologian
1241	Mongols conquer the Punjab, expand holdings in South Asia
1244	Almohads defeat the Marinids, ending their rule of Morocco; Christians lose Jerusalem to Ayyubids
1246	Death of the Delhi Sultan Ala ad-Din Masud, accession of Nasir ad-Din Mahmud
1248	Death of the Almohad ruler Abu al-Hasan during attack on Tlemcen
1250	Marinids re-occupy large portion of Morocco
1250–1517	Mamluk dynasty rules Egypt and central Middle East
1258	Mongols sack Baghdad; death of the Abbasid Caliph Al-Mustasim, effectively ending long-weakened Abbasid rule; Mongols under Genghis Khan's grandson Hulagu Khan establish rule in Iran and Iraq; death of Abu al-Hasan ash-Shadhili, founder of major Sufi order especially prominent in North Africa
1259	North African Hafsid ruler Abd Allah Muhammad declares himself Caliph and assumes name of Al-Mustansir
1260	Battle of Ayn Jalut in Syria; Mamluks defeat Mongols decisively, Baybars becomes new Mamluk Sultan
1262	Death of Baha ad-Din Zakariya in Multan; introduction of the Suhrawardiyya Sufi order in South Asia
1265	Death of Hulagu Khan; death of Farid ad-Din Ganj-i Shakar, preeminent saint of

the Chishti Sufi order in South Asia

1266	Death of Berke Khan, the first ruler of the Golden Horde to be converted to Islam; with the Eighth Crusade, crusaders fail attempt at invasion of Tunisia
1267	First Muslim state of Samudra Pasai in Indonesia; in Spain, Almohad Caliph Umar allies with Christians in taking back Morocco; Marinids expel Spaniards from Morocco; Umar assassinated and succeeded by Idris II
1269	Almohad Idris II overthrown by the Marinids, ending Almohad dynasty. The Marinids come to power in Morocco under Abu Yaqub.
1270	Death of Mansa Wali, founder of Muslim rule in Mali, West Africa
1272	Death of Muhammad I of Granada, founder of the Nasrid dynasty, last major Muslim presence in Iberia
1273	Death Jalal ad-Din Rumi, major Sufi poet, originator of "Whirling Dervishes" (Sufi order known officially as the Mawlawiya)
1274	Death of Nasir al-Din Tusi, famed Ismaili Shii theologian; Ninth Crusade, Edward I of England defeated and returns to England
1276	Death of Ahmad al-Badawi, founder of major Egyptian Sufi order
1277	Death of major Mamluk ruler Baybars
1281–1324	Reign of Uthman (Osman), beginning of Ottoman Empire
1290	End of the slave dynasty in India and rise of Jalal ad-Din Firuz Khalji
1291	Death of Iranian poet and wisdom author Sadi
1296	Mongol ruler Ghazan Khan converted to Islam
1299	Mongols invade Syria; Marinids besiege capital of the Zayyanid Kingdom of Tlemcen
1300s	Muslim merchants and missionary Sufis arrive in Southeast Asia
1300–1921	Ottoman Dynasty rules Turkey and much of gradually subsumes much of Byzantine Empire
1302	In Granada, Muhammad II dies and is succeeded by Muhammad III
1304	In the Mongol Ilkhanate, Ghazan dies and is succeeded by his brother Khudabanda Oljeitu
1304	In Algeria, Uthman dies and is succeeded by his son Abu Zayyan Muhammad
1305	In the Khilji Empire, Ala ad-Din Khilji conquers Rajputana, India
1307	In Morocco, assassination of Marinid Sultan Abu Yaqub Yusuf
1309	In the Chagatai Khanate (Central Asia), Taliku is assassinated and Kebek accedes
1309	In Granada, Muhammad III overthrown by his uncle Abul Juyush Nasr
1310	Ala ad-Din Khalji conquers the Deccan (Southern India)
1313	Ilkhanids invade Syria, but are repulsed
1314	In Granada, Abu al-Juyush is overthrown by his nephew Abul Wahid Ismail
1316	In the Ilkhanid realm (Iraq and Persia), Oljeitu dies and is succeeded by Abu Said; in the Khalji Empire (South Asia), Malik Kafur, a Hindu convert, seizes power
1320	Ghazi Malik founds the Tughluqid dynasty in South Asia; Bengali ruler Shams ad-Din Firuz dies, kingdom splits; Ghiyath ad-Din Bahadur becomes the ruler of East

411

Bengal with the capital at Sonargaon

1325	Ghiyath ad-Din Tughluq (South Asia) dies and is succeeded by his son Muhammad Tughluq; Nasir ad-Din over-throws Ghiyath ad-Din Bahadur and unites Bengal
1326	Ottoman "founder" Osman I dies, succeeded by Orhan, who conquers Bursa for his new capital as Ottomans expand hold over Anatolia
1327	Ottomans take Nicaea (Iznik)
1329	Muhammad Tughluq moves capital from Delhi to Dawlatabad in the Deccan (South India)
1337	In Persia, Ilkhanid dynasty (descendants of the Mongols) supplanted by the Muzaffarid regime; Ottomans capture Izmit; Marinids conquer Algeria, expanding their realm eastward
1347	Marinids take Tunisia. Muslim control of India expands southward with early Deccani Sultanates, first at Gulbarga
1352	Marinids re-capture Algeria; Abu Said Othman is taken captive and killed
1353	Ilkhanid dynasty ends; Muzaffarids conquer Shiraz (Iran) as new capital
1354	Muzaffarids annex Isfahan (Iran); in Granada, Nasrid ruler Abu Hallaj Yusuf is assassinated, succeeded by son Muhammad V
1361	Ottoman Sultan Murad I takes Edirne (formerly Adrianople) as Ottomans close in on Byzantine capital from two sides.
1366	Ottoman capital moved from Bursa to Edirne (near Bulgarian border)
1369	Amir Timur (Tamerlane) seizes power in Transoxiana, capital at Samarkand
1371	Ottomans take Bulgaria, advancing toward the Balkans
1381	Timur annexes Sistan (Iran), captures Qandahar (Afghanistan)
1389	Death of the Persian poet Hafiz; death of Sufi mystical poet Fakhr ad-Din Iraqi; death of Baha ad-Din Naqshband, founder of Sufi order prominent in Middle East and Central Asia. Ottoman Murad I wins Battle of Kosovo against Christian army, but is assassinated and succeeded by Yildirim Beyazid I
1390	Tunisian the city of Mahdiya besieged by a French crusader army
1396	Ottoman Sultan Yildirim Beyazid I defeats Christian Crusaders at Nicopolis
1400s	Islam reaches the Philippines
1400	Burji Mamluks lose Syria to Timur Lang, descendent of Gehghis Khan
1402–03	Timur defeats and captures Beyazid I at Battle of Ankara, beginning interregnum as Beyazid's sons vie for power
1405	Timur dies, succeeded by his son, Shah Rukh, the first "Timurid" ruler
1413	Ottoman Interregnum period ends and Mehmed I becomes Sultan
1444	Anti-Ottoman League formed; Sultan Murad II loses to Europeans at Varna and abdicates throne to son Mehmed II
1446	Murad II reclaims the throne
1448	The Ottomans are victorious at the Second Battle of Kosovo, annex Serbia and reduce Bosnia to vassalage
1453	Mehmed Fatih (r. 1451–81) conquers Constantinople, unites Ottoman Empire

1468	Timurids lose Battle of Qarabagh, Ak Koyunlu take over Persia and Khurasan
1469	Timurid Husayn Bayqara retains Khurasan
1475	Ottomans take Venice, rule Adriatic and Aegean Seas
1481	Sultan Mehmed II dies, succeeded by Beyazid II
1492	Fall of the Nasrid Dynasty in Granada to Castille and Aragon, ending major Muslim presence in Spain, expelling Jews and Muslims
1492	Death of Jami, major Sufi mystical poet of Herat (Afghanistan)
1496	Mamluk Qaitbay abdicates and is succeeded by his son, Nasir Muhammad
1499	Uzbek Shaybani Khan conquers Transoxiana
1501	Ismail I (1487–1524) establishes Safavid dynasty in Tabriz (NW Iran), claims to be the Hidden Imam and is proclaimed Shah (king) of Persia, proclaims Twelve-Imam Shiism state creed
1502	Golden Horde broken into a number of smaller khanates in Central Asia
1506	Death of Behzad, influential miniature painter from Timurid Herat (Afghanistan)
1516	Ottoman Selim I takes Syria from Mamluks
1517	Ottomans cross Sinai desert, defeat Mamluks and take Egypt; Selim I declared custodian of Mecca and Medina; last Abbasid caliph surrenders to Selim I
1520	Ottoman Selim I dies, son Sulayman I the Magnificent accedes to throne
1520–66	Reign of Sulayman I the Magnificent; Ottoman Empire reaches its zenith; Hungary and coastlands of Algeria and Tunisia come under Ottoman rule
1521	Sulayman I conquers Belgrade
1522	Sulayman I drives Knights Hospitaller from the island of Rhodes
1526	Sulayman I defeats the Hungarian army at the Battle of Mohacs, where Louis II of Hungary dies. Ottomans take Buda and Pest, make Hungary Ottoman vassal state
1526	Babur (Mongolian) wins Battle of Panipat in India, makes Delhi capital, takes control of northern India for Mughals
1526–1757	Mughal Dynasty rules much of India
1527	Fall of Majapahit empire, the last Hindu stronghold in South East Asia; Demak established as first Islamic sultanate of Java
1529	Unsuccessful Ottoman siege of Vienna.
1534	Sulayman the Magnificent defeats Safavid Shah Tahsmap, takes Van (eastern Anatolia), Baghdad, Tabriz
1533	Barbarossa Khayreddin named Admiral of Ottoman fleet, governor of Algeria
1550	Architect Sinan builds the Sulaymaniye Mosque in Istanbul; rise of Muslim kingdom of Acheh in Sumatra
1550	Islam spreads to Java, the Maluku Islands, and Borneo
1556	Akbar first major Mughal ruler in Northern India
1566	Sulayman the Magnificent dies, succeeded by son Selim II
1571	Ottomans lose naval Battle of Lepanto, ending Turkish dominance in Mediterranean

1578	Death of Sinan, chief architect of Sulayman the Magnificent, one of the Muslim world's greatest designers of religious space
1588	Safavid Shah Abbas I takes throne in Isfahan
1591	Mustali Ismailis split into Sulaymanis and Daudis
1604	In Dutch Indonesia, death of Ala ad-Din Rayat Shah, Sultan of Acheh, accession of Ali Rayat Shah III
1605	Death of the Mughal emperor Jalal ad-Din Akbar; accession of son Jahangir
1617	British East India Company begins trading with Mughal India
1625	Java comes under rule of Muslim kingdom of Mataram
1627	Death of Mughal emperor Jahangir, accession of son Shah Jahan
1629	In Persia, death of Safavid Shah Abbas; accession of grandson Safi
1631	Death of Mumtaz Mahal, wife of Mughal Emperor Shah Jahan, buried in Taj Mahal
1642	Death of Safavid Shah Safi, accession of Shah Abbas II; first Chinese book on Islam written by Wang Daiyu
1658	Mughal emperor Shah Jahan (builder of Taj Mahal) dies, succeeded by Awrangzeb
1667	Death of Safavid Shah Abbas II in Persia; accession of Shah Sulayman
1673	Awrangzeb builds Badshahi *Masjid* in Lahore, Pakistan
1683	Ottomans besiege Vienna under siege but lose Battle of Vienna, ending Turkish advance into Europe
1699	Treaty of Karlowitz marks substantial losses of Ottoman Empire in Europe
1600–1700s	Venetians, Habsburgs, and Russians divide European Ottoman lands among them
1700s	Muhammad Abd al-Wahhab rejects Sufism and all innovation, prepares foundations of what became "Saudi Arabia"; Hindus regain power from Mughals in northern India
1703	Birth of religious reformer Muhammad ibn Abd al-Wahhab
1707	Death of the Mughal emperor Awrangzeb, accession of his son Bahadur Shah
1711	War between Ottoman Empire and Russia (Russo-Turkish War, 1710–1711), Russia defeated
1712	Death of Mughal emperor Bahadur Shah I, accession of Jahandar Shah
1729	Origins of Wahhabi movement, collaboration between Abd al-Wahhab and Muhammad ibn Suud
1738	Mughal Empire invaded by Afghans
1739	Nadir Shah sacks Mughal capital of Delhi
1747	Ahmed Shah Abdali establishes native Afghan rule in Afghanistan
1750	Beginnings of Dutch presence in Java, Indonesia
1752	Death of Shah Abdul Latif Bhitai, major South Asian Sufi poet
1762	Death of Shah Waliullah of Delhi, noted Indian Muslim theologian
1779	Afghans ousted from Persia by Qajar dynasty, which rules Persia until 1925
1785	Muslim revolt against Chinese Emperor
1786	Uthman dan Fodio launches religious campaign in Nigeria

1788	First Chinese biography of Muhammad
1791	Death of Muhammad ibn Abd al-Wahhab, founder of Wahhabi movement in Arabian Peninsula
1797	Death of Agha Mohammad Khan Qajar, the Shah of Persia. Russia occupies Dagestan in Caucasus
1798	Napoleon's army takes Ottoman Province of Egypt, defeats Ottoman provincial army of Mamluks at Battle of Pyramids
1802	Wahhabi's take control of Karbala, major Iraqi Shiite goal of pilgrims
1803	Shah of Delhi declares war against Britain; Wahhabis control Mecca and Medina
1804	Uthman dan Fodio proclaims Islamic State of Sokoto in northern Nigeria
1805	Saud bin Abdul Aziz captures Medina from Ottomans; Muhammad Ali becomes Ottoman Pasha (governor) of Egypt, now independent of the Ottomans, gaining control of western Arabia and extends into the Sudan
1807	Darqawi Sufi order revolts against Turks
1807–76	Tanzimat period as Ottomans embark on extensive program of modernization in government, law, and medicine
1811	Birth of Sayyid Mirza Ali-Muhammad, known as the Bab, founder of Babi movement
1812	Egyptians capture Medina
1813	Egyptian troops take Mecca and Taif, expel Saudis from Hijaz (northwestern Arabia), Wahhabis regroup and defeat Egyptian forces
1814	Iran allies with British with Definitive Treaty
1816	British cede Indonesia to the Dutch
1817	Birth of Sir Sayyid Ahmad Khan, major Indian theologian
1818	Egyptian forces take on Wahhabis again in Arabia and occupy their capital
1830	French forces occupy Algeria, end 313 year Turkish rule; Greece regains independence from Ottomans
1831	Sayyid Ahmad Barelvi and Shah Ismail leaders of Jihad movement in India die fighting Sikhs in Balakot
1832	Turks defeated in the battle of Konya by Egyptian forces
1834	French acknowledge Abd al-Qadir of Algeria as ruler of part of Algeria
1842	Amir Abd al-Qadir ousted from Algeria by the French, goes to Morocco
1843	Sanusi establishes foundation of his Sufi order in Libya
1847	Amir Abd al-Qadir surrenders to France for safe conduct to a Muslim country of his choice, but France violates its pledge and sends him captive to France
1849	Death of Muhammad Ali of Egypt
1850s	Non-Muslim Ottoman citizens granted equality with Muslims
1852	Amir Abd al-Qadir freed by Napoleon III, exiled to Ottoman Empire
1857	British take Delhi, end Mughal rule in India after 332 years
1858	Last Mughal in India deposed as India comes under British rule

1859	Imam Shamil surrenders to Russia making Islamic State of Dagestan a Russian province
1867	Deobandi reform-minded college founded in India, major critics of Sufism
1869	Jamal al-Din al-Afghani exiled from Afghanistan to live in Egypt
1871	Tunisia recognizes suzerainty of Ottoman Empire through a *firman* (royal edict)
1873	Central Asian Emirate of Bukhara and Khanate of Khiva made protectorates by Russia
1874	Aligarh University (India) founded by Sayyid Ahmad Khan
1875–1902	Sanusi Sufi order major political force in North Africa
1876	Britain purchases shares of Khedive Ismail in the Suez Canal, more involved in Egyptian affairs; constitutional monarchy in Ottoman Empire (Turkey, first phase)
1876–1908	Reign of autocratic and religiously conservative Ottoman Sultan Abd al-Hamid II
1878	Ottoman Empire loses territories to Russia, Balkans gain independence; Ottomans cede Cyprus to Britain
1879	"Modernist" Jamal al-Din al-Afghani exiled from Egypt
1881	Tunisia acknowledges supremacy of France in treaty of Bardo; Muhammad Ahmad declared himself *Mahdi* in northern Sudan
1882	Britain occupies Egypt militarily (until 1952); Sudanese *Mahdi* wins military conflicts
1883	Death of Algerian anti-colonialist patriot and Sufi Amir Abd al-Qadir in Damascus
1885	Khartoum, Sudan, taken by supporters of anti-Sufi *Mahdi*
1891	Mirza Ghulam Ahmad of Qadian claims to be promised Messiah and Imam *Mahdi*, "founder" of the Ahmadiyya Movement
1901	Abd al-Aziz Ibn Saud captures Riyadh. French forces occupy Morocco
1902	Birth of Ruhollah Khomeini, founder of Islamic Republic of Iran
1903	Birth of Syed Abu al-Ala Mawdudi (founder of Jamaat-e-Islami)
1905	Death of Muhammad Abduh, modernist proponent of reason as source of knowledge; Rashid Rida advances cause of the Salafi movement in Egypt
1906	All India Muslim league established in Dhakka (East Bengal)
1907	Beginning of the Young Turks movement in Turkey
1908–18	Last decade of Ottoman rule
1912	Balkan wars, coalition defeats Ottoman Empire; founding of Islamic Union (Sareket Islam), a modernizing movement in southeast Asia
1913	Mohammad Ali Jinnah joins All India Muslim League
1914	Ottoman Empire allies with Germany in WWI
1915	Ottoman Empire defeats Allies in Çanakkale (Dardanelles)
1916	Arab revolt against Ottoman (Turkish) rule; Lawrence of Arabia leads attacks on the Hijaz Railway.
1917	British Balfour Declaration supports creation of Jewish national homeland

1918	Birth of Gamal Abd an-Nasser; after losing virtually their entire empire, the Ottomans capitulate on October 19 and sign the Armistice of Mudros with the Allies on October 30; World War I ends on November 11; Syria becomes French protectorate
1918	League of Nations grants Britain mandatory status over Palestine and Iraq, and France over Lebanon and Syria
1919	The first revolution in Egypt led by Sad Zaghlul against British occupation
1920–1922	Turkish War of Independence, groundwork for secular Republic; Wahhabis take last Ottoman holdings in Arabia, begin Saudi Kingdom
1921	Abdullah I of Jordan in made King of Transjordan; his father was the Sharif of Mecca; Faisal I of Iraq is made King of Iraq (was son of the Sharif of Mecca)
1922	Effective end of Ottoman Sultanate (and Empire) brought about by Mustafa Kemal and nationalists
1922	Britain unilaterally declares Egypt independent
1922–24	Mustafa Kemal Ataturk secularizes Turkish state
1923	Treaty of Lausanne recognizes independent Turkey; Mustafa Kemal declares Republic of Turkey with Ankara as capitol
1923	Republic of Turkey established under first president Mustafa Kemal (Ataturk)
1924	Turkish National Assembly dissolves Ottoman Caliphate, exiles last Ottomans
1924	King Abd al-Aziz Ibn Saud conquers Mecca and Medina, unifying Kingdoms of Najd and Hejaz
1925	Reza Khan seizes the government in Persia and establishes the Pahlavi dynasty
1927	Tablighi Jamaat reform movement founded in India
1928	Republic of Turkey declared secular state
1928	Hasan al-Banna founds Ikhwan al-Muslimun (Muslim Brothers) in Egypt
1930	Muhammad Iqbal raises hopes for a separate nation of Pakistan
1932	Iraq gains independence
1933	Chinese Muslim revolt leads to forming Republic of East Turkistan
1935	Iran ("Land of the Aryans") becomes the official name of Persia
1935	Death of Rashid Rida, founder of Egyptian Salafi movement calling for retrieval of pristine days of the Prophet
1936	Jewish immigration sparks Arab revolt in Palestine in the Great Uprising
1938	Mustafa Kemal Ataturk dies; succeeded by Ismet Inonu, second president of Turkey
1941	British and Russian forces invade Iran; Reza Shah abdicates to son Mohammad Reza Shah in Iran; Jamaat-e-Islami founded in Lahore, South Asian counterpart to the Muslim Brotherhood
1945–60s	Centuries after first Muslims came as slaves to America, Islam spreads to the West with mass migrations from Asia, Africa, and India
1945	Indonesia gains independence from Netherlands; Sukarno declines to implement Sharia as national law

1946	Jordan, Lebanon, and Syria gain independence from Britain and France
1947	India gains independence from Britain, with Pakistan partitioned as Muslim state led by Muhammad Ali Jinnah; dispute over Kashmir causes first Indo-Pakistani War, with Kashmir divided between India and Pakistan
1948	New state of Israel defeats Arab states, displacing thousands of Palestinians; "founder" of Pakistan, Quaid-e-Azam Mohammad Ali Jinnah, dies in Karachi
1949	Death of Hasan al-Banna, whose Muslim Brotherhood (1929) gains strength with failure of liberal Muslim governments and proclamation of the State of Israel; assassinated by Egyptian security forces; second East Turkestan Republic overthrown and re-incorporated into Xinjiang, China
1950	Chinese Muslims revolt against Communist indoctrination of their children
1951	Libya gains independence from Italy
1953	With CIA and MI6 support, Iranian General Zahedi leads a coup against elected Mohammed Mosaddegh, returning the Shah to power; death of King Abd al-Aziz Ibn Saud of Saudi Arabia. The foundation stone is laid to enlarge the Prophet's mosque in Medina
1954	Algerians begin War of Independence; Egyptian President Gamal Abd an-Nasser bans the Muslim Brotherhood
1956	Morocco and Tunisia become independent
1957	Tunisian Bey deposed, Bourguiba becomes president; dnlargement of the Haram in Mecca begins; Malaya (Malaysia) gains independence, with Islam as the official religion but guaranteed tolerance
1960	Mali and Senegal become independent; Turkish religious scholar Bedi-az-Zaman Said Nursi dies in Urfa (Turkey)
1960s	Muslim families from Southeast Asia and North Africa emigrate to Europe and the Americas
1962	Death of Zaydi Imam Ahmad of Yemen, succeeded by Crown Prince Bahr with title Imam Mansur Bi-Llah Muhammad
1965	American Muslim leader Malcolm X assassinated; the second Indo-Pakistani War results in a stalemate; Malaysia grants independence to Singapore; in Indonesia, anti-communist witch hunts give political Islamists an advantage over Communists; Catholic Second Vatican Council publishes breakthrough declaration concerning need for Christians to "regard Muslims [and their faith] with esteem."
1966	Death of Sayyid Qutb, influential theorist of Muslim Brotherhood movement
1967	Six-Day War leaves Israel in control of Jerusalem, the West Bank, Gaza Strip, the Sinai Peninsula, and the Golan Heights; massive dispersal of Palestinians
1968	Enlargement of the Haram in Mecca completed; Israel begins building Jewish settlements in territories occupied during the Six-Day War
1970	Death of Gamal Abd an-Nasser; Anwar Sadat becomes president of Egypt and continues preparation of the army for the next war with Israel
1971	Bengalis seek independence from West Pakistan, Pakistan responds militarily; India intervenes, sparks third Indo-Pakistani War, leading to creation of Bangladesh

1973	King Zahir Shah of Afghanistan deposed; Yom Kippur War, also known as 1973 Arab-Israeli War, leads to failed attempt of Egypt and Syria to recapture the Sinai Peninsula and Golan Heights from Israel
1975	King Faisal of Saudi Arabia assassinated; death of Elijah Muhammad, leader of Nation of Islam among African Americans in North America, son Warith Deen Muhammad, assumes leadership of Nation of Islam and shifts movement toward Islamic mainstream, renaming it American Muslim Mission
1978	Egypt becomes the first Arab nation to recognize Israel; Israel returns the Sinai Peninsula to Egypt
1979	Islamic Republic of Iran proclaimed after overthrow of second and last Pahlavi Shah
1979	Day One of Islamic year 1400—Ayatollah Ruhollah Khomeini establishes an Islamic government, calls Iran an Islamic Republic; religious students in Saudi Arabia seize control of the Haram of Mecca, sparking a two-week standoff with Saudi security forces; Soviets invade Afghanistan; death of Sayyid Abu al-Ala Mawdudi, Pakistan
1980	Muhammad Asad publishes his *magnum opus, The Message of The Quran.*
1980	Iraq invades Iran, beginning the Iran–Iraq War; Israel claims capital as united Jerusalem
1981	Egyptian Islamists assassinate President Anwar Sadat
1982	Israel invades Lebanon
1983	U.S. Marine barracks in Lebanon bombed
1988	End of eight-year Iran–Iraq War; President Muhammad Zia-ul-Haq of Pakistan killed in a plane crash caused by a mysterious mid-air explosion
1989	Death of Ayatollah Ruhollah Khomeini; accession of Ali Khamenei as the Supreme Leader of Iran; Afghan *mujahideen* force Soviet departure, but infighting follows
1990	Iraq invades Kuwait; North Yemen and South Yemen reunite
1992	400-year-old Babri *Masjid* in Ayodhya, India, is destroyed by Hindu extremists, sparking widespread religious rioting across India
1994	Jordan becomes the second of Israel's Arab neighbors to recognize Israel
1996	Taliban forces seize control of most of Afghanistan and declare the Islamic Emirate of Afghanistan
1998	Pakistan becomes first Islamic republic to have the nuclear power as it successfully conducted five nuclear tests on May 28, becoming the first Muslim nuclear power
1999	Death of Jordan's King Hussein; son Abdullah declared king of Jordan
late 1990s	Taliban come to power in Afghanistan
2000	Palestinians in the West Bank and Gaza Strip begin the Al-Aqsa Intifada, prompted by Ariel Sharon's visit to a disputed religious site holy to both Jews and Muslims
2001	Extremists claiming Islamic sanction attack the United States; September 11: terrorists attack the U.S. World Trade Center in New York City, and the

Pentagon, and attempt a third attack (thwarted by passengers) using hijacked passenger airplanes as weapons; September 27: major Muslim religious scholar in Egypt rules that Muslim members of U.S. military forces are allowed under Islamic law to fight against other Muslims if deployed to predominantly Islamic regions

2003	Saddam Hussein ousted by Western forces; he is executed three years later
2005	170 Muslim religious scholars and jurists meet in Amman, Jordan, and produce an important statement of Muslim religious/legal unity, insisting that Muslim violence against other Muslims cease
2006	Pope Benedict XVI's Regensburg address raises concerns for Muslim–Christian relations by suggesting the Islam is violent and "non-rational"; within weeks, three dozen Muslim scholars reached out in a letter to the Vatican seeking reconciliation
2007	International group of 138 Muslim religious leaders seek reconciliation with the Vatican with open letter to the Pope and other Christian leaders, emphasizing common bond in love of God and neighbor
2009	New Yorkers protest Muslim plans to construct a community center within blocks of "Ground Zero"
2010	Tunisian suicide in protest of injustice sparks early events in what came to be called the "Arab Spring"
2011	Amid popular uprising, Egypt's President Mubarak resigns after thirty years of dictatorial rule
2012	Muslim Brotherhood member Muhammad Morsi elected president of Egypt
2013	Major Egyptian protests against Muslim Brotherhood lead to arrest and deposition of President Morsi, eventual replacement by former army general Sissi
2014	So-called Islamic State in Iraq and Syria (or Levant—ISIS/ISIL) advances its cause of reviving the "Caliphate"; Muslim scholars and religious leaders across the world unite in condemnation of the organization as not only un-Islamic but anti-Islamic
2014	Global Muslim population exceeds 1.6 billion

Index

Note: (ill.) indicates photos and illustrations.

Stalin, Joseph, 51
State of the Union address, 85
Station of Abraham, 173, 199
Stephen, St., 331
Stories of the Prophets, 196
Straight Path, 115, 150, 222, 279, 282, 346
Straits of Gibraltar, 23
sub-Saharan African sphere, 32, 52–53, 68
suffering, views on, 218–19
Sufism
  aesthetics, literature, and the visual and spatial arts, 365, 367, 369, 378–79, 381–82
  authority, law, and ethics, 244, 255
  essential beliefs, 135, 155–56, 165
  growth of Islam, 42, 44, 46, 52–55, 64
  Islam and other faiths, 295
  knowledge, scholarship, and the Islamic humanities, 347–49
  photos, 233 (ill.), 235 (ill.)
  politics and contemporary global affairs, 72, 83, 89–90, 103, 105
  sacred sources and their interpretation, 126
  symbols, rituals, and observances, 175, 189–90, 200–201
  themes in Islamic spirituality, 209, 218, 228, 233–36
Suhrawardis, 42
suicide, 277
suicide bombings, 74, 78, 80–81, 216–17, 273, 277–78
Sulayman the Magnificent, 49, 89, 364, 380–81
Sulaymani Ismailis, 61
Sulaymaniye Mosque, 364
Sultan Ahmet mosque, 177 (ill.), 300
Sultanate, 43, 45, 54, 56, 86–87, 254
Summa Contra Gentiles (Aquinas), 324
Summa of Theology (Aquinas), 324
Sung dynasty, 51
Sunna, 124, 134, 142, 248–251
Sunni Muslims
  authority, law, and ethics, 245, 249–253, 255, 257, 260, 262, 277
  essential beliefs, 133, 139
  growth of Islam, 33, 36, 39, 41, 45–46, 52, 60–62, 65
  Islam and other faiths, 284
  knowledge, scholarship, and the Islamic humanities, 347, 349, 352, 354

origin and history of Islam, 3, 14, 16, 18, 27–29
politics and contemporary global affairs, 74, 77, 82, 86, 90
sacred sources and their interpretation, 121
symbols, rituals, and observances, 182–83, 193, 196–97, 199–200
themes in Islamic spirituality, 221, 225
surrogacy, 261–62
The Sustenance of Hearts, 366
Swahili language, 32, 52–53
symbols, 171–78, 172 (ill.), 173 (ill.)
syncretism, 293–94

T

Tabari, 339
Tablighi Jamaat, 349
Taj Mahal, 43, 43 (ill.), 303, 377
Tajiks, 51
takbir, 186, 204
Tales of the Friends of God, 367
Tales of the Prophets, 113, 155, 339, 367
Talha ibn Ubaydallah, 17
Taliban
  authority, law, and ethics, 277
  culture and religion, 318, 323
  essential beliefs, 134, 143
  politics and contemporary global affairs, 70–71, 77, 88, 100
Tamil Tigers, 80
al-Tantawi, Shaykh Muhammad Sayyid, 82
Taqi al-Din Ibn Taymiya, 326
Tariquas, 315
tawhid, 125, 135, 364
Tehran University, 367
Temple, 3, 12, 97, 286–87, 304
Temple Mount, 98, 286–87
Ten Commandments, 257
terrorism
  authority, law, and ethics, 256, 272–75, 277
  culture and religion, 325, 331–32
  essential beliefs, 143
  knowledge, scholarship, and the Islamic humanities, 350
  politics and contemporary global affairs, 75, 77, 101
Thalabi, 339
Thamud, 357
themes in Islamic spirituality, 207–39
themes in the Quran, 111–17

theological anthropology, 207–13
theology, Islam and, 342–47
theology, liberation, 347–351
theology, mystical, 356–58
theology and politics crossing in Islam, 64–66
Thirteen Articles of Faith, 138
Throne Verse, 120, 122, 152, 212
Tijaniyyas, 52
time, sacred, 179–181, 191–93, 229
Timur Lang (Tamerlane), 46, 89
Timurid dynasty, 42, 88, 362
Tito, Marshal, 292
Tomb of Abraham, 10 (ill.)
Topkapi Museum, 173
Torah, 116, 122, 154, 277
tradition, Islamic, 135–145, 293–94. See also Calendar
traditionalism, 133–34, 343, 347–351, 354
Traditions of Discord, 157
Treatise (or Epistle) of Light (Nursi), 82
Treatise on Government (Mulk), 368
Treaty of Hudaybiya, 17
Treaty of Zsitva Torok, 50
Trinity, 39, 282, 287, 293, 296, 305, 380
Tuanku Nan Tua, 55
Tuareg Muslims, 69, 69 (ill.)
Tughluq Shah, 43
Turkic sphere, 32, 42, 44–52, 68
Turkish Council for Religious Affairs, 254
Turkish language, 175
Turkish Republic, 89, 267
Twelver Shia
  authority, law, and ethics, 242, 244, 246, 255
  essential beliefs, 158
  growth of Islam, 41–43, 61–63
  knowledge, scholarship, and the Islamic humanities, 354
  origin and history of Islam, 28
  politics and contemporary global affairs, 74, 86, 90
  symbols, rituals, and observances, 180, 193
types of Islam, 3

U

Ubayd Allah, 41
Umar, *Mullah*, 71
Umar ibn al-Khattab
  aesthetics, literature, and the visual and spatial arts, 380
  growth of Islam, 61
  Islam and other faiths, 288